1983

3 0250 01037 8334

DATE DUE

NOW			
OCT 31 83			
NOV 1 0 1983		NOV 1 8 2003	
NOV 8 83			
MAY 11 1984			
MAY 24 84			
JUN 2 1986		OCT 2 9 2003	
JUN 3 86			
DEC 1 8 1986		dear 4	
DEC 15 86			
MAY 30 1989			
JUN 2 1989			
APR 25 1994		WITHDRAWN	
MAY 22 1994			
MAY 24 1994			
MAY 2 5 1995			
MAY 2 6 1995			

201-6503 Printed in USA

Civilization in the Ancient Americas

Gordon Randolph Willey

CIVILIZATION IN THE ANCIENT AMERICAS

Essays in Honor of Gordon R. Willey

Edited by Richard M. Leventhal and Alan L. Kolata

University of New Mexico Press
and
Peabody Museum of Archaeology and Ethnology
Harvard University, Cambridge, Massachusetts

Library of Congress Cataloging in Publication Data
Main entry under title:

Civilization in the ancient Americas.

    Includes bibliographies and index.
    1. Indians—Antiquities—Addresses, essays,
lectures. 2. Latin America—Antiquities—Addresses,
essays, lectures. 3. Willey, Gordon Randolph,
1913–   —Addresses, essays, lectures. I. Willey,
Gordon Randolph, 1913–   . II. Leventhal, Richard M.
III. Kolata, Alan L.
E61.C58   1983   970.01   82-25094
ISBN 0–8263–0693–4

© 1983 by the President and Fellows of Harvard College.
All rights reserved. Manufactured in the United States of America.
International Standard Book Number 0–8263–0693–4.
Library of Congress Catalog Card Number 82-25094.
First edition

Design: Barbara Jellow

Contents

Preface	vii
Introduction, *Alan L. Kolata and Richard M. Leventhal*	ix
Part 1 Historical Overview: Scholarship in the Maya Area	**1**
1. Lords of the Jungle: A Prosopography of Maya Archaeology, *Norman Hammond*	3
Part 2 Basic Data Interpretation	**33**
2. The Paleoecology of the Selin Farm Site (H-CN-5): Department of Colón, Honduras, *Paul F. Healy*	35
3. Maya Ritual Faunas: Vertebrate Remains from Burials, Caches, Caves, and Cenotes in the Maya Lowlands, *Mary Pohl*	55
4. Functional Analysis and Social Process in Ceramics: The Pottery from Cerros, Belize, *Robin Robertson*	105
Part 3 Iconography and Calendric Correlation	**143**
5. Altars 9 and 10, Kaminaljuyu, and the Evolution of the Serpent-Winged Deity, *Lee A. Parsons*	145
6. The Maya Calendar Correlation Problem, *David H. Kelley*	157

Part 4 Architectural and Spatial Patterns   209

   7. Cultural Reconstitution in the Late Moche Period:
      A Case Study in Multidimensional Stylistic Analysis,
      Garth Bawden   211
   8. Coast-Highland Relations in Northern Peru: Some
      Observations on Routes, Networks, and Scales of
      Interaction, *John R. Topic and Theresa Lange Topic*   237
   9. Deducing Social Organization from Classic Maya
      Settlement Patterns: A Case Study from the Copan Valley,
      William L. Fash, Jr.   261
  10. From Maritime Chiefdom to Agricultural State in
      Formative Coastal Peru, *Robert A. Feldman*   289

Part 5 The City and the State   311

  11. Rulership and the Ciudadela: Political Inferences
      from Teotihuacan Architecture, *George L. Cowgill*   313 ✓
  12. Chan Chan and Cuzco: On the Nature of the
      Ancient Andean City, *Alan L. Kolata*   345
  13. Ideological Adaptation and the Rise of the Aztec and
      Inca Empires, *Arthur Demarest and Geoffrey Conrad*   373

Part 6 Bibliography of Gordon R. Willey   401

  References   421
  Index   479

Preface

As students of Gordon R. Willey, we believe that his retirement represents a major transition in the field of New World archaeology. Over the past three decades, his teaching has helped shape an entire generation of scholars who now work throughout the world. His research and writing have provided new data, ideas, and insights for his colleagues.

The idea of a festschrift for Gordon Willey emerged more than three years ago. The date of his retirement was drawing near, and we wanted to prepare a volume of essays by his students. Learning that a Wenner-Gren conference in honor of Gordon Willey was being organized by Evon Vogt, we decided to join forces with Vogt in order to produce two volumes in time for Willey's retirement. The papers presented at the Wenner-Gren conference, which focused on settlement pattern studies, are published as a companion to this volume.

Contributors to this volume are all former students of Gordon Willey. They were chosen for their active fieldwork and new interpretations of data from Middle and South America—the primary focus of Willey's career. We feel that these essays well represent Gordon Willey's interests and ideas concerning the prehistory of civilizations in the New World.

A book of this kind does not come about without the support and hard work of many people. Luther Wilson and Elizabeth Hadas of the University of New Mexico Press were enthusiastic when we approached them with the idea of a two-volume festschrift. They were instrumental in overseeing the successful production of these volumes. Lorna Condon of the Peabody Museum provided invaluable assistance in the preparation of the final manuscript. We also wish to thank Nancy Lambert-Brown, for her work with the illustrations; Carle Lawton, who helped prepare several manuscripts; and Victoria Alexander, who was copy editor for the manuscript. Finally, we wish to acknowledge the contribution of C. C. Lamberg-Karlovsky, director of the Peabody Museum, who provided the necessary encouragement and financial support for this endeavor.

Richard M. Leventhal
Alan L. Kolata

Introduction

Alan L. Kolata, Field Museum of Natural History
Richard M. Leventhal, State University of New York, Albany

The essays in this volume are intended to honor one of the world's most productive and respected scholars of American archaeology: Gordon R. Willey. A companion festschrift, *Prehistoric Settlement Patterns,* has been published simultaneously with this set of essays. Taken in tandem, we hope, these two volumes will properly pay tribute to Gordon Willey and his remarkable professional career.

The companion volume includes various papers devoted to settlement pattern archaeology, as well as the editors' perspective on the scholarly career of Gordon Willey. In this volume we wish simply to present what we believe is a series of innovative and substantive essays covering virtually the entire spectrum of archaeological study. All of the authors of these essays are former students of Gordon Willey, and their work reflects in spirit and in substance his profound influence.

In soliciting contributions to this volume, we carefully refrained from imposing a thematic constraint. Each author was free to choose his or her own topic and mode of presentation. Despite the editorial difficulties inherent in such a free-form approach, we adopted it to insure that the contents of this volume would be emblematic of the tenor and breadth of Gordon Willey's own scholarly enquiries.

The effects of this editorial decision are apparent in the multiplicity of archaeological problems treated in these collected essays and in the broad array of methods used by the authors to extract significant cultural information from the imperfectly preserved and, at times, intractable remains of the prehistoric past. Underlying the diverse problems and approaches evidenced in these essays is a dual goal: to re-create, as graphically and as accurately as possible, the extinct landscapes and social formations of civilizations in the ancient Americas; and to explain the physical and social processes that account for the development and evolution of these civilizations.

Gordon Willey is one of the few anthropologists who has consistently achieved this goal in a satisfactory fashion. He is also one of the few students of prehistory willing to reevaluate his own methods and conclusions in the light of ongoing research in order to fashion new and more illuminating portraits of ancient civilizations. This characteristic, above all else, distinguishes Gordon Willey as an original, reflective, and undogmatic scholar.

It is fitting, then, that the following essays, at least in part, share this characteristic. They are an eclectic set—some broad in scope, others more narrowly focused—yet all of them are synthetic. They all present new and substantive bodies of data or hypotheses set within the frame of reference of prior research but reaching beyond the boundaries of these past studies to suggest new insights into prehistoric social processes.

Underlying the topical diversity of these essays is another kind of unity: that of geography. All of the works included here describe or explain some aspect of ancient societies in Mesoamerica or Peru. The bulk of the papers (Hammond, Healy, Pohl, Robertson, Parsons, Kelley, Fash, and Cowgill) are focused on Mesoamerica, with an emphasis on the Maya area. The other contributions are concerned with Peru (Bawden, Topic and Topic, Feldman, and Kolata) or with both of the two great centers of high civilization in the New World (Demarest and Conrad). This asymmetry in areal treatment is intended to reflect the trajectory of Gordon Willey's own career in the field.

Upon receiving the finished manuscripts, we fashioned a second, editorial organization for the collection. Of course, our scheme is in part arbitrary. We believe, however, that the volume's five sections—Historical Overview, Basic Data Interpretations, Iconography and Calendric Correlation, Architectural and Spatial Patterns, and The City and the State—represent an orderly progression and touch upon the principal themes of scholarly enquiry that characterize the work of Gordon Willey.

We open the volume with Norman Hammond's intellectual history of archaeological scholarship in the Maya lowlands. His urbane essay describes the growth of Maya studies and furnishes a perfect example of "back-looking curiosity" as a means of understanding the context and directions of scholarly research in that rich and complex field. Appropriately, Hammond locates the work of Gordon Willey within the broader cycles and trends that define the course of Maya archaeology. He further illustrates how Willey's work, in great part, initated and bridged the transition from the period of "institutional domination" to the current era of "problem orientation."

The next two sections of essays introduce a series of new data interpretations that range from paleoecology to calendric correlation. Healy discusses long-term coastal adaptation in southern Mesoamerica, as reflected in the Selin Farm site of eastern Honduras. Employing the concept of relative "subsistence risk," Healy deftly calls attention to the importance of diverse, closely packed ecozones (lowland forest, riverine, lagoonal, estuarine, and marine) in the subsistence strategies of Mesoamerican coastal inhabitants. Early maritime adaptations in Mesoamerica are increasingly coming under the scrutiny of ecologically oriented archaeologists. Perhaps stimulated by their colleagues in Andean archaeology, who have long debated the role of maritime adaptations in cultural evolution, these archaeologists, well represented here by Healy, are providing fundamental new data on the paleoeconomy of coastal Mesoamerica.

Mary Pohl's discussion of Maya ritual fauna explores yet another dimension of the sea's pervasive influence on the ancient cultures of Mesoamerica, an influence that penetrated far beyond the near-coast peoples. Marshaling considerable data on fauna discovered in "ritual" contexts, such as burials, caches, caves, and cenotes, she concludes that certain classes of animals—in particular, specialized forms of marine life—were of great ideological importance to the ancient Maya. These animals were intimately associated with and emblematic of ceremonies of agricultural fertility.

The coastal theme continues with Robertson's exhaustive analysis of Late Preclassic ceramics from the early Maya site of Cerros on Chetumal Bay in Belize. Robertson describes formal ceramic types, elicits some perhaps controversial functional classes, and then associates these two typological variables with differing "social contexts." In charting these changing ceramic patterns through time, she detects evidence at Cerros for the transition from an egalitarian to a stratified society. She concludes that "from the perspective of the ... pottery," the apparent process of increasing cultural complexity at Cerros ... and Robertson hints throughout the Maya lowlands ... was *sui generis*, and not attributable to foreign influence.

In the next section, *Iconography and Calendric Correlation*, the papers by Parsons and Kelley also present new interpretations of fundamental data, here in the special realm of cosmology and ideation. Parsons's paper is the first published analysis of two remarkable monumental stone sculptures from Kaminaljuyu: Altars 9 and 10. Parsons places these Izapa-style sculptures in the Arenal phase of Kaminaljuyu. Using the "Serpent-Winged Deity" motif as his principal evidence, he demonstrates their iconographic relationship with early Maya art. Parsons argues convincingly that these two altars were part of a corpus of late Izapa sculptures, some of which incorporated rudimentary glyphic passages, that can confidently be termed "proto-Maya." This conclusion, together with the iconographic analysis, offers significant implications for the nature and ultimate origins of Maya cosmology.

David Kelley's concern is not with the question of origins, but rather with the fully evolved Classic Maya calendric system and its correlation with the European calendar. His essay is unquestionably the most specialized of this collection, confronting head on the convoluted problem of correlating two calendars based on different number systems and divergent, seemingly alien, conceptions of time. Through a careful analysis of historical and astronomical data, Kelley fashions a new correlation of the Maya calendar that varies more than 200 years from the traditionally accepted G.M.T. correlation. Such a major shift in the chronologies will have a significant impact on our understanding of the Postclassic Period in Mesoamerica. It will also force us to reevaluate the relationship of the Maya with Central Mexico and other important cultures of the region.

From this formal consideration of time, the next set of essays (Architectural and Spatial Patterns) shifts to considerations of spatial patterning, ranging from the broad perspective of regional archaeology to the intrasite architectural use of space. Garth Bawden offers a critical methodological and empirical reconsideration of the hypothesis that the highland "Wari empire" invaded and conquered the indigenous Moche people of the Peruvian north coast, effectively destroying the political authority of the Moche state. Bawden disputes this "oversimplified view" of conquest and cultural replacement, arguing that it stems from a nonrigorous application of single-trait and overly generalized stylistic comparisons. He prefers a "multidimensional stylistic analysis" of architecture and ceramics, which reveals a considerably more complex political picture and permits a more sophisticated, "processual" explanation of events on the north coast of Peru during the Middle Horizon.

The same valleys of the Peruvian north coast are the setting for John and Theresa Topic's essay on roads, principles of routing, and networks of interaction between highland and coastal zones. Their essay provides a graphic example of the effects of physical landscape on social and economic formations. These effects are particularly important in regions such as the Andes, where there is tremendous vertical relief with concomitant compression of diverse ecological zones.

Networks of a different kind are the topic of Fash's essay on the Late Classic Maya settlement system of the Copan Valley in Honduras. He describes and discusses a hierarchical settlement network for the Copan pocket that ranges from the individual household to the "urban core" at the center of Copan. His greatest concern is defining the nature of an intermediate residential unit between these two extremes. Most often this intermediate unit has been referred to, somewhat ambiguously, as a "cluster." By comparing it to a similar residential unit, the *sian otot,* among the modern Chorti Maya of eastern Guatemala, Fash illuminates the true nature and function of the Late Classic settlement organization.

Robert Feldman uses his new data from the important Preceramic site of Aspero, on the central coast of Peru, to challenge the archaeological axiom that agriculture, particularly the cultivation of maize, was a necessary precondition for the development of complex societies. His work at Aspero indicates that some very precocious, large-scale structures, indicative of a high degree of social integration, were erected during the late preceramic period in the context of a predominantly maritime subsistence economy. Feldman provides solid empirical backing for the hypothesis of the maritime foundations of coastal Andean civilization.

The final set of essays in the volume (The City and the State) are concerned with the nature of political authority in some of the greatest native states of the ancient Americas. Cowgill explores and reconstructs plausible forms of government organization at the city of Teotihuacan from the perspective of the Ciudadela, one of the most prominent architectural complexes in that ancient city. He documents the construction and occupation sequences of the Ciudadela over several centuries of Teotihuacan's history and draws carefully reasoned inferences concerning the function of this monumental structure. Throughout his essay, Cowgill incorporates cross-cultural comparisons of architecture and advocates wider use of what he terms the "ethnoarchaeology of public architecture." His own successful use of architectural ethnoarchaeology to identify the Ciudadela as a royal residence should stimulate interest in this approach among Mesoamericanists and Andeanists alike. Cowgill and Joyce Marcus, in the companion volume, stress the "common denominators" underlying the forms and functions of preindustrial urban settlements. Both effectively invoke this cross-cultural commonality to examine the nature of pre-Columbian cities in Mesoamerica.

Of course, in the muddled realm of prehistory there is always the possibility of exceptions to the norm. Kolata argues that certain cities of empires in the ancient Andes were in fact exceptional examples of the preindustrial city. Drawing on ethnohistoric evidence and a new construction sequence for Chan Chan, Kolata draws out the salient, comparable features of political structure and economic organization at Chan Chan and Cuzco and contrasts these with preindustrial cities elsewhere. In effect, he points out the special character of these Andean cities and how it influenced their history.

In the final essay Demarest and Conrad criticize the almost exclusively materialist bias in archaeological explanations of cultural evolution. Carefully chronicling the rise of Aztec and Inca empires, they demonstrate that ideological factors (such as the conscious manipulation of state religion and the "official" cosmology) played critical roles in the transformation of these societies into the most powerful imperial states of the ancient Americas. Their paper, with its strong emphasis on the need for a synthetic approach to understanding cultural causation, provides a fitting conclusion to a volume honoring Gordon Willey.

Reflecting on the contents of this volume, with its multiple methods for discovering the nature of extinct societies, we would draw a modest moral, one with which we believe Gordon Willey would agree: for the archaeologist, as for any scholar, dogma is anathema.

Civilization in the Ancient Americas

PART ONE

Historical Overview: Scholarship in the Maya Area

One

Lords of the Jungle: A Prosopography of Maya Archaeology

Norman Hammond, Rutgers University

> "the Lords of the Jungle turn out to be the archaeologists themselves."—Clemency Coggins (1981:76)

It is doubly appropriate that an essay honoring Gordon Willey should consider the historical development of Maya archaeology as a subdiscipline: first, because his work marks an important phase in the advancement of Maya studies over the past thirty years, and second, because Willey has also stood back and examined the way in which American archaeology has emerged as a field of scholarly endeavor. His vision ranges from the broadest continental perspective (Willey and Sabloff 1974, 1980) to a topical advance within the circumscribed field of Maya archaeology (Willey 1968, 1977a, 1980).

Disciplinary maturity is marked by, *inter alia*, the crystallization of a body of explicit theory that shapes the practice of the particular discipline (Clarke 1968:xv, 3–13), and by what Leland called "a back-looking curiosity," a desire to examine the trajectory of past events and ideas that have resulted in the particular conformation of knowledge and notions now seeking identification as a discrete field of scholarship. In archaeology this second trait appeared in 1950 with the publication of Glyn Daniel's *A Hundred Years of Archaeology* and Sir Thomas Kendrick's *British Antiquity,* while the first gradually emerged through the following decade to find widespread acceptance (and disagreement) with the Binfords' *New Perspectives in Archaeology* (1968) and David Clarke's *Analytical Archaeology* (1968). Maya archaeology has lagged behind the field in both cases, with neither historiography nor theory arousing much interest until the 1970s: as the Classical archaeology of the

New World, it shared with the study of Greece and Rome an *embarrasse de richesse* of architecture, art, and inscriptions, which kept its practitioners immersed in fact long after those less well endowed materially had been forced to seek new ways of interpreting their material. However, Maya archaeology has caught up rapidly. Explicit models and testable hypotheses are now frequent, if not predominant, and the history of the subject has begun to attract attention (Adams 1969; Bernal 1977, 1980; Becker 1979; Graham 1971; Willey 1968, 1977a, 1980) as well as anecdotal biography (Brunhouse 1971, 1973, 1975, 1976). In this essay I draw on both sources to offer a model for the development of Maya studies, which is regional in its perspective and divisions and therefore differs somewhat in detail from the broader vision of Gordon Willey and Jeremy Sabloff (1974, 1980).

Such a model in effect declares the absence of any overarching theme to unify and direct its successive stages, and one of the salient characteristics of Maya archaeology has indeed been the extent to which personalities rather than ideas have dominated its development. Perhaps this is not surprising: the size of the active Mayanist community has always been modest, concentrated in a few centers and exchanging ideas in a restricted range of intellectual fora. Even so, these scholars were not insulated from the general academic climate of their times, and in their ideas we can often perceive, dimly and at several removes, the broad movements of Euroamerican culture.

Diego de Landa's careful description of the people he had persecuted tempers the intolerance of the Counter Reformation with the humanism of the Renaissance. The increasingly explicit instructions given to successive Spanish expeditions to Palenque in the eighteenth century reflect, first, the impact of science in Baroque Europe, an impact that had begun in the late seventeenth century; second, the tendency to adopt archaeology into the service of government, often for explicitly political purposes (Klindt-Jensen 1976); and third, the general interest in early human societies aroused by the Encyclopaedists and the new intellectual milieu of the Enlightenment (Harris 1968).

John Lloyd Stephens's vivid descriptions of jungle-clad ruins, which aroused strong interest in the Maya on both sides of the Atlantic, are a sober sidelight on the Romantic movement that had arisen as a response to Enlightenment rationalism. Books of travels were widely read—Kinglake's *Eothen* perhaps more widely than Stephens's own *Incidents of Travel in Egypt, Arabia Petraea and the Holy Land*—and although the literary taste for ruins had already fallen to parody in *Northanger Abbey*, the academic study of them was burgeoning with the foundation of national and regional archaeological societies in several countries.

The concerted attack on the mysteries of Maya hieroglyphic writing in the last quarter of the nineteenth century was a response to the successful decipherment of the Middle Eastern scripts. Champollion's elucidation of Egyptian hieroglyphics in 1822 was followed several decades later by the cracking of cuneiform by Rawlinson and others—ancient writing systems were clearly not insoluble problems.

After World War I the domination of Maya studies by the Carnegie Institution seems to have turned the field in on itself, in spite of the continuing infusion of people and ideas from North American archaeology. The *Kulturkreise* school, which had such an impact on European archaeology; the modified Marxism of Childe; the methodological revolution headed by Wheeler; and the ecological archaeology of Clark found no response among Mayanists. A preoccupation with art, architecture, and epigraphy created a massive data base devoid of explanatory models, a failing trenchantly criticized by Kluckhohn (1940). In some ways, however, this disciplinary solipsism was also definitive. Once a laggard imitator of academic fashions originating elsewhere, Maya archaeology became a distinct field of study in its own right, and since its intellectual reopening in the 1950s, it has increasingly been a donor rather than just a recipient of new ideas. The narrative that follows will, I hope, show how and by whom this was achieved.

The Spanish Travelers, 1548–1759

The interest in Maya ruins began shortly after the Spanish conquest of Yucatan (Bernal 1977), when the conquistadors and, more important, the priests who had come with them to save new souls, started to explore the land they had subdued. Because the controversy over the humanity of the inhabitants of the New World had been settled by Pope Paul III in 1537, the Spaniards were able to accept the Maya, who had fought them tenaciously for a generation already, as people like themselves. The Spanish capital, Mérida, was built on the ruins of Tihoo (as, in the highlands of Guatemala 20 years before, the Cakchiquel town of Iximche had become the first Spanish capital there), and it does not seem to have occurred to the Spanish that the older ruins derived from any people other than the ancestors of the sixteenth-century Maya. As a result, we have a number of casual mentions and descriptions of ruins but no record of a planned exploration of sites and no sense that the Maya past should be studied.

The first mention of a precontact period Maya site seems to be that of Lorenzo de Bienvenida, a Franciscan based at Mérida in 1548, who remarked on the "beautiful buildings" of Tihoo, saying that "in all the discoveries in the Indies none so fine has been found. Buildings of big and well-carved stones— there is no record of who built them. It seems to us they were built before Christ, because the trees on top of the buildings were as high as the ones around them. Amongst these buildings we, monks of the Order of St. Francis, settled" (quoted in Bernal 1977:21).

As Bernal notes, we have here an admiration for the vanished builders and an idea of great antiquity, with no attempt to attribute the ruins to any people, Maya or otherwise. The observation that the ruins must be old because of the size of the trees growing on them antedates by two and a half centuries Thomas Jefferson's circular on behalf of the American Philosophical Society. Discussing tumuli in the eastern United States, Jefferson suggests that "the diameter of the largest tree growing thereon, the number of its annulars, and the species of the tree, may tend to give some idea of their antiquity" (quoted in Willey and Sabloff 1980:29). Jefferson was, of course, more precise, and Bienvenida did not appreciate the speed at which tropical trees can grow, but Bienvenida's attribution of an age of more than one and a half millennia to a Maya ruin, at a time when the age of the world itself was not thought to exceed 6,000 years *(As You Like It,* IV, 1, 97–98), is remarkable. Judging from Bienvenida's remarks on the quality of the stonework, he was probably describing a Puuc-style building only seven or eight centuries old.

The following year Diego de Landa arrived in Yucatan and soon became Provincial of the Franciscan Order. His repression of Maya culture culminated in the Mani *auto-da-fé* of 1562, when, to destroy "superstitions and falsehoods of the devil," he had dozens of codices burned, even while acknowledging that they were used by the Maya to record "antiquities and their sciences." He was recalled to Spain to answer charges of overenthusiasm and was severely censured by the Council of the Indies before being acquitted by a jury of his friends and sent back to Yucatan as Bishop in 1573. As part of his defense Diego de Landa prepared, apparently from detailed notes, a briefing document describing the culture and customs of the Maya he was accused of oppressing. His *Relación de las Cosas de Yucatán* (Tozzer 1941) remained unread in the Madrid archives until 1863 and had no influence on the development of Maya studies until that date, yet it shows us, more than any other source of the period, a Spanish intellectual attitude to the Maya past.

Landa noted that the ruins he had seen indicated a former prosperity in Yucatan. He examined several theories that had been advanced for their construction, including religious devotion, frequent settlement shifts, and a way of absorbing surplus labor. Whatever the answer, he determined, the builders of the ruins were certainly the Maya, because there were sculptures in Maya clothing on some of them (probably an early reference to the Monjas at Uxmal), and because in a pot found in a demolished structure there were "three counters of fine stone, such as the Indians today use as money" (presumably a cache of jade beads). Here we have a cool deduction from the material evidence, to which Landa added the observation that the bones found in the pot were of a person larger than the contemporary Maya, and that this fitted in with the height of the steps on the staircases of the ruins.

The *Relación* also presented several rough plans of Maya sites, including Izamal, where Landa's monastery stood atop one of the major structures, and Tihoo (Mérida), where a plaza was surrounded by ranges of buildings, including one of circular plan. At Chichen Itza, Landa seems to have planned the Castillo on the spot: as Tozzer (1941:178, note 934) points out, the nine tiers, rounded corners, number of steps, and serpent heads at the base of the northern stair are all noted in his sketch or text. In his own way, Landa was the equal of the contemporary antiquaries of Tudor England (Kendrick 1950) and southern Scandinavia (Klindt-Jensen 1976), perhaps reflecting the same Renaissance stimuli. Like them, he recorded information from living informants, as well as describing monuments. The *Relación* is most widely known for Landa's outline of the Maya calendar and his attempt to transliterate a Maya "alphabet." These two aspects of the work were to have the greatest impact on Maya studies when it was published three centuries later.

Uxmal was certainly known by 1588, when Ponce visited it and remarked upon the "shapes of naked Indians with their loin cloths . . . which would seem to indicate the building to be Indian" (Ciudad Real 1872). His estimated age of nine hundred years was close to the truth. Twelve years earlier Diego García de Palacio had been sent to examine the ruins of Copan, far to the south, and had noted a cultural link with Yucatan: "They say that in ancient days a great gentleman arrived from the province of Yucatan and built these buildings . . . it seems among all the rubbish they talk this is the most certain" (1860). Here we have a notion of the cultural unity of the Maya area nearly three centuries before John Lloyd Stephens made a similar deduction on the basis of the hieroglyphic inscriptions of Copan, Palenque, and Uxmal and also, in the legend reported by García de Palacio, perhaps some folk memory of the Classic Period surviving for over half a millennium among the Chorti. Like Landa's manuscript, García de Palacio's report remained filed in the archives until 1840, when Stephens and Catherwood had already re-explored the ruins of Copan. Although descriptively far in advance of its time—Maudslay (1889–1902) remarking in the 1880s that "it might have been written by any intelligent visitor within the last ten years"—the Palacio document had no contemporary or later impact on the progress of Maya exploration.

The same can be said of all the sixteenth- and seventeenth-century friars and soldiers who were impressed enough to report on Maya ruins as "sumptuous . . . crowded with well carved figures" and as "beautiful buildings, so much art and sumptuousness . . . carefully carved stone" or who remarked on "the grandeur and beauty of Yucatan's buildings . . . the most remarkable of all the things discovered in the Indies," of which "Uxmal deserves great and special admiration." Their hard-headed ascription of the ruins to the Maya and their recognition of hieroglyphic writing for what it was—Ciudad Real's "characters and letters of those used by the Maya Indians in the old times," Landa's "characters that they use," and García de Palacio's "letters of unknown meaning"—did not excite any attention in the scholarly world.

Thus, initial European contact with the Maya past consisted of dissociated, often brief descriptions of individual sites or objects, among which Landa's compilation of ethnographic material and his own observations of ruins are outstanding. There was an overall assumption that the Maya had indeed built the ruins at some unspecified but not antediluvian time in the past, an appreciation of the quality of workmanship involved, and a recognition that these were the remains of a literate people. However, the reports had no specific archaeological or historical purpose (except perhaps for some of Landa's field notes on ruins); these prosaic and often incidental descriptions were made by men whose main thoughts were directed elsewhere.

Official Exploration, 1759–1840

A period of interest in archaeology throughout the Spanish Empire began with the accession of Charles III (1759–83) and continued through the reign of his successor Charles IV (1783–1808). While King of Naples and the Two Sicilies from 1735 to 59, Charles III had encouraged and sponsored the excavations at Pompeii, and during his reign the ideas of the Enlightenment spread through Spain (Bernal 1977:26), stimulating interest in the evolution of human society, as they had earlier in the century in England and France (Harris 1968).

Halfway through the reign of Charles III, Ramón Ordoñez y Aguiar, a rural priest in Chiapas, organized a small expedition to the "stone houses" that he had been told existed near Palenque, in the lowland rainforests in the north of the province. He reported his findings informally to Jose de Estachería, the governor of Guatemala, who in turn demanded an official report from his local subordinate, José Calderón. Calderón (Bernasconi and Calderón 1946) reported in December 1784 that there were 215 buildings, mostly ruined, including one which, "given its construction and magnitude could not be less than a palace"; he ascribed the ruins to the Romans.

Estachería's interest was aroused, and in the first part of 1785 he instructed Antonio Bernasconi (the royal architect who was at that time working in Guatemala on the new capital, following the disastrous earthquake of 1773) to establish the age of the site and its size, the origin of its people and size of population, whether it was fortified, the materials and style of the architecture, and why it had been abandoned. These remarkably detailed and explicit instructions may reflect some royal directive already extant.

Bernasconi's report in August 1785 noted the uniqueness of the architecture, though describing it as "somewhat gothic" (Bernasconi and Calderón 1946:39). The report was sent to Charles III, who insisted on further exploration, partly at the urging of the royal historiographer, Juan Bautista Muñoz, who at the time was working on a history of the Spanish American empire. The royal command demanded specific detail on the "shapes, sizes and cut of the stones and bricks, particularly in arches and vaults," distinction "between doors, niches and windows," and "samples of plaster, mixture, stucco, bricks (baked or otherwise), pots or any other utensils or tools that may be found, digging where necessary" (Muñoz 1946:43). Here for the first time we have a request for material to be sent back for analysis, clearly for its evidential value rather than for display, and also the first injunction to excavate for evidence. The commission also indicated the motive for the orders, to "illustrate the origins and history of the old Americans."

It took 14 months for the expedition thus authorized actually to reach Palenque, which it did on May 3, 1787, under the command of Captain Antonio del Río, and including the artist Ricardo Almendariz. Del Río took his orders seriously and reported, with some exaggeration, that "no window or blocked door, room, corridor, patio, tower, prayer room or crypt . . . has not been excavated." He determined that Palenque had been built by the same people as the ruins of Yucatan, on the basis of a description of Uxmal and other sites, and also fulfilled his commission by sending back a number of artifacts to Spain. Both the instructions given him and the way Del Río executed them represent archaeology as it was then recognized. His report and Almendariz's drawings, instead of being buried in the archives of Spain, reached London and a generation later were published as "Description of the Ruins of an Ancient City" (del Río 1822), with 16 plates engraved from the drawings by Jean-Frédéric Waldeck, who was working in London at the time.

Charles IV enlarged his predecessor's policy of official exploration of ancient sites within the empire, and in 1804 commissioned Guillermo Dupaix, a retired captain of dragoons with antiquarian interests, to survey the principal ruins of Mexico.

Dupaix worked eastward from the Basin of Mexico, and on his third and last expedition in 1807 reached the Maya lands. In Ciudad Real (now San Cristóbal de Las Casas) he met the aged Ramón Ordoñez y Aguiar and then proceeded with his artist, José Castañeda, to Palenque. There they worked methodically. Dupaix described the stucco sculptures in technical detail, noting the use of a core, the hardness and purity of stucco, and the traces of red pigment remaining in the folds. He also appraised them aesthetically, finding the figures "erect and well proportioned; all of them are in profile, portly and almost colossal, their height exceeding six feet. Their dress, though sumptuous, never wholly covers the body." In the Temple of the Cross Dupaix examined the intricate relief panel and decided "that it was not the holy Latin Cross which we adore, but a Greek Cross disfigured with various fantastical ornaments . . . we must therefore refer this allegorical symbol to the religion of the country. . . ."

His overall conclusions followed the same sober line: that the art of Palenque was probably original, with not even any close relationship to that of central Mexico. Castañeda's drawings were as responsible as Dupaix's descriptions and strove for accuracy. Dupaix's report, like Del Río's, ended up in London, where in 1830–31 it was published in Lord Kingsborough's massive compendium, *Antiquities of Mexico*. It also appeared in Paris in 1834, winning the prize offered by the Société de Géographie for work in Central America (and thus frustrating Waldeck, who had spent much of 1832–33 at the site gathering material and making drawings and molds of the sculptures). Dupaix's work aroused considerable interest in the United States and in Yucatan itself. Waldeck's *Voyage pittoresque et archeologique dans . . . Yucatan* (1838), the first fruits of his chagrin, led directly to the next major exploration in the Maya area, which transformed the public and scholarly attitude toward the whole subject.

This was the first expedition in 1839–40 of John Lloyd Stephens and Frederick Catherwood. Already a wealthy and well-known author of travel books (Von Hagen 1947), Stephens decided to visit the ruins of Palenque, Uxmal, and Copan, the three sites then widely known about (the last of these from the work of Juan Galindo [Graham 1963]), with further publication in mind. He recruited Catherwood, an English architect then practicing in New York, and bound him with a detailed contract that showed clearly how aware Stephens was of the value of his output. Catherwood would "not publish directly or indirectly the said drawings nor any narration of the incidents of his journey . . . and not in any way interfere with the rights of the said Stephens to the absolute and exclusive use of all the information drawings and material collected on the said journey." In return he was to receive his travel costs and a fee of $1,500, from which $25 a week would be paid to his family during his absence.

Stephens secured a diplomatic appointment from President Van Buren, and in October 1839 the two men traveled via Belize to Guatemala. Their brief stay in Belize stimulated a rival expedition to Palenque led by Patrick Walker, the colony's secretary, but it had no impact on Maya studies (Pendergast 1967). The first site Stephens and Catherwood visited was Copan, where the stelae impressed Stephens greatly:

> .. a square stone column, about fourteen feet high and three feet on each side, sculptured in very bold relief and on all four of the sides from the base to the top. The front was the figure of a man curiously and richly dressed and the face, evidently a portrait, solemn, stern and well fitted to excite terror. The back was of a different design, unlike anything we had ever seen before, and the sides were covered with hieroglyphics. . . . The sight of this unexpected monument put at rest once and for ever, in our minds, all uncertainty in regard to the character of American antiquities, and gave us the assurance that the objects we were in search of were interesting, not only as the remains of an unknown people but as works of art, proving, like newly-discovered historical records, that the people who once occupied the Continent of America were not savages. (Stephens 1841, I:102)

This passage epitomizes Stephens's style—literate, involved, yet both sober and precise—and Catherwood's drawings, done with a *camera lucida*, complement the text in detail and clarity. Even as they explored the site, however, Stephens was thinking ahead: he bought the ruins of Copan for $50 with the intention of shipping one of the stelae and casts of the others to New York "to be the nucleus of a great national museum of American antiquities." It would be another seven years before the Smithsonian Institution was founded.

Many of the views that Stephens formed during his two weeks at Copan and the subsequent three weeks at Palenque sound refreshingly modern. He observed that the people who reared [the hieroglyphic inscriptions] had published a record of themselves, through which we might one day hold conference with a perished race, and unveil the mystery that hung over the city" (Stephens 1841, I:152). There was "room for the belief that the whole of this country was once occupied by the same race, speaking the same language, or at least having the same written characters." At Palenque "there was no necessity for assigning to the ruined city an immense extent, or an antiquity coeval with the Egyptians or any other ancient and known people. . . . Here were the remains of a cultivated, polished and peculiar people, who had passed through all the stages incidental to the rise and fall of nations, reached their golden age and perished, entirely unknown" (Stephens 1841, II:356).

Stephens wrote up his travels swiftly upon returning to New York, and after delays caused by the difficulty of engraving Catherwood's extremely delicate drawings, *Incidents of Travel in Central America, Chiapas and Yucatan* appeared in June 1841. Fewer than 200 of the 900 pages were devoted to archaeology (Stephens had taken his diplomatic mission seriously and spent a fair portion of the ten months' journey trying to fulfill it), although most of the full-page engravings were of Maya sculpture and buildings, together with a map of Copan, a plan of the Palace at Palenque and architects' plans and elevations of the Temple of the Inscriptions there.

The book became a bestseller, racing through twelve printings in three months and bringing Maya ruins to the attention of a wide audience for the first time. Stephens's narrative was as lively as in his earlier books but spiced with the thrill of discovery. What made the book a landmark in the development of Maya archaeology however, was the sobriety of detail, as well as the intelligence and restraint of the speculation. Stephens observed:

> [there are] not sufficient grounds for the belief in the great antiquity that has been ascribed to thse ruins . . . they were constructed by the race who occupied the country at the time of the invasion by the Spaniards, or some not very distant progenitors . . . different from the works of any other known people, of a new order, and entirely and absolutely anomalous. They stand alone: we have a conclusion far more interesting and wonderful than that of connecting the builders of these cities with the Egyptians or any other people. It is the spectacle of a people skilled in architecture, sculpture, and drawing, not derived from the Old World but originating and growing up here without models or masters, having a distinct, separate, independent existence; like the plants and fruits of the soil, indigenous. (Stephens 1841, II:442–43)

Although Stephens had come to the same common-sense conclusion as the earlier Spanish travelers, in 1841 it was a refreshing change from the antediluvian antiquity suggested by Dupaix and the transoceanic inspiration argued by Waldeck. By putting ancient Maya civilization just beyond the limits of recorded history, Stephens made it a topic to be taken seriously. The widespread acceptance of his views ushered in a new phase in Maya studies.

The phase of official exploration had seen multiple expeditions to Palenque, which until Stephens's book appeared was the best known Maya site, with less attention paid to Copan and Uxmal. Stephens and Catherwood added a fourth major site, Quirigua, to the list, together with smaller sites at Utatlan and Ocosingo. Stephens decided on a more intensive survey to locate additional sites, and formed the notion of a museum of American antiquities to display the finds from the Maya lands. In 1839 John Lloyd Stephens had been a dilettante, an intelligent amateur pursuing antiquarianism and authorship together; by 1841 he had become a resourceful and well-read scholar, and it is entirely appropriate that his second expedition should mark a new period and a new approach.

Scientific Explorers and Major Scholars, 1841–1924

The 1841–1842 expedition was the first planned reconnaissance in the Maya area. Instead of visiting reported sites, Stephens and Catherwood were seeking new ones, confining themselves to the northern part of the Yucatan Peninsula, and setting out with explicitly archaeological and scientific motives. Catherwood brought along daguerreotype apparatus in order to record sculpture more objectively (although he soon found that his eyes and pencil were more accurate and discriminating), and Stephens recruited Samuel Cabot, Jr., a twenty-six-year-old Harvard medical graduate and amateur naturalist, to collect and identify the strange plants and animals noted on the previous journey.

They visited Mayapan on the way to Uxmal, where the previous expedition had been curtailed by Catherwood's malaria. While Catherwood drew the ruins, Stephens set out on horseback around the area, seeking other ruins and making copious notes on contemporary settlements. The proximity of many sites to existing villages led Stephens to speculate that the Spanish had settled on the margins of communities, and by a combination of ritual competition and killing off the Maya leaders had gradually made their own churches the foci of activity. Settlements had then clustered around them, leaving the old temples abandoned in the fields on the edge of town (Stephens 1843, I:274). Although incorrect, this model of settlement drift is a good example of the way Stephens's mind worked. Another is the way in which he deduced the function of the ball court at Uxmal on the basis of the structural evidence and excavation (Stephens 1843 I:298–99), linked it to the court at Chichen Itza on the basis of the stone rings and the parallel mounds, and then noted Herrera's description of the Aztec ball game and proposed a connection between the Aztec and Maya cultures, a "resemblance in manners and institutions," which is an early recognition of the unity of Mesoamerica (Stephens 1843, II:304–8).

They found a new major site at Kabah, and Stephens's interest in forming a museum in New York, having waned after the first expedition, was revived to the extent of extracting a carved lintel and several stone reliefs and sending them back; the reliefs survive in the American Museum of Natural History, but the lintel, together with the rest of their collection, was destroyed in the disastrous Broadway fire of 1842, which consumed Catherwood's famous Panorama of Jerusalem building.

From the Puuc sites they progressed to Chichen Itza and Tulum. Although Stephens thought that the Toltec-Maya hybrid architecture of Chichen was earlier than Puuc, he correctly surmised that Tulum was of late date, believing it to have been inhabited at the time of Spanish contact. Via Silan, Izamal, and Ake, the group returned to Mérida and then to New York.

Incidents of Travel in Yucatan was published within nine months of their return and emulated the success of the first book. Unlike the 1841 work, it was almost entirely concerned with archaeological exploration, used Spanish sources, such as Herrera and Cogolludo, intelligently, and included two appendices by the Yucatecan scholar Pio Perez (whom Stephens had met at Ticul) on the Maya calendar and the pre-Hispanic history of Yucatan.

Shortly after its publication, a young French priest, Charles Etienne Brasseur de Bourbourg, was posted to Boston. Having been introduced to Prescott's *History of the Conquest of Mexico* (1844), he traveled south in 1849 and became addicted to Mesoamerican studies. After returning to Paris (where he made full use of Aubin's magnificent library), he obtained leave to travel in Central America, and from 1854 to 1857 lived in Nicaragua and Guatemala, including a year as parish priest in the Quiche town of Rabinal. There he found a pre-Hispanic drama still alive in oral tradition and transcribed it: the *Rabinal-Achi* remains one of the few surviving fragments of Maya literature.

Another fragment, the *Popol Vuh,* survived in the capital but had already been recorded; Scherzer's Quiche edition with Ximénez's Spanish text appeared in 1857, Brasseur's French/Quiche version not until 1861. The work that made his reputation was the *Histoire des nations civilisées de Mexique et de l'Amérique Central* (1857–59), the four-volume synthesis of his accumulated knowledge and ideas.

It is not, however, for this magnum opus that we remember him, but for two discoveries made prosaically in the archives of Madrid a few years later: part of the Madrid Codex, and the copy of Landa's *Relación de las Cosas de Yucatán* (1864). Brasseur was essentially a library scholar, the first of the armchair Mayanists who were to make such an impact over the following half century or so—De Rosny, Thomas, Förstemann, Goodman, and Bowditch. As the heading of this section suggests, Maya scholarship in the second half of the nineteenth century split into two groups: the epigraphers working on the codices and monumental inscriptions as these were recorded in the field, and the field explorers in the tradition of Stephens, who sought and investigated new sites.

Although Leon de Rosny had by 1876 deciphered the directional glyphs, working with the Madrid and Paris Codices, and across the Atlantic in 1882 Cyrus Thomas showed that inscriptions were read by pairs of columns from the upper left corner, the most important of the epigraphers was Ernst Förstemann, librarian to the Elector of Saxony in Dresden. His library held the Dresden Codex, already published half a century earlier by Kingsborough and illustrated even earlier by Humboldt (1816, I:plate XVI) as being Aztec. Working with Brasseur's edition of Landa and with Pio Perez's calendric treatise so acutely published by Stephens, Förstemann (1880) was able to show that the Maya had used place notation to base 20, and also deciphered the signs for zero/completion. With these principles established, he unraveled the Venus tables in the Dresden Codex and, taking Landa's "calculation of ages" based on the *katun,* demonstrated the existence and structure of the Long Count. Field data provided by Alfred Maudslay from Copan enabled Förstemann to test his ideas on fresh material, and in 1894 he read seven Initial Series from the stelae there.

The structure of the Maya calendar was now clear, but it had not been correlated with the Christian calendar to anchor it firmly in time. This final step was taken by Joseph T. Goodman, a West Coast newspaper proprietor working from Förstemann's material and Maudslay's publications, together with historical information from Landa and others. From 1905 the Maya were part of dated history and Goodman's correlation survives in its essentials today.

Field archaeology in the Maya area in the last two decades of the nineteenth century was dominated by two men, Alfred Maudslay and Teobert Maler. Maudslay, the scion of an inventive middle-class English family (Graham 1977), had by chance become a colonial administrator in the South Pacific and was visiting Guatemala on vacation when he first saw Quirigua and Copan. He was astounded "how more important were these monuments... than any account I had heard of them led me to expect," and determined to record them fully. He returned again and again between 1883 and 1894, equipped with paper and plaster of Paris for making molds, surveying instruments, and a large plate camera, and explored Tikal, Palenque, and Chichen Itza after Quirigua and Copan. One of his earliest visits was to Yaxchilan, whence he removed under permit several sculptures to the British Museum and also had his celebrated encounter with the French explorer Désiré Charnay, who in 1858 had made a pioneering photographic record of Uxmal and Palenque.

Maudslay's assiduous and skillful work remains unmatched; he elevated the study of Maya archaeology to a new level of competence. His photographs and the drawings made from his casts by Annie Hunter (Maudslay 1889–1902) are still primary research tools, and the casts themselves are often in better condition than the original monuments. He did not claim to be a scholar, but his help to others, especially Förstemann and Goodman (whose work he had published as an appendix to his own), was instrumental in the advances they made in epigraphy. He was also responsible for encouraging Adela Breton (Carmichael 1973, Miller 1977), who made valuable contributions to the field. In his view of archaeology as a collaborative discipline, as well as in his rigorous technique, Maudslay thoroughly justifies H. E. D. Pollock's view of him as "the first modern archaeologist in the Maya field."

Teobert Maler worked in the Maya lowlands at the same time as Maudslay, in the later 1880s and 1890s, but apart from the common venue of their work, the two men were very different in their approaches. Whereas Maudslay operated like an army on the move, establishing a base camp and then blanketing a site with methodical efficiency, Maler moved like a guerilla through the rainforest, traveling light with his local workmen under taxing conditions that even he admitted were "a kind of immolation" (Maler 1903:105). From 1884 onward, he explored a series of sites in the Usumacinta basin, including Piedras Negras, Altar de Sacrificios, and Seibal, and also discovered the great center of Coba in northern Quintana Roo. His reports were published by the Peabody Museum of Harvard University (which had been founded in 1866 and became interested in Maya archaeology in the early 1880s) between 1901 and 1911 in Volumes II, IV, and V of the newly established *Memoirs* (Maler 1901, 1903, 1908a, 1908b, 1910, 1911). Until the 1930s, this series was devoted entirely to publication of Maya archaeology in a large format, and until Spinden's *A Study of Maya Art* (1913) appeared as Volume VI, it reported only the results of original fieldwork. Unfortunately Maler quarreled with the Peabody, which he decided was making a profit by selling these sumptuous volumes, and his work on Tikal had to be brought to press by Alfred M. Tozzer. Maler died in 1917, and as Brunhouse (1975) has noted, the anti-German jingoism of the time (Maler was an Austrian who had lived almost entirely in Mexico since 1865) left his contribution to Maya archaeology insufficiently appreciated. Although his records were careful and his photographs superb, both his tenacity and his achievement are still undervalued.

When it took on Maler's material, the Peabody Museum had already been involved in sponsoring and publishing fieldwork in the Maya area for some years. Volume I of the *Memoirs* contained six contributions: three on Copan (where Maudslay had taken over the 1894 excavations on the death of John Owens, the Peabody's director there); one on the Ulua Valley in northwestern Honduras, these mainly by George Byron Gordon; and two on work in Yucatan by Edward H. Thompson.

Thompson's entry into the Maya field differed from those of Maudslay and Maler: while the former had come from colonial administration and the latter from soldiering, Thompson was brought in as an enthusiastic young man specifically (if unofficially) to carry out exploration in Yucatan for the Peabody Museum. His advancement was due to the influence of Stephen Salisbury, Jr., a noted Massachusetts antiquarian, and his formal appointment, as United States consul in Mérida, was not a time-consuming one.

Working initially at Labna, Thompson concluded that the bottle-shaped subterranean chambers he called *chultunes* were used for storage and underscored the significance of the settlement area surrounding the large ceremonial structures. The small platforms were "once covered by the mud-walled, palm-thatched houses of these humbler classes.... Excavating these sites I find the ever-present *koben,* the three-stone fireplace, the broken pottery in the ashes, the fractured *metatl* and roller with which the corn was ground, and children's toys in the shape of polished sea-shells and bits of figured clay, hard-burned" (Thompson 1892:263). The ratio of corn-grinding equipment to houses was similar to that in contemporary Maya villages, and Thompson calculated that the diet must have been similar also: some 80 percent maize, 12 percent other vegetable crops, and 8 percent meat. The similarity of the dwellings led him to conclude in his 1892 paper that the "Ancient Structures of Yucatan [were] not Communal Dwellings." Viewing Maya culture as a whole, he thought that the "ruins indicate a considerable civilization ... above the communal pueblos of the Southwest, but not of that advanced state of progress that sends forth a far-reaching influence" (Thompson 1886:254).

The sensible conclusions of Thompson's early work have perhaps been forgotten in the subsequent notoriety that he acquired for his work at Chichen Itza. Having helped Maudslay there in 1889, he bought the site and in 1904 began to dredge in the Sacred Cenote. After modest initial results, gold and jade objects began to emerge, together with human bones, copal incense balls, and other unexpected finds. Much of the material was quietly sent to the Peabody Museum, where it was studied for many years (Lothrop 1952; Proskouriakoff 1974; Tozzer 1957), and much of it has subsequently been returned to Mexico. The finds gave a new aspect to Maya studies: for the first time a considerable quantity of diverse artifactual materials was available, and the human remains were the most substantial corpus of evidence on the physical traits of the ancient Maya themselves.

Other individuals were exploring the Maya area toward the end of the century with varying degrees of competence, adding to the foundations that were laid by Förstemann, Maudslay, and Maler. Maudslay had been preceded in the highlands of Guatemala by the Germans Bastian and Habel in the mid-

1870s (Bastian 1878–89; Habel 1878) and was succeeded by the German polymath Karl Sapper, whose early archaeological observations (1895a, 1895b, 1898) were followed over the succeeding 40 years by papers on ethnography, geology, and climate. Sapper's original contribution was in "using assemblage, orientation, construction practices and broad matters of design" to classify "the remains into architectural types associated with ethnographic and linguistic areas" (Pollock 1940:190)—a reflection, perhaps, of the notion of archaeological culture areas then current in his native Germany.

The work at Copan by Marshall Saville (1892) and George Byron Gordon (1896, 1898a, 1902) continued investigation of one of the best-known Maya sites, while in the Crown Colony of British Honduras a young Irish doctor, Thomas Gann, found and recorded the unusual Mixtec/Maya murals at the Postclassic site of Santa Rita (Gann 1897, 1900). In the first decade and a half of the new century the dichotomy between epigraphic study and field archaeology continued. The contributors to the *Papers of the Peabody Museum*, a smaller format monograph series that began in 1888 and printed its first Maya contributions in Volume IV, included Paul Schellhas (1904), who analyzed and systematized the deity representations in the codices; Förstemann (1906), in an English translation of his commentary on the Dresden Codex; and Tozzer (Tozzer and Allen:1910), on animal representations in the codices. Of these authors, Tozzer was the only one also to do fieldwork. He had already published his classic study of the Maya and Lacandon (1907), his report on work at Tikal (1911) was in press, and another report on Nakum (1913) was in preparation. These field reports set a high standard for later workers. Charles P. Bowditch, also at the Peabody, brought together the material on Maya writing in *The Numeration, Calendar Systems, and Astronomical Knowledge of the Mayas* (1910), the first synthesis in this field.

The Peabody also launched two talented field archaeologists in this period, who had different interests, however, and, as it turned out, contrasting careers. Raymond Merwin carried out a series of expeditions between 1910 and 1915 in the little-explored eastern lowlands, including Quintana Roo, Belize, and part of Peten (Merwin 1913). He was the first archaeologist to investigate or make an accurate record of several important sites, including Rio Bec and Lubaantun. At the latter center he excavated between two parallel mounds and found three carved markers depicting a ball game in progress (Hammond 1975:fig. 148)—the first identification of a ball court in the tropical forest zone of the southern lowlands. Merwin's most important work was at Holmul, in northeastern Peten, where in excavating a series of superimposed temples and their associated tombs he identified the first stratified ceramic sequence known in the Maya area. The first phase, Holmul I, dated to the end of the

Formative and is the type assemblage for the "Protoclassic" manifestation in the lowlands; Holmul V fell in the Late Classic. Unfortunately illness prevented Merwin from publishing his work, and it was eventually written up after his death by George C. Vaillant (Merwin and Vaillant 1932): by the time it appeared, the Uaxactun sequence was already known in outline and became the basis of ceramic comparison for the Maya lowlands. Much of Merwin's field work remains unpublished; his description of Lubaantun appeared only in 1975 (in Hammond 1975:260–267).

Slightly younger than Merwin, Sylvanus G. Morley had a passionate interest in Maya hieroglyphic writing, and much of his career was devoted to tracking down inscribed monuments in the Peten rainforest, assisted by *chicleros* and widely distributed notices saying "¡Ojo! ¡Ojo! ¡Ojo!" and offering $25 for each inscription reported. Morley's career has been exhaustively chronicled by Brunhouse (1971) and its incidentals noted in *Morleyana* (1950). He began fieldwork (after publishing a comment on the Tuxtla Statuette as early as 1907 and an article on the Naranjo inscriptions in 1909) as an assistant to Edgar L. Hewett at Quirigua in 1910–12 (a project which, incidentally, made some study of domestic structures and is of interest because of its sponsorship by the School of American Research and the publication of its report by the Archaeological Institute of America, both institutions that dropped out of the Maya field after World War I, apart from publishing occasional papers or books). Morley's bent toward epigraphy was already formed, however, and the *Introduction to the Study of the Maya Hieroglyphs* was published in 1915, the first nonspecialist compilation on this topic, although less general than Morley perhaps thought. Morley's interests were broader than that, however: in 1914 he had persuaded the Carnegie Institution of Washington to sponsor a program of field research at Chichen Itza. Had the war not supervened, the institutional period in Maya archaeology would have begun a decade earlier. As it was, Morley's work between 1914 and 1924 followed the pattern of the earlier scholarly explorers, Maudslay, Maler, Merwin, and Tozzer, mounting annual expeditions in search of sites and monuments. His major impact on the development of Maya archaeology came later.

The period just before the outbreak of war saw the publication of several other important syntheses, apart from Morley's epigraphic study. Herbert J. Spinden's *A Study of Maya Art* (1913), appearing as Volume VI of the *Memoirs of the Peabody Museum,* was an exercise in iconography and architectural analysis that remains in large part valid today, and Thomas Joyce's *Mexican Archaeology* (1914) was a pioneering synopsis of the available museum material and publications. Eduard Seler's monumental series, *Gesammelte Abhandlungen* (1902–23) used iconographic and documentary evidence to illuminate the archaeological data and construct culture sequences; his studies of Palenque and Uxmal were published in Berlin in 1915 and 1917, respectively. Between 1914 and 1919, William H. Holmes's series, "Masterpieces of Aboriginal American Art," appeared in the new journal *Art and Archaeology*, including his views on Maya architecture first advanced 20 years before (Holmes 1895–97).

As war engulfed Europe, and then in 1917 drew in the United States, Maya archaeology was moving from the period of individual achievement to one of topical synthesis. A major result of the war was the virtual withdrawal of European scholars and institutions from the field for a considerable time, and its domination by workers from the United States, and in particular from the Carnegie Institution.

Institutional Domination, 1924–70

Willey and Sabloff (1974, 1980), in their history of American archaeology, begin a third major classificatory-historical period with the introduction in 1914 of stratigraphic excavation and the emergent concern with regional chronologies. However, the complications of Mexican and subsequently of world politics delayed a new era in Maya archaeology for another ten years. The Carnegie Institution had committed itself to a Middle American program in 1914, but the exploring expeditions that Sylvanus G. Morley, the director of the program, was able to carry out during and after the war were essentially along the same lines as those of Maler, seeking new inscriptions and ruins.

The Carnegie Period, which has long been recognized as significant (Pollock 1940:194, Adams 1969), began in 1924 with the ambitious program of excavation and restoration at Chichen Itza under Morley's direction, which ran until 1933, and continued with the Uaxactun excavations of 1926–38. Its effective end came with World War II, even though a third major project at Mayapan began in the early 1950s and ended only in 1958 with the abolition of the Division of Historical Research. The division was based not in Washington, but next to the Peabody Museum on the Harvard campus, promoting cooperation between the two institutions (which included transfer of the division's archives to the Peabody after 1958). These two institutions, together with the University Museum of the University of Pennsylvania, dominated Maya research from 1924 until the end of the 1960s, although the Middle American Research Institute of Tulane University was also strong in Yucatan, the British Museum was briefly in the field at the beginning and end of the period, and the New World Archaeological Founcation began a long-term program in Chiapas in the mid 1950s.

Morley was one of the last major figures in the period of individual scholarly enterprise and small-scale expeditions, and he became the first manager of a large institutional project. The work at Chichen Itza was conceived on a grand scale, bringing into Maya archaeology some of the most noted figures of the period—J. Eric S. Thompson, H. E. D. Pollock, Earl Morris, Karl Ruppert, Oliver Ricketson, Robert Wauchope, and Frans Blom. Blom had set up the Uaxactun camp in 1924, for the second of Morley's major projects, but shortly thereafter was lured away to work for William Gates at the Middle American Research Institute.

The Chichen Itza project became multidisciplinary when Alfred V. Kidder was appointed to head the Division of Historical Research in the late 1920s. Natural scientists were hired to study the flora, fauna, and landscape of Yucatan; an experimental *milpa* was cultivated for several years to investigate corn productivity and the reasons for declining yields after the first two years; and Maya ethnology was studied for the light it could cast on the pre-Hispanic past. The Carnegie program also continued at Copan, where Gustavus Stromsvik was put in charge of another large-scale excavation and reconstruction project. Kidder himself directed one of the most significant excavations, at Kaminaljuyu on the outskirts of Guatemala City, where the strong Teotihuacan links with the Early Classic Maya were documented for the first time (Kidder, Jennings, and Shook 1946).

Through the 1930s the Carnegie Institution's program and personnel epitomized Maya research. The University of Pennsylvania project at Piedras Negras, begun under J. Alden Mason in 1929, was conceived along essentially similar lines (although unlike most Carnegie work, it was never adequately published). Site-centered projects were supplemented by further exploration, particularly in Campeche (Andrews IV 1943; Ruppert and Denison 1943).

The work at Uaxactun was of immense significance for Maya lowland archaeology: dated monuments were linked to architectural stratigraphy, and both stela caches and sherds in dumps and fill were thus placed in time. Although Merwin's Holmul sequence had been the first stratified ceramic sequence in the Maya area, Robert Smith's (1955) four Uaxactun phases represented an advance in that they were more accurately dated. They also extended much farther back in time than the Holmul sequence, because Uaxactun had yielded evidence of two Preclassic Periods, dubbed Mamom and Chicanel, which Smith estimated went back to about 600 B.C.

The importance of the Preclassic was also demonstrated at Uaxactun by the excavation of Structure E-VII-Sub, a late Chicanel pyramid adorned with colossal masks which demonstrated the existence of a complex religious iconography. In spite of this discovery, the Preclassic continued to be regarded as a village-farming culture for years afterward.

The ideas of Oliver G. Ricketson, Jr., one of the senior staff at Uaxactun, were often prescient, but his departure from the Carnegie Institution at the beginning of the war muted the impact of his theories compared with those put forward by men who remained part of the group. Carrying out the first systematic examination of settlement pattern, he advanced the empirical observations of Edward H. Thompson made nearly half a century before. Ricketson established a cruciform sampling area reaching out in the cardinal directions from the center of Uaxactun for a mile (1.6 km) and had the house platforms and chultuns within it counted (Ricketson and Ricketson 1937). On the basis of the 78 platforms recorded—an underestimate, according to more recent work in the region (Puleston 1974:305–306), by some 60 percent)—Ricketson calculated a density of 40 platforms per square kilometer and extrapolated population estimates for the whole of the lowlands. The inaccuracy of his data collection does not obscure the fact "that this was the first gathering and analysis of a large-scale sample of settlement data," and that "some of the essential elements of later settlement studies were there" (Ashmore and Willey 1981:9). Ricketson also followed up his survey by having a 6 percent sample—five of the mounds—excavated by Robert Wauchope (1934) to test the assumption of domestic function. Wauchope (1938) took the study of settlement further by carrying out an ethnological survey of modern Maya houses and examining the perishable components of dwellings.

A recruit in the third field season at Chichen Itza was J. Eric S. Thompson, an Englishman in his late twenties who had experienced the trenches in World War I and life as a *gaucho* in the Argentine, before studying at Cambridge University under A. C. Haddon and teaching himself Maya hieroglyphics (Thompson 1963, Hammond 1977b). Thompson was interviewed by Ricketson, accepted by Morley, and on his arrival at Chichen put to work under Earl Morris on the Temple of the Warriors. In 1927 he accompanied the Second British Museum Expedition to British Honduras, working at Lubaantun under the direction of T. A. Joyce, and at the end of the season exploring the new site of Pusilha to the southwest. Here, as at Coba the previous year, his epigraphic training proved useful.

While he worked in the bush on this new discovery, two of his most noted publications were already in press at the Field Museum of Natural History in Chicago, where he had taken up a position after leaving Morley. The first was his correlation of the Maya and Christian calendars (Thompson 1927), a modification of the 11.16. correlation put forward by Goodman at the beginning of the century and already corroborated by Juan Martínez Hernández from the documentary sources. Thompson's correlation remains in use, although he thought it might someday be superseded by one of greater accuracy.

Thompson's second publication was the first edition of *The Civilization of the Mayas,* a booklet still in print (7th edition, 1973), which demonstrated his ability to summarize and popularize his subject. This ability was most important in helping Thompson to get his ideas accepted by his colleagues (Becker 1979). (Morley's *The Ancient Maya,* published in 1946 at the end of its author's career, demonstrated a similar persuasiveness that had by then been at work for forty years in lectures and discussions.) One conclusion shared by Thompson and Morley was that the noncalendric glyphs on the monuments did not record history, as scholars from Stephens onward had assumed, but dealt with the cosmic progress of deified time and the movements of the planets, sun, and moon. Their agreement on this topic bottled up progress in decipherment for a generation.

Thompson was not only an epigrapher. Versatile as Kidder, his next major contributions were in excavation and ethnography, the twin fruits of his project in the western Maya Mountains in 1929. The work at Tzimin Kax resulted in definition of the house platform cluster on a common basal platform known as a *plazuela* (Thompson 1931:233) and "the concept of the interrelated ceremonial and residential components of Maya settlement" (Willey and Bullard 1965:364). The site also yielded ceramics comparable with those from Holmul I and confirmed Merwin's sequence (which was at that moment being edited for publication by George C. Vaillant).

Thompson employed Maya workers from Socotz on the Belize River. In the evenings in camp he drew from them folk tales, prayers, and descriptions of ritual practices, which he realized were survivals from the pre-Hispanic, perhaps even the Classic, period. He added to these observations those from San Antonio in southern Belize and concluded that "these modern descendants of the ancient Maya still preserved many ancient customs and religious ideas . . . it was clear that archaeological excavations were not the only means of learning about the ancient ways . . . pick and shovel would never reveal the many customs that had survived in San Antonio from an earlier age" (Thompson 1930:160). A perceptive melding of archaeological, documentary, and ethnographic data was to become a hallmark of Thompson's career, and this scholarship has endured better than much of his purely epigraphic work.

Thompson joined the Carnegie staff in 1936, and the Institution took over his current project at San José in British Honduras, an explicit study of a small and, he hoped, typical ceremonial precinct, which counterpointed the emphasis on major centers at Uaxactun, Piedras Negras, and Chichen Itza. Although the excavations and the analysis of pottery and artifacts conformed to a high standard (including a pioneering analysis of ceramic pastes by Anna O. Shepard), Thompson did not pursue his interest in settlement archaeology, and the report (Thompson 1939), "while one of the most admirable . . . of its time, is essentially a descriptive account" (Ashmore and Willey 1981:8). Thereafter, although he established an important Late Classic ceramic sequence at Benque Viejo (Xunantunich) in 1938 (Thompson 1940) and from 1954 to 1957 worked on the last Carnegie project at Mayapan (Thompson and Thompson 1955), he drifted away from fieldwork and spent the 1940s deciphering the noncalendric glyphs. This work resulted in *Maya Hieroglyphic Writing: Introduction* (1950), the outstanding codification of epigraphic progress to date. Thompson's work in this field in the next quarter-century adhered to his conception of the Maya writing system as nonphonetic, combining instead ideograms, verbal puns and homonyms, pictograms, metaphorgrams, symbolic forms, and determinatives. The thesis that the system was essentially phonetic, reiterated by the Russian Yurii Knorosov (1952, 1955) a generation after it had first been advanced by Benjamin Whorf (1933), was trenchantly attacked by Thompson and has begun to attain acceptance only in the past decade or so.

During the years of his "retirement" in England, Thompson produced two major epigraphic works: the *Catalog of Maya Hieroglyphs* (1962) and the *Commentary on the Dresden Codex* (1972a), as well as a brief guide to Maya writing, *Maya Hieroglyphs Without Tears* (1972b), and numerous papers. Until his death in 1975, he remained the most influential of Maya epigraphers, and his characteristic blending of epigraphic, iconographic, and ethnohistoric information culminated in the important studies of Maya deities in *Maya History and Religion* (1970). Thompson's career spans virtually the whole of the institutional period and beyond. Such professional longevity is exceptional even in the Maya field, where many productive scholars have contributed for up to forty years.

One of the most original of Thompson's contemporaries was Tatiana Proskouriakoff, whom Morley lured from the University of Pennsylvania's Piedras Negras project to work with the Carnegie Institution. Her studies of Maya architecture (1946), sculpture (1950), and jades (1974) are classics. Her most important single contribution is probably the 1960 *American Antiquity* paper on the historical nature of the Piedras Negras inscriptions, which is based on the realization that the monuments fell into sets that accorded with the life spans of successive rulers at the site. More than anything else, this paper restored the nineteenth-century historicist view of the Maya monumental inscriptions and opened the way for the important decipherments of the succeeding period. Almost as important, however, was the short paper by Heinrich

Berlin (1958) outlining the form and distribution of site-specific "emblem glyphs," which could sensibly be interpreted only as place or dynasty names and which thus implied at least some secular content to the texts.

Maya field archaeology began again some years after the end of World War II, but the Carnegie Institution never regained its old momentum; a change of central policy led to the abolition of the Division of Historical Research, although a final project was carried out at Mayapan in the 1950s (Pollock, et al. 1962). Two other institutions long active in the Maya field dominated the last twenty years of the period: the Peabody Museum of Harvard University and the University Museum of the University of Pennsylvania.

At Harvard the major impetus came with Gordon R. Willey's appointment to the Bowditch Chair of Mexican and Central American Archaeology and Ethnology. Willey had been working in Peru and Panama, but given Charles Bowditch's obvious intentions when endowing the chair, its holder was expected to work in the Maya field. Willey brought Maya studies the techniques of settlement archaeology that he had used in the Viru Valley of coastal Peru (Willey 1953). For his first project, he selected a rural settlement away from any major ceremonial center: the cluster of some 200 mounds at Barton Ramie, on the middle Belize River. The site was investigated in detail from 1953 to 1956, while at the same time Willey attempted to place the site within the wider context of the river basin, inaugurating the regional approach that has characterized Maya archaeology in the 1970s. At Barton Ramie a large sample (some 25 percent of the total) of house mounds was excavated for the first time, some almost totally and others by test pitting, and an occupation sequence running back to 600 B.C. or earlier was elucidated. The report on these excavations, like the project itself, was a landmark in the discipline (Willey et al. 1965).

Willey followed up this project with a sequence of investigations in the Pasión Valley in the western Peten. The first project, at Altar de Sacrificios, was designed to study the role of that site at the confluence of two rivers, with a view to understanding contact between the Maya lowlands and the highlands to the south. Although the results of the investigation were modest in this respect, Altar proved to have an occupation even earlier than that at Barton Ramie—the Xe phase yielded radiocarbon dates in the first half of the first millennium B.C. (Willey 1973).

The second phase of the Pasión Valley project was focused on Seibal, upstream from Altar, and on a sequence of monuments that reflected a Terminal Classic florescence similar to that found at Altar. Both sites had large quantities of Fine Orange temperless pottery of non-Classic Maya style. These ceramics and the sculptures at Seibal suggested an alien intrusion into the area that might be relevant to the vexed question of the Classic Maya collapse. From 1964 to 1968 Seibal was intensively investigated; a large-scale settlement survey (Tourtellot 1970) complementing the architectural investigations in the ceremonial precinct was the last field project directed by A. Ledyard Smith (Smith 1982). While the Terminal Classic florescence and its alien elements provided material for historical model building and a consideration of cultural process—a new approach in Maya archaeology deriving from the Binfordian Reformation in North America (Adams 1963, 1971; Sabloff and Willey 1967; Binford 1968)—the cultural sequence at Seibal produced evidence of occupation even earlier than that at Altar de Sacrificios (Sabloff 1975) and contact with the Olmec area to the west. Gordon Willey's three major projects had yielded, in addition to many of the intended results, an extended Formative occupation of the southern Maya lowlands, and a solid basis for the study of both rural and semiurban settlement systems through time.

Beginning just as the Belize Valley project was coming to an end and continuing for over a decade, the Tikal Project of the University of Pennsylvania was probably the most ambitious and costly Maya field program ever mounted. Under Edwin Shook and then William Coe, the largest of the tropical forest ceremonial centers was mapped, excavated, and substantially reconstructed (Coe 1965b). A series of royal burials linked to architectural construction documented the rising power of the Maya elite, and the developed nature of Maya society by the Late Formative Period could be appreciated for the first time. The detailed mapping of the surrounding settlement area (Carr and Hazard 1961) showed a vast and rather dense distribution of house platforms reaching to the limits of the survey, and suddenly the *milpa* model of Classic Maya subsistence, which had held sway for decades, began to seem somewhat at variance with the archaeological evidence (Hammond 1978). Although members of the Tikal staff sought ingeniously for solutions (Bronson 1966; Puleston 1968), for several years, "Maya civilization seemed to defy the principles of ecological possibility" (Culbert 1974:50). Most of the data and analyses from Tikal remain to be published, but the project has influenced Maya archaeology deeply in several ways. First, the essentially urban nature of Maya centers as preindustrial cities in their range of functions and in many aspects of form, was established (Haviland 1970), controverting the "vacant town" model advanced by Thompson. Second, the complex, multilayered nature of the society that lived in the city was made palpable by the archaeological evidence for rulers, bureaucrats, craft and ritual specialists, and a massive urban labor force. Third, the arcadian priest-peasant society portrayed by Thompson was shown to be an oversimplification. Finally, the complex nature, long persistence, and early rise of Maya civilization at Tikal were strong evidence

Lords of the Jungle   27

for its local emergence, rather than implantation by contact with the Teotihuacan-dominated highlands.

Tikal was important, too, in training a generation of Mayanists, and in bringing the art of restoration, successfully practiced for decades in the dry climate of Yucatan, into service to make a rainforest center permanently accessible as a public monument.

In Yucatan a third major project, at Dzibilchaltun, was conducted coevally with those in the Pasión Valley and at Tikal. It was directed by E. Wyllys Andrews IV (a Carnegie veteran) and sponsored by the Middle American Research Institute of Tulane University and by the National Geographic Society. Here also an extensive mapping program was undertaken (Stuart et al. 1979), and Andrews felt that the settlement was very large. Other Mayanists disagreed with his definition of the limits of a single site and also with his preference for a 12.9.0.0.0. correlation of Maya and Christian calendars, which he felt was necessary to contain the complex architectural development of the Florescent and Modified Florescent styles in Yucatan (Andrews IV 1965). A long series of radiocarbon dates run on inscribed Tikal lintels during the 1960s strongly favored the alternative 11.16.0.0.0. correlation. Andrews moved on to begin a more broadly multidisciplinary project at Becan, which, in some ways anticipated the projects of the 1970s.

Another ambitious program of excavation and restoration was directed by the Mexican archaeologists Alberto Ruz Lhuillier and (later) Jorge Acosta at Palenque. Only the major buildings in the ceremonial precinct were cleared of bush, but in the Temple of the Inscriptions Ruz Lhuillier (1973) made one of the most dramatic single discoveries in the history of Maya archaeology: the buried stairway leading down to the tomb of a ruler encased in a great stone sarcophagus. A second, slightly less dramatic find occurred sixteen years later, in 1968, at the small center of Altun Ha on the coastal plain of Belize: there, in a tomb set high in a pyramid, David Pendergast (1969a) found a jade head of the Sun God, made from a boulder and weighing more than 4 kilograms. The Royal Ontario Museum excavations at Altun Ha, carried out with a small staff but still focused on architectural excavation within the central ceremonial precinct, can be considered the last survival of the massive projects of the institutional period. They ended in 1970, four years after Tikal, three years after Palenque, and two years after Seibal. These last excavations also marked the end of a period in which Belize, the eastern margin of the southern lowlands, was almost ignored apart from Pendergast's work. In the succeeding period of problem-oriented small projects, Belize became, for various reasons, the locus of an unprecedented number of investigations.

The end of the institutional period also saw a gathering together of the rich harvest of factual data that had been extracted from Maya sites beginning with the Carnegie expeditions. The first volume of the *Handbook of Middle American Indians,* under the editorship of Robert Wauchope, appeared from 1964 onward. Gordon Willey edited the two volumes on the archaeology of southern Mesoamerica, which summarized by areas and topics all that was then known about the ancient Maya. Many of the contributors were former Carnegie staff, and the enduring value of the articles attests to the solid virtues of the institutional period.

Problem Orientation, 1970–1981

Two main factors influenced the direction of Maya archaeology from 1970 to 1981: economic stringency, resulting from global conditions, and the impact of the "New Archaeology" in North America, which enjoined the use of research design and hypothesis testing to examine discrete problems, rather than simply to continue gathering data and expanding the space-time framework of Maya studies. The main source of funding was the National Science Foundation, which favored problem-oriented proposals. Because major architectural excavation was unfashionable and seemed likely to solve few processual problems, there was a shift toward settlement and small-structure studies, toward intersite rather than intrasite perspectives. Regional archaeology in the Maya area came into its own in the 1970s.

The regional projects ranged from basic exploration, through studies of ecological and economic adaptation, to the testing of explicit models of ancient Maya society. Early in the period, projects such as that at Lubaantun (Hammond 1972, 1975) adopted Willey's procedure in the Belize Valley of focusing on a single site and conducting a less detailed study of the region around it. Others soon adopted a more even-handed approach, examining as many sites within the sampling region as possible before looking at a few in greater detail. This approach was used especially in areas where few sites were known, such as Quintana Roo (Harrison 1981) and northern Belize (Hammond 1973), but it was also the basis of operation for testing rather than formulating models, such as the Cozumel project (Sabloff and Rathje 1975).

This project was innovative in several ways: the entire island was taken as an easily defined sampling universe, the problem (of trading port/port-of-trade function) was elaborated in advance in terms of explicit research design and testable propositions, and the settlement system recorded was analyzed in terms of islandwide factors that included commerce and pilgrimage. The project was also organizationally innovative, in that it employed large numbers of students instead of the local labor force and small professional staff characteristic of the institutional period.

A coeval project designed to examine both regional archaeology and a specific problem—the emergence of complex society in the Maya lowlands in the Late Formative and Protoclassic—embraced northern Belize as its artificially defined sampling universe. Here the initial survey was already skewed toward finding sites with a strong Preclassic occupation, and excavation was swiftly directed to such sites, leaving many others unsampled except by surface collecting. The project also yielded a fine example of archaeological serendipity in the fortuitous discovery of Cuello, a site with stratified Early Formative occupation (Hammond 1977a). This discovery resulted in another project with a narrow spatial dimension, designed to recover data about this previously undetected period of Maya prehistory (Hammond et al. 1979).

Several other projects also sought to extend the Maya cultural sequence back in time. The developed nature of the earliest occupation at Cuello, dated to the early second millennium b.c. (in radiocarbon years), indicated the likelihood of an antecedent human presence in the region. This hypothesis was given substance by a survey of preceramic sites in coastal Belize, which was guided by an ecologically based model of likely settlement patterns (MacNeish, Wilkerson, and Nelken-Terner 1980). At the same time, preceramic occupations were reported in Loltun Cave in northern Yucatan (Velasquez V. 1980) and in the Quiche highlands of Guatemala (Gruhn and Bryan 1977; Brown 1980), and a widespread human penetration of all parts of the Maya area soon after the end of the Pleistocene became apparent. These preceramic and Early Formative discoveries suggest that the Maya were mainstream Mesoamericans, with as long a prehistory as Oaxaca or the Valley of Mexico, and that their complex society in the Late Formative is likely to have been of autochthonous development and not the result of cultural stimulus or population movement from other parts of Mesoamerica.

The complexity of the Late Formative has become apparent, to the extent that "Preclassic Maya civilization is no longer a contradiction in terms" (Hammond 1980:189), only in the last few years, with discoveries at Lamanai (Pendergast 1981), Mirador (Matheny 1980), Cuello (Hammond 1980), Cerros (Freidel 1979), Abaj Takalik (Graham 1979), and other sites. Monumental public architecture, large and dense populations at many sites and throughout several well-surveyed regions, facilities for intensive agriculture, evidence of external trade and internal social differentiation, and the emergence of a complex, communally accepted belief system and iconography of widespread occurrence all demonstrate that we are dealing with a civilized, possibly state-level society by around the time of Christ. Further investigation of the Late Formative and its Middle Formative antecedents promises to be one of the more intensively trod avenues of research in the 1980s.

The discrepancy between Classic Maya settlement size and complexity and the apparent inability of the swidden farming base to support it, which had become a serious interpretative problem by the end of the 1960s, was a productive area of research in the 1970s. Facilities for intensive agriculture were reported in several parts of the lowlands starting in 1972 (for example, Siemens and Puleston 1972; Turner 1974), and the discovery of large areas of apparent raised-field networks in several regions by the use of airborne radar (Adams 1980) indicated a new economic landscape in which wetland management was a significant factor. The rapidity with which the perception of ancient Maya economics changed can be seen in Harrison and Turner's *Pre-Hispanic Maya Agriculture* (1978), the incarnation of the new orthodoxy. Equally sophisticated animal-protein procurement techniques are not yet known but should be a focus of future research.

Other aspects of the Maya economic base have been examined by several projects. The industrial chert-working center of Colha has been intensively examined in the field, by Hester and his associates (Hester 1979, Hester et al. 1980), using a procurement-processing-distribution sequence model and paying less attention to the settlement aspects of the site. Smaller scale examinations of chert- and obsidian-working sites are included in Hester and Hammond (1976). Obsidian analysis for source characterisation has been a major field of research in the 1970s, with substantial samples examined from Tikal (Moholy-Nagy 1975), Seibal (Nelson, Sidrys, and Holmes 1978), and Palenque (Johnson 1976), among other sites, and various exchange models (for example, Hammond 1972, Sidrys 1976) put forward to explain the observed source distributions. Similar exchange studies have been carried out on jade and ceramics, and the impact of the natural sciences on the documentation and understanding of Maya local and long-distance trade networks seems likely to increase in the 1980s.

The superstructure of Classic Maya society, a focus of research for decades, continues to receive attention. The historicist interpretation of the monumental inscriptions, current since 1960, has led to detailed studies of dynastic genealogies at several sites, and the demonstration by Lounsbury (1973) and others that Maya writing was phonetically based has resulted in an increasing number of mutually coherent decipherments of texts. Probably the most extensive work has been done on the long texts of Palenque, where a Late Classic dynasty was documented in detail (Mathews and Schele 1974; Schele 1974, 1976). The interdependence between text and representation in the royal art of Palenque and the sheer richness of the iconographic referents has been elucidated in cooperative work by the troika of Lounsbury, Mathews, and Schele, as well as by Merle Greene Robertson and others.

A second focus of iconographic study is the neglected area of vase painting, long assumed to be restricted to genre scenes of Maya life with occasional portrayals of myth. Michael Coe (1973, 1978) has convincingly argued that the majority of figure scenes show episodes from a lost epic literature, of which the *Popol Vuh* is a surviving fragment, and Adams (1971, 1977c) has argued for a specific historical depiction on the "Altar Vase." Adams's argument depends on the wealth of associated material and the known circumstances of the burial from which the base was recovered. It demonstrates how much information has been lost in the acquisition of the majority of decorated vessels, which have come from looters' excavations and been laundered of any remaining associations in the dealers' network. Coe's work is limited in importance because virtually all his material comes from looted tombs, and thus lacks associations that might suggest the function of these decorated vessels in Classic Maya necrolatry.

The combined study of stelae, tomb contents, and texts by scholars such as Clemency Coggins (1979) has begun to tell us something about the nature of Classic Maya religion. It can no longer be seen as confined to the chaste worship of a celestial pantheon, with a tendency toward monotheism (Thompson 1970), but clearly embraces ancestor worship, human sacrifice (from at least the beginning of the Late Formative), and the use of mind-altering drugs: it is a darker, but more characteristically Mesoamerican, relationship with the supernatural than Thompson and Morley could conceive of, with their episcopalian tendencies.

The problem-oriented period has thus resulted in topical advances in the study of almost all areas of ancient Maya culture, with the more practical problems also being tackled. The rate of destruction of sites has increased alarmingly because of urban expansion and industrial development, on the one hand, and commercial looting of monuments and tombs, on the other. Salvage survey and excavation in the face of modern building was carried out at Kaminaljuyu (Michels and Sanders 1977–1979), and in several parts of Chiapas by the New World Archaeological Foundation, as part of a long-established regional program. On a smaller scale, surveys (E. Graham 1976) and single-site projects (for example, Chase 1981) have tried to rescue something in Belize. The merciless onslaught of the commercial looters has not been effectively countered at the political level. Archaeologists have less powerful vested interests, and less money, than the dealers and museum directors who oppose them. At the practical level, however, the Corpus of Maya Hieroglyphic Inscriptions project, under Ian Graham, has revived Morley's dream of attempting to record and publish all known texts and their associated sculpture, and some success has been achieved in stemming the flow of stelae from both known and unknown sites and recovering others from dealers and collectors. The diminishing number of monuments for sale has unfortunately led to a new phase of looting in which entire buildings are torn apart in search of tombs stocked with pottery vessels and jades. This problem seems likely to persist in the future, although the number of sites is itself limited, and some kinds of evidence may be destroyed totally before archaeologists ever become aware of them. Certainly the present period may be seen as one in which an unprecedented interest in Maya archaeology has been accompanied by an unprecedented rate of destruction.

Conclusion

In this essay I have examined the developmental trajectory of Maya archaeology over nearly four and a half centuries, from the Renaissance to the present day, describing five successive periods of, respectively, casual observation, deliberate exploration, scholarly investigation, institutional involvement, and problem solving. Each period saw both innovative studies presaging future approaches and attitudes that carried over from an earlier age. Some approaches were cyclical in popularity, so that hieroglyphic decipherment sometimes gave way to subsistence economics or iconography as a leading concern among Mayanists, but few were ever completely neglected. Two irreversible trends are the continued discovery and recording of new sites, making the map ever fuller, and the progressive pushing back of the beginning of Maya prehistory from the beginning of the Classic in the early institutional period to the end of the Pleistocene today. Another steady trend is the increased interest in the economic infrastructure of Maya society, the productive forces and economic organization that sustained the glittering superstructure of architecture, art, and religion. Initially viewed as unique, the Maya have been brought into the mainstream of Mesoamerican prehistory, the builders of a civilization no less fascinating for being better understood. For the past thirty years the progress of that understanding has been stimulated by, and illuminatingly synthesized in, the work of Gordon Willey.

PART TWO

Basic Data Interpretation

Two

The Paleoecology of the Selin Farm Site (H-CN-5): Department of Colón, Honduras[1]

Paul F. Healy, Trent University

Introduction

The 1976 field season of the Trent University archaeological project in northeast Honduras concentrated upon the H-CN-5:Selin Farm site. H-CN-5 is located in a present-day *potrero,* about 7.5 kilometers northeast of Trujillo, capital of the Department of Colón, and about 1 kilometer south of the Guaimoreto Lagoon, on low-lying terrain (less than 5 meters above sea level; Figs. 2.1 and 2.2). The site was first explored by Bird in 1931 as part of the Boekelman Shell Heap Expedition, and the results of this early effort have been described by Epstein (1957). Our preliminary investigation in 1973 included relocation of the Selin Farm zone and a brief reconnaissance of the site (Healy 1973). In 1976, aided by a crew of 6 students and as many as 15 local laborers, we mapped H-CN-5 and conducted test excavations in 4 separate mounds (Healy 1978a). There are at least 16 mounds dotting the H-CN-5 site; some of these constructions are solid earth; others are earth and shell mounds (Fig. 2.3). Three of the 1976 excavations (Pits 2, 3, and 4) were placed into earth-covered mounds of shell, which encased well-preserved faunal and molluscan remains. The following discussion of the paleoecology of the region is based upon these identified skeletal and shell remains, and on observations on modern ecology.

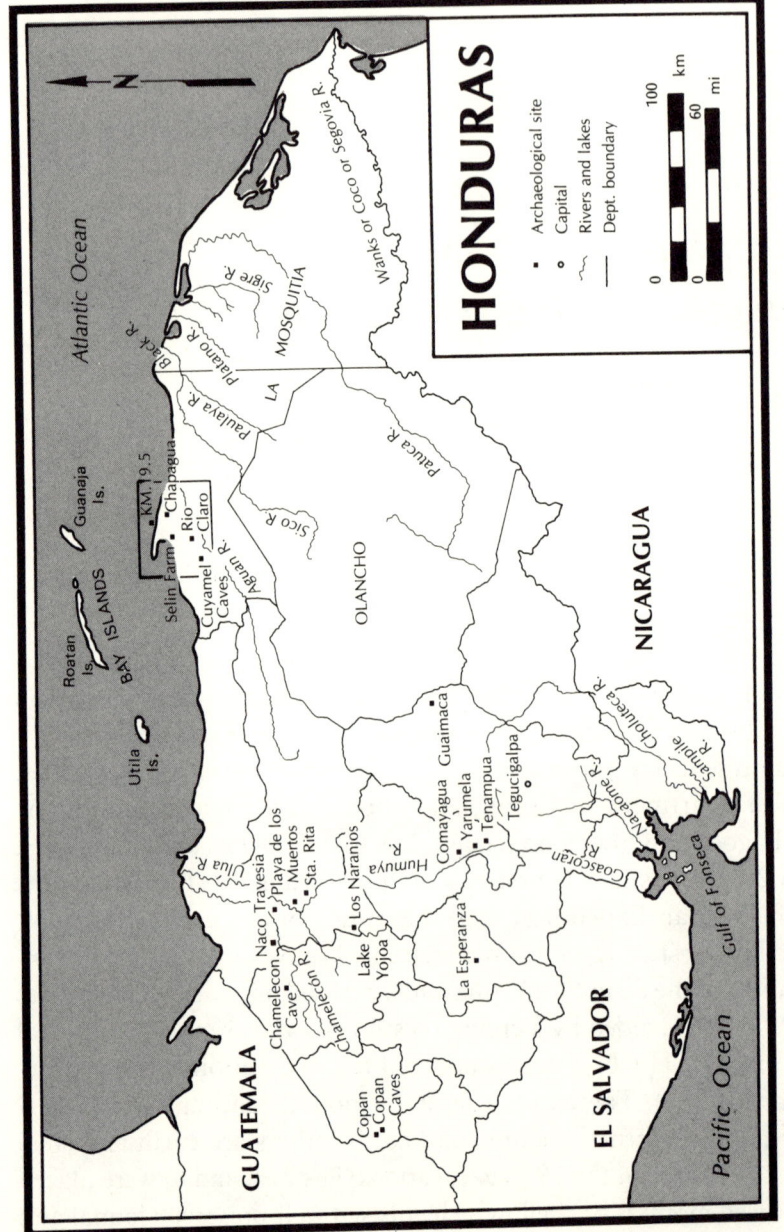

Figure 2.1. Map of Honduras noting some principal archaeological sites. Map inset of northeast Honduras is enlarged in Figure 2.2, and shows the region under discussion.

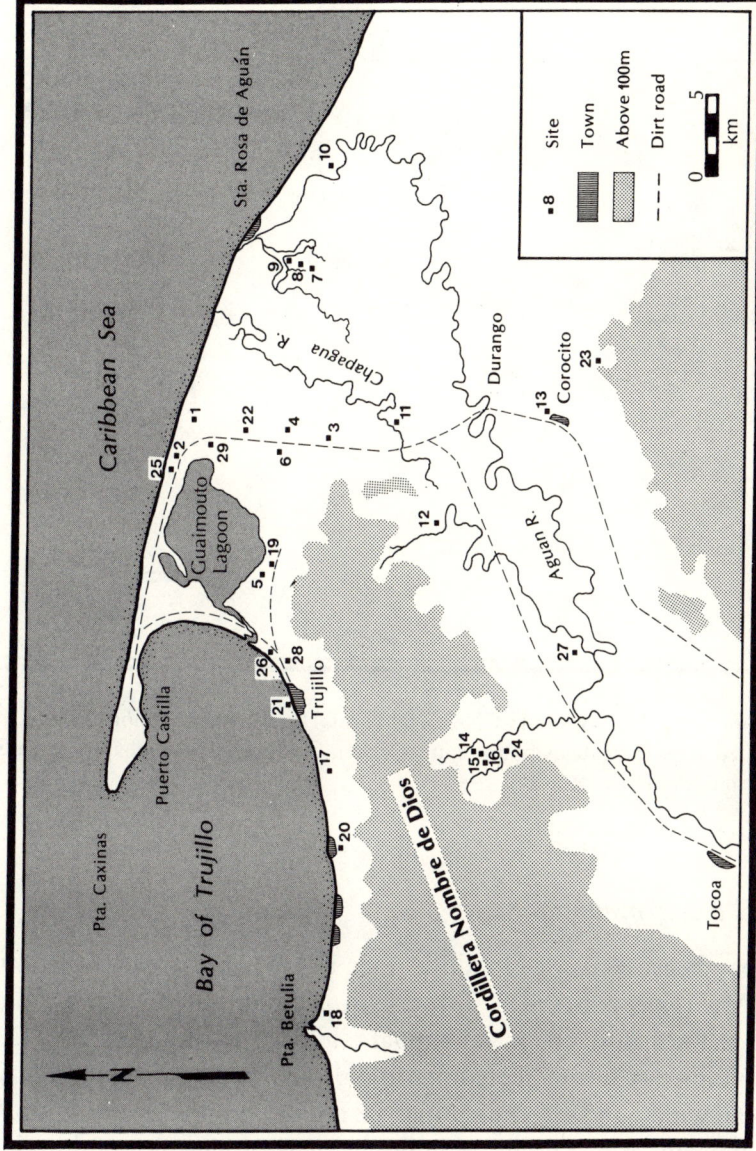

Figure 2.2. Map of northeast Honduras showing the location of H-CN-5:Selin Farm, and other archaeological sites in the Department of Colón survey area.

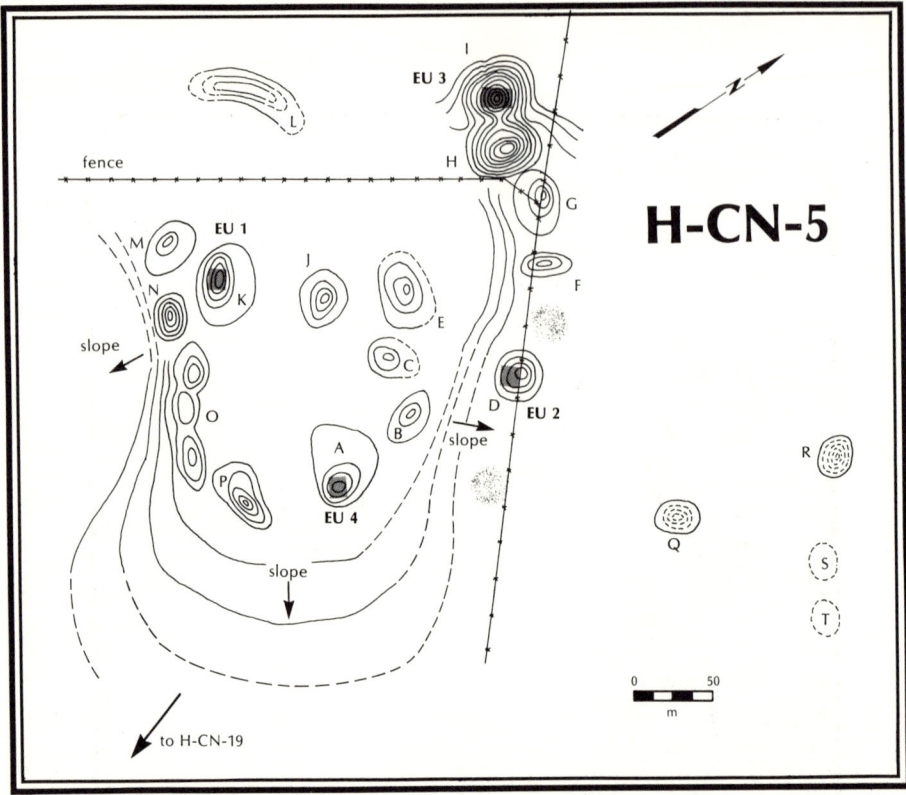

Figure 2.3. Map of site H-CN-5:Selín Farm, Department of Colón, 1976. Shaded areas indicate excavation units (E.U.). Contour lines equal approximately 30 cm each (or 1 foot).

General Environmental Setting

The northeast coast of Honduras falls in the climatological classification of Am-Afw (Koeppen 1948). Typically it is a hot, humid area with marked wet and dry seasons. The mean annual rainfall reaches a drenching 2,000 to 3,000 millimeters. From September to November, monsoonlike rains, heavy Caribbean winds, and even hurricanes are not uncommon (Vivo Escoto 1964).

The majority of northern Colón lies below 1,000 meters in altitude. Temperatures frequently reach 32°C (90°F); frosts are unknown. This largely underdeveloped region has a rich and diversified natural vegetation over wide areas today. Wagner (1964) has classed the region as a whole as "tropical rainforest formation." However along the coastal margins several mangroves (*Rhizophora*) grow in swamps and in saltwater tide pools. Tidal flats and estuaries produce a mangrove vegetation, and between the ports of Trujillo and Puerto Castillo today this zone extends inland nearly 2 kilometers in some spots, while a similar, estuarylike environment exists adjacent to the large, 9-kilometer-wide Guaimoreto Lagoon.

The lagoon, fed by several freshwater streams flowing out of the mountain range behind Trujillo, opens into the Trujillo Bay. This bay is a deep body of water created by a low-lying land mass that hooks out from the Honduran north coast into a cape terminating at Punta Caxinas. This spit of land is often termed the Cape of Honduras. Today fishing in the lagoon and in the Caribbean is actively pursued by the widespread coastal Carib population (Davidson 1976).

Several winding creeks lead from the lagoon to the east, a flatland that rapidly gives way to two larger river systems: the Chapagua River and the Aguan River. Both of these open to the Caribbean Sea and extend, in the opposite direction, a substantial distance southward and inland. This is especially true of the Aguan River, which has its headwaters in the Department of Yoro some 200 kilometers away. As one travels eastward from the Bay of Trujillo, beyond the Guaimoreto Lagoon, to the Aguan River and southward into the Aguan Valley, the vegetation becomes more luxuriant and forestlike along the valley edges, where clearing has been minimal. The valley itself, which has relatively rich alluvial soils, has been cleared for farming.

In historic times man-made savannas have been created through burning, cutting, and cultivation. Large portions east of the lagoon and into the center of the Aguan Valley are now savannas and for the last few decades have been utilized for cattle ranching. Earlier, several large fruit plantations were operated in the region. As early as 1860, bananas and *platanos* were being grown for export to North American markets. In the first half of the twentieth century several major fruit company conglomerates began sizable plantations on the Honduran north coast, including the area around Trujillo. These were largely abandoned around 1939 owing to a widespread banana blight.

Previous Archaeological Research

In the 1920s H. J. Spinden (1925) explored the region around Trujillo as part of an extensive archaeological survey along the north coast of Honduras and the adjacent Miskito coast of Nicaragua. Less than a decade later, J. B. Bird conducted a survey and excavations in the Trujillo region, particularly at the Selin Farm site in 1931, while the property was under cultivation by the United Fruit Company. The archaeology of the entire north coast of Honduras was described in an important early survey monograph by D. Z. Stone

(1941), although no clear time depth was elaborated for the region. In the 1950s J. F. Epstein utilized Bird's notes and ceramic collections, as well as other northeast Honduras collections in the American Museum of Natural History, to present the first ceramic (time) sequence for the region (Epstein 1957).

Between 1973 and 1976, I surveyed the region between Punta Betulia and the Aguan Valley in Colón, excavating at several chronologically distinct sites. Preliminary reports on these recent efforts have been published and a final report is in preparation (Healy 1974a, 1974b, 1975, 1978a, 1978b).

The H-CN-5:Selin Farm excavations have been described elsewhere (Healy 1977, 1978a). Briefly, four test excavations produced over 16,000 sherds, several hundred lithic artifacts (manos, metates, polished stone axes, and so forth), and several bone artifacts (especially needles). Initial analysis of this material, complemented by five radiocarbon dates, suggests that H-CN-5 was inhabited totally within the Selin Period, from approximately A.D. 300 to 1000, making it one of the longest continuously occupied sites known in Honduras (Healy 1977). The site history can be subdivided into three phases: Early Selin (a newly defined chronological unit), Basic Selin, and Transitional Selin (Healy 1978b). In this paper I examine the subsistence data for the Selin culture and the changes evidenced through seven centuries of habitation at H-CN-5.

Faunal Analysis

Faunal data can be classified in various ways. Identification and analysis of the more than 3,500 bones and dozens of shell remains in the H-CN-5 collections was carried out between 1976 and 1979. First, we divided the identifications into five major taxonomic units (fish, mammals, reptiles-amphibians, birds, and shellfish). Second, we ranked the individual species and genera represented in each of these larger taxonomic groupings by their overall representation at the site, using minimum number of individuals (MNI), to see how like animals compared (for example, white tail deer vs. peccary among the mammals, or jack vs. tarpon among the fish). Finally, we examined the changes in faunal representation at the site through time (that is, dominant species in the Early Selin phase, in the Basic Selin phase, and in the Transitional Selin phase).

The largest faunal category (in MNI) from H-CN-5 was fish: 13 genera of freshwater and saltwater fish were identified, as well as 5 identifications at the family level (Table 2.1). The second largest category was mammals: 10 genera of mammals were identified and 4 families (Table 2.2). Amphibians and reptiles have been combined in a third category of fauna (Table 2.3): 5 distinct genera were identified and 4 families. Birds (Table 2.4) were not heavily represented in the collection; generally they were fragmentary and often

Table 2.1. Ranked Order of H-CN-5 Fish (by MNI and period)*

Common Name	Scientific Name	E.S.	B.S.	T.S.	Total MNI	% of Fish MNI
Jack	Caranx hippos	5	20	30	55	53.39
Snook	Centropomus sp.	2	1	5	8	7.76
Snapper	Lutjanus sp.	1	2	3	6	5.83
Grouper (sea bass)	Serranidae	1	2	2	5	4.85
Tarpon	Megalops atlanticus		3	2	5	4.85
Barracuda	Sphyraena sp.		3	2	5	4.85
Houndfish	Tylosaurus sp.		1	2	3	2.91
Cartilaginous fish	Chondrichthys			2	2	1.94
Mullet	Mugil sp.			2	2	1.94
Cichlid (mojarra)	Cichlosoma sp.			2	2	1.94
Croaker	Micropogon sp.		1	1	2	1.94
Marine Mojarra	Eugerres sp.		1	1	2	1.94
Shark	Carcharhinidae		1		1	.97
Porcupinefish	Diodontidae sp.			1	1	.97
Rays/Skates	Rajiformes			1	1	.97
Catfish	Ariidae			1	1	.97
Porgie (sheepshead)	Archosargus sp.			1	1	.97
Puffer	Spheroides sp.			1	1	.97
					103	99.96

*E.S. = Early Selin Period
B.S. = Basic Selin Period
T.S. = Transitional Selin Period

Table 2.2. Ranked Order of H-CN-5 Mammals (by MNI and period)

Common Name	Scientific Name	E.S.	B.S.	T.S.	Total MNI	% of MNI
Deer (white tail)	Odocoileus virginianus	2	4	4	13	31.70
(brocket)	Mazama americana		2	1		
(sp. unidentified)	Cervidae		—	—		
Armadillo	Dasypus novemcinctus	1	3	3	7	17.07
Peccary	Tayassu sp.	1	2	2	5	12.20
(sp. unidentified)	Artiodactyla	—	—	—		
Manatee	Trichechus manatus	1	2	1	4	9.96
Agouti	Dasyprocta punctata	1	1	1	3	7.32
Paca (spotted cavy)	Agouti paca		1	1	2	4.88
Howler monkey	Alouatta villosa			2	2	4.88
Tapir	Tapirus sp.		1		1	2.44
Jaguar	Felis onca		1		1	2.44
Porcupine	Coendu sp.		1		1	2.44
Otter	Lutra annectens			1	1	2.44
Sm. unidentified rodent	———			1	1	2.44
					41	100.01

Table 2.3. Ranked Order of H-CN-5 Reptiles and Amphibians (by MNI and period)

Common Name	Scientific Name	E.S.	B.S.	T.S.	Total MNI	% of MNI
Iguana	Iguanidae	1	3	9	13	44.82
Sea turtle	Chelonidae		2	2	4	13.79
Green turtle	*Chelonia mydas*	—	—	—		
Crocodilians	Crocodylia	1	2	1	4	13.79
Crocodile	*Crocodylus* sp.	—	—	—		
Frogs/Toads	Anuran			2	4	13.79
Marine toad	*Bufo Marinus*		2			
Mud turtle	*Kinosternon scorpiodes*		2		2	6.89
Pond turtle	*Chrysemys* sp.		2		2	6.89
					29	99.97

unidentifiable as to species. Those represented (5 orders, 1 genus, 2 at species level) proved to be mostly large waterfowl (herons, cranes, and so on). Because bone preservation at H-CN-5 was excellent, I am inclined to believe that the infrequency of bird bones is an accurate reflection of Selin dietary preferences, and that fowl were only occasionally added to Selin daily foodstuffs.

Molluscan remains compose the last major category (Table 2.5): at least 29 species were tentatively identified. The importance of shellfish is apparent from the presence of numerous large mounds marking the site, composed almost entirely of discarded shells. Even recognizing the cautionary admonitions of Meighan (1969) and Parmalee and Klippel (1974) that the dietary significance of shellfish can be deceiving, it is obvious that they were an integral part of the Selin subsistence pattern. Though the quantities cannot be readily compared at present with the bony remains (all bones were kept but not all shells), examination in the field of molluscan remains sug-

Table 2.4. Ranked Order of H-CN-5 Birds (by MNI and period)

Common Name	Scientific Name	E.S.	B.S.	T.S.	Total MNI	% of Bird MNI
Heron	Ardeidae		3	5	10	45
Great blue heron	*Ardea heroidias*			2		
Wood stork	*Mycteria americana*		4	2	6	27
Turkeylike birds						
(guan, chachalaca)	Galliformes		2		2	9
Curassow	*Crax* sp.	—	—	—		
Shore birds (plover,						
gull, snipe)	Charadriiformes		2		2	9
Cranelike birds (coot,						
rail, trumpeter)	Gruiformes			1	1	5
Ducklike birds (duck,						
goose, swan)	Anseriformes			1	1	5
					22	100

Table 2.5. Unranked List of H-CN-5 Shellfish

	Common Name	*Scientific Name*
BIVALVES	Brazilian ark	*Anadara brasiliana*
	Cut-ribbed ark	*Anadara floridiana*
	Eared ark	*Anadara notabilis*
	Buttercup lucina	*Anodontia alba*
	W. I. pointed venus	*Anomalocardia brasiliana*
	Calico scallop	*Argopecten gibbus*
	Tiger lucina	*Codakia orbicularis*
	Mangrove oyster	*Crassostrea rhizophorae*
	Beaded venus	*Protothaca granulata*
	Prickly cockle	*Trachycardium isocardia*
	Magnum cockle	*Trachycardium magnum*
	Yellow cockle	*Trachycardium maricatum*
GASTROPODS	Striate bubble	*Bulla striata*
	Queen helmut shell	*Cassis madagascariensis*
	Alphabet cone	*Conus spurius spurius*
	Measled (zebra) cowrie	*Cypraea zebra*
	True tulip shell	*Fasciolaria tulipa*
	Superb gaza	*Gaza superba*
	Angulate periwinckle	*Littorina angulifera*
	W. I. crown conch	*Melongena melongena*
	Colorful moon snail	*Natica canrena*
	Punctulata nerite	*Neritina punctulata*
	Caribbean olive	*Oliva scripta*
	Scotch bonnet	*Phalium granulatum*
	Florida horse conch	*Pleuroploca gigantea*
	Pyramid shell	*Pyramidella dolobrata*
	Queen conch	*Strombus gigas*
	Rustic dogwinkle	*Thais rustica*
	Caribbean vase shell	*Vasum muricatum*

gests a reasonable approximation of the range of shellfish utilized and consumed in the Selin Period at H-CN-5.

Among the fish, the marine species far outnumber (and generally outweigh in body size and weight) the freshwater fish. All three freshwater species (catfish, freshwater mojarra, and houndfish) are well suited to fresh-to-brackish water environments, such as those encountered in parts of the Guaimoreto Lagoon. The majority of the marine species are large fish (reaching lengths of a meter or more), such as tarpon, barracuda, snook, grouper, and marine mojarra.

The most significant of all the fish recovered was the jack *(Caranx hippos)*. This fish is known to grow up to 113 centimeters in length and to weigh as much as 15.8 kilograms. It was found in substantial quantities (more than 50 percent of the MNI of fish). It is a fish that tends to run in schools, and is generally considered to be a good food fish. Modern marine fishermen consider the jack to be a hard-fighting fish when caught, suggesting that H-CN-5 inhabitants were skilled fishermen (Randall 1968).

Among the 14 mammal groups found at H-CN-5, deer *(Odocoileus virginianus)*, armadillo *(Dasypus novemcinctus)*, and peccary *(Tayassu* sp.) are well represented (composing over 60 percent of the mammalian MNI). The large and reclusive manatee *(Trichechus manatus)* accounts for about 10 percent of the mammalian MNI. Several other forest mammals were procured, including tapir *(Tapirus* sp.), paca *(Agouti paca)*, agouti *(Dasyprocta punctata)*, and perhaps even howler monkey *(Alouatta villosa)*, otter *(Lutra annectens)*, porcupine *(Coendu* sp.), and jaguar *(Felis onca)*. The latter undoubtedly had importance and value beyond its flesh.

Identifications and ranking of the H-CN-5 reptiles and amphibians revealed that turtles were quite prevalent in the site refuse. The sizable marine, or sea, turtle, particularly the green turtle *(Chelonia mydas)*, would have provided ample food, even if only occasionally taken. These creatures can weigh as much as 150 to 250 kilograms (Carr 1952; Carr and Giovannoli 1957). Smaller species of freshwater turtle included the pond turtle *(Chrysemys* sp.) and mud turtle *(Kinosternon scropiodes)*, which were almost certainly of less significance in the Selin diet. Iguana *(Iguanidae)* are amply represented in the collections (MNI = 13) and are a tasty, readily available source of meat. Crocodiles, or caiman (Crocodylia), and toad *(Bufo marinus)* were of less clear dietary importance.

Among the avifauna, herons (Ardeidae), especially the great blue heron *(Ardea heroidias)*, are found in significant quantities (45 percent of the avian MNI). Most other birds were aquatic, coastal species, with the exception of some forest, turkeylike birds (Galliformes), including an excellent game bird, the curassow *(Crax* sp.)

Examination of cross-temporal variations of H-CN-5 faunal types revealed several patterns. First, several species were present and clearly important to the Selin inhabitants throughout the 700-year span of settlement. Among the mammals, these long-term staples appear to have been armadillo, agouti, white tail deer, peccary, and manatee; among the reptiles, iguana and crocodile/caiman; and among the fish, snook, grouper, snapper, and jack. All of these fauna are present in deposits of each of the Selin phases.

Looking more closely at the relative levels of representation of different species through time, we can see some indications of possible changes in subsistence emphasis (Fig. 2.4). The smallest proportional representation of fauna of the three phases was found in Early Selin times (11 genera). This number is expanded considerably in the Basic Selin phase (30 genera). The Transi-

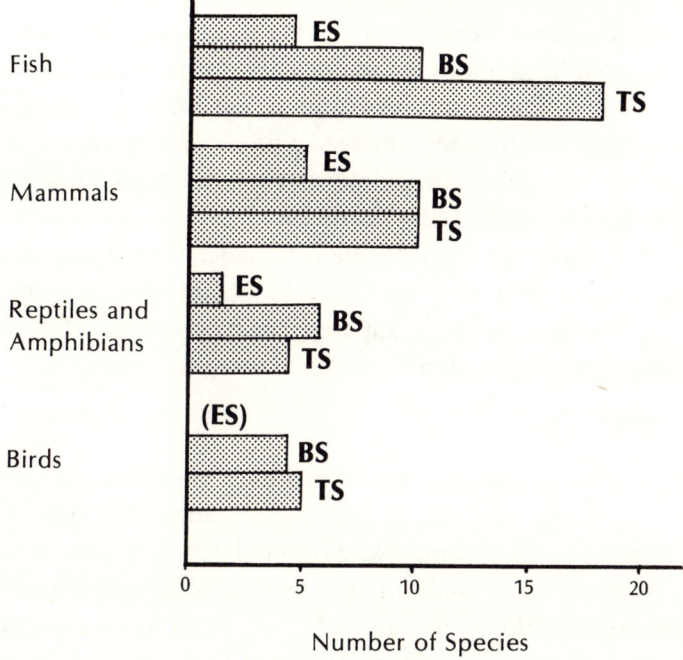

Figure 2.4. Diachronic comparison of H-CN-5 faunal diversity. ES represents Early Selin Period, BS is Basic Selin Period, and TS is Transitional Selin Period.

tional Selin phase sees an increase in faunal representation to 32 genera and the greatest overall diversity.[2] Thus, the species represented at H-CN-5 gradually increased over time, with an especially significant growth of marine fish in later times.

Discussion

Prior to the 1976 research at H-CN-5 there was virtually no evidence of prehistoric subsistence staples or preferences for the north coast cultures of Honduras. The early work by Spinden (1925) emphasized the presence of large shell middens in northeast Honduras, and therefore of shellfish for subsistence. Stone (1941:47–51) suggested that fishing may have been an important activity. My own earlier efforts at site H-CN-4:Williams Ranch in

1973 provided some limited indications of maize agriculture, as well as reliance on shellfish and deer (Healy 1975:66).

Aside from the direct archaeological data from the 1976 work at the Selin Farm site, we have contemporary ecological information to help reconstruct the probable native fauna that was hunted, fished, and collected. Knowing the respective habitats for these modern animals, we can draw some reasonable conclusions about Selin Period subsistence strategies (cf. Wing and Hammond 1974). Earlier I noted that northeast Honduras is a complex, dynamic area, which for study purposes, can be subdivided into three major biotopes: the lowland forest, the freshwater marsh-lagoon estuary, and the mangrove-coastal zone. The first and most apparent observation from the H-CN-5 faunal remains is that they are derived from all three ecozones.

TROPICAL FOREST

The lowland rainforest canopy would have provided refuge for various game birds, squirrels, and monkeys hunted by man. The howler monkey is still present today in this region, and it may have been important in prehistoric times. It shows up in small amounts at H-CN-5 and may have been hunted for its edible meat. Other forest animals that are common today in northeast Honduras and can reasonably be assumed to have been present in Selin times are opossums, kinkajou, raccoon, coati, and anteaters. In fact, opossum *(Didelphis virginiana)* and raccoon *(Procyon lotor)* are both present in the faunal remains of the coeval Selin Period site H-CN-4, located only 10 kilometers east of H-CN-5.

The forest floor was a natural habitat for several ungulates, which could have been an important food source for the pre-Columbian natives of the region. Among these is the peccary, especially the white-lipped peccary *(Tayassu* sp.), which is found at H-CN-5 and would have fed upon palm nuts and various forest roots. The small, reclusive brocket deer *(Mazama americana)* and the bulky tapir are only rarely seen in northeast Honduras today, but both are found in Selin Farm contexts. *Mazama* was clearly hunted for its meat, whereas the hide of the tapir may have been considered more desirable than its meat. The smaller game animals of the forest floor would include the nine-banded armadillo and the porcupine; each is represented in the H-CN-5 faunal remains.

In the wetter zones of the forest, particularly along river margins, large tropical rodents, such as the agouti and the paca (or spotted cavy), are the most common important game animals. These fleshy animals feed on the rich grasses and roots that grow along the water's edge, but they also range into open fields (and especially cultivated gardens), where food may be more abundant and readily available (Linares 1976). The raccoon, which is absent at H-CN-5, but identified from the faunal records of nearby H-CN-4, favors the river edges, where small fish and crustaceans can be obtained. Similarly, the otter would have been present along the many Colón rivers and streams in prehistoric times. Streamside reptiles include the ubiquitous iguana, which is still trapped today by local people; iguana eggs are another edible byproduct of this creature.

Preying upon all these forest creatures were the Central American felines. These are the most spectacular of the carnivores in the American tropics, and their range clearly extended beyond the forest environment. The jaguar, whose pelts were highly valued in pre-Columbian Mesoamerica, and the marguey *(Felis wiedii)* are present in the faunal collections from H-CN-5 and H-CN-4, respectively. These cats are rare today in northeast Honduras.

In the patches of lowland forest cleared by aboriginal groups (probably for slash-and-burn cultivation), several forms of wildlife would have been available (and probably relatively abundant). Aside from the agouti, paca, and armadillo mentioned earlier, the most important cleared-forest game was the white tailed deer *(Odocoileus virginianus)*. This very important ungulate tends to enjoy and inhabit the grasses and vegetation of second-growth forest (Cooke 1977).

Thus, the faunal remains provide solid evidence of tropical forest game at H-CN-5. Unfortunately, we still do not know how these mammals, some of them quite large, were actually hunted and killed. Aside from snares, deadfalls, and similar traps, we generally assume or infer hunting with the use of spears or bows and arrows. However, there are no indications of any of these implements in the H-CN-5 assemblages.

FRESHWATER MARSH-LAGOON ESTUARY

The second extensive ecological zone has many distinctive animals. Such a setting is particularly prevalent around the Guaimoreto Lagoon and the flatlands to the east. It is a zone which would have favored aquatic and semiaquatic wildlife. The fish of the northeast Honduras streams and lagoons were of some importance to the ancient Selin inhabitants, and freshwater fish, such as catfish (Ariidae), guapote or freshwater mojarra *(Cichlosoma* sp.), and houndfish *(Tylosaurus* sp.), are present (though represented in small numbers). The American crocodile *(Crocodylus* sp.) may have been found within this marsh-lagoon setting. The related caiman *(Caiman* sp.) is found today in the marshy area about the lagoon, but the larger crocodile has long since been hunted out for its meat and valuable hide.

Two unusual types of marsh-lagoon fauna that appear to have been utilized at H-CN-5 were the mud turtle and the pond turtle. There is a difference of opinion about the edibility of these two reptiles, but elsewhere in Central America they are known to have been sold openly in food markets. Even if they were not collected for their flesh, their shells may have been utilized. Frogs and toads (Anurans) were probably also residents of this habitat; again, they are found among the remains at H-CN-5 but in small amounts. Two large marine frogs *(Bufo marinus)* have been positively identified.

A small number of bird bones was recovered; most of these belong to waterfowl (storks, gulls, egrets, ducks, herons), which would have frequented this type of environment. Land, or blue, crabs *(Cardisoma* sp.) are also present and provide a significant seasonal food source for local Colón residents. The crabs are easily captured during their annual breeding period, when they swarm to the sea in large numbers. Several broken crab claws were found in the H-CN-5 collections, and dozens of crabs literally overran the site during the 1976 field season.

The most important animal of the entire marsh-lagoon ecozone was the sea cow, or manatee *(Trichechus manatus)*. This large yet passive creature weighs more than 350 kilograms and has an excellent, tough hide, as well as fat and meat. It is at home in brackish waters (such as those at the mouth of the lagoon) and in the lower courses of rivers (that is, the mouth of the Chapagua and Aguan Rivers). Probably it fed upon subaqueous plants and was hunted in prehistoric times with harpoons. Indeed, the important sixteenth-century account by Diego de Landa (Tozzer 1941:190–91) describes the Maya custom of procuring manatee with harpoons, and Gann reports similar manatee hunting practices off the Belize coast more recently (Gann 1925). Nietschmann (1973:91) reports that manatee is one of the most esteemed meats of the coastal Miskito Indians.

MANGROVE-COAST AND MARINE BIOTOPE

The third major ecozone extends from the mangrove swamp into shallow offshore waters, the bay, and deeper Caribbean waters. The zone has a somewhat specialized wildlife. With the exception of howler monkeys, which sometimes take refuge in the mangrove area, mammals are rare here. Iguana (Iguanidae) are present and dart about the *Rhizophora*. Large waterfowl, such as egrets and herons, occupy stream channels and mangrove clearings.

The saline pools that fringe the coast and the brackish waters of the lagoon mouth (a rich feeding ground) would have attracted some species of marine fish, while others were undoubtedly caught by more ambitious prehistoric deepsea fishing efforts. In addition to deer and manatee, the marine species of fish constituted the most important food source of the Selin Period. These included grouper, or sea bass (Serranidae); snapper *(Lutjanus* sp.); tarpon, or sabalo *(Megalops atlanticus)*; snook, or robalo *(Centropomus* sp.); and barracuda *(Sphyraena* sp.). Cartilaginous fish included sharks (Carcharhinidae) and rays, or skates (Rajiformes). Smaller saltwater species identified among the faunal remains were puffer *(Spheroides* sp.); porgie, or sheepshead *(Archosargus* sp.); mullet *(Mugil* sp.); porcupinefish *(Diodontidae* sp.); and croaker *(Micropogon* sp.). As I noted earlier, the most crucial marine species to Selin natives appears to have been the jack *(Caranx hippos)*; over 50 distinct specimens were positively identified.

Some of the smaller marine fish may have been caught with nets skillfully manipulated by boats. Occasionally some of the larger marine species are known to enter tidal zones, brackish water estuaries, and even freshwater, which may have facilitated lagoon fishing of some of these fish (Jordon and Evermann 1963; Meek 1907). It should be noted, however, that some of the larger pelagic fish found at H-CN-5 prefer deeper waters, which suggests that Selin natives' boats were capable of offshore travel. It is also likely that the natives used sophisticated fishing techniques to catch and land these sizable and fast-moving game fish. Again, we lack clear artifactual evidence of nets, fishhooks, and large ocean-going craft, but the faunal remains provide good, secondary-level inferences pointing to these types of procurement activities.

Other possible food sources from the mangrove-mudflats ecozone include the mangrove oyster *(Crassostrea rhizophorae)* and angulate periwinkle *(Littorina angulifera)*, which thrive in the shallow mangrove areas of all coastal bays and lagoons such as Guaimoreto. Oyster beds are known from the mouth of the Chapagua River and are undoubtedly present in several other nearby localities as well. The huge quantities of oyster shells at H-CN-5 attests to centuries of use of this staple. Additional important shellfish identified at the Selin Farm site in substantial quantities are queen conch *(Strombus gigas)* and West Indian crown conch *(Melongena melongena)*. Altogether, nearly 30 species of shellfish have been identified. Most of these species live in shallow or moderately shallow waters, although some, superb gaza *(Gaza superba)*, live in very deep waters—50 or more fathoms (Fig. 2.5).

The last major sea food from the shallow coastal zone is the marine turtle (Chelonidae), especially the green turtle *(Chelonia mydas)*, which occurs in both the Basic and Transitional Selin phases. The sea turtle feeds upon marine grasses *(Zostera* and *Thallasia)* often found in "pastures" some 10 to 20 fathoms deep (Nietschmann 1973). Although not represented in great numbers, this is a large sea creature producing on the average over 65 kilograms of tasty meat per 160 kilograms of animal (Nietschmann 1973:93). The meat of the green turtle is universally accepted as an excellent food and its fat produces oil. In historic times commercial hunting of the sea turtle has been an

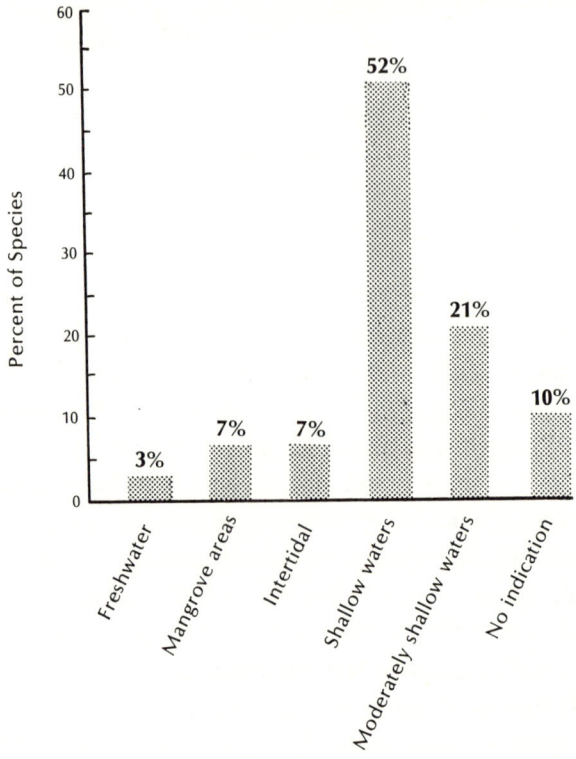

Figure 2.5. Histogram illustrating the zonal habitats of represented Selin Farm (H-CN-5) shellfish (after Moreau 1978).

important (if unstable) economic base for coastal groups of the nearby Nicaraguan-Miskito coast (Helms 1971; Nietschmann 1973).

Summary and Conclusion

In the last decade a growing number of paleoecological studies of prehistoric coastal sites have been carried out in both Mesoamerica proper and in lower Central America (Stark and Voorhies 1978; Linares 1979). These analyses have focused upon the relationships between ancient coastal groups and their environments. In pre-Columbian times the region of northeast Honduras provided an exceedingly rich, complex natural environment ideal for a broad-based, generalized subsistence strategy exploiting both land- and sea-based resources.

We can now be confident that in addition to some cultivated foodstuffs (particularly maize) Selin Period inhabitants of the site were hunting lowland forest mammals, especially deer, peccary, and armadillo. From the nearby lagoon-estuary zone, native settlers were actively pursuing the giant sea cow (or manatee), while fishing for game fish, such as jack, tarpon, grouper, and snapper, provided complementary portions of their dietary needs. Finally, from the Honduran coastal zone, collection of oysters, conch, scallops, cockles, and other readily accessible, shallow-to-medium-depth aquatic shellfish, along with the occasional sea turtle, was still another subsistence option relied upon by the Selin peoples between A.D. 300 and 1000.

During the seven-century span of the Selin Period, the archaeological data suggest that in addition to the above terrestrial and aquatic species, agouti, crocodile (or caiman), and iguana were all present in each of the Selin phases. Furthermore, there was a trend of increasing diversification of the fauna selected, with growing reliance upon marine species of game fish by late (Transitional) Selin times. Indeed, there was a 50 percent increase, from Basic Selin to Transitional Selin times, in the numbers of jack *(Caranx hippos)* represented in the faunal collection, and most other marine species show clear increases in minimum numbers (see Fig. 2.4).

The extensive exploitation of these varied environments, each with a very complex ecology, required broad technological knowledge and capabilities that can be reasonably inferred from modern faunal adaptations, habitats, and contemporary food-gathering strategies. As Porter (1965) and Nietschmann (1973:100) have pointed out, a primary concern of all societies is how to cope successfully with the economic difficulties termed "subsistence risk."[3] This risk can be reduced by careful settlement placement and knowledgeable scheduling of food-procurement activities to coincide with advantageous environmental circumstances.

In our three-season site survey of the Colón region, some six Selin Period settlements (H-CN-1, 3, 4, 5, and probably 19 and 22) were identified within approximately 5 kilometers of the Guaimoreto Lagoon, and it is likely that additional Selin sites will be identified with more intensive searching of this vicinity. This is an unusually high concentration, at least by northeast Honduras standards, and it probably reflects an early inclination by Selin natives to exploit more fully the abundant resources of the large marsh-lagoon-estuary environment, which not insignificantly abutted both the tropical forest and mangrove-marine ecozones as well. The Selin Farm (H-CN-5) site location, at the nexus of a trio of distinctive environmental zones, each with different associations of fauna and flora, offered numerous combinations of rich food-getting opportunities. The obvious advantage of living in such a locality was an overall lessening of the subsistence risk.

We have already documented the mosaic of species from these contiguous ecozones, the physical evidence of this exploitation, and through inference, the strong likelihood of a wide-ranging subsistence strategy in Selin times. Judicious settlement selection and diverse food-gathering techniques would have helped considerably to avoid the typical danger of overexploiting particular fauna or flora. The very richness of the region reduced the chances of severe ecological disruption by overhunting, disproportionate reliance on any one biotic region, or excessive gathering of any one species.

Living in an ecological setting much like that of the modern Miskito of eastern Nicaragua, the Selin natives probably made hunting and fishing activities the core of their village life. Like many Miskito settlements in coastal Nicaragua, the groups living about the Guaimoreto Lagoon were able to exploit, nearly simultaneously, both land- and sea-based food resources. To do this successfully, of course, they had to possess the knowledge and ability to utilize extremely different environmental zones, each with a complex ecology (Nietschmann 1973:89).

On the basis of comparison with the Miskito subsistence patterns, it is likely that the paleoecological evidence from H-CN-5 represents year-round habitation. The availability and location of food resources would have differed somewhat from the dry months to the wet months. Nietschmann (1973:121, table 13), discussing the Miskito coast, for example, noted that in the rainy season many brackish-water and ocean fish move out of the lagoons and away from the shore as river and creek runoff occurs. In the dry season the freshwater fish reenter the lagoons from river and creek retreats. Deepsea fishing and turtling also diminish in the rainy season. By contrast, hunting becomes more important than at other times of the year as the major meat-getting activity. Although paleobotanical data were lacking from the H-CN-5 excavations, I believe that the gathering of wild plants and fruits would have been especially important during the rainy season, when many of these plants were ripe for harvest. In sum, if we can use the Miskito of Nicaragua as an analogous group for comparison, during the dry season many of the food-getting activities are focused on marine resources and during the rainy season, on terrestial resources. Surveying the faunal representation from H-CN-5, it seems reasonable to conclude that both seasons (wet and dry) are well represented. However, due to the nature of the site, and the use of arbitrary level excavation techniques, it is not possible to determine which levels might be associated with wet season activities and which with dry season activities. Furthermore, the location of Selin Farm, its proximity to such different ecozones, would have allowed them nearly unrestricted gathering between resources and ecozones. This is an area of investigation, however, that might be profitably pursued in future studies.

In conclusion, in the northeast Honduras study area the close proximity of diverse microzones and their respective, culturally significant biota allowed the prehistoric Selin inhabitants extensive utilization of multiple ecozones, which lowered the subsistence risk and resulted in a lengthy habitation of H-CN-5. But if the subsistence resources and procurement systems of the Selin natives were so strong, why were their sites uniformly abandoned about A.D. 800 to 1000? The question cannot be answered adequately on the basis of our present knowledge of this remote area, but there is evidence in the succeeding Cocal Period (A.D. 1000–1530) of substantially altered settlement patterns, cultural remains, and subsistence strategies. These markedly widespread changes almost certainly represent the intrusion into northeast Honduras of different cultural traditions, which disrupted the Selin society and forced the abandonment of virtually all Selin sites by the end of the tenth century A.D.

Notes

1. I would like to acknowledge the financial assistance provided by the National Geographic Society of Washington, D.C. for the research in northeast Honduras in both 1975 and 1976. Additional support was provided by the Trent University Committee on Research. In Honduras we were aided by Dr. J. Adán Cueva V., director of the Instituto Hondureño de Antropología e Historia, and by Lic. Vito Véliz R., chief of investigations of the same institution. The latter's assistance in the field and his general cooperation between 1973 and 1976 deserve special mention and gratitude. Additional thanks go to Don Témis Ramírez for granting permission to excavate on the Selin Farm lands and for general aid to our field operations in Colón. Student assistants in 1976 were Sandra Alton, Joel Boriek, William Loker, Lori Oliger, David Payne, and Jill Yakubik. Research in Honduras would not have been possible without the cooperation and help of my wife, Doreen Healy; I am, as always, grateful for her aid. Dr. Junius Bird (American Museum of Natural History) and Dr. Jeremiah Epstein (University of Texas at Austin) have both generously provided notes, maps, and other unpublished data on their earlier work in this region, facilitating my more recent research. Dr. Elizabeth Wing (Florida State Museum), Arlene Fradkin (University of Florida), and Dr. Richard G. Cooke (Smithsonian Institution Tropical Research Institute) provided the faunal identifications, and Dr. Jean-François Moreau (University of Montreal) provided the molluscan identifications. Dr. Olga Linares (Peabody Museum and Smithsonian Tropical Research Institute) kindly read and commented upon an earlier version of this paper presented at the Forty-third Annual Meeting of the Society for American Archaeology in Tucson (May 1978). Finally, special gratitude goes to Dr. Gordon R. Willey (Harvard University) for introducing me to Honduras archaeology, and for years of encouraging and assisting my work there.

2. A comparison of excavated deposits, phase by phase, shows that the Early Selin remains were removed from 16.6 cubic meters, the Basic Selin from 8.3 cubic meters, and the Transitional Selin (with the greatest diversity of faunal remains) from 7.25

cubic meters. Thus, there is a decrease in the total volume of excavated deposits over time but an increase in faunal variability.

3. Porter defines subsistence risk as a "settlement negotiated between an environment and a technology. . . . A community has institutional and technical means of coping with [such] risk. . . . [The] danger to the individual can be decreased by sharing out risks, through dispersal of fields, timing of harvests . . . adjustment to risk is the essential element in the articulation of subsistence with environment" (1965:412).

Three

Maya Ritual Faunas: Vertebrate Remains from Burials, Caches, Caves, and Cenotes in the Maya Lowlands*

Mary Pohl, Florida State University

To the ancient Maya, animals symbolized the elements of nature, such as earth, rain, and sun, in addition to such abstract concepts as renewal and immortality. The Maya used animals in their agricultural and lineage ceremonies. They buried fauna in monument caches and in tombs, and they made blood sacrifices at sacred caves and cenotes. On ritual occasions they adorned themselves in status paraphernalia taken from animals. Because animals were the tangible manifestations of Maya religious thought, the bones provide unique insight into prehistoric ceremonies and the people who conducted them.

Moholy-Nagy (1963, 1978) reported on the social and ceremonial uses of mollusks among the Maya. Borhegyi (1961) wrote about shark teeth and stingray spines. An array of other vertebrate remains have turned up in special deposits. It has been difficult to discern meanings among these diverse materials. Nevertheless, enough data are now available to warrant an investigation of patterns in Maya ceremonial offerings. These can be compared with refuse from other contexts, such as middens, and interpreted by examining the animals depicted in ancient Maya art, including painted vases and sculpture of the Classic Period, as well as the Postclassic Dresden and Madrid codices (Villacorta and Villacorta 1930). Ethnohistoric and ethnographic descriptions

---

*I am indebted to Norman Hammond, Richard M. Leventhal, Hattula Moholy-Nagy, Evon Z. Vogt, and Elizabeth S. Wing for ideas, facts, and illustrations.

of Maya ceremonialism also have a bearing on the problem. Bricker (1981) has demonstrated the structured nature of religious syncretism, based on the Maya belief in cycles of time. Thus, ritual transformations that occurred after the Spanish Conquest can be identified and linked with prehistoric rites (M. Pohl 1981b).

This paper deals with pre-Columbian ritual from the Preclassic through the Postclassic Periods. At least from Late Preclassic times onward, Central Mexican culture traits appear in the Maya lowlands. My theory is that the same sort of transformations that have been documented for the historic era (Bricker 1981, M. Pohl 1981b) also occurred in prehistoric times; an example is the substitution of the Central Mexican rain god *Tlaloc* for the Maya *Chac* (see J. Pohl 1979). The fact that the religion of aboriginal peoples throughout Mesoamerica was similar no doubt facilitated such borrowings. Thus, Maya ritual from the Preclassic through the Postclassic Periods is treated as a unitary—though developing—belief system here.

The study demonstrates that caches and burials contain many of the same animal offerings as caves and cenotes. In the first section I interpret the ritual deposits at ceremonial centers, focusing on dynastic and renewal rites, which I believe to be representative of such deposits. The *cuch* rite has been specifically identified; other new year rituals were probably closely related to, if not the same as, the *cuch* rite. In the second section I show that the patterns of faunal remains in caves and cenotes correspond to the rites that the art and ethnohistory suggest were enacted.

Caches and Burials

Caches and burials may have been conceptually related (Moholy-Nagy 1978). Dedicatory and intrusive caches, some actually comprising burials, were placed in structures and below stelae. Many of the structures were built as mortuary monuments to dead rulers, and the stelae were erected to commemorate dynastic ceremonies. Most caches and burials may therefore be linked to ancient Maya rulership and lineage worship.

The vertebrate remains from these special deposits are listed in Table 3.1 in the order discussed in the text. No clear pattern in the associations of bones of different animals was detected, and thus no systematic data have been given. Because Borhegyi (1961) has analyzed the occurrence of stingray spines and shark teeth, this information is not reported in detail here.

Many of the objects found in special deposits have not been submitted for expert identification, and the details of elements that have been recovered are often vague. Thus, one of the greatest barriers to interpretation of Maya ceremonial activity is lack of information on the nature of the objects presented as offerings.

Table 3.1. Animals in Burials (Bu) and Caches (Ca) at Lowland Maya Sites
(numbers in parentheses indicate multiple occurrences at a site)

Key to Site Abbreviations

AH	Altun Ha	CZ	Cozumel sites	PN	Piedras Negras
AS	Altar de Sacrificios	D	Dzibilchaltun	PO	Pomona
B	Barton Ramie	G	Guaytan	S	Seibal
CA	Caracol	H	Holmul	SJ	San Jose
CO	Copan	HC	Hatzcap Ceel	T	Tikal
CI	Chichen Itza	L	Lamanai	TU	Tulum
CR	Cerros	M	Mayapan	U	Uaxactun
CU	Cuello	P	Palenque		

ANIMALS	Early Preclassic Bu	Early Preclassic Ca	Middle Preclassic Bu	Middle Preclassic Ca	Late Preclassic Bu	Late Preclassic Ca	Protoclassic Bu	Protoclassic Ca	Early Classic Bu	Early Classic Ca	Late Classic Bu	Late Classic Ca	Terminal Classic Bu	Terminal Classic Ca	Post-classic Bu	Post-classic Ca	Undated Bu	Undated Ca
MAMMALS																		
Odocoileus virgianus (white-tailed deer)	CU					CU			H		S CO(3)	U			M(3) CZ		U	
Mazama americana (brocket deer)															M			
Tayassuidae (peccaries)																		
Canis familiaris (domestic dog)											CO U D	U C(2)	CZ		M T CZ		CZ(4)	CZ
Felidae (cats)							AS		U(4) H		AH U U(2) AS PN	U AS			M(3) CZ(13) L		U	HC CO(2)
Felis concolor (puma)											U	U(2)						
Felis pardalis (ocelot)									H									
Didelphis sp. (opossum)									H		U				M			
Dasypus novemcinctus (armadillo)			AS								U	U(2)						
Cryptotis sp. (shrew)																CI		

Table 3.1. continued

	Early Preclassic		Middle Preclassic		Late Preclassic		Protoclassic		Early Classic		Late Classic		Terminal Classic		Post-classic		Undated	
ANIMALS	Bu	Ca	Bu	Ca	Bu	Ca	Bu	Ca	Bu	Ca	Bu	Ca	Bu	Ca	Bu	Ca	Bu	Ca
Chiroptera (bat)									U									
Carollia perspicillata (short-tailed bat)																		U
Artibeus jamaicensis (Yucatan leaf nosed bat)																		U
Desmodus rotundus (vampire bat)																		U
Rodentia (rodent)					CR				U	D		D						
Oryzomys sp. (rice rat)											U							
Sigmodon hispidus (cotton rat)											U							
Small animals					CR				H									
Tapirus bairdii (tapir)												SJ				M		
Urocyon cinereoargenteus (gray fox)														SJ				
Carnivore							AS		AH					D	TU			
Trichechus manatus (manatee)																		
FISHES																		
Siluriformes (catfish)					CR													
Rhamdia sp. (catfish)																		
Pristis sp. (swordfish)																		
Balistidae (triggerfish)					CR													CA

58

Table 3.1. continued

ANIMALS	Early Preclassic Bu	Early Preclassic Ca	Middle Preclassic Bu	Middle Preclassic Ca	Late Preclassic Bu	Late Preclassic Ca	Protoclassic Bu	Protoclassic Ca	Early Classic Bu	Early Classic Ca	Late Classic Bu	Late Classic Ca	Terminal Classic Bu	Terminal Classic Ca	Postclassic Bu	Postclassic Ca	Undated Bu	Undated Ca
Labridae (hogfish)					CR													
Cynoscion nebulosus (sea trout)																		
Chilomycterus sp. (burrfish)												D	D	D(2)				
Pogonias cromis (drum)														SJ	M			
Diodon sp. (porcupine fish)																		
Elopidae cf. Megalops atlanticus (tarpon)												AS						
Galeocerdo cuvier (tiger shark)																M(2)		
Carcharodon carcharias (great white shark)									AH	AH	PN	PN(2)						
Carcharodon megalodon (fossil shark)									T, AH, PO, U(2)		U(2), T	AS(4), PN, D(4)	P(2)					
Carcharhinus lamia (cub shark)													P					
Sphyrna sp. (hammerhead shark)											P						CZ	
Squaliformes (shark)					U, T, C		AS						CZ(3)		M		CZ(2)	
Dasyatidae (stingray)															M, CZ	M		
Dasyatidae (fossil stingray)																		

Table 3.1. continued

ANIMALS	Early Preclassic Bu	Early Preclassic Ca	Middle Preclassic Bu	Middle Preclassic Ca	Late Preclassic Bu	Late Preclassic Ca	Protoclassic Bu	Protoclassic Ca	Early Classic Bu	Early Classic Ca	Late Classic Bu	Late Classic Ca	Terminal Classic Bu	Terminal Classic Ca	Postclassic Bu	Postclassic Ca	Undated Bu	Undated Ca
Myliobatis sp. (fossil eagle ray)	CU																	
Fish			AS				AS	AS	D			P(2) AS D(3) PN	G		M			HC
REPTILES																		
Crotalus durissus (rattlesnake)													S					
cf. *Lampropeltis* sp. (king snake)									D				D					
Colubridae (colubrine snake)												U						
Crocodylus sp. (crocodile)									T	T(2)				D		TU		
Ctenosaura similis (black iguana)										AH								
Kinosternon sp. (mud turtle)								AS										
Dermatemys mawei (hicotea blanca)											CO B U				TU	CZ	U	
Turtle																	U	
BIRDS																		
Meleagris ocellata (ocellated turkey)																		
Ara sp. (macaw)										T						CZ		
Sarcoramphus papa (king vulture)										T						TU		

Table 3.1. continued

ANIMALS	Early Preclassic Bu	Early Preclassic Ca	Middle Preclassic Bu	Middle Preclassic Ca	Late Preclassic Bu	Late Preclassic Ca	Protoclassic Bu	Protoclassic Ca	Early Classic Bu	Early Classic Ca	Late Classic Bu	Late Classic Ca	Terminal Classic Bu	Terminal Classic Ca	Postclassic Bu	Postclassic Ca	Undated Bu	Undated Ca
Glaucidium brasilianum (ferruginous pygmy owl)												CO				CI		
Saltator sp. (finch)																CI		
Colinus nigrogularis (quail)									D U				D					
Cardinalis cardinalis (cardinal)									D									
Icteridae (blackbirds)									D									
Buteogallus urubitinga (great black hawk)												D	D					
Columba sp. (pigeon)															TU			
Ardeidae (heron)									U	PN	PN U	AS PN(2)			TU			
Birds							L AS										HC U	
AMPHIBIANS																		
Bufo sp. (toad)											D CZ(2) CZ				M(2) CZ(8)			
Smilisca baudinii (Mexican tree frog)																		
cf. *Leptodactylus* sp. (leptodactylid frog)															CZ			
Rana pipiens (leopard frog)															M			

Sources: Longyear 1952; Ricketson and Ricketson 1937; Merwin and Vaillant 1932; Kidder 1947; Ray 1956; Hamblin 1980; Lothrop 1924; A. Smith 1950, 1972; Wing and Steadman 1980; J. Thompson 1931, 1939; W. Coe 1959; Pendergast 1979, 1981; Maudslay 1889–1902; Ruppert 1935; Carr 1980; M. Pohl 1976; Borhegyi 1961; Moholy-Nagy 1963; Wing n.d.; Stuart 1934; Morris, Charlot, and Morris 1931.

61

DEER

Ethnohistoric data indicate that the deer supernatural was a significant figure in ancient Maya religion. It appears to have been associated with the sun. For example, in distance numbers, a deer appears as the sign of *kin*, meaning "day" or "sun" (Schele 1977:52–53). On Vault 2 of the East Subterranean passage in House E at Palenque, a deer and the sun both ride on the back of a saurian creature (Greene Robertson, personal communication, 1978). In the riddles of the *Book of Chilam Balam of Chumayel* "that which hooks the sky" is a deer (Roys 1933:127), and in the Dresden Codex (page 36a), a deer carrying torches hangs by his tail from a sky band.

The references cited above may throw some light on a much earlier funerary offering uncovered at Cuello. A terminal Early Preclassic crouched burial contained two bone hooks made of deer metapodials. One lay at the foot and one at the chest of the skeleton. We know that later Maya were fond of puns. If these funerary deer-bone hooks can be related to sun symbolism, they may represent prehistoric beliefs about the continuity of life.

The *Popol Vuh* relates that Tohil (Storm), one of the principal gods of the Quiche Maya, took the form of a deer and demanded young deer as a sacrifice (Edmonson 1971:186). During the Inquisition that Bishop Landa conducted in Yucatan in 1562, the Indians said that they sacrificed a small deer to Tabay, who was perhaps a female fertility deity (M. Pohl 1981b). These historic references suggest that immature animals were required for specific rituals.

The bones indicate that young animals were deliberately selected on occasion. In the Late Preclassic Period the Maya of Cuello deposited a double cache of deer mandibles (Fig. 3.1) in the course of renewing the surface of Platform 34 (Hammond and Wing, personal communications, 1981). Some upper molars and a few other cranial fragments suggest that the whole skulls had been deposited, but these may have rotted away. In Cache 363, 20 of 30 minimum numbers of individuals were juveniles (Wing, personal communication, 1981).

Other evidence dates to the Postclassic Period. An immature PM_2, the only subadult deer bone from Cozumel, turned up in a burial at El Cedral (Hamblin 1980:249–53). Deer were probably not native to the island, so the tooth offering must have been imported.

The deer was a primary player in the most important ritual drama of the Maya ceremonial cycle, the *cuch* rite marking year renewal (M. Pohl 1981b). The Late Classic style Calcehtok vase (Fig. 3.2) depicts this rite. As a vulture hovers overhead, celebrants remove the antlers of a stag before a sacred tree encircled by a serpent. The sound of a conch trumpet accompanies the ceremony. Because the men on either side of the stag bear spears, we can assume that the final act was to put the deer to death.

Maya Ritual Faunas 63

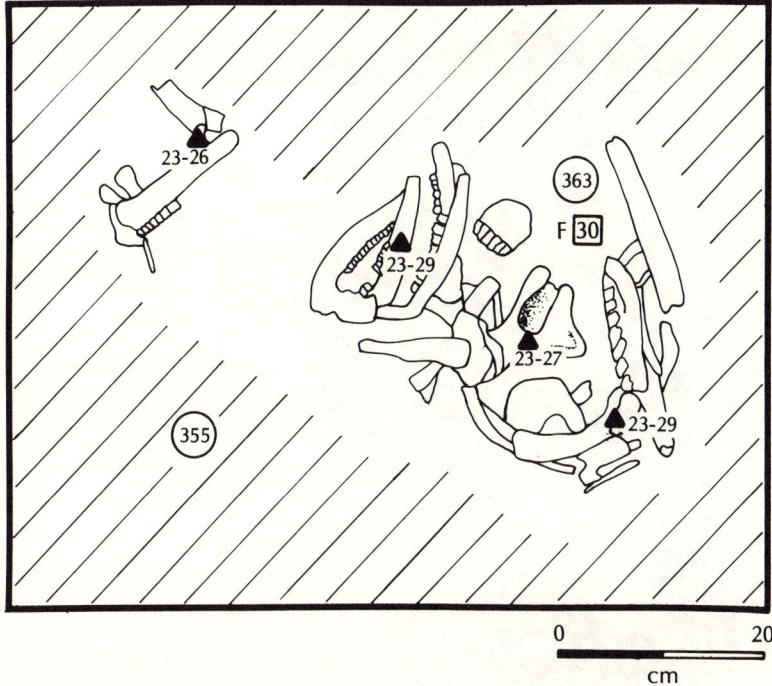

Figure 3.1. One of two caches of deer bones placed roughly on the midline of the east-west axis of Platform 34, Cuello, during the Late Preclassic Period. (Drawing courtesy of N. Hammond.)

Page 30b of the Postclassic Madrid Codex may be an allegorical representation of this *cuch* ritual. A deer, together with a peccary, dog, jaguar, and *Chac*, surround a gigantic female figure with water streaming from her body and a snake in her headdress (Fig. 3.3). The Maya continued to perform the *cuch* sacrifice shortly after the conquest. During the Inquisition of 1562, Yucatec Maya confessed to sacrificing deer, dogs, and peccaries at the foot of crosses (the equivalent of sacred trees) in churches and cemeteries. The Indians said that these blood offerings were petitions for rain and good crops.

Many Maya, following prophecies about the coming of great deer at the time the Spaniards arrived, substituted a bull for the aboriginal stag character after the conquest (M. Pohl 1981b). The Lacondones of Chiapas may have continued to observe the rite in its original form, however. Early in this century,

Figure 3.2. The Late Classic style Calcehtok vessel. Two men with spears flank a stag. The man to the right is removing the stag's antlers, while the figure on the left blows a conch shell trumpet. (Courtesy of Dumbarton Oaks, Washington, D.C.)

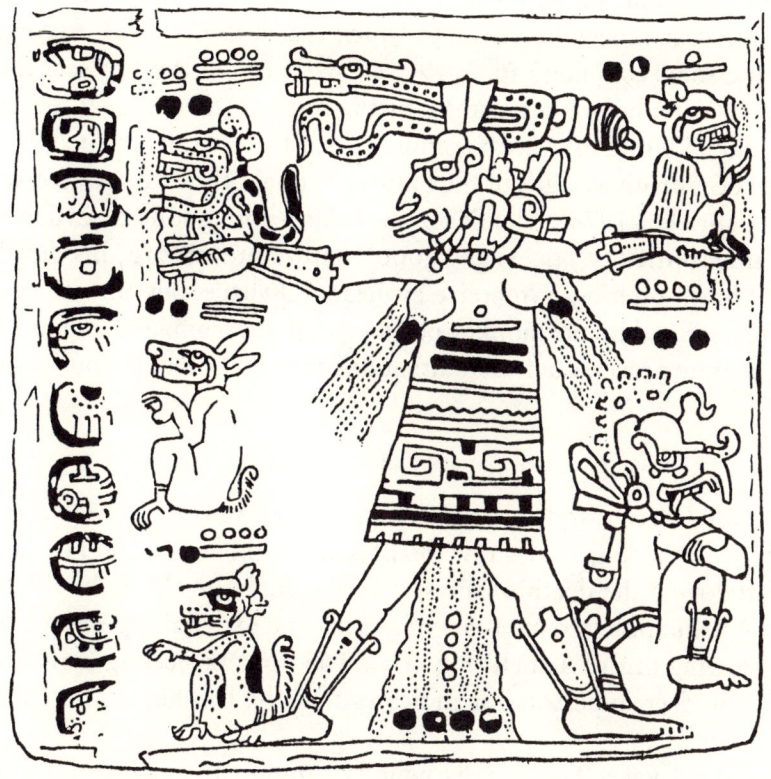

Figure 3.3. The deer and its cohorts associated with *Chac* and a female fertility figure in the Madrid Codex (page 30b) (Villacorta and Villacorta 1930).

Tozzer (1907:115) reported that the mandibles stuck in the thatch of the ceremonial *hermita* were mostly those of deer, along with peccary and some monkey.

According to ancient Maya art and ethnohistory, other animals associated with renewal rites were the monkey, peccary, dog, jaguar, snake, fish, opossum, armadillo, crocodile, and turtle, as well as the turkey in the Postclassic Period. The following discussion concentrates on these fauna, which illustrate the symbolism of animal offerings.

MONKEY

Monkey bones occur only rarely in ritual deposits, but this animal was clearly linked to the stag in ancient times. In Maya art monkeys often have deer antlers, and stags sport long tails (for example: Fig. 3.6). In present-day highland Chamula, the opposing forces of bull and monkey characters appear in the year renewal ceremony, which is tied to Carnival. According to Gossen (personal communication, 1978), a spectacular three-bull sacrifice takes place eight days before the climax of the festival (the Tuesday before Ash Wednesday). During four great communal feasts, thousands of people are fed chili and beef broth as a gift of the Pasión, a ritual official associated with the sun deity (Bricker 1973). The Pasión embodies both good and evil, and only with "ritual difficulty" does his "good" nature prevail over his "evil" side. The beef broth offerings symbolize his heat and virtue, but his malevolent aspect is represented by the monkey personages that accompany him at all times and perpetrate perverse acts that are opposite to the forces the bull signifies.

PECCARY

Two Late Classic–style vessels, one from San Agustín Acasaguastlan and the other from Nebaj, may show the presentation of a peccary head, which I believe followed the death of the stag in the *cuch* rite (M. Pohl 1981b). On the San Agustín pot, two men carrying sacrificial axes hail a peccary head and a tree growing out of a shell (Fig. 3.4). The bone projecting from the forehead of the deer impersonator indicates that the hatchet men are about to sacrifice him.

The second vase (Fig. 3.5) is usually thought to represent a traveling merchant. An alternative interpretation is that a lord is parading the peccary head, along with a dog skull. One of the characters in the procession wears a conch shell on his back; another carries a sacred bundle, the symbol of rulership.

The present-day equivalent of the *cuch* rite is a ceremony marking the close of one agricultural year and the beginning of the next. This event is expressed in allegorical terms in the modern Cakchiquel Maya belief that two deer pull the sun across the sky on short days, and two peccaries pull him on long days (Stoll, cited in J. E. S. Thompson 1970:370). Significantly, the hat worn by the anthropomorphic snail in the San Agustin Acasaguastlan vase (Fig. 3.4) bears the *tun* sign, symbol of the solar year (Taube, personal communication, 1981). The parading of the animal head (today a pig, probably substituted for the aboriginal peccary) accompanies the transfer of the burden, or *cargo* (*cuch* in Maya), from one fiesta sponsor to another. The act ensures continued economic viability in the coming year.

The distribution of bones at Maya sites provides evidence for ritual use of peccaries. Two incised peccary skulls came from Late Classic Period Tomb 1 at Copan (Fig. 3.6). The date carved on one of the skulls was earlier than the burial, suggesting that the object commemorated an important event or

Figure 3.4. Late Classic–style vessel from San Agustín Acasaguastlan, middle Motagua, Guatemala. The peccary head, lying in the jaws of a serpent, and a tree growing out of a shell are the center of attention (Smith and Kidder 1943:fig. 43b).

Figure 3.5. Late Classic–style polychrome vase from Nebaj, El Quiche, Guatemala. A lord on a palanquin parades peccary and dog heads. On the other side of the vessel, celebrants carry long trumpets, a conch shell, and a sacred bundle. (Photograph courtesy of the Museum of the American Indian, Heye Foundation.)

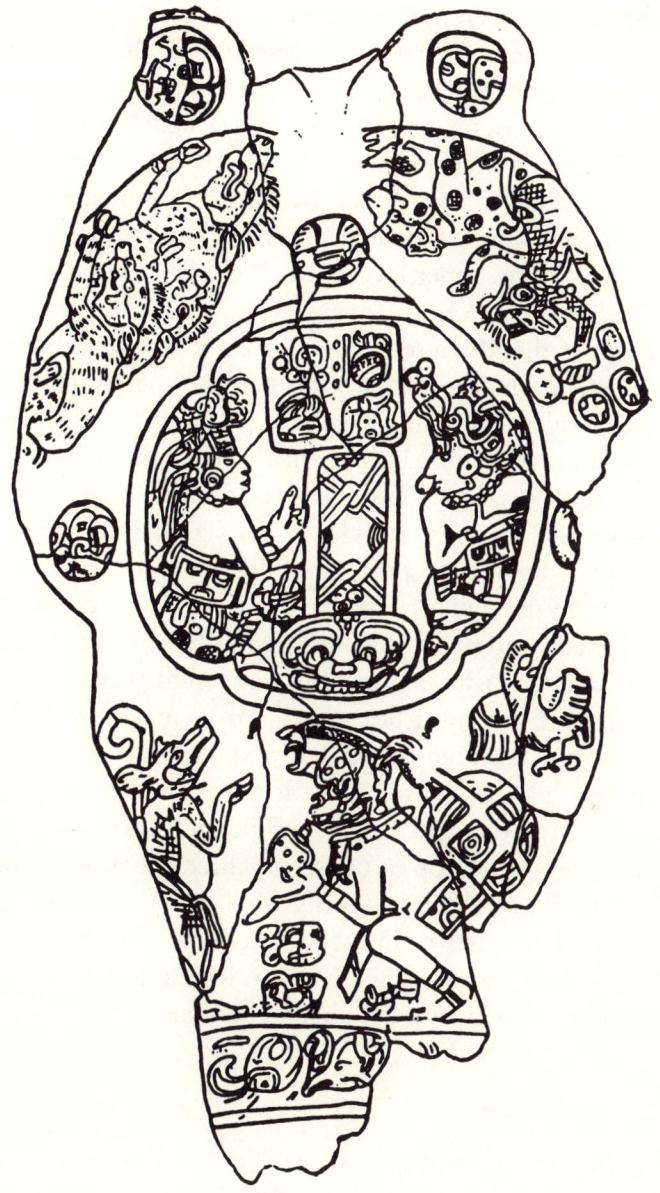

Figure 3.6. One of two incised peccary skulls from Tomb 1 at Copan. In the center the royal mat symbol rises behind a jaguar head, which may constitute a cave symbol. Below, a monkey with deer antlers blows on the conch trumpet and carries an immense burden on a tumpline, while a bird hovers overhead (Spinden 1913:fig. 210).

that the offerings were heirlooms (Longyear 1952:40–41). The skulls were found associated with deer, as well as with turtle bones.

Skulls were consistently treated differently from the rest of the body. At Cozumel's San Gervasio, peccary was represented in Postclassic burials primarily by postcranial elements, whereas skull fragments were most often in house mounds (Hamblin 1980:244). At Postclassic Mayapan (Pollock and Ray 1957) and at Late Classic Seibal (M. Pohl 1976) postcranial bones were associated with elite site contexts. Peccary skulls appeared juxtaposed with censor fragments in the upper levels of the middle Postclassic occupation of Flores, Peten (Cowgill 1963).

In ancient times the Maya may have performed a ceremony similar to the *cuch* rite not only each year but also at significant period endings and at the inauguration of rulers (Pohl and Pohl, n.d.), whose reigns were often correlated with cycles of time in Mesoamerica (see Klein 1976, 1980). Like the modern fiesta sponsor, it may have been the ruler's duty to assume responsibility for the well-being of the people, a duty symbolized by the burden. The carving on one of the Copan peccary skulls (Fig. 3.6) is of great interest in this connection. In the center of the composition is an altar or throne, which resembles a jaguar head but which also carries the circular markings characteristic of the *cauac* monster, a possible cave symbol (Taylor 1978:79). Above the head is an upright object bearing the royal mat sign (Robicsek 1975); below it is a stag with immature antlers and a long monkey tail. He faces a curious figure with a monkey skull head adorned with deer antlers and ears. This character blows the conch shell trumpet and carries an enormous burden on a tumpline. At the top of the scene, three peccaries cavort opposite a jaguar, and a monkey holds a rattle engraved with three crosses. Nearby is a *kan* cross, symbol of water or maize. The iconography may suggest that the Copan peccary skull was used in a Maya ruler's accession ceremony, which might have taken place in a cave (Pohl and Pohl, n.d.).

DOG

Both the ancient art and ethnohistorical data point to an association between the dog and year renewal. Landa (Tozzer 1941:145) reported that in the New Year's rite for the Muluc year, old women danced with pottery dogs with bread on their backs. A little dog with a black back was sacrificed to ward off calamity.

This description of a dog sacrifice is supported by the puppy bones found in late prehistoric archaeological contexts. At Tikal (Instituto de Antropología e Historia de Guatemala and University of Pennsylvania excavations), dog remains, many of very young animals, occurred in Terminal Late Classic refuse in abandoned palace rooms (M. Pohl 1980; Moholy-Nagy, personal communication, 1980). Standard ritual practices seem to have been abandoned at this time, but some of the dog bones may represent ritual offerings.

In recent times the Lacandones have made small figures of dogs to place in graves (Tozzer 1907:47). According to Sahagún, Central Mexicans believed that dogs helped their masters across the great river encircling the underworld, and at the time of the Spanish Conquest, the Indians customarily provided a dog as a burial offering (Tozzer and Allen 1910:360). Postclassic Cozumel and Mayapan may provide evidence for such a belief late in Maya prehistory. At Cozumel dogs were concentrated in burials (Hamblin 1980:127); at least 32 individuals were recovered from 14 burials at 5 sites. One burial dated to Pure Florescent times, and all of the other deposits that could be fixed chronologically were Postclassic in date. Tooth eruption and postcranial fusion of bones indicate that nearly 20 percent of the Cozumel dog elements came from animals no more than 21.5 months of age; many (14 percent) were puppies 5 months or younger. About one-third (32 percent) of these tiny puppy elements occurred with human burials (Hamblin 1980:210). Dog teeth were recovered from three Postclassic burials at Mayapan (Ray 1956), but there is little evidence of dog remains in funerary contexts dating to earlier periods in the Maya lowlands, even though dogs were common in middens at Cuello as far back as Early Preclassic times (Wing n.d.).

FELINES

The jaguar was a supernatural being in ancient Maya religion on a par with the deer. Noting that the jaguar had the water lily and symbol for night as ornaments, Thompson (1950:134) concluded that the jaguar was an underworld deity, perhaps the embodiment of the night sun on its journey below the earth. Thus, the Maya may have come to believe that the jaguar inhabited caves traditionally regarded as entrances to the underworld, as well as sources of life-giving water.

The cat is often depicted with the deer. A Late Classic Period dish, discovered by Diane and Arlen Chase at Santa Rita, portrays a jaguar and a deer (again with the long monkey tail) opposite one another. The jaguar deer dance, performed all over the Maya area in this century, centers on the jaguar's pursuit of his prey, the deer. Among the highland Tzutuhil Maya of Santiago Atitlan, this dance appears to be a rain-making ritual (Mendelson 1958:123).

In the Classic Period jaguars may have been connected with rulership and even with specific lineages. The jaguar glyph figures prominently in the names of Yaxchilan rulers (Marcus 1976). Cats are often depicted in contexts in which dynastic ceremonies are represented. For example, on Lintel 3 of Temple I at Tikal (Fig. 3.7), a gargantuan jaguar stands behind the enthroned ruler, who

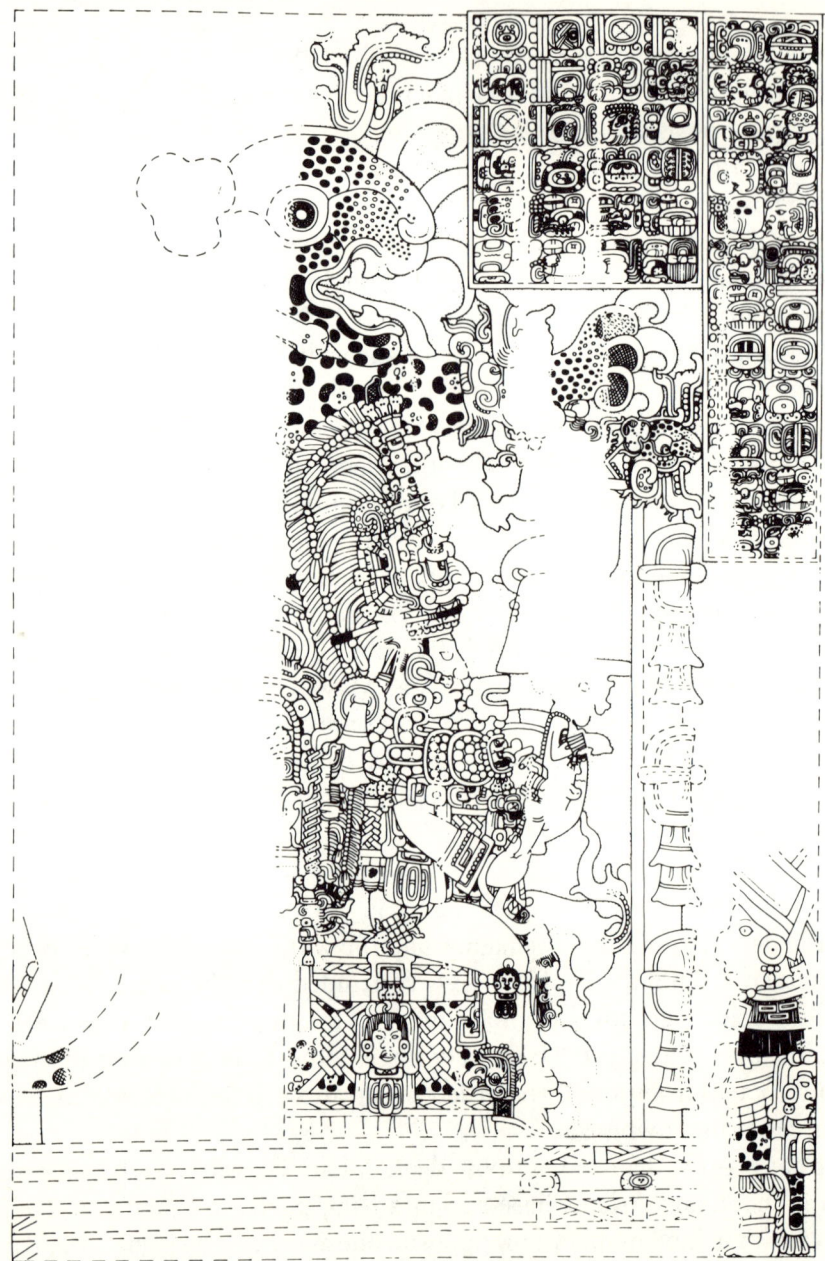

Figure 3.7. In Lintel 3 of Temple I at Tikal, a gigantic water-lily jaguar behind the new ruler, who is sitting on a throne adorned with mat symbols. (Drawing by W. Coe in Jones 1977:fig. 1. Reproduced by permission of the Society for American Archaeology.)

is being inaugurated (Jones 1977:29). Similarly, at Palenque in the Oval Palace Tablet, Pacal, the new ruler, is shown sitting on top of a double-headed feline throne. The cats lack spots, but a foliation motif on their foreheads may identify them as water-lily jaguars (Schele 1977:50–51). The jaguar's presence may have validated the lord's right to rule. The fact that the jaguar is so closely associated with caves supports the hypothesis that the accession ceremony, perhaps a variant of the *cuch* rite, took place in caves.

The association of jaguars with office and with lineage continued into the historic era in modified form. According to the Motul dictionary, *balam* ("jaguar") was a term applied to town officials and native priests in sixteenth-century Yucatan (Roys 1931:328). In the highlands Jaguar House was one of 13 secondary tribes listed in the *Popol Vuh* (Edmonson 1971:157, note 5106).

Maya art demonstrates that elites exploited jaguars for paraphernalia befitting their rank. Pelts were particularly sought after, and claws occur in burials. For example, ungual phalanges were found in two Early Classic burials at Uaxactun (A. Smith 1950:table 6). The position of these bones in Burial A-31 suggests that a skin, perhaps that of a jaguar, had covered the skeleton.

In the *Lineage of the Lords of Totonicapan,* "All of these titles/and ranks/ had their insignia/ and these were claws of jaguars/panthers . . ." (Edmonson 1971:232, note 7708). There is little faunal evidence for the jaguar claw ornaments described ethnohistorically, though a perforated *tumbaga* claw, evidently of Panamanian origin, occurred in an Early Classic cache at Altun Ha (Pendergast 1979:150–51).

The data do demonstrate that canines were status markers deposited in burials. Canines were found in six burials at Uaxactun, Altar de Sacrificios, and Holmul, ranging in date from Early to Terminal Classic period (A. Smith 1950:table 6, 1972:259, 268; Merwin and Vaillant 1932:figs. 30 and 36).

Jaguars appear to have denoted male activities. In the ancient art men wear spotted pelts. Traditionally a jaguar skin was spread in the marketplace as a sign of war *(Book of Chilam Balam of Tizimin,* quoted in Roys 1931:331), and the Motul dictionary defines *zin balam* ("spread the jaguar") as "to fight" (Roys 1933:154, note 2). Most cat remains occurred with male skeletons, where sex could be determined (A. Smith 1950; W. Coe 1959:24).

The Maya frequently cached whole or partial cat skeletons. At Altar de Sacrificios, the remains of an immature ocelot skull, together with the scapula and a caudal vertebra, were placed between two vessels in a Protoclassic cache (A. Smith 1972:239). A puma skull, painted red and accompanied by a few postcranial elements, was cached at Uaxactun during the Late Classic Period. What appears to be the complete skeleton of an ocelot on its right side, head to the west, was found in another cache of the same period (A. Smith 1950:

103–4). Such caches seem to have been a specialty of Copan. Beneath the main mound in the Great Plaza, a feline skeleton, said to have been a jaguar, was interred under a layer of charcoal. The teeth and some bones were covered with red pigment. A smaller mound, 100 yards to the south, yielded parts of another cat skeleton, together with fragments of human bones and some dog teeth (Maudslay 1889–1902:20). When Willey and Leventhal recently re-excavated Copan, they found the decomposed skull and partial skeleton of a young felid below the plaza floor of an important Late Classic house group.

FISH

Fish may have been involved in the *cuch* rite. M. Coe (1973:126) illustrates a *cuch* vase showing the hornless, dead deer with conch trumpet strapped to his back and fish below his hooves. In his description of the *cuch* fiesta (M. Pohl 1981b), Landa (Tozzer 1941:155–56) says that during the month of Zip, a dance with arrows and deer skulls was followed by a pole-raising rite and a communal fishing party. García de Palacio described a similar ceremony in the sixteenth century:

> They took a live deer to the courtyard of the *cu* or temple which they had outside the town and there they throttled and skinned him, collecting all his blood in a vessel and cutting the liver, lungs, and stomach into small pieces. They divided the heart, head and legs. They cooked the deer by itself and the blood, by itself, and while these were cooking, they had their dances. The high priest took the skull by the ears and the four priests each took one of the four feet, and the *mayordomo* put the heart in a brazier and burned it with *uli* and copal as incense to the idol of the god who was protector of hunting and fishing. When the dance was finished, the head and feet were scorched in the fire before the idol as an offering and afterwards taken to the house of the high priest and eaten. The priests consumed the deer and his blood before the idol; they gutted fish and burnt them before the same idol. (García de Palacio 1860:75–76; Tozzer and Allen 1910:349)

We do not know precisely where this fiesta took place. Palacio was most familiar with ancient Cuscatlan, now the republic of El Salvador, but he also visited Copan and the city of Chiquimula.

Artifacts found in prehistoric burials may relate to the *cuch* rite. A carved bone from Late Classic high-status Burial 116 in Temple I at Tikal (Trik 1963) shows *chacs*, perhaps wearing stylized deer ears, engaged in a ritual fishing expedition. The same burial contained a tripod plate in the shape of a conch shell (Moholy-Nagy 1978). In the codices whole fish and fish heads are portrayed as offerings in the new year ceremony (for example, see pages 27b and 27c of the Dresden Codex). In Dresden 27c the fish sacrifice is resting on two *kan* signs, which may symbolize water or maize (J. E. S. Thompson 1950:276; Tozzer and Allen 1910:308).

Fish bones occur much more frequently in burials and caches than in general refuse (see Tables 3.1, 3.2, and 3.4). Catfish were utilized for ritual offerings. A whole catfish *(Siluriformes)* occurred in a Protoclassic burial at Altar de Sacrificios (M. Pohl 1976), and unspecified catfish remains were reported in a Postclassic burial at Tulum (S. Lothrop 1924:97).

The Maya appear to have favored marine organisms of various sorts. In addition to the sharks and stingrays, other marine vertebrates include a swordfish *(Pristis)* rostrum from a cache associated with an altar at Caracol (Satterthwaite, cited in W. Coe 1959:64), one triggerfish *(Balistidae)* and one hogfish *(Labridae)* bone from a Late Preclassic burial at Cerros (Carr 1980), the skull portion (basioccipital) of a sea trout *(Cynoscion nebulosus)* from a Pure Florescent burial at Dzibilchaltun, dermal spines and beak of burrfish *(Chilomycterus)* associated with one Early Period II and two Pure Florescent caches at Dzibilchaltun (Wing and Steadman 1980:794), and seven drum *(Pogonias)* teeth from a Postclassic burial shaft at Mayapan (Ray 1956). About 70 complete and 50 broken spines of the porcupine fish *(Diodon)* were scattered in a Terminal Late Classic cache at San Jose (Thompson 1939:188). Carr (1980) warns that bones in Cerros burials might have been accidentally included with fill, but this is an unlikely explanation for sites located at a distance from the coast and where marine species are otherwise rare.

Sea fish form part of a whole complex of marine organisms that the Maya deposited in burials and caches, including crab claws, manatee bones, mollusks, coral, pearls, sand dollars, bryzoa, sponges, and gorgonian (for example, see Moholy-Nagy 1963, 1978; W. Coe 1959; Andrews 1969; Longyear 1952; Thompson 1931, 1939; Pendergast 1979; Kidder 1947; A. Smith 1950; Hamblin 1980). At Cuello, two Late Preclassic Period child burials included marine shells, which Hammond (personal communication, 1981) tentatively suggests were pubic shields for girls. *Spondylus americanus* had been stripped to reveal the pink interior and pierced in two places, presumably for suspension. One shell was located in the pelvic region of the skeleton.

This "cult of the sea" (Andrews 1969:53) may have been connected with renewal ritual. In Maya art the underworld deity, God N, is often depicted emerging from a conch (for example, see M. Coe 1975:no. 10). Ix Chel, goddess of childbirth, is also associated with this shell (J. E. S. Thompson 1950:133, Closs 1977). These contexts suggest that the shell symbolized both death and birth or rebirth. The interpreter of Vatican A observed, "just as the [shell]

Table 3.2. Minimum Numbers of Individuals of Selected Animals from Three Cave Sites in Belize Compared with Fauna from the Late Classic Elite Zone at Seibal

	Eduardo Quiroz	Actun Balam	Actun Polbilche	Seibal
MAMMALS				
Cryptotis mayensis (Yucatan small-eared shrew)			3	
Chiroptera (bats)	7		62*	
Dasypus novemcinctus (armadillo)	1			
Rodentia (*Heterogeomys hispidis, Sigmodon hispidis, Oryzomys couesi, Ototylomys phyllotis,* Sciuridae, etc.)	51		315	1
Canis Familiaris (domestic dog)			124	2
Felidae (cats)	1	1	2	5
Tarpirus bairdii (tapir)	1			
Tayssuidae (peccary)				4
Odocoileus virginianus (white-tailed deer)	1	1		18
Mazama sp. (brocket deer)	2		2	1
BIRDS**				
Ardeinae (egret or heron)	1			
Mellagris ocellata (ocellated turkey)				2
cf. *Penelope purpurascens* (crested guan)	1			
Psittacidae (parrot)				1
Colinus nigrogularis (black-throated bobwhite)	2	1*		

Table 3.2. continued

	Eduardo Quiroz	Actun Balam	Actun Polbilche	Seibal
Accipitidae cf. *Spitzaetus ornatus* (hawk eagle)				1
cf. Raillinae (rail or crake)	1			
Gallinula chloropus (common gallinule)	2			
Tyto alba (barn owl)	1			
Hiurndinidae (swallow)	1			
Emberizinae (sparrow)	1			
REPTILES				
Kinosternon sp. (mud turtle)	1	1*		
Dermatemys mawei				4
Chrysemys scripta (pond turtle)				1
Crocodylus sp. (crocodile)				1
FISHES				
Siluriformes (catfish)				1
AMPHIBIANS				
Anura (frog or toad)	1		2	
TOTAL	86	8*	516*	50

*Estimated MNI
**Birds were not analyzed at Actun Polbilche and were only partially studied at Eduardo Quiroz.
Sources: H. Savage 1978; Pendergast 1964, 1969b, 1974; M. Pohl 1976.

fish issues from the shell, so emerges man from the womb of its mother" (J. E. S. Thompson 1950:133).

Rain and underworld gods share certain traits, and the reason may be rooted in Maya ideas of renewal. For example, both God B, the rain god, and the underworld deity G 1 sometimes wear thorny oyster *(Spondylus)* shells over their ears (Moholy-Nagy 1978).

Today the Chorti of southeastern Guatemala decorate their altars with marine shells to celebrate the summer solstice. The shells symbolize rain, moisture, and fertility. Girard (1962:248) theorized that these decorations were used for this particular ceremony because it coincided with the period of maximum rainfall.

SNAKES

The snake is one of the characters of the *cuch* ritual. On the San Agustín Acasaguastlan *cuch* vase (Fig. 3.4) the peccary head rests in the jaws of a rattlesnake. The snake also appears in the headdress of the female deity associated with this ceremony (Fig. 3.3).

In recent times the Quiche Maya of highland Guatemala have used snakes, including coral snakes and rattlesnakes, in a ritual dance. The snakes are piled around the neck of a female impersonator (Schultze-Jena 1946:76–77). Schultze-Jena theorized that offerings of food presented in the dance indicated that the ceremony had originally been a petition for abundant crops.

The Maya may have practiced snake handling as part of their rites. The figure on the west end of the reviewing stand in the western court of the acropolis at Copan holds a snake between his teeth. A polychrome vessel from a Late Classic Period burial at Altar de Sacrificios depicts a dancer holding a snake high above his head.

Deadly snakes are most often depicted in scenes of blood sacrifice in Classic Period art. In the late sixteenth century, Ciudad Real reported that native priests traditionally used rattlesnake rattles in ceremonies and sacrifices (Noyes 1932:309). The Maya handled live snakes too: "They were great sorcerers and they had their books to charm and enchant them. With the few words they recited, they charmed and tamed poisonous serpents; they caught them and held them in their hands without injury" *(Relaciones de Yucatan* I, quoted in Roys 1931:335).

The Maya may have gone to some lengths to procure snakes for their ceremonies. At Seibal, a rattlesnake *(Crotalus durissus)* vertebra was placed in a Fine Orange pot, along with the partial skeleton of marine toad *(Bufo marinus),* and deposited in a Terminal Late Classic burial (Olsen 1978:173).

Rattlesnakes do not occur today in humid southern Peten (Duellman 1963; Lee, personal communication, 1978). Unfortunately, no direct evidence of past environmental conditions is available for southern Peten. Pollen data for central Peten (Vaughan 1979) suggest that climate during the Late Classic Period was about the same as it is now in that area. If the same were true of southern Peten, one might speculate that the Maya brought the rattlesnake to Seibal from a relatively dry habitat, such as the savanna zone of central Peten.

OPOSSUM

The books of *Chilam Balam* refer to the Bacabs as Tolil Och, the "Opossum Actors." Landa (Tozzer 1941:137–41) indicates that the Bacabs were involved in the new year rite, and Joralemon (cited in Klein 1980) points out that they were associated with God N, who presided over the Uayeb rites. The Bacabs may be the opossum year bearers in the upper register of pages 25 through 28 of the Dresden Codex (Fig. 3.8).

During Early Classic times at Holmul, 25 perforated opossum jaws *(Didelphis)*, along with 100 worked pieces of shell and a jade bead, were found scattered below six skeletons in Building B of Group II, the most impressive structure at the site (Merwin and Vaillant 1932:29). Perhaps the Holmul mandibles were sewn on clothing worn by the dead nobles.

ARMADILLO

The fossorial armadillo occasionally appears in Classic Period paintings. In one recurrent motif the armadillo participates in a musical procession led by a water lily jaguar or a stag (for example, see Dieseldorff 1926:plate 22). Perhaps this picture represents a parade that was part of a prehistoric jaguar deer dance.

The armadillo was a symbol of fertility in many areas of Mesoamerica. In the Madrid Codex, page 92d, an armadillo and a deer sit on mats facing women, an association that may represent fecundity.

The armadillo occurs occasionally in archaeological deposits. Two armadillo shells *(Dasypus novemcinctus)* were found in a Middle Preclassic child burial at Altar de Sacrificios (A. Smith 1972:266) and a Late Classic adult male burial at Uaxactun (A. Smith 1950:table 6).

CROCODILE

Seventeenth-century historian Lizana (Roys 1931:327) said, "They worshipped the crocodile, a creature without a tongue." In one manifestation the animal appears to have been a crocodile representing the earth; its celestial counterpart was Itzam Na[1], which Las Casas identified as "God the Father."

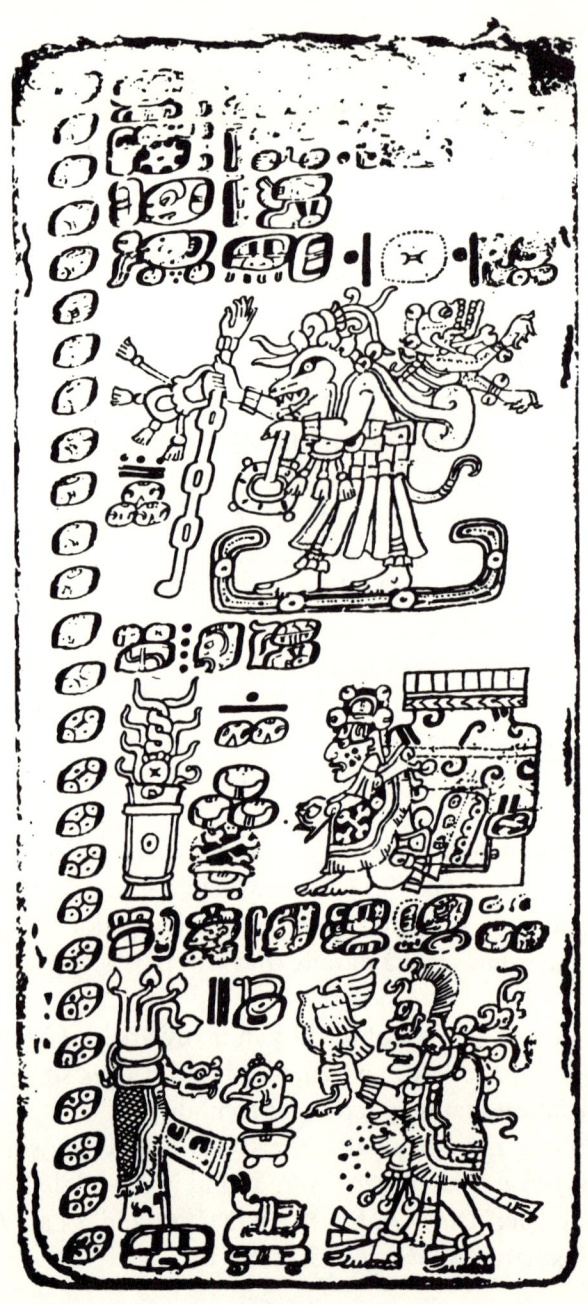

Figure 3.8. A new year's ceremony from the Dresden Codex depicts turkey and deer offerings before a sacred tree encircled by a snake. Above, the opossum acts as year bearer, and a ritual bundle lies ensconced in a temple decorated with the mat symbol (J.E.S. Thompson 1972a).

According to López Mendel's *Relación,* published in the early seventeenth century (Tozzer 1941:223), a crocodile emerged from the cenote at Chichen Itza to receive the sacrifices of women that the Maya offered as petitions for rain and maize.

The present-day Chorti of southeastern Guatemala see a connection among crocodiles, snakes, and fish. The Indians believe that the earth takes the form of a crocodile, and one aspect of the rain deity is a serpent. Their offspring is a fish representing the young maize god. Girard (1966:83–85) suggests that because these animals are associated in prehistoric art, the belief is ancient.

In Maya art the white-tailed deer is closely connected with crocodiles, as well as with snakes (J. E. S. Thompson 1939). Saurian and ophidian forms are depicted with antlers and cloven hooves, along with deer ears and molars (the so-called dragon teeth). Examples of the deer-crocodile combination are the Itzam Na (J. E. S. Thompson 1970:220, fig. 5) carved on Altar D at Copan (Spinden 1913:53) and the later clay crocodile from Postclassic Santa Rita (Gann 1918:fig. 18), which Thompson (1970:220) believes is another version of Itzam Na. This mingling of traits may be explained by the fact that both crocodiles and deer are associated with the earth.[2] Deer ears are often adorned with the query sign, which Landa reported was the earth symbol (Tozzer 1941).

At Tikal, entire skeletons of crocodiles were interred in two caches and a tomb, all dating to the Early Classic Period (Stuart, personal communication, 1977). The prevalence at Tikal and Uaxactun of aquatic fauna, such as crocodiles and also turtles, is surprising, because water is scarce in the vicinity of these sites today. The animals may have been procured from artificial *aguadas,* or water reservoirs. Alternatively, these fauna may have resided in canals excavated in the Bajo de Santa Fe, which Adams, Brown, and Culbert (1981) think are reflected in images obtained by side-looking, airborne radar.

We may have evidence that crocodile bones were used in dance costumes worn by impersonators of this supernatural. In a mound at Altar de Sacrificios excavators recovered a left crocodile mandible that had been drilled, grooved, and polished (Olsen 1972:245).

TURTLES

Testimony given in the Inquisition of 1562 indicates that idolators sacrificed deer and turtles in the church at Yaxcaba "in the ancient way" (Scholes and Adams 1938:104). The codices show that the Maya associated turtles with water and abundance. On page 19 of the Madrid Codex, a turtle is surrounded by five gods, including Chac, who are connected by a rope drawn through perforated penises. Joralemon (1974) relates such autosacrifice to fertility ritual.

The turtle or tortoise motif is so common in Yucatecan art that Ball (1979:34) suggests the animal was a tutelary or totemic of the Xiu lineage at Uxmal. At Mayapan, stone turtles or tortoises were associated with shrines that may have been devoted to lineage worship. The iconography of fertility and immortality may have been appropriate for elite lineages in a culture devoted to ancestor worship, such as that of the Maya.

Freshwater turtles, including the small *Kinosternon* and the large *Dermatemys*, occur in burial and more frequently cache contexts dating from Protoclassic to Late Classic times. The prehistoric art indicates that the Maya beat turtle shell drums with deer antlers in ceremonial processions, including the *cuch* rite (for example, see M. Coe 1975:fig. 16). Present-day Palencano-Chol insist that such drums be male river turtles (Greene Robertson, personal communication, 1978). In the future some attention should be paid to sexing these archaeological turtles.

TURKEY

At Seibal, the left first phalange of the forelimb of an ocellated turkey *(Meleagris ocellata)* was found in a Late Preclassic to Protoclassic cache vessel. This bone is often removed with the wing feathers; perhaps a single plume or a feather fan was actually the subject of the offering. Fans may have been symbols of rulership among the Maya (Roys 1965:xvii). Turkey feather fans were carried by Indians impersonating nobility in the *xtol* dance that Starr (1904) witnessed in Merida in 1901. Research suggests that this dance may have originally been part of the *cuch* ritual.

The codices, in conjunction with the archaeological evidence, demonstrate that turkey sacrifices became a requirement for new year's ceremonies in the Postclassic Period. Pages 25 to 28 of the Dresden Codex show turkey sacrifices (Fig. 3.8), along with offerings of deer haunches. On page 91 of the later Madrid Codex, a turkey is shown tied to the sacred tree in the same manner as hornless deer (M. Pohl 1981b).

Turkeys are most common at lowland Maya sites during the Postclassic Period. *Meleagris ocellata* remains were found in a Postclassic burial at Tulum (Lothrop 1924:97). Large numbers of ocellated turkey bones were strongly associated with elite site contexts at Mayapan (Ray 1956).

Archaeological evidence for the domesticated turkey *(Meleagris gallopavo)* appears first at the trade center of Cozumel, and its presence implies direct or indirect contact with northern Mexico. Wild ocellated turkeys do not occur on Cozumel today, although they may once have inhabited the island (Waide, personal communication, 1981). Perhaps increased demand for these birds in

Postclassic times decimated local populations and induced the Cozumel Maya to import domestic types to raise.

The codices and early historic data indicate that the Maya sacrificed turkeys by decapitating them (Tozzer 1941:141, 145; Tozzer and Allen 1910: 325–27). Of all the bird bones found on Cozumel sites, the only skulls were two specimens from an elite burial at El Cedral (Hamblin 1980:182).

OTHER BIRDS

Birds had immense ritual significance throughout the New World. Like fish remains, bird bones occur more often in caches and burials than in kitchen refuse. The lowland Maya exploited a variety of species, notably the owl, the macaw, the quail, and birds of prey (king vulture and great black hawk).

The macaws best demonstrate the extent to which the Maya engaged in long-distance trade to obtain objects for ceremonial devotion and ornamentation. In an Early Classic cache at Tikal, remains of a macaw *(Ara)* were found with four king vultures *(Sarcoramphus papa)* (Paynter, personal communication, 1974). The macaw is at home in remote regions, especially along watercourses (Land 1970:57). The king vulture is a forest bird that rarely lands in inhabited regions, though it may fly over them (Land 1970:124). The archaeological evidence for high population densities around Tikal at the time the caches were buried suggests that the birds might have been imported to the site for the ceremony.

At Cozumel sites, three species of macaw may be represented (Hamblin 1980:186). *Ara macao* has been seen only in Campeche but may have had a wider distribution on the Yucatan peninsula in the past (Waide, personal communication, 1981). One species was possibly a north Mexican type, *Ara militaris*, and another might be *Ara ambigua*, a Central American bird. A parakeet *(Aratinga)*, also not a modern Yucatecan species, may have been a trade item or an extinct bird. Cozumel psittacid bones were burned, suggesting that birds were used for ritual purposes (Hamblin 1980).

A macaw skull was found in a Late Preclassic to Early Classic votive deposit at Zacaleu in the Maya highlands (Woodbury and Trik 1953:115). This bird must have originated in the tropical lowlands. Taken together, these remains testify to a widespread commerce in macaws and probably also in their feathers.

The historic Maya kept flocks of macaws around their houses. A seventeenth century account of the Cholti-Lacandon settlement of Sac Balam contains the following description of tame birds: "At 5 o'clock in the afternoon, after having flown around, they came to roost on the ridge poles of all the houses, forming a delightfully beautiful landscape of various deep red colored clusters of flowers . . ." (Hellmuth 1977:426). Writing in the highlands in the eighteenth century, Ximénez (1967:90) also reported the custom of keeping domesticated macaws for their plumes, which were used to decorate altars and dance costumes.

In Maya religion the macaw may have symbolized the sun. One aspect of the sun god was Kinich Kakmo, "Sun-face Fire Macaw." Lizana wrote that a temple of Kinich Kakmo was located in the plaza of Izamal on the north side, the direction associated with the sun god. The deity was reported to descend at midday, flying like a macaw, to burn the sacrifice (J. E. S. Thompson 1970:240). In Classic Period sculpture the deity's glyph is the head of a macaw with the *kin* (sun) glyph in front (J. E. S. Thompson 1970:240). Macaws are shown in the Dresden (page 40b) and Madrid (page 12a) codices brandishing torches, symbol of burning heat.

The Motul dictionary lists the owl as an omen (Roys 1931:331). In the *Popol Vuh* four owls are the messengers of Hell (Edmonson 1971:96). Even today a popular Mexican saying is, *"Cuando canta el tecolote, el indio muere"* (When an . . . owl calls, an Indian dies") (Laughlin 1976:19).

Surprisingly, the owl is mentioned in passages in the codices that Tozzer and Allen (1910:338) interpret as referring to birth, baptism, and the naming of children. The Maya may not think of death as a terminal event in the sense that we do. For example, in Chorti fertility ritual a pair of turkeys is encouraged to copulate. The Chorti explain that coitus is like death: life springs from both (Girard 1966:31).

The owls depicted in Maya art appear to be the great horned owl *(Bubo virginianus)* and the screech owl *(Otus guatemalae)*, but owl caches usually consist of the ferruginous pygmy owl *(Glaucidium brasilianum)*. Excavations conducted by Willey and Leventhal at Copan uncovered a cache containing the partial skeletons (primarily wing and leg elements) of two ferruginous pygmy owls.[3] The bones of one specimen were covered with red pigment and lay in a *Spondylus* shell. The other bird bones were in a carved, polished, brown vessel dating to the Late Classic Period. Inside a limestone vessel found at Chichen Itza, wing and leg elements of pygmy owl, as well as finch *(Saltator)*, lay upon and around remnants of textile and a spectacular turquoise mosaic (Morris, Charlot, and Morris 1931:189).

The reason for the choice of pygmy owls in caches is unknown. The Copan specimens were both males, the smaller of the two sexes (Broadkorb, personal communication, 1980). A hypothesis concerning the significance of small size is discussed below.

SMALL ANIMALS

In addition to pygmy owls and other small birds, bats and rodents often occur in ceremonial deposits. Some of these animals may have entered on their own. According to Carr (1980), the character of the soil around a Late Preclassic Cerros burial suggested burrows. Other deposits, however, look intentional. For example, in the Late Classic Period an adult female skeleton was buried with a vampire bat skull *(Desmodus rotundus),* a cotton rat *(Sigmodon hispidis),* a rice rat *(Oryzomys),* a shrew *(Cryptotis),* and a small bird (A. Smith 1950:table 6). At the same site, in a cist in the corner of an altar of Temple E-II, many bones of a Yucatan leaf-nosed bat *(Artibeus jamaicensis),* a short-tailed bat *(Carollia perspicillata),* a cotton rat *(Sigmodon hispidis),* probably a rice rat, and the ulna of a small bird were closely packed around an offering of human bones placed between red ware bowls.

Perhaps the common denominator in these bone deposits is small size. The present-day highland Maya of Chiapas picture distant persons or objects as physically small (Morris, personal communication, 1980); deities are often diminutive in the lowlands. For example, the Zip, patron of deer, is a tiny stag about the size of a dog (Redfield and Villa Rojas 1962:118). Divine characters may be considered distant and hence small (Morris and Schele, personal communications, 1980).

The proposed relationship among size, distance, and divinity may be ancient. On the Tablet of the Temple of the Foliated Cross at Palenque, the dead ruler, Pacal, is small in contrast to his successor, Chan-Bahlum. A dwarf on the south side of Pier C, House C, at this site is painted blue, the color of things supernatural (Greene Robertson 1979:166). This evidence suggests that small size has traditionally been a trait of otherworldliness.

Bats, rats, and some birds inhabit caves, which the Maya believed were avenues to the underworld. Thus, the presence of these animals in ritual deposits might be sacred symbols of their deities and ancestors. The hypothetical significance of small size may also account for the frequency of young animals, including human babies, in ceremonial offerings.

Frogs and toads are another class of small animal that the Maya have traditionally revered. Today in Chan Kom, Yucatan (Redfield and Villa Rojas 1962:20), amphibians found in caves and cenotes are considered sacred because they consort with the *chacs.* Among the highland Tzotzil of Larrainzar, a frog guards the entrance to sacred caves, which are believed to be the home of the rain god and the source of clouds and lightning bolts (J. E. S. Thompson 1970:268; Vogt 1969:387). These beliefs about toads and frogs are deeply rooted in Maya culture. For example, the Madrid Codex (page 17c) shows a frog or toad, along with a turtle, in the rain.

Toads are also connected with women. In the highlands "toad" is the word for fetus. In ancient Maya art toad designs decorate women's ceremonial robes, as they do today among highland Tzotzil and Tzeltal Indians of Chiapas (Morris 1980). Like frogs and toads, female deities inhabit caves and cenotes.

The Maya of the northern lowlands put anurans in burials during the Postclassic Period. On Cozumel, 94 percent of the amphibian elements and 74 percent of the minimum numbers of individuals came from seven burials at four sites, ranging from Terminal Classic or Early Postclassic to Late Postclassic Period in date. Nearly all parts of the skeleton were present, suggesting that the animals were buried whole in many cases (Hamblin 1980:103).

Caves and Cenotes

The Maya may not have drawn a distinction between caves and cenotes. In the sixteenth century Indian informants probably pointed out to Ciudad Real that "in the wall of this well or *zonote* [of Chichen Itza] there is a cave that reaches far within" (Noyes 1932). Present-day highland Tzotzil Maya of Zinacantan classify all water holes, sinkholes, and caves as "openings" in the earth's crust. They are a means of communicating with the Earth Lord, and in rituals they are treated similarly (Vogt 1969:386–89).

Abundant historic data testify to the fact that cenotes figured in the rain cult. The Inquisition testimony of 1562 provides a great deal of evidence on the ritual. Describing a rite at the cenote of Tixpayan, one Indian reported that, "they made . . . that sacrifice in order to be provided with sustenance and good rainy spells." Sacrifice appears to have had a divinatory element. Alonso Chan's testimony given at Hocaba contained the following: ". . . Gaspar Chuc threw the said boy into the cenote, and they waited to see if he was coming out to give them the reply of what their gods had told him in order to know whether there was to be any pestilence or much food or sterility . . ." (Tozzer 1941:notes 948, 949).

In addition to this fertility cult, caves and cenotes may have been used for dynastic ritual. Present-day Mam Maya from the Guatemalan highlands report that caves are the centers of ancestor worship (J. Pohl, personal communication, 1980). Writing of the highlands of Chiapas in the early eighteenth century, Bishop Núñez de la Vega reported that the bones of the founders of the group that introduced the Maya calendar were kept in caves. The people presented them with flowers and copal and venerated them "as though they had been saints" (J.E.S. Thompson 1975:xxxiii). Even though Núñez ordered the bones destroyed, human remains have been found in many caves. Some bones may have belonged to sacrificial victims, whereas others might be related to a lineage cult.

Roys (1933:173) suggests that the cenote at Chichen Itza may have been inhabited by the spirits of the illustrious dead, as well as by the gods. The Postclassic figure Hunac Ceel, who lept into the cenote to receive the prophecy, later became head chief of Mayapan. The story of his jump may be allegorical, and his ability to communicate with the gods and the ancestors might be symbolically connected with his political ascendency.

One of the problems in analyzing cenote and cave faunas is distinguishing between animals that died naturally and those that were deposited by the Maya. Another difficulty is assigning dates. Cenotes are unsealed deposits, and cave offerings are often unstratified palimpsests of activity. Despite these analytical problems, the cave and cenote fauna demonstrate a clear resemblance to animal offerings from caches and burials.

CAVES

According to López de Cogolludo (1971, vol. I:410–11), the Inquisition of 1562 was touched off by the chance discovery of a deer sacrifice in a cave. The subsequent investigation of paganism revealed that the Maya worshipped about 100 idols in the cave, petitioning them for rain and good crops (J. E. S. Thompson 1975:xxxv). Deer appear to have been prominent figures in prehistoric cave ceremonials. Carvings of deer have been found on the wall of Actun Ceh (Mercer 1975:fig. 10).

A Late Classic Period polychrome vessel from Actun Balam Cave (Fig. 3.9) depicts hunters spearing stags. Glyphs associated with the hunters might be interpreted as referring to water and God B *(Chac)* (Pendergast 1969b:50). A female figure rides one of the stags, and behind her is a dwarf holding a spindle with unspun cotton hanging from it. The same substance may decorate the hats of some of the hunters. Cotton is a fertility symbol. It is equated with clouds in both highland and lowland Maya folklore (J. E. S. Thompson 1970:251, Morris 1980). Spinning is also a metaphor for both sexual intercourse and civilization in Mesoamerica (Sullivan 1977). In the Madrid Codex, page 30a, Ix Chebel Yax, the Creator's spouse, wears spindles of spun cotton in her headdress.

At the cave of Balankanche, Andrews (1970) found a formation resembling a tree surrounded by censors (perhaps also used as water collectors) in the shape of *Tlalocs,* Mexican rain gods. Maya caves with their "trees" and deer carvings recall the paintings of the *cuch* ceremony on the Calcehtok and San Agustin Acasaguastlan vases. Appropriately, other cave finds included hoards of miniature manos and metates and tiny food vessels, as well as spindle whorls.

Pendergast (1969b, 1971, 1974) has provided systematic data on animal remains dating primarily to Late Classic times from three caves in Belize:

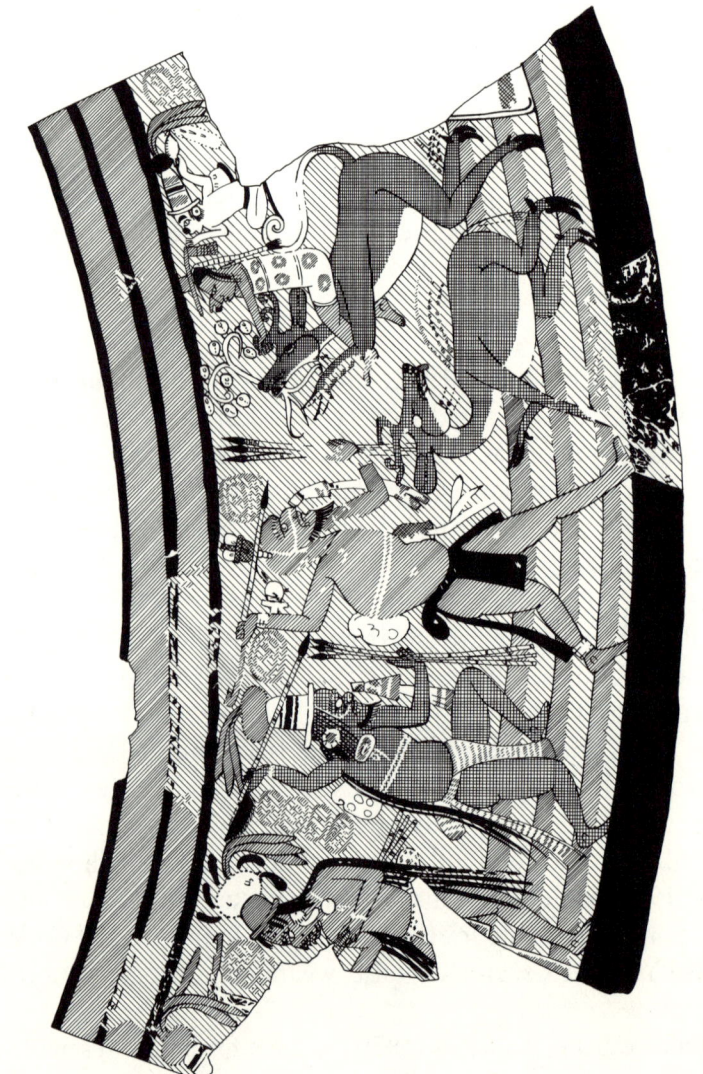

Figure 3.9. Late Classic Period polychrome vase from Actun Balam depicting a ceremonial stag hunt. (Roll-out drawing courtesy of D. Pendergast.)

Eduardo Quiroz, Actun Balam, and Actun Polbilche (Table 3.2). The cave faunas reveal that the Maya were using the animals in much the same way they used those in other special deposits, though the details of the ritual practices appear to differ somewhat.

Remains of brocket and white-tailed deer occurred in the caves. Bones of deer from Belize caves tend to be antlers and skull parts, in accordance with the description of the deer ceremonies by Landa and Palacio. The meatier parts of the deer may have been removed for ritual consumption.

As in other ritual deposits, peccary remains are rare in caves. Pendergast found none in the Belize caves. A few elements of collared peccary *(Dicotyles tajacu)* have been reported in caves in Yucatan (Mercer 1975; Hatt 1953:72), but these are undated. Ceremonial disposal of peccaries appears to have taken place primarily around habitation sites rather than in caves.

At Actun Polbilche, Pendergast uncovered 873 dog teeth, representing at least 124 medium-sized and small dogs (Luther 1974:76–77). Many of the teeth were perforated, and all animals were adult. The incisors were most abundant, in contrast to the concentration of canines and carnassials in Cozumel fauna and in cenote deposits in Mayapan. Other animals, including large cats (jaguar or puma), brocket deer, and *Homo sapiens,* were also represented by teeth, especially incisors. The reason for this preponderance of teeth is unclear.

Eduardo Quiroz Cave yielded several birds. Some, including the barn owl and swallow, might have flown into the cave on their own. The common gallinule *(Gallinula chloropus),* black-throated bobwhite *(Colinus nigrogularis),* and heron or egret (cf. snowy egret, *Leucophoyx thula,* or Louisiana heron, *Hydranassa tricolor)* are another story. The closest suitable habitat for these birds would have been located 60 to 65 kilometers from the cave (Savage, cited in Pendergast 1971:84). The fact that the gallinule and egret or heron are water birds may be meaningful. In Yucatec Maya, *bac ha,* the word for white heron, also means to pour out water (J. E. S. Thompson 1972a:100). The Maya may have brought these birds to sacrifice to the *chacs,* whom the Yucatecans have traditionally believed inhabit caves (Villa Rojas 1945:103).

Of the 14 bird bones that could be assigned to right or left position, 11 wing or leg elements were from the left side. This occurrence of left bones is greater than one would expect by chance, according to the chi square test. This finding at Eduardo Quiroz may parallel a statistically significant association of left elements of white-tailed deer with elite and ceremonial areas of the site of Seibal (M. Pohl 1976). At Copan, Willey and Leventhal uncovered a left deer haunch buried near an early house floor. The turkey wing bone from the Late Preclassic to Protoclassic cache at Seibal was also a left element.

Directional symbolism pervades Maya life today, especially in the highlands. In Chamula right is the direction of the rising sun, and left signifies the underworld (Gossen 1974). Evidence that the ancient Maya ordered their lives similarly can be found in the art. In nearly all instances, the most important figure in a painted or carved scene faces left. Likewise, heads in almost all glyphs face left. In the archaeological deposits, however, we cannot determine whether the left bone elements were the side that was selected or the side that was discarded.

Bird bones commonly occur in caves. An unidentified small bird was cached in the rim of a vessel at Actun Polbilche (Pendergast 1974:70). Fisher (Hatt 1953:87) found remains of pigeon, quail, chachalaca, and parrot, perhaps *Amazona xantholora* or *A. albifrons* (Wing and Steadman 1980:789), in caves in Yucatan and suggested that the Maya brought the birds into the caverns. Skulls of all birds are underrepresented. Wing notes the prevalence of leg bones of chachalaca *(Ortalis vetula)* both in Yucatecan cave contexts and at the site of Dzibilchaltun. She believes that the pattern of elements reflects human exploitation of the bird. A noticeably large number of *Icteridae* (blackbird, oriole, grackle) occurred in caves in Yucatan. Because birds of this family have been found in other ritual deposits, their presence in caves may have cultural significance.

Freshwater turtles have often been found in the caves of Belize and Yucatan. The mud turtle *Kinosternon* is frequently represented here, as well as in caches and burials. Although it may have been used for ritual purposes, the mud turtle was not eaten by Late Classic elite residents of Seibal, who showed a marked preference for *Dermatemys* (M. Pohl 1976). However, a small amount of mud turtle was found in elite refuse at Mayapan (Ray 1956).

Snakes, including the poisonous *Crotalus* and *Bothrops,* have been recovered from caves (Hatt 1953). At Petroglyph Cave, Caves Branch, Belize, the Maya had cached snakes in crannies along the cave walls. Excavators Reents and MacLeod also found remains of child sacrifices in ancient pools (now dry), paraphernalia for autosacrifice, manos and metates, and apparent cloud symbols on cave walls (MacLeod and Puleston 1978:72; Reents, personal communication, 1978). Activity in the Caves Branch caves of central Belize appears to extend from Late Preclassic to Postclassic times.

A large number of bats, rats, and shrews have been reported from Petroglyph Cave, Eduardo Quiroz Cave, and Actun Polbilche (Savage 1978). These bones are probably natural deposits. Nonetheless, in Cave 3 at Copan, Gordon (1898a:11) came upon three jars with partially cremated bones of children, together with small rodent remains, also charred.

Shells found in caves reinforce the idea that rituals held there were directed toward renewal and regeneration. At Petroglyph Cave, millions of freshwater and terrestrial snails paved a pathway to an underground river (MacLeod and Puleston 1978:74). Many caves also contained marine shells indicating a connection with the "cult of the sea" (MacLeod and Puleston 1978:72; Pendergast 1969b:55, 1971:110, 1974:59).

CENOTES

The early historic Inquisition testimony from Yucatan (Scholes and Adams 1938) indicated that the Maya sacrificed deer, dogs, and peccaries at the foot of crosses, probably representing the pre-Columbian sacred tree, while they crucified children and threw them into cenotes. The archaeological data from Mayapan and Chichen Itza suggest that the Indians deposited animals in cenotes as well. Researchers have found human bones in cenotes, especially at Chichen Itza (Hooton 1940; Fry 1956; Saul 1975), but most of the remains are animal bones (Ray 1956; Littlehales 1961:561; Andrews and Andrews 1980; Moholy-Nagy 1982). Mayapan yielded a large sample of fauna from cenotes X-Coton and Ch'en Mul. The associated ceramics suggest that the Maya made most of these sacrifices in the Late Postclassic Period (R. Smith 1953, 1954). The frequencies of selected animals, calculated according to minimum numbers of individuals, are shown in Table 3.3. Dog *(Canis familiaris)* and deer *(Odocoileus virginianus),* along with some peccary *(Tayassuidae),* constitute 58 percent of the cenote fauna. The strong emphasis on deer and dog can be demonstrated by comparing the cenote fauna with bones from high-status contexts at the site. Elite midden refuse yielded only 9 percent deer and dog, while ocellated turkey *(Meleagris ocellata)* and black iguana *(Ctenosaura similis)* made up 73 percent of the latter sample. Clearly these bones reflect different activities.

An examination of bone elements of deer and dog in the Mayapan cenote sample (Table 3.4) indicates that these animals were treated in different ways. Most deer bones were elements of the hind limb, as we would expect from examining pictures of offerings in the codices (Fig. 3.8). The Madrid Codex, page 65a, depicts a haunch in front of God B or D (Tozzer and Allen 1910:350), and in describing a sixteenth-century year-renewal rite, Landa says, "they gave the priest the leg of a deer" (Tozzer 1941:141). The high numbers of astragali and calcanea may indicate that the Maya deposited these bones as tokens of the sacrificial haunch, while other elements of the hind limb were sometimes saved, perhaps for ceremonial feasting or as raw material for tools.

The dog is represented by a large number of mandibles, along with maxillae, carnassials (lower first molars and upper fourth premolars), and cervical vertebrae, including a few atlases and axes. Other skull fragments may have

Table 3.3. Frequencies of Selected Animals From Cenote and Elite Contexts at Mayapan, Yucatán*

	Elite		Cenote	
	MNI	%	MNI	%
MAMMALS				
Canis familiaris (domestic dog)	7	(1)	37	(31)
Felis onca (jaguar)	1	—		
Felis concolor (puma)	1	—	1	(1)
Tayassuidae (peccary)	5	(1)	3	(3)
Odocoileus virginianus (white-tailed deer)	40	(8)	28	(24)
Mazama sp. (brocket deer)	8	(2)	5	(4)
BIRDS				
Meleagris ocellata (ocellated turkey)	170	(33)	13	(11)
Ortalis vetula (chachalaca)			3	(3)
REPTILES				
Chrysemys scripta (pond turtle)	4	(1)	2	(2)
Ctenosaura similis (black iguana)	210	(41)	16	(14)
FISHES				
Squaliform (shark)	3	(1)		
Galeichthys felis (sea catfish)	9	(2)	1	(1)
Epinephelus sp. (grouper)			1	(1)
Cichlasoma sp. (moharra)	18	(3)		
TOTAL	517		118	

*Eight cow *(Bos)* and horse *(Equus)* bones have been omitted from the cenote calculations, because these animals do not reflect prehistoric Maya activity.
Source: Ray 1956.

Table 3.4. Mayapan Cenote Fauna: Number of Deer *(Odocoileus virginianus)* and Dog *(Canis familiaris)* Bones.

	Odocoileus virginianus	*Canis familiaris*
Antler	5	
Skull	9	8
Maxilla		17
Mandible	3	66
Upper Fourth Premolar		11
Lower Fourth Premolar		4
Upper Molars		10
Lower First Molar		42
Lower Second Molar		3
Incisors		1
Canines		44
Atlas		3
Axis		5
Cervical Vertebrae	6	17
Thoracic Vertebrae	2	4
Lumbar Vertebrae	8	17
Scapula	5	4
Sacrum	1	2
Pelvis	20	8
Rib		1
Humerus	9	26
Radius	13	6
Ulna	4	29
Femur	29	18
Tibia	22	25
Patella	5	
Cuboid	9	
Lunar	1	
Astragalus	46	1
Calcaneum	50	14
Metapodials	20	18
Phalanges	84	2

suffered from lack of preservation. The data suggest that dog heads, or parts thereof, were thrown into the cenote as offerings. The osteological finds conform to the picture of the *cuch* rite on the Nebaj vase (Fig. 3.5).

The Mayapan cenote evidence for dog utilization parallels the evidence found at habitation sites. At Cozumel, skull bones, mandibles, maxillae, and loose teeth comprised 42 percent of all dog elements. Of the loose teeth, canines and carnassials constituted 69 percent of the total. These teeth are three to four times their expected frequencies (Hamblin 1980:212). At Dzibilchaltun, 21 of 28 dog bones found in midden contexts ranging from Formative to Decadent times were skulls, jaws, teeth, atlases, or axes. No concentration of head elements was noted at Dzibilchaltun's Cenote Xlacah, however (Wing and Steadman 1980:782). Though skull elements were not overrepresented in general refuse at Mayapan, almost all teeth were canines and carnassials (Ray 1956). This distribution of dog bones at Maya sites suggests that ceremonial use of dogs was not confined to cenotes.

At Mayapan, peccary bones, though rare, were closely associated with elite and cenote contexts. Peccaries are less abundant than deer and dogs in the cenote sample. Except for two skull fragments and a dentary, the bulk of the bones, 36 in number, were postcranial elements. Most peccary fragments were not distinguished to the species level. Nonetheless, three head elements were identified as white-lipped peccary *(Tayassu pecari)*, a high forest animal (Ray 1956). Its presence implies either the existence of considerable forest cover in the vicinity of Mayapan or the practice of bringing in animals specifically for ceremonial purposes (Pollock and Ray 1957:640).

The Maya have traditionally associated female fertility figures with bodies of water (J. E. S. Thompson 1970:244). Even today Indians living near Cenote Xlacah claim that their patroness St. Ursula lives at the bottom of the sinkhole (Marden 1959:120). As previously suggested, page 30b of the Madrid Codex (Fig. 3.3), which was probably painted right after the fall of Mayapan, may be a metaphorical depiction of animal sacrifices, such as those connected with the *cuch* rite. These rites may actually have taken place at cenotes. The remnants of dog skulls and deer haunches in Mayapan cenote fauna support this theory. The scarcity of peccary head elements might be explained by the fact that skulls were decorated, some eventually being deposited in tombs, as at Copan.

The iconography of archaeological finds from cenotes provides further evidence that the Maya may have performed the *cuch* ceremony, or a closely related rite, at these natural wells. At Chichen Itza, a gold disc depicts the spear sacrifice of the deer impersonator (Fig. 3.10). The same cenote yielded wood and gold spear throwers, parts of spear shafts and stone knives, and projectile points (Willard 1926; Sheets and Bathgate 1982; Coggins 1982b). Such finds also occur at other cenotes; for example, R. Smith (1954) recovered a flint point from Cenote Ch'en Mul.

Representations of the *cuch* rite show that the conch shell trumpet was a key element in the ceremony. At Chichen Itza, Thompson dredged up such a trumpet (Moholy-Nagy 1982). On some pots the conch is shown tied to the back of the deer (for example, see M. Coe 1975:fig. 6). A jade bead (Fig.

Figure 3.10. The spear sacrifice of the deer impersonator depicted on a gold disk from the Cenote of Sacrifice at Chichen Itza (Lothrop 1952:fig. 32). J. Pohl points out that a *Tlaloc* plate occurred in Cenote Xlacah (see Andrews 1959), paralleling such imagery at Balankanche Cave.

3.11) with a carving of a deer emerging from a conch shell also occurred in the cenote at Chichen Itza (Proskouriakoff 1974). Many of the jades were probably parts of necklaces, and they may have symbolized accession. In present-day Zinacantan a transfer of office is marked by a exchange of necklaces (Bricker 1973:42).

Throughout Mesoamerica, renewal ceremonies generally included disposal of used objects and new fire rites. At Chichen Itza, many artifacts of stone and wood were broken and burned (Sheets and Bathgate 1982; Coggins 1982b); many of the textiles were tattered (Lothrop 1982).

Even though the remains of relatively few human sacrifices have been recovered from cenotes, we have evidence that autosacrifice accompanied these ceremonies. Mayapan archaeologists found that 70 percent of the artifacts from the cenotes were obsidian blades (Smith 1954). At Cenote Xlacah, bone needles may have served as bloodletters (Taschek 1982).

Cenote Xlacah, located in the center of the site of Dzibilchaltun, provides further data on cenote ritual. The majority of the artifacts from the cenote date to Early Period II and Pure Florescent. Among the fauna (Wing and Steadman 1980) deer, dog, and peccary were represented by only a few individuals. However, 16 of the 21 bones were elements of the skull or mandible, suggesting that the bones were deposited in the course of ceremonial activity.

Cenote Xlacah yielded the entire shell of the terrestrial black-bellied turtle *(Rhinoclemys areolata)*, which was covered with scratch marks (Wing and Steadman 1980:791). In modern-day Chan Kom an animal identified as a "tortoise" is said to weep in times of drought. His tears are thought to draw rain (Redfield and Villa Rojas 1962:207).

Cenote Xlacah fauna is distinguished by a variety of birds comprising 30 percent of the total minimum number of individuals (Wing and Steadman 1980). These include the ocellated turkey *(Meleagris ocellata)*, neotropic cormorant *(Phalacrocorax olivaceous)*, great egret *(Casmerodius albus)*, blue-winged teal *(Anas dicors)*, turkey vulture *(Cathartes aura)*, great black hawk *(Buteogallus urubitinga)*, collared forest falcon *(Micrastur semitorquatus)*, and rare great-horned owl *(Bubo virginianus)*. Most of these birds could have been incorporated into the cenote deposit naturally, or they may have been ceremonially thrown into the deep well. The elements recovered, as well as the biotopes they represent, lend support to the latter theory. The bones of cormorant, egret, and turkey vulture consist of skulls, along with some wing segments. The turkey was represented by most elements of the body *except* the skull (Wing and Steadman 1980:786–90). The collared forest falcon lives in relatively undisturbed forest (Paynter, personal communication, 1981). Perhaps

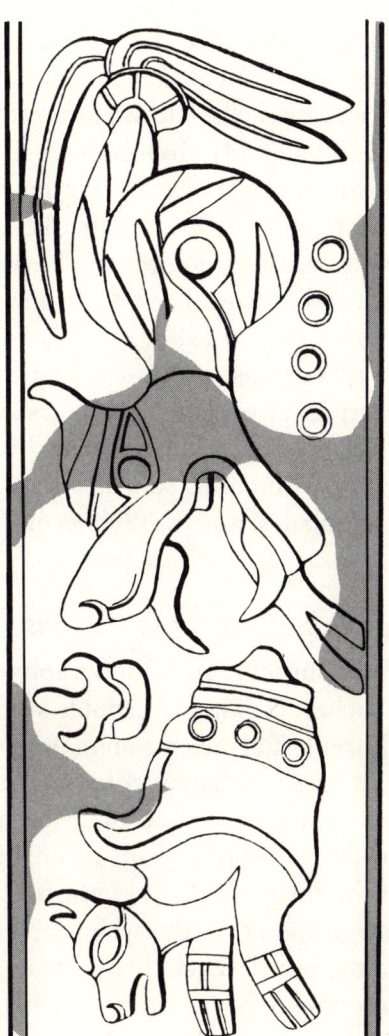

Figure 3.11. A small deer emerges from a conch shell, while a menacing serpent with deer horns opens his jaws, on a carved jade bead from the Cenote of Sacrifice at Chichen Itza (Proskouriakoff 1974:104).

this bird, like other fauna, was procured for special use in an ancient cenote ceremony.

Marine biota demonstrate that cenotes were linked to the "cult of the sea." The complete skull of a green turtle *(Chelonia mydas)* and the maxillary of a jack *(Caranx hippos)* (Wing and Steadman 1980), along with gorgonian, were recovered from Cenote Xlacah (Andrews 1959:92). Sea catfish *(Galeichthys felis)* and grouper *(Epinephelus)* were among the cenote fauna at Mayapan. Shark teeth, marine shells, and sea fan were taken from the cenote at Chichen Itza (Piña Chán 1970:54; Moholy-Nagy 1982).

The cenotes contained objects conveying fertility symbolism remarkably similar to that found in caves. Manos, textiles, spindle whorls, needles, awls, and other possible weaving equipment have been recovered from cenotes at Dzibilchaltun and Chichen Itza (Willard 1926; Littlehales 1961; Andrews and Andrews 1980; Lothrop 1982; Moholy-Nagy 1982). An Early Classic burial at Altun Ha (Pendergast 1979) demonstrates the strong parallelism between funerary offerings at ceremonial centers and activities at caves and cenotes. The Altun Ha grave contained 22 eyed bone needles and miniature dishes and jars, along with coral, conch, a shark tooth, a manatee bone figurine, obsidian flake blades, and an "Olmecoid" pendant, perhaps once part of a necklace.

The Meaning of Maya Ritual Faunas

The art, ethnohistory, and ethnography suggest that the animals deposited in burials, caches, caves, and cenotes symbolized sun, earth, water or rain, and agricultural fertility. Some animals had ties to the underworld, and on a more abstract level, the fauna represented concepts such as renewal.

The Maya may have shared the Mesoamerican concept of "bone soul." The present-day Huichol Indians of northwest Mexico regard bones as the source and the focus of life (Myerhoff 1974:83, 201). They carefully save deer remains in the belief that the deer does not die but is endlessly resurrected from the bones. These beliefs may account for the prevalence of animal bone offerings in Maya ritual deposits. Even today in the Maya highland community of Santa Eulalia, Indians gather up all bones and place them on altars so that the animals can return to nature (Davis, personal communication, 1974).

Ritual deposits go back to the Early Preclassic Period at Cuello, where deer and fish are the earliest animal offerings. Although fauna may originally have served as metaphors in the rain cult, animals, particularly those of the *cuch* rite, probably became increasingly central to lineage worship as systems of rulership developed. The elaboration of ceremonial offerings appears to parallel the emergence of elite lineages in the Late Preclassic and especially the

Classic periods, though we must bear in mind that more data are available for these periods. Perhaps the adoption of Tlaloc imagery from Central Mexico, which began in the Early Classic Period, increased the power of the symbolism.

The veneration of ancestors appears to have been a significant component of ancient Maya religion. The chroniclers of the conquest insisted that the Maya of Yucatan believed in the immortality of the soul and life after death. The extent to which these ideas were native to the New World is unknown. Lizana and López de Cogolludo reveal that Itzam Na, the supreme Maya diety, had the power to resurrect the dead (Ruz Lhuillier 1968:66, 183–185). A trip to the underworld and back is the theme of the *Popol Vuh*. The idea of rebirth was probably a native Maya concept. Some support for this view is found in the propensity for covering burials and cache offerings with red pigment (Ruz Lhuillier 1968:186). For the Maya, red was the color of the east, the direction associated with the rising or "resurrected" sun. Adams (1977a, 1977b) has theorized that in the Classic Period ancestor worship was transformed into a "royal cult" in which the dead ruler was thought to live on as a semidivine being. If these theories about Maya religion are correct, funerary offerings symbolizing rebirth would seem highly appropriate.

The dead rulers may have entered the underworld through caves. The Maya have traditionally regarded such natural features as avenues of communication with their deities and divine ancestors. Some Maya ceremonial centers provide a connection with caves. The so-called High Priest's Grave at Chichen Itza consisted of a pyramid and temple built over a natural cavern that the Indians had enlarged (E. H. Thompson 1938). Tomb 6 at Copan, which may date to the Postclassic Period, contained stalactites (Longyear 1952:43).

It may have been the living ruler's duty to assume responsibility for the economic welfare of the people and to guide the world through another cycle of time. Maya iconography suggests that the lord took up his burden when he was inaugurated; the *cuch* rite appears to have been performed at accession (M. Pohl 1981b). Each year, as well as at important period endings, the ruler may have presided over the rite. Public performance of the *cuch* ritual at ceremonial centers was probably meant to reaffirm the lord's lineage.

The most sacred part of the ceremony may have been the point at which the ruler descended into a cave to receive the prophesies of the gods. Cave findings support this idea, and certain aspects of ceremonial centers may symbolize the cave ritual. At Yaxchilan, Maler (1903:158) found that stalactites had been placed as columns in front of structures. One stalactite had vertical rows of glyphs incised in its depressions. At Copan, 24 stalactites, along with a stingray spine, 2 lumps of coral, and 2 marine shells with traces of red pigment, were cached with Stela I and Stela N (Longyear 1952:51–52). Girard (1962:197–205) suggests that elaborate cruciform, substela vaults at

Copan and cross-shaped rooms below temple floors at Palenque were meant to represent caves. He draws parallels with present-day Chorti ritual assemblages consisting of foliated cross and altar with a pit in front. The pit, or "cave," is said to represent the umbilical cord of the world.

In addition to the development of a cult of rulers, militarism came to characterize Maya society (Webster 1977). Definite fortifications first appear in the Late Preclassic or Terminal Preclassic Period (Webster 1977; Rice and Rice 1981). Rulers may have sought to control their subjects, and in addition to guaranteeing good crops, they may have assumed the responsibility of defending their territory from neighboring groups that were conducting raids for land, along with slaves and sacrificial victims. Elites probably exacted payments for these services, and at least some foodstuffs may have been redistributed in feasts such as the *cuch* rite.

Many Mayanists think that Classic Period art portrays scenes of warfare. However, the iconography of these pictures, which includes the symbols of the *cuch* rite, suggests that they depict ritual sacrifices instead of the actual conflict (Pohl and Pohl 1981). The Classic Period may, therefore, be the period of most intense public ceremonialism, which was designed to attract a worshipful following, as well as to control surpluses. In the Postclassic Period Maya lords or Mexicanized foreign elites appear to have dropped the showy trappings of rulership—the massive funerary pyramids, the stela cult commemorating accession, representations of ceremonies such as the *cuch* rite on fine ceramics, and eventually ball courts. From Terminal Classic times on, they concentrated on caves and cenotes. The use of physical coercion continued in the Postclassic Period. The high incidence of fortifications and pictures of raids at Chichen Itza, together with Spanish accounts, testify to the militaristic nature of late prehistoric Maya society. Elites intensified commercial competition (Sabloff and Rathje 1975) and were supported by wealth extracted from dependent populations.

The ethnohistoric and ethnographic data suggest that animals figured in personal, as well as public, ritual. The Maya have traditionally used animals as alter egos *(naguals)* and as remedies for ailments. Unfortunately, the antiquity of these practices, which were applied to individuals rather than to the community, are difficult to document in the archaeological record.

Characteristics of Maya Ritual Faunas

The procurement of fauna for ritual purposes appears to have been a specialized activity. In many cases biota that occur in ceremonial offerings are species that are rare in midden deposits. The sea turtle may be one example.

Marine turtle bone was identified in cenote fauna inland at Mayapan, yet at Postclassic Cozumel Island sites, these reptiles amount to only about 1 percent of all turtle remains (Hamblin 1980:126). The scarcity of sea turtle remains in Cozumel refuse is surprising, because the southeastern coast of the island is a habitual haunt of the green turtle *(Chelonia mydas)*. The Maya may have considered marine turtles sacred. Alternatively, methods of butchering or cooking the animals may account for the low numbers of bones in archaeological contexts (Hamblin 1980:155).

Elites at Mayapan made a concerted effort to procure marine organisms for their ceremonies. Sea catfish and grouper occurred in the cenote fauna, and the freshwater *Cichlasoma* was found in elite refuse (Table 3.3).

The difference in emphasis between ritual and subsistence faunas is most evident in the case of amphibians, snakes, birds, and fishes. These animals occur much more frequently in ceremonial contexts, particularly during the Classic Period.

The interpretation of fish remains presents a special problem. The lack of fish bones in middens at inland Maya sites, even those located on rivers, such as Seibal, may be due to factors of preservation and recovery. With the introduction of flotation, archaeologists have recovered fish bones from Preclassic sites, such as Cuello, and Postclassic to early Historic sites, such as Macal-Tipu. So far, however, we have little new information on Classic Period centers. Using window screen to water-sieve samples of Terminal Late Classic refuse that had been protected in abandoned rooms in Group G at Tikal, I found only one tiny catfish spine. The presence of freshwater turtle in the same deposit suggests that a suitable habitat, in the form of *aguadas* or canals, was still available in the area, even though the site was allowed to fall into ruins in Terminal Classic times. We cannot assume that Classic Period Maya ate fish. Perhaps their attitude was similar to that of the Blackfeet Indians of Montana: the Blackfeet believed that fish was the food of the underwater people and therefore did not eat it, despite its abundance. Nevertheless, bracelets manufactured from fish vertebrae have been noted in museum collections (Olsen 1971:3), suggesting that fish bones had ritual uses.

Birds had enormous religious importance among all native peoples of the New World. Many birds found in Maya ritual deposits are small passerines whose significance is baffling. Avian remains are not abundant in midden contexts at lowland sites until the Postclassic Period, when wild and domesticated turkeys were heavily exploited.

Felid remains are relatively rare both in ritual and in midden contexts. Cats may have been scarce in the lowlands, especially during the Classic Period, when human population was very dense, and demand for both the predators and their prey, such as deer, was high. Perhaps the Classic Maya had to import jaguar pelts, as well as resort to the less esteemed ocelot and puma. The animals may have been so precious, their bones were given special treatment. Debris from a Late Classic workshop at Tikal suggests that the Maya used felid bones to make high-status artifacts.

The vertebrates found in ritual deposits can be linked with invertebrate offerings, particularly the mollusks. At Lubaantun, Gann (1925:199), Joyce (1926:299), and Hammond (1975:384–85) uncovered substantial caches of freshwater *Pachychilus*, which were consistently larger than those encountered in middens and seem to have been deliberately selected for size. These caches were associated with the northern and southern ball courts at the site. Research suggests that the ball game was performed during the *cuch* or accession ritual (J. Pohl, personal communication, 1981).

The conch was central to the *cuch* rite and appears to have symbolized its message of rebirth. Appropriately, conchs have turned up in burials of the Classic and Postclassic Periods at such sites as Altun Ha (Pendergast 1979: 48–54), Mayapan (Pollock et al. 1962), and Tulum (Lothrop 1924:97), as well as in such cenotes as Chichen Itza (Moholy-Nagy 1982).

Summary

Burials, caches, caves, and cenotes were probably conceptually linked, and ritual faunas found in these contexts might be analyzed as a unit. Ceremonial offerings, particularly during the Classic Period, for which we have the most evidence, were characterized by an emphasis on snakes, toads, birds, and fish, in contrast to fauna found in middens. However, this observation may be biased by factors of preservation and recovery. The Maya made a special effort to procure animals for their ancient rites, and they often imported fauna, sometimes from considerable distances. A significant percentage of biota in ceremonial deposits was marine in origin.

The prehistoric Maya used fauna as metaphors for sun, rain, and earth. Some animals symbolized the underworld, as well as more abstract concepts, such as fertility and renewal. The ancient rites were allegorical dramas performed at agricultural rituals and at dynastic and calendric ceremonies honoring the lord whose divine lineage was to live on and whose duty it was to guide the world through various cycles of time. These beliefs, and the *cuch* rite through which they were acted out, were intended to invest Maya rulers with power, which was probably backed by physical coercion starting in Late Preclassic times.

Notes

1. J. E. S. Thompson 1970:217–18. The Vienna dictionary defines *itzam* as *lagartos,* or iguanas of land and water. Thompson (1970) believed that iguanids contributed to the deer-snake-crocodile composite animal. In my opinion, however, all the *lagarto* components in the pictures resemble crocodiles. Iguanids appear as sacrifices in the Postclassic codices, often lying on top of the *kan* sign and in association with *Chac.* Bishop Landa mentions iguana offerings, including sacrifices made during the year renewal ceremony complex. Iguanid bones, like turkey bones, are most common at Postclassic sites and are associated primarily with elite ceremonial and administrative contexts.

2. Karl Taube wrote an undergraduate thesis on the deer as a symbol of the earth, though I have not as yet had an opportunity to read his work.

3. Identified by Pierce Brodkorb, University of Florida.

Four

Functional Analysis and Social Process in Ceramics: The Pottery from Cerros, Belize

Robin Robertson, Southern Methodist University

The site of Cerros is situated on the southern edge of Chetumal Bay, near the mouth of the New River, in Corozal District, Belize (latitude 18° 21' 00", longtitude 88° 21' 10"). The center at Cerros (Fig. 4.1) consists of a concentrated area of monumental pyramids and plazas occupying approximately 5.5 hectares. Two distinct settlement zones are directly associated with the center. The first is a nucleated residential village underlying the main plaza (Feature 2A) at the site (Cliff 1981). The second consists of dispersed house mounds surrounding the center and demarcated from the rest of the peninsula by a canal (Scarborough 1980). Six seasons of excavation at the site have revealed that it was occupied and abandoned during the Late Preclassic Period (300 B.C.–A.D. 150) of lowland Maya prehistory. Evidence for Postclassic and Classic activity within the area enclosed by the canal is limited. Thus, the focus of ceramic research at the site has been on the Late Preclassic material. This research has been concerned with two principal objectives: (1) dividing and refining the ceramic chronology for the Late Preclassic in northern Belize and possibly, by comparison, in other areas of the Maya lowlands; and (2) identifying the ways in which the inhabitants of the site utilized pottery. Although this paper is primarily concerned with the second objective, a few words must be said about the first prior to considering it.

The potential for accomplishing the first objective became apparent in the 1976 field season. The first two seasons of work at the site (1974 and 1975)

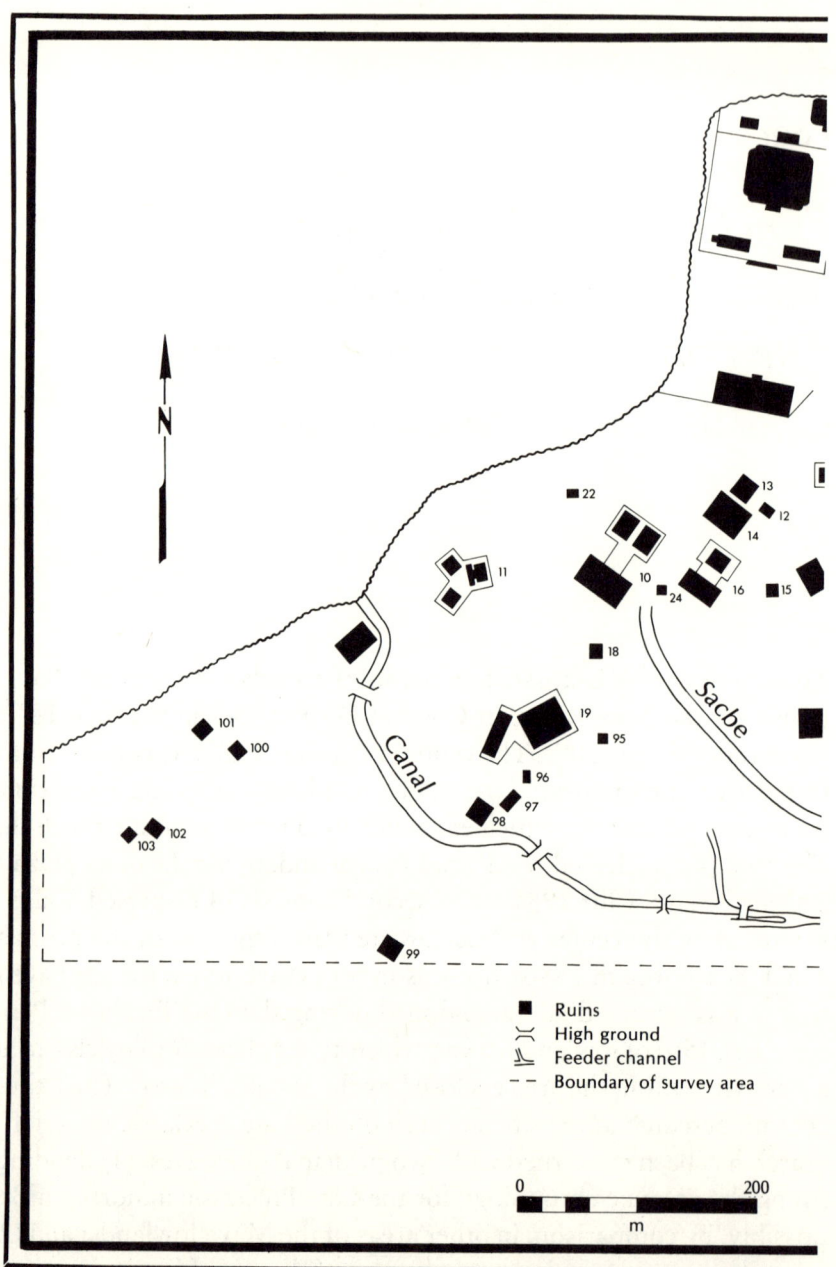

Figure 4.1. Map of Cerros.

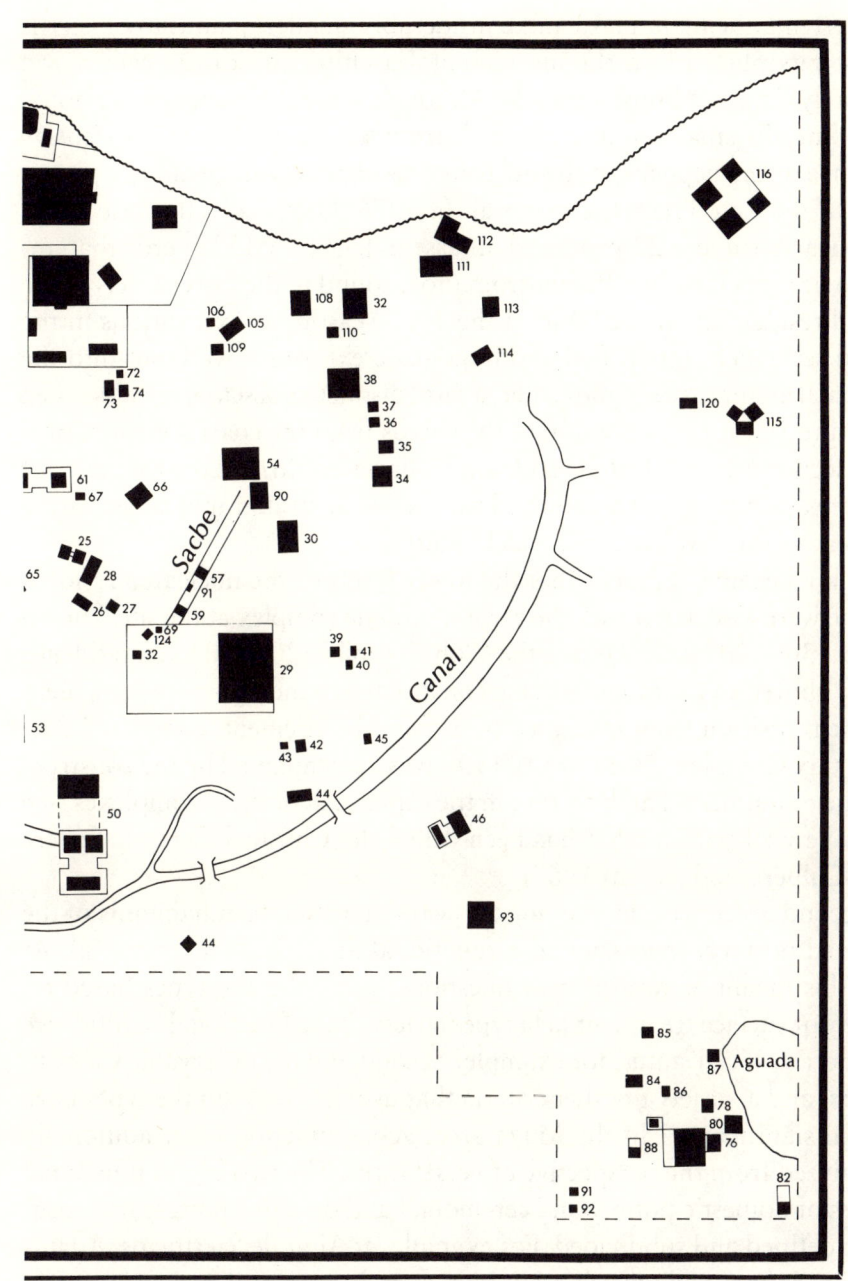

produced large quantities of sherd material from the nucleated residential village underlying the main plaza and considerably smaller quantities of sherds from test pits placed into the monumental architecture of the center and immediately adjacent house mounds. Although some differences were noted at that point, the small number of sherds from the test pits and the extensive disturbance of the deposits in the nucleated residential village did not permit division of the Late Preclassic material. In 1976, however, a flat test into a tree fall near Structure 22 produced an assemblage of 5,153 sherds that appeared to be significantly different from those found in the lower levels of the nucleated residential village. During the 1977 season, as excavations in the dispersed settlement intensified and large-scale exposures were put into the monumental architecture of the center, a third distinctive assemblage was noted on Structure 5C. Re-examination of the sherds from the coastal erosion profile that sections the nucleated residential villages confirmed the existence of these three assemblages and provided the means of stratigraphically relating them to each other (Robertson-Freidel 1980).

It quickly became apparent that the lower levels of the nucleated residential village were associated with the earliest ceramic complex at the site, known as Ixtabai (300–200 B.C.). During the C'oh Complex (200–50 B.C.), residence gradually shifted to the mounds being constructed in the dispersed settlement zone. The transition from nucleated to dispersed settlement, completed during the Tulix Complex (50 B.C.–A.D. 150), was accompanied by the construction of the monumental architecture in the center. All of these complexes (see Fig. 4.2) lie well within what has been called the Chicanel Ceramic Sphere (Willey, Culbert, and Adams 1967).

The second objective—identifying the ways in which the inhabitants of the site utilized pottery—necessitated a functional analysis of the material. At Cerros, this meant answering two questions. First, did the types based on variability of surface treatment (à la type-variety) have functional significance with respect to social status, for example? Second, did the observable variability in form and a variety of other criteria that usually cross-cut the types have functional significance? In the Maya area, vessel function has traditionally been analyzed from the perspective of vessel form. The two broad functional categories of domestic pottery and ceremonial and/or status pottery have usually been defined and subdivided. For example, at Altar de Sacrificios, Adams (1971:138) defines two type classes within domestic pottery: necked jar forms used as water carriers and open bowls, and plate forms used for serving and storing prepared foods. Ceremonial and status pottery is defined as "all finely made pottery whose decoration, by its symbolic nature, may indicate ritual or status functions" (Adams 1971:139) and includes the following type classes:

1. mortuary vessels,
2. drums,
3. incense burners,
4. cult effigies, and
5. trade exotics.

Adams then goes on to examine functional modes, such as handles and medial flanges, and their distribution in the various ceramic complexes at Altar.

In the Mayapan ceramic report, R. Smith (1971:103–13) also addresses the question of vessel function but from the perspective of what inferences can be made about the architectural features in which the functional classes occur. Like Adams, he distinguishes between utilitarian and ceremonial pottery. Drawing heavily on R. Thompson (1958), he relates general shape classifications to generalized functions, such as serving, grating, storing, and cooking. These functions are then correlated with contexts to identify kitchens, dwellings, oratories, shrines, and other structures, as well as to support the ritualistic characterization of colonnaded halls, for example.

In a study of pottery from the central highlands of Chiapas, Culbert (1965:43) also uses form to determine function and then examines the distribution of functional classes over various kinds of deposits. Unlike Smith, however, he finds no difference between the ceramic inventories from ceremonial contexts and those from domestic contexts.

More recently, Sharer (1978b:119–20) has classified the pottery from Chalchuapa as subsistence or nonsubsistence, but he cautions that the two categories are not mutually exclusive. Subsistence pottery includes vessels used for transporting water; storing water, food, and nonfood materials; processing, cooking, serving, and eating food; and drinking water. Nonsubsistence pottery includes vessels for ritual offerings, burials and caches, and incensarios. Sharer defines 31 forms for Chalchuapa, assigns each to one or more functional categories (Sharer 1978b:table 8), and examines these functional categories for each complex over time (Sharer 1978b:table 9). He concludes that throughout the Preclassic there is an increasing elaboration of vessel form in each category. In the Early Classic the number of forms per category decreases dramatically and then begins to increase again in the late Classic. The Postclassic sees another decline.

Lischka (1978) has gone a step further in attempting not only to relate functional classes of pottery to specific areas of the site, as did Smith and Culbert, but also to correlate the ceramic functional classes with other types of artifacts in the Late Classic occupation at Kaminaljuyu. First, Lischka groups the pottery into form types and determines probable uses and associations for

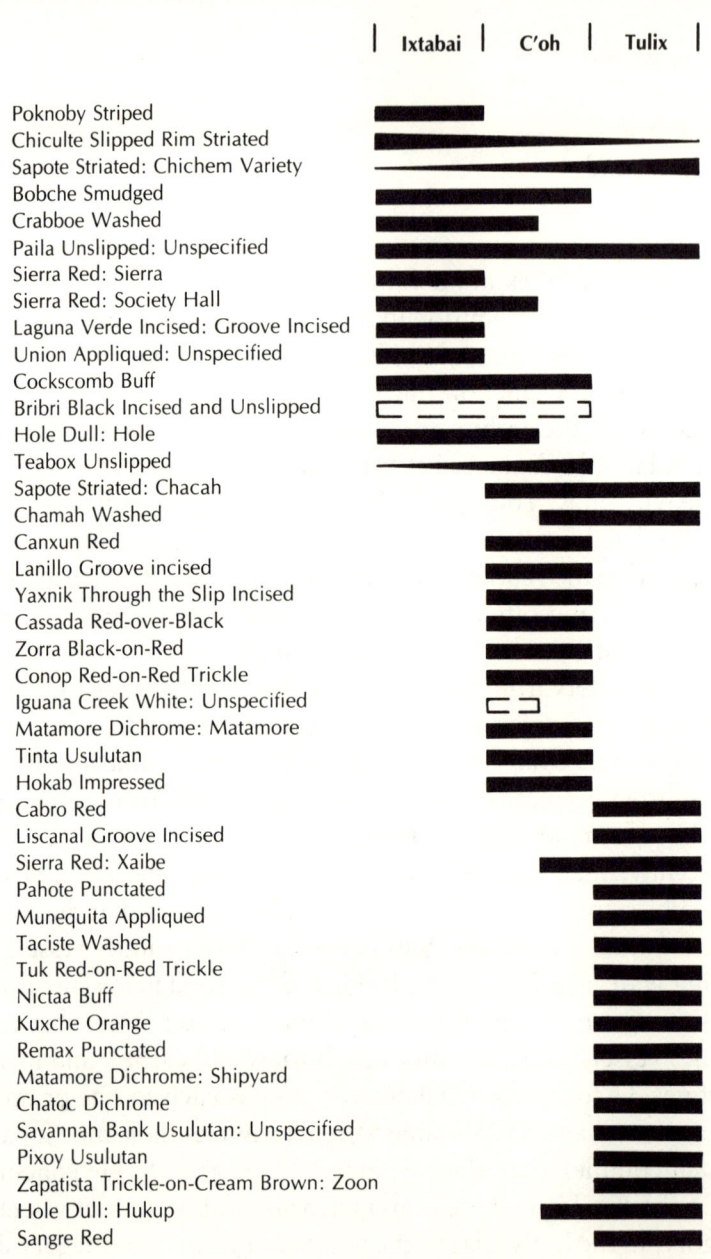

Figure 4.2. Chronological placement of the ceramic types from Cerros.

110

each type. Then, he outlines the nonvessel artifact categories (including figurines, incensarios, candeleros, metates, and manos) and predicts their associations. These two sets of data are integrated with the excavation data and subjected to a variant of factor analysis, called key-cluster analysis. Lischka functionally interprets the four resulting factors in terms of the activity sets they represent and the social contexts in which these activities were carried out.

Again, at Cerros the question of function was approached from two directions: the types themselves and the forms and other criteria that usually crosscut the types. We hoped that a synthesis of these two approaches would lead to a better understanding of how the Late Preclassic Maya utilized the vessels they produced.

The Functional Nature of the Cerros Type-Variety Types

The analysis began with the types enumerated using the type-variety system of classification commonly used in the Maya lowlands (see Culbert 1965; Smith and Gifford 1966; Willey 1970; Sabloff 1970, 1975; Matheny 1970; Adams 1971; R. Smith 1971; Gifford 1976; Ball 1977, 1978; Sharer 1978b). An attempt was made to determine whether or not these types (as opposed to the forms in which they occurred) had any functional significance. Rather than working from the ceramic categories to the contexts in which they occur, as all of the above analyses have done, this analysis proceeded from the contexts to the ceramic categories. Consequently, the first step in the analysis was to classify the various contexts into categories that reflected patterns of deposition and, in one case, collection. Six such categories were defined at Cerros:

1. caches and burials;
2. primary habitation debris;
3. ritual interment of the monumental architecture;
4. secondarily deposited occupational debris, such as that found on the corners of structures;
5. construction fill; and
6. surface collections.

Category 1 contexts are found primarily in the monumental architecture of the center and in the nucleated residential village.

Category 2 contexts are found in the nucleated residential village and in the flat test put into a tree fall near Structure 22. This flat test provided the largest pure corpus of C'oh Complex material found at the site. It should be emphasized that primary habitation debris means exactly that—the trash deposited by the inhabitants either inside or outside their houses and not subsequently moved.

The Category 3 contexts are found in the monumental architecture and were initially defined on Structure 5C. On the terrace and in the lower levels of the wash in front of the façades on Structure 5C-1st, the excavator (Garber, personal communication) noted the presence of burned areas and an unusually high frequency of charcoal. When the ceramics were analyzed, the size of most of the sherds, the number of reconstructable vessel forms, and the amount of burned sherd material (25 percent) were notable. Moreover, the burned material increased in frequency as one approached the façades. The large number of sherds that could be glued together suggests that the vessels were broken in the vicinity of the façades and subsequently deposited on the terrace in front of them. Additionally, the forms represented were primarily large, high-flaring-necked jars with three strap handles, "beer mugs," and large medial-angle dishes with usulutan decoration, arguably representing ceremonial serving vessels associated with the Tulix Complex (see below). The material was then probably burned in situ, although this cannot be demonstrated conclusively, because the sherds were not point plotted.

Additional examples of similar patterns were found in front of the façades on Structure 29 and on the staircase in front of Structure 2A-Sub. 4-1st (Cliff, personal communication, 1979). These represent the only major horizontal exposures in the monumental architecture to date. Future excavations will probably reveal that this behavior pattern was associated with the ritual interment and renewal of all the monumental architecture at the site.

Categories 4 and 5 were obtained in test pitting and trenching operations conducted in the monumental architecture and the house mounds. Material from Category 6 is relatively difficult to find at Cerros because of the heavy undergrowth that covers the site. This material comes primarily from the coast, where large, unusual sherds were collected when they were seen.

In a functional analysis that relies on context to infer ceramic use, it is essential that the sherds and/or whole vessels being analyzed come from primary deposits that reflect ancient usage patterns rather than construction or erosional events. Because Categories 4, 5, and 6 represent the latter, secondary events, the material in these categories was not used in this analysis. Categories 1, 2, and 3, on the other hand, arguably do reflect usage patterns, and the material in these categories provides the data for this analysis.

In addition to this categorization, a second typology is based on location within the community and degree of elaboration in the associated features and artifacts. The excavators have used these two sources of variability as a

Table 4.1. Source Classes, Complex Assignments, and Functional Interpretations of the Contexts Used in the Ceramic Typology

Op Number	Source Class	Ceramic Complex	Excavators' Hypothesized Function for Deposit
1	2	Ixtabai	Domestic/Nonelite
		C'oh	Domestic/Nonelite
33	2	C'oh	Domestic/Nonelite
	2	Tulix	Domestic/Elite
34 east	2	Ixtabai	Domestic/Elite
		C'oh	Domestic/Elite
		Tulix	Domestic/Elite
107	2	C'oh	Domestic/Elite
35	3	Tulix	Ritual
111	3	Tulix	Ritual
34 west	3	Ixtabai	Ritual
		C'oh	Ritual
		Tulix	Ritual

means of distinguishing elite from nonelite and domestic from ritual areas of the site (Freidel, personal communication, 1979). These determinations have been applied to the Category 2 and 3 material in this analysis, as Table 4.1 illustrates.

Category 1 contexts, which are restricted to caches and burials, are regarded as ritual in nature and thus are not included in the table. Category 2 contexts come from Ops 1, 33, and 34 in the nucleated residential village and Op 107, the flat test near Structure 22 (see Fig. 4.1). Op 1 has been interpreted as an ordinary domestic locus containing Ixtabai and C'oh Complex pottery. The Tulix Complex material for the most part was removed when the area was leveled to construct the main plaza (Feature 2A). Although Op 33 contains deposits from all of these complexes, the Ixtabai material occurs in construction fill and thus is considered to belong to Category 5 rather than 2. The C'oh and Tulix deposits are domestic in nature. Op 34, like 33, contains deposits from all three complexes. Given the presence of the dock or projecting plaza (Fig. 4.1) in the western part of the exposure and a masonry platform in the eastern portion, the eastern portion of the deposit is thought to be elite in nature (Cliff 1981). The dock itself has been interpreted as a ritual ceramic dump (Cliff, personal communication, 1980). Op 107 is some distance from the waterfront nucleated village (see Fig. 4.1) and has a higher quality and quantity of associated artifacts. Consequently, it has been interpreted as an elite residential area (Scarborough, personal communication, 1980). Unfortunately, the elite Category 2 deposits from the Tulix Complex house mounds have not yet been found. Instead, the excavated housemound deposits (Structures 11, 15, 16, 19, 21, 26, 54, 65, 66, 77, 84, 115, and 118) invariably belong to Categories 4 and 5. Because of the dearth of Category 2 deposits, the Category 4 material has been used informally in this analysis to confirm patterns observed or predicted for elite ceramics, based on the information from the excavations outlined above.

In addition to the Category 1 ritual deposits, the Tulix Complex has a large sample of ritual pottery from the ritual interments of Structures 29 (Op 111) and 5C (Op 35). As discussed above, these deposits make up Category 3. Because none of the monumental architecture at the site is earlier than the Tulix Complex, comparable deposits from the Ixtabai and C'oh Complexes have not been recovered.

Thus, three kinds of contexts were identified for each complex: domestic nonelite, domestic elite, and ritual. The pottery types and their frequencies were plotted over these contexts.

With regard to frequencies, Foster (1960), David (1972), and Deboer (1974) have discussed the problem of differential breakage in pottery. Because some pots break into large pieces and some into small, they argue that raw counts may be misleading. Moreover, how does one deal with whole vessels? Various solutions have been proposed, including the use of weight (cf. Baumhoff and Heizer 1959; Solheim 1960), reconstructed vessels, and "batches" for typological purposes (Newell and Krieger 1949).

The ceramicist presumably has some impression of how large the average fragments in a given type are and how the fragments relate to the whole vessels. Therefore, instead of complicated ratios, which would have required a great deal of time to calculate and given only the appearance of being objective, the subjective terms "uncommon" and "common" were used in this analysis. Within the ritual contexts, a type was shown as being present or absent, because there was no way to determine how common or uncommon it was over the limited number of Ixtabai and C'oh Complex contexts of this nature. The tabulated types and their frequencies are listed in Table 4.2. The type name is used as a shorthand referent when it is the same as the variety name.

Within the Ixtabai Complex there appears to be little difference in the material from various locations within the primary habitation debris and between it and the ritual deposits. Although this may be due to the fact that the Ixtabai sample is smaller than that from the C'oh and Tulix Complexes, other factors may be contributing to the lack of variability. The pottery from the elite area of Op 34, for example, does not differ from the pottery recovered from the domestic nonelite area of Op 1, whereas in the C'oh Complex there are differences in the types found in the two areas. Moreover, despite exten-

Table 4.2. Occurrence of Types over the Functional Loci at Cerros			
	Nonelite	Elite	Ritual
Poknoboy Striped	c	c	x
Chiculte Slipped Rim Striated	c	c	
Bobche Smudged	c	c	
Crabboe Washed	c	c	
Paila Unslipped	c		
Sierra Red: Sierra Variety	c	c	x
Sierra Red: Society Hall	c	c	
Laguna Verde Incised	c	c	x
Union Appliqued	r		
Cockscomb Buff		c	
Bribri Black Incised and Unslipped	r		
Hole Dull: Hole Variety			x
Teabox Unslipped	c	c	x
Sapote Striated: Chacah Variety	c	c	x
Sapote Striated: Chichem Variety	c	c	
Chahmah Washed	c	c	
Canxun Red	c	c	x
Lanillo Groove Incised	c	c	x
Yaxnik Through-the-Slip-Incised	r	r	x
Cassada Red-over-Black			x
Zorra Black-on-Red	r	r	x
Conop Red-on-Red Trickle		c	x
Iguana Creek White	?	?	x
Matamore Dichrome: Matamore Variety	r	r	x
Hokab Impressed			x
Cabro Red	c	c	x
Liscanal Groove Incised	c	c	x
Sierra Red: Xaibe, Form 1	c	c	
Sierra Red: Xaibe, other forms	c		
Pahote Punctated	c	c	x
Muñequita Appliquéd			x
Taciste Washed			x
Tuk Red-on-Red Trickle		c	x
Nictaa Buff		c	x
Kuxche Orange			x
Remax Punctated			x
Matamore Dichrome: Shipyard			x
Chactoc Dichrome			x
Savannah Bank Usulutan	r	r	x
Pixoy Usulutan	r	r	x
Zapatista Trickle-on-Cream-Brown: Zoon			x
Hole Dull: Hukup Variety			x
Sangre Red			x
Tinta Usulutan	r	r	x

r = rare.
c = common.
x = present.

sive tests and horizontal exposures in the dispersed settlement zone, no material relating to this complex has been recovered from the house mounds. Thus, it is highly likely that during the life span of this complex, pottery was not used to express status differences, and ritual pottery types apparently were not present as distinct entities. As Table 2 illustrates, a different pattern characterizes the slipped wares in the C'oh and Tulix Complexes.

Yaxnik Through-the-Slip-Incised, Cassada Red-over-Black, Zorra Black-on-Red, Matamore Dichrome: Matamore Variety, and Tinta Usulutan occur in small amounts in all of the C'oh Complex deposits. Although they may be interpreted as rare domestic types, it seems more likely that they represent what can be called special occasion pottery types.

Special occasion types would have been used during weddings, household santification rites, and other individual or family rituals by all members of the community. A modern analogy for these types can be found in Reina and Hill's (1978:246–47) discussion of a properly equipped modern Quiche Maya kitchen. Four of the nineteen forms they identify have special occasion counterparts to the everyday domestic vessels. These are differentiated from the everyday domestic *tamaleros, jarros, apastes,* and *batidors* by surface treatment, size, or source. The special occasion *jarro*, for example, is glazed, whereas the domestic version is not. The special occasion *tamalero* is differentiated from the domestic one on the basis of size. The domestic *tamalero* cooks 25 tamales, whereas the special occasion one cooks 400 tamales or 100 pounds of corn. The special occasion *batidor* and *apaste* were purchased in San Cristobal. These vessels are used at fiestas, to deliver *atole* to relatives, to serve food at weddings or funerals, and to deliver cooked food to godparents. Although the specific contexts probably were different in the past, the nature of the contexts in which special occasion vessels were used was probably similar. R. Thompson (1958:119–120) also describes ceremonial basins *(ocliz)* specially ordered for rituals in Yucatan and cites Rendon's statement that the pottery vessels used at a fiesta must be new. The sponsor of the fiesta usually has the pots made to order (R. Thompson 1958:115). Moreover, despite the widespread use of iron cooking vessels in domestic contexts, food for fiestas and religious ceremonies is usually prepared in pottery vessels.

One elite type, Conop Red-on-Red Trickle, also appears in this complex. This type is restricted to Op 107 and the C'oh Complex ritual deposits. During the C'oh and Tulix Complexes, elite types apparently were also used in ritual contexts. Perhaps this use of what were otherwise regarded as ritual types strengthened the group identification of elites and emphasized their status. The elites would be demonstrating they had the wherewithal to procure and use in a domestic context vessels that were normally only available for ritual

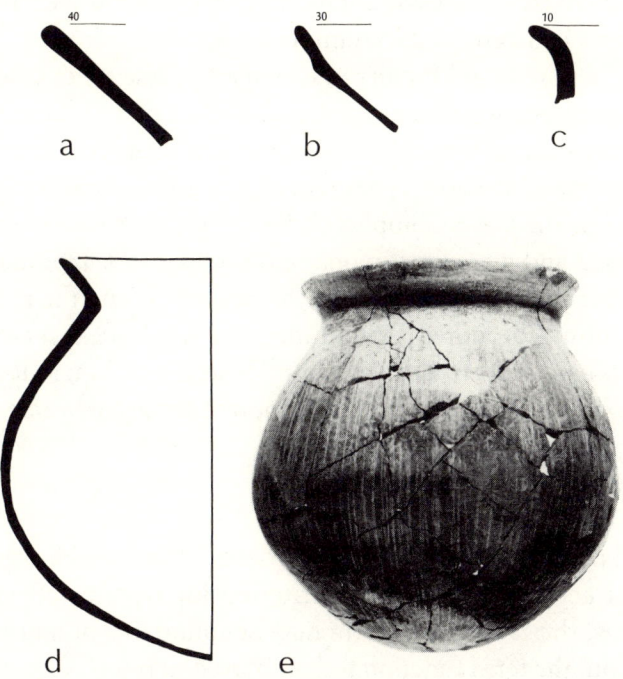

Figure 4.3. Sierra Red and Poknoboy Striped vessel profiles. *a:* Sierra Red: Xaibe Variety, Form 1; *b:* Sierra Red: Xaibe Variety, Form 3; *c:* Sierra Red: Xaibe Variety, Form 5; *d* and *e:* Poknoboy Striped: Poknoboy Variety.

use. However, at least two types were reserved strictly for ritual use in the C'oh Complex: Hole Dull: Hole Variety and Hokab Impressed.

In the Tulix Complex the number of special occasion pottery types seems to decrease while the number of exclusively ritual types increases dramatically. Although all the occupants of the site had access to Cabro Red, Liscanal Groove Incised, Pahote Punctated, and Form 1 of Sierra Red: Xaibe Variety (Fig. 4.3a), the number of special occasion pottery types decreases from five to three: Pixoy Usulutan; Savannah Bank Usulutan: Variety Unspecified; and Sierra Red: Xaibe Variety, Forms 3, 4, and 5 (Fig. 4.3b, c). Moreover, Sierra Red: Xaibe Variety, Forms 3, 4, and 5, were apparently used only by nonelites. The number of elite types remains the same.

The most notable difference between the C'oh and the Tulix Complexes is the dramatic increase from two to nine ritual types. However, the identification of Chactoc Dichrome and Matamore Dichrome: Shipyard Variety as ritual types may be due to a difficulty in classifying these types when the sherds are from the upper portion of the vessel, and the fact that Matamore Dichrome: Shipyard Variety occurs primarily in whole vessels. Even if they are eliminated, however, the remaining seven types represent a substantial increase over the number found in the C'oh Complex. It would seem that as communitywide rituals developed and were institutionalized (Freidel 1981), pottery types were created to perform them. In support of this argument and the ritual nature of the types, it should be noted that Muñequita Appliquéd, Tascite Washed, Zapatista Trickle-on-Cream Brown: Zoon Variety, and Sangre Red occur only in ritual contexts, and there is a 1:1 correlation of surface treatment with form.

Functional Classes of Vessels

The second portion of the analysis was devoted to vessel function. Because form does not generally constitute a criterion for type membership in type-variety analysis, the same vessel form may be found in a number of types. To avoid confusion, the term functional class is used to refer to a group of vessels sharing a given function, whereas type is restricted to the type-variety groupings. It should be noted that at Cerros some of the functional classes (for example, stationary cooking vessels) show a 1:1 correlation with a type in a given complex. However, these 1:1 correlations are generally limited to the unslipped utility types, which are more finely divided at Cerros than elsewhere in the lowlands (see Robertson-Freidel 1980:appendix 3).

In the literature two approaches have been used to investigate the relationship between form and function. The first (often used in conjunction with the second) involves defining the universalistic, common-sense requirements of use that determine the morphology of a vessel. The second approach is based on ethnographic analogy and ethnohistoric studies.

Recent attempts have been made to explicate the rules that provide the basis for the first approach explicit and to quantify the relationship between use and form. Ericson, Read, and Burke (1972) propose 17 explicit relationships between morphology and function. For example, if cooking and wet storage vessels were supposed to be impermeable, they will have relatively high values of hardness and density. If a vessel designed for long-term storage of liquids had to be relatively stable, with limited access to the interior, it will have a high center of gravity, because a high center of gravity increases leverage and decreases access to the interior. Ericson, Read, and Burke have calculated numerous ratios to quantify such things as center of gravity, access to the interior, and stability. They have also proposed various means of measuring such factors as hardness and density.

Braun (1976), on the other hand, establishes sets of relationships based on the shape of the vessel orifice and its size. He regards these variables as particularly important in determining use, because they restrict or permit frequent access to the contents of the pot and determine whether or not the contents will spill.

In addition to these general rules, ethnographic studies have been used to investigate vessel function. In the Maya area these include R. Thompson's (1958) study of modern pottery production and use in Yucatan, and Reina and Hill's (1978) and Arnold's (1978) discussion of vessel use in the highlands of Guatemala. Landa (Tozzer 1941), Redfield and Villa Rojas (1962), and Villa Rojas (1945) also provide some useful information about vessel function. Farther afield, Linton's (1944) study of cooking vessels among North American Indians, Fontana et al.'s (1962) examination of Papago Indian pottery, Chapman's (1970) investigation of the pottery from San Ildefonso Pueblo, Solheim's (1965) consideration of vessel use in Southeast Asia, Birmingham's (1975) discussion of use in Kathmandu, India, and David and Hennig's (1972) archaeological interpretation of Fulani pottery can be used on a general analogical level to infer primary use from vessel form.

In this study the common-sense rules and ethnographic information were combined with an analysis of surface treatment, wear patterns (see Matson 1965:205), fire blackening and its location, fire clouding, paste differences, distribution over the site, and frequency to determine the primary use of vessels. This was done on a type-by-type basis. The functional attributes present were examined and then interpreted using the explanation that seemed to account for all of them most effectively and efficiently.

The following functional classes were identified as a result of this analysis:

1. stationary cooking vessels;
2. soaking vessels;
3. mixing bowls;
4. water vessels;
5. dry storage vessels;
6. serving dishes for hot and cold foods;
7. buckets;
8. eating and ritual offering bowls and dishes; and
9. ritual vessels.

Before proceeding with the discussion of these classes, it should be noted that the pottery at Cerros does not fulfill all the necessary cooking or storage functions. Lischka (1978) points out that in humid climates baskets are usually preferred for storing most foods, because a certain amount of ventilation is required to keep the food fresh. R. Thompson (1958:146) and Redfield and Villa Rojas (1962:39) indicate that this is the case among modern lowland Maya. Additionally, gourds of all sorts can be and are used for many of the functions fulfilled by pottery (cf. Gann 1918; J. E. S. Thompson 1930; Tozzer 1941; Redfield and Villa Rojas 1962; Villa Rojas 1945; R. Thompson 1958).

From the perspective of modern pottery use, the only major gap in the functional classes represented at Cerros is the absence of small cooking vessels and *comales*. None of the smaller vessels at the site that would be appropriate for cooking show any indication of fireblackening. If the fire had been hot enough and sufficient oxygen had been present, then the carbon might have burned off, leaving no deposit on the vessel (cf. Lischka 1978:228). However, two other alternatives need to be considered: the Late Preclassic Maya may not have cooked food in small amounts, or some other material, such as stone, may have been used for small cooking vessels. The first alternative seems unlikely, and the second is not supported by the other data categories at the site (Garber, personal communication, 1980). Complete combustion of the carbon thus seems the most likely of the three explanations, but other, more probable explanations have been offered for these vessels (see below). Nonetheless, cooking cannot be eliminated as a possible function for these small vessels; the signs of it may simply be invisible.

Comales, which the modern Maya use to cook tortillas, are relatively rare in lowland Maya archaeological sites. After evaluating the ethnohistoric as well as the archaeological evidence, J. E. S. Thompson (1930) and Tozzer (1941:90) concluded that tortillas were not a staple of the diet in the past. If their conclusion is correct, *comales* would not be expected to occur frequently in the Cerros assemblages.

STATIONARY COOKING VESSELS

The large, round-bottom jars with outflaring necks and direct, rounded rims (Fig. 4.3*d, e*) found in Poknoboy Striped (Ixtabai Complex) and the later, related type, Teabox Unslipped (C'oh and Tulix Complexes) appear to have functioned as large, stationary cooking vessels in all the domestic contexts at the site. Both types have "zoned" areas of fire blackening on the exterior of the vessel but not on the round bottom. If the pots were stationary cooking vessels sitting in a depression and embers were heaped up around the exterior, the base of the pot would have been protected from the fire and remained unaltered, whereas the exterior areas in contact with the embers would have been blackened. The dramatic contrast between the 0.9–1.1 centimeter thick rims and upper bodies and the 0.6 centimeter thickness of the basal portions of the vessels supports this hypothesis. Sitting in a depression, the round base would have been supported and not subjected to blows from use. Moreover, a thin base would aid in the transmission of heat from the embers surrounding the vessel. The rim and upper body would need to be thicker to withstand everyday use and to prevent heat loss.

The occurrence of carbon deposits and blackening on the interior surfaces of the basal and lower body sherds suggests that the contents were stone boiled. The heat of red hot stones and the carbon associated with them would discolor the lower interior portions of the vessel and also make them impervious to water (see Harrington 1909).

Stone boiling would be an ideal way to cook the shellfish that seem to have formed such an important part of the diet at Cerros (Andrews, personal communication, 1978). The occurrence of depressions large enough to hold the stationary pots and of piles of small, fire-cracked rock in association with large quantities of shellfish in the village area of the site (Cliff, personal communication, 1980) provides further support for this argument. The shells do not appear to be burned as they would have been had they been cooked over an open fire. Additionally, the mammal bones from the primary habitation debris show little evidence of spit cooking or barbecuing (Robertson 1973). The meat they bore was probably boiled or stewed.

SOAKING VESSELS

Corn and beans, two essential foodstuffs in the Maya diet both today and in the past, can or must be soaked overnight or for long periods of time before they can be eaten. It has been argued that the flaring-walled dishes (Fig. 4.4a) found in Crabboe Washed (Ixtabai and Early C'oh) and the later Chahmah Washed (Late C'oh and Tulix) at Cerros served as containers for soaking these or similar foods. Crabboe Washed and Chahmah Washed are the most common unslipped types at Cerros, suggesting that whatever domestic function they served, it was essential to every household.

The interiors of these pots bear a wash that is usually stained on the base and lower 4 centimeters of the wall, suggesting that they contained a liquid. If that liquid, in turn, contained lime, then an unusual feature of the pastes found in these two types, as well as the staining, can be explained.

The pastes in both variants are friable, producing a diagnostic attribute of this type: cleavage along a plane running parallel to the body of the vessel. As a result, the exterior surface frequently has been separated from the interior. In fact, sherds were initially sorted into two ceramic units until this character-

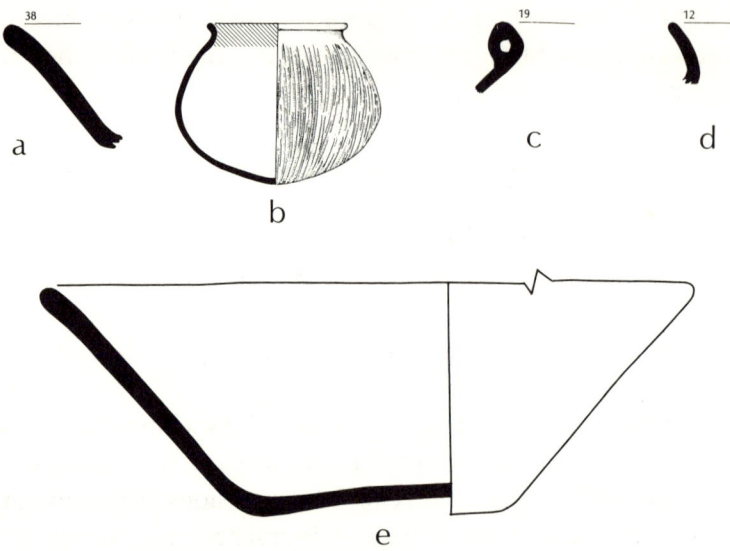

Figure 4.4. Soaking, mixing, storage, and water transportation vessels. *a:* flaring walled dish; *b* and *c:* water transportation vessels; *d:* low-necked jar; *e:* mixing bowl.

istic was identified. The cleavage plane can be located anywhere in the cross-section of the sherd, but it occurs most commonly about 0.2 centimeters in from the interior surface. This cleavage plane may be explained by the fact that the lime penetrated only part way into the walls before the basic ph of the solution eroded the wash on the interior and made the pots useless. Postdepositionally portions of the lime-saturated paste would absorb water differentially from the nonsaturated areas of the paste, resulting in a cleavage plane. In fact, the rims show less tendency to cleave than do the body and basal portions of the pot.

These fairly crude but common vessels were probably disposable, compared to other types at Cerros. They nonetheless are uniform in size and shape, indicating they were produced to serve a specific function. In the absence of metal, which would be less susceptible to a corrosive lime solution, it makes sense that a relatively disposable kind of pottery would have served this function (see R. Thompson 1958:117). It should be noted that elsewhere wooden pots may have served a comparable function. Given the prevalence of good quality clays all over Lowry's Bight (Morrison, personal communication, 1976), it may have been more efficient at Cerros to make such pots out of clay rather than wood.

MIXING BOWLS

The large, flaring-walled dishes found in Sierra Red: Society Hall Variety (Ixtabai and Early C'oh) and the later Sierra Red: Xiabe Variety (Late C'oh and Tulix) have direct rims and rounded lips. The bases are always convex (Fig. 4.4e). Such a form would be inappropriate for storage, and the convex bases suggest a function other than serving. The exterior basal break is clearly and unusually worn in all cases, probably through contact with a hard surface. Such a wear pattern would be produced if pressure were applied to the vessel while it was rotated, as is commonly done when mixing food. The convex base would reduce the area in contact with the surface on which the vessel rested, making it easier to rotate. The frequency of this form in domestic contexts supports this interpretation of function.

WATER VESSELS

Three types of unslipped pottery at Cerros appear to be related to water usage: Chiculte Slipped Rim Striated, Sapote Striated: Chacah Variety, and Sapote Striated: Chichem Variety.

Chiculte Slipped Rim Striated is most common in the Ixtabai Complex but small amounts are present in the other complexes. The small size, globular shape, and presence of striation, as well as small strap handles (Adams 1971:138), on these vessels (Fig. 4.4b, c) supports the argument that they were used to transport water over short distances. This function is fulfilled by similar vessels available in the markets of Oaxaca today (Cliff, personal communication, 1980). Because the primary focus of occupation during this complex is on the waterfront (see Freidel 1979, who argues that Corozal Bay was a freshwater lagoon), it seems unlikely that there would have been much need to store water. The inhabitants could have taken water from the lagoon as they needed it. With the movement of part of the population away from the water during the C'oh Complex, however, water storage would have become important, because there are no other water sources in the immediate vicinity of the site. As predicted, large vessels with rim diameters of 26.0–37.0 centimeters suitable for this function appear for the first time during the C'oh

Complex in Sapote Striated: Chacah Variety. These vessels increase in frequency over time and as more and more people move away from the water. This increase correlates with a decrease in the number of Chiculte Slipped Rim Striated vessels, which would have been used less frequently under these circumstances to remove water from the storage vessels.

Sapote Striated: Chichem Variety is found in all three complexes but is more common in the C'oh and Tulix than it is in the Ixtabai. These vessels, along with Sapote Striated: Chacah Variety (Light Red), were used for heating and/or boiling water. The exterior surface of almost every sherd shows signs of fire blackening or calcination produced by direct contact with an open fire. Moreover, the thin walls (0.4–0.6 centimeters) would promote rapid transmission of heat. The low frequency of the type may be explained by the fact that a household would not have needed more than one of these vessels.

DRY STORAGE VESSELS

The functional class of dry storage vessels includes three types: jars, *floreros*, and *lec-i-uah*.

Jars (Fig. 4.4d; 4.5a, b). Throughout the sequence at Cerros, jars undergo increasing elaboration in form and function. In the Ixtabai Complex they occur only as low, slightly flaring-necked vessels with direct rims in Sierra Red: Sierra Variety and Laguna Verde Incised: Groove Incised Variety. Although the rim diameters of the low flaring-necked jars with direct rims in all the complexes are within the range (10.0–20.0 centimeters) of jars used for water transport today (R. Thompson 1958), the modern vessels are not globular and usually have two or three strap handles in addition to high necks. All of these attributes would facilitate storage or transport, but they are more characteristic of the unslipped vessels for which these functions have been suggested (Sapote Striated: Chacah Variety and Chiculte Slipped Rim Striated). The vessels in this functional type, which are globular in shape and lack handles, would be more appropriate for dry storage. Moreover, their low necks would make it difficult to pour liquid contents and would not inhibit spilling. This same form occurs in the C'oh Complex in Canxun Red but a new, small (10.5 centimeters), carinated jar form occurs as well in Hokab Impressed (Fig. 5a).

By the Tulix Complex, thick-walled jars (Cabro Red) and large decorated jars (Pahote Punctated and Remax Punctated) have been added to the inventory. The carinated jars continue in the new type, Pahote Punctated, and possibly in Sierra Red: Xiabe Variety.

The carinated jars cannot contain more than two or three cups of anything and thus would not be efficient for water storage. Their rim diameters are

The Pottery from Cerros, Belize 125

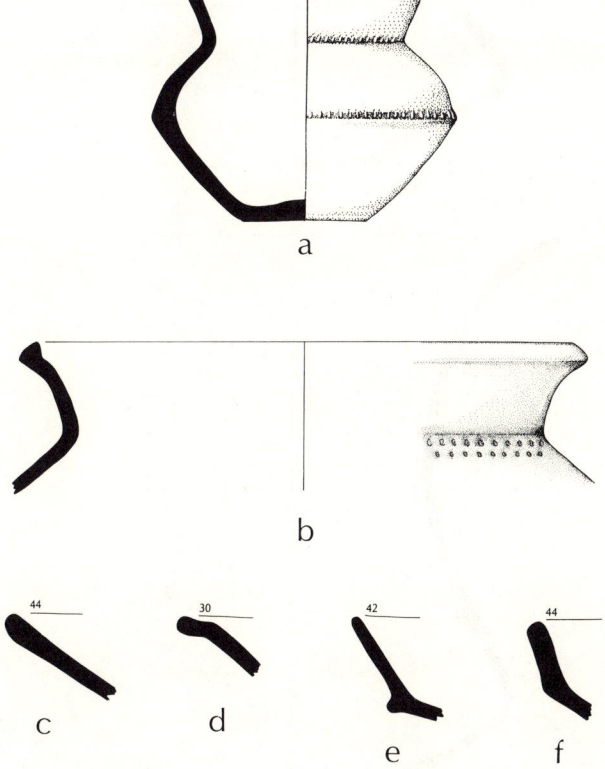

Figure 4.5. Jars and dishes. *a:* carinated jar; *b:* large decorated jar; *c:* flaring-walled dish with simple rim; *d:* flaring-walled dish with flanged rim; *e:* medially ridged dish; *f:* medial-angle dish.

too small to permit easy access to their contents. Consequently, the contents would have to be removed in small quantities ("pinches") or completely removed by pouring. These jars would be ideal for storing dry substances used only in small amounts, such as seasonings. The wear on the rims of Vessel 122 (Hokab Impressed) from the C'oh Complex and Vessel 499 (Pahote Punctated) from the Tulix Complex suggests that some of the vessels were used in conjunction with lids. This storage function was probably fulfilled by perishable vessels in the earlier Ixtabai Complex.

The large, decorated jars in the Tulix Complex (Fig. 5b) seem to represent larger, more elaborate versions of the more common storage vessels found in all three complexes. Their distinctly globular shape would make it very difficult to lift them, and the large rim diameters (29.0–30.0 centimeters) would

Figure 4.6. *Lec-i-uah* and florero.

definitely promote evaporation of any liquid. The increase in size and elaboration of this functional type may be related to the greater size of consumption groups (see the discussion of dishes), as well as to increasing status differentiation. This latter phenomenon is supported by the appearance of a common storage jar form in Nictaa Buff, which may well be an elite ceramic type.

Floreros. During the Tulix Complex, the florero form (Fig. 4.6b) occurs for the first time in Cabro Red and Matamore Dichrome: Shipyard Variety. These vessels were probably used for storing liquids. The large rim diameters would permit easy access to the contents, and the constriction in the vessel walls would inhibit evaporation. The presence of an interior slip supports this contention. One vessel in Matamore Dichrome: Shipyard Variety was apparently reused as grave furniture in Burial 3, as were at least three floreros from Tikal (Coe 1965a:20–21).

Lec-i-uah. These incurving sided vessels with incurving sides, relatively unrestricted orifices, and direct rims with rounded lips (Fig. 4.6a) are similar to the spherical *lec-i-uah* used by the Maya today to keep tortillas warm and soft (Villa Rojas 1945:53; Redfield and Villa Rojas 1962:36; personal observation, Chunux Village, 1978). Although it is possible that the ancient Maya did not eat tortillas (see Tozzer 1941:90), Landa observed, "they make good and healthful bread of different kinds, except that it is bad to eat when it is cold" (cited in Tozzer 1941:90–91). These vessels would have kept their contents warm, and their size and relatively unrestricted orifice are appropriate for holding bread. The distribution of these forms over domestic contexts and their occurrence only in domestic or elite types indicate that they were used in household contexts.

DISHES

At Cerros dishes come in four basic forms:

1. flaring walls with a simple rim (Fig. 4.5c),
2. flaring walls with an everted or flanged rim (Fig. 4.5d),
3. a medially ridged vessel (Fig. 4.5e),
4. a medial-angle vessel (Fig. 4.5f).

The majority of vessels in these classes have fairly large rim diameters (greater than 20 centimeters), relative to their height (less than 15.0 centimeters). R. Thompson describes a series of water basins with rim diameters comparable to the Class 1 and 2 vessels that are used "for washing and cooking, preparing food which does not require cooking and general storage" (1958:117–119). Redfield and Villa Rojas (1962:36) also point out that similar vessels are used to store *balche*. These ethnographic vessels, however, are proportionally much taller than the Cerros vessels and have rounded, lower bodies and larger bases. Moreover, with the exception of washing, these functions may be served by mixing bowls (see above), the Bobche Smudged storage jars (see below), and the Crabboe Washed and Chamah Washed vessels discussed above. Washing activities, on the other hand, could have been carried out directly in the bay or the canal or on washboards similar to those found in Yucatan today (Redfield and Villa Rojas 1962:plate 5a). The class 3 and 4 vessels, with their medial ridges and angles, would be inappropriate for all of these activities, and the Class 1 and 2 vessels, given that these functions are fulfilled by other forms, could have been more appropriately used for serving food or transporting it from the cooking to the eating area.

The form of these vessels may also permit some speculation as to what was served in them. For example, none of these vessels is particularly suited for serving anything with a high liquid content, as it would spill over the sides in transport. However, pieces of meat, whole or parts of fish, salads, or vegetables could be effectively transported in these vessels. In the eating area the wide orifices would permit easy access to the contents.

One of the functional advantages of an everted or flanged rim or a medial flange is what might be called "graspability." (See Adams 1971:141 for a discussion of the function of medial flanges.) These forms can be carried or moved with only the finger tips (as opposed to both hands) in contact with the vessel. Graspability would be highly desirable if the vessel and/or its contents were hot. The flaring-walled dishes with simple rims and/or medial angles, on the other hand, could be moved only by supporting the vessel with both hands. Clearly cold contents and/or vessel surfaces would be advantageous when these latter forms were used.

Within these broad classes, the vessels are also divisible on the basis of size. With the exception of the vessels with rim diameters under 20 centimeters (see the discussion of individual eating vessels), two sizes are represented, medium (20.0–40.0 centimeters in diameter) and large (40.0 centimeters or more in diameter). These are proportional sizes based on rim diameter as well as vessel height. Whallon (1969) and Turner and Lofgren (1966) have suggested that a distinct bimodality within a functional class may indicate that two consumption groups of different sizes were using the vessels. This suggestion receives support from Reina and Hill's (1978:246) work among the Quiche Maya. Thus, the medium-size vessels at Cerros could be called family serving vessels, and the large vessels appear to have been used by suprafamily groups.

The functional class "dish" cross-cuts a large number of types. Consequently, it would seem to be a good test of the usefulness of relating various functional divisions based on form to the more broadly defined functions of the type-variety types. The distribution of the type-variety types over the functional classes of cold and hot serving vessels and the family and suprafamily size ranges is presented in Table 4.3. The letters enclosed in parentheses following the type name indicate whether the type as a whole has been interpreted as domestic (D), elite (E), special occasion (SO), nonelite special occasion (NSO), or ritual (R).

Throughout the sequence, family-sized dishes for serving cold food occur in Paila Unslipped: Variety Unspecified. The dishes in this type apparently were used in domestic contexts in the Ixtabai Complex, but as social stratification increased during the C'oh and Tulix Complexes, they came to be associated with the nonelite occupants of the site.

In the Ixtabai Complex there do not appear to be any special types limited

Table 4.3. Distribution of Types Including Dishes over Functional and Size Classes*

Type Name	Cold Serving Vessels Family	Cold Serving Vessels Suprafamily	Hot Serving Vessels Family	Hot Serving Vessels Suprafamily
Sierra Red: Sierra (D)	x	x	x	x
Laguna Verde Incised (D)			x	x
Cockscomb Buff (E)				x
Canxun Red (D)	x		x	x
Lanillo Groove Incised (D)		x		x
Cassada Red over Black (R)				x
Conop Red-on-Red Trickle (E)	x		x	x
Cockscomb Buff (E)	x	x		x
Zorra Black on Red (SO)				x
Matamore Dichrome: Matamore (SO)			x	x
Tinta Usulutan (SO)			x	
Yaxnik Through the Slip Incised (SO)	x			
Cabro Red (D)	x	x	x	x
Liscanal Groove Incised (D)	x	x	x	x
Pahote Punctated (D)			x	
Tuk Red-on-Red Trickle (E)		x	x	
Nictaa Buff (E)	x			
Sierra Red: Xaibe (NSO)		x	x	
Savannah Bank Usulutan: Variety Unspecified (SO)		x	x	
Pixoy Usulutan (SO)		x	x	
Matamore Dichrome: Shipyard (R)		x		
Chactoc Dichrome (R)		x	x	

x = present in type.
D = domestic.
E = elite.
SO = special occasion.
NSO = nonelite special occasion.
R = ritual.
*Paila Unslipped: Variety Unspecified not shown.

to suprafamily serving vessels, with the exception of a single late Ixtabai, Cockscomb Buff, suprafamily serving vessel. Otherwise, both sizes and all the suggested functions are fulfilled by Sierra Red: Sierra Variety and Laguna Verde Incised.

In the C'oh Complex the types comparable to Sierra Red and Laguna Verde Incised, Canxun Red and Lanillo Grorve Incised fulfill the entire range of serving functions outlined above, but specialized types are introduced as well. For example, Cassada Red-over-Black, which has been interpreted as a ritual pottery type, occurs only in large, suprafamily vessels for serving hot food. This complex also sees the introduction of elite pottery types that were used in ritual contexts. Conop Red-on-Red Trickle and Cockscomb Buff contain family-sized vessels for serving hot and cold food, as well as suprafamily-sized serving vessels for hot food. Within the special occasion pottery types, Zorra Black-on-Red, Matamore Dichrome: Matamore Variety, and Tinta Usulutan seem to have been used to serve hot food to family and suprafamily groups.

The restriction of Yaxnik Through-the-Slip-Incised to average-sized, medial-angle vessels and the elaborate decorative motifs found on the interiors of the vessels suggest that this special occasion type was used to serve a specific kind of cold food. What that might have been is open to speculation, but it should be noted that the incised decoration on the interior makes the vessel difficult to clean.

In the Tulix Complex the monochrome red type (Cabro Red) and the incised (Liscanal Groove Incised) and punctated (Pahote Punctated) red types continue to fulfill the entire range of serving functions.

Within the special occasion, elite, and ritual pottery types, however, there is a difference in size distribution not reflected in the earlier complexes. Among the elite pottery types, Tuk Red-on-Red Trickle occurs in suprafamily serving vessels for cold food and family-sized vessels for hot food. Among the special occasion types, Savannah Bank Usulutan: Variety Unspecified and Pixoy Usulutan include both hot and cold serving vessels, but the hot vessels are family-sized, whereas the cold ones are suprafamily-sized. Similarly, within Sierra Red: Xiabe Variety, which may have been a special occasion type used by nonelites, cold food vessels are large and hot food vessels are family-sized. The ritual type Matamore Dichrome: Shipyard Variety is restricted to large serving vessels for cold food, whereas Chactoc Dichrome has large serving vessels for cold food, as well as medium-sized ones for hot food. The only exception to this pattern is the elite type Nictaa Buff, which is represented by family-sized vessels for cold food.

The significance of this distribution pattern could be explained in several ways. It may indicate that as the ritual and elite structures developed and were elaborated, the inventory of foods increased, necessitating more serving vessels for small amounts of different kinds of foods rather than for large amounts of one or two kinds. Another possibility is that hot foods were consumed only in rituals or on special occasions by a limited number of people, perhaps those with special powers. (See Villa Rojas [1945] for distinctions between hot and cold people and objects.) A third possibility is that the forms that seem to be dictated by function in the earlier complexes are now simply symbolic. Supporting this last suggestion is the later prevalence of the basal

The Pottery from Cerros, Belize 131

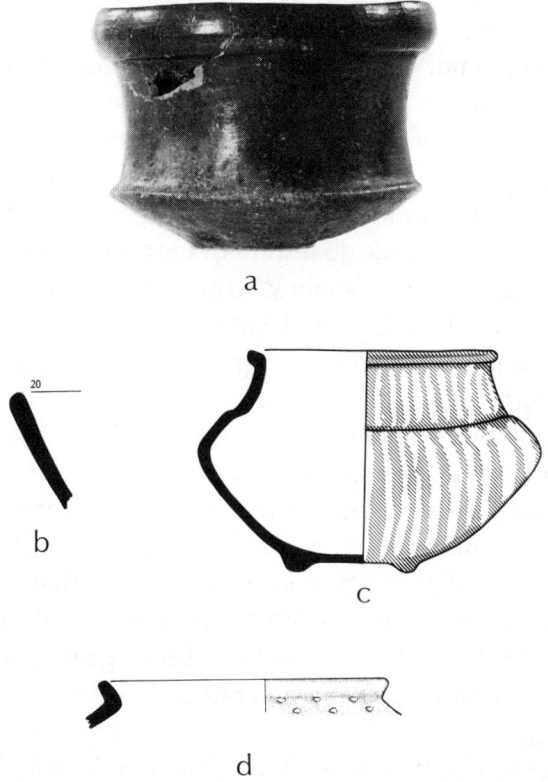

Figure 4.7. Buckets and individual eating vessels. *a:* medium-sized bucket; *b:* flaring-walled bowl with direct rim; *c:* S-Z angle bowl; *d:* collared bowl.

flange in ritual contexts. If it developed out of the Late Preclassic medial flange (Adams 1971:141), it seems likely that by the Early Classic it has become synonymous with ritual vessels, providing a larger exterior surface for the inconographic themes painted on the vessels (Freidel, personal communication, 1980). These ideas must remain speculative until comparable analyses have been undertaken at other sites.

BUCKETS

Complementing the dish form are medium-sized buckets (Fig. 4.7*a*). These vessels have low medial angles, high flaring walls above the angle, and flaring or everted rims. From a functional point of view, the unrestricted orifices of these vessels make them less than ideal for storage. The flaring or everted rims, however, would make it easy to carry the vessels, even if the contents were hot. In contrast to the dishes discussed above, the high walls insure that liquid contents would not be spilled while being transported. Moreover, the high walls would conserve heat more efficiently than would the low walls of the dishes. The absence of fire blackening indicates that these vessels were not used as cooking pots.

On the basis of their morphological traits, it appears that these vessels were used for serving relatively large quantities of food with a high liquid content, such as soups or stews. The Poknoboy Striped (Ixtabai and Early C'oh) and the Teabox Unslipped (Late C'oh and Tulix) vessels have been interpreted as stationary cooking pots for stews or soups (see above), suggesting a need for such serving vessels.

The ethnographic and ethnohistoric record provides some support for these hypotheses. Landa says, "they prepare stews of vegetables and flesh of deer and wild and tame birds of which there are great numbers and of fish of which there are large numbers" (cited in Tozzer 1941:91). Redfield and Villa Rojas (1962:40) note that in Chan Kom meat of all kinds is usually boiled for domestic consumption, as it is in Quintana Roo (Villa Rojas 1945:55). Although Gann (1918:21) discusses only barbecuing and smoking, he is concerned primarily with food preservation rather than preparation for immediate consumption.

In Cache 1 Vessel 132 (Savannah Bank Usulutan: Variety Unspecified), an unusually large example of one of these vessels with a rim diameter of 52.0 centimeters, was used to contain various offerings (see Freidel 1979:fig. 5). Its unusual size, usulutan decoration, and groove hook rim suggest it was specially made for this purpose.

The distribution of buckets over the types in which they occur is presented in Table 4.4.

EATING AND RITUAL OFFERING BOWLS AND DISHES

Within the forms at Cerros, there is a residual category of relatively small bowls and dishes that may have been used as containers for small amounts of things. These bowls and dishes occur in three forms: vessels with slightly insloping walls above a shoulder; vessels with flaring walls, direct rims, and rounded lips; and S-Z angle bowls (Fig. 4.7*b, c*). Over time they increase both in frequency and in the number of types in which they occur.

In the Ixtabai Complex this functional class is represented by vessels with flaring sides, direct rims, and rounded lips. It is found only in Hole Dull: Hole Variety, which has been interpreted as a ritual type.

In the C'oh Complex the class occurs not only in the dominant red mono-

Table 4.4. Distribution of Buckets over the Types In Which They Occur Correlated with the Nature of the Types

Type Name	Nature of the Type			
	Domestic	Special Occasion	Elite	Ritual
Sierra Red: Sierra	x			
Canxun Red	x			
Matamore Dichrome: Matamore		x		
Conop Red-on-Red Trickle			x	
Cassada Red-over-Black				x
Cabro Red	x			
Sierra Red: Xaibe		x		
Liscanal Groove Incised	x			
Savannah Bank Usulutan		x		
Pixoy Usulutan		x		
Nictaa Buff			x	
Tuk Red-on-Red Trickle			x	
Chactoc Dichrome				x

x = present in type.

chrome type, Canxun Red, in the form of small, medial-angle bowls with slightly insloping walls above the angle, but in the special occasion Matamore Dichrome: Matamore Variety and in the elite Cockscomb Buff. In Matamore Dichrome: Matamore Variety the vessels are bowls with incurving sides and in Cockscomb Buff they have slightly recurving walls.

The Tulix Complex sees a dramatic increase in both the number of these vessels but the types in which they occur. In Cabro Red and Pahote Punctated, for example, these vessels are represented by four-collared forms, none of which has a rim diameter greater than 18.0 centimeters (Fig. 4.7d). The elite types in this complex, Nictaa Buff and Tuk Red-on-Red Trickle, occur as collared bowls and medially ridged bowls with insloping walls above the ridge, respectively. Three of the ritual types in this complex also have these vessels. In Kuxche Orange they occur in bowls with restricted orifices and in bowls with flaring walls. Remax Punctated has collared bowls, and Matamore Dichrome: Shipyard Variety has bowls with flaring walls, direct rims, and rounded lips. Special occasion Savannah Bank Usulutan: Variety Unspecified vessels are bowls with flaring walls and S-Z angle bowls.

Because these vessels are first represented as a ritual type in the Ixtabai Complex and show the greatest proliferation of ritual types, it seems likely that they were used primarily for a ritual purpose. These forms are somewhat analogous to the gourds that the modern Maya use as eating dishes.

Although gourds probably were used for these purposes in normal domestic contexts, the use of pottery in a ritual context may have signaled a sacred occasion, much as the modern Maya differentiate between factory-made vessels and gourds for everyday use and clay dishes for ceremonial use (Villa Rojas 1945:108; see also the discussion in R. Thompson 1958:105–7). Culbert (1965:43), however, points out that only a limited number of small vessels are used to serve food in modern Maya villages. Nonetheless, as Lischka (1978:230) notes, probably the number of ritual contexts was greater in the past than it is today.

The occurrence of these forms in the dominant monochrome and elite types confirms their use in domestic contexts possibly as eating bowls instead of the usual gourd vessels among the wealthier members of the community (Redfield and Villa Rojas 1962:36).

RITUAL VESSELS

This functional class consists of small jars for storing dry substances used in mortuary and sanctification ritual, three forms associated with liquids used in rituals, and four miscellaneous vessels.

Small jars. Small jars, either vertical or with slightly flaring necks, occur in Hole Dull: Hole Variety, Hole Dull: Hukup Variety, and Sierra Red: Sierra Variety (Vessel 501). They are characterized by moderately high necks, small rim diameters, and very thick walls (Fig. 4.8*a*). At first glance, the thick walls appear to be anomalous because the occupants of Cerros were capable of making thin-walled small jars. The pastes, however, are usually dense and hard, making the pot relatively impermeable to moisture, and thick walls definitely would contribute to this end. Following this line of reasoning, the presence of an exterior slip would seem to indicate that the vessels were intended to keep the contents dry. The rims, which are small in diameter, simple, and direct, would prevent easy access to the contents but facilitate sealing with a stopper of wood or stone. These pots are similar in size to the modern cosmetic powder containers described by R. Thompson (1958:107 and fig. 31a, b), which are used in a domestic context by women. Few of the Cerros vessels have been found in domestic contexts, but many have been found in burials (15, 22, 20 and 2), pits (F8, 22, 19, and 1b-6), and along the dock. According to Cliff (personal communication, 1979), these pits may have been caches associated with houses in the nucleated village. The low volume of material these vessels could contain and their relatively low frequencies outside ceremonial contents suggest that they contained a dry substance probably used in mortuary and sanctification rituals. This type of intermittent use corresponds to the ex-

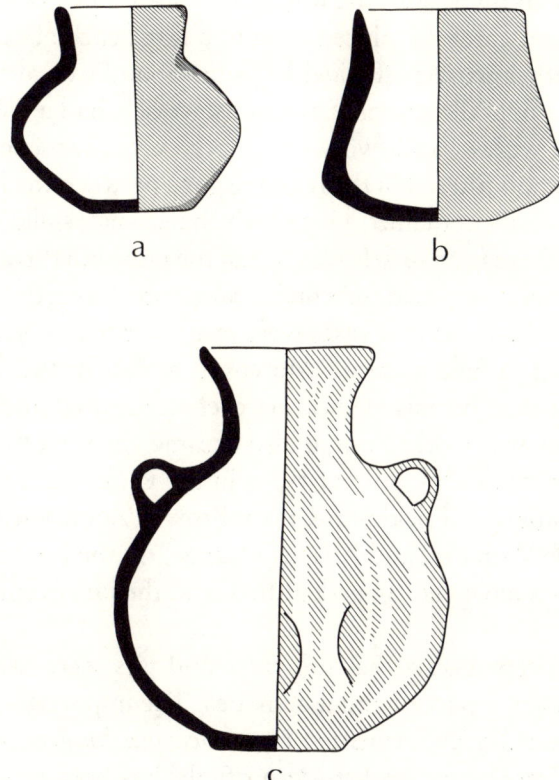

Figure 4.8. Ritual vessels. *a:* small jar; *b:* beer mug; *c:* jug with three strap handles.

tended storage function indicated by the dense, hard pastes and thick walls (Ericson, Read, and Burke 1972:90).

Liquid containers. In the Tulix Complex two forms repeatedly occur in contexts associated with the ritual interments and renovation of structures (for example, Structures 5C, 6, 29, and 2A-Sub. 4-1st). The first is a small vase with a well-rounded, low medial angle (Fig. 4.8*b*) and a rim diameter between 8.0 and 12.0 centimeters. The second form is a globular jar with a high, flaring neck and three strap handles (Fig. 4.8*c*).

In the field the vases were referred to as "beer mugs," because they are the perfect size for drinking cups or mugs. During the first season, four of these vessels came out of Burials 2, 3, and 4 in the nucleated residential village, suggesting a ritual function. This supposition was strengthened by the discovery of four more of the vessels the following season in Cache 1 on Structure 6B. They had been carefully placed around a large cache bucket containing jade heads and other artifacts (Freidel 1979:fig. 5) and were oriented approximately to the cardinal directions. Each of the vessels had a worked sherd lid on or associated with it, and two were empty except for a small amount of fine sand, which had filtered in through the gaps between the lid and the rim. These vessels may have contained a liquid which had since spilled or evaporated. Associated with these four vessels was one of the jars with three strap handles.

As work continued in the monumental architecture during the 1976 and 1977 seasons, more of these jars and vases were recovered together, indicating that the two forms were a functional set. Moreover, to date neither has been found in contexts other than burials, dedicatory caches, or ritual interments.

As the typology was worked out, it also became apparent that the jar forms occur only in ritual or elite pottery types in the C'oh and Tulix Complexes (for example, Zapatista Trickle-on-Cream Brown: Zoon Variety, Hole Dull: Hukup and Hole Varieties, and Kuxche Orange). In the Ixtabai Complex ritual and elite types have yet to be identified, and the jars occur in Sierra Red: Sierra Variety.

All this evidence suggests that the vases and jars were used to hold and consume a liquid as a part of ritual activities. The importance of *balche*, the intoxicant produced from fermented *Lonchocarpus longistylus*, Pittier bark, and honey in ethnohistoric and modern rituals, has been repeatedly emphasized by Landa (cited in Tozzer 1941:92), Redfield and Villa Rojas (1962:128), J. E. S. Thompson (1930:82–82, 85), Villa Rojas (1945:110), and Gann (1918:47). The descriptions of the ceremonies in which *balche* was and is used provide some surprising parallels to the archaeological forms.

Redfield and Villa Rojas (1962:36, 129) state that today *balche* is always offered in vessels made from oval gourds with a small opening at the stem end. These are stood on end. The vases replicate this form in pottery. Gann (1918:43–44) records that a jar of *balche* is placed beneath the altar in the *Chac chac* ceremony. His drawing of the altar (1918:fig. 11) shows a jar very similar to those found at Cerros. Landa (cited in Tozzer 1941:92) speaks of cup bearers who poured the drink from great tubs for the celebrants of rituals, implying that cups were used to consume the drink. Elsewhere, also in reference to the *Chac chac* ceremony, Landa (cited in Tozzer 1941:104) records that *balche* is poured into a vessel and carried out of town. Later in the same ceremony, "they then took a large vessel of wine, and having placed it in the middle they offered it to the gods" (cited in Tozzer 1941:106).

An even more striking parallel can be found in Landa's discussion of the *Pacum Chac* ceremony in the month of Pax (cited in Tozzer 1941:165). The

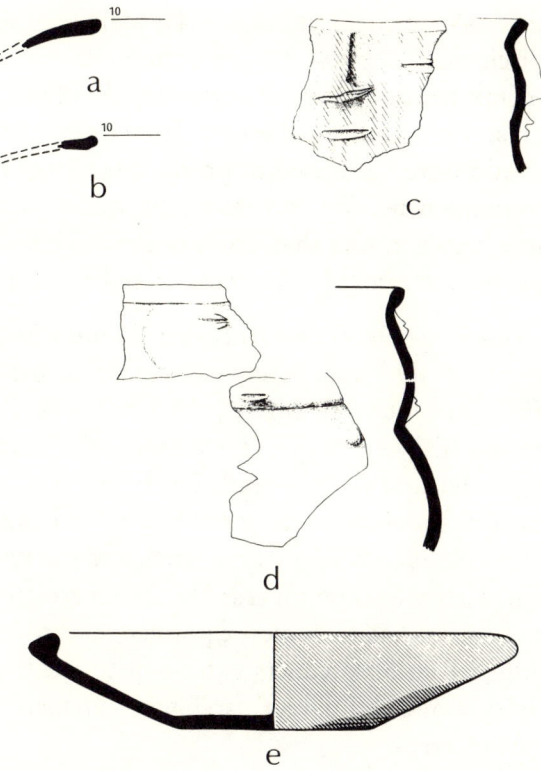

Figure 4.9. Ritual vessels. *a* and *b:* fermentation vessels; *c* and *d:* effigy jars; *e:* plate with internally folded rim.

ceremony ends with the smashing of a large jar filled with drink. Perhaps this explains why most of the jars in the interment deposits have been smashed.

Despite the amount of time separating the occupation at Cerros and these various accounts, it seems likely that the basic function of *balche*—to sanctify and make safe—would have been fulfilled by this drink or a comparable one in the Late Preclassic. The occurrence of these forms in contexts requiring sanctification or safety supports this assumption. Whether or not that liquid was *balche* cannot be determined at present. The term *balche* mugs and jars is simply used as a shorthand referent.

The hypothesis that it was an intoxicant is supported to some extent by the unslipped type Bobche Smudged. These large bowls with thin walls and restricted orifices, would be ideal for the fermentation of a liquid (Fig. 4.9*a, b*).

Their smudged interiors make them impervious to water, and the orifices (8.0–10.0 centimeters) are small enough to be sealed for fermentation but large enough to be cleaned. These vessels were probably used to produce small amounts of the drink for domestic consumption (Redfield and Villa Rojas 1962:129) as both an intoxicant and a purge (Tozzer 1941:92). Large wooden vats, however, would have been used to produce the large quantities necessary for rituals. Presumably the domestic intoxicant was consumed from gourds or other perishable vessels rather than from pottery. This distinction would serve to emphasize the difference between the sacred and the profane.

Miscellaneous ritual vessels. Four forms that do not cross-cut other types seemingly occur only in the ritual contexts assigned to the Tulix Complex. These are the effigy jars found in Muñequita Appliquéd (Fig. 4.9c, d), the censers of Taciste Washed (Fig. 4.10b), the plates with internally folded rims in Cabro Red (Fig. 4.9e), and the thin-walled dishes in Sangre Red (Fig. 4.4a). With the exception of the plates with internally folded rims in Cabro Red, each of these forms occurs only in the type cited, and the type occurs only in the forms mentioned in earlier complexes. This 1:1 correlation between form and type seems to be restricted to domestic pottery, such as Poknoboy Striped and Chiculte Slipped Rim Striated. Its extension to ritual pottery, coupled with the advent of specialized ritual forms, suggests an increasing elaboration of ritual over time at Cerros.

SPECIAL FORMS

What has been interpreted as a paint pot occurs in Bribri Black Incised and Unslipped (Fig. 4.10a). This fragment of a bowl with an exterior, thickened rim and rounded lip is unslipped on the exterior below the rim. The unslipped area is decorated with three preserved rows of groove-incised lines (0.9–1.3 centimeters in length), which are oriented vertically. Traces of red ochre are still present in some of the incisions. The presence of red ochre in the incisions on these pieces may indicate that they were used to store this substance, as it was not a common practice to decorate incised areas in this manner in the Late Preclassic. Although in later periods red ochre was used to make the red paints found on the Protoclassic and Classic polychromes, red ochre may have been added to the Late Preclassic slips to produce the bright red pottery or the reds found on painted stucco in this time period. If so, it may have been stored in larger quantities, thus explaining the large size of these vessels (rim diameter approximately 24.0 centimeters), compared to the paint pots from earlier periods in Mesoamerica (for example, see Gordon 1898b:plate XII, fig. 1d), which tend to be considered miniatures.

A miniature dish in Cabro Red may represent a toy (R. Thompson 1958:60).

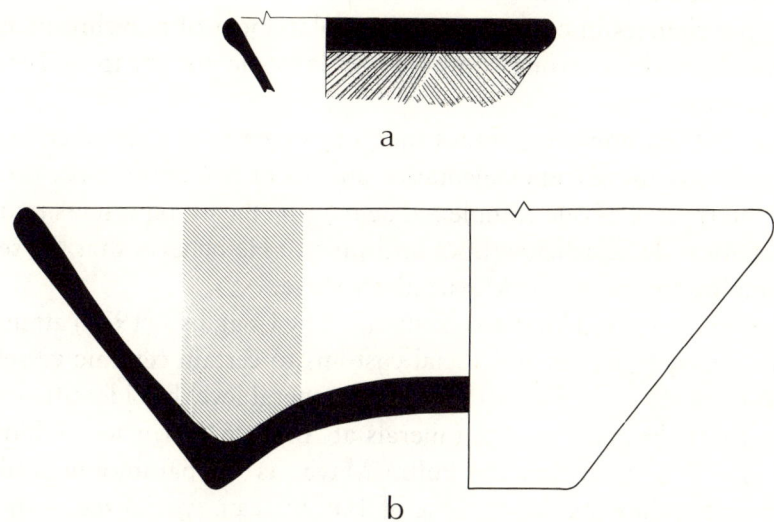

Figure 4.10. Paint pot and censer. *a:* Bribri Black Incised and Unslipped paint pot; *b:* Taciste Washed censer.

Interpretations

In the first portion of this paper I presented the data that now needs to be interpreted from a broader systemic perspective. Other attempts to do likewise in the Maya area have concentrated on identifying either intrusive elements at a site or broad functional types as a means of determining specific social customs or institutions. With the exception of Willey and Gifford's (1961) model for the Floral Park Ceramic Sphere and later elaborations on it (for example, see Adams 1971; Sabloff 1975; Willey 1977b; Pring 1977), these studies have focued on Classic and Postclassic complexes.

For example, Sabloff and Willey (1967), and Sabloff (1970) use the occurrence of similar motifs on Pabellon Modeled-carved and on the tenth cycle sculpture at Seibal as evidence for a takeover of the site by non-Classic Maya in the ninth century A.D. As further evidence, Sabloff cites the distribution of pottery, the changes in censer types, the replacement of polychrome by fine paste vessels, and the strong continuity in domestic pottery from Tepejilote to Bayal times.

Adams (1973), however, argues that, on the basis of a disjunction in ceramic traditions, usage complementarity, and the origins of fine paste ceramics, what is interpreted as one complex at Seibal (the Bayal) represents two complexes at Altar de Sacrificios (Boca and Jimba). He believes that the second, later complex represents the Mexicanized Maya.

Studies of the second kind are exemplified by Coggins's (1975) attempts to relate mortuary practices and social customs to certain ceramic vessels and types. Adams (1971:159–160) on a more general level has identified vessels that were gifts brought to elite funerals at Altar de Sacrificios. Sabloff and Rathje (1975) suggest that the Putun Maya, as the paramount traders in Mesoamerica following the collapse of Teotihuacan, specialized in the mass production of simple shapes designed for ease of shipment.

The functional analysis of the pottery at Cerros has combined both of these objectives and really differs from previous work only in detail. Through an examination not only of vessel form but of paste, contexts, modes (such as medial ridges), and diagnostics of use (such as fire blackening and wear patterns), specific functions have been advanced for almost all the vessels. These in turn have been used to define functional classes. The distribution of types over functionally distinct loci at the site has been used as the basis for suggesting the social functions of the types. A correlation between the distribution of functional classes of vessels over the types and the functional nature of the types themselves may signify internal changes in the ceramic inventory at the site. These changes include an increase in the number of formal types, as well as the gradual restriction of certain types to specific groups of individuals. Additionally, there is an increase over time in the number of functionally specialized types and in the number of 1:1 correlations between formal types and functional classes defined on the basis of form, particularly within the class of ritual pottery.

These changes in the ceramic inventory seem to be indicative of social processes that were operating during the Late Preclassic. The appearance and increase in the number of elite types during the C'oh Complex can be interpreted in two ways. This phenomenon seems to indicate either that elites began to use pottery to express social differences or that social differentiation itself was occurring and being expressed materially. The other data bases at the site support the latter interpretation. There is abundant evidence in the Maya lowlands, for example, that variability in social status is expressed in variability in domestic architecture (A. Smith 1962; Haviland 1963; Willey et al. 1965; Freidel 1976). However, the five Ixtabai structure loci identified at the site show no such variability. The structures all appear to be pole and thatch buildings daubed with white marl. This is also true of the locus next to the docking facility (Cliff, personal communication, 1979), which, if analogous to the C'oh and Tulix occupations of this area, would be expected to show some differentiation. Moreover, there appear to be no differences in the artifact inventories from the five loci. Thus, it can be argued that the early deposits, which apparently are restricted to the coastal erosion cut, represent a relatively egalitarian community.

More positive support for the second hypothesis comes from the fact that at the time when the elite ceramic types first begin to appear, people begin to move from the nucleated village to the house mounds presently found in the dispersed settlement. Although people continue to reside in the village along the coast, they do not seem to have access to the material culture associated with elitism at Cerros. An exception is found in the residential locus next to the dock. During the C'oh Complex, a low platform was constructed next to this dock. This platform contrasts with the areas farther east (Op 1) along the profile, where houses are raised above ground level not intentionally through construction activities, but unconsciously as a result of the continuous rebuilding and refurbishing of pole and thatch dwellings on the same spot (Cliff 1981). If the development of an elite at Cerros can be attributed to trade (Freidel 1979), these elites apparently found it necessary to keep a careful eye on this source of their power.

The pattern of materially expressing status differences continues in the Tulix Complex but is only slightly intensified. The number of elite types in the assemblage does not increase; instead, a nonelite type, Sierra Red: Xaibe Variety, is introduced.

This seeming lack of intensification may be related to the other major change in the ceramic inventory. The number of special occasion types present in the C'oh Complex decreases in the Tulix Complex from five to three, whereas the number of exclusively ritual types increases dramatically from two to at least seven and possibly nine. These changes may reflect a change in the nature of ritual activities in Maya communities at this point in the Late Preclassic. It has been argued that special occasion types were used primarily for rites focused on the individual or the family, whereas ritual types were used in the context of communitywide rituals, particularly those associated with the sanctification and dedication of monumental architecture. If the appearance of elite types in the C'oh assemblage does indeed signify the appearance of social stratification at Cerros, it would seem that the divisive elements of such stratification would have to be counteracted by an integrating force. Personal or private activities and/or rituals would only serve to exacerbate the situation, as would an intensification of the material expressions of social differences. On the other hand, communitywide rituals focusing on corporate activities, such as the construction of monumental architecture (see Mendelssohn 1971), would provide an integrating force. Not only would the existence of an elite class be justified and reinforced, but these public rituals and activities would also help relate community activities to regional activities, encouraging the local inhabitants to view themselves not as Cerrosaños, but as Maya. The importance of such regional integration is indicated by the standardization of public architecture in the Maya lowlands during the Late Preclassic (Freidel 1981). The use of similar iconographic themes on the stucco façades of every known Late Preclassic site with such façades suggests that a regional, if not universalizing, religious ideology underlies the communitywide rituals and integrates them into a regional framework. This phenomenon is accompanied by the decline and eventual disappearance of figurines presumably related to private ritual activities. Assuming that the economic life of Cerros was dependent on trade (Freidel 1978, 1979), increasing social stratification, accompanied by community-oriented rituals and activities that facilitated regional integration, would seem to have benefited all members of the community.

From the perspective of the Cerros pottery, these social changes are internal and gradual. With respect to this site at least, it seems there is no need to postulate that external groups were responsible for the inception of Classic Maya civilization. The most popular argument for such external influences, like the one offered here in opposition, is based on ceramic evidence. The appearance of the Floral Park Ceramic Complex (Willey, Culbert, and Adams 1967; Sharer and Gifford 1970; Pring 1977) in the Maya lowlands has been characterized as "the arrival of groups with an elite social class organization who subjected the simpler resident Lowland Maya and, in effect, lifted them up to the status of civilization" (Willey 1977b:404).

If the arguments represented above are valid, then the Maya already had an elite social class, which expressed itself materially in the form of differential access to certain kinds of pottery. Willey's assessment of the Floral Park Complex as simply "an indication of extraterritorial trade and contact" (1977b:405) seems to be correct. Incorporation of these diagnostics into the ceramic repertoire as elite or ritual types (see Sabloff 1975:232; Robertson 1980) seems to have followed an already established pattern of ceramic usage in the Maya lowlands. If this is the case, then the importance of the influence of highland Maya societies in the florescence of civilization in the lowlands is called into question by the very data base from which it arose.

PART THREE

Iconography and Calendric Correlation

Five

Altars 9 and 10, Kaminaljuyu, and the Evolution of the Serpent-Winged Deity[1]

Lee A. Parsons

The sprawling, two-hundred-mound site of Kaminaljuyu in the southern highlands of Guatemala is now fully recognized for its innovative role in southeastern Mesoamerica during the Late Preclassic Period, as well as for its importance during Teotihuacan colonization in the Middle Classic Period. Although Maudslay, Gamio, Lothrop, and others brought the site to scholarly attention between 1896 and 1926, it was not until the masterful monograph on Esperanza-phase Mounds A and B appeared (Kidder, Jennings, and Shook 1946) that Kaminaljuyu became known to every archaeologist. The report on Miraflores-phase Mound E-III-3 (Shook and Kidder 1952) focused on the richness of the Late Preclassic occupation of the site. Finally, William Sanders initiated a comprehensive survey of the region in 1968.

One of the predominant features of Kaminaljuyu is the quantity of monumental stone sculpture, uncovered partly in professional excavations, but more commonly in suburban Guatemala City housing projects since World War II and in previous surface finds. There are now some 125 numbered monumental stone sculptures assigned to Kaminaljuyu (Parsons n.d.), many of which have never been documented before.

The styles represented by this corpus of sculpture range from the outset of the Late Preclassic through the Middle Classic, or from about 500 B.C. to A.D. 700. The majority, however, are Preclassic. Significant aspects of this early material were analyzed, seriated, and published for the first time by Suzanna Miles in a much-referred-to article in the *Handbook of Middle American Indians* (Miles 1965). Two especially important Kaminaljuyu sculptures, Altars 9 and 10, deserve special attention, because they have not been described elsewhere, except for a photograph of Altar 9 in an exhibition catalog when the object was sent to Europe from the Guatemala National Museum (Fig. 5.1; Lehmann 1968:item 37).

The iconography of this pair of monuments reflects the greater Izapan horizon, which I consider Terminal Preclassic, dating roughly to the period 200 B.C. to A.D. 200. Izapan-related sculpture is frequently cited as a developmental transition between Olmec and Maya, a view that I share (Parsons 1967, 1973). However, the contemporary Miraflores (Verbena) and Arenal phases at Kaminaljuyu produced substyles that are more clearly "proto-Maya" than anything at the site of Izapa on the Pacific coast of Chiapas. Altars 9 and 10 are specifically assigned to the Arenal substyle and are dated to the early half of the Izapan horizon. My purpose here is to point out the salient iconographic features of these complex sculptures, with minimal comparative references, for an exhaustive synopsis of associated sculptures at Kaminaljuyu or elsewhere is beyond the scope of one paper. The principal motifs I will discuss are the Serpent-Winged Deity and accompanying glyphlike emblems.

Altars 9 and 10 were accidentally unearthed in 1961 during municipal bulldozer operations for housing projects at the junction of 23rd Avenue and the road to San Juan Sacatepequez on the western fringe of Guatemala City, in the central sector of ancient Kaminaljuyu. Suzanna Miles and Joya Hairs were soon on the scene, but not before a large slice of Altar 10 had been sheared off by the bulldozer (Fig. 5.3, right). Six stone carvings were found together in what was apparently a prehistoric sculpture dump; the latest associated potsherds in the fill are of Arenal type, though I place the carvings in the Verbena time phase, 200–1 B.C. The other four sculptures are small but exquisitely carved full-round effigies: a kneeling human figure, a seated pisote, a double monkey, and a spherical stone ball bearing a puffy human face (the last two are illustrated in Easby and Scott 1970:items 53 and 54).

The two altars[2] are cylindrical, or drum shaped; stand on low, cylindrical, tetrapods and are about 2 feet in height (for exact dimensions, see captions, Figs. 5.2 and 5.3). They were carved from a light-green, soft, volcanic stone, and when discovered bore traces of red pigment. The sides are intricately carved in low relief around their circumferences. The friezes are framed by raised plain bands at the top and bottom. The two compositions are essentially mirror images of one another (see Figs. 5.2, 5.3). Their form is not unique in this region; another cylindrical altar, with geometric carving, was found at Finca

Figure 5.1. Cylindrical, tetrapod, Altar 9, Kaminaljuyu. (The form of Altar 10 is identical but damaged.) See roll-out renderings, Figure 5.2 and 5.3. This view captures the far left portion of Figure 5.2. (Photo taken from Lehmann 968: item 37.)

Figure 5.2a. Composite roll-out photos of Altar 9, Kaminaljuyu (Guatemala National Museum #6368a). Dimensions: height, 59 centimeters; diameter, 26 centimeters; circumference, 78 centimeters. (Photographs courtesy of Joya Hairs, Guatemala City.)

Figure 5.2b. Drawing by the author of the complete low-relief composition on Altar 9, rendered from the composite photographs. Note the serpent-winged monster facing right.

Figure 5.3a. Composite roll-out photos of Altar 10, Kaminaljuyu (Guatemala National Museum #6368b). Note recent damage to stone, upper right. Dimensions: height, 65.5 centimeters; diameter, 27 centimeters; circumference, 83.5 centimeters; height of tetrapod supports, 6 centimeters. (Photographs courtesy of Joya Hairs, Guatemala City.)

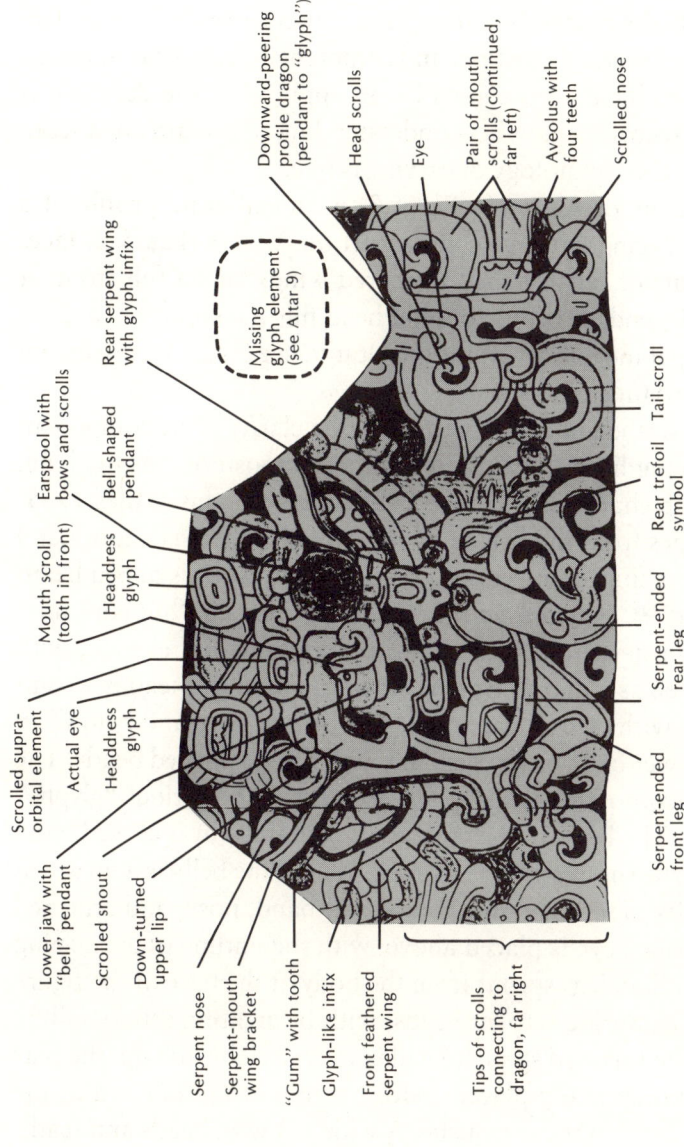

Figure 5.3b. Drawing of the complete low-relief composition on Altar 10, rendered from the composite photographs. Note the serpent-winged monster facing left. The component elements are labeled.

Solola, Tiquisate, on the Pacific Coast. It was discovered not far from a line of three small Preclassic potbelly sculptures.[3]

Even though Altars 9 and 10 were conceived as a pair and are equally well preserved, they differ in the quality of execution and in the details of motifs. Altar 10 was probably the first to be carved, and it was certainly by the master sculptor; each motif is crisply distinct and comprehensible. Altar 9, on the other hand, appears to have been copied by an apprentice; the detailing is relatively casual and seems to show less understanding of the intended iconography, even though the technology of carving is fine.

Dominating the theme of Altar 10 (Fig. 5.3) is an elaborate profile of a serpent-bird monster facing left. His counterpart on Altar 9 (Fig. 5.2) faces right. Both have a pair of outstretched feathered wings facing full front. A glyphlike sign with dependent profile dragon head fills a column of space at the rear of the principal monsters (extant on Altar 9; see Fig. 5.1; missing on Altar 10 owing to the damaged stone).

Altar 10 will be described in detail because of the clarity of its component elements. The left-facing head in the center of the composition has the long, down-turned upper lip characteristic of certain Izapan dragons (Miles 1965: fig. 3). A scroll emerges from the rear of the mouth; also there is a tooth and an attenuated, double-chinned, lower jaw. A bell-shaped motif is appended to this jaw ("false beard"?). Perched on the long upper lip is a "human" nose from which a scroll projects, an eye, and a supraorbital ovoid element with infixed U motif, as well as a pair of trailing scrolls. Behind the head is a compound ear ornament with central ear spool, tied bows above and below, an upper scroll, and a lower bell-shaped pendant with three attached beads. The headdress structure incorporates two glyphlike elements. (The various "glyphs" are discussed below.) The body of the creature is contained by a curved band connecting the tip of the snout with the rear leg. Within the belly is a forward-facing profile head. Its mouth area has a diagonal band, nose, and attached scrolls. An ovoid scrolled eye is placed above, with the outline of an earplug to the right. Two reptilian legs sprout from the body at the base of the figure and are tipped with elaborate serpent heads, with bifurcating scrolls falling from their mouths (the forward serpent head is viewed right side up, the rear is upside down). A horizontally placed trefoil symbol at the tail end of the body has a diagonal band in the cartouche. A wide tail with beads and feathers curls out behind.

Of special interest is the treatment of the monster's wings, of which the forward wing can be viewed most clearly. The tiers of feathers are contained and held by a profile serpent-mouth bracket, which substitutes for the wing bones. The back corner of this abstract mouth turns in a scroll; above the front of the serpent mouth is the typical humanoid dragon nose. Lining the mouth is an alveolar element containing one molar and ending in a tight volute. Below, in the center of the wing, a half-cartouched glyphic element is featured. The back serpent wing also contains a glyph, but of another type.

Isolated behind the serpent-bird monster may be seen an Izapan-type profile dragon head, which is placed vertically, facing downward, with mouth opening to the right. (The glyph to which it is appended is missing on the damaged Altar 10, but its counterpart is preserved on the upper left side of Altar 9.) Separating that cartouched symbol from the pendent dragon is a knotted bow tie (see Figs. 5.1 and 5.2). This dragon is agnathous, with a projecting upper alveolus containing four teeth. A pair of large scrolls spews from its mouth. A lobed element attaches to the front of its snout, and scrolls emerge from the eye region and also surmount the dragon head.

It is not necessary to describe the minor variations of Altar 9, except to note the differing central earplug pendant and the absence of the bell-shaped element below the mouth of the Serpent-Winged Deity's head.

Both altars incorporate six rounded-square cartouches with infixes that may be considered proto-Maya day sign glyphs. They occur in the same relative positions on the two altars, with only slight variations in the manner of draftsmanship; again, the cartouches on Altar 10 seem to be more accurately rendered. The two wing glyphs are mutually discrete: the forward wings contain the basic sign for "day," or *Kin;* the rear wings contain one-half of the *Kan* cross symbol, which might possibly be a prototype here for the Classic Maya day glyph, *Chuen*.[4] The frontal headdress glyph of the Serpent-Winged Deities is graphically similar to the latter, but its specific rendering on Altar 10 suggests an early form of *Akbal*. A related glyph appears on the headdress frontal of Miraflores Stela 11, Kaminaljuyu (Miles 1965:fig. 15a). At the back of the same headdresses is a sign which may be interpreted as *Muluc*. Trefoil symbols on tail bustles are extremely prevalent in Late Preclassic monuments, but they are too generalized to be traced as ancestral to any particular Maya glyph. Also, there is the isolated cartouched element behind the principal creature, extant on Altar 9. The infix is a profile of an unidentified animal, but insofar as the same animal appears in the monster's belly, this profile may symbolize the Serpent-Winged Deity himself.

Finally, note the distinctive bell-shaped earplug pendant with its three beads in the center of Altar 10. An identical pendant occurs on four other Kaminaljuyu low-relief monuments (Stelae 1, 22, 25; and Silhouette Relief "X"), all of the Miraflores-Arenal period. Furthermore, it is worn by the seated figure on a stone pectoral from southeastern Mexico (Coe 1966:fig. 7). The latter sculpture has an ancestral Maya text on the reverse, and Coe argues that it dates to the period immediately following that which I propose for Altars 9 and 10. Related bell-shaped ear pendants continue to occur in Classic Maya art.

I have been concerned here primarily with the identification of a fully developed Serpent-Winged Deity, and its complex symbolism, in the context of the Terminal Preclassic Izapan horizon. It remains to place this mythic creature in the broader evolution of Maya art. Altars 9 and 10 at Kaminaljuyu depict a profile composite monster with full-front serpent wings, serpent feet, plumed tail, and raptorial down-turned snout. The basis of this identification is the serpent-framed wing motif, which occurs widely in Izapan art (Quirarte 1976:235).[5] Bardawil (1976) named the same creature the Principal Bird Deity and traced its development from some Izapan prototypes to prolific Late Classic Maya manifestations. (The latter were originally called the Serpent Bird by Maudslay.) There is no need to repeat or amplify Bardawil's excellent exposition of the deity in Classic Maya art. However, certain comparative examples should be reviewed to place Altars 9 and 10 in their Late Preclassic and Protoclassic setting.

In Olmec art, prior to the Izapan period, both the serpent and the bird were frequently represented (see Joralemon 1971). There even is evidence for the amalgamation of serpents and birds in Olmec and post-Olmec iconography in the form of plumed serpents or serpents with raptorial beaks.[6] However, the Serpent-Winged Deity with its crucial serpent wings was apparently not represented until the early part of the Izapan horizon, ca. 200–1 B.C. For example, at Izapa itself the anthropomorphic figures on Stelae 2 and 4 (Norman 1973:plates 4 and 8), shown diving in an upside-down position from the celestial zone, have spread wings framed by profile serpent jaws. Furthermore, their wings also incorporate glyphic emblems (in these cases, the St. Andrew's cross). Stela 25 at Izapa (Norman 1973:plate 42) depicts a full-profile Serpent-Winged Deity in the celestial region of its narrative composition. This is a more literal depiction, with a recognizable bird wearing a long-lipped head mask and a diagnostic serpent wing. Stela 60, Izapa (Norman 1973:plate 52), shows a fallen Serpent-Winged Deity at the base of the scene.

The remaining examples to be cited are more in the Miraflores art tradition, which was centered at Kaminaljuyu. A low-relief panel from Chocola on the Pacific coast of Guatemala (Kidder and Samayoa 1959:plate 91) has, as a subsidiary motif on the right side, a damaged bird-headed creature with a recognizable serpent-framed wing. (Incorrect restoration of this section of the stone makes any further description impossible.) At Kaminaljuyu itself, the elegant Miraflores Stela 11 (Miles 1965:plate 15a) includes a peering, long-lipped, celestial being at the top of the scene (see Quirarte 1973:fig. 13g). Attached to its shoulders are the serpent wings, one of which contains a St.

Andrew's cross (a sky-band symbol in Classic Maya art). Also, Michael Coe (1973:26–27) has described a carved stone bowl that he feels was made at Kaminaljuyu in the Protoclassic Period (A.D. 50–200?). One of the two elaborately adorned human figures carved on this object wears serpent-framed wings on both arms. He also has a dragonlike mouth mask, so he may be impersonating the Serpent-Winged Deity in what is a somewhat more Maya-like interpretation.

One Early Classic Maya example of the evolving deity (Bardawil cites others) occurs on the cover of a polychrome Tzakol second- or third-phase basal-flanged bowl (Hellmuth 1978:208). A frontally splayed, anthropomorphic figure on the bowl has serpent wings attached to the back of his arms, and his head is in the guise of a snouted dragon. At Kaminaljuyu itself, several Maya-like painted cylindrical tripod vases from tombs in Mounds A and B show fully developed serpent-wing motifs from the Early Classic (A.D. 400–550) Esperanza phase (Kidder, Jennings, and Shook 1946:fig. 97c, f, h).

In Late Classic Maya art the Serpent-Winged Deity (or, by this period, the "Principal Bird Deity," according to Bardawil) is perhaps most characteristically found perched on the top of the cross motifs in the Temples of the Cross and Foliated Cross at Palenque (Bardawil 1976). Bardawil correctly observes that the long-lipped serpent bird is primarily a celestial deity in Maya iconography (as he is so often depicted in Izapan and Miraflores art), which also has a terrestrial counterpart (as shown on Stela 60 at Izapa). This form of cosmological dualism is certainly established by the Izapan horizon, as evidenced by two of the emblems on Altars 9 and 10 at Kaminaljuyu: *Kin* (sun or day) and *Akbal* (earth or night). This elegant pair of early sculptures elucidates the development of the Serpent-Winged Deity more profoundly than any other known examples.[7]

Notes

1. This paper was originally presented at a 1977 symposium in Guatemala City, organized by the Foundation for Latin American Anthropological Research. The significance of these sculptures and the excavation data were first brought to my attention by the late Suzanna Miles. I am also grateful to Joya Hairs for supplying me with eight photographic views of both monuments, making the roll-out photos and drawings possible. The actual monuments are located in the Guatemala National Museum of Anthropology (no. 6368 *a* and *b*).

2. The designation "altar" for this form of sculpture is equivocal, as we do not know the function. Some may prefer the term "cylindrical stela," though the tetrapod supports indicate a portable, freestanding monument more akin to a conventional altar than a stela.

3. Information and photographs supplied by Joya Hairs. In addition, for an example of a Late Classic Maya cylindrical "altar" of similar size and form, with carved hieroglyphic inscriptions, see Parsons (1980:item 325).

4. Linda Schele (personal communication, 1982) prefers an *Akbal* identification for the rear wing glyph, thus accurately associating the Serpent-Winged Diety with opposing day-night symbolism. (Is this, therefore, a prototype of the legendary "sun vulture" descending from the sky to the underworld in the west, to become the night sun?) We might also note the early use of the *Akbal* glyph in the headdress of a painted figure on structure 5D-Sub.10-1st at Tikal, dated to the time of Christ (W. Coe 1965a:19).

5. Although I noticed this important symbolic feature many years ago, Jacinto Quirarte, who has contributed vastly to the interpretation of Izapan iconography, was the first to identify in print what he called "feathered serpent wings" in Izapan art and also to relate them to the Maya "celestial dragon." However, he did not refer to the two Kaminaljuyu altars, which further clarify these interpretations.

6. Monument 6 from Abaj Takalik on the Guatemalan coast, dating to the last part of the Middle Preclassic (700–500 B.C.), bears a grooved image of a double-winged reptilian-bird monster realistically rendered on its upper and rear surfaces (Parsons in press:fig. 11).

7. Although I am not convinced that there is a direct iconographic relationship between the early Chavin horizon of northern Peru and the Izapan horizon of southern Mesoamerica, as Badner (1972) proposes, I am tempted to point out a common feature that Badner overlooked. The raptorial fanged deity from the round monolithic columns at Chavin de Huantar definitely has feathered wings supported by multi-fanged "dragon" jaws, in the manner of the Serpent-Winged Deity in Mesoamerica (Badner 1972:fig. 23).

Six

The Maya Calendar Correlation Problem

David H. Kelley, University of Calgary

Maya monuments and books contain dates in an intricate but well-understood calendar system in which dates can be fixed precisely to days over as long a period as desired. Dates commonly count from an era base (usually a day 4 Ahau, 8th of the month Cumku) giving the number of days that have elapsed since that date. This number of days can be converted to our system of Julian day numbers by the addition of a constant number of days, known as the Ahau equation or correlation constant. The correct solution to this problem of conversion has occupied many scholars since it first became possible to read the dates.

Previous Solutions

No reasonably complete discussion of the correlation problem has been published since J. Eric Thompson's *Maya Chronology: The Correlation Question* (1935), although E. Wyllys Andrews IV published an important discussion in 1940, and Thompson himself returned to the problem in 1950. Dan Wolfman's study (1973) of paleomagnetism in Mesoamerica includes a discussion covering many aspects of the problem, but it is far from complete. J. D. Schove (1980) has also examined several correlations. Thompson's (1935) conclusions continue to dominate Maya studies, yet many scholars who have made a careful study of the problem are dissatisfied with his correlation constant of 584285. The most influential support for Thompson's correlation came from Sylvanus G. Morley, whose comprehensive book on the Maya served as an introduction to Maya studies for many Mayanists. John Teeple and Linton Satterthwaite also provided support, followed more recently by Floyd Lounsbury, Michael Closs, Gregory Severin, and, with some reservations, Daniel Wolfman.

No professional astronomer has continually supported Thompson. Maud Makemson started with the assumption that the Thompson correlation was correct (1943), but became dissatisfied with it and developed a correlation of her own (1946):489138. Working with the Carnegie Institution, Alexander Pogo (1937) developed the correlation 588626, but the details of his reasoning have never been published. If Thompson was familiar with it, he deliberately ignored it, along with other astronomically based correlations, because of his insistence on the continuity of the calendar. Hans Ludendorff (1938) supported the correlation 489384, advocated by H. J. Spinden (1924). R. W. Willson (1924), professor of astronomy at Harvard, partially developed the correlation 438906, which has been largely ignored. Charles Smiley (1960), a specialist in eclipses, developed the correlation 482699, as well as a possible alternate, 500210.

E. Wyllys Andrews IV, one of the few scholars who knew the documentary materials, the dirt archaeology, and the astronomy, was never convinced that the problem had been solved, and Robert Wachope, with a good knowledge of the archaeology and of documentary sources, felt that the Thompson correlation was incorrect, although he sometimes used it. In 1947 he argued for a correlation (679183) first advanced, on purely archaeological grounds, by George Vaillant. On the basis of his work in Honduras, where the pottery seemed to show an unbroken development from the Classic Period wares to the time of the Spanish Conquest, Joel Canby (1951:84) argued for a late correlation, but did not specify a correlation constant ("some point between 11.3 and 10.10" and "the 10.10 or say 10.15 dating is reasonable").

Besides those already noted, there has been a plethora of other solutions. Most of the early solutions, suggested before the era base or the true length of the katun were known, cannot be stated as precisely as a correlation constant. For discussions of the early correlations, see Spinden (1928:5–6, 1930:35–41) and Escalona Ramos (1940:64). Among those who proposed correlations, now usually long forgotten, were Brasseur de Bourbourg, Valentini, Pio Perez, Thomas (1882), De Rosny (1904), Forstemann, Seler (1895), Lehmann (1912), Sapper, and Bowditch (1901) (followed and slightly modified by Joyce [1914:359 and appendix III), Goodman (1905): 584280, Martínez (1926): 584281, Teeple (1926): 492622, Kreichgauer (1927): 626927, Dittrich (1936):

698164, Mukerji (1936): 588466, Bunge (1940): 449817(?), Escalona Ramos (1940): 679108, Weitzel (1945): 774078, Makemson (1946): 489138, Schulz (1955): 677723, Dinsmoor (see Satterthwaite and Ralph 1960): 497879/8, Kelley (1967): 553279. At various times other possible correlations have been proposed: Hochleitner (1974): 507994, 508362, 525698, 609417, 660205, 674265, Hochleitner (1972): 578585, Owen (1975): 487410, Cook de Leonard (1973): 585789, Vollemaere (1972): 577264, Schove (1976): 594250, Schove (1977): 615824.

Correlations proposed at the end of the last century or early in this century differ by more than 1,200 years. Of more recent correlations, Smiley dates all Maya monuments 278 years earlier than the widely accepted Thompson correlation, whereas Escalona Ramos would date them 260 years later. Positions near these extremes have been acceptable in the recent past to well-trained and well-informed dirt archaeologists (E. Wyllys Andrews IV 1968, 1973; Ball 1979:48). It seems highly likely that the true correlation falls within these extremes but not near the centre.

With varying degrees of thoroughness, I have examined most of the correlations cited and have worked on all aspects of the correlation problem, but the present paper is limited in scope. Such interesting but minor problems as the possible use of the 24-year katun; variations in the days naming the year (except for the calendar reform of 934 to be discussed) (see Jiménez Moreno 1961; Caso 1967; Kirchhoff 1950, 1955; Davies 1973); the special leap-year calendar found in Alva Ixtlilxochitl; whether Aztec and Mixtec years began or ended on their naming date; when the day began and whether it was or was not the same for the 260-day cycle and the 365-day year will not be considered here, save for occasional cursory mention.

Finally, the most important omission in this paper is a detailed discussion of the many particular correlations listed above. Instead, I discuss the various criteria that have been used; their strengths and weaknesses, and what criteria or evidence must be ignored, rejected, or explained by various correlations, particularly those that have been widely accepted or that seem to me especially strong on particular points.

Tests of the correlation problem fall into five categories:

1. geophysical dating techniques, which can indicate a probable range within which a solution might be found;
2. dirt archaeology, which can indicate approximate contemporaneities and sequences (here used only in conjunction with historical evidence, because an adequate consideration would require another paper as long as this simply to define the limits more closely);

3. documentary evidence referring to the structure of the calendar and how various parts of it correlate with the Julian or Gregorian calendar;
4. historical tests to establish a framework of Mesoamerican chronology, which can sometimes be tied to dirt archaeology by inscriptional evidence (this paper presents a new historical chronology for the Toltec and later periods);
5. astronomical tests, which seem to be the only way to reach a correct day-for-day correlation, if there was a break in calendrical continuity.

In my opinion, both historical evidence and astronomical tests strongly suggest that there was a break in A.D. 934. Astronomical tests may also indicate that previously accepted correlations are wrong. On both the documentary evidence and the astronomical evidence (except the lunar evidence), the Thompson correlation does markedly less well than the Spinden correlation. This is true both of older evidence and of new tests that I have developed. As I have pointed out previously (Kelley 1976:32, Kelley and Kerr 1973), no correlation based on continuity is in agreement with evidence for equinoxes and solstices in the inscriptions, which I regard as very strong.

Since I first became dissatisfied with the Thompson correlation in 1949, I have examined many other correlations, about 20 in considerable detail, and have worked out several possibilities that satisfy some but not all of my criteria. In 1980, I worked out a new correlation, 663310, which meets all of my criteria. However, by that time much of the work on this paper had already been done, and it seemed better to present the paper as originally designed, criticizing accepted criteria, suggesting new criteria, and showing which correlations best meet particular criteria and which are incompatible with particular criteria. Thus, rather than a polemical defense of the correlation 663310, this paper is a general study of the correlation problem. The evidence that led me to think that the Thompson correlation was impossible emerged long before I developed a personally satisfactory correlation.

Geophysical Dating Techniques

A comprehensive examination of C-14, paleomagnetic dating, obsidian dating, or other specialized techniques that have occasionally been used, such as dendrochronology, is beyond the scope of this paper. Obsidian dating can contribute little to the correlation problem because of the remarkable variations in the results obtained thus far, though largely understood, and the dependence on outside chronological controls, usually C-14, to determine the local rate of hydration, as well as the possibility that the rate changes somewhat with varying climatic conditions. (The premise of regularity of rate clearly controls the chronological conclusions. See Michels and Sanders [1973:79, mound B-V-6, dates from 1040 B.C. to A.D. 911; 195, mound B-V-8, dates from A.D. 32 to A.D. 1199; 230, mound B-V-2, dates from 262 B.C. to A.D. 1067; 234, feature 4, dates from 364 B.C. to A.D. 1264.] For a sanguine view of the technique and results, see Michels [1973], Michels and Bebrich [1971].) The assumed chronological controls offered by the acceptance of the Thompson correlation have served as a yardstick for obsidian dating rather than the reverse.

Palaeomagnetic dating, in principle, offers a more consistent and potentially more important set of controls. Again, however, some outside method of dating is necessary to establish the period when the magnetic pole lay in a particular direction. This control has been through all available methods, but with a heavy reliance on C-14 (Wolfman 1973:235, 240–241, passim).

In the ultimate analysis, the precision and reliability of C-14 are crucial to geophysical dating methods in the new world. For the present purpose, the central question is the extent to which C-14 dates provide reliable limits within which a true correlation should lie. Individual dates support correlations across the entire range of possibilities for more than 1,200 years. In terms of general theory, if the one-sigma limits of C-14 dates are correctly determined, then one date in three should fall outside those limits. However, there is no marker to tell which date it is, and it makes a substantial difference in our chronological interpretations which dates we accept and which we throw out. Johnson and MacNeish (1972) based their chronology on 84 Tehuacan samples and "about 200" "compatible" dates, but rejected "almost 300." (Elsewhere, Johnson says that 214 were regarded as acceptable, and 166 were rejected, sometimes "because they duplicate the chronological record.") If the division between those accepted and those rejected had been made differently, it would certainly have been possible to create a different chronological scheme. A further problem is the possibility that there is some sort of systematic local variation in C-14 samples. Three samples from Barton Ramie, carefully collected as the best available (Willey et al. 1965:26, 29) provide the most remarkable example of this variation. A sample of maize from the Spanish Lookout phase was dated to 1452 B.C., about 2,200 years earlier than expected. Both the other samples contained mixed Jenney Creek and Barton Creek materials and were dated to 2054 B.C. and 2193 B.C., overlapping at the one-sigma range (the central dates reversed the not-too-firm stratigraphic expectations). This is a mean of 671 years earlier than the Spanish Lookout date, and about 1,400 to 1,500 years earlier than expected.

A similar problem is posed by the possibility of systematic differences between dates from the Peten and dates from Yucatan. A beam from the Casa Colorada at Chichen Itza gave a date of 609 ± 60. The inscription, which probably dates the structure, gives the date 10.2.0.1.9 (correctly read first by

Knorozov, [1963: fig. 81]). In the Spinden correlation it is A.D. 610, and in the Thompson correlation it is A.D. 870, in the 5-sigma range. This is one of a series of dates from Yucatan that fit much better with correlations near 490,000 (Smiley, Spinden, Owen, Makemson, or Dinsmoor) than with those near 580,000 (Mukerji, Pogo, Thompson, Cook de Leonard, or the first Schove correlation) at the middle range. E. Wyllys Andrews IV, in completing the work of his father, E. Wyllys Andrews V (1980:284–85), indicates that the samples that support the Spinden correlation are from beams, whereas those that support the Thompson correlation come from other materials such as twigs. The latter, however, usually do not come from as tight a context. They calculate that 9 dates support a 12.9.0.0.0 correlation (one near Spinden), 7 dates are intermediate, and 11 support an 11.16.0.0.0 correlation (near Thompson). Matheny has a series of 11 dates from Edzna, 9 of which he thinks may have been contaminated by modern carbon from farming. He blames the relatively thin deposits of surface soil in the area (Matheny, personal communication). This may affect some of the samples supporting Thompson, as well. However, some of the beam dates favoring Spinden may not have been taken from the outer rings of the tree, as they should have been.

A carefully selected series of samples from Tikal, associated more or less directly with dated monuments, would support a middle range correlation, probably 50 to 80 years earlier than Thompson for the best possible fit. Most of the other Peten dates fit reasonably well with the Thompson correlation.

Highland and coastal Guatemalan dates are not as closely associated with Maya calendrical dates as are those of Yucatan and the Peten, but a date from Bilbao for the Late Classic Santa Lucia phase was 1447 ± 70 (Parsons 1967–1969:48; he assumed either laboratory error or contamination by surface carbon, although the sample seemed undisturbed and was more than 3.5 feet below the surface). Another probably Late Classic date from Nebaj was 1189 A.D. ± 60 (Foncerrada de Molina 1964:151). This fits most reasonably with dates at the upper end of the currently proposed correlations. Other dates from highland Guatemala could be interpreted as supporting a late correlation but are not as clear-cut.

The majority of C-14 dates would support a correlation between 470000 and 605000, but if there are systematic differences between areas (even if these are only in probability and kind of contamination), a "majority vote" is not a useful approach. If systematic regional differences in C-14 production can account for variations as great as those of the Barton Ramie dates, then C-14 is useless for the present problem, at least until the nature of local variation is fully worked out. At the present state of our knowledge, I do not think that the discriminatory power of C-14 is adequate to allow us to choose even between the Spinden correlation and the Vaillant correlation, separated by 520 years. No one has ever supposed that it could differentiate between, say, the Thompson and first Schove correlations, only 27 years apart.

Documentary Evidence—The 52-Year Cycle

The Mesoamerican calendar has long fascinated scholars because it is so different from our own. Some components of the system still survive today among Indian groups in Mexico and Guatemala. The 260-day count and the year of 18 "months" of 20 days, plus a 5-day period (which combine to give the 52-year cycle) have been recorded repeatedly, sometimes together, more often separately. Colonial sources also include references to the 260-year katun counts of Yucatan. Criticism of the nature and relationships of these documents has been almost nonexistent, yet they are crucial to all the correlations that have ever been supported by competent archaeologists. The extent of calendrical agreement among widely scattered groups has been the most important single factor in suggesting continuity between the modern calendars and the Classic Maya.

Among Spinden's notable contributions to the study of the correlation problem was the discovery that the 52-year cycle was in step, with a discrepancy involving no more than a 3-day range, from Yucatan to Guatemala and highland Mexico. This includes areas that were never part of the Aztec empire but that probably were all parts of the Toltec empire at its greatest extent. John Molloy and I would put this from about A.D. 1200 to 1240, whereas others would put it earlier, and Davies (1977:312–28) goes so far as to deny the existence of a Toltec empire even as large as that of the Aztecs.

A wealth of additional evidence now supports Spinden's arguments for a unified calendar (Miles 1952; Carrasco, Miller, and Weitlaner 1961; Caso 1967). Spinden's discovery is the backbone of the argument for calendrical continuity between the Classic Maya and later calendars. All correlations based on the principle of continuity must differ from Spinden by multiples of 18980 days ± 1 day. All correlations that are not multiples of 18980 ± 1 day from Spinden must assume that the calendar spread so widely by the Toltecs was a revision and modification of the Maya calendar—or possibly that the Classic Maya calendar was a revision and modification of the prototype of the Toltec calendar. Such a structural break in continuity requires explanation, whether it amounts to only a few days, as in the Goodman and Martinez correlations, or an extensive shift.

In short, it is now clear that a uniform 260-day cycle existed from Yucatan and Guatemala to Michoacan at the time the Spaniards arrived. All Classic period correlations must account for this cycle, unless there was a deliberate break in continuity, as I believe there was (see below).

Documentary Evidence—The Katun Count

The documentary cornerstone of the Thompson correlation is the *Crónica de Oxkutzcab*, p. 66, translated and annotated by Gates for Morley (1920: 506–11). It gives 13 tun-endings and 12 year-bearers from 1533 to 1545 and was copied "from an ancient book" "in characters" in 1685 by D. Juan Xiu. Since all tuns end on the day Ahau, they can fall on only four days of the month: 3, 8, 13, and 18 of the old long count or 2, 7, 12, and 17 of the colonial calendar; 7 and 2 appear correctly on four tuns; however, 1, 6, 11, and 16 account for six entries; 11 Ceh appears where 12/13 Yaxkin would have been expected, 7 Yaxkin appears where 17/18 Yaxkin would have been expected, and 18 Yaxkin appears where 2/3 Mol would have been expected. The crucial katun ending for the Thompson correlation is 11.16.0.0.0 4 Ahau 13 Xul and 4 Ahau 13 Xul of the intertribal calendar round fell in 1539. The entry reads "1540 11 Ix on Pop 1st, 13 Ahau the tun on 7 [Xul]." The year 1540 does not agree with other evidence for the year-bearers but does agree with other evidence for the katun endings, although it cannot be correct if it is a katun ending of the long count of the Classic Period. The scribe was writing 140 years after the latest date he gives; apparently, he did not realize that a given day name, such as Ahau, can fall only on four days of the month; he makes the year 2 Ix followed by the year 13 Cauac, although it has to be 3 Cauac (his other year-bearers are correct); and he puts the beginning of Christianity and the founding of Merida in this year 13 Cauac in 1545. 13 Cauac would actually have been either 1529 or 1581, but neither of these dates nor 1545 is correct for the founding of Merida. Such ignorance on the part of the scribe does not inspire confidence that he correctly interpreted his sources.

Spinden (1924:92) suggested that D. Juan Xiu had a codex with katun endings and that he "naively identified the recognizable year-bearers with those of the same name and number falling in the first years of the Conquest and naively adjusted to this calendrical mechanism the known events of the years in question." Spinden's interpretation seems to me entirely likely, and I find the Oxkutzcab chronicle negligible support for the Thompson correlation. The Oxkutzcab chronicle is in strong contrast to the prophecies for the tuns of a katun 5 Ahau (Roys 1949). These were apparently written in the 1590s or slightly later by someone who understood the mechanism of the calendar thoroughly. Although the scribe was probably contemporaneous with the katun, Ralph Roys calls it a "fictitious" katun 5 Ahau (1949:158), because it makes the katun begin with a year 13 Kan, corresponding to 1593–94, which does not agree with the Thompson correlation. I prefer to accept the writer's statements and assume either that the correct correlation is in agreement with this or with some modified interpretation of it, or that it is evidence for a break in the katun count, perhaps due to the establishment of several parallel katun counts.

There are numerous problems with the dates of the katuns. The third chronicle of Chumayel differs markedly from other sources. Most notably, it puts the arrival of Bishop Toral in the 6th tun of Katun 9 Ahau. Toral arrived in Yucatan in August 1562, which puts the first tun of katun 11 Ahau in 1537, rather than in 1536, as demanded by the Spinden correlation, or in 1539, as demanded by the Thompson correlation. The arrival of Toral is also connected with a peculiar entry in the *Chronicle* of Nakuk Pech, where he says that he was baptized by Bishop Toral when Christianity first arrived in the land in 1513. Why Pech, who must certainly have known who baptized him, was so confused about the Christian date as to write 1513 for 1562 remains a minor mystery. Another entry in the third chronicle of Chumayel indicates that Christianity began in the seventh tun of Katun 11 Ahau, in 1519; calculated from Bishop Toral's arrival, the true intended date would have been 1543. A statement in the Mani–Tizimin–Chumayel I chronicle (three copies, markedly different in minor details, of a single chronicle) puts the arrival of the Spaniards in katun 11 Ahau in 1513. According to Landa, the Spaniards arrived in Mérida in the first year of katun 11 Ahau, in 1541, which disagrees with the chronicles, with other colonial documents, and with all correlations based on a concept of continuity. I think that Nakuk Pech's confused statements are probably the basis of the chronicle entries and that there is no historical basis for the 1513 and 1519 dates. There is a statement in the Chumayel I—Mani—Tizimin chronicle that the first Spaniards arrived in the 13th tun of katun 4 Ahau, which would be 1513 in the Thompson correlation. The statement was apparently lacking in the common original of this chronicle and the third chronicle of Chumayel, which postdated the death of Landa in 1579. I think it is a back calculation and that these statements have little historical value and tell us little about the katun count (for a contrary view, see Closs 1976).

It seems clear that in general events assigned by the second chronicle of Chumayel to katuns 4 Ahau are assigned by the first chronicle to katuns 8 Ahau. Other variations indicate either the marked unreliability of our Maya historical sources or the use of multiple calendars, or both. The Mani text puts the seizure of Mayapan by the Itzas in a katun 11 Ahau (1284–1303, according to the usual interpretation), whereas the Chumayel I text of the same chronicle puts the event under 4 Ahau (1225–44), and the Tizimin text (which inserts an entire cycle of 260 years *after* the first arrival of the Spaniards, giving some idea of the degree of care the scribe put in his work) puts it in 4 Ahau (968–87). According to the Chumayel I–Mani–Tizimin, the ruler Hunac Ceel conquered Izamal in katun 8 Ahau (1185–1204). The third chronicle of Chumayel puts the same event in 5 Ahau (1087–1106). The Itza fled from Chichen Itza, according to the third chronicle of Chumayel, in the third tun of 1 Ahau (1127, for this source), but according to the second chronicle of Chumayel, in 4 Ahau (probably intended for 968–87). There are too few chronicles and they give too little detail to reconstruct various calendars with any assurance, but the nature of the variations suggests calendrical differences, as well as copying errors and confusions. Kirchhoff, in an unpublished 1949 study, maintained that 13 separate katun counts were operating in Yucatan; that is, every katun would have every possible name in some part of the area. It is true that Avendaño says "These thirteen ages are divided into thirteen parts which divide the kingdom of Yucatan, and each age, with its idol, priest and prophecy, rules one of the thirteen parts of the land . . ." (cited in Spinden 1930:16). However, I know of remarkably little evidence that any katun 11 Ahau began in 1539, as demanded by the Thompson correlation, or, in 1536, as demanded by the Spinden correlation. In my opinion, the available evidence, scanty as it is, suggests that at least three or four distinct ways of naming katuns were in use in Yucatan and that we have no assurance that any of them represented a continuous series from the old long count. I therefore reject the criterion that correlations should put a katun 13 Ahau of the old long count near 1540.

Historical evidence

MIXTEC CHRONOLOGY

Beginning in 1949, Alfonso Caso presented the results of his extensive studies of Mixtec genealogy and chronology. More recently, Emily Rabin has shown that Caso's chronology prior to the time of Eight Deer (born, according to Caso, in 1011 and died in 1063) has many inconsistencies. She has pointed out (Rabin 1981 and personal communications) that the interval between the birth of Six Deer, king of Tilantongo (in 1357, according to Caso) and of his great-grandson, Four Deer, about 1468, is a very long period and implies long generations not only at Tilantongo but at several other places. She therefore rejects two dates in the Bodleian codex and one in the Selden codex and eliminates one calendar round, making much shorter average generations. This enables her to accept two other dates in the Selden codex which must be rejected with the Caso chronology. In both interpretations the balance between the sources is quite even. In the Caso chronology several lines show improbably long generations, and in the Rabin chronology several of them show improbably short generations, yet one of the two must be correct. The Rabin chronology has been tentatively accepted by most of the scholars now working on these problems. I still favor the Caso chronology but regard the Rabin chronology as almost equally probable.

From the birth of Seven Water of Teozacoalco to the birth of his descendant, Six Deer, of Tilantongo, is a period of 260 years (Caso: 1097 to 1357; Rabin: 1149 to 1409), according to everyone familiar with the problems. Rabin and I independently developed a genealogy for "Cerro de la Mascara," modifying Caso's genealogy in the same way at the same points. The new genealogy gives better chronological control and verifies Caso's overall chronology, though requiring occasional modification of some of his individual dates. If we are correct in our interpretation and if the Bodleian scribe had access to correct data on this genealogy, then this period can neither be extended nor reduced.

Caso puts the birth of Eight Reed, king of Tilantongo, in 7 Rabbit, A.D. 1110, correcting 8 Rabbit of his source, the Bodleian, which would give 1098. He regarded this as "impossible," because he put the marriage of Eight Reed's grandfather, Six House, in 1086, only 12 years earlier. Eight Reed was the brother-in-law of Thirteen Snake, born in 1100, a younger brother of Three Vulture, born in 1096. Caso identified them as maternal grandchildren of Eleven Flower, of "Flames" (now identified as Achiutla) and his sister-wife, Five Wind, whose births Caso put in 1080 and 1082. This allows only 14 years: 1082 to 1096) for two generations, which is impossible. Thus, either the genealogy or the chronology must be revised. Unfortunately, this is one of the few places where the genealogy given by the Bodleian scribe is ambiguous. I prefer Caso's interpretation of the genealogy, which means correcting Caso's chronology by pushing it back 52 years. Rabin prefers the Caso chronology and a corrected interpretation of the genealogy. The current evident makes either position plausible. It was my conclusion that lines from Eight Deer's children, Four Crocodile of "Flint," Ten Flower ♀, Ten Earthquake of Tula, Six House of Tilantongo, and Four Dog of Teozacoalco all permit, support, or demand that Eight Deer be moved back to 959–1011.

Thus, at the present time, there are three possible interpretations of the Mixtec chronology. Caso's would put the life of Eight Deer from 1011 to 1063, Rabin's would make Eight Deer's dates 1063 to 1115, and I would place him from 959 to 1011. Table 6-1 shows my interpretation of the major Mixtec genealogies and their chronology. The table includes my reinterpreted ancestry of the dynasty of "Cloud-belching Mountain" (probably Jaltepec), recorded in the Selden codex. The revision makes that dynasty agree much better with other evidence. It does not allow us to choose one of the three possible chronologies. My chronological revision is of major importance for the date of the calendar reform established by Eight Deer's father, Five Crocodile, and for the dates of the Toltec emperors, Mixcoatl and Quetzalcoatl, which furnish important data for developing a correct correlation.

TOLTEC HISTORY AND ARCHAEOLOGY

The most crucial period for the correlation problem is the length of time between the end of the Classic Maya and the well-dated beginnings of Aztec history. During much of this period, Mesoamerica was dominated by the Toltec empire.

John Molloy and I (1981) have attempted to establish a firm dynastic sequence and genealogy of Toltec emperors, which is shown in Table 6-2. This differs widely from previous attempts but cannot be justified here. In general, the traditions of highland Mexico and Guatemala seem to start with the emperor Mitl or later. Molloy and I have identified this emperor, Mitl, with a certain Seven Lizard Mitl in the Bodleian codex, a younger son of Five Water, king of Tilantongo, by Ten Reed, daughter of Eight Deer Quetzalcoatl of Tula. This Mitl married his aunt, Two Rain, daughter of Quetzalcoatl.

Two Toltec traditions appear to deal with a period earlier than Mitl. The first is the mass of Mixtec-Chocho data already partly considered. The second is a list of joint conquests of the Toltec emperors, Mixcoatl and his son, Quetzalcoatl, preserved in the *Leyenda de los Soles*. Among their conquests were Zapotlan (Teozapotlan, Zaachila), the Zapotec capital in Oaxaca, and Acallan near the Laguna de Términos. We argue that these emperors are the Toltec leaders whose name glyphs are a giant cloud-snake (Mixcoatl) and a Feathered Snake (Quetzalcoatl). They are depicted in Chichen Itza in the Upper and Lower Chambers of the Temple of the Jaguar, in the North Temple of the Ball Court (the Temple of the Bearded Man, that is, Quetzalcoatl), and on the pillars of the Castillo. Miller (1977:212–213, 220) has drawn attention to murals at Chichen Itza showing attacks by these leaders, whom he lumps as "Captain Serpent," in a dry, hilly area, which he regards as Oaxaca, and in a jungle area, which he suggests may be Seibal. We think these are probably Teozapotlan and Acallan of the *Leyenda de los Soles* list.

It does not seem unreasonable that the *Leyenda de los Soles* has preserved a list of conquests from two or three generations before Mitl, but it does seem most unlikely that such a fragment should have been preserved in isolation from a much earlier period, referring to otherwise unknown rulers. For this and other reasons, Molloy and I (1981) have identified the *Leyenda de los*

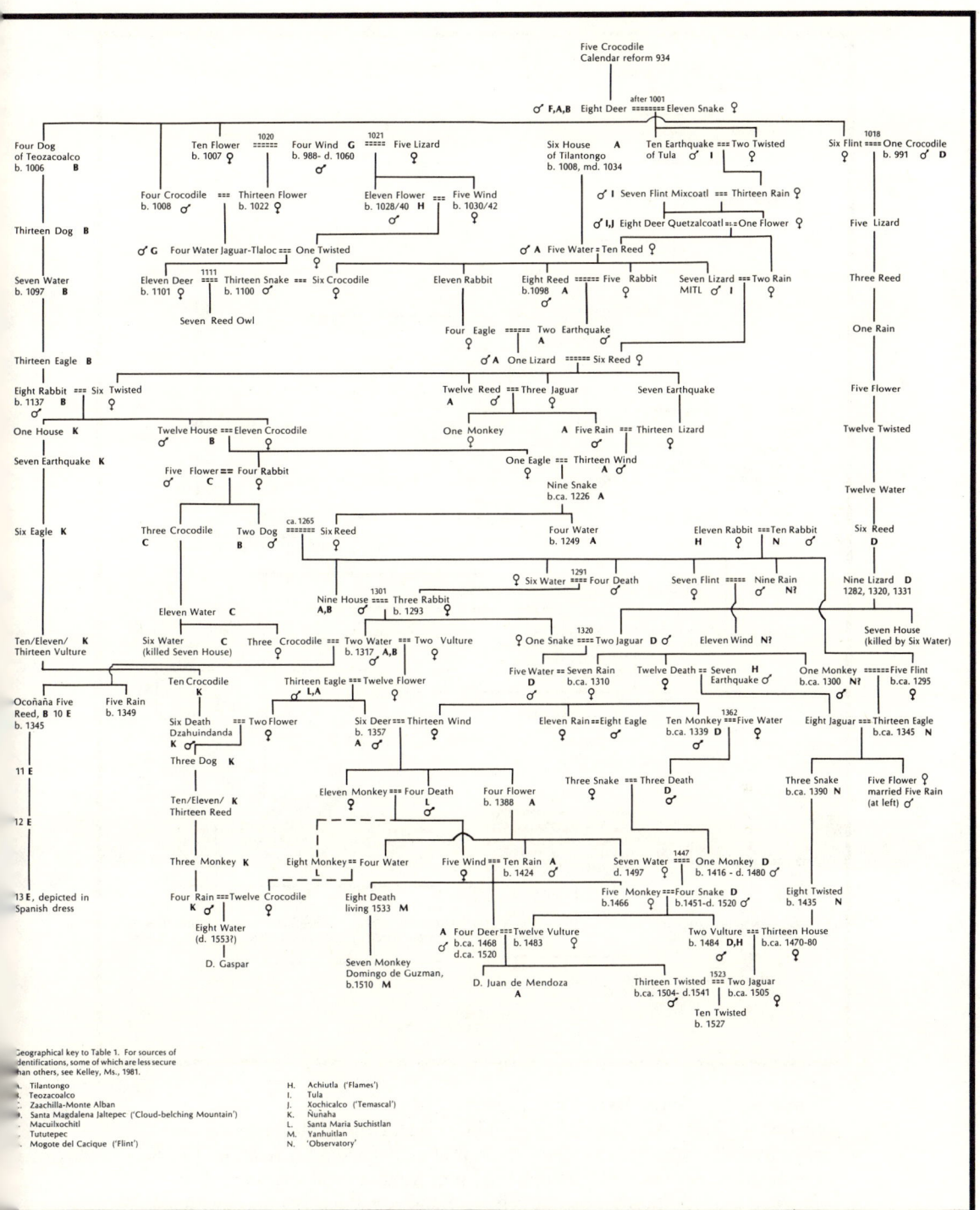

Table 6.1. Mixtec Genealogy and Chronology.

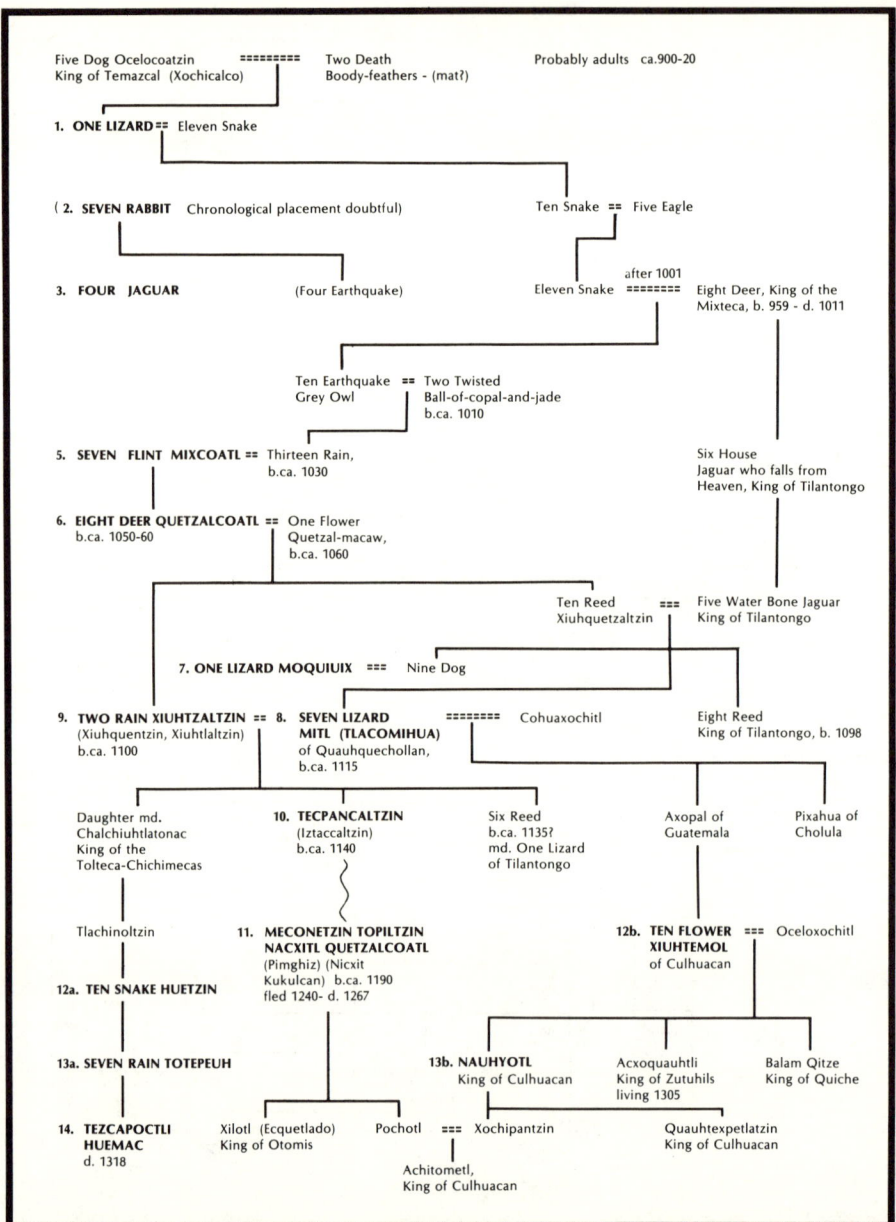

Table 6.2. A Toltec Dynastic Sequence*
*Based on the work of John Molloy and David H. Kelley Toltec rulers are in capitals and numbered. The numbers are provisional and other rulers of Tula may eventually be determined. The conquest list of Mixcoatl and Quetzalcoatl in *Leyenda de los Soles* is believed to refer to 5 and 6, and most of the other material on "Quetzalcoatl" is either mythical or refers to number 11. Seven Rabbit (2) conquered Xochitepec in the Mixteca where a son succeeded him. Mixcoatl (5) and Quetzalcoatl (6) are believed to have been the conquerors of Yucatan, and Mitl (8) was the conqueror of Guatemala.

Soles list as pertaining to Eight Deer Quetzalcoatl of Tula, the father-in-law of Mitl, and to Quetzalcoatl's father, Seven Flint Mixcoatl. The invasion of Yucatan must have occurred when they were both alive. In terms of the previous chronology, Eight Deer Quetzalcoatl must have been born about 1050 or 1060, and a reasonable date for the invasion would be between 1070 and 1090. I suspect that the erection of the Great Ball Court dates from shortly after the peace treaty depicted in the Lower Temple of the Jaguars, where Quetzalcoatl is shown wearing ballplayer's garb, that the Castillo-sub may be a funerary monument for Mixcoatl (or possibly his opponent, Captain Sun), and that the Castillo proper may be a similar monument for Quetzalcoatl.

The earliest clear evidence of Toltec penetration of Yucatan in the monuments of Chichen Itza that can be dated in Maya terms seems to be the construction of the Caracol. I have read the date on the Caracol band, belonging to a late stage of the structure, as 10.3.0.15.1 (Kelley, n.d.). I am inclined to regard this as an early result of either the invasion of Quetzalcoatl and Mixcoatl, about 1070–1090, or the invasion of Tlillan Tlapallan (the Maya country) by Four Jaguar of Tula and Eight Deer of Tilantongo, in 994. Spinden's date of 629 seems much too early, and Thompson's date of 889 seems nearly a century too early for even the earlier of these two interpretations.

I have pointed out that all but one of the monuments at Chichen Itza that can be dated with certainty fall between 10.2.0.1.9 (the accession of Kakupacal, given in the Casa Colorada) and the Caracol Stela at 10.3.17.0.0, a period of about 37 years when most of the Puuc structures of Chichen Itza were constructed. The rulers during this period were Kakupacal and Yax T'ul, whose relationship has not yet been determined. The last dated monument that can be read with assurance and that seems to be contemporary is the Toltec column from the "High Priest's Grave" (El Osuario), dated 10.8.10.11.0 2 Ahau 18 Mol. The date is fully integrated into the design of the column, and I can see no indication that it is reused. The associated grave materials seem to belong to a late Toltec period. I think this date is a very good marker for a later Toltec period at Chichen Itza and probably elsewhere. It falls a mere 93 years after the date of the Caracol stela. Most archaeologists have been unwilling to accept or even consider the implications of the shortness of this period as indicated epigraphically. I have also been reluctant to accept them, but I think this evidence suggests that the Toltec period started considerably later, and lasted for a shorter time, than has usually been believed.

I am inclined to think that One Lizard, the first Toltec king we have been able to determine, who may have been living around A.D. 940, should be associated with the founding of Tula. Metepec trade sherds from Teotihuacan have been found at Tula in association with Coyotlatelco wares (Matos

Moctezuma 1978), which probably started in the Tula regions and were introduced at Teotihuacan when that site was taken over by the expanding Toltec empire.

The implications are similar at Xochicalco, whose king was the father of the first king of Tula. As Caso pointed out and as I discuss more fully later, the temple of Quetzalcoatl, the Piedra del Palacio (now in Cuernavaca), and the stelae discovered by Saenz all show the calendrical changes associated with the calendar reform that I date to A.D. 934. The associated archaeological materials have been assigned to the Middle Classic, the equivalent of the Metepec phase of Teotihuacan, and the monuments show both Teotihuacan and Toltec characteristics (Davies 1977:66–67). To put these materials in the mid or late tenth century, as I now think the epigraphy demands, implies a correlation at least 150 years later than the Thompson correlation, in accordance with the evidence from Chichen Itza.

Astronomical Evidence

Although correlations based on documentary evidence and the concept of calendrical continuity have shown some correspondence with astronomical evidence, astronomers have seldom been completely convinced. Ludendorff wrote an extensive series of papers on Maya astronomy in terms of the Spinden correlation. These have generally been ignored in the comfortable conviction that the Spinden correlation was wrong. Makemson (1943) wrote one paper using the Thompson correlation but then decided Thompson was wrong and began looking for a better solution. Thompson himself made no (published) attempt to show that any specific Maya inscriptions had important astronomical content, and he did not reply to Spinden's suggestion that astronomical inscriptions fit the Spinden correlation better than the Thompson correlation, save for a brief attack on Ludendorff (Thompson 1935). For all the phenomena except lunations, I find the Spinden correlation fits the astronomy better than the Thompson correlation. Spinden's important papers (1928, 1930) are seldom cited in the literature, although they are full of valuable insights on Maya astronomy. To be sure, many of these insights are incompatible with the Thomspon correlation, as was Willson's identification of the Mars table and the independent identification by Escalona Ramos, Smiley, Hochleitner, and myself of equinoxes and solstices.

Thompson's attitude toward the astronomical evidence is well illustrated by his willingness to shift from a 584285 correlation, which fits the lunar and eclipse evidence moderately well, to a 584283 correlation, which does not fit that evidence nearly as well, because his interpretation of the documentary evidence and surviving calendars fitted better with 584283. With the exception of one general article, Thompson's efforts in Maya astronomy were largely devoted to trying to show that the Dresden Venus and eclipse tables could be interpreted in ways that did not conflict with his correlation. Smiley's far more important studies of these tables were published in sketchy form in sources that are obscure to most archaeologists and in terms of a correlation they were unprepared to accept. Because of the astronomical anomalies, certain scholars rejected the Thompson correlation, but most of them simply tried to find a correlation that fit better with the particular items that had disturbed them.

I think that the greatest problem posed by astronomical interpretations is the existence of structural realities that are interlocked and that may fit several correlations. The Maya use of intervals with multiple properties leading to dates of multiple astronomical phenomena means that a correlation based on one sort of valid criterion will include some other phenomena, even if the correlation is incorrect. To the scholar proposing the correlation, this seems to be good evidence that his or her correlation is correct; to others, it suggests that chance can do very strange things; to me, it suggests that the particular supporting evidence probably points to a valid phenomenon. A correct correlation should fit all such phenomena.

I shall discuss in particular interpretations of the Dresden Venus, eclipse, and Mars tables, including both the older interpretations and possible new ones. I shall also consider evidence from the inscriptions for tropical year anniversaries of equinoxes and solstices, as well as detail evidence from Caracol Stela 3 relating to Jupiter-Saturn conjunctions, Mars conjunctions with the sun, Mercury conjunctions with the sun, and other possible conjunctions. Although I have discussed some of these possibilities before, Mesoamericanists generally do not seem to realize that acceptance of many of these criteria is impossible if the Thompson correlation is correct. I shall also discuss the astronomical import of Dresden Ring Number dates and the astronomical identities of various Maya gods, as calculated from a 12 Lamat 1 Pop base, which should be reflected in references to these deities in the inscriptions in appropriate astronomical contexts. Finally, I shall consider the historical and astronomical evidence for a calendar reform in A.D. 934 as well as the Eurasian evidence relating to the date of invention of the Mesoamerican calendar as a limiting factor on the correlation.

THE DRESDEN VENUS TABLE

The Dresden Venus table is well described by Spinden (1930:87–93), by Thompson (1972a:62–71), and by Lounsbury (1978:776–789). It is a table of mean motion, not an ephemeris, covering 104 Maya years. The table has 5 pages with one Venus period of 584 days repeated 13 times on each page and with 3 lines of month dates on each page. Structurally, the base of the middle line of month dates is a day 1 Ahau 18 Kayab. The table is prefaced by the dates 12.19.13.16.0 1 Ahau 18 Kayab (2,200 days before the Maya era base) and 9.9.9.16.0 1 Ahau 18 Kayab. After Förstemann (1906:182) recognized that the table gives formal approximations to Venus intervals, it was assumed that 9.9.9.16.0. 1 Ahau 18 Kayab was the base of the table until various real-time correlations were checked against this. Dittrich (1936) found that the only time in 1,800 years that a day 1 Ahau 18 Kayab of the intertribal calendar round coincided with a heliacal rising 4 days after an inferior conjunction was on Julian day number 2062524, 19 November (Julian) A.D. 934. The Spinden correlation makes 9.9.9.16.0 correspond with J.D. 1853744, 11 April 363 (Julian), with the sun in 21° and Venus in 14°, 26 days before a superior conjunction. The Thompson correlation (584283) makes the same Mayan date correspond to J.D. 1948643, 4 February 623 (Julian), with the sun in 318° and Venus in 341°, some 16 days before an inferior conjunction of Venus and 20 days before a heliacal rising. Thompson (1972a:63) refers to the error as 16 days before heliacal rising rather than 18, which is correct for the 584285 correlation, or 20, which is correct for 584283. This invalidates his argument for a 16-day correction based on the table itself. Proponents of the Spinden and Thompson correlations have tried to explain how their correlations could be made to fit these awkward facts by suggesting that 19 November 934 was the intended date and that some sort of correction of the table was involved. For Thompson, the "real base" is 10.5.6.4.0 1 Ahau 18 Kayab. For Spinden, it is 10.18.9.15.0 1 Ahau 18 Kayab. Neither is mentioned in the table. Since Thompson and Spinden both thought that Maya calculations of the synodic period of Venus were accurate to at least three decimal places, the contorted explanations of why the Mayas should have chosen a base they knew to be incorrect are unconvincing.

It makes no sense to suggest that elaborate tables were constructed with extremely precise correction formulae, accurate to a small fraction of a day, and that the base of these tables was deliberately set inaccurately by 15 to 20 days so that the tables could be used repeatedly without correction until they finally came into step with reality. The alternative—that they were deliberately set at an inaccurate base in the past so that a derivative table (which is not given) would be in step at a contemporary date (which is not mentioned) —seems equally unconvincing, although the sophistication with which this view has been presented has tended to obscure its basic implausibility. Thompson (1935:66–67) said that "no evidence has ever been produced" in favor of Spinden's view that the Maya would have used a lunar calendar according to a formula which slowly got out of step with reality without correcting it. Spinden's explanation seems far more plausible than Thompson's explanations for the poor fit between the Venus and eclipse tables with reality in his correlation.

There are alternate explanations of the table. The interval from 12.19.13.16.0 1 Ahau 18 Kayab to 9.9.9.16.0 1 Ahau Kayab is 1,366,560 days, or (20 x 117 x 583.92166) plus 183.34 and (3741 x 365.24219) plus 188.97−. Allowance for secular variation would change these values slightly, and we do not know if Maya values would agree with ours in detail. However, the Mayas must have known that both Venus and the sun would have been about half a year off from reality over such an interval. They may have intended the table to run in 584-day periods, perpetually, from the calculated early base, noting the error and developing tables for calculating it but not shifting the tables. Thus, the difference between observation and table would serve as a constant check on the proper value of the correction. This makes sense to me in a way that a back calculation to a date known to be half a year in error does not. If this interpretation is correct, one might expect to find a true correlation giving a heliacal rising of Venus about half a year earlier than 9.9.9.16.0.

Another possibility is suggested by the relationship of the three lines of month dates to each other. Spinden (1928:44–45) pointed out that it is 11,960 days, the exact length of the eclipse table, between 9.9.9.16.0 1 Ahau 18 Kayab and 9.11.3.2.0 1 Ahau 13 Mac, the closest recurrence of a date 1 Ahau 13 Mac. The same relationship, of course, holds for all dates in the middle row with respect to the dates directly above them in the top row. Smiley, recognizing these relationships, looked for a correlation that would put 9.9.9.16.0 1 Ahau 18 Kayab at an eclipse, at an equinox or solstice, and at a heliacal rising of Venus. Smiley was the first to point out that the bottom row is separated from the middle row by a minimal interval of 9,360 days, also an eclipse interval. The total interval between the bottom row and the top row is 21,320 days, or (36 x 584) + 296. A mean interval of 292 days separates inferior and superior conjunctions of Venus. An interval of 4 days goes from inferior conjunction to heliacal rising but has no relevance to superior conjunction. In a Venus table using these values, it is hard to believe that the 296-day interval is accidental. If it is not, it would suggest that 9.8.3.16.0 1 Ahau 13 Xul of the bottom line was a superior conjunction of Venus and that 9.11.3.2.0 1 Ahau 13 Mac was a heliacal rising of Venus. At any rate, it seems likely that 1 Ahau 13 Mac represented some sort of current reality when the table was constructed, for past-tense suffixes accompany all verbs of the table, except those associated with 1 Ahau 13 Mac and the three following positions.

Of the various possible interpretations of the table, I would prefer that which puts 12.19.13.16.0 at a calculated heliacal rising of Venus, followed by that which makes 9.11.3.2.0 1 Ahau 13 Mac an observed heliacal rising of Venus, that which makes 9.9.9.16.0 1 Ahau 18 Kayab an observed heliacal rising of Venus (such as Dittrich, Smiley, Schove), one which makes 9.8.3.16.0 1 Ahau 3 Xul an observed heliacal rising of Venus, and finally those which add corrections to 9.9.9.16.0 to reach a heliacal rising (Spinden 1928; Thompson 1972a).

THE DRESDEN ECLIPSE TABLE

Pages 51–58 of the Dresden codex give a table of 69 real or formal eclipse syzygies, covering a period of 11,960 days. In nine cases a picture follows a short eclipse interval of 148 days and a tenth picture ends the table. A short text accompanies each eclipse, and slightly longer ones accompany the pictures. Several of the texts accompanying pictures show glyphs for eclipses of both sun (at new moon) and moon (at full moon). Hence they must refer to the period reached rather than the date. Some of the glyphs are verbs with past-tense suffixes, showing the references to be past, although this table is usually presumed to have had a predictive function as well.

The introductory passage contains a reference to the date 13.0.0.0.8 12 Lamat 16 Cumku (parallel to a ring number statement, but 8 days after the Maya era base rather than before it). It is followed by some multiplication tables; a peculiar number (probably a date) composed of 13 successive 13s; and finally, immediately preceding the table proper, four dates, one of which is incorrect as it stands. The table immediately follows with an interval of 177 days leading to the sequent days 6 Kan, 7 Chicchan, and 8 Cimi. Counting back 177 days from these days, one reaches 11 Manik, 12 Lamat, and 13 Muluc. The four dates that precede the table include only one date 12 Lamat and no days 11 Manik or 13 Muluc. That date is 9.16.4.10.8 12 Lamat 1 Muan. I have recently suggested (Kelley 1980:S33) that 12 Lamat 1 Muan was the calendar name of the Maya eclipse cycle at the time of the invention of the Mesoamerican calendar, which is one reason for its presence here.

Teeple (1930b:99) studied the positions of the 148-day intervals in the table and argued that the base of the table was a day 12 Lamat at, or one day past, draconitic node passage. Teeple (1930b:98) suggested that the multiplication tables were designed as correction formulae and that the true base was at some time between 10.12.0.0.0 and 10.15.0.0.0. It seems to me that the text clearly says that the table is calculated from 9.16.4.10.8. The Thompson correlation (584285, not 584283) puts an eclipse syzygy at 9.16.4.10.8 12 Lamat 1 Muan (not given in Oppolzer's tables but calculable from Schram's tables), but it is about 18 days before the draconitic node passage. The Teeple suggestion seems to me tortuous and unconvincing, but it has appeared to be the only way of accepting Teeple's arguments about node passage and also accepting the Thompson correlation. When she was still convinced of the Thompson correlation, Makemson argued for a base at 10.12.16.14.8 12 Lamat 1 Ch'en (1943:193–94); Satterthwaite (1965:623, 629) preferred 11.6.2.10.8, and Thompson (1972a:73) preferred 10.19.9.12.7—.9. None of these dates are given by the codex, and only the presumed parallel with the Venus table has given them even minimal plausibility. Such ad hoc manipulations of the multiplication tables can offer little support to any correlation. If one accepts that 9.16.4.10.8 12 Lamat 1 Muan was within a day of draconitic node passage, then the Thompson correlation must be wrong.

However, as in the case of the Venus table, it is possible to interpret the eclipse table as a formal table designed to measure differences between observation and the formal structure of the table. My own interpretation of the table looks back to the base 13.0.0.0.8 12 Lamat 16 Cumku. The age of the moon at 13.0.0.0.0 4 Ahau 8 Cumku (the Maya era base) is given at Macanxoc as 23 days (Satterthwaite 1947:131), which means that the Maya calculated that 13.0.0.0.8 was within a day of a new moon. Its position at the introduction to the eclipse table strongly suggests that it was also calculated as a solar eclipse. The interval from 13.0.0.0.8 to 9.16.4.10.8 is 1,412,840 days (118 x 11,960) + 1,560. Spinden's calculations show that the mean difference of the eclipse season and the 11,960-day cycle is 1.6752 days per cycle and that the mean difference of the lunations if .1115 days per cycle. Over 118 cycles, the eclipse season would have dropped back 197.6736 days (plus .21 for 1,560 days), and lunations would have dropped back 13.1570 days (− 5.12 days for 1,560 days). Because the half eclipse seaeon is 173.3092 days, the draconitic node passage would have receded to 24.5744 days before 9.16.4.10.8, and the lunation would have receded to 8.0570 days earlier. Although this calculation is probably very close to a true value for the interval given, we have no idea how close it is to the Maya value.

I have argued that a structure analagous to this one was in use when the Mesoamerican calendar was invented and that the eclipse god was "born" 11,960 days (one eclipse cycle) after a 12 Lamat 1 Pop at node passage, at 12.8.19.0.8. This would put the "birth" at 12.10.12.4.8 12 Lamat 1 Muan, 78 calendar rounds before 9.16.4.10.8. During the Classic Period, there is no concordance of this calendar round date with a multiple of 11,960 days from 12.10.12.4.8. However, going forward 9,360 days, one reaches another day 12 Lamat at 11 Mol (12.11.18.4.8—in the Dresden analogue it is at 9.17.10.10.8), where the node passage interval and the mean lunation are less than three days apart, the mean lunation being on the following day, 13 Muluc. If the earlier date was an eclipse near node passage, this would also have had to be an eclipse. The fact that 12.11.18.4.8 is exactly 123 eclipse cycles of 11,960 days before 9.16.4.10.8 12 Lamat 1 Muan strongly suggests that the Mayas were using a formal table with back-calculated values. We still do not have a clear understanding of the correction values implied by the multiplication tables, hence the Maya parameters may vary substantially from ours. Adoption of the principle of a formal eclipse table does not have as clear results for the correlation problem as the parallel case of the Venus table, and probably many correlations might be justified by suggesting minor changes in the Maya values for lunations or draconitic node passage intervals. A slight preference might be given to correlations that agree precisely with our formulae, but a lack of agreement should not be considered significant.

THE DRESDEN MARS TABLE

The Mars table of the Dresden codex was first recognized by Willson (1924:22–26), who used it as one of the bases in reaching his correlation. In spite of criticism from Thompson (1950:257–58, 1972a:107–9), I have argued that Willson was correct in regarding this as a Mars table (Kelley 1980:S30). The base date of the Mars table is 12.19.19.0.8 3 Lamat 1 uayeb, which is 352 days before Maya zero at 13.0.0.0.0 4 Ahau 8 Cumku. The terminal date of the series is 9.19.7.15.8 3 Lamat 6 Zotz. The 352-day interval is a close approximation of the interval from Mars conjunction to the first stationary point (where it stands before beginning retrograde motion) or from the second stationary point to conjunction. The mean synodic period of Mars is 779.93651 days, so that 780 days is a very close approximation; 780 days is also 3 x 260 days, so that the mean date of Mars shifts only slowly from a given tzolkin date, although actual conjunctions may vary up to about plus or minus 30 days from the mean. Although Thompson's arguments against regarding this as a Mars table are general in nature, the fact that the crucial terminal date seems to be far removed from any important Mars phenomena in his correlation may also have influenced him.

I have argued that the day 12.8.19.0.8 12 Lamat 1 Pop was a mass planetary conjunction and that the "birth" of Mars was 780 days later (Kelley 1980:S30). It is 100 x 780 days to 13.0.0.0.8 12 Lamat 16 Cumku, 8 days after the Maya era base, which was thus both a formal position of eclipses and a formal position of Mars. With the value 779.93651 for the mean synodic period of Mars, the mean conjunction would have receded 6.41249 days from 12 Lamat 16 Cumku, so that it would have occurred a day and a half after the era base by our calculation. Hence the 352 days back to 3 Lamat 1 uayeb must go back to the secondary stationary point, which was the interpretation indicated by Willson's analysis, although not what he himself preferred (see Kelley 1976:32). The agreement of the two kinds of calculations in suggesting that the Maya calculated 13.0.0.0.0 4 Ahau 8 Cumku as a Mars conjunction is further strong support for regarding this section of the Dresden codex as a Mars table.

If the same sort of explanation is suggested for the Mars table as for Venus and eclipses, then the Ring Number 12.19.19.0.8 3 Lamat 1 uayeb would have been calculated by the Maya as a true second stationary point, and the day 3 Lamat would have been the "name" of this point. From the Ring Number to the terminal date is 1,435,980 days, or 1,841 x 780 days. Since the mean error on each synodic period is .06349 days, the error over this period (ignoring secular variation) would be 116.88509 days. The correction is very close to one mean synodic period of Mercury (115.8774 days), suggesting that Mercury may have been involved in a predominantly Mars calculation.

I have not systematically checked correlations for this possibility. The correlation 663310, to be discussed shortly, makes the terminal date J. D. 2098938 (31 July 1034, Julian). At this date, the sun was in 133°, Mercury in 139° (6 days past conjunction), and Saturn in 125°, 8 days past conjunction with Mercury and 10 days past conjunction with the sun. Subtracting a correction of 117 days, one reaches 2098821, 5 April 1034, with Mars in 144° at the second stationary point. The sun was in 21° and Mercury in 13°, 6 days before conjunction. Going forward the mean 352 days to an expected Mars conjunction, one reaches 2099173, six days before a conjunction of Mercury and Mars in 17° with the sun in 14°. The conjunction of Mars and the sun was 17 days off from the mean interval after second stationary, occurring on J.D. 2099190, 9 April 1035, Julian, in 25°.

This new interpretation of the Mars table, supported by both the Ring Numbers and my calculation of the "sky peccary" as a Mars animal, gives a new structural test for correlations. This interpretation is incompatible with many previously suggested correlations, including those of Spinden and Thompson. The new correlation 663310 is in better accord with the data, although not nearly as good as the Kaucher correlation, which, however, was developed as a "best fit" for this particular data set.

THE TROPICAL YEAR

The structural relationship of many dates in the Maya inscriptions and in the Dresden codex shows the importance of an emphasized series of dates that approximately divides the year in quarters. Table 6.3 lists a considerable number of such dates and their transcriptions in various correlations which make them either equinoxes or solstices. Because of the inequality of the seasons and because the Maya apparently liked to use intervals with multiple

Table 6.3. Equinoxes and Solstices in the Maya Inscriptions*

Source	Maya Long Count Calendar Round Decimal equivalent	Hochleitner 674265 (rejected)	Schove 615824	Kelley 663310	Escalona Ramos 679108	Smiley 482699	Kelley 553279 (rejected)	Spinden 489384
Dresden RN	12.19.15.7.14 9 Ix 2 Ch'en -1646	672619 ca. -2871 87	614178 ca. -3031 85	661664 ca. -2901 89	677462 ca. -2858 178	481053 ca. -3396 271	551633 ca. -3202 359	487738 ca. -3177 21
Maya era base	13.0.0.0.0 4 Ahau 8 Cumku 0	674265 ca. -2867 269	615824 ca. -3027 267	663310 ca. -2897 271	679108 ca. -2854 0	482699 ca. -3392 93	553279 ca. -3197 181	487738 ca. -3373 203
Palenque TC	13.0.1.9.2 13 Ik *tun* Mol 00542	674807 ca. -2865 84	616366 ca. -3025 82	663852 ca. -2895 86	679650 ca. -2852 175	483241 ca. -3390 268	553821 ca. -3196 356	489926 ca. -3371 18
Palenque TFC	1.18.5.4.0 1 Ahau 13 Mac 275480	949745 5 Ap. -2112 358	891304 4 Ap. -2272 356	938790 8 Ap. -2142 360	954588 9 July -2099 88	758179 ca. -2637 177	828759 7 Jan. -2443 269	764864 ca. -2618 289
Dresden Venus table probable LC position (implicit, Palenque)	9.11.3.2.0 1 Ahau 13 Mac 1376320	2050585 13 Mar. 902 357	1992144 12 Mar. 742 355	2039630 15 Mar. 872 360	2055428 16 June 915 89	1859019 19 Sep. 377 177	1929599 15 Dec. 570 266	1865704 8 Jan. 396 289
Dresden Venus table	9.9.9.16.0 1 Ahau 18 Kayab 1364360	2038625 14 June 869 87	1980184 13 June 709 85	2027670 17 June 839 89	2043468 17 Sep. 882 179	1847059 21 Dec. 344 271	1917639 18 Mar. 538 359	1853744 11 Ap. 363 21
Dresden Venus table RN	12.19.13.16.0 1 Ahau 18 Kayab -2200	672065 ca. -2872 258	613624 ca. -3032 256	661110 ca. -2902 260	676908 ca. -2859 354	480499 ca. -3397 86	551079 ca. -3104 174	487184 ca. -3178 193
Copan Stela C	10.19.14.17.0 6 Ahau 18 Kayab -217820	456445 ca. -3658 89	398004 ca. -4818 87	445490 ca. -3688 91	461288 ca. -3645 181	264879 ca. -4183 272	335459 ca. -3989 1	271564 ca. -4165 22
Base of Dresden eclipse table	9.16.4.10.8 12 Lamat 1 Muan 1412848	2087113 16 Mar. 1002 1	2028672 15 Mar. 842 359	2076158 18 Mar. 972 3	2091956 19 June 1015 93	1895547 22 Sep. 477 181	1966127 18 Dec. 670 270	1902232 11 Jan. 496 293
End of Dresden eclipse table	9.17.17.14.8 12 Lamat 16 Yax 1424808	2099073 13 Dec. 1034 267	2040632 12 Dec. 874 265	2088118 15 Dec. 1004 270	2103916 17 Mar. 1048 3	1907507 21 June 510 91	1978087 16 Sep. 703 176	1914192 9 Oct. 528 198

Site	Long Count / Maya date / LC							
Tikal T4, L2	9.15.12.11.13 7 Ben 1 Pop 1408553	2082818 12 June 990 86	2024377 11 June 830 84	2071863 14 June 960 88	2087661 15 Sep. 1003 177	1891252 19 Dec. 465 270	1961832 16 Mar. 659 358	1897937 8 Ap. 484 20
Tikal TI, L2-3	9.13.2.7.18 11 Etz'nab 11 Ch'en 1390838	2065103 11 Dec. 941 265	2006662 10 Dec. 781 263	2054148 14 Dec. 911 267	2069946 16 Mar. 955 0	1873537 19 June 417 89	1944117 14 Sep. 610 174	1880222 8 Oct. 435 196
Palenque TC	8.19.6.8.8 11 Lamat 6 Xul 1291128	1965393 14 Dec. 668 266	1906952 13 Dec. 508 264	1954438 17 Dec. 638 269	1970236 19 Mar. 682 1	1773827 22 June 144 89	1844402 17 Sep. 337 175	1780512 11 Oct. 162 197
Palenque TC	8.19.19.11.17 2 Caban 10 Xul 1295877	1970142 15 Dec. 681 267	1911701 14 Dec. 521 265	1959187 18 Dec. 651 270	1974985 20 Mar. 695 3	1778576 23 June 157 90	1849156 18 Sep. 350 178	1785261 12 Oct. 175 198
Tikal MT 28B	9.12.6.2.19 11 Cauac 17 Mac 1383259	2057524 12 Mar. 921 357	1999083 11 Mar. 761 355	2046569 15 Mar. 891 359	2062367 15 June 934 88	1865958 18 Sep. 396 178	1936538 14 Dec. 589 265	1872643 7 Jan. 415 288
Tikal MT 28B (reading and LC arguable)	9.12.2.11.13 1 Ben 11 Cumku 1383353	2057618 14 June 921 87	1999177 13 June 761 85	2046663 17 June 891 90	2062461 17 Sep. 934 179	1866052 21 Dec. 396 272	1936632 18 Mar. 590 360	1872737 11 Ap. 415 22
Yaxchilan L41	9.16.4.1.1 7 Imix 14 Zec 1412661	2086926 10 Sep. 1001 173	2028485 9 Sep. 841 171	2075971 13 Sep. 971 175	2091769 14 Dec. 1014 268	1895360 19 Mar. 477 0	1965940 14 June 670 85	1902045 8 July 495 107

*0° or 360° are equivalent to the spring equinox, 90° to the summer solstice, 180° to the fall equinox, and 270° to the winter solstice. A few of the dates that led to this conclusion are listed in the table. Numbers associated with Maya dates are transcriptions into our system of the Long Count date. Numbers associated with Christian dates are Julian day numbers. The ealier Hochleitner correlation is somewhat closer on the tropical year than the one that he now prefers and is used here to illustrate the tropical year positions. 2501 B.C. = −2500. All references before that date are approximations of a lower degree of accuracy. All later data are read or extrapolated from Stahlman and Gingerich 1963.

properties in their calculations, so that some dates are approximations, not all the dates are precisely at equinoxes or solstices in any of the correlations. The importance of these anniversaries has been recognized independently by Escalona Ramos, Hochleitner, Smiley, and myself.

No correlation based on the principle of continuity is in accord with this material (Kelley 1976:32) and this evidence was the final factor in convincing me in 1965 that neither the Thompson nor Spinden correlations could be correct.

A full discussion and critical appraisal of the dates of this set would require a lengthy article. It should be pointed out that all the dates of these quarter-year sets occur in a nonchance proportion in an astronomically sorted list, but only the position identified by Spinden as April 9 occurs in much more than chance proportion throughout a long list containing most Maya dates, where each of two sequent dates approximating this position recurs more than twice as often as any other tropical year date recurs. Calculations frequently move from one position of this tropical year set to another position within a single inscription. It should also be pointed out that the dates most clearly associated with these positions show the displacement from exact quarter-year intervals that one would expect from the inequality of the seasons. This supports the view that these dates are the equinoxes and solstices rather than some other quarter-year phenomenon of an undetermined nature (as the Thompson correlation, for example, must assume). It also suggests that the dates identified by Spinden as April 9 should in fact be summer solstices (Kelley and Kerr 1973:194–95), although this conclusion is not as strong as the conclusion that the dates mark equinoxes or solstices. (See a slightly fuller but still incomplete discussion in Kelley and Kerr 1973.)

These tropical year anniversaries include 1.18.5.4.0 1 Ahau 13 Mac at 754 years after the Maya era base, when the Maya year of 365 days had progressed halfway through the tropical year, and its repetition at 9.11.3.2.0, after the Maya year had progressed entirely through the tropical year twice (2 x 29 calendar rounds = 3,016 Maya years = 3,014 tropical years). The date 9.11.3.2.0 is my preferred position for the calendar round date 1 Ahau 13 Mac, where this date appears in the *Dresden* Venus table, in association with 9.9.9.16.0 1 Ahau 18 Kayab, also one of this set of dates. The *Dresden* eclipse table is set so that both ends are approximations to the putative equinoctial-solstitial positions. Another date is a Maya New Year's date, 9.15.12.11.13 7 Ben 1 Pop, from Tikal Temple 4, Lintel 2, associated with star glyphs and other indications of astronomical interest. On Stela C at Copan, a lengthy interval goes back from 9.14.0.0.0 6 Ahau 13 Muan to 10.19.14.17.0 6 Ahau 18 Kayab, some 4,532 Maya years earlier than 9.9.9.16.0 1 Ahau 18 Kayab (3 x 29 calendar rounds plus 8 years), putting that date also within 2 days of the same position in the tropical year. Spinden recognized one of the four points as an important tropical year anniversary, April 9 in his correlation, which he thought of as the beginning of an otherwise unknown "farmer's year." Most recently, Schove (1977) has adopted a correlation approximating these points of the tropical year as one of his criteria.

Table 6.4 shows the recurrences of 7 Ben 1 Pop in the later intertribal calendar round from A.D. 120 to A.D. 1419. The date approximates equinoctial and solstitial positions of the tropical year during this period only four times. If the concept of continuity is valid and if the interpretation of 7 Ben 1 Pop at Tikal as a tropical year position is correct, this results in possible correlations of 375503, 527345, 660205, and 793065 (using the plus-or-minus one day

Table 6.4. Recurrences of the Date 7 Ben 1 Pop in the Intertribal Calendar Round from A.D. 120 to A.D. 1419*

Julian Day Number	Julian Date	Position of the Sun in Degrees	Resultant Correlation Constant	
1765076	7 July 120	103	356523	
1784056/7/8	24/25/26 June 172	92/93/94	375503	
1803036	11 June 224	80	394483	
1822016	29 May 276	68	413463	
1840996	16 May 328	56	432443	
1859976	3 May 380	42	452423	
1878956	20 April 432	31	470403	
1897936	7 April 484	19	489383	(489384, Spinden)
1916916	25 March 536	7	508363	
1935896/7/8	12/13/14 March 588	355/356/357	527345	
1954876	28 February 640	342	546323	
1973856	15 February 692	329	565303	
1992836	2 February 744	317	584283	(Thompson)
2011816	20 January 796	304	603263	
2030796	7 January 848	291	622243	
2049776	25 December 899	278	641223	
2068756/7/8	12/13/14 December 951	266/267/268	660205	
2087736	29 November 1003	253	679183	(Vaillant, No. 1)
2106716	16 November 1055	240	698163	(698164, Dittrich)
2125696	3 November 1107	227	717143	
2144676	21 October 1159	214	736123	
2163656	8 October 1211	202	755103	
2182636	25 September 1263	189	774083	(Vaillant, No. 2)
2201616/7/8	12/13/14 September 1315	177/178/179	793065	
2220596	30 August 1367	164	812043	
2239576	17 August 1419	152	831023	

*One of these dates should correspond with 9.15.12.11.13.7 Ben 1 Pop, if the principal of calendrical continuity is accepted. For convenience, the first of three sequent dates that might match this date is given, except for those that approximate equinoxes or solstices (90° summer solstice, 180° fall equinox, 270° winter solstice, 360° spring equinox).

of the intertribal calendar round to give the best fit with the equinox or solstice in each case). 793065 would put 10.2.9.1.9 9 Muluc 7 Zac of the Initial Series lintel of Chichen Itza in 1450, reducing the entire Postclassic history and archaeology of Mesoamerica to less than 70 years, which can safely be considered impossible. 375503 would put the same lintel in A.D. 305, which is far outside what any modern scholar would be willing to accept. Thus, only 527345 and 660205 can approximate both the tropical year positions and the intertribal calendar round. All other correlations must reject either the interpretation of these dates as equinoxes and solstices or the continuity of the intertribal calendar round. This tropical year criterion was the final factor in convincing me that neither the Spinden nor the Thompson correlation could be correct. Correlation 660205 puts all dates 208 years later than Thompson does. On general archaeological and historical grounds, it fits well with the interpretations suggested in this paper.

If the criterion of calendrical continuity is rejected, a tremendous number of possible correlations fit the tropical year data, because there are four possible coinciding positions in every year, and a shift of a day or two would be possible on most of them, and they could still pick up a number of the dates of this set.

CARACOL STELA 3

One of the most remarkable monuments of Maya astronomical knowledge is Stela 3 from Caracol, Belize. The dates of this monument were worked out and circulated in an unpublished memorandum by Linton Satterthwaite, who was also kind enough to send me a drawing of it by William Coe. Later, Peter Mathews and I were privileged to examine the original monument in the Denver Museum of Natural History, through the courtesy of the Museum officials. I have published three studies including material from this monument (Kelley and Kerr 1973; Kelley 1975, 1977), and it will provide material for many more studies.

Satterthwaite thought that the monument was primarily dynastic, a view also espoused recently by other scholars (Stone, Reents, and Coffman 1980, who cite the work of Carl Beetz). I agree that the initial series date was probably the birth of an important local ruler, as well as a date of astronomical importance. No doubt it was this combination that led to the erection of a monument with so much astronomical information. Astronomical events are phrased in terms of life, death, warfare, and so forth, and the same phrases tend to appear both in astronomical and historical contexts. However, I have suggested five criteria, any of which may identify astronomical inscriptions (Kelley and Kerr 1973:181), and Caracol stela 3 meets four of them. The monument has star glyphs and other astronomically associated phrases; it contains an extensive series of astronomical intervals; it includes the days 5 Cib, 8 Ahau, 3 Lamat, 4 Eb, 3 Chicchan, 9 Kan, and 1 Ahau, which tend to recur in astronomical contexts; and it also includes the month positions 0 Pop, 18 Zip, 13 Pop, 14 Uo, 6 Pax, and 16 Muan, which also recur in astronomical contexts (Kelley and Kerr 1973:199, Kelley 1977; tables 5.1–5.4). The initial date itself, 9.6.12.4.16 5 Cib 14 Uo, is a formal position of the 13 Mac table of Venus dates in *Dresden*, being 56 Venus rounds of 584 days before 9.11.3.2.0 1 Ahau 13 Mac; the date 9.7.10.16.8 9 Lamat 16 Ch'en is a comparable date of the *Dresden* 3 Xul table, being 8 Venus rounds of 584 days before 9.8.3.16.0 1 Ahau 3 Xul. There are no formal positions in the 18 Kayab table, but 9.9.13.4.4 9 Kan 2 Zec is 2 days after 7 Ik 0 Zec of that table, and 9.9.18.16.3 7 Akbal 16 Muan is 3 days before 10 Cimi 19 Muan of that table.

Stone, Reents, and Coffman have suggested that a second "birth" glyph with the date 3 Lamat 16 Uo is that of a ruler who may have been the son of the one whose birth is marked by the Initial Series. This date differs by 22 Maya years and 2 days from the Initial Series. It is exactly twice the length of the interval from 9.9.13.4.4 9 Kan 2 Zec to 9.10.4.7.0 8 Ahau 3 Zec. Moreover, 9 Kan 2 Zec of this last interval is exactly 33 tropical years (33 Maya years and 7 days) after 9.7.19.13.12 8 Eb 15 Zotz. All these dates are on the monument. It seems unlikely that the Maya fitted their historical relationships quite so neatly to astronomical and numerological patterns, although they may occasionally have tried to do so. In any case, Stone, Reentz, and Coffman admit that the ruler associated with the Initial Series is mentioned after the "accession" of his son, but they try to associate him with a different site. They also suggest that a frequently repeated phrase on the monument refers to human warfare, although it contains no clear references to known sites or rulers. In my opinion, this lengthy series of dates refers only to astronomical matters, except for the birth of the principal ruler.

The content of the monument parallels glyphically and with respect to some of the dates the inscription of the Hieroglyphic Stairway of Naranjo. Table 6.5 shows the dates of these monuments together with phenomena reached on the dates by several different correlations. The table emphasizes two related characteristics. First, the structural relationship of the dates is such that correlations picking up one class of astronomical or calendrical phenomena tend to pick up others. Second, different correlations tend, with many notable exceptions, to pick up comparable phenomena on the same date. Thus, correlation 525698, based on putting the birth of Chan Bahlum of Palenque at the time of a notable eclipse visible in Tabasco, puts 9.6.18.12.0 8 Ahau 8 Mol at J.D. 1871618, 18 March 412, with Jupiter in 61° and Saturn in 59° (28 days past conjunction), and it puts 9.9.17.11.14 13 Ix 12 Zac on 1893352, 19 September 471, with Jupiter in 88° and Saturn in 80°. The Thompson

Table 6.5. Dates of Caracol Stela 3 and the Naranjo Hieroglyphic Stairway;
Astronomical Phenomena in Various Correlations*

Maya Date--LC	CR	Decimal Equivalent
9.6.12.4.16	5 Cib 14 Uo	1343616
		2304
9.6.18.12.0	8 Ahau 8 Mol	1345920
		4408
9.7.10.16.8	9 Lamat 16 Ch'en	1350328
		1320
9.7.14.10.8	3 Lamat 16 Uo	1351648
		1864
9.7.19.13.12	8 Eb 15 Zotz	1353512
		9050
9.9.4.16.2*	10 Ik 5 uayeb	1362562
		306
9.9.5.13.8	4 Lamat 6 Pax	1362868
		1377
9.9.9.10.5	3 Chicchan 3 Ceh	1364245
		155
9.9.10.0.0	2 Ahau 13 Pop	1364400
		1164
9.9.13.4.4	9 Kan 2 Zec	1365564
		341
9.9.14.3.5	12 Chicchan 18 Zip	1365905
		1249
9.9.17.11.14+	13 Ix 12 Zac	1367154
		449
9.9.18.16.3	7 Akbal 16 Muan	1367603
		397
9.10.0.0.0	1 Ahau 8 Kayab	1368000
		1580
9.10.4.7.0	8 Ahau 3 Zec	1369580

☉ Sun * Calculated back from end date
☿ Mercury + From parallel text of Naranjo
♀ Venus   Hieroglyphic Stairway
♂ Mars
♃ Jupiter
♄ Saturn

Spinden 489384	**Kreichgauer 626927**	**Kelley 663310**
☉93 ☿98 ♃99	☉304 ♀301	☉161 ☿163 ♃156
	☿37 ♀42	
☉90 ♂89/ ☿116 ♀118		☉158 ♂153
♃186 ♄184		♃243 ♄243
☉49 ☿47 ♂51	♃108 ♄108	☉116 ♀116
	☉114 ☿119 ♄113	♀291 ♂296
☉60 ♀63	☿287 ♃287	
☉125 ♀127 ♃124/ ☿150 ♂152		☿218 ♂219/ ♀179 ♃181
	☿330 ♀335	♀199 ♃199 ☿196
♂273 ♄273		
☿332 ♀332/ ♃293 ♄293	☉183 ☿186/ ♀193 ♃198/ ♂216 ♄220	♃356 ♄356
☿14 ♂17	☿235 ♃229 ♄234	♀84 ♂85
☉123 ♂122/ ♀108 ♃103		♀158 ♃160

Table 6.5. continued

Kelley 562080 rejected	Thompson 584283	Hochleitner 674265
☿131 ♄130	☿23 ♀24	
☿235 ♂237/♃208 ♄208	☿130 ♀125	☉272 ♀272/♂343 ♄347
	☉164 ☿159 ♂162	♂193 ♃192
♀59 ♂60	☿50 ♄54	☿143 ♂143
☿121 ♀120	♀51 ♂52	☉192 ☿188 ♀184
☿44 ♄39		☉114 ♀114 ☿118 ♃121
		☉57 ♀60
☿49 ♀52	☉358 ♂351 ♃353	♃258 ♄253
☿121 ♀124 ♂124	☿85 ♃88	
	☿63 ♂59	
☉351 ♀351/♃217 ♄218	♂234 ♄238	
♀338 ♂340		☉75 ♂74
		☉190 ☿189/♀173 ♂175

Schove 615824	Mukerji 588466
☉157 ♀153	
♂127 ♃123	♀169 ♂174
♃103 ♄107	
☉190 ♂191 ♃189	
☉320 ♂316 ♃320	♂125 ♃120
	☉355 ♄351/ ♀10 ♂14
	☉107 ♂103

*Mercury-solar conjunctions are omitted except when part of multiple phenomena.

The Mukerji correlation picks up few structural realities and is probably close to what would be expected by chance. All other correlations shown pick up a nonchance degree of structural reality.

correlation (584283) puts 9.9.17.11.14 13 Ix 12 Zac on 1951437, 29 September 630, with Jupiter in 213° and Saturn in 218°, 50 days before conjunction. The Spinden correlation (489384) puts 8 Ahau 8 Mol at 1835304, 15 October 312, with Jupiter in 271° and Saturn in 278° (farther apart in degrees than Thompson but closer in time); puts 9.7.19.13.12 8 Eb 15 Zotz at 1842896, 29 July 333, with Jupiter in 186° and Saturn in 184°; and puts 9.9.18.16.3 7 Akbal 16 Muan at 1856987, 26 Feb. 372, with Jupiter and Saturn both in 293°. The Kreichgauer correlation, based partly on colonial evidence and partly on astronomy, puts 9.7.19.13.12 8 Eb 15 Zotz on 1980439, 23 February 710, with both Jupiter and Saturn in 108°. Jupiter-Saturn conjunctions occur irregularly at intervals of about 19 to 20 years and remain close together up to a year in one of three conjunctions but separate in a couple of weeks in the other two conjunctions—impressive evidence that at least some of the dates of this set are indeed associated with Jupiter-Saturn conjunctions.

Examining a set of dates on Caracol Stela 3 that seem structurally related to Mars, Carl Kaucher (1980) found only one place where four dates fit closely, with a correlation constant of 626660 or 626664. The latter is slightly less accurate on Mars but picks up the intertribal tzolkin exactly. Correlation 626660 makes 9.7.14.10.8 3 Lamat 16 Uo fall on 1978308, 24 April 704, with the sun in 37°, Mercury in 32°, Mars in 37°, and Saturn in 34°. An expectation of Mars on this date was based partly on other correlations and partly on the fact that 3 Lamat is the day of the Mars table of the *Dresden*. The correlation puts 9.9.4.16.2 10 Ik 5 uayeb at 1989222, 12 March 734, with the sun in 355°, Venus in 350°, and Mars in 353/4° (the 626664 correlation makes the end of the Maya year at 5 uayeb correspond with the day before a spring equinox, with Mars in 356° and Venus in 355°); it puts 9.10.0.0.0 1 Ahau 8 Kayab at 1994660, 30 January 749, with the sun and Mars in 315° and Mercury in 317°; and it puts 9.10.4.7.0 8 Ahau 3 Zec at 1996240, 29 May 753, with the sun in 71°, Venus in 69°, and Mars in 72°. Although the Mars conjunctions are the criterion for the correlation, the fact that two of them are also Venus conjunctions is a separate structural feature picked up by the correlation. It is impressive to be able to find such a match for a set of dates on a single monument. Based exclusively on Mars, the correlation also picks up a paired set of Venus-Jupiter conjunctions and a paired set of Venus-Mercury conjunctions. At 9.6.18.12.0 8 Ahau 8 Mol, 1972580, 18 August 688, Venus was in 171° and Jupiter in 173°; at 9.7.10.16.8 9 Lamat 16 Ch'en, 1976988, 12 September 700, Venus was in 177° and Jupiter in 182° (with the sun in 173°). At the Initial Series date, 9.6.12.4.16 5 Cib 14 Uo, 1970276, 28 April 682, Mercury was at 16° and Venus at 20°; and at 9.9.9.10.5 3

Chicchan 3 Ceh, 199905, 20 October 738, Mercury was at 192° and Venus at 189°.

In no sense are such correspondences random. They reflect the fact that most correlations have been based on some kind of relevant data, which are structurally related in ways that have little to do with the criteria on which the correlation is based. They also reflect the Maya tendency to use standardized intervals with multiple properties where possible.

Because of this latter factor, some structurally similar sets are incompatible with each other, so that no correlation could possibly pick up all the intervals as real phenomena. Thus Caracol Stela 3 shows an alternate Mars set besides that picked up by the Kaucher correlation. In the Thompson correlation (548283) there is a paired set of near conjunctions of Mars and the sun at 9.7.10.16.8 9 Lamat 16 Ch'en, 1934611, 4 September 584, with the sun in 164° and Mars in 162°, and at 9.9.10.0.0 2 Ahau 13 Pop, 1948683, 16 March 623, with the sun in 358° just before the spring equinox, Mars in 351°, and Jupiter in 353°. The same set is picked up, a bit father from reality, by the correlation 525698, based on the birth of Chan Bahlum at an eclipse and already mentioned in connection with Jupiter-Saturn conjunctions. This puts 9.9.10.0.0 2 Ahau 13 Pop at 1890098, 22 October 462, with the sun in 211° and Mars in 221° (37 days before conjunction); it also puts 9.9.5.13.8 4 Lamat 6 Pax at 1888566, 22 August 458, with the sun in 140°, Mercury in 141°, and Mars in 146°, while 9.7.19.13.12 8 Eb 15 Zotz became 1879210, 30 December 432, with the sun in 281° and Mars in 285°. It might be possible to find a set of Mars conjunctions that would fit these dates and intervals as well as the Kaucher correlation picks up the other set, but the interval between the two sets means that it is completely impossible that both sets can be tied to a Mars conjunction, although one set might be attached to some other Mars phenomenon.

Conjunctions of Mercury with the sun, omitted from Table 6.5, are shown in Table 6.6 in a considerable number of correlations. Because the mean interval between an inferior and superior conjunction of Mercury is only 58 days and the movements, as observed from earth, are extremely variable, it is hardly surprising that every date on the monument shows Mercury within 5° of the sun in one correlation or another. The Spinden correlation picks up six dates on the monument on which Mercury was within 5° of the sun, more than any other correlation, and including the Initial Series date. Three of the same dates are also near conjunctions of Mercury in the Thompson correlation, which picks up five dates on which Mercury was within 5° of the sun. The Kreichgauer correlation picks up four dates within this degree of accuracy, three of which are identical with Thompson Mercury dates; for the fourth (7 Akbal 16 Muan).

Table 6.6. Caracol Stela 3 and Mercury Conjunction in Various Correlations*

Maya date—LC	CR	Decimal equivalent	Spinden 489384	Thompson 584283	Kaucher 626660	Hochleitner 674265	Kelley 663310
9.6.12.4.16	5 Cib 14 Uo	1343616 2304	1833000 93/98				2006926 161/163
9.6.18.12.0	8 Ahau 8 Mol	1345920 4408			1972580 148/151		
9.7.10.16.8	9 Lamat 16 Ch'en	1350328 1320	1839712 228/223	1934611 164/159			
9.7.14.10.8	3 Lamat 16 Uo	1351648 1864			1978308 37/32		
9.7.19.13.12	8 Eb 15 Zotz	1353512 9050				2027777 193/188	
9.9.4.16.2**	10 Ik 5 uayeb	1362562 306	1851946 48/47	1946845 346/342		2036827 114/118	
9.9.5.13.8	4 Lamat 6 Pax	1362868 1377		1947151 287/291			
9.9.9.10.5	3 Chicchan 3 Ceh	1364245 155	1853629 267/265	1948528 202/204			
9.9.10.0.0	2 Ahau 13 Pop	1364400 1164			1991060 7/3		
9.9.13.4.4.	9 Kan 2 Zec	1365564 341				2039829 192/188	
9.9.14.3.5	12 Chicchan 18 Zip	1365905 1249			1992565 49/49		
9.9.17.11.14 +	13 Ix 12 Zac	1367154 449					2030464— 325/326
9.9.18.16.3	7 Akbal 16 Muan	1367603 397	1856987 338/333				
9.10.0.0.0	1 Ahau 8 Kayab	1368000 1580	1857384 9/14				
9.10.4.7.0	8 Ahau 3 Zec	1369580				2043845 190/188	2032890 193/198

*Sun first, Mercury second, position in degrees, without symbols. European dates are identified only by Julian day numbers.
**Calculated back from end date.
+From parallel text of Naranjo Hieroglyphic Stairway.

Thompson puts Mercury 8° from the sun. The Kaucher correlation picks up five dates within 5° of the sun. One (8 Ahau 8 Mol) is picked up by Thompson with Mercury 10° from the sun and one agrees with Spinden. Hence the general lack of overlap of the Kaucher and Thompson Mercury sets does not show a clear incompatibility. This is also demonstrated by correlation 507994, which I have proposed as a possibility (Kelley 1974:143). It picks up one of the Thompson dates and two of the Kaucher dates within 5°. The Schove 2 correlation picks up one Thompson date, one Kaucher date, and one date not picked up by any of the other correlations considered here. The Hochleitner correlation (674265) picks up two of the Thompson dates and two of the Kaucher dates.

This overlap of dates suggests that a "best fit" correlation of Mercury might show Mercury within 5° of the sun for most or all of the dates on the monument, but I doubt that this was intended by the astronomers who observed or calculated the monument dates. Instead, I think it suggests that most of the intervals incorporated widely used approximations for the Mercury synodic period.

This preliminary analysis of Caracol Stela 3 shows that many dates on the monument are separated by known astronomical intervals. Many correlations pick up some of the dates in connection with expected astronomical phenomena. Jupiter-Saturn conjunctions, occurring once in 20 years, are found on one of three indicated dates by the Spinden and Kreichgauer correlations. The intervals between two of these dates led to the development of a new correlation, 663310, based on Jupiter-Saturn conjunctions.

The Thompson correlation is weaker than many others with respect to the presumed astronomical import of this monument. In this regard, the Spinden correlation is probably the strongest astronomically of any correlation based on the principle of continuity.

DRESDEN RING NUMBER DATES

In the Dresden codex several dates before the Maya era base are marked by a distance number with a knot around its lower section. Calculations show that the distance number marks the amount by which these dates are earlier than the Maya era base. The intervals have been called "Ring Numbers" because of the ringlike appearance of the knot. In the Venus table the Ring Number base is 12.19.13.16.0 1 Ahau 18 Kayab, and a long-distance number goes forward to 9.9.9.16.0 1 Ahau 18 Kayab, the base of the Venus table. The table has four "standard" positions: heliacal rising; disappearance at superior conjunction after 236 days; reappearance after 90 days; and disappearance after 250 days, 8 days before the next heliacal rising. The 1 Ahau 18

Kayab date corresponds to heliacal rising, in a structural sense. Another Ring Number is 12.19.18.13.4 3 Kan 17 Mac. This is 3 x 584 less 8 days, and hence is a formal position of disappearance before heliacal rising, both by calculation and in the Dresden table. Two other Ring Number dates approximate the other two formal positions. The date 12.19.19.7.12 4 Eb 20 Yaxkin is 240 days after 3 Kan 17 Mac, so that it would be 240 days after heliacal rising, rather than the standard formal interval of 236 days. Finally, 12.19.19.11.19 13 Cauac 7 Ceh is 87 days after 4 Eb and 91 days after the standard position, corresponding to reappearance after superior conjunction.

The date 12.19.14.7.14 9 Ix 2 Ch'en is a Ring Number that is 4 years and 186 days before the Maya era base and corresponds to an equinox or solstice, according to my interpretation of that data. I have previously drawn attention to the fact that this date is at a Mercury interval from other 9 Ix dates that are Ring Numbers (Kelley and Kerr 1973:197) and that the equivalent 9 Jaguar is a name for Tlaloc, whom I have identified with Mercury (Kelley 1980:S12).

The date 12.19.19.0.8 3 Lamat 1 uayeb is the Ring Number base of the Mars table. Modifying slightly Willson's original analysis, I have suggested that this date, rather than the terminal date, was the second stationary point of the Mars cycle, 352 days before conjunction at 13.0.0.0.0 4 Ahau 8 Cumku.

The eclipse table shows a similar pattern of a set of early and late dates, but the early date is 8 days after the Maya era base, and hence is not marked with the ring, which seems merely to mean "count back" or "before." The count goes forward to several late dates rather than one. Again, the early date 13.0.0.0.8 12 Lamat 16 Cumku was calculated by the Mayas as a new moon and occupied a calculated formal position as an eclipse (probably calculated as a real eclipse but not matching our calculations).

The pattern revealed by these relatively well-understood Ring Numbers (see Table 6.7) suggests that all the Ring Numbers relate to astronomical phenomena. Further analysis should help clarify the meanings of Ring Numbers that have not been discussed here. An extremely small sample of dates have given the results summarized above, hence it is unlikely that they have been improperly fitted to astronomical realities that were not intended.

Historical and Astronomical Evidence

A CALENDAR REFORM IN A.D. 934

If there was a break in calendrical continuity, it probably occurred because of a deliberate calendar reform. In Mesoamerica such a reform would have had tremendously important theological implications, even if the change were only a day or two. One would expect both historical and astronomical evidence of any such reform, which would be strong evidence against *any* correlation based on continuity, such as Spinden, Thompson, or Vaillant correlations. There is, in fact, both astronomical and historical evidence for a major calendar reform in A.D. 934, establishing the 52-year cycle as it is attested in later periods.

Alfonso Caso has repeatedly drawn attention to the evidence for an important calendar reform in the Mixtec and Zapotec areas during the reign of Five Crocodile, father of Eight Deer, of Tilantongo, which is referred to in the Bodleian (pp 7–8); in the Nuttall (p. 25); in the Vienna (reverse, p. 6); and, Caso argues, on a golden pectoral from Monte Alban (Caso 1977:69–71). Five Crocodile is shown in the Nuttall either wearing a skull in his headdress or with a fleshless lower jaw. The human figure shown on the pectoral also has a fleshless lower jaw. Caso concludes—and I agree—that the two figures, both associated with calendar reforms, represent the same individual.

The reform seems to have been marked by ceremonies celebrated by Five Crocodile; certain curious anomalies in the dates of these ceremonies first suggested to Caso that they involved a calendar reform. The Nuttall mentions only ceremonies on the day 7 Earthquake of the year 12 House and the day 1

Table 6.7. *Dresden* Ring Number Dates			
12.12.17.3.1	13 Imix 9 Uo	—51419	
12.19.13.16.0	1 Ahau 18 Kayab	—2200	Venus table base, near an equinox or solstice
12.19.15.7.14	9 Ix 2 Ch'en	—1646	Tropical year (equinox or solstice) and Mercury base
12.19.18.5.14	9 Ix 7 Xul	—606	Mercury base
12.19.18.10.9	13 Muluc 2 Zac	—511	Long text, including 'fire'
12.19.18.13.4	3 Kan 17 Mac	—456	Venus table disappearance before inferior conjunction
12.19.19.0.8	3 Lamat 1 uayeb	—352	Mars second stationary
12.19.19.5.9	13 Muluc 17 Zec	—251	
12.19.19.6.5	3 Chicehan 13 Xul	—235	
12.19.19.7.12	4 Eb 20 Yaxkin	—208	
12.19.19.11.19	13 Cauac 7 Ceh	—121	
12.19.19.13.14	9 Ix 2 Kankin	—86	Mercury base
12.19.19.16.10	13 Oc 18 Pax	—30	
12.19.19.17.3	13 Akbal 11 Kayab	—17	
(13.0.0.0.0	4 Ahau 8 Cumku	0	Mars conjunction near an equinox or solstice)
(13.0.0.0.8	12 Lamat 16 Cumku	+8	new moon, eclipse table base)

Crocodile of the year 4 Reed. The Bodleian mentions the day 7 Earthquake of the year 13 House and the day 1 Crocodile of the year 6 Reed, agreeing on the days but giving different names to the years. This suggests the possibility but not the certainty that the same dates were intended and that there is a systematic variation between the sources underlying the Nuttall and the Bodleian. The Vienna gives the day 7 Earthquake of the year 13 Owl. This date, 13 Owl, makes it clear that a calendar reform is involved rather than a mere copying error, for there is no year Owl in the later Mixtec calendar nor indeed any day Owl.

The pectoral shows two years, 10 Wind and 11 House, associated with a day 2 Flint. 10 Wind belongs to the year-bearer series Wind–Deer–Twisted–Earthquake, known to have been employed by various highland Mexican groups during the early Classic; 11 House, the following day, belongs to the year-bearer series House–Rabbit–Reed–Flint used by Aztecs, Mixtecs, and other groups during the Postclassic period. The purpose of the pectoral is clearly to indicate a change in the year-bearer system. Caso (1977:70) suggests that the day 12 House, which named the year, was followed by the day 13 Lizard, and hence that 13 Owl might correspond with 13 Lizard. However, Lizard belongs to the series Lizard–Water–Jaguar–Rain, which follows the House series, and there is no evidence that any Central Mexican group ever used this series (it was used in colonial Yucatan). It is completely inconsistent with the evidence from the pectoral, which indicates a change from the Wind series to the House series. The day Owl is known as the 16th day name among the Pipils and Cakchiquels of Guatemala and appears in an unknown position in Zapotec inscriptions. There is no evidence that a day name in the 16th position was ever part of a year-bearer series.

The structure of the Mixtec year is still not entirely known, hence we cannot make positive associations with Christian dates. I have assumed congruence with the intertribal tzolkin and have used the general chronological framework of Table 6.1, putting Five Crocodile 52 years earlier than Caso does. Caso's useful tables showing correspondence between Mixtec and Christian year names treat the Mixtec years as if they were of the same length as the European ones, rather than exactly 365 days long. Over the time period with which we are concerned, the Mixtec year would have shifted about 140 days later, and I think that the actual correspondence is about a year later than that given by Caso for this period. The day 12 House in the intertribal tzolkin fell on 6 May 934 (Julian calendar, Julian day number 2062327) and at 260-day intervals later and earlier. This date may be the yearnamer for a Mixtec year of which it was the first day. I regard the year 12 House, 934, as the effective date of the calendar reform. The next most likely structural interpretation is that the year was named by the day 260 days later and that it was the last day of the last month (excluding the five "extra" days). The problem will almost certainly be solved when all available Mixtec dates have been analyzed. It should be understood in the following discussion that I have picked the dates that seem to fit a consistent pattern and that the sources do not allow exclusion of dates 260 days from those given.

The Bodleian shows Five Crocodile participating in a ceremony on the frequently recurring date 1 Crocodile of the year 1 Reed. This corresponds to 15 March 936, with the sun in 360°, the only time it fell at a spring equinox in 1,508 Mesoamerican years. The day 1 Crocodile is also repeated with the year 5 Reed, becoming 22 June 940, with the sun and Venus in conjunction in 96°, six days past the summer solstice.

The day 1 Crocodile, year 1 Reed, appears on page 21 of the Nuttall in connection with the god Four Crocodile, the "war with heaven," and a great deal of explicit solar symbolism. Red and white striped gods, markings elsewhere given to the sun god, dive from heaven on the days 7 Crocodile and 8 Wind of the year 12 Flint, 14 and 15 March 921, with the sun in 359° and 360°, at the spring equinox. These dates also recur on page 4 in a similar scene, where one of the gods is given the calendar name Four Earthquake, a name of the sun god (see Kelley 1980:S43–S44). There they are followed by the day 12 Earthquake of the same year, 18 June 921 with the sun in 91° (one day past the summer solstice) and Mercury and Venus in conjunction in 108°.

On this page, Four Crocodile's wife, One Death of Sun Mountain, has a simplified sun disk as her name. She is presumably the goddess born on the day 1 Death, J.D. 2062551, 16 December 934, the year of the calendar reform, with the sun in 270° (at the winter solstice). Her husband, Four Crocodile, corresponds to 15 December 937 (exactly three Mesoamerican years later, but with the sun in 269° rather than 270°—the solstice actually occurred on the following date, Five Wind). Four Crocodile is shown with two faces, each within an eagle headdress, one facing forward and one facing backward, which is appropriate for a winter solstice god. His name is shown above a sky band on the right and that of Four House appears above a sky band on the left. On the previous page, Four House and his "brother," Three Monkey, wearing the red and white striped face paint of sun gods are shown being killed and put in bundles for cremation. 4 House is 15 June 938, with the sun in 88° and Mercury in 92°, just after conjunction and just before the summer solstice. Three Monkey would have been born on the day 3 Monkey, 15 March 938, at the spring equinox (with the sun in 360°). A god Ten Crocodile, wearing an eagle headdress that faces in two directions and holding the goddess Three Flint, is shown in *Nuttall* (p. 16) in the year 7 Rabbit. The date is apparently the year 955, in which 3 Flint fell on the 18 December, the day after the winter solstice, with the sun in 271°.

Because these "families" seem to behave in thoroughly human ways and are described in terms of genealogical relationships to historical figures, Mixtec scholars have generally regarded them as historical. I think this is an error, comparable to thinking that Apollo, another sun god, is human because he is described in human ways and is said in some sources to be the ancestor of the human Asklepiads.

Four House, Three Monkey, and a third "brother," Ten Eagle, are shown together in the Bodleian (p. 3), where Ten Eagle seems to be born after they die in the war with heaven (shown as a sky band with a red and white chevron, symbolizing war, attached). In the Baranda, Four House and Three Monkey recur with Four Crocodile and are connected with the Hill of the Parrot (Caso 1958:381–83). The Palacio tablet from Xochicalco (Caso 1967:166) shows the brothers Three Monkey, Four House, and Ten Eagle going from Parrot Temple to see the ruler Two Earthquake. Their "grandfather," Four Rabbit, of the Mixtec sources, is also mentioned on this tablet. Two Earthquake might be intended for 2 Earthquake, 14 June 937, with the sun in 87°, although the solstice actually occurred three days later on 5 Flower. The latter may be the Five Flower associated with Three Monkey and Four House in the Baranda and regarded by Caso as another brother. Still another possible "brother" in the Baranda is Two Water, who is probably named from 2 Water, 17 June 935 (J. D. 2062734), with the sun in 90° (at the summer solstice) and Mercury (retrograding) in 86°, about three days past conjunction.

Although the placement of these names at particular points in real time is conjectural, the structural relationship between the names, the solar symbolism, the connection with the war with heaven, and the consistent pattern shortly after the date of the calendar reform are not conjectural. In any case, the correspondence of the Palacio tablet from Xochicalco with personages of the war with heaven clearly supports Caso's view that the monuments of Xochicalco refer to the calendar reform, whether one thinks that the individuals are historical or mythico-astronomical. The fact that the monuments of Xochicalco use the same system of year-bearers as that introduced by Five Crocodile in 934 is also strong evidence of some connection. A similar demonstration for the three stelae found with Metepec phase materials at Xochicalco must be left for a subsequent paper, but I will point out here that year-bearers of the reform system are shown on the monuments. This, in turn, means that the monuments of Xochicalco should postdate the year 934, an important historical-archaeological conclusion.

The Mixtec evidence pointing to the year 934 as the date of an important calendar reform is supported by Maya evidence, which I recognized several years ago, long before I had made the 52-year revision of Mixtec chronology followed in this paper. The most obvious evidence is the heliacal rising of Venus on 20 November 934 (J. D. 2062525), with the sun in 243° and Venus in 237°. The date in the intertribal calendar round was 1 Ahau 18 Kayab, the base date of the Dresden Venus table. This was the only time during the historical period that the later calendar round was in step with a heliacal rising of Venus. Only the Dittrich correlation, which identifies this date with 9.9.9.16.0 1 Ahau 18 Kayab, fits the intertribal calendar round and does not require a posteriori juggling of alleged "corrections." In this respect, it is superior to the Spinden and Thompson correlations, but it does not fit many other classes of evidence. I believe that the most likely explanation is that at this date a repeating 104-year table, which had been allowed to get far out of step with reality, was "reset." 1 Ahau is not only a calendar date but a deity name. It was impossible to maintain the structure of the calendar and pick up all appropriate deity names at appropriate points, but many of them could be "set" in the new scheme. Thus, it was impossible to put 12 Lamat 1 Muan, the base of the Dresden eclipse table, at an eclipse within a reasonable interval and even 11 Manik or the following date, 12 Lamat, could not be set at an eclipse in the year 934. However, Spinden (1930:56–58) drew attention to a series of 12 Lamat eclipses. (In the form of the intertribal tzolkin used here, which seems to be supported by the Mixtec evidence, they became 11 Manik eclipses.) They start with the lunar eclipse of J. D. 2064212, 4 July 939, and continue for 13 repetitions of the Maya eclipse cycle of 11,960 days. These are offset from a series of 11 Manik solar eclipses by the ideal interval of 4,680 days (13 tuns), starting with 2068892, 1 May A.D. 952. The one-day shift to the 12 Lamat positions suggested by Spinden fits easily with the Venus evidence, for the Borgia codex and other highland books show the Venus tables with a series beginning with Crocodile rather than Flower/Ahau; however, the tropical year dates seem to fit better as I have given them.

In the same way, Dresden tables dealing with Mercury emphasize the day 9 Ix, the equivalent of 9 Jaguar (a name of Tlaloc, the rain god, whom I have equated with Mercury) (Kelley and Kerr 1973:197, Kelley 1980:S12–S13). Mercury and the sun were in conjunction in 278° on 24 December 934 (J. D. 2062559), 9 Ix 7 Pop. Elsewhere I argue that 1 Death was back calculated as a winter solstice and equated with Tezcatlipoca—God K (Kelley 1980:S41–S43). I have already pointed out that the winter solstice of the year 934 was a day 1 Death and that this was apparently given as a name to a sun goddess, as a partial replacement for the old sun god or as a way to distinguish the early and late placements of 1 Death. The date was 1 Cimi 4 uayeb of the later Maya calendar, almost at the end of the Maya year. The day 4 Earthquake, which I equate with the winter solstice that began the present world age (Kelley 1980:S42–S43), corresponds to 4 Caban 5 uayeb, the last day of the Maya year, on 16 December 936 (J. D. 2063282) with the sun in 270° at the winter solstice. The effect was to make the Maya New Year's day, 1 Pop, fall on the winter solstice for the four years beginning with 9 Etz'nab 1 Pop, 16 December 940. Most of the other older names of gods of the tropical year stations could be "rejuvenated" in the same way.

Thus, Five Crocodile and his associates were able to maintain the structure of the old calendar and to set mythically important dates and tables in step with astronomical reality for Venus, Mercury, eclipses, and the tropical year. Even though they apparently were not able to achieve the combination of appropriate dates and astronomical reality for Mars, Jupiter, or Saturn, it seems to me that they could not have accomplished what they did without a substantial shifting of the calendar structure. There is one possible exception to this. My date 12.8.19.0.8 12 Lamat 1 Pop is 3591 B.C. in the Spinden correlation. The date A.D. 934 is (3 x 1,507 tropical years) + 3 beyond that base. The period of 1,507 tropical years, equal to 1,508 Mesoamerican years, is a basic calculation period, within which several astronomical features come back in step, though others remain out of step. This interval means that the Spinden correlation is the only one in which one might conceivably have achieved this degree of harmony between the naming dates of the gods and the later intertribal calendar round. Therefore, I think that, unless the Spinden correlation is correct, the criterion of continuity between the later intertribal calendar round and that of the Classic Period must be rejected, along with all other correlations based on it, such as those of Thompson and Vaillant.

THE KALIYUGA ERA BASE

I have argued that the Mesoamerican calendar represented a remarkable new approach to calendar making and was the most ingenious and useful calendar ever devised (Kelley 1980). I have also argued that the ideas and calendar systems incorporated in the new calendar were largely of Eurasian origin and that they probably first came together not earlier than the first century B. C., probably in northern India (Kelley 1960, 1972, 1974, 1975; Moran and Kelley 1969). Among the knowledge built into the calendar was the concept of a series of four world ages. In India the last of these was thought to have begun at a date used by astronomers as an era base, the so-called Kaliyuga era of 17 February − 3101 (3102 B.C.), calculated by the Hindus as a mass planetary conjunction in zero degrees of Aries (Ginzel 1906/58, vol 1:

337–38) and regarded in the conjunction astrology of the Persians as the date of the great Flood (Pingree 1963:243, Kennedy and Pingree 1971:187–89).

Mukerji (1936) thought that the Maya had adopted this base without change, so that 13.0.0.0.0 4 Ahau 8 Cumku of the Maya was identical with the Kaliyuga era, giving the correlation 588466. Pogo's correlation (588626) differs from this by a mere 160 days, putting the base at 27 July of the same year. Pogo's base could be considered a minimal correction of the Kaliyuga era.

The Thompson correlation also agrees remarkably with the Asian evidence. The 60-year Jupiter cycle was widespread in Asia. The Hindus used a set of 60 names to identify years of the cycle, whereas the Siamese used a combination of 10 numbers and 12 animal names, starting 3 years later than the Hindu set. The Kaliyuga era base of 3102 B.C. corresponded to the thirteenth year of a Hindu Jupiter cycle and to the sixteenth year of a Siamese cycle, a year 6 Hare (calculated from Ginzel 1906/58, vol. 1:410–12, 406–7). Thus, the Thompson correlation puts the Maya era base as the first year of the Hindu Jupiter cycle in which the Kaliyuga era base fell and puts the Kaliyuga era base in a Maya year beginning with 7 Ben, the general Mesoamerican 7 Reed. One of Chimalpahin's dates for the flood, 2935 B.C., corresponds to a Mixtec year 6 Rabbit, the year before 7 Reed; another, 2973 B.C., corresponds to an Aztec year 8 Flint (the year after 7 Reed); and a third, 2944 B.C., is 2 years after a Maya year 7 Ben (3 calendar rounds, or 156 years after the Thompson 7 Ben date) (see Kelley 1980:S45–S46, where the Mixtec and Aztec years are both given but without pointing out that they are in different calendars).

A full discussion of the complex correspondence between the Asian and Mesoamerican systems as era bases and flood dates must be deferred. The Thompson correlation certainly corresponds remarkably well with this evidence. It might be argued that the Chimalpahin dates, in the third or fourth calendar round after the Kaliyuga date, represents a Mesoamerican modification of the Kaliyuga era base, supporting correlations in the latter range. Of these, 641223 is exactly three calendar rounds later than Thompson, and 660205 is four calendar rounds later than Thompson. They will play an important role in the fuller discussion I hope to write eventually. The correlation 663310, which I think is probably the correct correlation, puts dates 216 years later than Thompson. I have suggested that 12.8.19.0.8 12 Lamat 1 Pop was the base from which the birth of the gods was counted (Kelley 1980:S17, S46). This base is 217 years before the Maya era; hence in 663310 it is somewhat over a year earlier than Thompson's date for the 4 Ahau 8 Cumku base.

At a preliminary level of analysis, I would suggest that Mukerji, Pogo, Thompson, 641223, 660205, and 663310, in a descending order of probability, show adequate correspondence with the Asian materials.

A New Correlation

During the past 30 years, I have examined a wide range of possible correlations and have tried to obtain new criteria for testing them as I have gradually discarded the most commonly accepted criteria. My eventual rejection of all criteria based on continuity meant that possible correlations needed to be examined in the light of archaeological, epigraphic, and historical data, but only astronomical evidence seemed adequate for ultimate proof or disproof.

If it is true that the inventor of the Mesoamerican calendar incorporated Eurasian ideas of approximately known history, then correlations much earlier than Thompson's are unlikely. Recognition of Mixcoatl and Quetzalcoatl as the principal figures of the Toltec invasion of Chichen Itza, their identification with the eleventh and early twelfth century rulers mentioned in the Bodleian codex, and the clear presence of Toltec elements in the Caracol, coupled with a new reading of a date from the hieroglyphic band of the Caracol, suggest a possible date about 200 years later than the Thompson correlation. The contemporaneity of the date from the High Priest's Grave with the late Toltec pottery also suggests a later correlation, with some leeway, because the text seems to have no legible glyphs to indicate whether the date marked a birthday, an accession, a conquest, a death, or some other event.

With respect to the astronomical criteria, the evidence for equinoxes and solstices in the inscriptions seems particularly strong. Other intervals between associated dates, especially on Caracol Stela 3, suggest possible solar conjunctions of Mercury and Mars, as well as Jupiter-Saturn conjunctions. I was willing to consider correlations that put either the Ring Number dates or the terminal dates of the Dresden Venus tables and other tables in step with reality. The birth of Chan Bahlum of Palenque at an eclipse visible in Mexico seemed likely, particularly after correlations based on eclipses with paths of centrality across Tabasco picked up other structurally likely features. I would also have favored correlations that picked up an eclipse at 9.17.0.0.0.

It would of course have been nice to find a correlation that fitted the tropical year stations; picked up at least six Mercury conjunctions on Caracol Stela 3 as Spinden did; fitted Mars Phenomena on that stela as closely as the Kaucher correlation; picked up at least two and probably three Jupiter-Saturn conjunctions on Caracol Stela 3; put the birth of Chan Bahlum, the base of the Dresden eclipse table, and 9.17.0.0.0 all at eclipses visible in Mexico; fitted near the central range of the majority of C-14 dates; and matched the Kaliyuga era base or chronologically close bases of the 60-year Jupiter cycle, either with the Maya era base or my newly found 12 Lamat 1 Pop base.

Unfortunately, it is clear that there is no such correlation. However, the best entry point for finding one that would fit as many of these criteria as possible and as closely as possible seemed to be the potential Jupiter-Saturn conjunctions of Caracol Stela 3. Both the intervals on the monument and the way various correlations pick up certain dates on the monument suggestded this possibility. In view of the rarity of Jupiter-Saturn conjunctions (19 to 20 years apart) and the variability of the period, such conjunctions seemed to suggest possible correlations more than such short-term variable phenomena as lunations, Mercury conjunctions, specified tropical year positions, or even eclipses. Therefore, I checked all Jupiter-Saturn conjunctions between A.D. 273 and A.D. 1027 (having earlier made a less systematic check of numerous earlier possibilities), looking for intervals of 7592 (from 8 Ahau 8 Mol to 8 Eb 15 Zotz), of 14091 (from 8 Eb 15 Zotz to 7 Akbal 16 Muan), and of 21683 from 8 Ahau 8 Mol to 7 Akbal 16 Muan. In approximately one Jupiter-Saturn conjunction in three, the two planets may remain in near conjunction for periods up to about 250 days. Naturally, it is easier to find an approximate match in such cases. I found no intervals approximating 7592 during this period, three exact intervals of 14091 (not involving long periods of near conjunction), and eight approximating 21683, most involving a couple of degrees difference in the position of the planets at one end or the other, a period of long near conjunction at one end or the other, or both.

Of these eleven possible correlations, all but two were excluded by at least three of my own criteria and also by conventional interpretations of the Venus or eclipse tables. Because of the slow motion of the planets, even the short periods of conjunction usually last for about two weeks, hence some leeway is possible with correlations based on Jupiter-Saturn conjunctions. The correlation constant 518590 picked up on Caracol Stela 3, within a 5° limit; four conjunctions of Mercury and the sun; three Venus-Saturn conjunctions; two Mars-Saturn conjunctions; two conjunctions of Jupiter and the sun (one of which was also a conjunction with Mercury and Saturn); and one summer solstice. This correlation seems to show a common Saturn theme running through most of the dates of that monument. It puts 9.9.9.16.0 1 Ahau 18 Kayab 20 days before a Venus superior conjunction, and it might be fitted to one of the alternate interpretations of that table. A shift of six or seven days would allow it to pick up my tropical year positions (though losing the one on Caracol Stela 3). It would also pick up the Maya month positions exactly 80 Maya years later than Spinden does, on the same day-name series, but changed; for example, a day that would be 3 Lamat 1 Pop of the later intertribal calendar round would instead have been 5 Lamat 1 Pop. The correlation does not fit eclipses and lunations in terms of either present interpretations or my suggested alternative, but there is enough leeway with the latter, considering our ignorance of the Maya parameters involved, so that the explanation might be adjusted to the correlation.

518590 suffers most of the archaeological and historical disadvantages of the Spinden correlation, but it corresponds to the views of the late E. Wyllys Andrews IV on the archaeology. If the only available information came from Caracol Stela 3 and the modern calendar round, I would regard this correlation as an extremely strong possibility; it clearly picks up some important structural realities. However, it does not fit many of my interpretations of the archaeological and historical evidence.

The remaining correlation, 663310, is the only one that seems to fit, though sometimes rather roughly, all the criteria I accept at this time. Table 6.8 shows how the correlation meets the various criteria. The birth of Chan Bahlum, of Palenque, expected as an eclipse, was an eclipse visible in Mexico very close to draconitic node passage. Many of the expected equinoxes and solstices appear as such. Conjunctions of Mercury and the sun and of Mars and the sun occur at some, but not all, expected points. 663310 matches my explanations of the Dresden Venus and Mars tables. All dates are 216 years later than they are in the Thompson correlation, closely matching my estimate, based on the historical epigraphic evidence, of about 200 years after Thompson. It also fits the Eurasian evidence nearly as well as Thompson does. Katuns 4 Ahau of the old long count in this correlation correspond to katuns 8 Ahau of the colonial long count, in accordance with the clearest evidence on multiple katun counts in Yucatan. If the 14091 interval between 8 Ahau 8 Mol and 7 Akbal 16 Muan is accepted as a Jupiter-Saturn interval, acceptance of any two of the other criteria I have just mentioned would eliminate all possibilities but 663310. The other criteria, in conjunction, would lead to a 663310 correlation, even if 14091 were not accepted, a priori, as a Jupiter-Saturn conjunction interval. However, it is much harder to check the possible combinations of these other criteria; for some of them, which represent alternate possibilities, I was not certain which was preferable. The wide range of possible correlations that have been suggested indicates that it is unwise to proclaim 663310 as the correct solution to the problem. Nevertheless, it is th only one that meets all of my own expectations, and I shall be very surprised if it is not eventually supported by additional evidence.

Effects of the New Correlation

Gordon Willey has long maintained that an important element in the Maya collapse was invasion from other areas of Mesoamerica. The principal evidence for this was the presence of apparent foreigners in ruling positions at Seibal. The shortened Postclassic period and the new Mixtec-Toltec dynastic sequence and chronology now indicate that the Maya collapse followed a series of Toltec attacks upon the Mayas, beginning with one by Four Jaguar and Eight Deer in 994 (ca. 9.17.7.0.0 of the Maya calendar) and culminating with the attacks of Mixcoatl and Quetzalcoatl about 1070 to 1090. Approximately a century later, Axopal, probably acting for his father, Mitl, was finally able to incorporate highland Guatemala into the Toltec empire, but by then the Maya lowlands had been largely abandoned.

The most crucial factor in the collapse was probably the attack by Mixcoatl and his son, Quetzalcoatl, upon Acallan and the Maya (Itza) ruler of Chichen Itza, Kakupacal, with the incorporation of his nascent Puuc state into the rapidly expanding Toltec empire. The dates make it clear that Miller's "Captain Sun," the opponent of "Captain Serpent" (Mixcoatl and Quetzalcoatl), must be Kakupacal, whose name recurs in inscriptions throughout Maya Chichen Itza. It is almost certainly Kakupacal whose figure is shown in a large disk on the end of the Monjas, with stylized smoke curls coming from it. This is probably a Maya prototype of the Toltec sun disk that names Captain Sun, which is also marked by smoke curls. Glyphically, smoke curls were sometimes read *kak* (Kelley n.d.), although probably also sometimes *budz*. In this context, they probably help to identify the name of Kakupacal.

Miller has suggested that Captain Serpent was actually responsible for the invasion of Seibal. With the Thompson correlation, this would mean separating the Mixcoatl and Quetzalcoatl of the wall paintings from those in the Mixtec codices and making a very length Toltec period at Chichen Itza largely unconnected with events in highland Mexico. The invasion of 994 would have been an attack on an already thoroughly Toltec city. With the 663310 correlation, Toltec expansion coincides with Maya defeats. Both the genealogical details and the general historical situation support the view that the Toltec conquest, by cutting off the peninsula and probably the Tabasco plain, made Maya trade with the coastal zone impossible. It has become increasingly evident that such trade, which may well have included substantial amounts of fish and other basic resources, was an important factor in the survival of Maya culture. Coupled with direct invasion of some parts of the area, it is not surprising that the Maya civilization of the Peten, already facing many internal problems, could not survive.

The dates of the beginning of Toltec expansion and the relationship of Toltec Chichen Itza to the Maya settlement there also throw light on the "Middle Classic" concept and the obscure problem of the relationships of Teotihuacan and Tula (Pasztory 1978). It seems clear that at Chichen Itza, Toltecs invaded and dominated an already existent Maya city but that they did so during the latter stages of the Classic Period, and individual Toltec structures might easily antedate some Puuc structures. Continuity from Tectihuacan to Tula is much more understandable and likely with the earlier emergence of the Toltec

Table 6.8. How Correlation 663310 Meets Various Criteria

Expectations	Results, 663310
A. General archaeology and physical dating techniques: within the range ± 300 years of the Thompson correlation (584283)	Thompson plus 216 years
B. 1. Continuity of calendar round broken by reform of A.D. 934*	Continuity broken
2. Continuity of katun count broken; Katuns 8 Ahau of some sources equivalent to katuns 4 Ahau of other sources	Continuity broken; katuns 4 Ahau of the Classic Maya overlap katuns 8 Ahau of the Spanish period
C. 1. Toltec influences in the Caracol (Kelley reading 10.3.0.15.1) should correspond either to Four Jaguar in 994 or to Mixcoatl and Quetzalcoatl about 1080–1090	10.3.0.15.3 is 6 July 1106, during the reign of Quetzalcoatl
2. The High Priest's Grave at 10.8.10.11.0 should be late in the Toltec sequence	10.8.10.11.0 is A.D. 1214, 26 years before the major breakup of the Toltec empire in 1240
3. Metepec-related materials at Xochicalco should be equivalent to Maya Late Classic and after A.D. 934	A.D. 934 is equivalent to 9.14.6.0.0, which is Late Classic Maya
D. Astronomical criteria	
1. Lunations and eclipses (solar eclipses have to be at new moon, so any eclipse expectation must also be a new moon expectation, but the reverse is not true), the following dates should all be at or very near to new moon:	
a. eclipse at birth of Chan Bahlum	Birth of Chan Bahlum on 2032156, 28 Sept. 851, solar eclipse, near node passage, path of centrality along west coast of Guatemala and Mexico
and/or b. eclipse at 9.16.4.10.8 12 Lamat 1 Muan base of eclipse table (counter-indicated if formal table)	J.D. 2076158, 18 Mar. 972; no eclipse
and/or c. eclipse at 9.17.0.0.0 13 Ahau 18 Cumku	2081710, 31 May 987; no eclipse
and/or d. eclipse at 9.17.19.13.16 (Santa Elena Poco Uinic) (Thompson 584283 is 3 days off from an eclipse with path of centrality across Chiapas)	2088826, 23 Nov. 1006; eclipse, not visible in Mesoamerica; very close to node passage
2. Tropical year (see Table 3) 9.11.3.2.0 1 Ahau 13 Mac; Expected equinox or solstice, probably spring equinox	2039630, 15 March 872; sun in 360° (spring equinox)

*All dates are in the Julian Calendar

Table 6.8. continued	
Expectations	*Results, 663310*

3. Venus
   a. preferred explanation of *Dresden* table as a formal table—12.19.13.16.0 1 Ahau 18 Kayab calculated as a heliacal rising; slipped back by 183.3 days on Venus and 188.9 days on the sun from 9.9.9.16.0 1 Ahau 18 Kayab

   9.9.9.16.0 is equivalent to 2027670, 17 June 839, sun in 89° (day before summer solstice) (Mercury in conjunction in 88°)—minus 183 days is 2027487, 16 Dec. 838, sun in 269° (day before winter solstice), Venus in 269° (at conjunction, four days off expected heliacal rising) (Mars and Saturn in conjunction, 245° and 248°)

   b. shell star, Tikal T4, L2; expected Venus and tropical year, doubtful. 9.15.12.11.13 7 Ben 1 Pop, New Year's day

   2071863, 14 June 960, sun in 88°, Venus in 88° in conjunction, 2 days before summer solstice

4. Mars
   a. preferred explanation of *Dresden* table as a formal table—12.19.19.0.8 3 Lamat 1 uayeb calculated as second stationary point; slipped back by 116.8+ days from 9.19.7.15.8 3 Lamat 6 Zotz

   9.19.7.15.8 is equivalent to 2098938, 31 July 1034—minus 117 days is 2098821, 5 April 1034, Mars in 144° at the second stationary point

   b. the accession of Pacal of Palenque is associated with the Mars beast, so Pacal is expected to be associated with Mars phenomena

   Pacal was born on 9.8.9.13.0 8 Ahau 13 Pop, 2020410, 1 August 819, with the sun in 132° and Mars in 131°, in conjunction

   c. Kakupacal of Chichen Itza acceded on 10.2.0.1.9 6 Muluc 12 Mac (the day after 5 Lamat—a day 5 Lamat was the accession of Pacal of Palenque); name and date suggest possible Mars connections

   10.2.0.1.9 is equivalent to 2117739m, 29 Jan. 1086, Mars 356° in conjunction with Jupiter in 357°; Nine-tun anniversary was Initial Series lintel, 10.2.9.1.9 9 Muluc 7 Zac, 4 Dec. 1094, Mars in 264°, in conjunction with Jupiter in 268° and with the sun in 259° (Jupiter also in conjunction with Mercury in 273°)

   d. various correlations suggested that the following four dates on Caracol Stela 3 might have Mars connotations:
   9.7.14.10.8 3 Lamat 16 Uo (3 Lamat also suggests Mars)

   Equivalent to 2014958, 27 Aug. 804, Sun 158° in conjunction with Mars, 153°

   9.9.4.16.2 10 Ik 5 uayeb

   Equivalent to 2025872, 15 July 834, Sun 116° in conjunction with Mars, 116°

   9.10.0.0.0 1 Ahau 8 Kayab

   Equivalent to 2031310, 4 June 849, Sun in 77°, near conjunction

Table 6.8. continued

Expectations	Results, 663310
	with Mars in 84°, in conjunction with Venus in 85°
9.10.4.7.0 8 Ahau 3 Zec	Equivalent to 3032890, 1 Oct. 853, Sun in 193°, Mars in 187°, 20 days after exact conjunction
5. Because of intervals and associations in other correlations, expected that from 1 to 3 of the following dates on Caracola Stela 3 should be Jupiter-Saturn conjunctions:	
9.6.18.12.0 8 Ahau 8 Mol	Equivalent to 2009230, 21 Dec. 788, sun in 274°, 4 days past winter solstice, Jupiter in 334°, Saturn in 340°, 50 days before conjunction
9.9.17.11.14 13 Ix 12 Zac	Equivalent to 2030464, 9 Feb. 847, far from Jupiter-Saturn conjunction
9.7.19.13.12 8 Eb 15 Zotz	Equivalent to 2016822, 4 Oct. 809, Jupiter and Saturn in conjunction, both in 243°
9.9.18.16.3 7 Akbal 16 Muan	Equivalent to 2030913, 3 May 848, Jupiter and Saturn in conjunction, both in 356°
6. Mercury is so erratic that suggestions based on mean intervals or on results in other correlations are probably misleading; "hits" seem little more than chance and would probably be misleading to cite (see Table 6.6)	
E. 1. Asian parallels suggest that the earliest dated monuments with the full Mesoamerican calendar system should be not earlier than the first century B.C.	Chiapa de Corzo Stela 3, the monument with the earliest presently known long count inscription, would date from A.D. 182
2. The Kaliyuga era base of 3102 B.C. or the Jupiter cycle beginning in 3114 B.C. should be connected either to 13.0.0.0.0 4 Ahau 8 Cumku or to 12.8.19.0.8 12 Lamat 1 Pop, directly or conceptually	The 12 Lamat 1 Pop base was apparently calculated as a mass planetary conjunction (mean), as was the Kaliyuga era base; it would date from 3115 B.C.

empire relative to the Classic cultures. The near contemporaneity of Cotzumahualpa and early Toltec structures, suggested by Parsons and supported by Cohodas, is assured in the new correlation by a considerable amount of external chronological control, though details of the interpretation would be markedly different. Toltec Chichen Itza began late in the Classic Period, but its roots are firmly based in the Middle Classic tradition, and Tula itself was the intermediary between the Middle Classic and the later period.

PART FOUR

Architectural and Spatial Patterns

Seven

Cultural Reconstitution in the Late Moche Period: A Case Study in Multidimensional Stylistic Analysis

Garth Bawden, Peabody Museum, Harvard University

Introduction

Archaeological research in Peru has been marked by a series of attempts to formulate the definitive culture-historical synthesis. These endeavors have produced a variety of regional integrative schemes based on cultural developmental stages and relative chronological periods. Criteria used in such formulations include aspects of technology (Bennett 1948; Bushnell 1957; Collier 1962; Mason 1968), sociopolitical structure (Strong 1948; Steward 1948, 1949) and ceramic art style (Uhle 1903; Kroeber 1925, 1944; Willey 1948; Rowe 1962). The one common feature of these varied approaches is investigation into the nature of temporal and spatial change in selected cultural traits. Recognition and tracing of formal modification, functional development, or spatial variation of the traits being studied yield the information used to detect cultural change and identify the nature of this development.

The trait-based methodology is clearly apparent in the integrative scheme now widely accepted in Peruvian archaeological studies. The synthesis of J. H. Rowe (1962), building on the horizon-style concept originated by Uhle (1913) and Kroeber (1930), specifically uses ceramic style analysis to observe the interrelationships of the Andean cultures. In this scheme stylistic traits become the prime indicators of cultural contact, development, and territorial variation. Although such an approach is useful in formulating a relative chronological framework, it can oversimplify and thus misinterpret cultural dynamics.

The main problems associated with this methodology are inherent in applying a specific stylistic approach to wide cultural research. First, this approach is somewhat restrictive. Although a careful analysis of style can often identify trait diffusion, and through it cultural contact, it will not by itself explain the nature of the contact. Only broader investigation of the cultures involved can fully reveal the implications of relationships identified through stylistic analysis.

A second problem is invalid selection of comparative stylistic traits. To be analytically meaningful, traits must be of such a functionally or decoratively specific nature that their occurrence through time and space can reasonably be assumed to mark continuity (see Rowe 1966). A common mistake in the archaeological application of stylistic analysis, especially in diffusional studies, is to select general diagnostic traits whose widespread occurrence should be more satisfactorily explained by multiple innovation than by diffusion.

A third problem may occur when two styles that are being compared resemble one another superficially. Care must be taken not to assume a relationship on grounds of general similarity. It is important to identify not only traits that appear identical but also those that differ, and this requires attention to the slightest nuances of variation. Recognition of these nuances is often essential to an understanding of stylistic relationships, and thus effective application of stylistic analysis to cultural research.

Given the tradition of stylistic analysis in the archaeological research on Peru, it is not suprising that the problems associated with this methodology are common. Analysis of Peruvian cultural development and diffusion are usually oversimplified. Ceramic art styles become the exclusive focus of research and almost seem to exist apart from their associated cultures. Wider cultural issues are then fitted into these stylistic patterns. As a result, theories of dramatic political expansion and cultural replacement dominate studies of culture-historical development. This view of culture change permeates both the early archaeological studies (see, for example, Bennett 1948), and also more recent research (Rowe 1963; Lanning 1967; Lumbreras 1974).

Nowhere are the results of stylistic interpretation, both positive and negative, more evident than in the research on the north coast of Peru. From the time that Uhle excavated the extensive Huaca del Sol cemetery collections, stylistic studies have dominated research. A succession of "ceramic cultures" based on these collections (Uhle 1913; Kroeber 1925, 1926, 1930, 1944) was supplemented by similar ceramic studies elsewhere (Larco Hoyle 1938–1939, 1944, 1945a, 1945b, 1946, 1966; Bennet 1939) to produce the cultural framework now accepted for the region. This consisted of a series of indigenous cultures, Salinar, Gallinazo, Moche, and Chimu, interspersed by expansion from outside the region, manifested by the Coastal Chavin (Cupisnique), Tiahuanacoid

(Wari), and Inca styles, the latter constituting the three "horizons" of Rowe's synthesis. In the absence of broader, settlement-based cultural research, these stylistic studies suggested a simple pattern of cultural expansion, contraction, and entrenchment, with little understanding of the extent or nature of such developments.

The lack of comprehensive cultural study is especially apparent for the period that forms the focus of the present study. The early Middle Horizon on the north coast is marked by the spread of ceramic styles related to the dominant style of a supposed southern-highland-centered Wari empire; this is the phenomenon labeled the Tiahuanacoid horizon by earlier scholars (Kroeber 1925, 1926, 1944; Bennett 1939; Ford 1949; Strong and Evans 1952; Collier 1955). Menzel (1964, 1968, 1977), in an exhaustive study of the Wari-related ceramic styles, traces these styles to the north coast and assumes that they indicate political domination by the Wari empire over at least the south and central sections of the region (also see Isbell and Schreiber 1978). Extending stylistic analysis to wall mural painting, Donnan (1972) projects the Wari area of hegemony into the northern portion of the region. The proposed Wari expansion into the north coast region is believed to have crushed the existing Moche state, indigenous to the area, and supplanted it.

Similarly, other scholars have linked various architectural traits to the ceramic cultural development of the northern coastal Middle Horizon. However, these traits—general architectural forms and settlement configuration—are far less precisely defined than the ceramic stylistic elements, and this imprecision makes them less accurate as diagnostic markers of cultural development. Using this approach, first Schaedel (1951a) and then Kosok (1965), Lanning (1967), and Lumbreras (1974) argue that urban settlements were introduced to the north coast during the Middle Horizon Wari imperial expansion. Specifically, the pattern of formally planned, multiroom compounds, surrounded by large adobe walls visible at the site of Wari (Lumbreras 1974:159) is seen as a settlement style carried by the Wari conquerors through most of Peru (Bennett 1944:15, McCown 1945:267–73, Rowe 1956:142–43, Thatcher 1972–1974:119).

Thus, according to the traditional picture of the Middle Horizon on the north coast of Peru, based on the analysis of ceramic and architectural style, vigorous imperial expansion into the region was accompanied by abrupt artistic, architectural, and settlement modification. I believe that this model has been largely determined by an unsound application of stylistic analysis, resulting in an overly simplistic view of cultural development. The present study demonstrates that the same approach applied more rigorously reveals a more complex cultural pattern on the north coast of Peru during the early

Middle Horizon, one in which the element of foreign intrusion is considerably less dominant.

Chronological Implications and the Ceramic Record

The theory of Wari expansion into the northern coastal region suggests that the Moche state, represented archaeologically by the Moche V phase, was replaced politically by the invaders. Wari domination introduced the southern phenomenon of urbanism to the region, with its characteristic configuration of huge compounds within large, intensively built settlements. The Moche V ceramic style was replaced by several Wari-Tiahuanacoid styles. This complex of stylistic traits formulated on purely morphological bases comprised a formidable cultural intrusion, one that on the surface fully justifies the concept of rapid military expansion. However, if the actual relationships and development courses of these component traits are carefully examined, the theory appears untenable.

The traditional explanation of Middle Horizon cultural development on the north coast of Peru is based primarily on analyses of ceramic styles. The original theory of Wari hegemony in the north was formulated on the basis of the Uhle burial collections from the Huaca del Sol at Moche (Fig. 7.1). Later scholars merely refined the model and added to it the results of research on architectural and settlement patterns. Because the chronological framework for the region remains predicated on ceramic analysis, it is essential at the outset to review the evidence of these studies.

The Moche V cultural phase is defined by its ceramic attributes. In essence the Moche V ceramic style stands solidly within the earlier Moche tradition, although it does demonstrate marked modifications from the preceding Moche IV phase. The principal changes are a tendency toward proliferation of stlylized decorative motifs and the near disappearance of naturalistic representation in iconography. Nevertheless, in its overall formal, decorative, and technological aspects the Moche V style marks the continuing development of a strong indigenous tradition. In terms of distribution, however, continuity between the Moche IV and Moche V ceramic phases is not so apparent. Whereas Moche IV pottery has been found in large amounts from Nepena to the Lambayeque Valleys, Moche V distribution is more restricted (Fig. 7.1). This style occurs in quantity only north of the Viru Valley, although small, isolated lots appear farther south (Donnan 1973:126). It thus seems clear that significant Moche presence disappeared in the fifth phase from the southern third of the area previously occupied. However, it must be emphasized that in the Moche V phase, during the early Middle Horizon, Moche ceramic art continued to flourish in the Moche Valley and farther north.

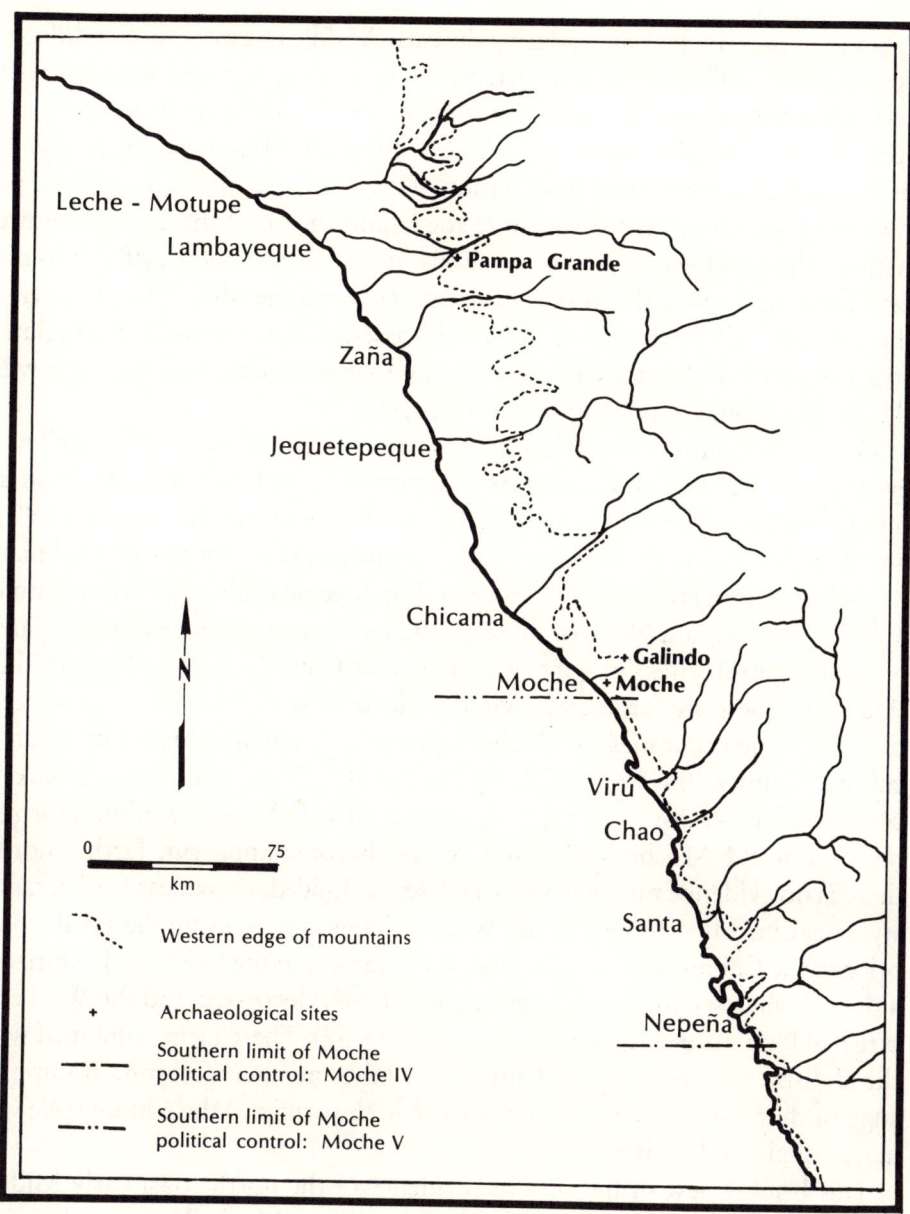

Figure 7.1. North Coast of Peru.

South of the Moche Valley, during the early Middle Horizon, several different ceramic styles, all of them purportedly Wari-related, replaced the Moche IV style (Kroeber 1944:66; Menzel 1964:36, 1977). Most of these styles are sparsely distributed (Collier 1955:112; Proulx 1973) and cannot be clearly linked to actual settlement distribution. This confusing situation spans a period of at least four centuries before the solidification of the Chimu culture, with its clear archaeological associations. It is thus extremely difficult to discern the actual cultural configuration that replaced the Moche IV presence in the southern valleys. The most that can be asserted is that various Wari-related styles and their associated cultural complexes were possibly contemporary with the Moche V phase on the upper north coast.

The ceramic basis for a Wari-related presence north of the Viru Valley is even less secure. The total corpus of evidence is derived from a relatively small number of burials in a terrace of the Huaca del Sol at Moche (Kroeber 1925) and a single lot from the Chicama Valley (Donnan 1968). Moreover, the Huaca del Sol collection is diversified, representing three possibly related but distinct Tiahuanacoid styles. None of these small, localized collections are associated with occupation sites. In contrast, the site of Galindo in the Moche Valley (Fig. 7.1), the only large early Middle Horizon settlement identified there, contains large quantities of Moche V pottery, clearly identifying its ceramic cultural affinity (Bawden 1977, 1982a:289 ff.). Thus, while there is strong ceramic evidence for positing a significant Moche V early Middle Horizon presence in the Moche Valley and, as will become apparent, farther north, there is no evidence for such a Wari presence. Indeed, no widespread ceramic style bearing any affinities to the Wari varieties is present on the north coast prior to the Chimu style, which dates at the earliest to the late Middle Horizon, a period when stylistic exchange had apparently decreased and the Wari empire had long since disappeared (Menzel 1964:62). These facts, combined with the stylistic affinity between Chimu and other northern ceramic traditions, suggest that the degree of Wari influence in the origin of the Chimu style was at best slight and indirect.

This brief review of the ceramic evidence of the north coast early Middle Horizon shows the Moche V style prevailing in the Moche Valley and farther north, while various Wari-related styles, differing between valleys, were present to the south. Isolated Wari-style ceramic lots of uncertain chronological identity appear on the north coast, unassociated with known occupation sites, just as similarly small Moche V lots appear south of the Moche Valley. This ceramic distribution indicates a drastically reduced area of Moche political hegemony north of the Viru Valley (Fig. 7.1), bordered to the south by regionally diverse cultural units, possibly exhibiting a loose and ill-defined

Wari association. There is no ceramic evidence to posit expansion north of the Viru Valley by any force originating from outside the north coast.

The Form of North Coast Urbanism

Proponents of the Wari invasion theory, lacking adequate ceramic evidence, cite the appearance of cities on the north coast as evidence of such an invasion. They also suggest that certain architectural characteristics are of Wari derivation, thus supporting the expansion theory. Careful examination of these points, however, leads to a different, more complex picture of early Middle Horizon development.

Although the data on north coastal settlement are not abundant, intensive work in the Viru and Moche Valleys indicates a general evolution of urbanism in this area. The Early Intermediate Period in the Viru Valley saw the development of large accumulations of people living close together in residential areas of considerable size. The largest of these is the site of Gallinazo (Bennett 1950), which had an estimated population of several thousand people (Willey 1953:396). Clearly such intensive settlements required a high level of social integration and administrative control, prerequisites for an urban situation.

This settlement pattern continued through the Moche occupation of the Viru Valley, which ended at the close of the Moche IV phase. Subsequent occupation of the valley in the early Middle Horizon evidenced no significant increase in the size of urban settlements, although new architectural components appeared at this time.

The urban settlement pattern of the small, politically peripheral Viru Valley is repeated in its more important neighbor, the Moche Valley. The political center of the Moche state for much of its duration, as well as that of the Late Intermediate Chimu empire, the Moche Valley reflects an early development of urbanism. Urban occupation is clearly present by the Early Intermediate Period, when the Salinar settlement of Cerro Arena covered several square kilometers and consisted of numerous agglutinations of residential dwellings interspersed with more formal architectural complexes (Brennan 1980). Following the rise of the Moche policy in the latter part of the Early Intermediate Period, a large settlement appeared centered around the Huacas del Sol and de la Luna at Moche (Fig. 7.1). It was located near the sea athwart intervalley communications routes and probably constituted the capital of a multivalley polity. This settlement has traditionally been regarded as an immense ceremonial center lacking significant associated population (Schaedel

1951a:232ff.). Recent research clearly shows that this assessment in part derives from the fact that all architecture adjacent to the focal *huacas* is deeply buried by aeolian sand. Extensive excavations during the past few years (Topic 1977, 1982) have revealed a significant residential component at this site. Although the site as presently identified does not show the degree of density or planning formality apparent in later, Moche V, urban settlements on the north coast, most architectural forms and their related functions seen in the latter sites are present at Moche. There is thus little doubt that the site of Moche is formally and functionally antecedent to the Moche V cities within the continuing north coast urban traditions.

At the commencement of the Middle Horizon and the Moche V cultural phase, the great settlement surrounding the Huaca del Sol was abandoned and the settlement of Galindo became the urban center of the Moche Valley (Figs 7.1, 7.2). This site, often mistakenly labeled as Chimu (Lumbreras 1974:183; Schaedel 1951a:235; Willey 1953:417), covers over four square kilometers of ground and contains large areas of domestic residential architecture, as well as elaborate complexes that mark the centers of social control. However, in size and grandeur, Galindo does not approach the other known Moche V city, Pampa Grande, in the Lambayeque Valley (Shimada 1978) (Figs. 7.1, 7.3). This settlement, with its great platform mounds, has been regarded as the possible successor to the site of the Huacas del Sol and de la Luna as capital of a Moche V state. However, in the absence of archaeological evidence from the intervening valleys, this identification is at best tentative.

It seems apparent that large complex cities were indeed present on the north coast during the early Middle Horizon but that urbanism in the region did not commence with their construction. Examination of the regional settlement pattern through time reveals that the roots of urbanism reach back at least to the initial portion of the Early Intermediate Period. Moreover, the early Middle Horizon northern coastal cities, Galindo and Pampa Grande, are associated only with Moche ceramic styles, showing no evidence of southern influence. The Wari ceramic phenomenon, with its loosely identified settlement associations, is present south of the Moche Valley, but it is diverse in nature and its origin is unclear. The cities of the north coast Middle Horizon are thus seen as standing temporally in a long-continuing urban tradition. Spatially they represent the northern expression of an urban evolutionary process that involved the whole Andean culture area. Although cultural traits from other areas of Peru probably did influence the north coast within the overall framework of an evolving Andean civilization, there is little firm evidence to suggest that urbanism in the region was imported from the central and southern Andes.

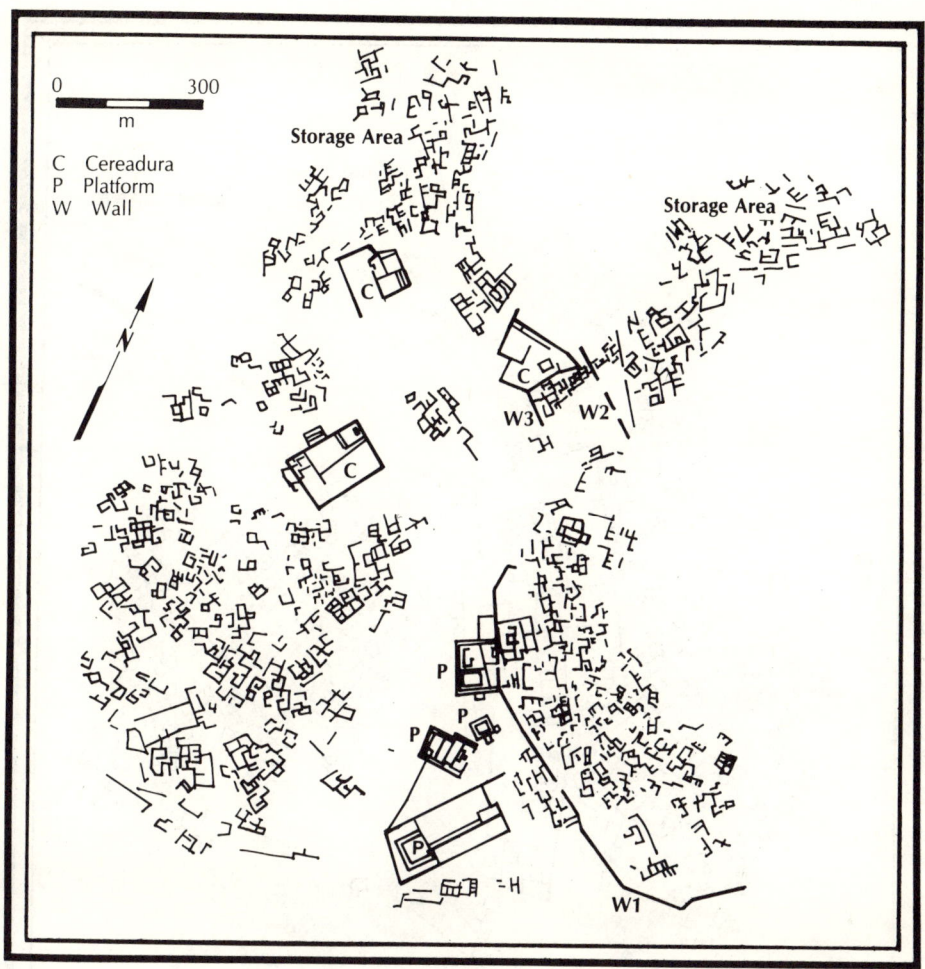

Figure 7.2. Plan of Galindo.

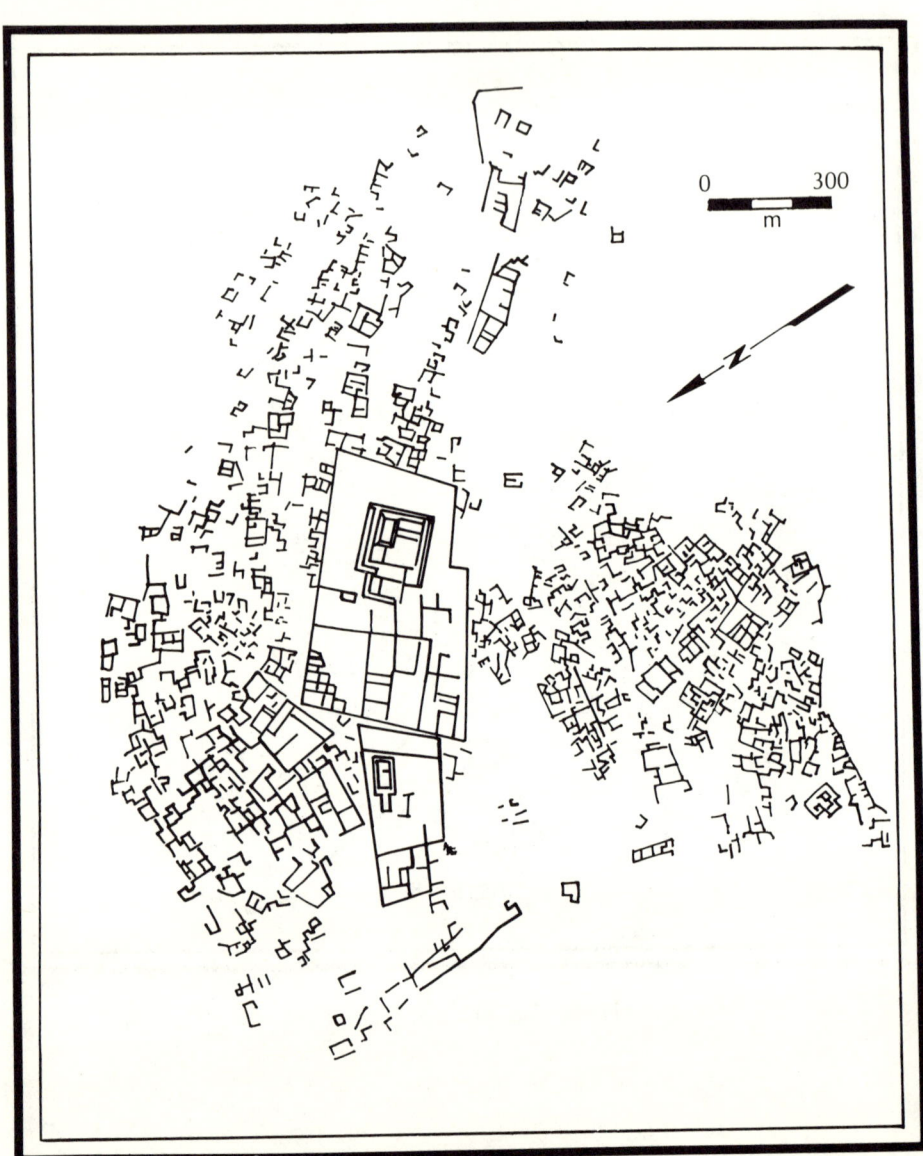

Figure 7.3. Plan of Pampa Grande.

Urban Innovations in the Moche V Cultural Phase

Even though it is apparent that urbanism did not commence on the early Middle Horizon north coast as the result of a military conquest, some innovations in settlement configuration do appear in the Moche cities at this time. Proponents of Wari expansionism assume that these innovations originated at the city of Wari. Various explanations are affoered, but most of these writers agree that the appearance in the region of large, planned settlements, composed of houses, compounds, and streets subdivided by tall walls into sections, is an important manifestation of Wari intrusion (Lumbreras 1974:165). Within this general pattern, the construction of rectangular enclosure complexes is considered the most significant innovative trait (Willey 1953:412; Schaedel 1951a:232; Rowe 1963:14; Lumbreras 1974:166). Careful investigation of the nature of early Middle horizon architectural modification on the north coast suggests that although there were indeed significant changes, previous research, by comparing very generalized stylistic traits and omitting rigorous examination of their origins, has produced an oversimplified explanation of the innovative process.

As a basic architectural form, the compound-enclosure has a long history on the north coast. The numerous examples that have been described extend through the Early Horizon and into the first portion of the Early Intermediate Period (for example, see Bennett 1950; Willey 1953:figs. 10, 14, 26, 32). The compound continued as a common architectural element in the latter part of the Early Intermediate period within the cultural context of the Moche I-IV phases (Fig. 7.4). It should be noted that during the Moche occupation of the north coast, the compounds, where present, were usually attached to large platform mounds. Thus, large compounds adjoin the Huaca de la Luna at Moche (Kroeber 1930), the large platform complex at Panamarca (Schaedel 1951b:fig. 3), and similar structures, in the Santa Valley (Donnan 1973:24, 31, figs. 6, 9) and in the Viru Valley at Huancaco (Willey 1953:205ff., fig. 44). The mere appearance of compound architecture in the early Middle Horizon Moche V cities of Galindo and Pampa Grande does not connote change. It is the wider architectural association of these compounds that must be examined for discontinuity in the meaning of this basic form, which would signify innovation.

The compound architecture of the Moche V cities does not exhibit a simple formal or functional pattern. At Galindo the compound is used in two different ways. First, there is a single example of a platform mound (Bawden 1982a:293, Conrad 1974, Moseley 1978:58) standing at the rear of a rectangular compound (Fig. 7.5). Second, three large rectangular compounds of mod-

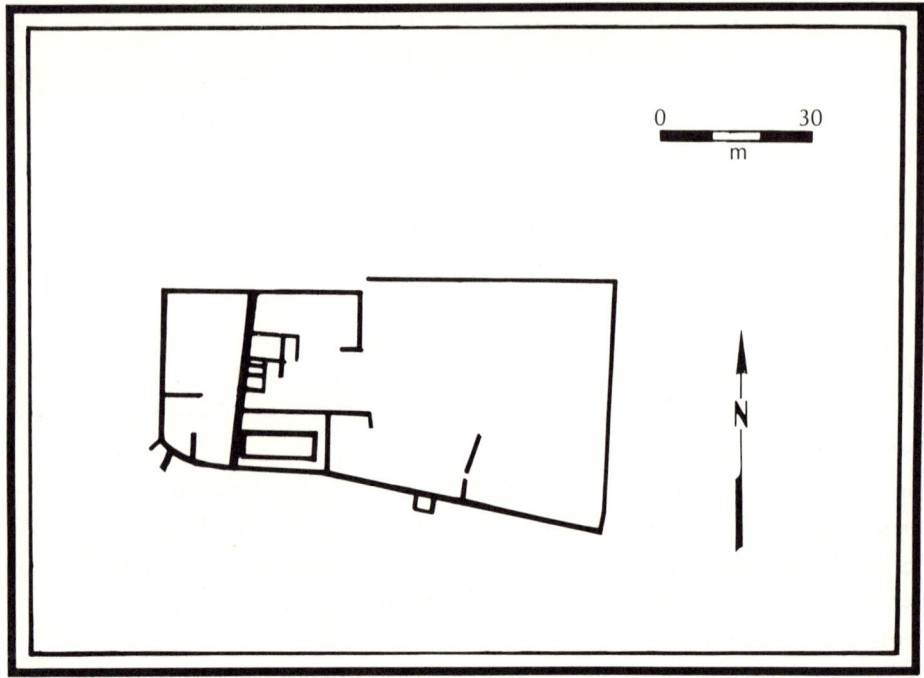

Figure 7.4. Plan of Site V-10, Viru Valley (after Willey 1953: fig. 37).

erate size stand isolated in the center of the settlement, containing complexes of rooms and small courts (Fig. 7.6). Three platform mounds of traditional Moche form, with attached terraces and a complex architectural superstructure, have no associated compounds. This use of the rectangular compound to contain a complex of small enclosures focused on a burial platform is new to the Moche settlement pattern on the north coast, as is the appearance of a large, subdivided enclosure as the central architectural feature (Bawden 1982a:296).

The situation at Pampa Grande is quite different. At this Moche V capital, huge platform mounds of traditional form stand in large enclosures (Fig. 7.3), repeating a pattern similar in its composition and configuration to such earlier Moche examples as Panamarca and Huancaco. The rectangular compound complexes found at Galindo are absent at Pampa Grande as is the burial platform enclosure. It appears that with the advent of the Middle Horizon, vari-

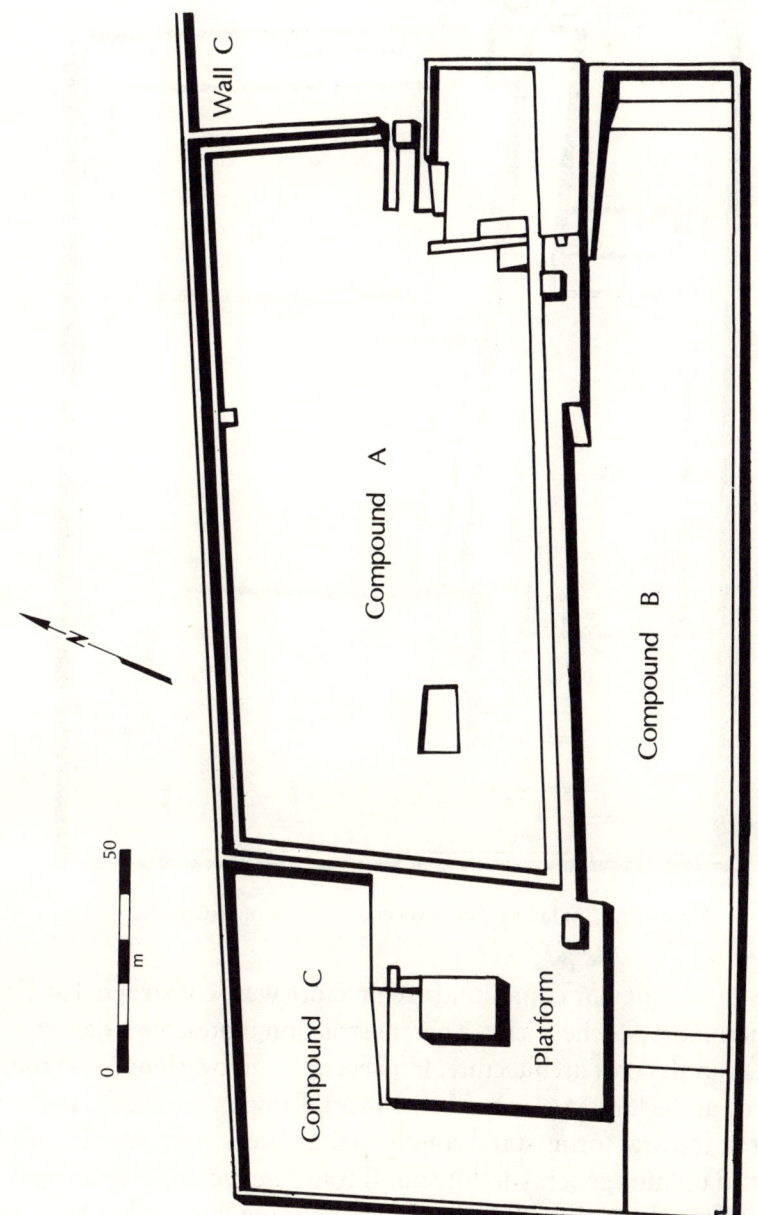

Figure 7.5. Plan of Galindo platform-compound complex (isometric projection).

Figure 7.6. Plan of Galindo *cercadura* (isometric projection).

ous types of rectangular compound architecture were constructed at Galindo, the southernmost Moche V city. This construction represents a departure from traditional north coast architecture. However, the innovations at Galindo were not utilized at the largest Moche V settlement, Pampa Grande, far to the north, whose architectural forms stand solidly in the Moche tradition. It is therefore incorrect to use this general architectural trait, the rectangular compound, to trace contact with southern Peru, without analyzing the nature of its use. Such an analysis reveals a range of use, from continuing construction of traditional forms to innovative occurrence. Architectural innovation based on the compound is spatially limited and varied in nature. Obviously a simple theory of regional military expansion is inadequate for explaining such complex phenomena.

This type of overgeneralized stylistic comparison is even more apparent when a broader settlement configuration is used to support the theory of military expansion on the north coast. The urban pattern at the imperial capital of Wari has been described by Lumbreras (1974:161) as consisting of thick-walled, rectangular enclosures containing streets, plazas, platforms, compounds, and other features, which in turn were surrounded by higher and thicker walls delineating areas or districts. The site is large and sprawling (see Lumbreras 1974:fig. 171), its configuration reflecting a long-developing city with generally defined functional units rather than a tightly planned entity. Although Willey (1953:415) long ago warned of the danger of using this little known site as either the single point source or the diagnostically typical settlement for Middle Horizon urbanism, this has in fact largely occurred in terms of both overall settlement diffusion and specific settlement characterization. This definitional problem has been compounded by incorporating the formal traits of two other, quite different sites into the Wari urban diagnostic complex. Pikillaqta, in the south-central highlands, and Wiracocha Pampa, in the northern highlands (Fig. 7.7), are small, totally planned settlements assumed to represent Wari provincial centers (Lumbreras 1974:168). They comprise rectangular walled sites containing complexes of small rooms and rectangular enclosures (Fig. 7.8). These are small, specialized sites separated by many hundreds of kilometers, and their relationship to the settlement of Wari has yet to be confirmed through intensive archaeological investigation. Yet they are characterized as prototypes of the planned rectangular enclosures that appear on the Peruvian coast in the Middle Horizon, purportedly of Wari origin.

The incorporation of settlements so different in form, function, and location, with uncertain chronological equivalence, into a single formal trait complex used to trace the spread of Andean urbanism reveals a stylistic methodology of doubtful validity. Probably no more than a handful of Middle Horizon Peruvian cities possess even a superficial likeness to the Wari "source settlements." The contemporary central coastal city of Cajamarquilla, although originating prior to the Middle Horizon, displays the rectangular compounds and long internal dividing walls purported to derive from the site of Wari (Lumbreras 1974:166). Elsewhere on the central coast (Fig. 7.7), sites such as Manchan (Thompson 1964:93) and Pampa de las Llamas (Tello 1956a) in the Casma Valley and Chimu Capac in the Supe Valley (Lumbreras 1974:166) are assumed to show Wari influence. It is significant that this influence assumes different forms in the various settlements. For instance, Pampa de las Llamas is almost totally planned, whereas Manchan is characterized as Wari largely because of its massive tapia walls, and Chimu Capac, a complex of platform mounds and terraces, is identified on the basis of its Wari ceramic affiliation.

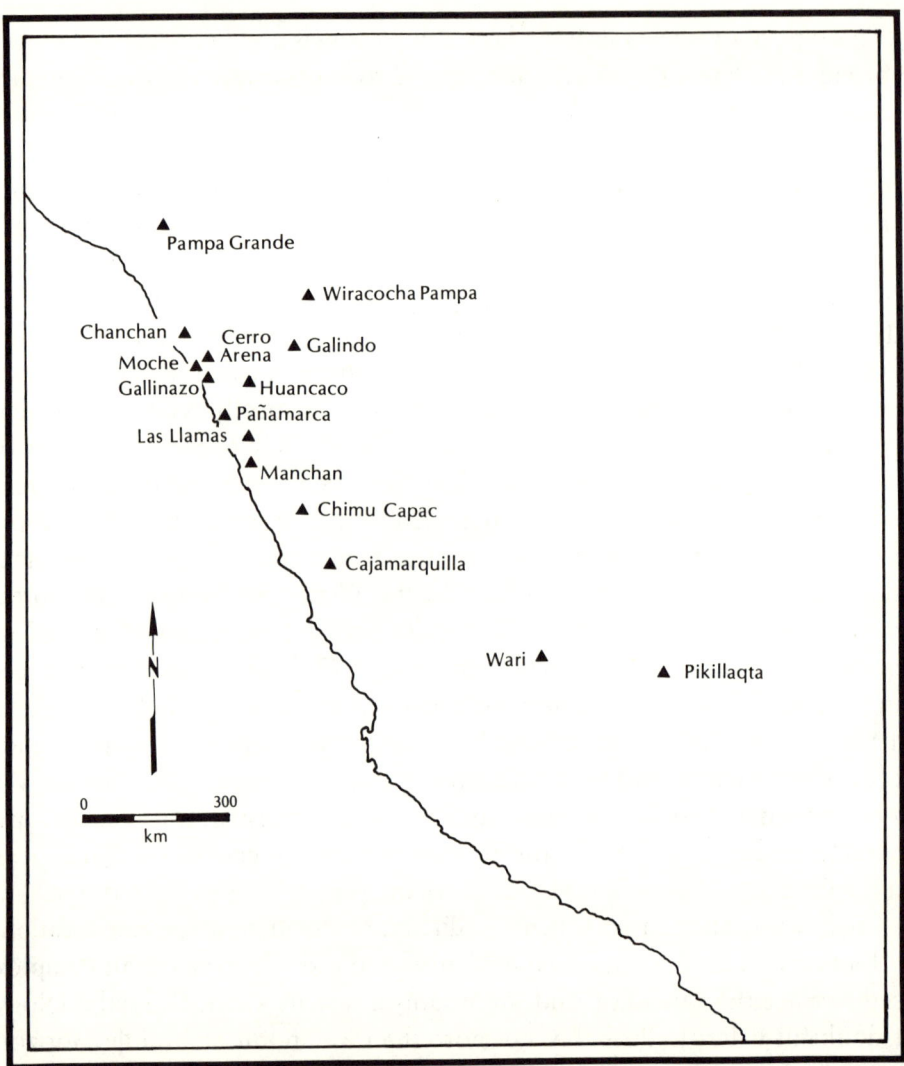

Figure 7.7. Map of Peru showing sites mentioned in text.

Cultural Reconstitution in the Late Moche Period 227

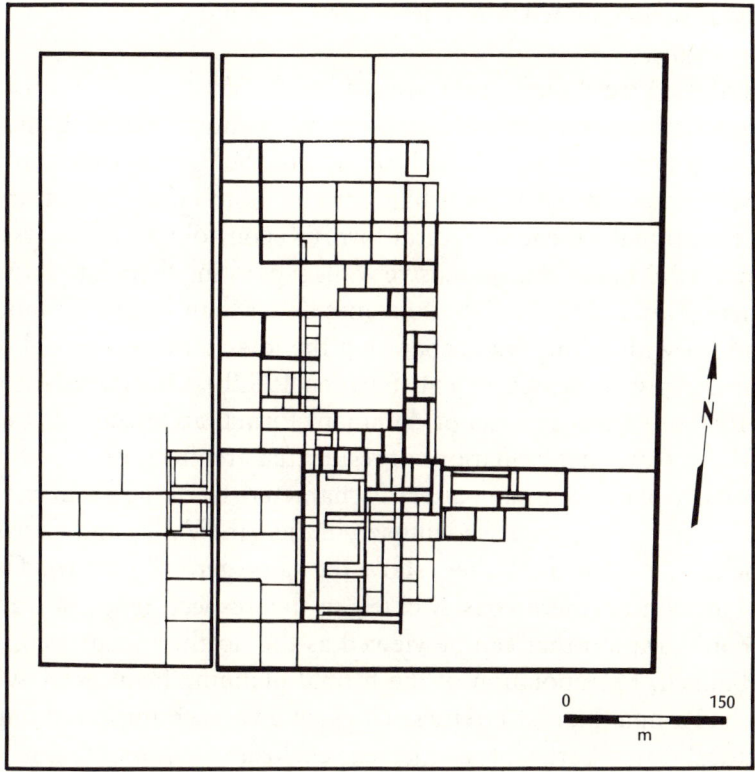

Figure 7.8. Plan of Wiracocha Pampa.

Farther north in the Viru Valley, the Wari presence is manifested by the advent of planned enclosures, structures that were present earlier but now become the dominant formal architectural structures in the valley (Willey 1953:412), although the small, unplanned residential settlements of earlier periods continue.

Thus, it seems certain that urban changes in the Middle Horizon took differing forms in those areas that can most feasibly (on the basis of ceramic evidence) be placed within the bounds of a polity centered on the southern Peruvian highlands. These changes range from new, planned settlements to various types of architectural intrusion into existing patterns. No simple trait complex diffusion occurred. Wide difference in traits used to relate the coastal sites to their highland antecedents and the looseness of their formal similarity to such assumed antecedents casts even more doubt on this theory of urban origins.

North of the Viru Valley, in the area of Moche V hegemony, both Galindo and Pampa Grande contain evidence of strict functional planning and strong centralized control, yet they show little sign of the formal architectural features associated with the Wari urban pattern. Both cities used strategically located, traditional Moche structural forms to control internal access routes (Bawden 1982a) rather than extensive walls separating them into large, regular districts (Figs. 7.2, 7.3). Galindo comes closer than Pampa Grande to the Wari pattern with a long wall separating the low-status residential occupation from the rest of the settlement (Bawden 1982b). Otherwise, the general pattern for both cities consists of dominant formal architectural complexes surrounded by large agglutinations of residential architecture.

This loosely planned urban pattern is characteristic of the north coast. Earlier urban settlements, such as Gallinazo in the Viru Valley and Cerro Arena and Moche in the Moche Valley, show the same general pattern. The early Middle Horizon northern coastal cities, in this respect, repeat a traditional overall configuration that can be viewed as the northern expression of Andean urbanism. Extrapolation of the formal planning features of Wari and Wiracocha Pampa (Fig. 7.8) to these cities involves a confusion of important architectural traits. Large intrasettlement enclosures representing whole city districts are equated on the north coast with rectangular compounds that in fact comprise functionally and architecturally discrete structures (Figs. 7.2, 7.5, 7.6). The combination of formally similar but functionally distinct stylistic traits into a single analytic class results in interpretational errors.

Although much of the earlier evidence of architectural and settlement innovations on the north coast in the early Middle Horizon period is invalid, certain important innovations do occur. In terms of their general character, the new Moche V cities continue the tradition of regional urbanism, and there is no firm evidence for the appearance of an intrusive urban type in the area. However, the abandonment of the earlier Moche state capital surrounding the Huacas del Sol and de la Luna, the creation of a huge new center at Pampa Grande much farther north, the loss of the valleys south of Moche, and the appearance of certain architectural innovations at the settlement of Galindo in the Moche Valley indicate significant changes at the commencement of the Middle Horizon.

In addition to modifications in the settlement and architectural continuum, it must be remembered that changes also occurred in ceramic iconography and function. The disappearance of the naturalistic Moche IV ceramic decoration was accompanied by developments that cannot be explained by simple stylistic evolution. Thus, the entire thematic concept manifested by the realistic "portrait heads" of Moche IV art appears to have been rejected, together with various motifs that dominate earlier art. This development occurs concurrently with the restriction of all representational art to ritual and burial settings (Bawden 1978) and what appears to be innovation in burial practices—small groups of burials scattered within the settlement rather than large, peripheral cemeteries (Bawden 1977:362ff.).

Although a framework of continuity has been identified in Moche V culture, it is apparent that within this framework an important change occurred in the early Middle Horizon. It remains to examine the meaning of this change.

The Nature of Moche V Cultural Innovation

MOCHE V MODIFICATIONS

The magnitude of disturbance in the Moche V phase cannot be minimized. The disappearance of Moche ceramic and architectural presence from the valleys south of the Moche Valley denotes political withdrawal from an area that had constituted more than a third of the total Moche IV cultural sphere (Fig. 7.1). Just as significant is the abandonment of the great Moche IV center located at the Huacas del Sol and de la Luna at Moche and removal of settlement from the strategic coastal area, with its potential for controlling intervalley communication. Emerging from this massive occupational retreat is an entirely new settlement pattern, one that must reflect a different system of social and political integration. Moche V sites are located in the neck of the river plains, away from coastal access and in a very unfavorable location for exerting multivalley political authority. Moreover, the site of Galindo, while displaying important internal settlement innovations, is less formal and imposing than its great predecessor at Moche. The new settlement of Pampa Grande, located far to the north in the Lambayeque Valley (Fig. 7.1), bears a much greater resemblance, with its huge platform mounds, to the late capital of the Moche IV state, but it is not yet possible to determine if it in fact replicates the political functions of the earlier site or is the center of one of several smaller Moche V successor polities.

These profound modifications and innovations in the settlement pattern reflect large-scale cultural trauma. Obviously the Moche polity at the end of the Moche IV phase was in such a state of disruption that a complete reorganization of administrative structure and settlement configuration was required. Thus, the southern valleys were abandoned, leaving the Moche Valley, traditionally the center of an extensive state, on the southern border of a greatly diminished area of Moche hegemony.

INTERPRETATION

Considering the inconsistent chronological and stylistic data pertaining to the "Wari empire," it is unlikely that simple military expansion occurred in the northern regions of Peru, in the earliest Middle Horizon Period. However, events external to the Moche V culture area obviously were involved in the drastic modification undertaken at this time. In light of the present evidence, it appears more likely that Moche political withdrawal from the valleys to the south of the Moche Valley resulted from a local resurgence against a northern intruder rather than from a Wari invasion. The definitive solution to this problem awaits further investigation, but it would appear that either cause of the Moche retreat involves the existence of a hostile presence directly to the south of the Moche Valley in the early Middle Horizon.

Therefore, architectural innovation in the Moche V settlements should probably be studied within a context of external threat and internal reorganization. Innovation represented by previously unknown forms of compound architecture occurs at Galindo, the southernmost Moche V settlement. Such innovation does not appear at the much larger site of Pampa Grande, which in general replicates the traditional architectural forms of the now-abandoned Moche IV capital centered around the Huacas del Sol and de la Luna in the Moche Valley. It is a common cultural phenomenon that change is most manifest in areas under greatest stress. Such modification as a response to danger is commonly seen in archaeological and historic studies of ancient states. Border settlements contain defensive and administrative components not present in protected centers, and their settlement patterns are often tightly organized and formally planned, reflecting their vulnerable position. Conversely, settlements under no external threat, especially those that represent important political centers (as Pampa Grande apparently did), are likely to maintain dominant architectural forms that symbolize continuity and stability, thus bestowing legitimacy on the governing authority. Architecture filling this role tends to retain strong traditional ties, both functionally and formally.

The huge platform mound at Pampa Grande closely resembles in form its architectural predecessor, the Huaca del Sol at Moche, in this regard, and can be viewed as its symbolic and functional descendant. It is of course tempting to regard Pampa Grande as the lineal successor to the site of Moche, the capital of a unified Moche V state. Certainly its great size and formality, together with the apparent functional continuity of its most elaborate architectural components with the earlier site, indicate such a relationship. However, the lack of research on Moche V settlements in the many valleys intervening between Pampa Grande and the only other investigated Moche V site, Galindo, makes such an identification premature, although feasible. At the very least, Pampa Grande must have been an extremely important political center, probably the most prominent settlement in the Moche V phase, and as such its architecture reflects much of the traditional authority of its great ancestor in the Moche Valley. Galindo, on the other hand, was a small settlement on the exposed border of the Moche V culture area, and its architecture reflects adaptive innovations stimulated by the external pressure that had led to the loss of the more southern valleys.

The innovations in Galindo architecture suggest the diminished importance of traditional religion and the growth of a more secular administration. The religious connections of the traditional Moche platform mounds are clearly depicted in ceramic art. They were large structures and were usually located so as to dominate the surrounding countryside. At Galindo, however, they are greatly diminished in size and peripherally located (Fig. 7.2). The settlement is dominated by three centrally located rectangular compounds, or *cercaduras* containing complexes of small rooms and courts with little evidence of residential activity (Figs. 7.2, 7.6). In addition, a single large compound contains a burial platform and habitation refuse (Figs. 7.2, 7.5). These architectural features evidently reflect a major functional departure from traditional administrative patterns. The Galindo innovation is clarified by comparison with the later Chimu architecture of Chanchan, in the same valley. At the latter site, the two earlier forms are combined in the huge *ciudadelas*—the palace compounds of the Chimu kings and the centers of state bureaucracy (Conrad 1974; Moseley 1978:58). Galindo marks the first appearance of these architectural expressions of a centralized, secular government.

The major administrative reorganization at Galindo may be seen as a functionally adaptive response to massive cultural disruption. The evidence of Moche withdrawal to the Moche Valley in the early Middle Horizon indicates that this period was marked by political disruption and breakdown. The large scale of the disturbance probably required drastic measures to stem further loss including creation of a centralized, secular administration to replace the traditional, more religious system.

Examination of the ceramic inventory shows that the disruption of the Moche state evidenced by settlement pattern change and architectural innovation was not limited to the political and administrative systems. In order to provide cultural information beyond stylistic development and distribution, this examination takes into account the physical contexts of Moche V ceramics and thus their functional significance.

In their basic form and technology, Moche V decorated fineware ceramics reflect continuing artistic evolution on the north coast. However, the iconographic content represents a major departure from earlier ceramic phases. Moche IV ceramic art is characterized by large-scale design and naturalistic, representational themes. The realistic class of "portrait vessels"—molded heads showing all aspects of human facial physiognomy—represents the ultimate expression of this type of art. A wide range of human, animal, and anthropomorphic forms is depicted. Ritualistic scenes are often represented. Donnan (1976) has analyzed this large religious component of Moche ceramic art, and he concludes that most of the art has ideological connotations.

Moche V ceramic art differs significantly from the preceding phase. The dominant decorative style consists of elaborate, small-scale, formal designs repeated over the bodies of vessels. Representational art is rare and, when it does occur, is extremely sytlized. The class of modeled representational art that characterizes Moche IV art totally disappears in Moche V. Moreover, it is difficult to ascribe religious implications to much of the Moche V decorated pottery. Most of this material is covered with abstract design and was recovered archaeologically from all social classes of residential architecture and all contexts within this architecture (Bawden 1978). The small class of stylized representational ceramic art appears almost exclusively in ritual or burial settings, representing the only pottery that can reasonably be related to religious practice or belief. There is little evidence of the extensive complex of apparently mythological scenes that appear frequently in earlier Moche painting (Donnan 1976). The few examples at the site of Galindo occur in association with burials, indicating a specialized function related to mortuary ideology (Bawden 1978). The earlier widespread distribution of representational ceramic art through all strata of Moche society appears to have narrowed in the Moche V phase, replaced by nonrepresentational, decorated pottery.

These changes in artistic content and context in the Moche V phase cannot be satisfactorily ascribed to normal stylistic evolution. Although such a development could reasonably explain the increased elaboration and stylization of Moche V representational art, it does not explain the total abandonment of naturalism in modeled ceramics, the apparent restriction of mythological representation to burial contexts, or the large-scale replacement of representational art by abstract motifs as the basis for design. These changes go beyond modification of existing style, reflecting the abrupt rejection of an entire thematic concept and the expansion of one quite different. The usual development from simple naturalism to elaboration or stylization is here overlaid by abrupt change in decorative composition and content. Such profound changes in a strong art tradition must be explained by factors that extend beyond the range of stylistic evolution to more general cultural considerations.

The ideological changes reflected in the shift to a centralized, secular administration help explain the radical disruptions indicated in the ceramic record. Restriction of ceramic vessels bearing traditional Moche mythological and ritual iconography to burial contexts and abandonment of naturalistic portrayal suggest a narrowing in the scope of traditional beliefs and a change in the mode of representation of these beliefs. This trend, expressed in both architecture and ceramic art, may well reflect identification of traditional ideological beliefs with the profound disturbances that occurred at the end of the Moche IV phase and a consequent reaction against them. Iconographic change in this sense accompanies modification and restriction of discredited beliefs perceived to have been unsuccessful in guarding against disaster. The apparent alteration of the Galindo burial patterns may represent an additional aspect of this ideological modification. Thus, divergence and innovation in Moche V ceramic art reflect the ideological component of a disruption that involved all Moche cultural systems in the early Middle Horizon.

A less identifiable factor in the events leading to the Moche V disruption is internal decline. No comprehensive study of the Moche polity in the early Middle Horizon should ignore the possibility that this phenomenon contributed to the cultural modifications occurring at the time. Indeed, the rejection of traditional administrative and ideological forms may in part reflect their stagnation and ineffectiveness in a time of stress.

Even a cursory study of ancient states reveals that they pass through discernible developmental phases. Although the course of evolution varies in each individual state, they all pass from formative phases to maturity and at some later period appear to decline in strength, ultimately giving way to some new, more vigorous cultural integrative form, either generated from within or imposed from without. In some cases flourishing states were destroyed by direct foreign invasion, but this is one of the least common forms of culture change. Much more common is gradual internal development leading to the emergence of new cultural forms, often in the presence of foreign pressures. If such cultural assessment and adaptation did not occur, the state and its culture would be unable to adapt to a changing environment and would give way to viable alternative forms. This complex process of adaptation is continuous throughout the existence of the state and involves periodic crises—the apparent historic events through which adaptive change is accelerated and most obviously visible to the historian and archaeologist.

Given this view of cultural development as expressed in the state, a study of the drastic modification of Moche sociopolitical structure in the early Middle Horizon must take into account the historic process that preceded it. Within this conceptual context, it seems clear that the Moche state at the commencement of the Middle Horizon was no longer able to resolve the problems that it confronted. These problems may well have included both internal stagnation and external pressures. Moreover, it is possible, given the form of subsequent response, that the problem of stagnation was initially paramount. An internally stagnant and weak Moche state would have been unable to confront internal social or external political problems. These problems ultimately led to the loss of the southern Moche territories. Perhaps the smaller area of Moche political hegemony was less culturally diversified and thus easier to reorganize.

Conclusion

In this study I have used information from recent archaeological research on the north coast of Peru, together with previously acquired data, to examine cultural developments during the early Middle Horizon in the region. Although I have readily utilized the important results of older scholarship, I have avoided the single-trait stylistic comparison prevalent in such work. I have examined architectural and ceramic traits within their formal and functional settings rather than isolated from them. This procedure facilitates detection of valid temporal and spatial modifications of form. It is thus possible to observe the total cultural context of the innovations apparent in the Moche V archaeological record. These innovations should be viewed as cultural adaptations resulting from broad and complex pressures rather than as primary denominators of simple diffusional events.

The results of this multidimensional study do not absolutely contradict the conclusions of traditional scholarship. Rather the study reveals that limited stylistic analysis, while identifying some general cultural contacts during the Middle Horizon, has exceeded its interpretational capacity, resulting in oversimplification of these relationships. The traditional view that Wari expansion into the north coast region brought with it the concept of urbanism and a distinct architectural configuration must be rejected. However, the events reflected by the chronologically and spatially diverse appearance of Wari-related and Wari-derived ceramic styles elsewhere along the coast probably did exert a profound influence in the north. Although this confusing picture appears more likely to represent localized action against foreign intrusion at the outset of the Middle Horizon, rather than imperial invasion, there seems little doubt that it does reflect elimination of Moche political hegemony from the southern portion of its erstwhile territorial domain. In addition, it is quite possible that this withdrawal was at least in part caused by internal weakness in a 400-year-old polity, which could not overcome the combination of external and internal pressures. The only recourse in the face of such pressures appears to have been a major reorganization of the Moche polity, touching all important aspects of cultural integration—political, administrative, and ideological.

This explanation of the events that transpired on the north coast of Peru at the commencement of the Middle Horizon can most aptly be understood in terms of A. L. Kroeber's evolutionary term, "cultural reconstitution" (Kroeber 1963:39ff.). Here, an apparently declining state undergoes profound, internally generated structural modifications in order to remain adaptively viable. Although in part speculative, this interpretation of events on the Peruvian north coast fully accords with the complex archaeological record, unlike the traditional theory of simple diffusion. While further comprehensive archaeological investigation can confirm and refine this explanation, it seems extremely likely that the events analyzed in this study represent one of the first cases of cultural reconstitution identified in Andean pre-Columbian history.

Eight

Coast-Highland Relations in Northern Peru: Some Observations on Routes, Networks, and Scales of Interaction

John R. Topic, Trent University
Theresa Lange Topic, Trent University

Introduction

The nature of relationships between prehistoric complex societies and their neighbors is an intriguing and important area of study. Even a superficial familiarity with written history tells us that we cannot draw boundaries around a society and expect it to grow and change only in response to internal conditions; interaction between societies unarguably affects the trajectories of individual cultures. Such interaction can take various forms, including conflict, trade, alliance, migration, and pilgrimage. The remains of prehistoric fortifications and roads offer direct evidence of cultural interaction. Fortifications close off a territory, and roads open it up; together, they define boundaries and control permeability.

Between 1977 and 1980 we directed a project that studied the role of prehistoric fortifications in northern Peru.[1] The Fortifications Project surveyed a zone in northern Peru reaching from the Pacific Ocean to the Continental Divide, with an emphasis on the area intervening between the major centers of the coast and the sierra. In effect, we surveyed the natural and cultural buffer zones through which communication between core areas was routed. The central area of the survey zone (about 4,000 square kilometers) comprised the Moche and Viru drainages, with some "spot" survey in contiguous zones (see Figs. 8.1 and 8.2).

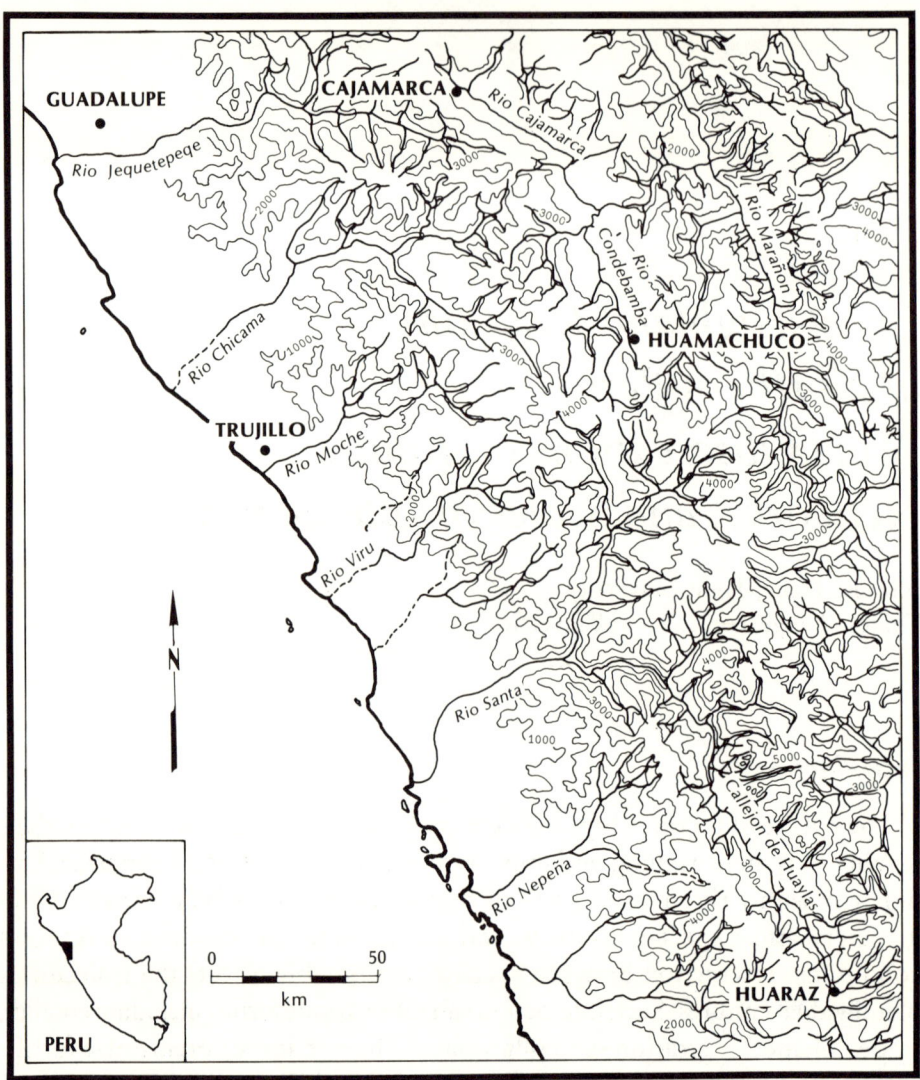

Figure 8.1. A portion of northern Peru.

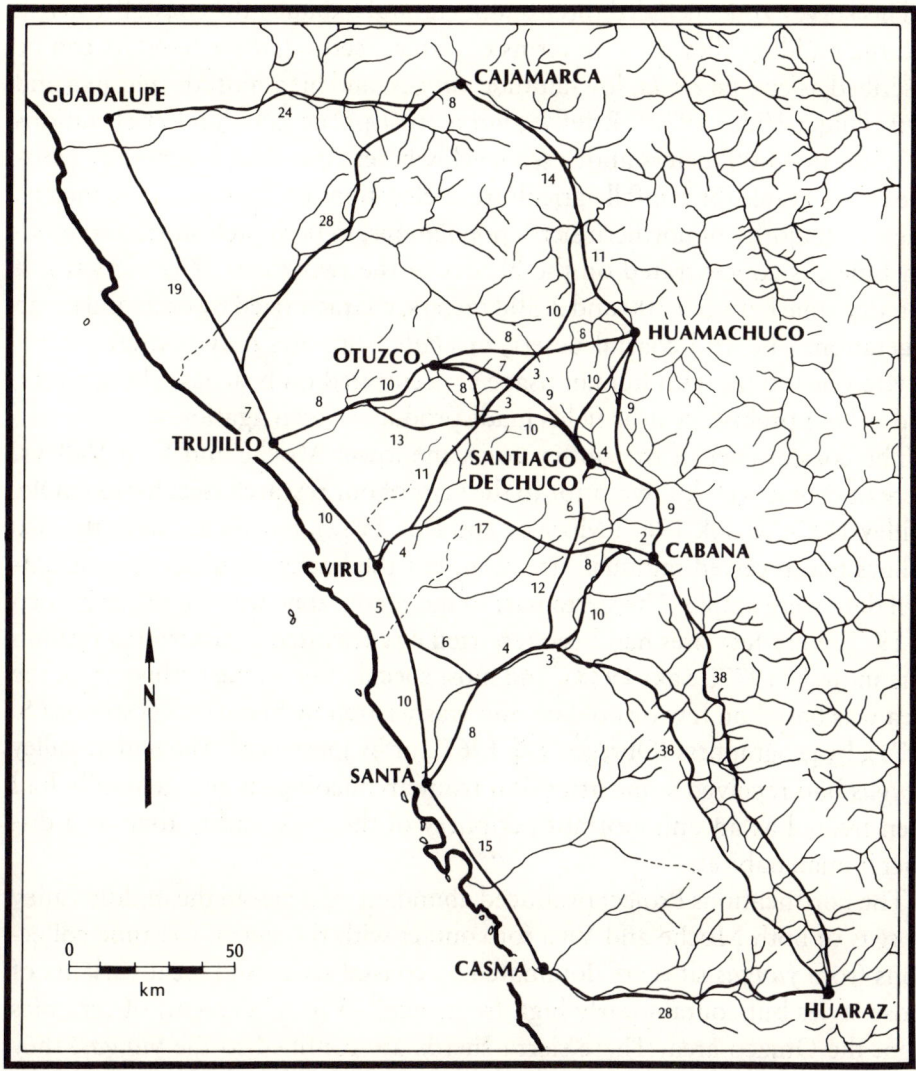

Figure 8.2. The shortest routes between 11 points in northern Peru. These routes are derived from principles of route location rather than from empirical evidence. Many, however, do correspond to actual prehistoric routes. The numbers along the routes express distances in hours of travel time.

This survey zone included three major cultural habitats: the coast, the sierra, and the middle valley area. In terms of natural setting, these habitats can be described as coastal *chala*, low-altitude *yungas*, and high-altitude *quechua* and *suni* (Pulgar Vidal 1972). Briefly, *suni* is frost-prone grassland at elevations of 3,500 to 4,000 meters above sea level, whereas *quechua* is generally frost-free land suitable for rainfall agriculture at elevations of 2,300 to 3,500 meters. The vast majority of northern sierra populations, in both prehistoric and modern times, is concentrated on the border of the two zones. The *yungas* is a hot, dry zone between 500 and 2,300 meters, characterized by cacti and scrub vegetation. The arid coastal desert, or *chala*, supports only scattered xerophytic vegetation, with human usage concentrated on beaches, along rivers, and in later prehistory near fields made productive by irrigation.

The coastal part of the survey zone, the lower Moche and Viru Valleys, were of course well-known prior to the start of our research (see, for example, Willey 1953; Kosok 1965; Moseley and Day 1982). Fortifications in the two valleys had received minimal attention, but the background settlement pattern data were ample. The sierra part of the survey zone was almost unknown in 1977. Very few sites had been reported or excavated in controlled fashion (Krzanowski 1977; Zaki 1978), and most speculation on the prehistory of the area was based on few or no data and was written by historians (Espinoza S. 1971), by geographers (Obregoso R. 1967), or by journalists. The middle valley *yungas* had received some attention from archaeologists but generally had been treated as an unimportant periphery of the coast rather than as a distinct human habitat.

The Fortifications Project produced abundant evidence in the middle valley *yungas* of both Moche and Viru for contact with the sierra. Ceramic collections from *yungas* sites are dominated by coastal styles and local variants of those styles but contain fairly high frequencies (5 to 25 percent) of ceramics from the Otuzco area. These sierra sherds are confined to the *yungas*, they rarely percolate down to the lower valleys. Less frequent and more episodic in the *yungas* are ceramics from more distant sierra locales. When they do occur, these exotic sherds are concentrated at a few large *yungas* sites. In view of these ceramic distributions, as well as the tendency throughout the survey zone for roads to be associated with fortifications, we decided to examine the general problem of interaction between the coast and the sierra.

This paper concentrates on the role of roads rather than on fortifications. We will discuss some principles of routing that allow a comparison of travel times and a uniform measure of distance applicable across several zones. We will also examine the various ways in which routes are combined to form networks and, using the idea of minimum distance, explore the implications of several network designs. The efficiency of a network design will be related to both the scale of interaction and the form of interaction. Using a fortified Gallinazo site in the *yungas,* we will illustrate how a variety of different networks, operating over varying distances, were actually combined in practice.

Principles of Route Location

The rural areas of Peru are criss-crossed by a bewildering maze of footpaths. Our survey in the sierra around Otuzco has shown that many of the paths still in use today are of considerable antiquity; many of them pass by or through prehistoric settlements, and ancient embankments, gates, and checkpoints are clearly visible. On the coast, differences in preservation tend to leave the major intervalley roads as evidence of prehistoric communication, and in the *yungas* the local paths connecting adjacent sites are most frequently preserved.

It was via these complex networks of paths and roads that travel, exchange, and communication between distant points occurred in prehistoric times. Of special interest here are the communication routes between major centers in northern Peru. Although the culture history of the zone is only partially known, certain foci of influence containing first-rank centers can be identified on the basis of site size and wide dispersal of ceramic styles. The lower Moche Valley, the Lambayeque Valley, Cajamarca, Huamachuco, and the Callejón de Huaylas are examples of such core areas, and theories of optimum route location can be tested against data pertaining to actual routing among the various centers.

The theory of route location is not well developed (Haggett, Cliff, and Frey 1977:64), but some basic principles can be discussed. The optimum location of any route is determined by the points to be served, the cost of construction of the route, and the cost of moving goods along it. When applied to pre-Hispanic northern Peru, these principles interact to (1) minimize the length of a route through uninhabited territory, (2) minimize changes in elevation along the length of a route, and (3) minimize the overall length of a route, consistent with the first two factors.

The reasons for these "minimization" rules are quite straightforward, relating to the realities of topography and travel. Because we are dealing only with foot and camelid traffic, route construction costs per unit length are low. Usually, very little construction is necessary to provide a usable path. The major costs involve construction of bridges across large rivers and canals, and retaining walls on very steep slopes. The most used and the best-maintained routes will service population concentrations and will tend to favor population increase in their immediate vicinity. Routing across uninhabited areas (very high elevations, very steep slopes, coastal desert, and so forth) will be infrequent and as direct as possible. The cost of moving goods is dependent on travel time, which is in turn dependent on the length and gradient of the route.

A route connecting two points along most sections of the north coast will tend to run along the coastal plain. Here the changes in elevation are minimal, and the ever-broadening fan of the irrigated area reduces the distance traveled across the desert. Between certain valleys, notably Moche, Viru, Chao, and Santa, a second route exists farther inland on or near the transition between *chala* and *yungas*. In these valleys the configurations of the courses of the rivers and a series of passes between rivers combine to provide short routes with little change in elevation.

It is much more difficult to generalize about routing in the sierra, because local topographic and population patterns are idiosyncratic. In the major northwest-southwest trending basins, two points within the basin can usually be connected by a route that stays within a single linear stretch of *quechua* or *suni*, passing through populated areas and encountering few obstacles or altitudinal changes; clearly such a route is ideal. Interbasin communication between distant sierra points will require routes that make substantial ascents and descents. Route selection will reflect the minimizing principles discussed earlier and in general must compromise between the ideal of shortest distance and the ideal of least possible climb.

The result is that routes connecting two distant points can be expected to make some deviations from a straight line. These deviations are of two major types (Haggett, Cliff, and Frey 1977:65–68). Positive deviation, made to avoid uninhabited areas or areas of low population density, has the effect of increasing traffic along the route. Negative deviation is made to avoid the natural barriers posed by changes in elevation. In general, both types of deviation result in the same routing, because both in the sierra and on the coast areas of high population density tend to occur within specific altitudinal zones. In effect, optimum routes in the sierra will be channeled through the *quechua* and *suni*, and those on the coast will follow the *chala*. In both cases, the choice of an optimum route is relatively restricted, and routes trend northwest-southeast.

Routing problems between the coastal *chala* and the large sierra basins are more complicated. Such transverse routes must climb the western slopes of the Andes, passing through several different environmental zones from sea level to high altitude passes of 3,800 meters or more before dropping down into the highland valleys. Because this change in elevation cannot be avoided by negative deviation, the choice of route is determined largely by positive deviation. Ascending/descending transverse routes have two options: they can run alongside rivers or they can follow ridges. Where a floodplain along a river permits agriculture, the route will parallel the river. Often, however, the middle course of a river is steeply V-shaped, encumbered by boulders, and lacking a floodplain, resulting in an area with low population potential. In these cases—for example, in the Moche Valley above Poroto or in the Cañon del Pato in the Santa drainage—a ridge offers the advantage of more direct passage between the populated areas of the *yungas* and *quechua*. In fact, there are many possible and actual transverse routes on the western slopes of the Andes of northern Peru, but they tend to occur in clusters. The overall effect is to funnel coast-sierra communication through a few transverse corridors.

The 3,000 meter difference in altitude between coast and sierra in northern Peru adds to the travel time and the cost of moving goods. In order to compare route distances in the area, we transformed airline distances to travel time distances by estimating a walking pace of 5 kilometers per hour on level terrain. Each time a 1,000 meter contour was crossed, we added another 1.5 hours to the travel time.[2] Although not definitive, these figures are useful for estimating the optimum amount of deviation around high-cost areas, as well as for comparing alternate routes between two points. We used Tobler's multidimensional scaling technique (Hagget, Cliff, and Frey 1977:327) to transform the map of a portion of northern Peru (Fig. 8.1). The method involved plotting a series of possible routes between the 11 modern towns shown and determining the shortest route (Fig. 8.2) between each pair of points. The route distances, expressed as travel times, were then manipulated by Tobler's technique to reposition the 11 points. The coastline and rivers were interpolated (Fig. 8.3).

This map shows that on the coast the ratio of travel time distance to airline distance is 1, in the sierra the ratio rises to approximately 1.3, and between the coast and sierra it is approximately 1.46. In other words, travel along the coast is easiest, travel within the sierra is somewhat difficult, and travel between the coast and the sierra is most difficult. The effect, of course, is to distance the two regions.

Network Design

A network exists whenever more than two points are interconnected by routes. Because pre-Hispanic communication usually involved several major and minor points, it is useful to consider the possible problems and solutions in network formation between points. Optimal network design is determined by the points linked, the construction costs, and the costs of movement along

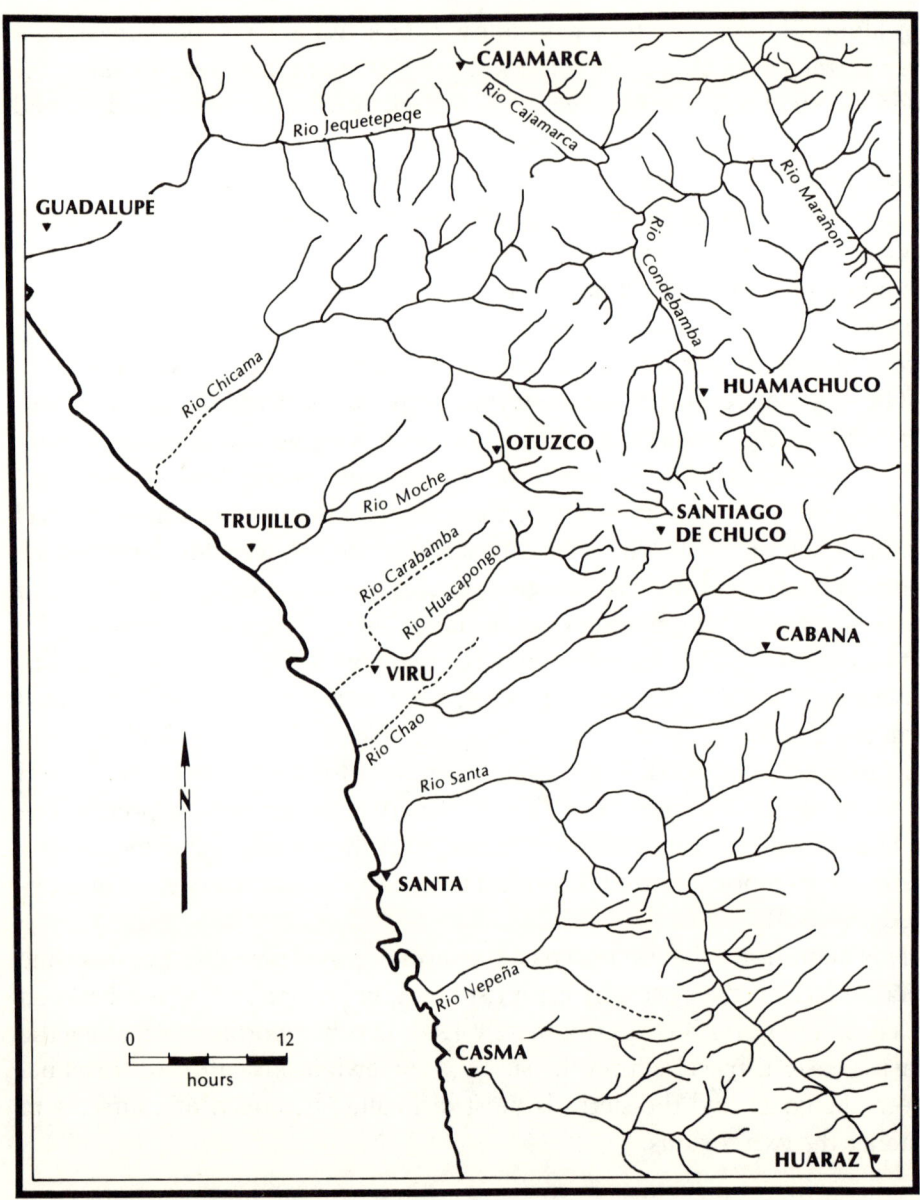

Figure 8.3. A spatial transformation of a portion of northern Peru, derived from Figures 8.1 and 8.2.

the route; in effect, optimal networks incorporate optimal routes. In addition, network design is affected by the size or importance of individual nodes and the use for which the network is intended. Ignoring for the moment the differential importance of individual nodes, optimal network design can be related to optimal route location and the use of the route. Optimal networks are based on the idea of minimum distance, and minimum distance can be defined according to the use of the route. We will discuss here only four variants of minimum distance (Bunge 1962).

One variant, often termed the "traveling salesman" solution, is illustrated in Figure 8.4a. This solution minimizes the total distance traveled when one wishes to begin and end a journey at the same node and visit all other nodes on the route only once. As the name implies, the traveling salesman solution to the minimum distance problem is well suited to certain types of exchange activities, and in the Andean context it would be the logical solution to pilgrimage routing problems. As is obvious from the illustration, the traveling salesman solution minimizes distance around the circuit but often takes a roundabout route between two nodes (for example, Trujillo and Huamachuco).

The second variant, which might be called the hierarchical solution, overcomes this problem for a single node. This solution is logical only when one node is of inordinate importance. In the example illustrated in Figure 8.4b, that one node is Trujillo. The network minimizes distance to it from all other nodes but results in inconvenient routing between most nodes.

Both solutions can be incorporated into a single general solution, the completely connected network (Fig. 8.4c). The advantage of the completely connected network is that it minimizes distance between any two nodes; its disadvantage is its overall length, which might involve prohibitive construction costs.

Figure 8.4d illustrates one type of solution in which construction costs are an important consideration. This shortest set solution is characterized by junctions at angles of 120° or greater and by the use of floating nodes (junctions that do not coincide with any of the connected nodes). Although the overall length of the network is minimized, distance between any two nodes (for example, Trujillo and Huaraz) may not be minimal.

We cannot expect a real network to conform perfectly to any of the ideal patterns, but it is interesting to see which models are approximated in specific situations. The type of network linking pre-Hispanic centers suggests the kind of interaction occurring along the routes and the relationships among the centers being joined. However, the network is best studied not in the centers, but in the intervening hinterlands and buffer zones through which the routes comprising the network actually pass.

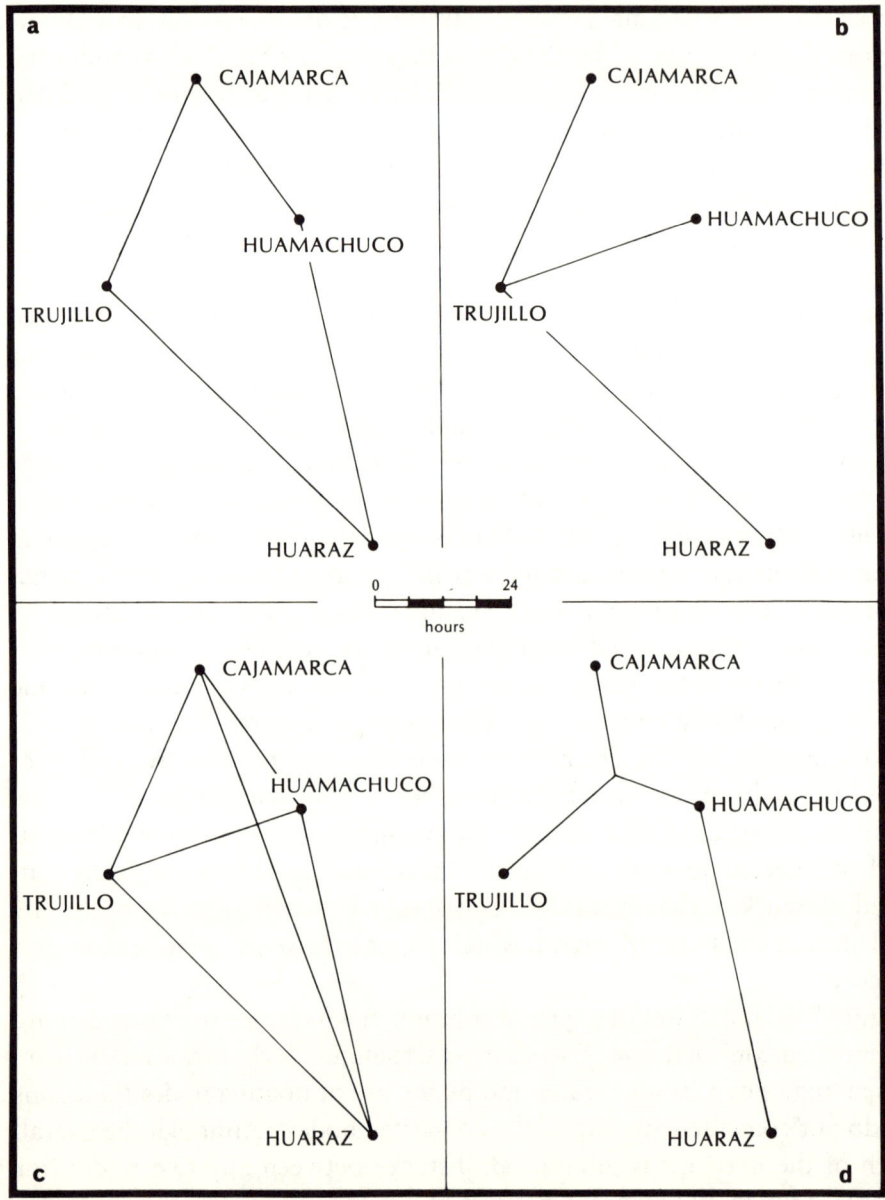

Figure 8.4. Four examples of minimum distance networks linking four centers in northern Peru. The centers are shown in their transformed locations.

Network Evolution and Node Primacy

Examination of modern topographic maps of northern Peru on which footpaths are indicated shows elements of both the completely connected and the shortest set networks in operation. A labyrinth of footpaths connects any given house in a district with any other house, any small town in a region to all other towns in the region. Although these local and regional networks tend to be poorly preserved, we can assume that they have great antiquity. The better-known roads, such as the Inca highway system, are major interregional communications networks overlaid on the local and regional networks. These interregional networks evolved over time through a dynamic process of selection and emphasis of specific route segments in response to such factors as changes in traffic flow as particular points grew or interacted more frequently or minor changes in route location as large centers forged more direct links with one another (Haggett, Cliff, and Frey 1977:95–96). Thus, the actual design of a network will reflect political and economic events in the first-rank nodes and, to a lesser extent, route manipulation by small-scale polities in the buffer zones through which routes pass.

One factor that effects changes in a network is change in the relative importance of the nodes. Of course, the importance of any node or center depends on several variables, but certainly the general importance of an area and its center will be affected by ease of travel and population potential. Not surprisingly, in northern Peru there is a strong tendency for outstanding political, economic, and artistic achievement to occur in locales that are favored by both large expanses of arable land and easy communication. The principles of route location discussed above illustrate that the large northwest-southeast trending basins of the sierra and the relatively level coastal plain have the best internal travel conditions. Both kinds of zones are also characterized by especially large expanses of arable land. Generally in the north sierra the optimum location for habitation, as well as for centralization of authority, is near the head of major river valleys where the belt of *quechua* and *suni* doubles back in a boldly drawn U-shaped configuration. Such locations, exemplified by Cajamarca, Huamachuco, and Huaraz, approximate a von Thunen-like landscape that often incorporates a slice of high *yungas* zone, permitting intensive cultivation of some fruits; a large expanse of *quechua* land suitable for extensive cultivation of subsistence products; and an outer ring of *suni* pasture land.

The amount of arable land in any given coastal drainage is dependent on both topography and river flow. Because of the need for irrigation, the ideal situation is a broad area of relatively level land coupled with a river flow adequate to water the area. This combination is not found in all drainages, but where it occurs, it is at lower elevations, usually near the ocean. Certain portions of the *chala,* then, as well as certain locations in the large highland basins, are more likely to contain major centers that will serve as primary nodes in communication networks. On the basis of empirical evidence, we know that first-rank centers arose in locations such as the lower Moche Valley, the Callejón de Huaylas, Cajamarca, Huamachuco, and the Lambayeque Valley.

We can expect to find numerous secondary centers located in less favored portions of the *chala* and the highland basins. Because optimum routes in both the sierra and on the coast trend northwest-southeast, the secondary centers form secondary nodes on networks connecting large population centers within the coastal region or within the sierra. A general and perduring pattern of interaction results, in which especially strong links are formed among various coastal nodes and among various sierra nodes. However, the small pockets of habitable land on the western slopes of the Andes will tend to be isolated from these major networks. Difficult access and relatively low population densities favor only small centers of local importance, which achieve regional importance only through involvement with external centers. If routing changes make a small west slope center a secondary node on a major coast-sierra network, the importance and wealth of that center will increase dramatically, but generally only local communication networks are developed.

Scale of Interaction

The western slopes of the Andes are interesting because interaction on a variety of scales can be studied there. Interaction between the first-rank centers of the coast and the sierra must pass through the area, and the close juxtaposition of ecological niches will favor exchange on a more local level. Because of the topography, interaction tends to occur on three discrete scales. The traveling salesman circuit can be used to illustrate this. A small-scale traveling salesman circuit, confined to an area of about 20 kilometers on a side, is ideal for the local exchange of products from different ecological zones that are vertically stratified. A circuit of this magnitude can begin in the *quechua,* climb to the *suni,* descend again through the *quechua* to the *yungas,* and thence back to the *quechua.* Every link in the circuit allows for an exchange between zones. The length of the circuit is beneficial to the extent that it is minimal, but has the drawback in most cases of not including a first-rank center. A first-rank center either on the coast or in the sierra can accomplish the same exchanges, but the scale increases to about 75 by 75 kilometers. Again, in terms of the exchange of produce from diverse ecological zones, the length of the route is minimal, but a circuit begun in the sierra would probably not include a coastal center and vice versa. It is only when the scale of the circuit is increased to about 150 kilometers on a side or greater than contact between coastal and sierra centers of first rank can be assured. At this scale, however, the circuit is so long that it is better suited for movement of elite goods or pilgrimage than for transport of subsistence commodities from one zone to another.

Our survey of the Moche and Viru drainages has documented interaction on all three scales, though a traveling salesman network is rarely indicated. The most general pattern is small-scale interaction between *yungas* and *quechua* on the western slopes. It is difficult to tell whether this interaction involves the traveling salesman circuit or a simpler point-to-point route (Haley 1979; MacKenzie 1980). The intermediate-scale pattern is much less common. Huamachuco reached southwest on this scale in the Early Intermediate Period, and the Chimu in the Late Intermediate Period interacted with the western fringes of the *quechua*. In both cases, the actual interaction pattern corresponds more to a hierarchical network than to the traveling salesman circuit. Large-scale coast-sierra interaction (that is, interaction involving both coast and sierra first-rank centers) also can be documented in our survey zone only during two time periods. One case in which the network approximates a shortest set solution occurred during the Early Intermediate Period and will be discussed in more detail later. The second case, Inca expansion during the Late Horizon, probably approximates the completely connected network, although the evidence from our survey could be accounted for by a combination of the earlier Huamachuco and Chimu networks (DeHetre 1979).

Interestingly, there is evidence for interaction in the survey zone, but it rarely involves domination of extensive portions of the area. The idea of scale, when applied to the transformed map, bears on this fact.

In the competitive landscape of complex societies, ease of communication is one factor that affects the economic and political success of a polity. A territory is more easily governed and controlled when all parts of it are easily accessible to the central place through its heirarchy of administrative centers. Because of the topography of northern Peru, densely populated areas occur as islands surrounded by seas of sparse or nonexistent population. Thus, political expansion will tend to occur in discrete increments. Many factors affect the nature, speed, direction, and mechanics of expansion; here we will discuss the influence that travel time can be expected to exert on political expansion.

A coastal center, for example, the lower Moche Valley, which is intent on expansion will have three options. Within one day's travel time, it can either go north, south, or east. The first two choices will usually provide access to other dense *chala* populations, and hence a good return in terms of taxable labor. The third option will lead to the less populated *yungas* and the fringes of the *quechua* on the western slopes, resulting in less tax revenue but providing access to greater ecological diversity. A two-day journey in each direction allows access to the *chala* from Jequetepeque to Santa, the *yungas* of the Moche Valley, and most of the *quechua*, as well as part of the *suni* at the headwaters of the Moche River. In addition, however, a two-day journey starting from the lower Viru and the Chicama Valleys will lead into the *yungas* and to the lower edge of the *yungas*, respectively. As this reiterative procedure continues, it is apparent that any attempt to equalize travel times to the edges of the political unit will result in a very elongated boundary with a bulge extending inland only in the immediate vicinity of the dominant center.

In fact, the recent survey by the Fortifications Project in the upper Moche and Viru drainages tends to document this restricted eastward expansion by polities based in the lower Moche Valley. The Moche civilization of the late Early Intermediate Period directed its major expansion north and south; eastward expansion absorbed the *yungas* zone but left no detectable evidence in the *quechua*. The major thrust of Chimu conquest in the Late Intermediate Period was again north and south. The *yungas* to the east were conquered, but the Chimu had access to *quechua* and *suni* products only through gateway middlemen (Coupland 1978, MacKenzie 1980). Clearly travel times alone cannot account for the shape of coastal polities, but the jump in the ratio of travel time distance to airline distance from 1 to almost 1.5, which occurs between the *yungas* and *quechua*, affects expansion.

The case of an expanding sierra center is quite different for two reasons. First, the jump in the ratio of travel time distance to airline distance is not as great between "normal" travel and a major descent to the coast. Second, obviously a sierra center can expand in all four cardinal directions. Although the northwest-southeast trend of optimal routes will favor some elongation, these factors lead to a more rounded shape for the territory and access to ecological diversity, and in some cases densely populated land, in several directions.

In the case of the survey zone, the nature of both Huamachuco and Inca influence is still unclear. Certainly Huamachuco influenced the *quechua* and *suni* portions of the upper Moche and Viru Valleys, but evidence of influence is lacking in the *yungas*, perhaps because similar zones are located closer to Huamachuco in the upper Chicama and on tributaries of the Marañon. Inca expansion was on a scale so vast that it really constitutes a special case outside the bounds of discussion of this paper.

What our survey of the hinterland between major centers of influence on the coast and in the highlands has shown, then, is that political expansion can generally be classified as an intermediate-scale phenomenon when viewed in terms of coast-highland relations. Such major centers as Huaca del Sol, Chan Chan, and Marcahuamachuco attempted to control only portions of the closest hinterlands. The concept of equalizing travel times to the farthest nodes of a hierarchical network helps to account for this pattern; the hierarchical network is optimal only up to a point, after which a link with a combination of small-scale and large-scale networks of other types becomes more efficient.

An Application

The principles of route location and network design can be illustrated with an example drawn from the Early Intermediate Period in northern Peru. Interaction between several sierra and coastal points of the area via routes descending through the intervening west slope buffer zone will be discussed. The time period in question is the equivalent of the Gallinazo and Moche I–II phases in the Moche and Viru Valleys, approximately 200 B.C. to A.D. 200.

Between the deeply incised middle courses of the Chicama and Santa Rivers, a westward projection of the Andes reduces the airline distance between coast and sierra. On this plateaulike projection there are no exceptionally high peaks, the *quechua* and *suni* zones are characterized by relatively level topography, and the *quechua* communicates quite directly with the middle valley *yungas* below via several ridge routes. Furthermore, the *yungas* of the Moche, Viru, Chao, and Santa Valleys intercommunicate easily. In combination, these factors make the west slope buffer zone a natural crossroads for interaction between the north coast and the various sierra centers to the northeast, east, and southeast. For example, the shortest point-to-point routes for Trujillo-Huamachuco, Trujillo-Cabana, Cajamarca-Santa, and Cajamarca-Casma all pass through the area.

Unusual ceramic distributions in the middle Moche Valley encountered by the Fortifications Project in the 1980 survey can be accounted for by hypothesizing a combination of small-scale networks of indeterminant type, an intermediate-scale hierarchical network, and a large-scale shortest set network. In general, ceramic collections from the *yungas* of both Moche and Viru show close similarities to coastal assemblages. *Yungas* collections also contain significant quantities of ceramics from the adjacent western slope, and there is a marked tendency for these local sierra sherds to become more frequent as one moves upvalley within the *yungas*. These ceramics represent the small-scale coast-sierra interaction alluded to above. Ceramics from more distant sierra centers, indicative of large-scale interaction, are found only during some time periods. These ceramics tend to be found at the larger *yungas* sites and are far more common in the Moche *yungas* than in its Viru counterpart. There is also a sort of filtering effect at work within the *yungas*, as very few ceramics from either nearby or distant sierra centers are found in the lower valleys.

In the Moche Valley *yungas* several sites with major and minor Gallinazo equivalent occupations were identified by the survey. Ceramic assemblages were similar to but distinct from classic Gallinazo assemblages in the lower Viru Valley, reported by Bennett (1950). There was significant admixture of a ceramic style from the Otuzco area, typified by large, flaring jars with a hard, buff-colored paste and decorated with sloppily painted red lines along the interior and exterior jar lip. To the best of our knowledge, this style has not been found in the lower valleys of either Moche or Viru.

Most important, however, in the problem of long-distance communication is the presence of significant quantities of fragmentary kaolin bowls in Gallinazo sites of the *yungas*. Kaolin vessels are common in the north sierra, and kaolin was used in the fabrication of pottery at least from Cajamarca south to Huaraz. The dates of many of the kaolin styles are still imprecise, but it appears that from the beginning of the Early Intermediate Period kaolin vessels were being produced at one or more places in the north sierra. Some of these styles, such as Cajamarca Cursive and Recuay, are very distinctive and can be recognized wherever they occur. Other, less important styles are not nearly as widespread or as well documented. The kaolin ceramics from the Moche Valley *yungas* fall into this latter category, and it is somewhat difficult to assign sources.

Style A (Fig. 8.5a) consists of a simple hemispherical bowl, well finished, unslipped, with thin (3 to 4 millimeters) hard walls. There is a tendency for all or part of the vessel surface to take on an orange hue, probably as a result of firing. The only decoration on these bowls, occurring on about 40 percent of the sample, is a single incised line running 1 centimeter below the exterior lip.

Style B vessels (Fig. 8.5b) are of similar shape, but are painted, usually on their exterior surfaces, with simple geometric designs in red paint. Style C bowls (Fig. 8.5c–f) at times have a slight angle but are usually hemispherical. Decoration is painted on the exterior in red, black, orange, brown, or white; rarely are two or three colors combined. Motifs are simple and geometric, and are usually repeated in a band below the exterior lip.

Style C has been identified as Early or pre-Cursive Cajamarca (R. Matsumoto and Y. Onuki, personal communication). Specimens from the Moche Valley *yungas* are identical to ceramics from Huacaloma, a stratified site with a long occupation near Cajamarca, excavated by the University of Tokyo Scientific Expedition to Nuclear America. The source of Style B is undoubtedly the Callejón de Huaylas. Bowls with identical shape, paste, and decoration are abundant in pre-Recuay collections from Balcón de Judas near Huaras (Stephen Wegner, personal communication). Style A is most similar to vessels from the Callejón de Huaylas to the best of our knowledge. Kaolin bowls with inci-

Coast-Highland Relations in Northern Peru 253

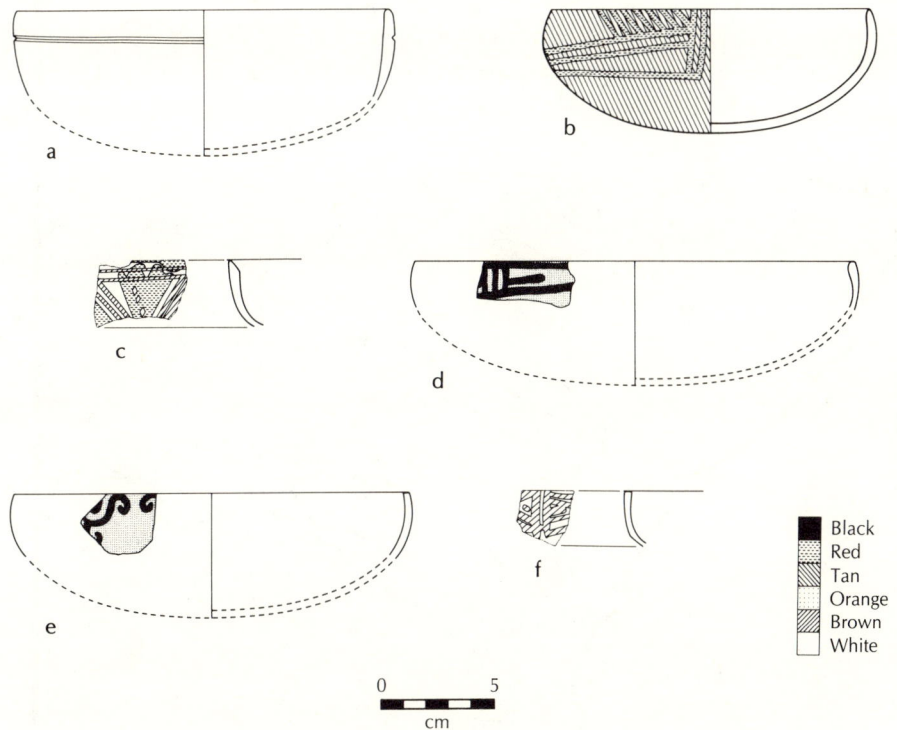

Figure 8.5. Kaolin bowls from Moche Valley *yungas* sites. *a:* simple bowl with incised line, unslipped, probably from the Callejón de Huaylas. *b:* red painted bowl from Callejón de Huaylas. *c–f:* bowls with painted decoration on exterior, pre-Cursive Cajamarca.

sion are also found at Balcón de Judas, but the incision tends to be more complex and is often combined with painting (S. Wegner, personal communication).

The three kaolin styles are found in small quantities in the Otuzco area. Styles B and C are somewhat difficult to identify there, especially in surface collections, because of the tendency for painted decoration to be eroded away. Both styles are present at two large sites of Gallinazo-equivalent age. Style A is found at a wider range of sites. Frequencies of the three styles are much lower in the Otuzco area than in the Moche Valley *yungas*. Within the middle valley, the highest frequencies come from the site complex of Cruz Blanca.

The Cruz Blanca complex is located 30 kilometers inland from the Pacific Ocean, well into the hot dry *yungas* zone (Fig. 8.6). It occupies a strategic point where two major tributaries, Rio la Cuesta and Rio Sinsicap, join with the Rio Moche. The location facilitates control of traffic along all three tributaries, as well as through an inter–*yungas* pass connecting the Moche

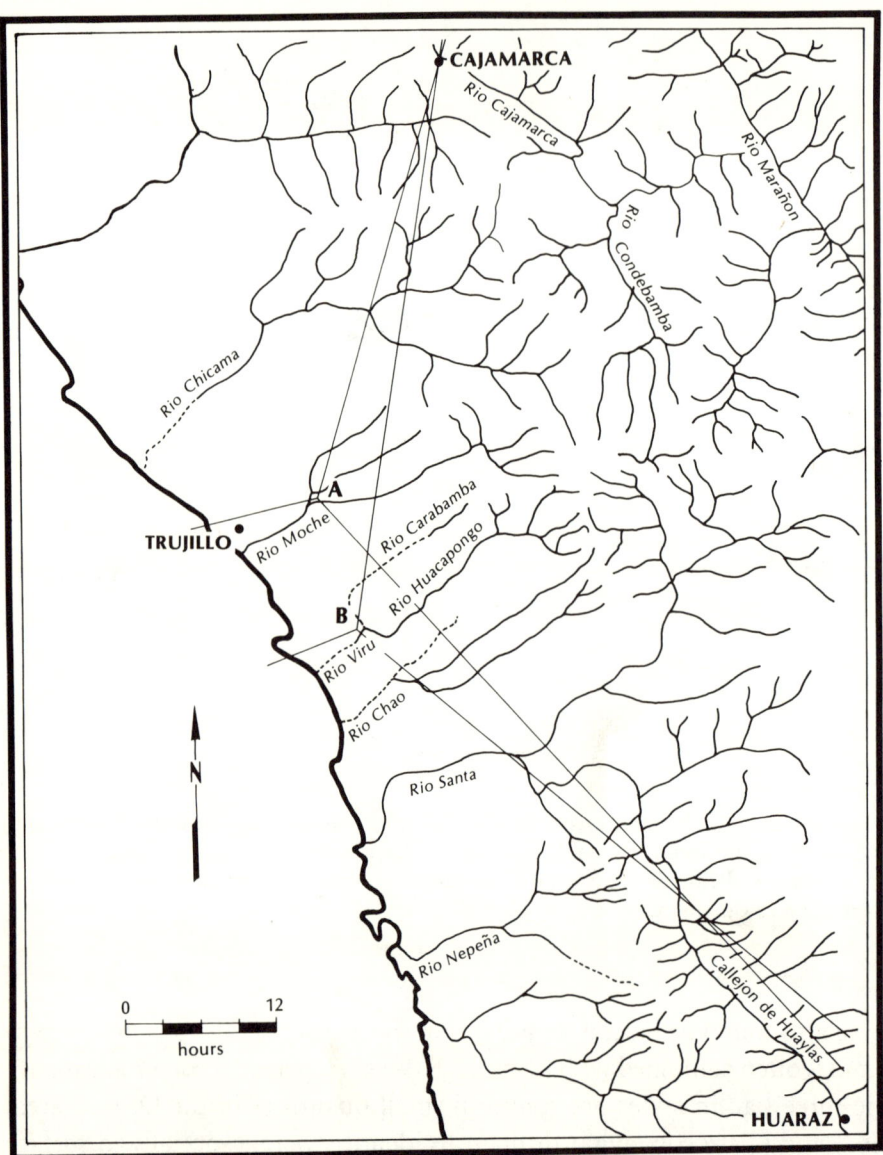

Figure 8.6. Two examples of a minimum distance network connecting three equal centers. Actual routes would not necessarily be straight lines. Evidence, in fact, suggests that in Case A the route from the Callejon de Huaylas would have been located much farther east, passing through Cabana and Santiago de Chuco (see Fig. 8.2). The routes from the lower Moche Valley and Cajamarca would have paralleled the straight lines more closely. All three actual routes were the shortest possible to Cruz Blanca. Evidence indicates that Node B was not used.

254

and Viru Valleys. Moreover, the ramifying drainage pattern maximizes the amount of arable land that can be exploited from the site. The site occupies a steep, rocky slope north of the Rio Moche; there is an elevational difference on the order of 400 meters between the lowest and highest preserved architecture at the site. The site complex extends over 2 square kilometers and consists of several discrete segments.

The main occupation is on the south-facing slopes of the hill, where hundreds of domestic structures constructed on stone-faced terraces have slid downslope. Partially overlapping this occupation is a walled and terraced area with controlled access and a Moche V reoccupation. From these densely occupied lower slopes, a narrow ridge rises to join the main ridge that separates the Moche and La Cuesta drainages. The narrow ridge is blocked by two man-made ditches, cut 2 to 3 meters into the rock. Above the site complex, two small sites of Gallinazo date are located on high points along the main Moche–La Cuesta ridge. These sites command excellent views of the entire area and probably functioned as a watch station and fortress. Both were protected by ditches.

Although the three kaolin styles are found quite frequently in both the densely occupied and fortified areas of Cruz Blanca, they are especially common on ridges adjacent to the densely occupied zone. There is very little architecture, either preserved or destroyed, on the slopes, but small surface collections (12 to 30 sherds) from various sectors contain 20 to 50 percent kaolin sherds. Kaolin materials in general are common enough to suggest that *serranos* were residing at the site. The distinctive buff paste jars from the sierra of Otuzco are uncommon at Cruz Blanca.

Fifteen kilometers downvalley, at Cerro Blanca del León, a second, lesser concentration of kaolin sherds occurs. Again, the sherds are in association with Gallinazo ceramics but are in a cemetery context. Because this site in a quebrada has been almost completely destroyed by flooding and looting, little can be said about the Gallinazo occupation. Both Cerro Blanco del León and Cruz Blanca are located at Moche Valley termini of inland routes linking the Moche and Viru *yungas* zones.

For Cruz Blanca, we have documented the presence of four foreign styles co-occurring with a local variant of a nearby coastal style, at a site in the coast-sierra buffer zone. This situation could be interpreted in several ways, of course. The presence of four foreign styles and their prevalence in the outlying areas of Cruz Blanca make conquest an unlikely explanation. It is clear that some sort of exchange model must be invoked.

Recent discussion of exchange within the Andes have relied heavily on Murra's (1972) model of verticality, which is the most important explanatory model of prehistoric land use in the Andes. The verticality model posits that, given the broken nature of Andean terrain and the need of Andean communities for agricultural products from a variety of altitudinal "floors," it behooves a community to control as many as possible of the zones from which it seeks products. The rationale is that it is more efficient for community members to exchange products through mechanisms of redistribution or reciprocity than to trade for those products in the marketplace.

Murra (1972) documents the model with ethnohistorical examples, the best of which are drawn from the central and southern sierra of Peru. Social anthropologists studying traditional communities in the sierra have found variants of verticality in widely dispersed parts of the sierra (see, for example, Brush 1976, 1977; Custred 1977; Mayer 1977). Archaeologists have also found the model useful for interpreting data from the sierra and from the coast-sierra interface (Dillehay 1979; Topic and Topic 1979).

In an especially lucid article on verticality, Brush (1976:161–63) describes three types of verticality:

1. compressed, in which steep gradients place altitudinal floors so closely that they can be controlled and exploited by a single community;
2. archipelago, where discontinuous spacing of desired resource zones requires a community or ethnic group to colonize "islands" separated from the parent center by several days' walk; at times, several different ethnic groups will share an island's resources,
3. extended, in which the large size and gentle gradients of some valleys require that communities distribute themselves over the entire landscape, specialize in the products of only one or two resource zones, and trade for the products of other zones.

Both Huancayo Alto, the site studied by Dillehay (1979), and Cruz Blanca lie within the *yungas* zone. This zone is especially important because coca can be grown here. The *yungas* zone around Cruz Blanca, in fact, was an important coca-growing area during the late prehistoric period (Rostworowski de Diez Canseco 1973). The verticality model, then, emphasizes the importance of the fact that foreign sherds are found in the *yungas* zone, and the situation at Cruz Blanca could be simply interpreted as a case of multiethnic exploitation of the archipelago type.

In contrast, network models emphasize factors such as distance and scale, the rank of the interacting nodes, and the efficiency of different types of networks. Ecological zonation and topography enter into network models as they affect routing choices and potential rank of individual nodes. In terms of network models, the multiethnic presence at Cruz Blanca is not necessarily related to the site's location in the *yungas*.

The network and verticality models are not mutually exclusive but can be combined to interpret the situation at Cruz Blanca. The presence of ceramics from the Otuzco area, for example, can be viewed as evidence of archipelago or extended verticality, or it can be interpreted as a case of small-scale, point-to-point interaction. Otuzco area ceramics are not confined to Cruz Blanca but occur in a number of smaller sites in both the Moche and Viru *yungas*. This small-scale interaction tends to link nodes of generally similar rank in the *quechua* or *suni* and in the *yungas*. The choice of nodes and the scale of the networks suggest that the purpose of the interaction is the exchange of products from different ecological zones.

Similarly, the presence of Gallinazo ceramics at Cruz Blanca can be interpreted as a sign of either compressed verticality or a node in a hierarchical network of intermediate scale. In the latter case, the presence of fortifications at Cruz Blanca and the site's strategic location—facts which are duplicated at other sites in or along the fringes of the *yungas* in the Viru Valley (Willey 1953)—indicate that the site is located near the end of the network. The Gallinazo presence at Cruz Blanca can be partially explained by a desire to exploit the *yungas* and partially by the strategic advantage of fortifying a few points of access in the middle valleys rather than all sites in the lower valleys.

In these first two cases, interpretations using the network and verticality models are essentially similar. It is much more difficult, however, to see the relevance of verticality in the case of large-scale interaction involving major sierra centers in the Cajamarca and Callejon areas. Sierra centers would certainly have sought to exploit lands in the *yungas* and *chala*, but efficiency would dictate that the closest zones be exploited most intensively. Instead, the evidence indicates that the *yungas* of the distant Moche Valley was the focus of the most intensive interaction. If we consider Cruz Blanca a floating node in a network connecting three equal partners, rather than a trading partner in its own right, the third, coastal, partner is probably either Cerro Oreja (Moche Valley) or the Gallinazo group (Viru Valley). In this case, the correlation of foreign sherds with the *yungas* is de-emphasized, and the purpose of interaction is probably not the exchange of products from different ecological zones.

The inevitability of a floating node in the *yungas* of either Moche or Viru can be demonstrated by generating the shortest set solution to the network design problem. The solution would posit three straight links joined at angles of 120° to form a floating node. It is difficult to specify the exact source area of Style A; therefore, the floating node is first placed over Cruz Blanca, with one link passing through Cajamarca (Fig. 8.6, Node A). The transformed map is used, because it is more representative of real distances than is a standard topographic map. The resulting network adequately serves the lower Moche Valley and the Callejón de Huaylas.

Although the actual routes used would not be straight lines, the hypothetical straight links are guidelines for locating evidence of routes. The coast–Cruz Blanca link is straightforward; not surprisingly, there is Gallinazo material along this route. Because the Cajamarca route lies outside our survey zone, we should not find much pre-Cursive Cajamarca (Style C) material within the zone. In fact, the vast majority of Style B sherds from the survey zone come from Cruz Blanca; they are not present on the coast and are very rare in the Otuzco area. In contrast, sherds in the Callejon style (Styles A and B) are common in the sierra portion of the survey zone, but their distribution on both the north and south banks of the Upper Moche, as well as in the Upper Viru, indicates a major eastward deviation from the idealized route.

This case posits that one node of the three-point network is located in the lower Moche Valley. If the two sierra nodes are unchanged but the coastal node is moved to the Gallinazo group in the lower Viru Valley, the floating node is moved to Castillo de Tomoval (Fig. 8.6, Node B). Such a network would offer advantages to the two sierra partners, because each would have access to three *yungas* areas, as well as the *chala* partner. The data, however, do not support this interpretation. Although classic Recuay pieces are reported from Viru, kaolin sherds are generally uncommon in the valley. Pre-Cursive Cajamarca sherds are not present, and the Callejón bowls are found in the upper *yungas,* but only rarely.

It should be noted that the shortest set solution to the network location problem predicts the presence of a floating node at Cruz Blanca but does not predict the behavior of the node. Clearly Cruz Blanca is operating in different ways at different scales. Most clearly, on the intermediate scale it serves as one of a series of Gallinazo boundary fortifications. In terms of small-scale interactions, Cruz Blanca functions as one of several points that control the permeability of the boundary, and in terms of large-scale interactions, it constitutes a uniquely permeable point.

Conclusion

A complex maze of routes, and therefore the potential for interaction, existed in pre-Hispanic Peru. We have attempted to simplify this situation by generalizing different patterns of interaction in terms of scale. However, the network patterns we discuss at different scales are in fact overlaid, one on top of the other. Any site has the potential for interaction at any scale, and interpretations of intersite relationships must take this fact into account.

As Bilbo used to say, "there was only one Road; that it was like a great river: its springs were at every doorstep, and every path was its tributary.... You step into the Road, and if you don't keep your feet, there is no knowing where you might be swept off to." (Tolkien 1965:110)

Notes

1. This paper is based on fieldwork funded by the Social Sciences and Humanities Research Council of Canada (formerly Canada Council) and by Trent University. Permission for the research was given by the Instituto Nacional de Cultura, Lima.

2. These figures are only approximate and only roughly based on our own experience. They are useful for our purposes here but are not intended to be interpreted as actual travel times. Widely divergent figures have appeared in the literature; compare, for example, Smith (1978) and Flores Ochoa (1977). Ethnohistoric sources may provide useful information on travel times. Susan Ramirez-Horton is amassing figures for northern Peru.

Nine

Deducing Social Organization from Classic Maya Settlement Patterns: A Case Study from the Copan Valley

William L. Fash, Jr., Harvard University

Recent studies of settlement patterns in the Maya lowlands have attempted to elucidate the social organization of pre-Hispanic societies using archaeological data in conjunction with ethnohistoric and ethnographic analogy (Kurjack 1974; Haviland 1977, 1981; Kurjack and Garza 1981; Sanders 1981b; Willey 1981). Now that the Copan pocket of the Copan Valley has been mapped—a project initiated by Gordon R. Willey in 1976 and completed in 1980 by the Proyecto Arqueológico Copan, under the direction of Claude F. Baudez—we can examine the social and political organization of another Classic Period Maya community. In this paper I will attempt to explain the forms of Maya settlement in the Copan Valley, from the level of the individual household to that of the entire community. An intermediate level has been "emically" identified in the Copan pocket. An ethnographic correlation, derived from Wisdom's (1940) work among the nearby Chorti Maya, shows the deep-rooted nature of this type of grouping and can aide interpretation of Copan's social organization.

The Problem

The recent School of American Research Advanced Seminar volume *Lowland Maya Settlement Patterns* (Ashmore 1981) underlines the progress to date in our understanding of ancient Maya social groupings during the Classic Period. Ashmore defined three basic forms, or "levels," of social groups in the archaeological data: the "minimum residential unit," the "group residential unit," and the "cluster." As Sanders (1981a) and Willey (1981) pointed out, however, serious disagreements among the seminar participants arose when the discussion turned to the cluster level of organization. There was no clear consensus on the universality of the cluster or on how these groupings related to each other or to larger polities of which they may have formed a part. How were the minimum residential and group residential household units grouped together? Were these clusters somehow representative of a higher level of social organization? Was there a consistent pattern of clusters? Willey notes: "In seminar discussions, Haviland referred to such clusterings at Tikal as 'multiplaza' (more than one patio group) residential units, stating that each consisted of 8 or 9 groups clustered together and separated by empty spaces from other such clusters" (1981:390). Similarly, Kurjack and Garza (1981) describe the Dzibilchaltun settlement pattern as consisting of concentric zonings, each of which focused on its own architectural nucleus of temple-palace or "special-purpose" buildings. These have been referred to in other regions as "minor (ceremonial) centers." Willey concludes: "The function of these minor or lesser centers remains speculative; however, the hypothesis that they might have been residential complexes of the heads of important lineages, outranked only by the center's high ruler, is supported by Haviland's excavation of one of them at Tikal" (1981:399). Kurjack (1974) and Sanders (1981a) further suggest that the building complexes constituting the core, or "center," of all Maya sites were the residences of the most important lineage heads, in concordance with more recent opinion regarding the secular nature of public buildings in the southern Maya lowlands. Is it possible that this represents another case of "structural replication," with the smaller, outlying multiplaza or concentric groupings merely imitating the patterns of the center? Or, perhaps more to the point, is it the other way around, with the center being merely a lineage cluster writ large? Data from the Copan pocket accord well with the latter view.

The Setting

The fertile Copan Valley represents a marvelous working area for the settlement pattern specialist because it has been cleared of virtually all its mature tropical forest growth by modern agriculturalists (Turner et al., forthcoming). Although rainy-season growth and occasional patches of immature forest present considerable obstacles to mapping, these are miniscule in comparison to the difficulties faced by archaeologists attempting to do systematic surveys in the Peten.

The Rio Copan cuts through a region of rolling hills and mountains, forming a series of small valleys, or pockets (Willey and Leventhal 1979), along its length in western Honduras and eastern Guatemala, before draining into the Rio Motagua just north of Zacapa. From an agricultural point of view, the most ecologically rich and diverse of these small valleys is the Copan pocket. It offers both the largest expanse of river bottomlands (low terraces as well as floodplain) and the most extensive zone of foothills of any of the pockets. This double advantage is bolstered by the fact that the lands of this pocket are both well drained and constantly renewed, a circumstance still recognized and taken advantage of today. The ecological superiority of the Copan pocket is attested by the density of the pre-Columbian settlement there and by the antiquity of its occupation in comparison to the adjacent, less well-endowed pockets of the Copan River drainage system.

From 1975 to 1977, under the aegis of the Peabody Museum, Harvard University, Gordon R. Willey conducted a mapping program in the Copan pocket, combining a general walking survey and intensive mapping. The field mapping and subsequent preliminary analysis were the responsibility of Richard M. Leventhal (1979). In 1978 the Honduran government continued the archaeological investigations in the Copan Valley, with Claude F. Baudez as director and Edward B. Kurjack as principal investigator of the survey. In 1979 mapping was resumed under my leadership, along with the excavation program, which had been initiated by Kurjack. The final map of the 24 square kilometers will be published as part of the report on the first phase of the Honduran project (Fash n.d.a). Further mapping has been undertaken during the second phase of the Honduran government's Proyecto Arqueológico Copan, with William Sanders heading the project and David Webster in charge of the survey. Webster and Sanders are expanding the coverage to include regions outside the Copan pocket, for it has long been Sander's position that regional surveys should be conducted on a much larger scale than has been accomplished in the Maya area to date in order to understand the whole picture of Maya sociopolitical organization.

Willey and Leventhal (1979) identified a series of micro-regions, or "zones," within the Copan pocket, based on the walking surveys and intensive mapping completed in the first two seasons' work. In his examination of the maps (surveyed by Willey, Leventhal, Fash, King, and Wrotenbery), Leventhal (1979) described the settlement patterns within the individual zones. The reader is referred to Willey and Leventhal (1979) for a definition of the zones and to Turner et al. (n.d.) for a more comprehensive treatment of each zone's ecological characteristics. In this paper I will examine both the zones and the emically defined social groupings within them. In general terms, the density of occupation in the different zones is roughly comparable, with the marked exception of Zone I, the modern floodplain that is devoid of archaeological deposits, and Zone II, the low river terrace north of the Copan River. This second zone contains more than one-fourth the total number of mounds within the mapped area, and considerably more than that in terms of the total volume of construction. This is the zone in which the main group, or center, is located, with dense residential settlement to the east, west, and south. Sanders (n.d.) refers to this sector as the "urban core" of Copan and views the remainder of the settlement in the pocket as a notch lower, or more rural (Sanders, personal communication; Sanders and Webster, n.d.). The three remaining zones are more varied ecologically than the first two. The foothill areas or high river terrace sections contain the vast majority of the ancient settlements within these three remaining zones. For a discussion of the relationship of settlements to topographic and ecological areas of the valley, see Fash (n.d.a).

Modern Maya Domestic Groups and Social Organization

> Patrilocal residence and patrilineal inheritance of land ideally construct domestic units each generation that are composed of fathers and their married sons, who live with the fathers in the same houses or in houses in the same compound. And in fact, most Zinacanteco domestic groups are patrilocal extended families living in one or more houses constructed around a common terrace and sharing a single house cross. On the other hand, at any given point in time, many Zinacanteco domestic units are found to be "nuclear" families or combinations of widows and young unmarried sons or even, rarely, matrilocal extended families, again with one or more houses in a compound. (Vogt 1969:128–29)

This passage suggests a model for the "ideal" Maya domestic group, and at the same time shows that deviations from the ideal are not uncommon. Most of the ethnographic studies conducted during the present century have shown that Maya residential groups most commonly consisted of extended families. Where the nuclear family predominates, informants remember with remorse a "better" time when such was not the case (Reina 1967:223). Although the sample is too small to be conclusive, the few ethnohistoric examples also represent extended, rather than nuclear, families (for example, Scholes and Roys, 1948:470–71). The vast majority of the extended families that have been recorded are patrilocal and reckon descent patrilineally.

There has been some discussion as to whether or not the pre-Hispanic Maya reckoned descent exclusively through the male line, and also whether they were predominantly patrilocal. A passage in Landa discussing name reckoning has been interpreted by most authorities (Eggan 1934; Roys 1943; Vogt 1969:152) as indicating that a matrilineal reckoning of descent paralleled the socially more important patrilineal system in Yucatan. Significantly, however, land inheritance and hereditary offices were passed down the male line. Although present to some degree in several modern groups, bilateral descent is the proscribed system only among the Yucatec Maya (Redfield 1941; Villa Rojas 1969a:265). Villa Rojas is convinced that this modern Yucatec system is a bastardized one, and in no way representative of the indigenous form (1969a:265). He bases this judgment on his own work among the Tzeltal of Oxchuc and Cancuc and their system of exogamous patrilineal clans (Villa Rojas 1947). Traces or hints of the existence of patriclans have been encountered among the Tzotzil (Vogt 1969:150; Laughlin 1969:213), at Santiago Chimaltenango (Wagley 1949:14), among the Chol (Villa Rojas 1969b:236), among the Lacandon (Tozzer 1907), and possibly among the Chontal of Acalan (Scholes and Roys 1948:478). There is some variation in the degree to which the clans (or remnants thereof) are localized, but the patrilineages that comprise the larger unit definitely are localized.

The residential pattern of the patrilineal, patrilocal extended families shows many similarities from group to group (Holland 1963:50; Vogt 1969:140–44; Reina 1969:123; Villa Rojas 1969b:216; La Farge 1947:22; Oakes 1951:34; Wagley 1949:11; Redfield 1941:191; Bunzel 1952:28). In addition to the main dwelling, several subsidiary structures have been identified, including sweathouses, corn cribs or granaries, storage houses, kitchens, chicken coops, pigpens, and aviaries (Wauchope 1938; Laughlin 1969:162; Villa Rojas 1969a:257; La Farge and Byers 1931:47). The following description of residences of the Chorti might easily describe communities in other Maya groups:

> With the exception of the few distant milpas which the *aldea* family may own, its house sites and cultivated land form a contiguous area. Trails connect all the households with one another and with the chief household, and a larger trail runs from the latter to the main trail which connects with other families, with other *aldeas,* and with the pueblo.
> The chief household of the (extended) family usually consists of two or three sleeping-houses, a kitchen, several storehouses for maize, vegetables, and agricultural equipment, an altar

house, and the family burial plot. The principal houses and
sheds are set in a rough circle, thus enclosing a central courtyard
which is kept free of weeds and useless shrubs. The whole is
enclosed usually with a fence-like row of tall spiny plants.
(Wisdom 1940:119)

An integral part of these residence groupings is the family shrine, which takes the form of a cross among many modern Maya groups. This cross identifies the members of a patrilineage with a specific plot of land:

> Connected with this is the cult of the ancestral cross, *kurus ko mam* or *ko mam kurus*. This cross, more than any individual, is the center of the family group. Where it has been established—it can never be moved—is the place where the family "is planted," even though it may no longer own that piece of land. Even after such a group has broken up, it will for some time continue to pay respect to the original ancestral cross, which may remain in the former patriarchal house, in the possession of the head of the central, but now smaller, unit; or, if that house has been abandoned, in a specific shelter upon its site.
> Meantime, the heads of subordinate families have made their own house-crosses, to which, in time, antiquity attaches. . . .
> (Wagley 1949:24)

Although the phenomenon of the household cross is widespread, it is by no means universal. Often an altar (which may or may not contain icons or sacred objects of some sort) or shrine structure serves the same purpose, for what is needed is a sacred context in which to make offerings to the ancestors (Bunzel 1952:39). The actual placement of the altar, shrine, or cross varies from group to group. In Zinacantan the cross is placed just outside the door of the patio, an area of some importance in the house plot. In Quintana Roo the cross (and occasionally images of saints) is also kept outside of the house itself, whereas in Chan Kom and other Yucatec communities it is placed on an altar inside the house (Redfield 1941:242). Wauchope (1938) often encountered altars during his survey of modern houses, and they are reported in many communities in the highlands and elsewhere. Among the Lacandon, the "ceremonial hut," purportedly the best construction in the house compound, provides the necessary sacred context for the family group (Duby and Blom 1969:285).

Kin groupings larger than the extended family have been identified at Zinacantan by a series of cross shrines maintained and utilized in periodic ceremonies (Vogt 1969:141–47). Unfortunately, most other Maya groups have not been as carefully studied in terms of the composition and responsibilities of these larger polities. It is possible that equivalents of the *sna* and waterhole groups exist elsewhere. For the present purposes, the most thought-provoking and potentially relevant example of a grouping larger than the extended family is documented by Wisdom among the Chorti Maya of eastern Guatemala and, today, far-western Honduras. This is the social grouping referred to as the *sian otot* ("many houses"), whose Spanish translation is the word *aldea*: "An *aldea* Indian is *ah sian oto*; a small and unimportant *aldea*, or *caserio*, *ut sian oto* or *om-p'ihk e oto tar* ('few houses place'); a large *aldea*, *noh sian otot*, and the *aldea* area, *ta sian otot*, or *sian otot tar* ('many houses place'). The Indian refers to his own *aldea* as *ni sian otot* ('my aldea'), or as *ni tur-tar* ('my place, locality, or neighborhood')" (Wisdom 1940:216, fn. 17).

Some might argue that the *aldea* and town settlements represent impositions of Colonial policy rather than indigenous groupings, yet the turn-of-the-century Chorti may well have been one of the more conservative of Maya tribes. A particularly striking manifestation of this conservatism is that, until 1890, dried cacao seeds were used as a medium of exchange among the Indians in the Jocotan and Olopa markets (Wisom 1940:60–61). Furthermore, the possibility that ancient Copanecos were Chorti speakers (Morley 1920; Thompson 1938, 1970; Wisdom 1940) makes the Chorti data particularly relevant. Bertold Riese (1981, personal communication) has adduced evidence that Copan hieroglyphic writing contains Chorti elements of speech, adding additional archaeological weight to the hypothesis previously derived from ethnohistoric materials. Perhaps most significant, the area occupied by the Chorti, studied by Wisdom, is geographically contiguous with the Copan pocket and in fact, contains the lower reaches of the Copan Valley itself before reaching the Motagua drainage. The environment of the Chorti-occupied region is more xerophytic and rugged than the Copan pocket because it has less rainfall (Turner et al. n.d.). However, the upland nature of this region, with intermittent and permanent stream systems criss-crossing mountains and rolling terrain, is more similar to the environment of the Copan pocket than to the habitats of the other modern Maya groups. Chorti adaptation to such an environment may be very useful as an analogy in the analysis of the foothill and upland sectors of the Copan pocket settlement. In view of these parallels, it seems worthwhile to review Wisdom's (1940) data in some detail:

> Each *aldea*, which is no more than a rural settlement, is made up
> of a number of fairly self-sufficient families, each with its group
> of houses and surrounding milpas, gardens, and orchards. Most
> of the families are of the single-household type, consisting
> usually of a man, his wife, and their own and adopted children;
> but a few are of the multiple-household type, containing the

chief household of the headman and his wife, and the subsidiary households of his married sons and daughters who have remained as members of his family group. These live and work together as a physical, social and economic unit. (p. 18)

Each *aldea* occupies a single geographical area, and it considers all the land and resources within that area as its own. The land is made up of house sites, milpa and garden land, orchards, unused milpa land which may or may not be lying fallow at any given time, and land which is too rough or rocky to be used for any purpose except grazing. There are no actual boundary marks which separate one *aldea* from another, and yet any Indian knows with some accuracy where his own *aldea* ends and the others which surround it begin. Trails sometimes divide them, but not usually. To this area the Indian feels a strong emotional attachment, since he was born within it, most of his friends and relatives live there, and he himself has probably lived there all his life. It is his neighborhood, the habitat of his family and kin, and the area in which his domestic life and productive work go on throughout the year. (p. 216)

Since marriage is most usual among the families of a single *aldea*, most of the people are interrelated by blood or marriage or both. But there are cases of marriages outside, so that each *aldea* has a few individuals brought up in other *aldeas*. . . . (p. 218)

The average *aldea* of Jocatan and Olopa *municipios* contains about twenty-five families, made up of sixty to eighty households, although some are three or four times larger than others. The average population seems to be between two and three hundred individuals. (p. 219)

Within the *aldea*, the families often cluster together in small groups, thus leaving large spaces nearly unoccupied. There is no plan in the *aldea* layout—nothing that could be called streets or a central plaza. The trails connecting the households and families simply wind through them on their way to other *aldeas*, and the families are located as near these trails as possible. (p. 219)

The Archaeological Data

It is my contention that specific social/geographical units akin to the *sian otot (aldea)* groupings of the modern Chorti can be defined among the Late Classic settlements in the Copan pocket. A review of the data on lower level settlements and the valley settlement system as a whole will be presented in order to document this position. Based on the results of intensive excavations of three architectural compounds, or "groups," by the Harvard University–Copan Valley Project and the test-pitting program initiated in 1976 by that project and greatly expanded during the first phase of the Proyector Arqueológico Copan, the ancient structures currently visible in the valley—those recorded on the archaeological map—are probably all Late Classic (Coner phase) in occupation. All of the earlier remains, and even a significant portion of the Late Classic ones, have been obscured by postabandonment soil deposition (Fash 1980). These same excavations have shown that Postclassic occupation in the valley is limited to a few scattered remnants in the Acropolis and nearby groups (Fash and Lane, n.d.). As a result, the visible archaeological remains in the Copan pocket represent the number of settlements in the late part of the Late Classic occupation; the community has been frozen in time. The question of whether all the settlements (that is, residential units or groups, as well as isolated mounds or minimal residential units) were indeed occupied contemporaneously during the Late Classic has not been definitively answered yet. The second-phase excavations of the Proyecto Arqueológico Copan should help provide an answer.

Both the minimum residential unit and the group residential unit are well represented in the Copan Valley settlements, with groups far outnumbering isolated individual mounds. Copan's residential units differ from other Late Classic households in several ways. First, individual house platforms tend to be much smaller at Copan compared with those in other areas of the Maya lowlands, a feature first noticed by Leventhal during his study of the Harvard maps (Leventhal 1981, personal communication). In fact, Ashmore's figure of 20 square meters as an estimate of minimum roofed space might exclude a substantial portion of Copan pocket structures, if this criterion were considered in isolation. The second significant difference between the Copan residential units and those of Seibel or Tikal is that a large percentage of the Copan groups contain more than a single patio, or enclosed space. In fact, many have numerous patios within one agglutinated unit (Fig. 9.1). This phenomenon could be explained in many ways. The most likely explanation is that extended families in Copan were allowed, or perhaps encouraged, to remain together rather than having the married sons establish separate groupings. A second possibility is that the proportion of nonresidential structures at Copan is much higher than at most Maya sites. The third difference is that Copan may be unique in terms of the high proportion of "informal groups," as opposed to "patio groups" (Ashmore 1981:49). It is unclear if this difference is culturally significant or merely the result of slow, unplanned expansion of individual residential units.

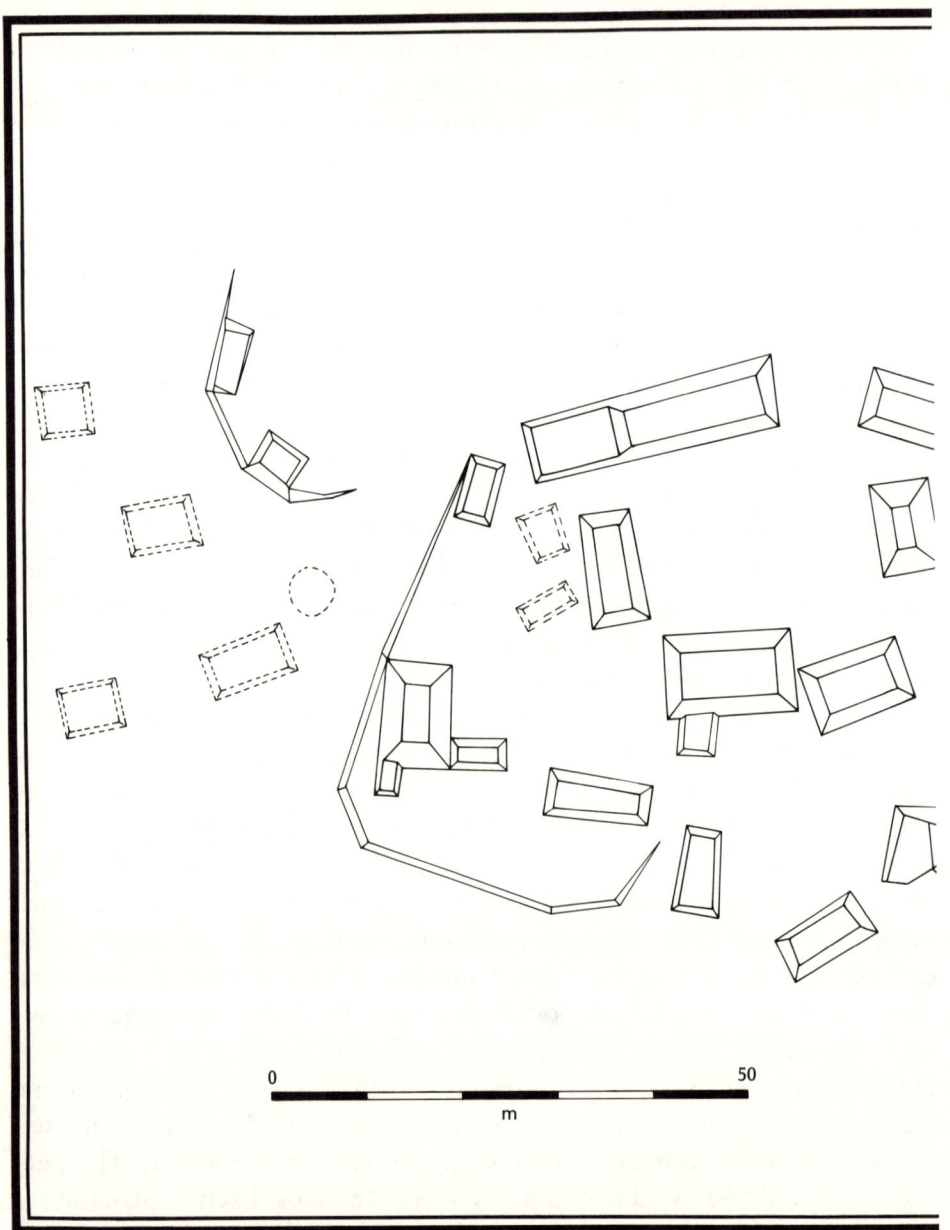

Figure 9.1. Group 11K-11, a Type 2 site in the El Bosque Quadrangle.

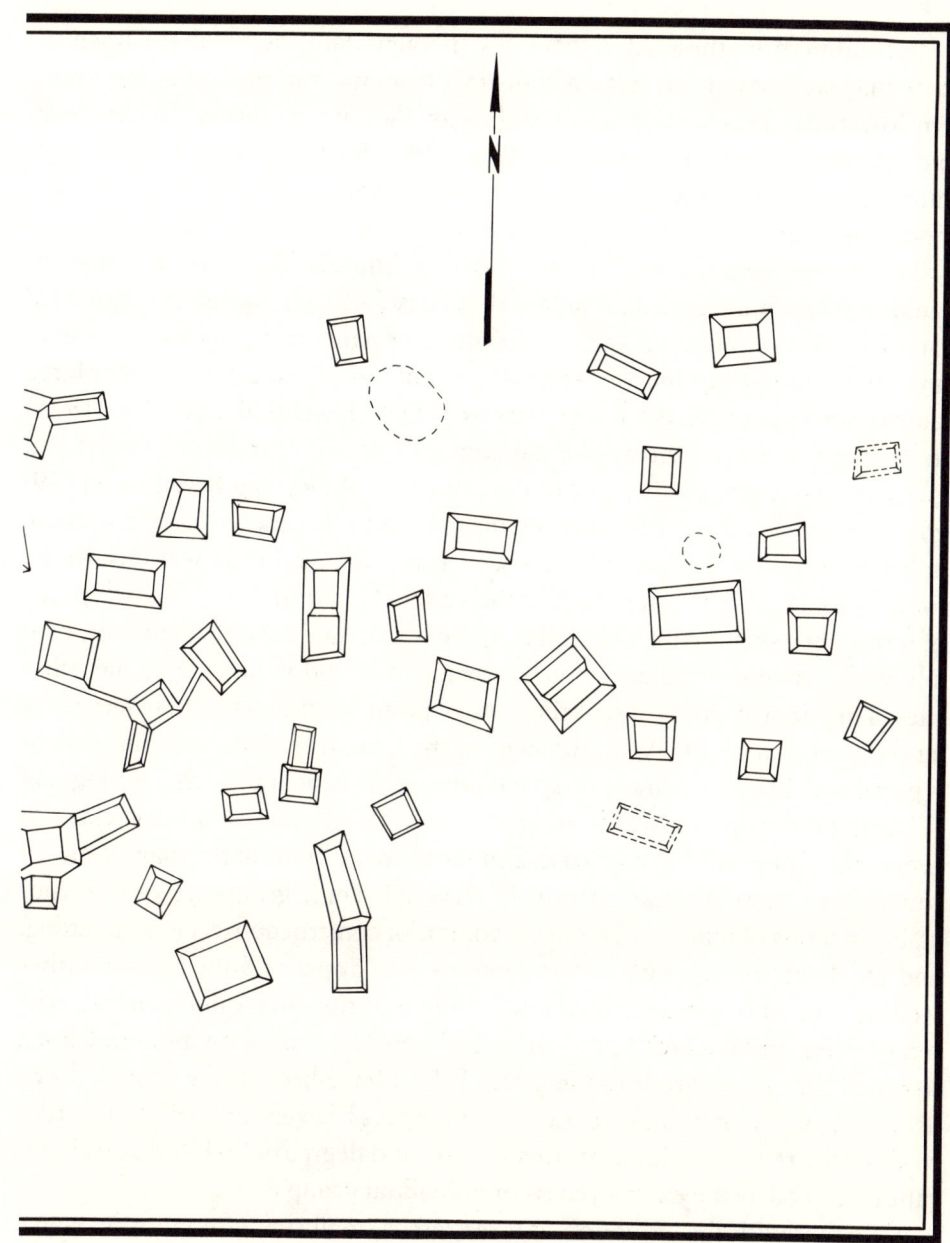

In combination, these differences in settlement data suggest that Copan society may well have been culturally distinct from most of the rest of the southern lowlands. This view accords well with the interpretation derived from hieroglyphic data that the Copan Maya were Chorti speakers. Copan's culture may represent a dialect, as well as a regional, variant of the Classic Period continuum.

Moving up from the level of the individual household, where both nuclear families (minimum residential units—that is, isolated platforms) and extended families (group residential—that is, informal or patio groups) are represented, it is necessary to examine the larger settlement unit, the cluster. A rather large cluster unit was implicitly recognized by Willey, Leventhal, and Fash (1978) in their discussion of the residential zone of Las Sepulturas, with individual groups laid out along either side of the causeway. Willey and Leventhal (1979) go into more detail regarding the organization and content of this sector. Also, in his dissertation, Leventhal discusses clusters, or quebrada sections, in the foothill zones of the eastern half of the valley. He argues that for each patch of terrain between major quebradas, there is a definable settlement unit, usually with a single site that is much larger in size and volume than the other sites. This site would represent the control point for that particular section of land (Leventhal 1979). With the map of the Copan pocket now complete, it is possible to better document these and other settlement units within the region.

During the mapping season of 1979 and 1980, numerous other social and geographic units were recognized, and these are evident on the map of the 24 square kilometers thus far intensively surveyed. These groupings vary considerably in terms of number of mounds, volume of construction, ecological setting, and areal extent, but with two exceptions they appear on the map as rather well-defined and self-contained units.[1] Some of the outstanding characteristics of these units, which I propose to call *sian otot,* based on modern Chorti usage of that term, are listed in Table 9.1.[2] I have broken the groups down according to the typology devised by Willey and Leventhal (1979), in order to show the relative volume of construction and degree of architectural elaboration (as well as the extensiveness of individual groups).

Note that with the exception of three rather small *sian otot* units (Yaragua, El Puente, and Titoror) and three relatively large units (Salamor/Comedero, Las Sepulturas, and El Bosque), all part of the urban core, most of the units contain between 15 and 36 groups, giving an average close to Wisdom's (1940) figure of 25 groups (1940) for modern *sian otot*. In fact, the mean number of groups for the 20 units defined is 27. The estimation of numbers of households per unit is based on the assumption that each Type 1 group represents one household, a Type 2 is two households (or minimally two extended

Deducing Social Organization from Classic Maya Settlement Patterns

Table 9.1. Characteristics of *Sian Otot* Defined for Late Classic Copan Pocket Settlements

Zone Sian Otot	Number of groups	I	Type II	III	IV	Isolated Mounds	Estimated Number of Households
Zone 1 (modern floodplain) No extant archaeological deposits							
Zone 2 (low river terrace north of river, east half of pocket)							
Grupo Principal	"1"		Great Plaza/Acropolis				?
Las Sepulturas	44	22	9	9	4	5	86
El Bosque	55	28	17	4	6	9	102
Zone 3 (foothills north of river, east half of pocket)							
Salamar/Comedero	70	41	22	5	2	19	116
El Pueblo	12+	8+	2+	+	2(+?)	3(+?)	21+
Chorro	47	34	11	2	—	18	71
Rastrojon	24	21	3	—	—	14	34
Mesa de Petapilla	36	25	9	2		10	54
Bolsa de Petapilla	17	13	4	—	—	12	27
Plan del Moro	17	14	3	—	—	3	21
Titoror	7	7	—	—	—	4	9
Zone 4 (foothills, high and low river terraces south of river, east half of pocket)							
San Lucas	20	16	4	—	—	7	27
San Rafael	36	34	2	—	—	20	40
Titichon	31	27	4	—	—	29	49
El Puente	11	10	1	—	—	4	14
Zone 5 (west half of pocket)							
Algodonal	15	14	—	1	—	9	21
Estanzuela	24	19	4	1	—	3	31
Tapescos	15	14	1	—	—	14	23
Rincón del Buey	15	13	2	—	—	4	19
Ostuman	25	19	3	2	1	9	39
Yaragua	11	10	1	—	—	2	13

families), a Type 3 is three households (nuclear families), and a Type 4, four households. This represents a considerable over-simplification, especially when considering the occasional Type 4 with very few structures (Fig. 9.2) or the Type 1 or 2 with multiple plaza arrangements (Fig. 9.1). In the Bosque and Las Sepulturas sectors, this method definitely underrepresents the total number of households. However, it may be useful as a working model of the situation.

The limited excavation data for isolated mounds have not, as yet, yielded definitive answers as to whether these buildings were full-time residences, part-time residences (field houses used during the growing season by men whose actual residence was at a considerable distance from the *milpa*—such structures are in use today in the Copan Valley), or storehouses with no residential functions. As a result, I have arbitrarily halved the number of isolated

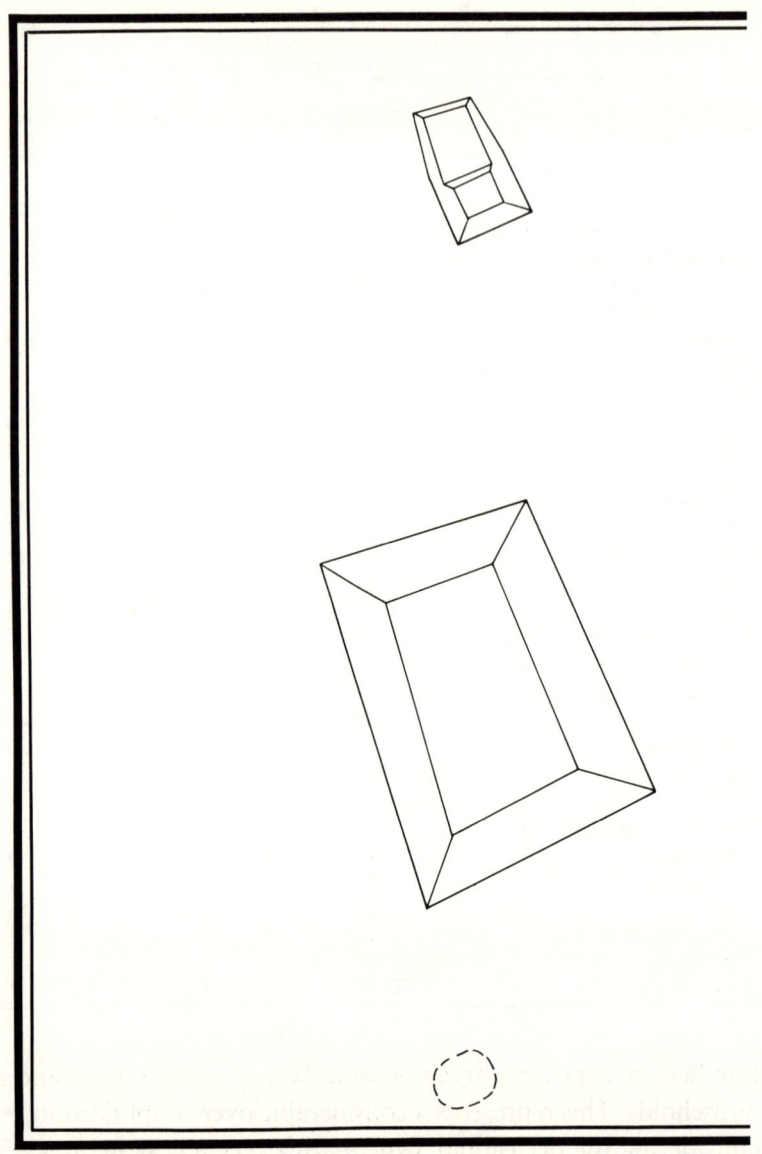

Figure 9.2. Group 10K-4, a Type 4 site in the Grupo Principal Quadrangle.

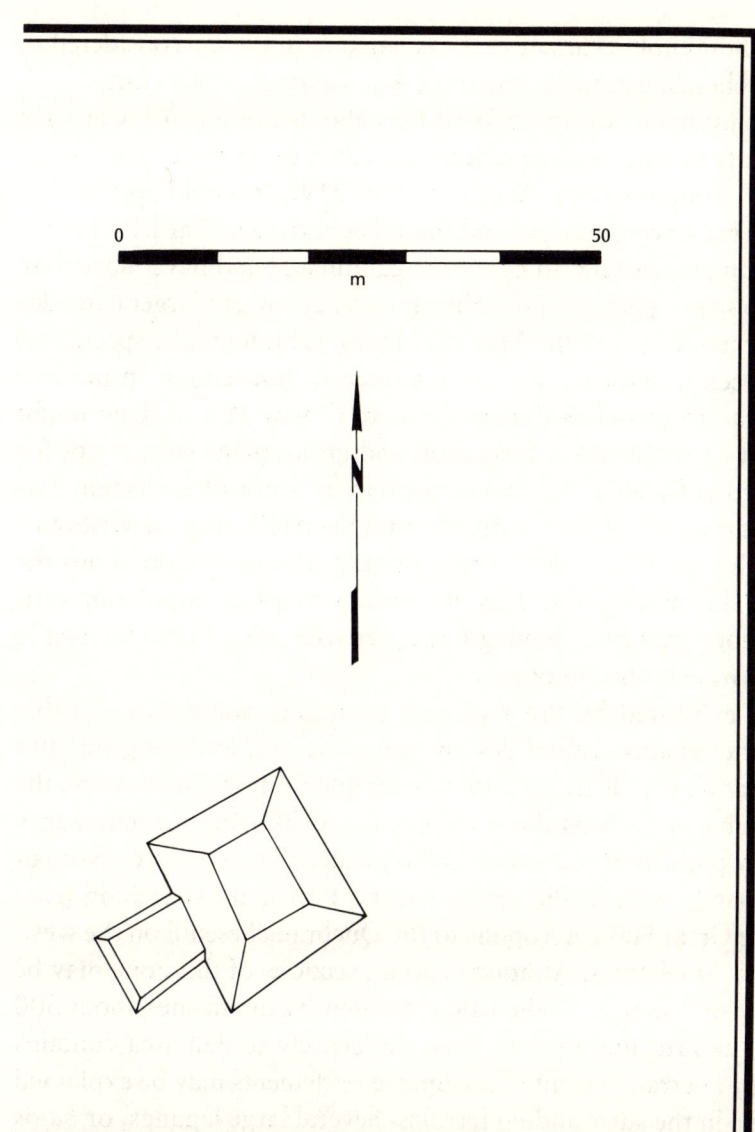

mounds for the household estimates—17 isolated mounds are considered to represent 8 households, 8 mounds represent 4 households, and so forth.

Note that my estimates of numbers of households are much lower than Wisdom's estimate for the modern *aldeas:* a median of 43 for Copan versus 60 to 80 for the modern Chorti (Wisdom 1940:219). It would appear that my estimates are rather conservative and should be revised upward. As I noted earlier, the Copan groups tend to be more agglutinated and have more than one shared patio space, perhaps indicating a tendency toward larger extended family units than elsewhere in the Maya lowlands. Or it might be speculated that there has been a tendency for more numerous households in modern Chorti residential groups than during the Late Classic Period. One might bemoan the lack of settlement information and group plans were it not for the fact that Gordon R. Willey's breakthrough in the study of settlement patterns did not occur until well over a decade after the publication of Wisdom's monograph. Although it provides a great amount of information about the modern Chorti, this monograph does not include maps or population estimates of the Chorti *sian otot,* having been prepared prior to the interest in settlement patterns in anthropology.

The patterns exhibited by the *sian otot* groupings show considerable variability, as I noted above. Brief descriptions of several of these groupings will make this variability clear. To take an example from the urban core, the El Bosque grouping is perhaps the most populated (though not necessarily the most *densely* populated) *sian otot* in the pocket (Fig. 9.3). It consists of the area immediately west of the center (Grupo Principal), stretching from the border of the Great Plaza/Acropolis to the Quebrada Sesemil on the west, an area of about 50 hectares. Although certain sections of this zone may be the most densely settled areas in the valley, the density diminishes about 300 meters west of the Principal Group. Even the densely settled area contains several seemingly aberrant vacant areas. Sparse settlements may be explained by poor drainage in the surrounding terrains. Several large lagunas, or *bajos* (seasonal swamps), exist in the densely settled area, and vast stretches of the western section of this unit, near the Quebrada Sesemil, are swampy even in the dry season. Although it contains the largest number of Type 4 sites of any of the *sian otot,* the El Bosque sector may be less prestigious than the grouping of Las Sepulturas, because the proportion of Type 1 and 2 households is far greater in El Bosque than in the latter area. Also, the breakdown of sites is more gradual and even in Las Sepulturas than in the El Bosque grouping.

Whereas the El Bosque *sian otot* is entirely confined to the low river terrace north of the Rio Copan, the Mesa de Petapilla is restricted to a relatively level sector of the foothills in the northeastern section of the valley (Fig. 9.4). This

Deducing Social Organization from Classic Maya Settlement Patterns 277

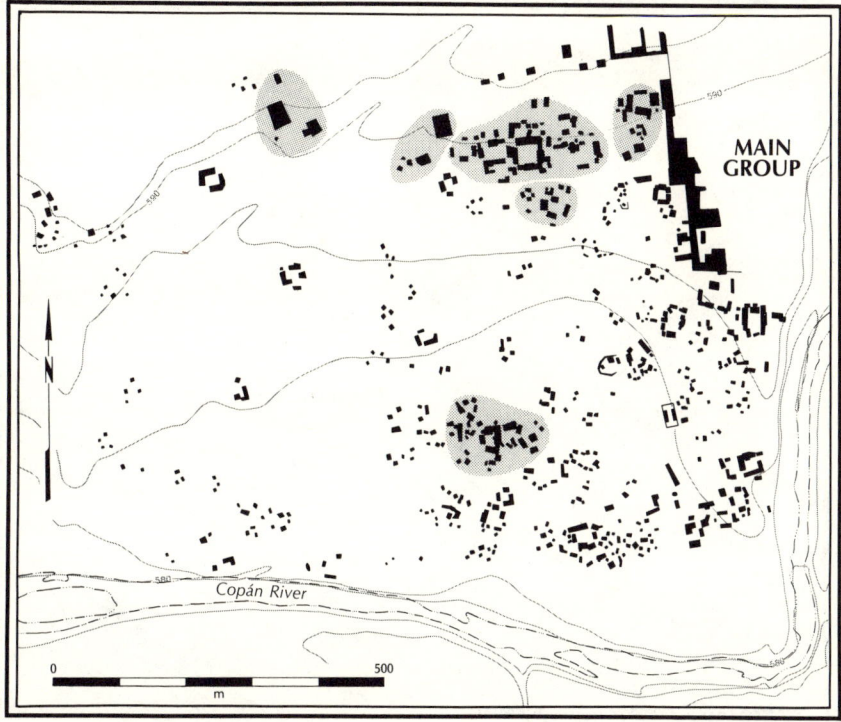

Figure 9.3. Map of the El Bosque *sian otot*. Type 4 sites are marked by stippling.

is one of the larger outlying *sian otot* in the pocket and an example, *par excellence,* of Leventhal's quebrada section (1979). This grouping is clearly demarcated by the Quebrada Seca on the west side, the Quebrada Petapilla on the east, and a steep dropoff to the river below on the south. The northern limit is marked by a steep hill, which divides this grouping from the intermontaine pocket and Bolsa de Petapilla *sian otot* to the north. The breakdown of sites by type shows a rather gentle gradation from small to large (25 Type 1, 9 Type 2s, and 2 Type 3). Of special interest is the fact that the two Type 3 sites are within 250 meters of each other, with no settlement between them, as if they were meant to stand out from the other residential units.

Unlike the Mesa de Petapilla grouping, which is between two major watercourses (Fig. 9.5), the *sian otot* of Titichon straddles a major quebrada. Here

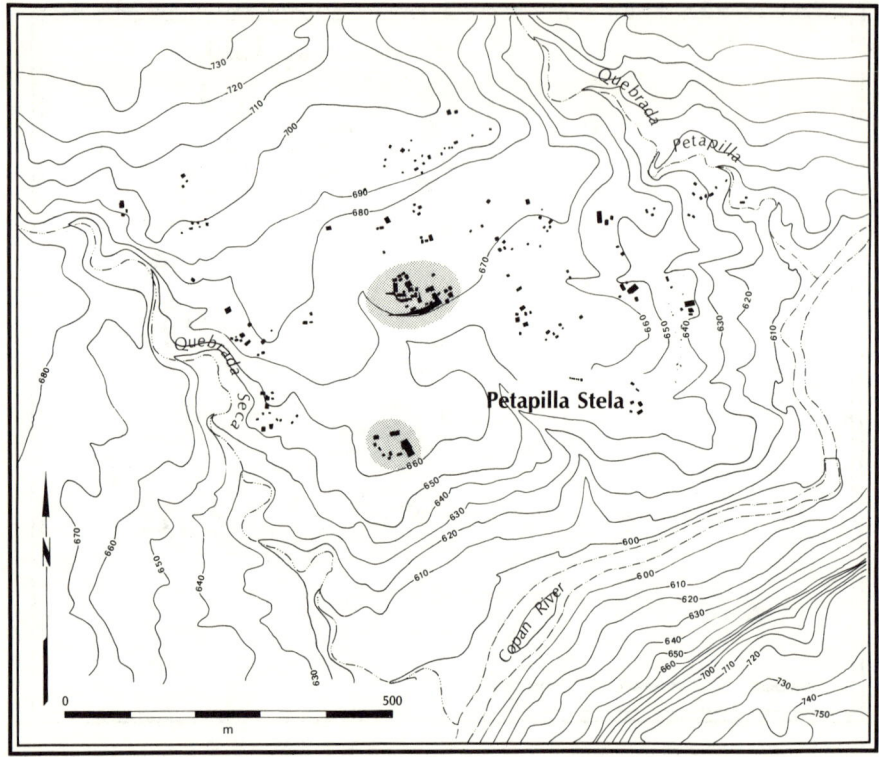

Figure 9.4. Map of Mesa de Petapilla *sian otot*. The two Type 3 sites are marked by shading.

the terrain ranges from rugged, mountainous areas on the north and east sides to a fairly substantial tract of river bottomland, or *vega*, at its far northern end. This layout brings to mind the ideal pattern for *sian otot* described by Wisdom:

> *Aldeas* are often located on the side of a hill which has a large stream, varying in width through the year from a few inches to eight or ten feet, running through the narrow valley below it. On both sides of it are the family sites, each from a hundred yards to a half-mile from its nearest neighbor, the former distance being the more usual. The land between the family milpas is usually rough and precipitous and often too rocky for cultivation. (Wisdom 1940:218)

Deducing Social Organization from Classic Maya Settlement Patterns

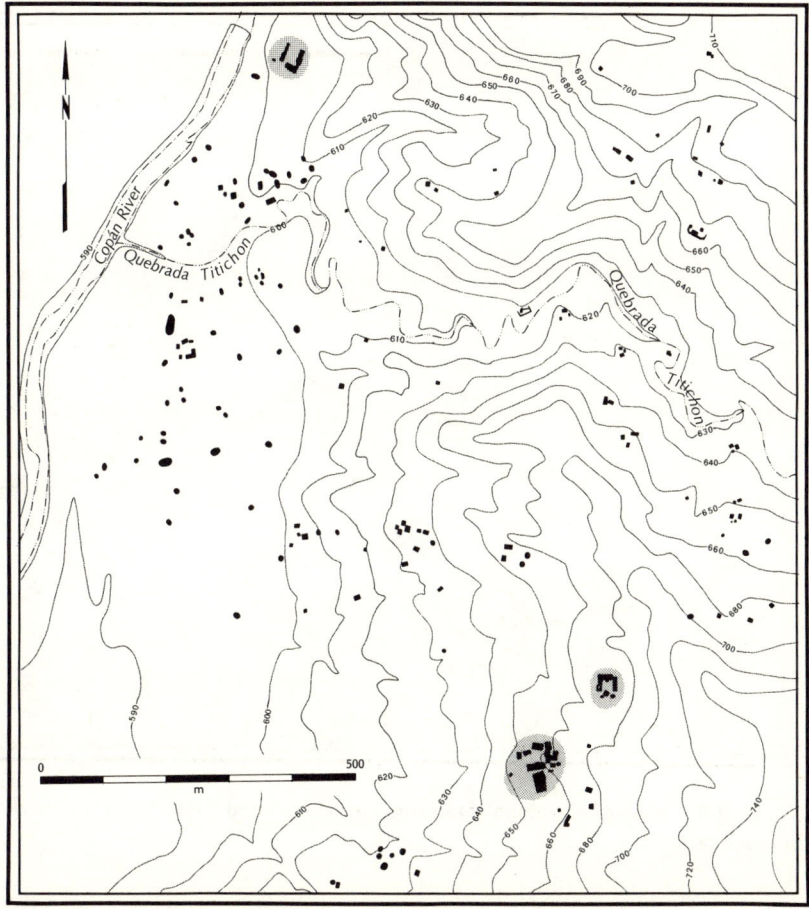

Figure 9.5. Map of Titichon *sian otot*. The Type 2 sites are marked by shading.

The sites in the Titichon grouping are generally on the smaller end of the typology. In fact, there is nothing larger than a Type 2 site in this or any other *sian otot* in the area south of the river, in the pocket's eastern half (Zone 4). Again, however, we find the phenomenon of a pair of large (in this case, fairly impressive Type 2) sites on the southeastern edge of the *sian otot*.

The intermontaine pocket of Ostuman contains a moderate number of sites, but is distinguished by three rather large sites (one Type 4 and two Type 3). The settlements are primarily located in the bottomlands of the small pocket, the richest agricultural land in the area (Fig. 9.6). This is analogous to the situation in Zone 2 (the bottomlands north of the river in the eastern half of the pocket), where the extent and richness of the agricultural land initially drew people to the area. However, attraction eventually became more social

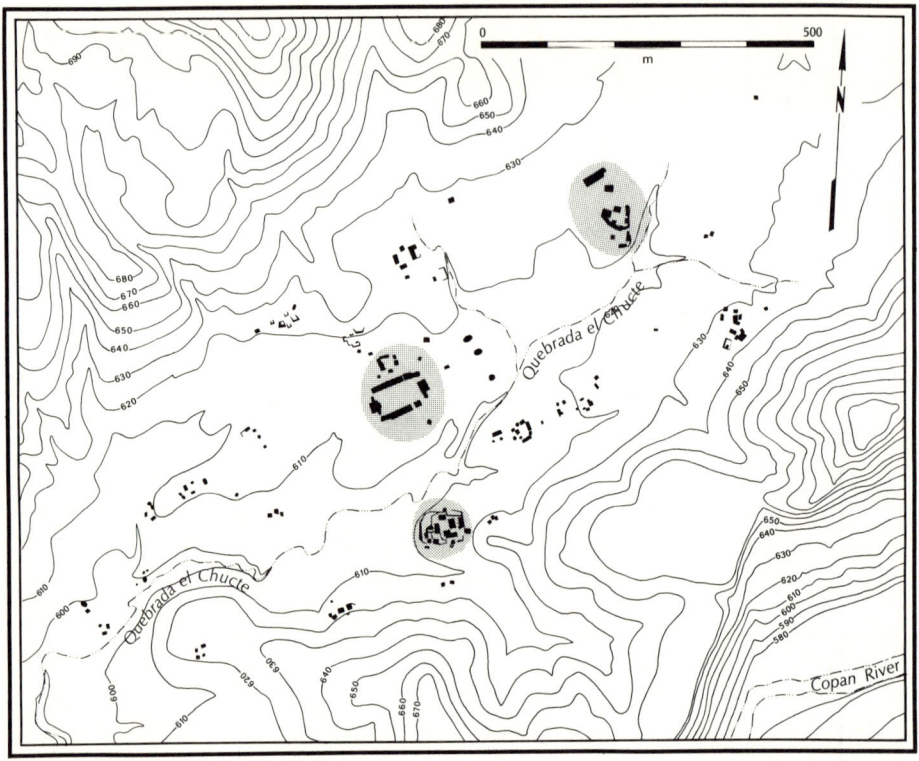

Figure 9.6. Map of Ostuman *sian otot*. The Type 3 and Type 4 sites are marked by shading.

and political as the land available for cultivation was diminished (Sanders and Webster, n.d.). In Ostuman the size and extent of the large constructions indicate a fairly long occupation at the three large sites. Because of the increasing importance and drawing power of these sites, they were built in close proximity, despite the cost in terms of loss of productive agricultural land. One of the Type 3 sites lies at the eastern extremity of the social/geographic unit, and the other is situated within 200 meters of the largest site in the western end of the valley, the Type 4 main group of Ostuman. As with the Mesa de Petapilla and Titichon examples, there is virtually nothing in the way of visible settlement between these two groups, and their pairing is made all the more obvious as a result. What is the meaning of this pattern?

Again, we have a provocative datum from Wisdom's (1940) monograph:

> It has been stated that the family is the unit which arranges the marriage of its members to the members of another family in its *aldea*. Usually, only two families intermarry, the children of the one tending to marry the children of the same generation level in the other, but there are many exceptions to this rule. (p. 253)
>
> The system of kin classification is consistent with and can best be understood in connection with the Chorti preferential marriage system. Whether or not it may have been based upon a cross-cousin marriage institution of the past, now prohibited as incest, the kinship system today fits the preferred marriage based on sibling and cousin exchange better than it would one based on cousin marriage. (p. 266)

Could it be that this pairing of large sites is the physical representation of another kind of pairing or bond, namely, that between two extended families that tend to intermarry? If so, the large sites could represent the residences of the oldest segments of the family, with the families that broke off occupying the groups scattered through the rest of the *sian otot*. As Leventhal (1983) indicates, these large sites presumably contained the most important lineage shrines for their respective sections of the valley (that is, *sian otot*), adding to their importance not only within their respective areas, but for the valley (pocket) community as a whole.

Given this hypothesis for the largest sites within individual sectors or *sian otot*, some data obtained from the testing of these sites is of particular interest. As part of the sampling program of the first phase of the Honduran Proyecto Arqueológico Copan, all of the larger sites were tested through limited excavations for longevity (both individually and as a corpus) vis-à-vis the other visible (mound) sites in the pocket (Fash 1980; n.d.b). The large sites tested in the bottomlands all had remains dating to the Middle Classic and in most cases to earlier periods, whereas the large sites in the outlying areas (including in the sample the sites tested as part of the Harvard test-pitting program) were exclusively Late Classic (Coner Phase). Thus, although the bottomland sites developed accretionally through time, the outlying area's large sites were relatively late phenomena. This is in fact consistent with the settlement history of the valley as a whole, in that the bottomlands seem to have been occupied first. These bottomlands were the most densely occupied area in the valley during all periods for which we presently have evidence. Following the bottomlands, the foothills north of the river were the next most favored zone for settlement through time. During the Late Classic, the foothills, including the spur of land on which the modern village now sits, were densely occupied. Finally, the foothills south of the river add the bottomlands of Ostuman were the last to be intensively occupied.

Accepting, as a working hypothesis, the idea that a feudal model is the best explanation for the distribution and form of the Late Classic settlement in the Copan pocket (Leventhal 1979, 1981; Leventhal and Fash 1981), this information on longevity of site and zone occupation can be used to predict shifts in land usage from intensive agricultural activity to residential terrain. For example, during the Coner phase, the richest sector of the valley, from the point of view of agricultural productivity (the bottomlands of the eastern half of the pocket, north of the river), was no longer available for extensive cropping, because most of the area was taken up by residences. It was at this earlier time that extensive cropping had to shift up into the foothills, intermontane pockets, and perhaps even outside the pocket itself, in response to increasing demographic pressure. Of considerable interest from this perspective is whether there was a deliberate colonization of these outlying areas in (and outside?) the pocket, or whether their growth was simply the result of the same factors producing notable population increases in the bottomlands. These two processes could produce significantly different results in terms of the societal make-up of the individual *sian otot*. The first process might result in more diversified subcommunities and the latter probably in more homogeneous groupings, where the majority of the families could be traced to two or more lineages that first colonized that particular pocket sector. I believe that the latter is the more likely possibility, except in large *sian otot,* such as Mesa de Petapilla.

Of course, the bottomlands of the eastern half of the pocket were much more complex than any of the outlying sectors in terms of social/lineage composition. Again, the layout and constituent parts of this sector may provide clues as to what kinds of groupings are represented, and how these are organized. A starting point for this analysis is to ask how communication flow was organized in the central, largest settlement zone in the pocket. The Las Sepulturas *sacbe*, first mapped by Robert Burgh as part of the Carnegie Institution of Washington's investigations at Copan (see Longyear 1952:fig. 1) but not described or otherwise noted until the Harvard University–Copan Valley Project (Willey, Leventhal, and Fash 1978: Willey and Leventhal 1979), is clearly the main artery of communication between this residential sector and the main group, or center. Recent excavations have revealed that the *sacbe* continues directly into the main group, and intersecting it at or near Stela J, just south of Structure 3 of the Carnegie map (Structure 10L-3 on the Harvard and Proyecto Arqueológico Copan maps). At the opposite (eastern) end of the Sepulturas *sacbe* is the large Type 4 residential compound Group 8N-11 (CV-68 in Willey and Leventhal 1979; Willey, Leventhal, and Fash 1978), with the *sacbe* apparently leading up to the site and terminating at that locus.

Although not very large or massive in terms of bulk (the majority of the *sacbe* stands only 50 centimeters above the surrounding ground level) compared to other causeways in the Maya area (such as those of Tikal, Coba, and other sites in the northern plains), the Sepulturas *sacbe* nonetheless was significant within its own area not only in terms of the connection with the main group, but also in terms of the numerous "side *sacbes*" that connected the individual residential compounds of this sector to the causeway, and thus to each other (Willey, Leventhal, and Fash 1978).

Another *sacbe*, encountered in the Comedero sector of the valley, was subjected to preliminary test excavations. Located just west of another Type 4 site, Group 9J-5 (CV-177), this *sacbe* apparently abuts directly against a large hill, locally known as "Cerro Chino." A small, dispersed site stands atop the unusually flat summit of this hill, which presumably must have had some ritual importance for the Maya, given this *(sacbe)* connection. The southern limits of the Comedero *sacbe* were not well defined during the preliminary excavations, and the possibility remains that some connection exists between this foothill section of causeway and the main group in the bottomlands below. The reasons for this assumption are numerous. There is a long, level stretch of land immediately south of the southern (mapped) limit of the Comedero *sacbe*, which is still used by modern campesinos as a walkway. This stretch terminates at the locus of the large Type 4 site of Group 10K-7, known to have a sculpted hieroglyphic bench panel dating to the reign of the last Copanec king. The path southeastward from this site toward the main group (a path still followed by thousands of mostly non-Maya pilgrims each year) passes next to two other Type 4 sites (Fig. 9.3) before leading into the great plaza area exactly opposite the entrance to the main group from the Sepulturas *sacbe* (Fig. 9.7). This symmetry is intriguing, particularly if one views the modern walking trails and path of Type 4 sites as evidence of an ancient artery in the exact same locus as the modern one. There is a remarkable similarity in the layout and length of this western communication route with that of the Sepulturas *sacbe*. Both extend approximately one kilometer from the main group, and both bend slightly northward rather than being perfectly linear. The fact that both end at or next to Type 4 sites is of added interest considering that yet another Type 4 site, Group 8L-12, is also located at a 1 kilometer radius from the center of the main group. (Not coincidentally, this central point in the Main Group coincides almost exactly with the location of the main ball court.) It would appear that the Maya again have provided us with an emic definition of the maximum extent of their core area, 1 kilometer from the geographic (and perhaps ritual) center of the main group. How deliberate this phenomenon is—an extreme view would see the 1 kilometer distant Type

Figure 9.7. Map of proposed limits of Copan urban core, showing the Sepulturas and Comedero *saches*. The proposed extension of the Comedero *sache* is delineated by a dashed line.

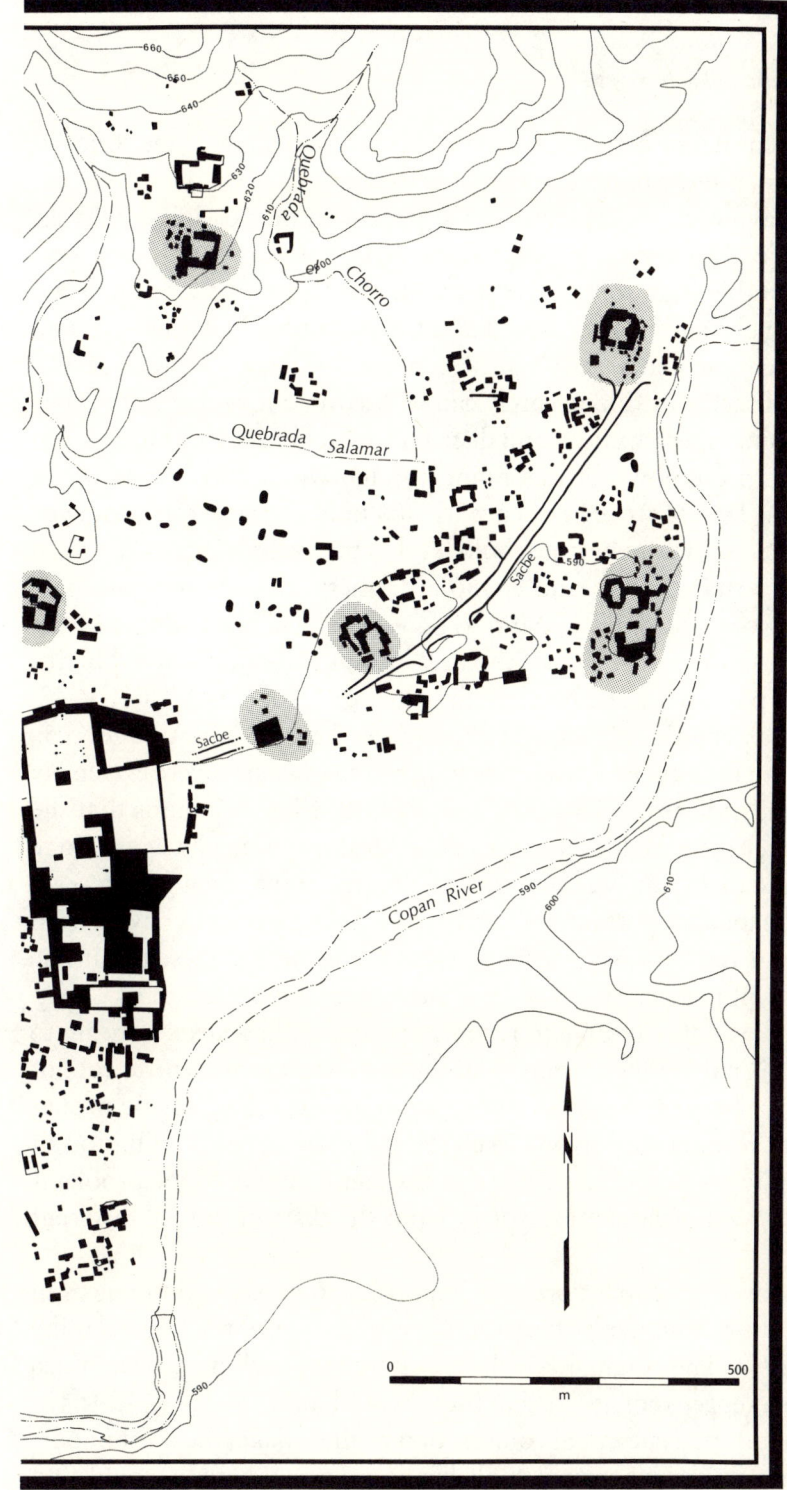

4 sites as representing the east, north, and south cardinal limits of the zone—is open to question, but the pattern undeniably exists.

Given these layout characteristics, one is faced with the possibility that the *sian otot* units of El Bosque, Salamar/Comedero, and Las Sepulturas were but one rung on the organizational scale, with all three plus the main group representing a single unit. If (and I would take this as a rather large qualification) one can consider Zaculeu a "city" in Mesoamerican terms (Marcus 1983), then this central sector of Copan surely can be accorded the same status. The degree of economic specialization and distribution of lineages within this sector is virtually an unknown at this point, though we do have some initial impressions. The lack of strong evidence for any kind of marketplace or even economic specialization on the household level in the excavations undertaken to date suggests that market and economic functions were not the most important functions of Copan, as Marcus notes for the majority of the Mesoamerican cities. On the other hand, the presence of elaborate, carved hieroglyphic bench panels, or thrones, at the sites of Group 9M-18 (CV-43; Willey, Leventhal, and Fash 1978) and 9N-8 (Fash, Agurcia, and Abrams, n.d.) indicates that ritual or actual lineage ties to the ruling dynasty were extremely important status indicators. This is in keeping with Marcus's thesis that the most important element in the definition of the Mesoamerican city was "where the king is." In Copan, during the Late Classic, ties to the royal family seem to have been the most important "in" an individual lineage could have. Given the propensity of the Coner phase Copanecos for recording these ties in the form of hieroglyphic inscriptions at even such an unimposing site as Group 9M-18 (CV-43), we may be able to recover enough of these texts to begin to interpret the internal layout of individual lineages within this central core of the city. Until we have such textual information, however, we should probably not attempt to infer this layout solely on the basis of the distribution of sites of varying types (see Chang 1983 for another example of the problems of identifying social organization solely from the distribution of different size groups).

On another level of abstraction, it is important to note the differences in density and internal complexity between the core and even the largest of the outlying *sian otot*. The original Pueblo grouping may well have been much larger than the meager remains at that locus would indicate. (The oldest villagers recall that during the initial colonization of the village, the most important factor determining where one built his house was where he could find space between the mounds that covered the entire area.) However, it is doubtful that this group matched the magnitude of either the Las Sepulturas or El Bosque *sian otot*. Had Copan survived another century, however, the urban core of Copan might have included a much larger area and several of the other *sian otot*. The Chorro grouping, for example, was well on its way to being included within the core in terms of both the density and magnitude of its residential groups. Recall Willey's words in this regard: "On the simplest interpretive level, this settlement scene looks like a stage in a process of urbanization, with available outlying living space gradually being filled up by expanding populations" (1981:397).

Why was this process of urbanization not continued to its logical conclusion? The reason for the collapse at Copan, and the form it took, may never be understood in its entirety, and in any case it is beyond the scope of this paper. However, what the Maya themselves had to say about the subject may offer some valuable leads. I refer to the hieroglyphic inscriptions dealing with Copan's political alliances toward the end of its Classic Period apogee. The most famous (and hotly debated) textual references on the subject are the so-called capture clauses at the site of Quirigua. Proskouriakoff (1973:168), Marcus (1976), and Sharer (1978a) interpret this as a statement that the Quirigua dynast "Two-Legged Sky" or "Cauac Sky" captured the contemporary Copan dynast 18 Jog (or Rabbit) and declared himself and his center sovereign as of that date. Riese (personal communication) is less convinced and points to other alternatives, based on his readings in key clauses in Copan's Hieroglyphic Stairway and other inscriptions. In any case, Quirigua does seem to go its own way as of that point in time (Sharer and Jones 1980), or at least show some independence on the symbolic level (for example, its own emblem; see Marcus 1976). It is possible that the same sort of breaking-away process was occuring on a local level at the site of La Canteada (Morley's Rio Amarillo), according to at least one student (Pahl 1977). If, as has been suggested here and elsewhere (Vlcek and Fash 1980), Copan was exceeding the subsistence base possible within the confines of the Copan pocket during the later part of the Coner phase, these ties to the outside may have been critical to the Copan state, particularly as the population grew. The severing of relations within the region and especially within its own valley system may have been the straw that broke the camel's back. More dependence on political ties rather than self-sufficiency made for a more "hyper-coherent" system, to use Flannery's (1968) term. Other factors, currently unknown or poorly understood, probably also figured in the breakdown of Copan's Late Classic system. Here we are reminded of Gordon Willey's thoughs on the subject: "The fill story of the Maya decline has not yet been told; but, in one sense, it might be considered as a failure in adaptation to the full urban order" (1974:141). The case of Copan fully accords with this interpretation.

Notes

1. Two exceptions are sections located south of the river.
2. Note that parts of several communities fall outside our grid of the 24 square kilometers and thus do not appear in Table 9.1. Other such units can be defined outside the Copan pocket as well.

Ten

From Maritime Chiefdom to Agricultural State in Formative Coastal Peru

Robert A. Feldman, Field Museum of Natural History

One of the outstanding characteristics of Gordon R. Willey's scholarly career is his willingness to consider new data and their implications for his work. In contrast to some of his contemporaries, Willey is not afraid to admit that some of his past interpretations are no longer supported by recent findings. However, instead of simply shifting to accommodate the new data, he assimilates them and reaches a new understanding of the events of prehistory.

So it was with his work at Aspero. As part of the Institute of Andean Research's coastal survey, Willey, along with John M. Corbett and Marshall T. Newman, conducted excavations in late 1941 at several sites in the Puerto de Supe area (Willey and Corbett 1954). These excavations were designed to expand on the work done by Max Uhle in 1905 (Uhle 1925). Uhle had discovered an early pottery-using culture, which Tello (1943) subsequently showed to be related to the Chavin tradition. Willey sought to obtain information on the stratigraphic position and relationships of the Early Supe pottery.

Willey was able to obtain stratigraphic samples of pottery from two sites near Puerto de Supe—the Lighthouse site and Li-31—and to define their temporal position. However, the work at the Aspero midden was not as successful: no pottery and very few artifacts were found.

Aspero presented a problem. It could not comfortably be lumped with Li-31 and the Lighthouse site as part of the "Early Supe Culture," yet it could not be linked to another period or culture. At the time of Willey's work at Aspero, there was no clear conception of a preceramic period in Peru (Moseley and Willey 1973). Aspero was caught in this theoretical gap (viz., Bennet 1946:88–91).

Aspero could not be satisfactorily interpreted until 1971, when Willey, accompanied by Michael Moseley, revisited the site. In the intervening time, Bird (1948), Wendt (1964), and Engel (1967), among others, had identified and defined a coastal preceramic culture capable of producing monumental architecture. Having just visited Wendt's old excavations at Rio Seco de Leon, Willey realized that the "hillocks" at Aspero (Willey and Corbett 1954:22) were actually artificial mounds (Moseley and Willey 1973:455).

Willey recognized the gap in his earlier work and thus promoted my 1973–1974 re-excavation of Aspero, which sought to define the nature of the artificial mounds and to gather data on the subsistence base of the society that built them. The excavations have been described at length elsewhere (Feldman 1980); in this paper I will concentrate on analyzing and interpreting the results of the excavations.

Excavations were undertaken at three sites: Aspero, Li-31, and As8 (Fig. 10.1). The latter site, located about 1 kilometer inland from Aspero, is the oldest of the three. A piece of gourd rind found near the middle of its depth (the 99–117 centimeter level) yielded a radiocarbon date of 6085 ± 180 B.P. (Table 10.1); using the method of Damon et al. (1974), this corrects to 4964 ± 190 B.C. Six radiocarbon dates from Aspero place its upper levels between 4360 ± 175 B.P. and 3950 ± 150 B.P. (uncorrected). The site Li-31 is an Early Horizon midden located immediately inland from Aspero. No radiocarbon dates were obtained from Li-31, but on the basis of its pottery it should date to no earlier than 3000 B.P., or more likely to about 2500 B.P.

One additional preceramic site, Piedra Parada, was examined but not excavated. It is located about 7.5 kilometers from Aspero, on the southern margin of the Supe Valley, 2.5 kilometers inland. On the basis of its architecture and textiles, Piedra Parada should date to late in the preceramic period, or about 3750 B.P.

Subsistence

Food remains from excavations at Aspero and two nearby sites were collected and analyzed (Feldman 1980). One of these sites, As8, precedes Aspero by some 2,000 years, and the other, Li-31, follows it by at least 1,000 years. Thus, the three sites give a picture of subsistence changes that occurred during the late preceramic and early ceramic periods in the Puerto de Supe area.

As8 consists of midden covering about ½ hectare to depths of up to 2 meters.

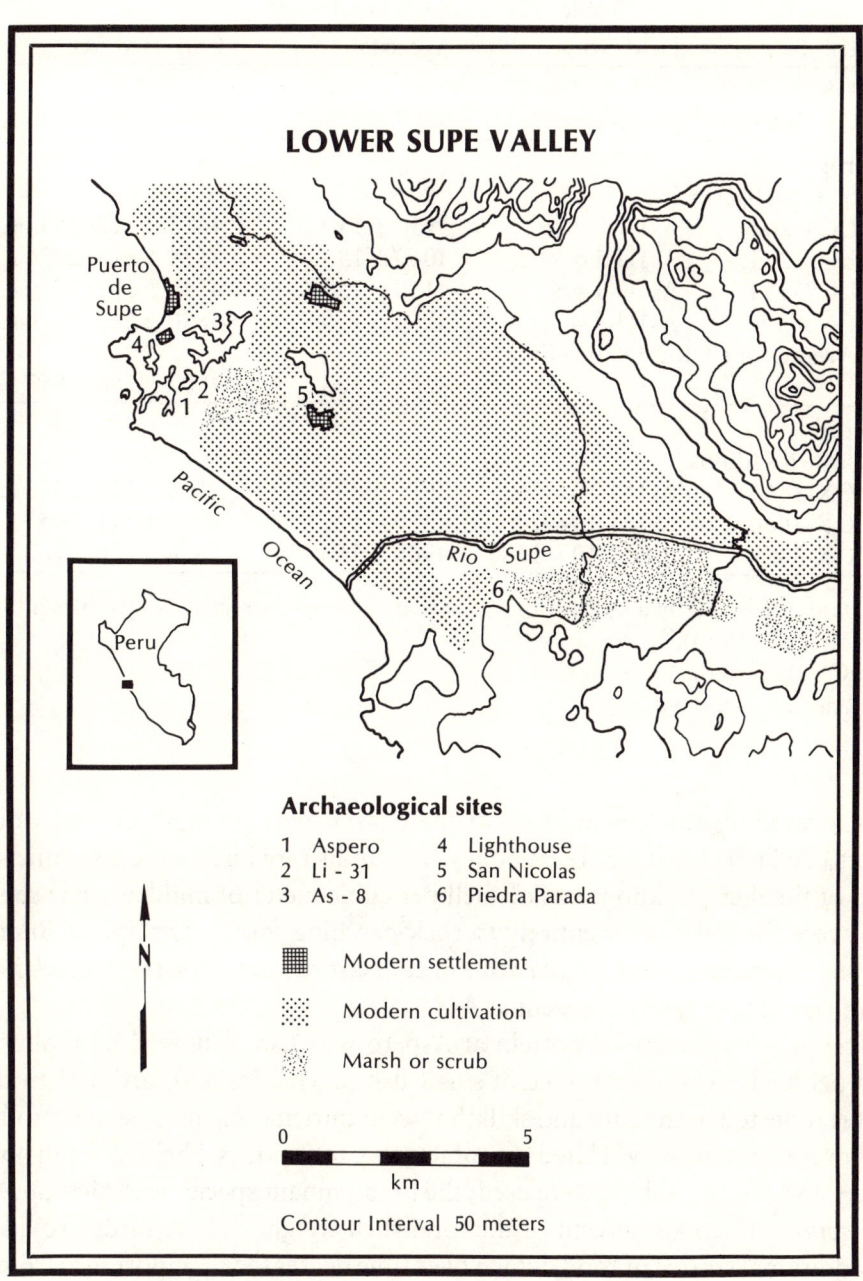

Figure 10.1. The Lower Supe Valley.

Table 10.1. Radiocarbon Dates*

Lab No.	Field No.	Age, B.P.	Corrected Age
Site As8			
GX-3863	As8A-14 = 25	6085 ± 180**	6914 ± 190; 4964 B.C.
Aspero:			
Huaca de los Sacrificios			
UCR-242	As1U-5 = 26	3950 ± 150	4483 ± 217; 2533 B.C.
UCR-243	As1U-5 = 62	4060 ± 150	4624 ± 217; 2674 B.C.
UCR-244	As1U-8 = 5	4150 ± 150	4740 ± 217; 2790 B.C.
GX3862	As1U-8 = 5	4260 ± 150	4880 ± 225; 2930 B.C.
Average of UCR-244 and GX-3862		4205 ± 106	4807 ± 156; 2857 B.C.
Aspero:			
Huaca de los Idolos			
GX-3861	As1M-10 = 263	3970 ± 145	4508 ± 210; 2558 B.C.
GX-3860	As1M-10 = 200	4360 ± 175**	5005 ± 211; 3055 B.C.
GX-3859	As1M-10 = 198	4900 ± 1600***	5658 ± 220; 3702 B.C.

*Dates are based on a half-life of 5,570 years and are corrected using tables in Damon et al. (1974).
**δC^{13} corrected.
***Rejected as too old.

It is located on the leeward side of the coastal hills (Lomas del Puerto) by Puerto de Supe. Shellfish, large boney fish, and shore birds were a significant part of the diet (21 kilograms of shell per cubic meter of midden). The shellfish were limited almost entirely to rock-perching forms, principally *Brachidontes purpuratus* and *Tegula atra;* in contrast to later sites, the *Mesodesma* clam was almost entirely absent at As8.

The primary source of protein at Aspero was fish, followed by molluscs and penipeds. The importance of small fish (anchovies and sardines) to the diet is reflected in the care and skill that went into making nets, which exhibit elaborate, functionally related manufacturing techniques. Shellfish from both rocky and sandy habitats were used; the predominant species was *Mesodesma donacium* (17 to 48 percent of the total shell weight). Shore birds provided an additional source of food, which over time decreased in importance from a significant role at As8 to a minor one at Li-31.

Agriculture—for industrial uses—was evident at all three sites. It was not clear if cotton was present at As8, but that site did have *Cucurbita* and *Lagenaria*. The variety of plants cultivated increased over time. Legumes *(Phaseolus* and *Inga)* appear at Aspero, as do *Capsicum, Psidium, Canna,* and possibly *Zea*. With Li-31 we jump more than 1,000 years forward; the intervening period saw not only the adoption of pottery, but also the increased importance of agriculture. New species appeared—*Manihot, Canavalia, Persea, Arachis,* and *Lucuma*—and old ones—*Phaseolus* and *Zea*—increased greatly in frequency. Fishing, hunting, and shellfish gathering continued, and agriculture represented an additional source of food rather than a substitute for old sources.

In general, the Aspero subsistence analyses indicate a gradual development of agriculture, following rather than preceding the rise of corporate organization. It should be noted that most, if not all, of the cultivated plants used on the Peruvian coast are not native to that area, but were domesticated in other areas (as near as coastal Ecuador or as far away as Argentina or Mexico) and then adapted to coastal use. The staggered appearances, as well as the varied origins, of the different crops show that they were not introduced as a unified complex, but were adopted as needed by the coastal peoples.

We may be underestimating both the role of certain cultivated plants—the legumes in particular—that have a long history of use and the possibility of a wider range of settlement types (including inland agricultural villages) than has been found to date. Recent research indicates that there have been major changes in valley landscape involving river sedimentation, sand dune encroachment, and severe erosion, all of which adversely affect the preservation of sites located to exploit riverine resources (Nials et al. 1979a, 1979b; Moseley, Feldman, and Ortloff 1981; Moseley 1983). Also, pollen studies by Kautz (1976) show significant amounts of wetland plant pollen at coastal sites. As Cohen (1972–74) points out, plant preservation might not be as complete as we think, and it is possible that we have misread the role of plants.

However, we must not assume on *a priori* grounds that agricultural villages, now destroyed, were contemporaneous with the coastal settlements. If there were such settlements, we might reasonably expect to see: (1) more agricultural produce in the coastal middens (as indeed we find at Li-31); and (2) monumental architecture (more likely to be preserved than midden or residential architecture) inland, reflecting the importance of these sites. We find neither indication of the importance of agriculture. I do not mean to say, however, that agriculture was not present or that it was entirely unimportant; it simply was not a significant factor in the origin of the large, sedentary coastal communities. In the model presented in this paper, agriculture does become an important factor in the expansion and solidification of political power implied in the developments that occurred at the end of the preceramic and during the Initial Ceramic Period.

It can be demonstrated that marine resources are in some ways inferior to terrestrial resources (Osborn 1977a, 1977b). Some have taken this condition to mean, by implication, that marine resources could not have supported the large coastal communities observed in the archaeological record (Wilson 1981). Although the first part of the argument is true, the conclusion overlooks certain important features of the Peruvian littoral and does not correspond to archaeological reality.

Using caloric and protein values of various marine foods and estimates of marine production, Osborn (1977a) calculated the theoretical, marine-based, preceramic population for the coast of Peru (4°–18°S), arriving at a figure far exceeding any derived from known sites and middens. He estimated a population of over 375,000 (compare to Lanning's 1967 estimate of 50,000–100,000 people) by assuming that the sea was tapped at the fourth trophic level and the population was at 60 percent of the calculated carrying capacity. However, midden analyses suggest substantial exploitation of the second and third levels. Correcting for this error would increase the estimate by at least tenfold.

Wilson (1981) has suggested that El Niño current reversals would have severely limited the maritime population, but his analysis suffers from the same problems as Osborn's, and then some. El Niño does disperse the anchovy schools, but this dispersal is often preceded by a concentration of the fish in nearshore waters, where they can be taken in great numbers. Such abnormal concentrations would signal a Niño, allowing the coastal peoples to store up additional food in the form of dried fish.

Anchovies were not the only fish caught. Certain types of shellfish increased in the warm waters of El Niño, and seabirds, weakened by lack of food, could be easily caught. Moreover, if rains accompany a Niño, plant life on land flourishes (often for several years after the rains), allowing replacement of marine by terrestrial foods (Murphy 1926).

Although a Niño does not destroy the marine food base to the extent implied by Wilson, it does adversely affect the food supply. Let us grant, for the sake of argument, that it reduces the food supply to one-sixth of the normal amount, as assumed by Wilson. Applying this figure to Osborn's (1977a) population estimate of 375,000 people, we arrive at a Niño-limited population of 62,500, which falls within Lanning's estimate. It should be noted again, however, that Osborn and Wilson do not include anchovies in the food supply, which is clearly an error. Correcting for this error would put the population back in the 300,000 to 600,000 range, once again amply covering the observed population, even without accounting for wild terrestrial foods.

Thus, the argument that the marine subsistence base was inadequate does not stand up to theoretical or archaeological scrutiny. Note also that subsistence agriculture experienced a long latent period between its introduction and ultimate acceptance, during which time marine resources continued to be the cornerstone of the diet (Pozorski and Pozorski 1979b).

Theoretical calculations of caloric production and trophic levels do point out differences in various resource bases, but cannot tell us which of several satisfactory modes a given people chose to exploit. We must examine the archaeological record and try to explain what we find, regardless of what the numbers tell us might be more "efficient."

Corporate Architecture

Although the primacy of the maritime subsistence base might still be open to debate, the material accomplishments of the coastal populations are quite clear. The 150,000 to 200,000 cubic meters of cultural deposit at Aspero suggest a large, stable resident population. The most prominent features of this extensive midden are its irregular, pitted surface and several large artificial mounds. Fully one-third of the site's area is occupied by some type of construction, including small domestic structures, stone-lined pits, terracing, plazas, and monumental mounds.

The most interesting constructions are the mounds (Fig. 10.2, see also Moseley and Willey 1973): there are at least eight recognizable mounds and six smaller, moundlike structures. The mounds are formed of conjoined rooms that were eventually filled in—either partially or completely—to form a raised platform for a new phase of wall and floor construction. Most of the walls were built using rounded boulders set in mud mortar or angular basaltic blocks set in mud or in mud and grass mortar. Handmade adobes were occasionally used, but always in combination with stones. Freestanding walls were plastered on both faces with light-colored clay. Floors were formed of mud plaster over a compacted mud and gravel layer that rested on the fill.

Major excavations were undertaken in two of the mounds, Huaca de los Idolos and Huaca de los Sacrificios. In Huaca de los Idolos individual rooms varied considerably in size, the largest being 11 by 16 meters (Fig. 10.3). This room, or more likely an open court, was the main entry area of the complex, reached by a stairway leading to a 2-meter-wide doorway at the top of the highest mound face, the eastern one. From this first room, passages led back to smaller rooms at the rear and sides. The central room, measuring 5.1 by 4.4 meters, was divided by a low wall, friezed with a clapboardlike design on the eastern side and broken by a narrow doorway in the shape of a double-topped T (T). The walls of this room, as well as those of the rooms to the north and east, had niches in them, which were roughly cubical and averaged 30 centimeters on a side.

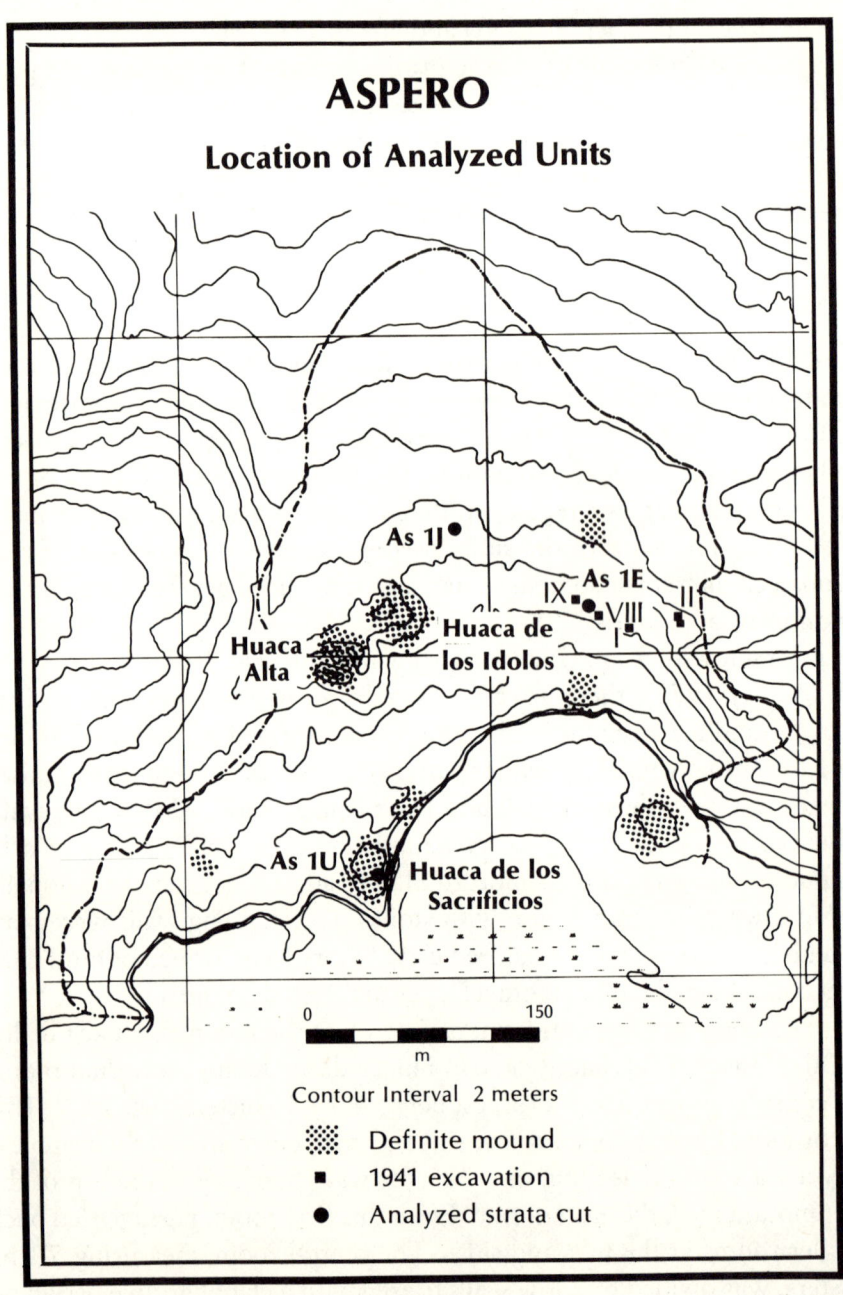

Figure 10.2. Locations of analyzed units, Aspero.

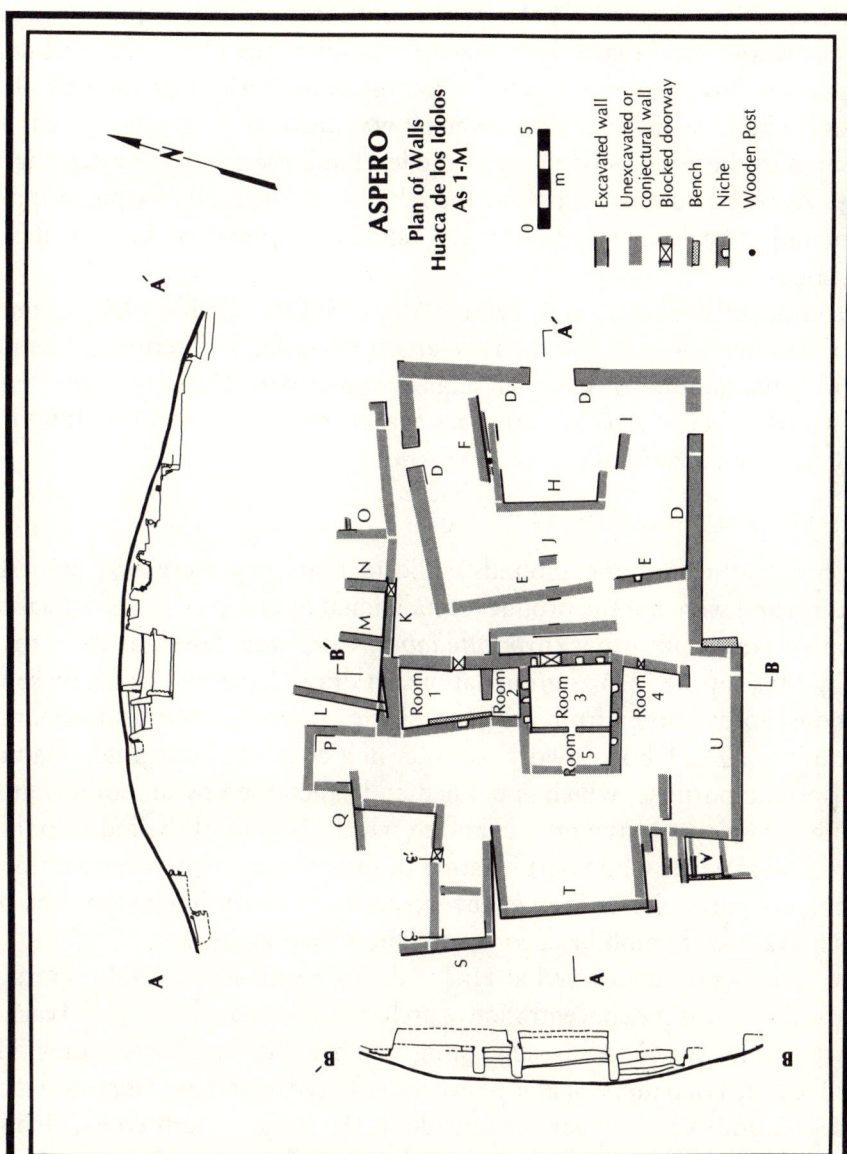

Figure 10.3. Plan of walls, Huaca de los Idolos, Aspero.

The central rooms of Huaca de los Idolos quickly underwent a series of refloorings and rebuildings that ultimately buried the level of the friezed wall under five floors. A similar pattern of rooms and reconstructions emerged from excavations in Huaca de los Sacrificios. Disrepair of the old level does not appear to have been the reason for reconstruction. Although the wall plaster was broken and missing places when it was uncovered, the damage can be attributed to the process of filling in the level and the subsequent settling of the fill. As will be discussed below, the rebuilding suggest a conspicuous display of authority designed to assert and validate the power of the central corporate body.

The radiocarbon dates range from 3950 to 4360 B.P. (Table 10.1). Coming from the upper 1/4 or 1/3 of the two largest mounds, they represent the upper end of the mound construction sequence at Aspero. The earliest construction probably began 250 to 500 years earlier, or around 4600 to 4800 B.P. (uncorrected radiocarbon years).

INTERPRETATION OF ARCHITECTURE

Several features of the mounds indicate that they were not domestic structures and were not the product of individual or unorganized group labor, but rather were built using *corporate labor*. Corporate labor, as the term is used by Moseley (1975b), is group labor that draws its work force from separate households, either from within a single community or from separate communities. The laborers work together in a collective, integrated manner for a specific purpose, which is defined and sanctioned by an authoritative body that coordinates the project and to which the will of the individual laborer is subservient while participating in the project. As an organizational concept, corporate labor implies the existence of an authority that has the rights and ability to mobilize people and direct their actions.

The architecture uncovered at Huaca de los Idolos has several important features. The first is the concentration of architectural ornamentation and cached artifacts in the central rooms, suggesting a higher status for these rooms. The second feature is a pattern of graded access, reflected in part by doorway width: the largest doorway is from the outside to the large eastern court, smaller doorways lead to the central rooms, and the smallest controls passage from Room 3 to Room 5 (Fig. 10.3).

The patterns of ornamentation and graded access suggest more and more restricted ceremonial areas. This pattern is evident at slightly later ceremonial centers, such as Huaca de los Reyes in the Moche Valley, with its three plazas arranged in increasing elevation, decreasing size, and decreasing access (T. Pozorski 1976).

In Huaca de los Idolos the most restricted space—in terms of physical access—is Room 5: its doorway is only one person wide (40 centimeters). The greatest concentration of ornamentation is in Rooms 3 and 5, but mainly in Room 3. The friezed wall physically divides these two rooms, but because it is only 1.25 meters high, it does not block the view from one room to the other. It is decorated on the Room 3 side, the side that would be seen by people able to enter Room 3 from the eastern court. It thus appears that most of the select group able to enter the inner sanctum of Huaca de los Idolos had to remain on the outside of the friezed wall, mere observers of the even more select few who were permitted to pass through the doorway, enter Room 5, and participate in the ceremonies conducted there.

THE ASPERO CHIEFDOM

The presence of an elite group, or a group with special functions and privileges, is one indication of a nonegalitarian society. Aspero was the type of nonegalitarian society that Service (1962) labeled a "chiefdom." As originally defined by Service, a chiefdom is a ranked society with population centers that coordinate its religious, social, and economic activities. A chiefdom is usually larger in size and population than an egalitarian society (a band or tribe), but it is smaller, less stratified, and less centrally organized than a state, the next level in Service's scheme. Despite the pitfalls in using such a simple, discontinuous typology to describe a complex spectrum of social forms, the term chiefdom does serve to distinguish certain types of societies from others and provides a convenient term for further discussion.

The chiefdoms of Polynesia make useful analogies because of the similarities in degree of social stratification, size, technology, and to a lesser extent, subsistence. One of the principal features of the Polynesian chiefdoms that left distinct material remains is the pooling of labor for corporate construction projects (Sahlins 1958). The structures at Aspero could be interpreted as products of an ad hoc organization, but their size, detail, and continuity of formal concept through time reflect organized control; we can clearly see evidence of corporate labor.

Colin Renfrew infers a chiefdom type of organization from third millennium Maltese "temples," though he notes that the only physical evidence for this designation is the structures themselves, which "clearly required for their construction (a) the mobilization of large labor forces, and (b) the exercise of architectural and artistic skill." He acknowledges that egalitarian societies can build large structures by accretional growth, but notes the "purposive nature" of the temples, a "central unifying concept" that signals the hand of a corporate body (Renfrew 1974:77). Several features at Aspero show the purposive and unifying hand of corporate control.

The first is the size of the constructions. While no domestic structures that could serve as direct comparisons were excavated at Aspero, habitations at other sites are much smaller, both overall and in room size (Engel 1963, Pozorski and Pozorski 1979a, Wendt 1964). Huaca de los Idolos has a base of about 30 by 50 meters; Huaca de los Sacrificios was of similar size. Rooms within these structures are over 10 meters square; walls are up to 1 meter thick and 2.5 meters in height; some of the individual stones are almost 1 cubic meter in volume.

The second feature is the use of *shicra* or bagged fill (Huapaya Manco 1977–1978). This construction technique is also found at the Supe Valley preceramic site of Piedra Parada (Figs. 10.1 and 10.4) and was later used at such ceremonial sites as Las Haldas (Fung Pineda 1969), Huaricanga (Ishida et al. 1960), and Huaca San Jose (a 100 meter square mound with a 50 meter circular plaza, in the Pativilca Valley), among others. In domestic structures fill accumulates principally through natural action, whereas shicra signals intentional, organized abandonment of a structure prior to rebuilding it in a more prominent, elevated position.

The third feature is special architectural decoration: niches, friezes, and wall paint. Again, this feature is not found in domestic contexts but is associated with ceremonial structures and corporate construction.

The fourth feature is the general lack of domestic refuse within the structures, both on the floors and within the fill. What artifacts were found occurred most often in the context of caches placed on the fill prior to the laying of a floor.

The above features, singly and in combination, point out the corporate nature of the Aspero mounds, and direct our attention beyond the structures to the social system behind them. Renfrew recognized two extremes on the continuum of chiefdoms: (1) the "group-oriented" chiefdom, which shows little evidence of accumulated personal wealth but clear indications of communal or corporate activities; and (2) the "individualizing" chiefdom, characterized by evidence of marked differences in personal possessions and symbols of prestige, which greatly outweigh expressions of communal authority (Renfrew 1974:74). Malta is cited as an example of the former, and the pre-Mycenaean Aegean as an example of the latter.

Using Renfew's scale to place Aspero in particular, and the Peruvian late preceramic in general, we note the predominance of community works over personal wealth, though status differences have been found. Moseley (1975b: 76) noted a bimodal distribution of grave textiles in the burials Engel (1963)

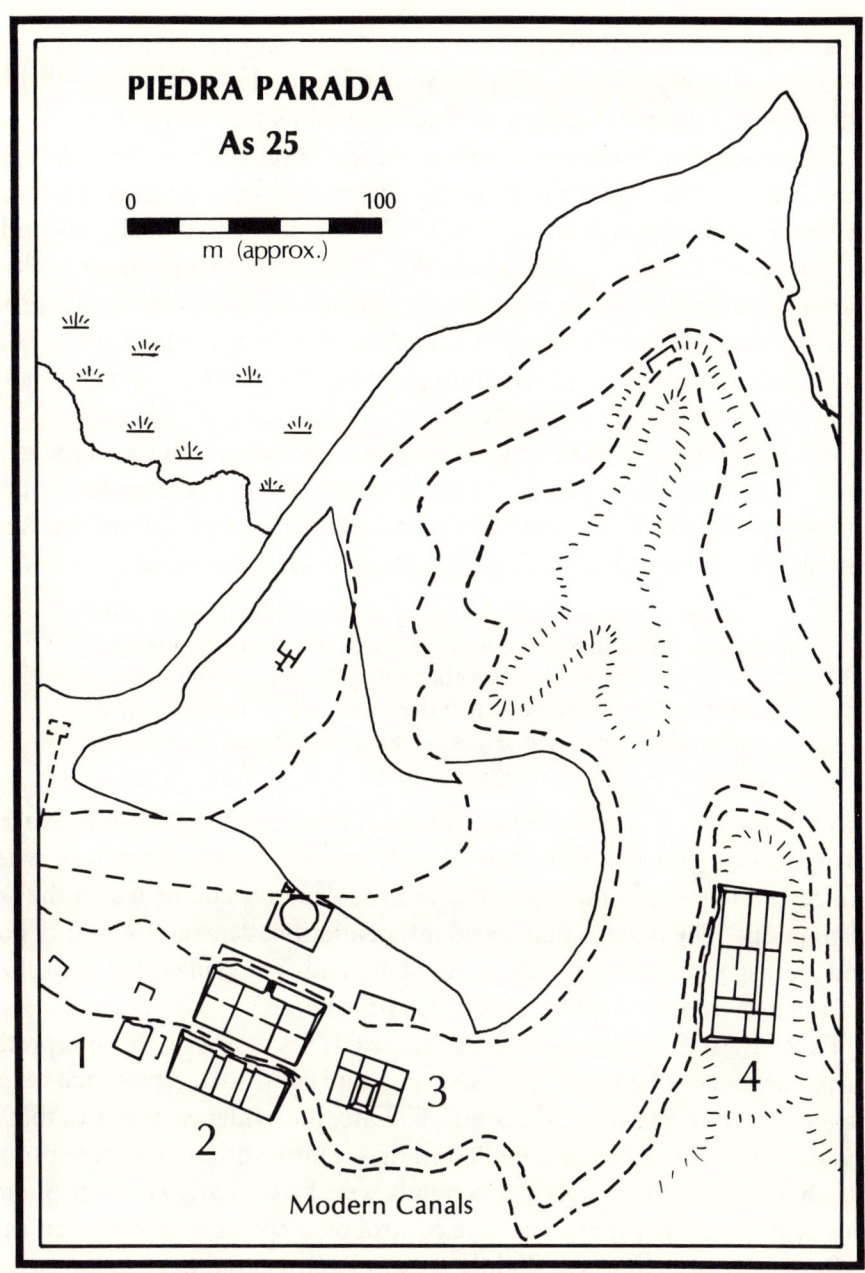

Figure 10.4. Piedra Parada.

excavated at Asia and interpreted these differences as evidence of a social hierarchy. A richly adorned infant burial on Huaca de los Sacrificios (Feldman 1980:114) might indicate the presence of hereditary status differences.

The presence of luxury trade items (beads, spondylus) at Aspero suggests differential access to wealth and goods (Feldman 1980:157), another characteristic of ranked societies (Service 1962). Members of the elite group have the means to acquire special goods that mark and enhance their rank. The demand they create for prestige goods encourages specialized craft production and trade in luxury goods. Conversely, the ownership of special or exotic goods can distinguish emerging classes. Demand can create a supply *and* supply can create a demand.

Rathje (1970) saw trade in prestige goods as a major factor in the genesis of the Maya chiefdoms. Similarly, Renfrew (1974) noted the probable interrelationships between the expansion of metallurgy and the rise of the Aegean chiefdoms. He has called this interaction the "multiplier effect":

> Changes or innovations occurring in one field of human activity (in one subsystem of a culture) sometimes act so as to favour changes in other fields (in other subsystems). The multiplier effect is said to operate when these induced changes in one or more subsystems themselves act so as to enhance the original changes in the first subsystem (Renfrew 1972:37)

It becomes a "chicken-or-egg" question, then, whether demand created by changes in social structure influenced craft specialization (and trade) or whether the development of new crafts created the demand and/or led to the social distinctions. The point is that social differentiation, demand for luxury goods, and craft specialization developed hand in hand. The evidence of craft specialization and trade at Aspero reflects this process.

The pattern of restricted access at Huaca de los Idolos can be interpreted as further evidence of differences in access to, and control of, ceremonial/religious activity by a small group of people. To date, the evidence indicates that during the late Cotton Preceramic Period these status differences were probably not sharply defined, though they certainly were by the Early Horizon. Similarly, this evidence shows that corporate control over construction was not as well defined at Aspero as it was slightly later at Piedra Parada.

Three features of Piedra Parada are important. The first is the regularity and formality of its monumental architecture (Fig. 10.4). All three main complexes are three rooms wide by two rooms deep, a pattern repeated at several Initial Period and Early Horizon sites in the mid-valley area. This regularity indicates a greater degree of central planning and control at Piedra Parada than at Aspero. The second feature is the size of its midden, which is smaller in both relative and absolute terms than the midden at Aspero, suggesting that the labor force at Piedra Parada was drawn from outside the site. The third feature is a circular, semisubterranean plaza centered in front of one of the mounds.

The circular plaza phenomenon, first noted by Kosok (1965), was incorrectly assigned to possible Middle Horizon status. Williams Leon (1972) expanded on Kosok's work and correctly noted that the circular plaza was a Formative trait. In addition to Piedra Parada, circular sunken plazas occur at two other definite preceramic sites: Alto Salaverry, in the Moche Valley (Pozorski and Pozorski 1979a), and Salinas de Chao, in the Chao Valley (Alba Alba 1978; Cardenas Martin 1977–78). The trait is more characteristic of the Initial Period/Early Horizon of the northern central coast; at least 36 examples are known from the Lurin to the Santa, 21 of them in the Supe-Pativilca-Forteleza valley complex, and 10 in the Supe alone. Circular sunken plazas also are found in the highlands: one is associated with the Old Temple at Chavin de Huantar (Lumbreras 1977).

The traits found at Piedra Parada indicate the existence of a strong corporate authority, with continuity in time and space. A great amount of labor was under the control of the various local bodies: mounds ranging from 60 to 100 meters on a side and from 5 to 15 meters high are common. One of the largest mounds in the New World, the 250-by-300-by-35-meter Sechin Alto (Tello 1956b; Fung Pineda and Williams Leon 1977) is part of the tradition.

Predominantly an inland phenomenon, the circular plaza complex must have been supported to a significant degree by irrigated agriculture. However, the tradition began at the coastal preceramic sites, where many of its physical features (such as bagged fill, friezes, wall paint, niches, and the circular plaza); organizational concepts (corporate labor, labor tax?); and, by inference, religious beliefs and practices (offering caches using textiles, mythological animals, hierarchical access to rooms and rites) were started or nurtured. Although agriculture certainly was a major factor in the growth and spread of the tradition, it was based on a maritime subsistence in the preceramic communities of coastal Peru. Agriculture had been known to these peoples for centuries, but only after uplift had altered the coastal environment was it adopted as an integral part of the subsistence system.

The Shift to Agriculture

Many scholars have pondered the question of why agriculture developed. Some have suggested that increased awareness of the environment led to experimentation and domestication (for example, see Braidwood 1960); others, that environmental changes forced the invention of agriculture (for example, see Childe 1951); and still others, that population pressure led to the search for new food sources, resulting in the domestication of plants and animals (for example, see Binford 1968, Cohen 1977).

We can readily dispose of the first explanation, for several reasons: it is untestable, "primitive" man had wide knowledge of the plants and animals in his environment, and there were no biological changes in man at the end of the Pleistocene that would prevent us from extending this capability back in time (see further Cohen 1977:19–23).

Parts of the second model are useful, in spite of the fact that Childe's "oasis theory" has not been supported by the data from the Middle East or from other parts of the world. Major environmental changes did take place at the end of the last glaciation. However, similar changes probably took place earlier, and although these changes might in some sense have been "necessary" conditions, they were not sufficient in themselves to trigger domestication.

Of the three explanations, versions of the third remain the most viable, but they do have problems. Barbara Bender (1978) has criticized the population pressure model for ignoring the underlying social structure of the groups that did or did not shift to agriculture: she views population pressure as an intermediate result rather than a primary cause.

Bender makes an important distinction between *intensified* food production (increased productivity per unit area, not necessarily involving any increase in the total amount produced) and *increased* food production (increased total yield, with or without changes in the area exploited). She notes that intensified productivity need not entail increased labor costs. Therefore intensification need not be a response to outside environmental stress or population pressure, two common explanations of why people would choose to exploit "less efficient" resources. She concludes: "The inquiry into agricultural origins is not, therefore, about intensification *per se,* not about increased productivity, but about increased production and about why increased demands are made on the economy" (Bender 1978:206).

SOCIAL FACTORS AS PRIME MOVER

Bender argues that the causes of increased demand are social, not techno-environmental changes or population pressure. In her view, population pressure is not simply a relation between numbers of people and resources, but rather "an expression of how these, the numbers and the resources, are culturally organized (Bender 1978:208). That is, demographic pressure is what a society perceives as stressful, and may not involve any increase in the population number or density.

In Bender's model the principal motivating factors are social obligations and ceremonial exchange, which generate pressure to increase social stratification and demands on production. These factors, in turn, promote what she calls "sedentism." (Bender argues that social exchange encourages group cohesion, because members reap the return benefits of their earlier gifts.) Increasing sedentism causes intragroup friction, which can promote a stronger leadership role, as the leader gains more power to mediate disputes. Conversely, the presence of a leader who has the power to resolve conflicts facilitates a shift to sedentism. Increased leadership may be accompanied by an increase in ceremonial demand, putting greater pressure on production: "On the one hand, sedentism, through concentrating labour in a more circumscribed area, tends to encourage increased productivity, and, on the other, through feeding back into the system and promoting hierarchization, encourages increased production" (Bender 1978:213).

A SYNTHESIS OF CAUSES

As the syntheses of Flannery (1972, 1973) have made clear, monocausal models for the origin of agriculture and complex society are unsatisfactory. To justify the timing of her model, Bender (1978:209) finds it necessary to invoke "the particular mental and physical changes that occurred 40,000 years ago," which allowed the development of hierarchical communities—a proposition difficult to substantiate. Rather than acting as simple dependent or secondary variables, techno-environmental change and population increase probably interact with and influence the social variables.

We might express this relationship in terms of the proportion:

$$P \propto \frac{CN}{RA}$$

where P is the pressure to increase production, C is the cultural demand or perception of need, N is the number of people, R represents the resources exploited, and A is the area exploited. Thus, pressure increases with increasing population or increasing cultural demand, and decreases when the exploited area is enlarged or more resources are exploited. The population size, N, is not entirely independent of the other variables, but because we are trying to illustrate rather than achieve mathematical precision, this point can be overlooked for the moment.

A group of people can respond to pressure to increase production in several ways, some of which do not result in any significant modification of their way of life. First, if there is additional area to exploit, intensified food production need not result. However, the distribution of currently known sites suggests that the Peruvian coast was fully occupied by the late preceramic period, and that expansion within that habitat was not possible.

Second, pressure can be controlled or reduced by controlling the population size. Evidence from La Paloma, in the Chilca Valley, shows that female infanticide was practiced before 5000 B.P. (Robert Benfer, personal communication). Thus, it is evident that population control was a factor in limiting pressure on resources.

Third, pressure can be controlled by reducing cultural expectations. This response has limited utility, however, and probably would not be resorted to by choice, but rather would be forced on the group by the threat of famine.

The final response to pressure—increasing the resource base—can take several forms: more intense exploitation of the same species; utilization of formerly unexploited species; movement into new areas to exploit different habitats; or creation of new resources either by modifying the habitat, importing new species, or domesticating existing species (generally accompanied by both increased yield per individual and increased crop density). The adoption of agriculture by the coastal population represents both importation of new species and expansion into new habitats: the river flood plain and the near-river desert (through irrigation).

A MODEL FOR THE END OF THE MARITIME PRECERAMIC

By 4500 B.P., the peoples of coastal Peru had successfully adapted to the littoral environment and were living in sedentary communities along much of the central and northern coast. Yet within the short span of several centuries at the end of the third millennium, the importance of marine foods decreased and agricultural became the primary means of subsistence. At roughly the same time a major shift in settlement location occurred—from coastal to inland sites—and the use of pottery became widespread.

Why did these changes occur? The answer, obviously is not simple. Our knowledge of this crucial time period has increased to the point where it is evident that these changes did not occur simultaneously or instantaneously, so we can rule out population replacement as the cause, as Engel (1966) and others once argued.

I would suggest that the three observed changes—subsistence base, settlement pattern, and ceramics—are interrelated, and that the primary change was in the subsistence base. The shift in subsistence was brought about, in large part, by changes in the sea level relative to the coastal plain, which reduced both the resource base and the area exploited, adding to the pressure to increase productivity. The subsistence base and settlement pattern changed relatively rapidly because of the prior existence of a developed chiefdom pattern of centralized corporate control and mobilization of labor and resources.

I am not suggesting, as Binford (1968) did, that a rise in sea level was responsible for the shift to an agricultural subsistence base. First, I am not concerned here with the "invention" of agriculture, for this occurred earlier than the time in question and in other areas of the hemisphere rather than coastal Peru. Second, the land rose relative to the sea level. The changes caused by coastal uplift modified the coastal habitat and led to profound changes in the life of the preceramic communities of coastal Peru.

It should be noted here that the changes in subsistence base that occurred at the end of the preceramic were not absolute nor were they instantaneous (Richardson 1981). Marine food continued to be a significant part of the diet for a considerable time (S. Pozorski 1976, Pozorski and Pozorski 1979b). Problems with differential preservation of shell versus bone versus plant material and with sampling biases make quantification of changes difficult at best, but I suspect that the dietary shift involved a small reduction in marine foods coupled with a large increase in agricultural foods, resulting in an overall increase in the subsistence base.

COASTAL UPLIFT

The major coastal preceramic sites of the third millennium B.C. (Ventanilla Bay sites, Bandurria, Aspero, Culebras, Los Gavilanes, Salinas de Chao, Alto Salaverry, and Huaca Prieta) are found near what are now, in the main, dry bays, lagoons, or marshy areas. When they contained shallow water, these areas provided a varied habitat for fishing, shellfish gathering, hunting, and wild plant harvesting. Additional fishing, hunting, and plant gathering took place along the rivers and their flood plains, together with the cultivation of cotton and gourds for industrial uses. Some food plants were also cultivated.

Data from a variety of areas, including Talara (Richards 1962, Richardson 1974), Chicama and Viru (Bird 1948), Ancon/Ventanilla (Moseley 1968), and Otuma (Craig and Psuty 1971), indicate the episodes of tectonic uplift have occurred along the Peruvian coast. Radiocarbon dates from hearths on a sequence of beach ridges in the Talara region (Richardson 1974) show that the earlier ridges were occupied around 4255, 3500, 3490, and 2685 B.P. The earliest occupation was preceramic, the latest ceramic; the affiliations of the two intermediate occupations are uncertain. The uplift occurring between 4255 and 3500 B.P. is of interest here. Another dated uplift episode comes from Otuma (Craig and Psuty 1971), on the south coast, where dates on charcoal and shell from aceramic middens indicate that a rapid uplift of about 9 feet occurred about 3600 B.P. Although too late to be of direct importance to this discussion, the episode does illustrate the magnitude of uplift possible in a single event. The observations of Craig and Psuty are also relevant. They note that the uplift, by stranding the shellfish beds of Otuma lagoon, was probably responsible for the abandonment of the middens and may have been responsible for the disappearance of potable water from the area.

The best recent synthesis of the uplift data is the work of Kautz (1976). Citing unpublished data and his own studies of pollen from Huaca Prieta and sites in the Ancon area, Kautz states:

> ... evidence of tectonic uplift at both Huaca Prieta and Ventanilla Bay is conclusive. The consequence of this relatively minor geomorphological event was the loss of brackish lagoonal habitat which had formerly provided a wealth of vegetational, shellfish, fish, and animal resources. The loss of this habitat, in so abrupt a manner, may well have caused the human populations to abandon the shorelines in favor [of] the river plains, an area which duplicated many of the same kinds and categories of resources. (1976:150)

To Kautz's observations we may add several other factors. First, an uplift could have affected potable water sources (Craig and Psuty 1971). An uplift of the coast could easily alter the flow of groundwater, cutting off springs or moving the water too deep for human use without technological advances, such as wells or sunken gardens. A lowering of the coastal water table (relative to the ground surface) would also have put the moisture out of reach of many of the plants that were utilized by the human and animal populations. Second, uplift would have modified the flow of the coastal rivers, promoting downcutting and entrenchment of the rivers in restricted flood plains. This change could have aggravated the changes incurred by loss of the lagoonal habitat, because it is likely that the flood plain areas were already being used to cultivate cotton, gourds, and other crops, and thus were not virgin areas that the people could penetrate.

One solution to this crisis would have been to create new "river-flooded" land by canal irrigation. It is likely (but with the present data, entirely speculative) that prior to uplift some irrigation was practiced by the preceramic peoples in order to expand cultivation beyond the flood plain. If so, then the changes required by the uplifted landscape would simply have been a matter of degree rather than kind. Be this as it may, irrigation agriculture was adopted at some point in time, and other evidence indicates that this change occurred before the close of the Initial Period (Pozorski and Pozorski 1979b).

Under the model proposed by Willey (1953) and reiterated by Moseley (1972), canal irrigation began in the valley neck areas, where a steeper gradient allowed for shorter lead-off canals and made it easier to control the water's movement. These conditions would have encouraged the preceramic peoples to move away from the diminishing coastal habitats toward inland areas. Just such a shift in site location can be seen in the archaeological record.

PREADAPTATION THROUGH CORPORATE LABOR

Canal construction generally requires investment of substantial amounts of labor, as well as planning and direction. Thus, expansion of agricultural land by canal irrigation would have been most feasible in those communities that had the largest available work force and had developed the greatest degree of corporate control over that force (subject to the availability of suitable inland areas).

The social factors emphasized by Bender (1978) would also have favored this change. It is evident that hierarchical differences had developed at Aspero, to the extent that it could be classified as a chiefdom. The increased demand generated by social obligation, corporate construction, and status-enhancing trade would have created pressure to increase production. Canal-irrigated agriculture would have increased not only productivity, but also the power and authority of the hierarchy. Thus, government control of farm land and irrigation was a basic fact of agricultural life from the beginning, not a subsequent development. Control and central authority led to irrigation agriculture rather than vice versa.

The social changes accompanying the shift from coastal hunting and gathering to inland farming must have been substantial. Here again, a central corporate authority would have provided an impetus for the move and facilitated it by mediating disputes.

The change to agriculture did not involve the adoption of any fundamentally new traits (except, pottery later): it was a shift of emphasis, though admittedly one of large proportion. The biological term for a condition in which a preexisting trait, selectively neutral in the environment where it developed, becomes advantageous in a new or changed environment is "preadaptation." Both corporate organization and experience with agriculture preadapted the coastal populations to the new environmental conditions brought about by tectonic uplift.

In the preuplift coastal environment of Peru, food-producing agriculture was of limited value. Over time, however, the combined effects of continued population concentration and increasing power of the corporate elite probably would have made agriculture more important until it became the principal source of food. (This gradual shift appears to have been under way when uplift accelerated the pace of the change.)

The elite's ability to organize and control labor and resources had an important role in the maritime societies, but this power increased dramatically as a result of the changes brought about by uplift. Agriculture blossomed as well, because it offered a ready replacement for the diminishing littoral and riverine resources. The speed with which the changes took place testifies to the preadaptive advantage possessed by the coastal chiefdoms.

PART FIVE

The City and the State

Eleven

Rulership and the Ciudadela: Political Inferences from Teotihuacan Architecture

George L. Cowgill, Brandeis University

Introduction

This paper is one of a series of publications growing out of the Teotihuacan Mapping Project, directed and inspired by René Millon.[1] I will not attempt to review the major results of that project and other recent work bearing on Teotihuacan. For an overview, see especially R. Millon (1973, 1974, 1976, and 1981); Millon, Drewitt, and Cowgill (1973); Cowgill (1974, 1977, and 1979); Cowgill, Altschul, and Sload (n.d.); Wolf (1976); Sanders, Parsons, and Santley (1979); and Sanders (1981a). All these new data, from many sources, have transformed our basis for understanding Teotihuacan. We are still in the process of digesting and absorbing all the new evidence and still in the midst of reassessing old assumptions and thinking through new implications about the ancient city. Moreover, large-scale fieldwork, directed by Rubén Cabrera Castro of the Instituto Nacional de Antropología e Historia (INAH), is in progress as I write. It will vastly expand our understanding of the Ciudadela and other architectural complexes that are central for the arguments of this paper (Cabrera Castro 1981). Nevertheless, it is never too early to reflect on data already accumulated, to question some old ideas, and to suggest problems for future research.

My purpose here is to attempt to further our understanding of political authority and governmental organization at Teotihuacan. Not long ago,

Mesoamerica was often characterized as "theocratic" during the Middle Horizon (roughly A.D. 200 to 750, according to the Goodman-Martinez-Thompson correlation), and Teotihuacan was believed to have been a "ceremonial center," with a relatively small resident population, consisting primarily of priests and their assistants. It seemed reasonable then to think that the Teotihuacan state, as well as the city itself, might have been governed by priests and priestly hierarchies. That is, in the thought of the Teotihuacanos themselves there might have been little or no recognition of a category of "secular" governmental offices conceptually differentiated from priestly offices. Activities that members of our own society would label political or governmental must of course have been carried out, but such activities might have been simply among the tasks appropriate for offices that primarily involved ritual and mediation between humans and deities.

Today, other parts of Middle Horizon Mesoamerica, such as the Maya lowlands and the Valley of Oaxaca, look much less "theocratic" than they seemed a few years ago. We now know that the population at Teotihuacan was very numerous throughout the Middle Horizon—probably between 100,000 and 200,000 during much of that period. A substantial proportion of the population was involved in craft production, often quite specialized. Such a large and varied population must have generated a relatively large and complex government apparatus. On rather vague general principles, it seems less likely than it did that there was no contrast between primarily political offices and primarily ritual offices.

This is not to suggest that offices with primarily political functions were likely to have been "secular" in anything like the sense of that term in many twentieth century states. No doubt all offices were more or less sacralized, even if there were important distinctions between more and less "priestly" offices. Such a general observation, however, does not carry us very far into the specifics of Teotihuacan government.

Since evidence about contemporary texts at Teotihuacan remains exceedingly scanty (C. Millon 1973), the attempt to learn much about Teotihuacan political organization may seem nearly hopeless. Certainly we need all the help we can get from every possible nontextual source of evidence. Nevertheless, the attempt does not seem unprofitable. We do not have to be content with plausible conjecture and unsubstantiated speculation. Surely, by striving to formulate specific hypotheses tightly connected to good evidence by explicit and logically valid arguments, and by making good use of knowledge about other political systems, we can improve our understanding of Teotihuacan government and politics.

It is important to emphasize that we should not simply attempt to infer *the* political system, but should seek evidence about trajectories of political change. It is highly unlikely that the political system of Teotihuacan remained static for the six to eight centuries during which the city was a metropolis of primary importance for Mesoamerica.

Two other matters deserve emphasis, because I believe they involve strategies widely applicable in scientific reasoning. First, I operate in part by making inferences that I consider most probable (among various alternatives) and in part by sketching *ranges* or *varieties* of models that I find reasonably plausible. This is roughly analogous to two kinds of procedures that complement one another in statistical inference. One can use sample data as information for a "best guess" about the specific value of a population parameter (for example, using the sample mean to estimate the population mean), and one can also ask what plausible range of true values is suggested by the sample by computing a *confidence interval* (for example, computing the standard error of one's estimate of the population mean). In thinking about Teotihuacan, it is useful to offer best guesses, but it is also useful to consider limits of plausible models. This is important because it is important to see how far we can go, and the points beyond which we *cannot* plausibly go, in postulating features of Teotihuacan society that are not contradicted by strong evidence. In this paper I present some best guesses, but I am also concerned with ranges of plausible alternatives. I have tried to make clear which are best guesses and which are plausible alternatives. I hope that, with this preparatory discussion, the structure and aims of my arguments will be clear. Above all, it should be understood that I suggest some things that may have been true of Teotihuacan, without necessarily advocating these possibilities. My intention, instead, is to test the data for "play." How far can one push interpretations this way, and how far that way, before limits of plausibility are reached? For what questions do we have relatively unambiguous evidence, which admits little variety in its reasonable interpretation? For what other questions do we have highly ambiguous evidence, consistent with very diverse possibilities, and thus badly in need of improvement?

Second, for those aspects of Teotihuacan for which we have no evidence or highly ambiguous evidence, there is a reasonably good chance that features or phenomena known to have been very common in other nonindustrialized complex societies were also present at Teotihuacan. Conversely, models that postulate features or phenomena at Teotihuacan that are unknown or very unusual in other broadly similar societies must be considered quite improbable, unless the models are supported by strong and unambiguous evidence from Teotihuacan itself. If this strategy is seen as simply filling in the gaps in our evidence about Teotihuacan by postulating the presence of whatever is common elsewhere and the absence of what is rare elsewhere, then it would be rightly condemned as pernicious and profoundly unscientific. I hope, however, that I use this strategy in a better way: more as an aid in judging limits of plausible ranges and less as a questionable source of support for specific best guesses. I also use knowledge of other societies heuristically to suggest questions and problems concerning Teotihuacan politics.

Although a full study of Teotihuacan politics should make the most of as many diverse kinds of evidence as possible, including iconography and symbol systems, in the present paper I will concentrate on one relatively neglected kind of evidence. I will try to draw out some of the political implications of some of the very large architectural complexes that (although they may include pyramids, rooms, or both) cannot be considered simply temples or ordinary dwellings.

My primary focus will be on the Ciudadela, generally believed to have included the residence of the rulers of Teotihuacan (for example, see Armillas 1964:307, R. Millon 1973:55). It also includes the extraordinary Pyramid of Quetzalcoatl, and Millon refers to the Ciudadela as "the religious and political center of the city...." It seems generally accepted that the Ciudadela combined political and religious significance, and that the cult or cults associated with the Quetzalcoatl Pyramid were intimately connected with rulership of Teotihuacan. More detailed discussions, however, tend to be concerned with identification of the deities represented and the calendrical or other rituals that may have been performed in the Ciudadela (for example, see Armillas 1947; Caso and Bernal 1952; Drucker 1974; Coe 1981; Coggins 1982a). Little seems to have been said about political aspects, beyond stressing the close connections between religious symbolism and political authority. However, as I will show, the Ciudadela differs in several significant ways from the residences of many heads of nonindustrialized states, both in Mesoamerica and elsewhere. These unusual features do not lead me to seriously doubt that the Ciudadela was politically important; indeed, I think it highly probable that many heads of the Teotihuacan state occupied the room complexes in the Ciudadela, at least part of the time. However, I suspect that, during much of its history, the Ciudadela served mainly for ritual and for state occasions. I think that much of the day-to-day business of political management, even at very high levels, may have been carried out elsewhere. This prompts me to take a fresh look at other large architectural complexes in Teotihuacan, generally thought of as primarily temples, and to consider their possible political uses. One group of structures in particular, the "Calle de los Muertos Complex," stands out as a likely candidate for the locus of much high-level governmental activity.

The Ciudadela

The Ciudadela is a great nearly rectangular structure, bounded by platforms about 400 meters (approximately 1,300 feet) on a side, on the east side of the Street of the Dead and on the axes of the major east and west avenues of Teotihuacan (Figs. 11.1 and 11.2, no. 3). Perhaps the firmest fact at our disposal is that it is architecturally unlike anything else in the city. It shares numerous features with many other structures, including such elements as platforms, *talud-tablero* pyramids, and plaster-and-concrete-faced masonry room complexes. However, the combination of size, relative proportions, and configuration of these elements results in a unique architectural complex. Although pyramids are prominent in the Ciudadela, it is quite unlike any other pyramid complex at Teotihuacan. Its architectural distinctiveness, in itself, argues that it was intended for activities different from those appropriate for any other place in the city.

In spite of the name now applied to it, the "citadel," I do not know of anyone who believes that it served primarily as a citadel or fortress. Marquina (1922:145) and R. Millon (1973:33) explicitly doubt that this was its primary function. Figure 11.2 includes a plan of the Ciudadela. Millon, Drewitt, and Cowgill (1973:76) show it at a larger scale and with additional information. For photographs, see especially R. Millon (1973:figs. 4–8a, 30–36, 38, and 39a). Marquina (1951:81–88) shows profiles and plans. Marquina (1922) provides the principal report of excavations at the Ciudadela, prior to those now in progress. Drucker (1974) has made a detailed study of many aspects of the complex.

Immediately to the north of the Ciudadela there is an enclosure about 380 meters long and 80 meters wide (Fig. 11.2, 2:N1E1). Its north, west, and east sides are formed by a freestanding wall, and its south side is the north platform of the Ciudadela itself. It is clearly an adjunct of the Ciudadela complex. It seems clear that there was nothing similar on the east and south sides, and 2:N1E1 is the *only* substantial structure directly adjoining the Ciudadela.

On the north, east, and south of the Ciudadela the great surrounding platforms are each about 400 meters long, about 80 meters wide, and 7 to 8 meters high. Four pyramids are set atop the north platform, another four on the south, and three on the east. Walls connect all these 11 pyramids on the north, east, and south, effectively separating interior and exterior space on these platforms (R. Millon 1973:figs. 30–31). Stairways on all these pyramids face toward the interior. Two other stairways, however, connect the Ciudadela

---

Following pages: Figure 11.1. Archaeological and topographic map of Teotihuacan. Map 1 of R. Millon (1973).

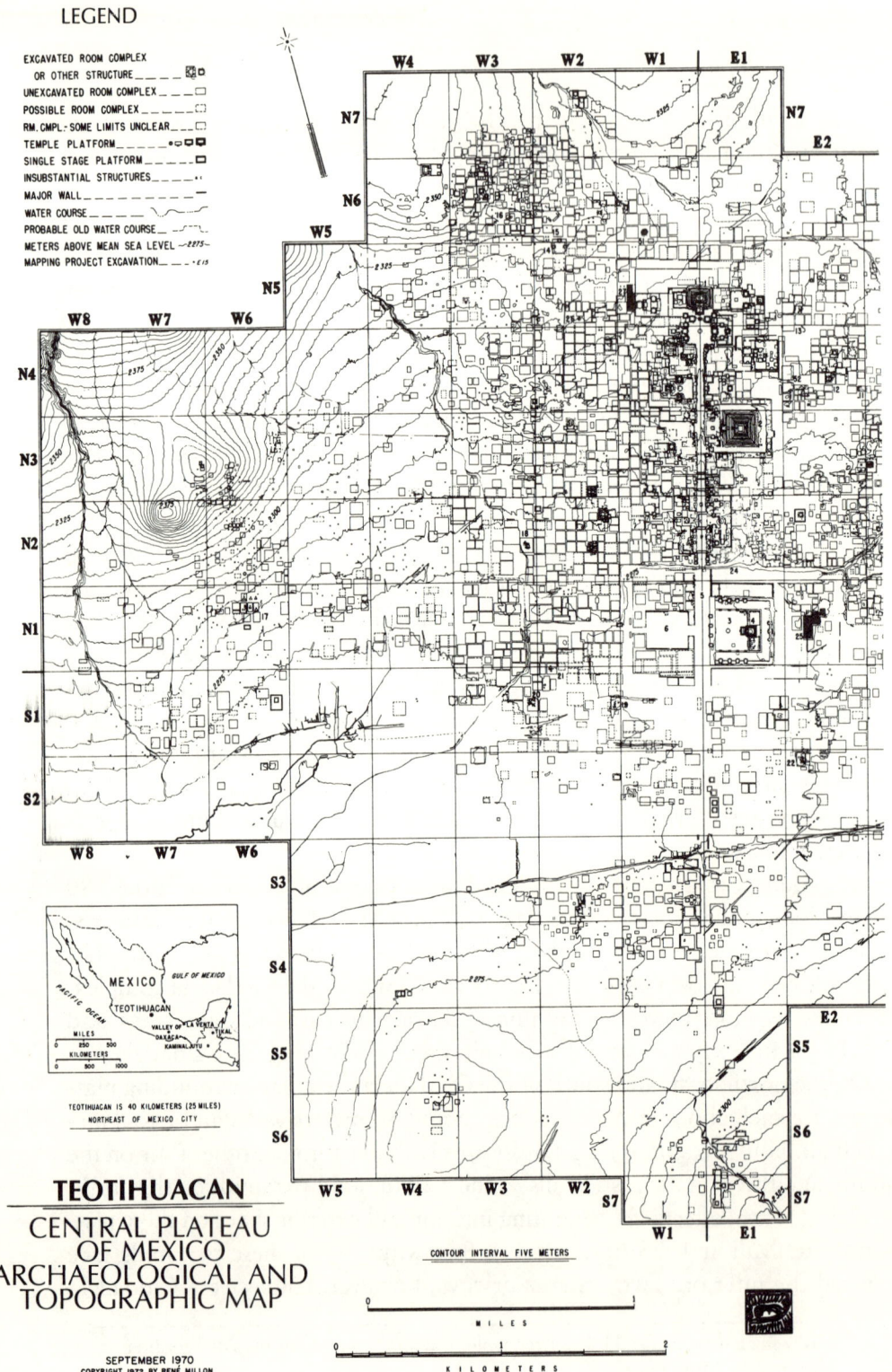

TEOTIHUACAN
CENTRAL PLATEAU OF MEXICO ARCHAEOLOGICAL AND TOPOGRAPHIC MAP

SEPTEMBER 1970
COPYRIGHT 1972 BY RENÉ MILLON

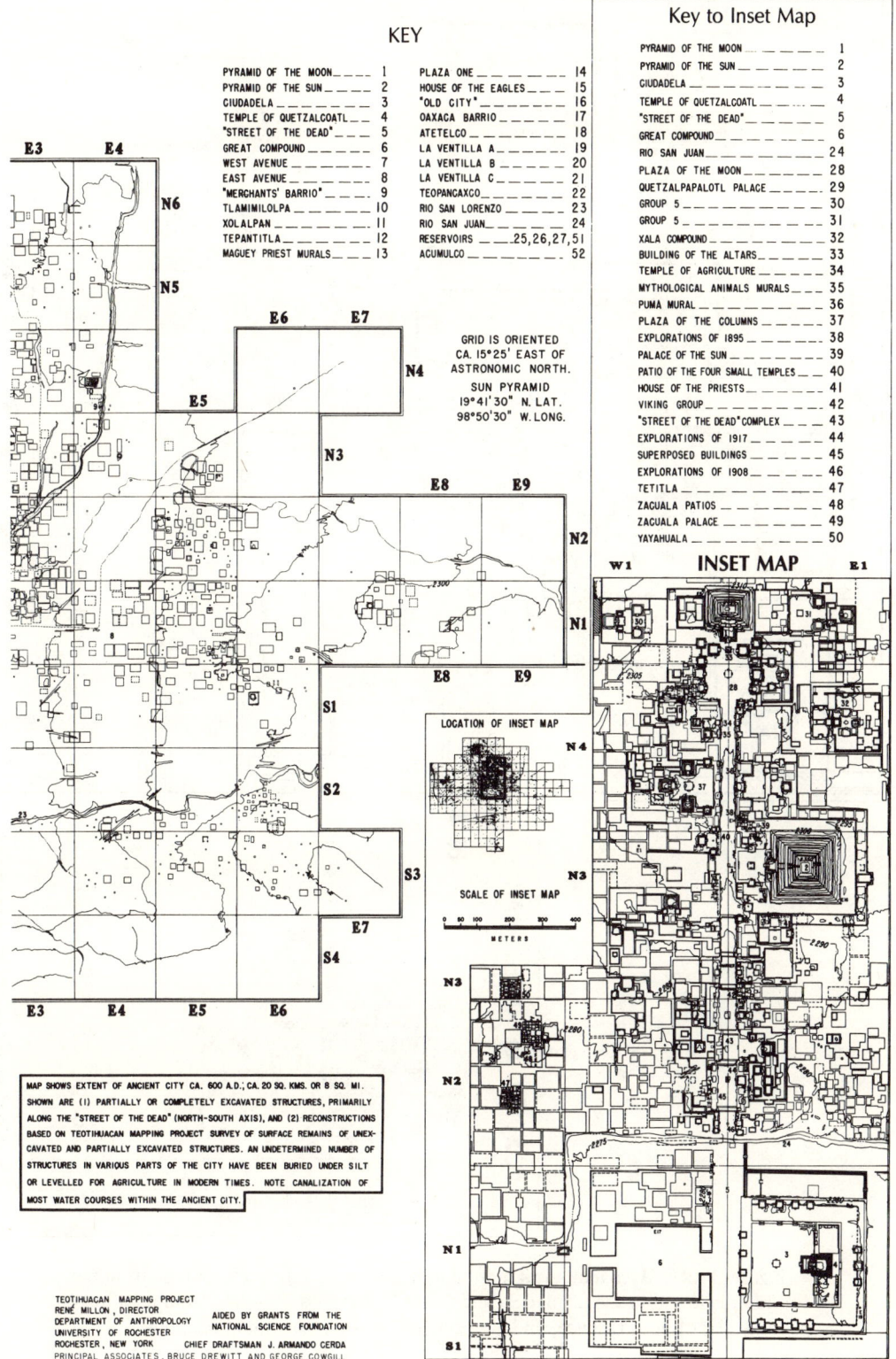

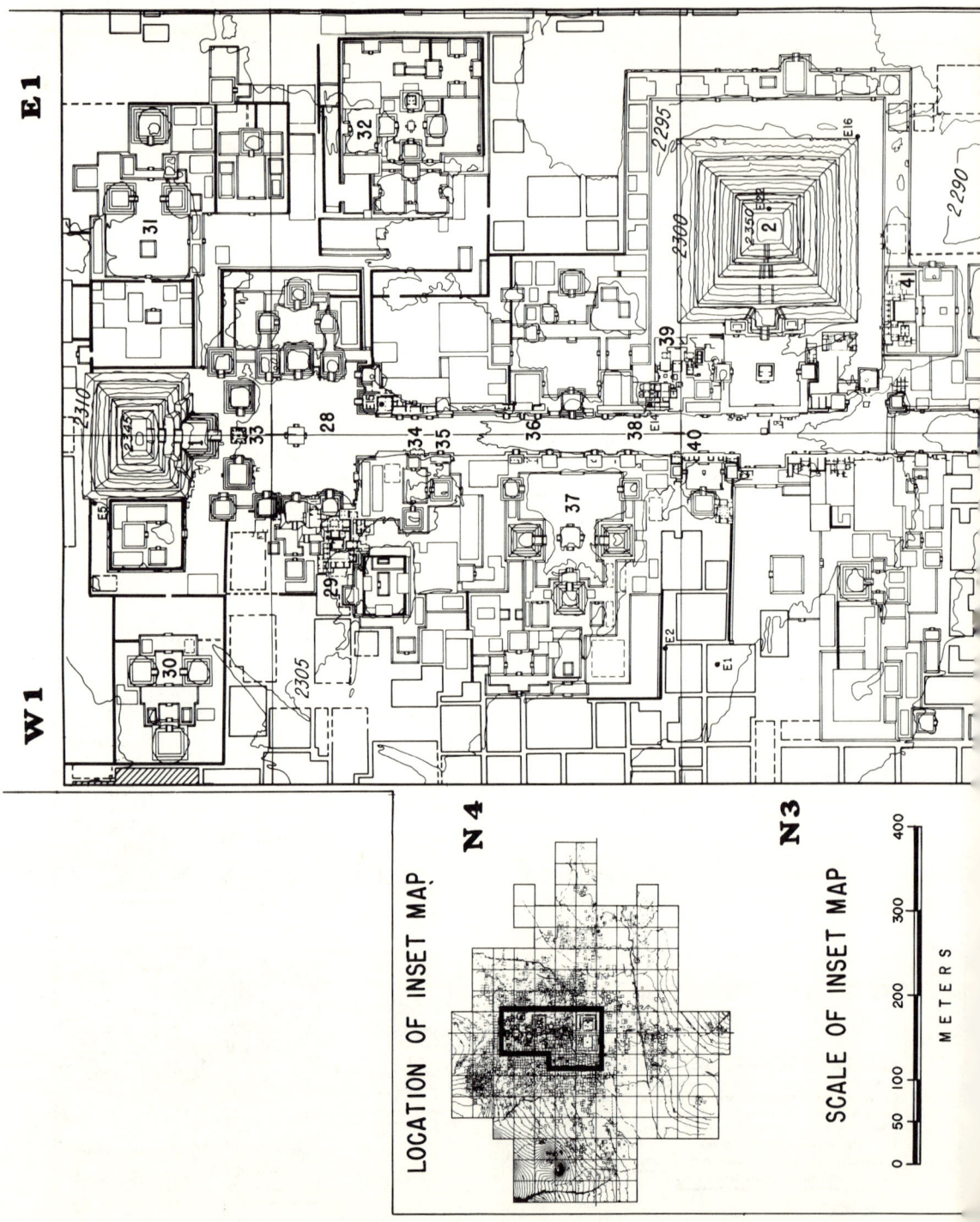

Figure 11.2. Archaeological map of a section of Teotihuacan running from the Moon Pyramid to the Ciudadela and Great Compound. Reduced from inset map in Map 1 of Millon, Drewitt, and Cowgill (1973), with some modifications.

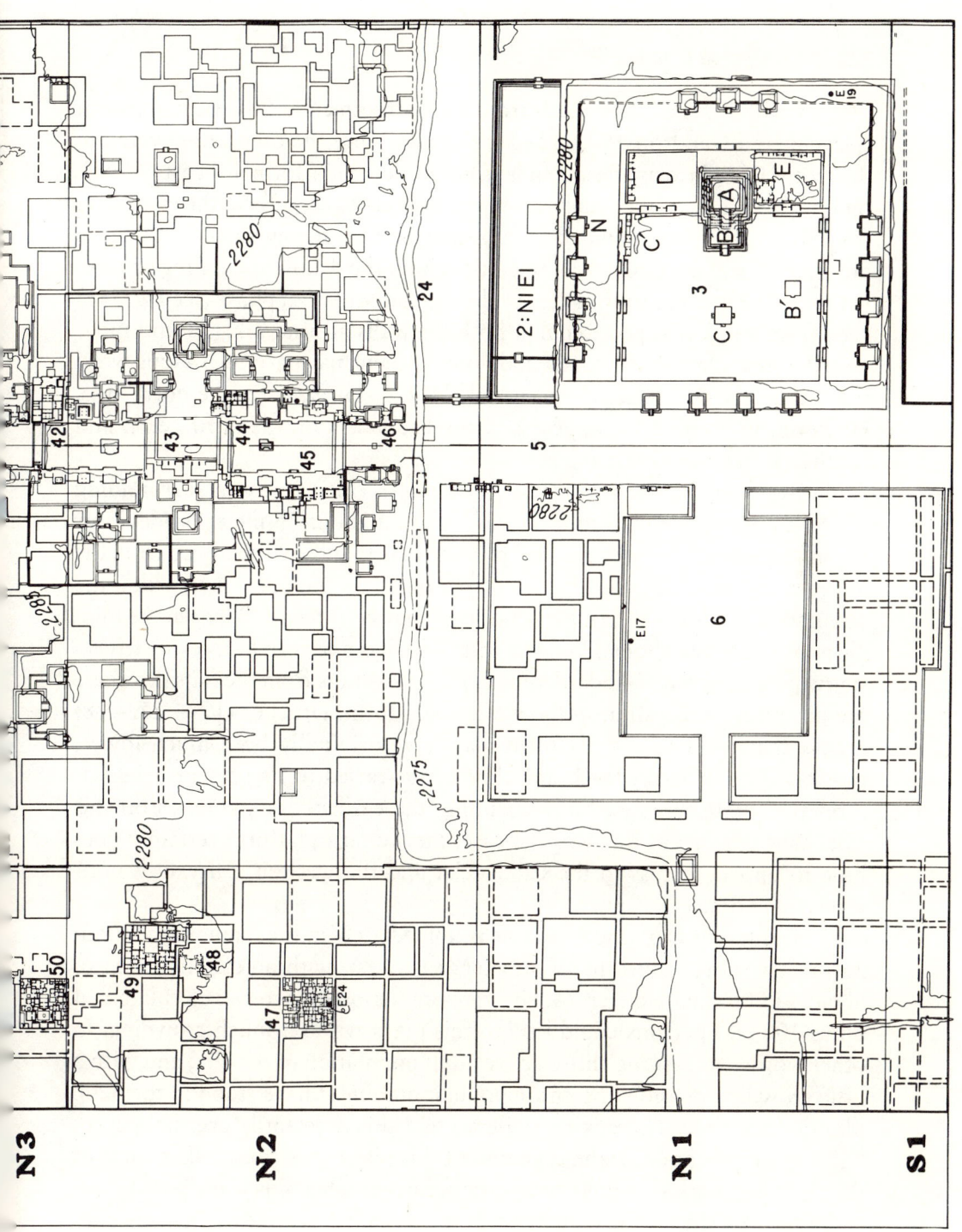

directly with 2:N1E1. One leads from the northern end of the west platform (Heyden and Gendrop 1975:32–33, plate 25), and the other, discovered in the recent INAH excavations, leads from the north platform just east of Pyramid N (Fig. 11.2; neither stairway appears in this figure). Nevertheless, access from elsewhere into the Ciudadela through 2:N1E1 is somewhat indirect. There are a number of unresolved complexities about the details and dating of these features. The great platforms clearly date to the Miccaotli phase (see Fig. 11.3 for chronology). It is possible that both the walls around 2:N1E1 and those atop the great platforms are later additions, so there may have been a time when the Ciudadela was relatively accessible by the stairways on the north side. However, in its final form, access to the Ciudadela on the north, east, and south sides was restricted at best.

On the west the situation is very different. There is also a surrounding platform, but it is only 3 to 4 meters high and about 35 meters wide. Four pyramids project above it, reached by stairways that lead directly up from the Street of the Dead. In contrast to the pyramids on the other three sides, the orientation of these western pyramids is primarily outward. Between the middle two, a stairway about 32 meters wide, which is not steep (as Mesoamerican stairways go), permits—indeed, almost invites—access from the outside. There are no traces of a wall atop the western platform. Drucker (1974:272–78) argues that the western platform may have originally been much lower, possibly even at street level, and that it was raised to its present height at a relatively late time, partially engulfing the earlier four pyramids on this side. Whether or not this was the case, the western platform certainly does little to impede access to the Ciudadela, and the western stairway was its principal entrance.

Upon entering from the west, one is immediately in the main plaza, about 250 meters north-south by 200 meters east-west, with an effective area of about 44,000 square meters (4.4 hectares, or almost 11 acres). I calculate that up to 100,000 persons could fit into this plaza without much crowding. In other words, at least the entire active adult population of the city, and with a little crowding possibly the entire population, *might* have stood in the main plaza at one time. There is no evidence that this necessarily ever happened, but it is an indication of the potential of this plaza to accommodate most of the city's population, if there were ever occasions when this was desired.

On the east side of the main plaza is the so-called Temple of Quetzalcoatl, a pyramid about 65 by 65 meters at its base and about 17 meters high (Fig. 11.2A). It is the third largest pyramid at Teotihuacan. Build up against its front (western) side is a large *talud-tablero* platform, the *plataforma adosada* (Fig. 11.2B). Formally, this is a fore-platform analogous to the platforms built

Fig. 11.3. Valley of Teotihuacan Chronology, Table of Concordances

			Phase Names [1]		Phase Numbers [2]		
LATE HORIZON	A.D. 1500		Teacalco		Aztec IV		
	1400		Chimalpa		Aztec III	POST-	
	1300						
	1200		Zocango		Aztec II	CLASSIC	
SECOND INTER-MEDIATE PERIOD	1100		Mazapan		Mazapa		
	1000					PERIOD	
	900		Xometla		Coyotlatelco		900 A.D.
	800		Oxtoticpac		Proto-Coyotlatelco		
	700	T	METEPEC		Teotihuacán IV	CLASSIC	
	600	E			Teotihuacán IIIA		
MIDDLE HORIZON	500	O	XOLALPAN	Late Early	Teotihuacán III		
	400	T				PERIOD	
	300	I H	TLAMIMILOLPA	Late Early	Teotihuacán IIA-III Teotihuacán IIA		300 A.D.
	200	U	MICCAOTLI		Teotihuacán II	TERMINAL	
	100	A C	TZACUALLI	Late Early	Teotihuacán IA Teotihuacán I	PRE-CLASSIC	
	A.D. B.C.	A					
	100	N	PATLACHIQUE	Chimalhuacán *		PERIOD	
	200		Terminal Cuanalan; Tezoyuca	Cuicuilco *	Proto-Teotihuacán I	LATE	
FIRST INTER-MEDIATE PERIOD	300		Late Cuanalan	Ticoman III *		PRE-CLASSIC	
	400		Middle Cuanalan	Ticoman II *		PERIOD	
	500		Early Cuanalan	Ticoman I *			
	600			Middle		MIDDLE PRE-CLASSIC	
	700		Chiconauhtla	Zacatenco *		PERIOD	
B.C.	800						

[1] Phase names used by personnel of Teotihuacán Mapping Project (Millon and others) and by personnel of Valley of Teotihuacán Project (Sanders and others).

[2] Phase numbers used by personnel of the Proyecto Teotihuacán, of the Instituto Nacional de Antropologia e Historia (see Acosta 1964: 58-59).

* Pre-classic phases elsewhere in the Valley of Mexico.

NOTE: The absolute chronology shown is that used by the Teotihuacán Mapping Project. Terminology for the Teotihuacán phases is based on the Armillas classification (1950) with modifications.

TEOTIHUACAN MAPPING PROJECT
UNIVERSITY OF ROCHESTER

J.A.Cerda

RENÉ MILLON
9/64
REVISED 5/79

up against the fronts of the Sun and Moon Pyramids. In absolute size, it is larger than the Sun *adosada* and smaller than the fore-platform of the Moon. Relative to the pyramid it fronts, however, its size is drastically different. The Sun and Moon platforms are clearly subordinate to the structures behind them, but the platform fronting the Quetzalcoatl Pyramid is so large, relative to it, that one's first impression is that is must have obscured the entire western face of the latter pyramid. However, as René Millon has emphasized, it is both lower and narrower than the Quetzalcoatl Pyramid and would have left much of its west face visible (see Fig. 11.2 and R. Millon 1973:fig. 32). Perhaps the *adosada* is the size it is because it was intended for activities that required that amount of space. Certainly it offers no evidence of a shift away from the cult (or cults) associated with the Temple of Quetzalcoatl itself.

Preserved by the frontal platform, the western face of the Quetzalcoatl Pyramid is a series of cut stone *tableros* and *taludes*. The vertical panels bear repeated carvings of a feathered serpent, alternating with another being that is more difficult to identify. Serpents with feathered bodies appear in profile on the *taludes,* and serpent heads emerge from the balustrades of the staircase. Because of this feathered serpent, the pyramid has been linked to Quetzalcoatl. However, as Armillas (1947) pointed out, there is no good reason to think that the full Quetzalcoatl complex of Aztec times is represented here. The other being, which prominently displays pairs of circular rings, is often linked to Tlaloc, the Aztec earth and rain deity. However, the rings are in the headdress and do not encircle the eyes, which can be seen very plainly lower down (for example, see R. Millon 1973:fig. 33). Caso suggested that this being may be related to the Aztec Xiuhcoatl, or fire serpent (Caso and Bernal 1952: 113–16). Drucker seems inclined to accept this idea and notes the connection of the Xiuhcoatl with the god Xiuhtecuhtli, although he mentions other possibilities as well (Drucker 1974:13–14, 212–13). Besides the two serpent beings, a variety of marine shells appear. Surviving colors include red, white, and green (Drucker 1974:155). Michael Coe hypothesizes that these reliefs "represent the initial creation of the universe through a series of dual oppositions" (1981:168). He suggests that the rulers of Teotihuacan "established for themselves an identity with the dual creator divinity and the power emanating from him/her." Coggins, however, noting analogs in the Maya area, suggests that the two beings are the paired heads of bicephalic serpents, with the heads representing the daily rising and setting of the sun. She says that the Quetzalcoatl Pyramid's facade "may be considered to have been decorated with a sculptural program symbolic of days" (Coggins 1982a:66). This possibility deserves serious consideration, although at present I am not fully convinced.

Similar decorations probably covered all four faces of the pyramid originally, although the only stairway was on the west (Marquina 1951:85, lámina 19). Drucker (1974) questions whether more than the west face had carvings, but INAH excavations in 1980 revealed similar stone carvings in place at the base of the south face, which greatly strengthens the evidence that they were on all four sides. This adds weight to the point that many of these figures would have remained visible even after the frontal platform was added.

Running north and south from the Quetzalcoatl Pyramid are transverse platforms that define the eastern edge of the main plaza. East of these transverse platforms, in the areas bounded by them, the Quetzalcoatl Pyramid, and the great outer platforms, are room complexes referred to as the north and south "palaces" (Fig. 11.2D and E). Each is about 80 meters north-south by 60 meters east-west. Thus, the area of each is about 4800 square meters; somewhat above average for a Teotihuacan apartment compound, but far from exceptional.

There are also rooms on the transverse platforms themselves, but these apparently face onto the main plaza and do not seem to connect directly with the palaces. It is unlikely that these rooms were residential. More problematic are rooms outside the transverse platforms in the northeast corner of the main plaza itself (Fig. 11.2C'). Probably there are more rooms than have been excavated in this area, but not many more. The present land surface near the excavated rooms is 1 or 2 meters higher than the general plaza level. Neither *cascajo* (fine volcanic scoria that have proven a good surface indicator of decayed Teotihuacan concrete construction) nor other building debris or sherds are at all abundant in the main plaza, except in the vicinity of known structures. The relatively few rooms for which there is good evidence in the northeast of the plaza almost surely date to Teotihuacan times, but at present a date anywhere from the Tlamimilolpa through the Metepec phases seems possible.

Finally, there is a small area on our map between the north and south palaces and just east of the Quetzalcoatl Pyramid. The INAH work now in progress should reveal whether any part of this area was residential. Assuming that it was, and adding the areas of the north and south palaces, the rooms on the transverse platforms, and a generous allowance for unexcavated rooms in the C' area, I calculate an absolute maximum of 15,000 square meters of residential space within the Ciudadela, but it is much more likely that the residential space did not exceed 11,000 square meters. Millon (1973:45) estimates that Teotihuacan apartment compounds of 3,600 square meters, occupied by people of intermediate status, may have housed an average of about 60 to 100 inhabitants. Blindly extrapolating these figures, one arrives at estimates of 160 to 270 for the two palaces, and 180 to 420 for the entire Ciudadela. Many of the residents of the Ciudadela were presumably of very high status, and their quarters would probably have been exceptionally spacious, so these figures should be regarded as maximum estimates. A resident population of around 400 is at the extreme upper limit of plausibility, but a figure of 250 or even less is more probable.

Highly relevant features of the Ciudadela in its final form can now be summarized. It was architecturally monumental; it covered about 16 hectares, and the surrounding platforms alone have a volume of at least 700,000 cubic meters (70 percent of the volume of the Pyramid of the Sun). It included a number of pyramids, among which was the third largest in the city, with exceptional carved stone decoration. It included a main plaza of about 4.4 hectares, in which an enormous crowd might have assembled. Although a sharply defined space is created by the Ciudadela and although access is impeded on three sides, the west side is relatively open. Defense against armed attack seems at most a secondary objective of its design. In spite of the overall monumentality of the Ciudadela, residential facilities are quite limited. It is unlikely that it housed more than two to four times the number of people in an average Teotihuacan apartment compound and probably it housed fewer.

To understand the Ciudadela fully, it would be necessary to know the history of its construction. Unfortunately, reports of earlier excavations provide very incomplete information on this history (Marquina 1922, Rubín de la Borbolla 1947). However, much has been learned from close study of surface evidence by members of the Teotihuacan Mapping Project (especially René Millon, Bruce Drewitt, G. R. Krotser, and David Drucker) and from Mapping Project excavations. These excavations were located near the southeastern outer corner of the eastern surrounding platform (TE 19, a long trench shown schematically as a dot labeled E 19 in Fig. 11.2), in the south palace (TE 25N), and on the south transverse platform (TE 25S). These last two excavations were done after completion of the map and do not appear in Figure 11.2. The INAH work now in progress will add greatly to our knowledge of the Ciudadela, but I doubt that the new results will contradict any of the essential elements of the picture I will present here.

To summarize what we know of the architectural history of the Ciudadela, it is clear that there were Patlachique and Tzacualli occupations at, or at least in the immediate vicinity of, the Ciudadela, because substantial quantities of ceramics from both phases were found in our surface collections (Table 11.1). The Patlachique occupation on the site of the Ciudadela seems to have been several hundred meters outside the main Patlachique settlement, to judge from our map of Patlachique sherd densities (Cowgill 1974:382, fig. 3).[2] The Tzacualli ceramic density on the Ciudadela is also higher than elsewhere in the immediate vicinity, but ceramic densities are high enough throughout the

Table 11.1. Counts of Ceramic Categories in Teotihuacan Mapping Project Surface Collections from the Ciudadela and 2:N1E1*

Totals of Phased Ceramics and Thin Orange	Proveniences				
	Surrounding Platforms	Pyramids on Platforms	Palaces	All Ciudadela Collections	2:N1El
Patlachique	171 (14)	92 (5)	3 (2)	273 (8)	21 (2)
Tzacualli	157 (13)	247 (14)	16 (13)	460 (14)	43 (3)
Miccaotli	426 (36)	482 (28)	11 (9)	1,000 (30)	114 (9)
Tlamimilolpa	193 (16)	447 (26)	37 (30)	731 (22)	287 (22)
Xolalpan	71 (6)	79 (5)	11 (9)	178 (5)	334 (26)
Metepec	20 (2)	62 (4)	12 (10)	106 (3)	67 (5)
Regular Thin Orange	98 (8)	196 (11)	20 (16)	337 (10)	247 (19)
Coarse Thin Orange	20 (2)	22 (1)	4 (3)	48 (1)	70 (5)
All Post-Teotihuacan	40 (3)	121 (7)	9 (7)	228 (7)	110 (8)
TOTALS	1,196	1,748	123	3,361	1,295

*Based on ceramic reanalyses supervised by Evelyn Rattray. Figures in parentheses are percentages of column totals. Thin Orange Ware is unphased.

region between the Ciudadela and the main focus of Tzacualli settlement in the northwest to suggest strongly that the vicinity of the Ciudadela was, by this time, within the large region of contiguous settlement (Cowgill 1974:386, fig. 4). These ceramic densities suffice to show that there was some sort of significant occupation at the site of the Ciudadela as early as the Patlachique phase, but unfortunately we still know nothing of the structures that were present then.

By the end of the Miccaotli phase, the great surrounding platforms on the east, north, and south had been constructed on their present plan and to within a meter of their present height. This is shown by Mapping Project excavation TE 19, which, at the top of the east surrounding platform, encountered several concrete floors in the top meter dating ceramically from Early Tlamimilolpa through Late Xolalpan. Below that was over a meter of adobes that incorporated nothing later than Miccaotli phase ceramics, with a high proportion of Tzacualli ceramics. This excavation had to be terminated at a depth of about two meters, some five or six meters above the underlying land surface, so the earlier history of the eastern platform was not revealed. It may well have been built as a single massive operation in the Miccaotli phase, incorporating sherds from quite different earlier structures. Our work could not rule out the alternative possibility that the Miccaotli platform may have greatly enlarged an earlier enclosing platform. Tunnels from Mexican excavations still traverse the south and north platforms, so it should be relatively easy to resolve this question. In any case, the eastern platform was already close to its present dimensions by the very beginning of Early Tlamimilolpa at the latest. This must also have been true for the northern and southern platforms, because it would have made no architectural sense to build the eastern platform by itself. The western platform, as noted earlier, might have been much lower in Miccaotli than it is now, but we have no stratigraphic evidence bearing on its construction history.

The currently visible Quetzalcoatl Pyramid probably dates to the Miccaotli phase and cannot be later than Early Tlamimilolpa, as shown by architectural evidence on the south side, where it links with the south palace (R. Millon, personal communication). There is good evidence for at least one earlier pyramid (Rubín de la Borbolla 1947:62–63, Drucker 1974:158), but we cannot say how much earlier it is. The *plataforma adosada* was obviously built later than the now visible Quetzalcoatl Pyramid. A burial and offering associated with it, discussed sketchily by Rubín de la Borbolla (1947), suggests a Tlamimilolpa date (R. Millon, personal communication).

Mapping Project excavations in the south palace and the south transverse platform revealed no layers earlier than Early Tlamimilolpa (Rattray 1981: 46–47; Drucker 1974:48, 113–14, 126). If there were any earlier structures in these areas, they must have been razed in the process of Early Tlamimilolpa construction. The south palace was evidently built and then extensively remodeled several times during the Early Tlamimilolpa phase. After this, there are no layers earlier than Metepec. During Late Tlamimilolpa and all of the Xolalpan phase, a period of some 350 years, the palaces may well have been kept in good repair, but all the evidence suggests that there was no major rebuilding and no significant alterations. This is the time that saw the widest and strongest evidence of Teotihuacan influence throughout Mesoamerica, and it includes the ceramic phases best attested in most excavations in residential structures elsewhere within the city.

Subsequently, there was at least some rebuilding in the palace areas during the Metepec phase, but earlier plans apparently were not altered. The upper layers excavated on the south transverse platform are Metepec, and Drucker (1974:115) argues that one set of rooms in the north palace (D4–D7), which are markedly higher than the others, are probably also Metepec.

After Early Tlamimilolpa few, if any, additions to the Quetzalcoatl Pyramid and its *adosada* seem to have been made. Later additions to the great surrounding platforms were also relatively minor, although the floor was raised and rebuilt several times from Early Tlamimilolpa through Late Xolalpan. The 15 pyramids atop these platforms may have had much earlier antecedents, but their present form is probably Xolalpan or Metepec, and I know of no certain evidence for more than one earlier construction stage. The walls connecting the pyramids join their latest stages and so are also late. It is not clear if earlier walls existed.

All this presents us with two problems. First, the area of the Ciudadela devoted to rooms is surprisingly small, especially in comparison with palaces for heads of other nonindustrialized states comparable in size to Teotihuacan. Usually quarters are provided for the activities of many hundreds or even thousands of retainers, servants, guests, and officials of many sorts. In the Ciudadela the facilities provide for a few hundred at most. Second, the architectural sequence confronts us with the picture of 15 or 20 generations of sovereigns who somehow resisted the temptation to make drastic changes in the structures inherited from their predecessors, during the very centuries when the Teotihuacan state was in its prime.

The Ciudadela in Cross-Cultural Perspective

The term "ethnoarchaeology" calls to mind studies of the living circumstances and technologies of hunter-gatherers, pastoral nomads, and villagers. To understand the politics of complex societies, it is necessary and should be highly productive also to study and reflect on the "ethnoarchaeology" of public architecture. This has not received nearly the attention it deserves, at least not by Mesoamericanists. Extensive cross-cultural investigation of the architectural facilities and spatial settings for governmental activities is needed, with particular attention to correlations between specific kinds of activities or political arrangements and specific architectural forms and configurations. Such a comparative perspective is especially necessary for understanding Teotihuacan, for which textual information is almost unavailable.

My own reading on this topic remains incomplete and unsystematic but reasonably extensive and varied. Some relevant points can be briefly summarized. Structures often tend to remain in tightly fixed locations when they are of central symbolic significance for a society. Instances range from the main temple precincts of Eridu and Uruk to the Aztec Templo Mayor in Tenochtitlan and Canterbury Cathedral (seat of the heads of the English church since the introduction of Christianity to the Anglo-Saxons in A.D. 597). There is also a tendency to resist frequent conspicuous change in the appearance of structures of such symbolic significance. Most of the examples that come to mind are directly connected with religion. In some cases, the residences of heads of state also show stability in location and appearance, but this seems most likely to happen when there is no religious cult strongly identified with the state, for example, the White House, the Kremlin). Such residences of heads of state often serve as major physical foci for, and expressions of, symbolism significant for the state as a whole. Where, instead, cult centers or temples serve this function, the residences of rulers may be far more variable, both in form and location. The pattern at Chan Chan, the Chimu capital on the north coast of Peru, may be a rather special case. Here, the residences of rulers were central symbolic foci, but because each residence was forever identified with a specific individual, each new ruler had to construct a new residential complex (Conrad 1981). More often, it seems that when residences of heads of state are not of central symbolic importance, they have shifted rather freely, in response to a variety of ad hoc political and personal considerations. Rulers, especially of expanding states, have often deliberately set out to outdo and overshadow their predecessors, drastically rebuilding and often at least partially destroying older palaces or locating their residences in different places altogether. Strong rulers are certainly not uninterested in creating residences of dazzling splendor and awesome majesty. However, it seems that the intention is often to symbolize the wealth, power, and authority of the individual ruler, or a specific dynasty, as long as there are *other* magnificent structures (such as religious monuments) that can serve as stable symbols for the society as a whole.

In spite of variability in the residences of heads of state, many of them share some rather obvious features. Very often in theory, in fact, or both, the ruler's household commands more wealth than any other in the state, and this is conspicuously demonstrated by the number of people involved as well as the splendor of their surroundings. The ruler's residence will accommodate a very large number of functionaries and perhaps numerous relatives, as well as servants, guards, various kinds of officials, and honored guests. The ruler's household is often a prime consumer of craft products, and the ruler may be deeply involved in their production and in commerce. Facilities for large-scale manufacture of textiles and other goods (although not necessarily residences of the workers) may be in or fairly close to the ruler's residence. Often the ruler has many wives and concubines, and he provides space for them in his residence. There may also be space for storage of valuables and perhaps for stores of grain and other staples, potentially available for wide distribution in times of shortage.

Some of the above features are far more common than others, and I do not mean to suggest that any one of them, still less the combination, is nearly universal. However, it does seem a well-founded generalization that the rulers of complex societies tend to reside in structures that are complex, as well as large. In addition to being splendid and monumental, they tend to have many rooms and a variety of other architectural features, providing facilities for diverse activities by a large number of people. This description, incidentally, seems to apply to the palaces of Moctezuma and his predecessors in Tenochtitlan.[3]

In contrast, although the Ciudadela is splendid and monumental, its room complexes do not cover a very large area, and they show little variety—the plans of the apartments are quite similar to one another.[4] The Ciudadela is also unusual in that throughout Late Tlamimilolpa and all of the Xolalpan phase—a period of about 350 years—only minor alterations seem to have been made. During the Metepec phase, not long before the collapse of the city, there was probably an increase in new construction in the Ciudadela. But the long period with little change is an unexpected finding of the Mapping Project investigations.

In the light of the previous discussion, it is extremely unlikely that the Ciudadela merely symbolized the wealth and power of a specific ruler or ruling dynasty. The evidence is very strong that it was one of the central symbols of the Teotihuacan state, as distinct from any specific persons who headed that state. This point has been explicitly stated by René Millon (1973:37, 55). My contribution here is twofold. First, I want to emphasize how difficult it is to interpret the Ciudadela as merely symbolic of a specific person or dynasty—to point out that such an interpretation is outside the range of plausible alternatives. Second, I want to underscore and elaborate on the implications of the Ciudadela for Teotihuacan political organization. The most important point is that the Ciudadela does not seem to provide enough facilities for much of the day-to-day government of either the city or the state of Teotihuacan. The recent INAH discovery that 2:N1E1 was directly linked by two stairways to the Ciudadela and that there were rooms and other features in parts (though probably not all) of this compound somewhat weakens this argument. However, even if 2:N1E1 is an annex of the Ciudadela, the space and facilities are unexpectedly limited.

It has always been obvious that much lower-level political and governmental activity must have been carried out elsewhere. René Millon (1973:20, as well as in earlier publications) has long since pointed to the flanking platforms of the Great Compound (Fig. 11.2, no. 6) as likely loci for fairly high-level bureaucratic activities. However, relatively little systematic attention seems to have been given to the many hectares of pyramids, platforms, and room complexes that stretch for nearly 2 kilometers along the northern Street of the Dead, from the Ciudadela to the vicinity of the Moon Pyramid. Indeed, it would scarcely have been possible or profitable to have given much attention to this region before having available the detail revealed by the Mapping Project survey and the extensive INAH excavations of the 1960s and later. Even today, however, there is a tendency to view this large zone mainly as the site of temples and priests' residences, where most activities were rituals. Nevertheless, it has always been a logical possibility that many governmental functions and much relatively high-level political activity were carried out in this zone, although it remains unclear how much of this activity was performed by persons whose primary identities were sacerdotal, and how much by persons whose roles and offices were conceived as not primarily priestly. My emphasis on the limited facilities of the Ciudadela provides a reason to look more closely at possible governmental functions of structures along the northern Street of the Dead. I will do this in a later section. First, however, I will summarize some evidence and offer some conjectures about changes over time in Teotihuacan government.

Politics and the Development of Teotihuacan

In the Patlachique phase the population of Teotihuacan grew very rapidly from practically nothing to perhaps as many as 20,000 to 40,000 (Cowgill 1979). The settlement seems unrelated, spatially, to earlier Cuanalan phase settlements (Cowgill 1974: figs. 2 and 3). The Mapping Project survey revealed a broad distribution of Patlachique phase ceramics in most of what was to become the northwestern quadrant of the city, and extending outside the later city to include a concentration west of Cerro Colorado, nearly 4 kilometers west of the Sun Pyramid (around squares N3W8 and N3W7 of Fig. 11.1). Within the city, the highest Patlachique sherd densities were collected around squares N4W2 and N5W2, some 500 to 1,000 meters west of the site of the Moon Pyramid. Both the Moon and Sun Pyramids are well within the region of high to moderate Patlachique sherd densities, although closer to the edge than the center. Although we cannot be sure, it is quite possible that important temples already stood on these spots. We have no evidence for the Moon Pyramid, where attempts by the Mexican government to drive tunnels were thwarted by cave-ins. A relatively small platform and other constructions are exposed in the lower tunnel through the base of the Sun Pyramid. While these have never been adequately tested, there is a good chance that the platform dates to the Patlachique phase (Millon, Drewitt, and Bennyhoff 1965: 10, 15, 21–25, 34–35).

South of the Sun Pyramid, Patlachique sherd cover decreases very rapidly, and there is very little south of about the Viking Group apartment compound (Fig. 11.1 and 11.2, no. 42). A significant quantity of Patlachique ceramics was collected from the Ciudadela itself, but this site is nearly a kilometer outside the main Patlachique phase settlement. Nearly 3 kilometers farther south, in square S6E1, is a second small concentration of Patlachique ceramics.

The Patlachique ceramics indicate that the site of the Ciudadela was occupied during this time, but the nature of that occupation remains unknown. The remoteness of the location suggests that the spot was not of great economic or political importance. It may have already had some special religious significance. Later the Ciudadela was on the axis of East and West Avenues and adjacent to the intersection of that axis with the Street of the Dead, and there is every reason to believe that this location signified not only the center of the four quarters of Teotihuacan, but the intersection of cosmic axes. However, I know of no strong evidence that the Street of the Dead already existed in Patlachique times (although at least its northern end may have), and there is no reason to think that East and West Avenues existed this early, because their courses are almost entirely outside the Patlachique settlement. Whatever significance the site of the Ciudadela had in Patlachique times, it is unlikely that it was already believed to be the center of the world.

An alternative possibility should be mentioned, although I think it is exceedingly improbable. It is conceivable that the Ciudadela was already the site of a ruler's residence and that it was placed well outside the city in order to be less susceptible to threats from unruly elements within the city. There are many instances of this, such as Westminster and Versailles (where in 1789 this strategy proved not very successful). However, it seems most probable where cities have developed strong identities and relatively autonomous organs of government, and where all authority is not strongly concentrated in a single, highly centralized state hierarchy. More often, among nonindustrialized states, rulers' residences are located centrally within major cities, as in traditional China and ancient Mesopotamia. I think it extremely unlikely that Patlachique phase Teotihuacan had the kind of political system in which it would have made sense to locate the ruler's residence nearly a kilometer outside the main settlement.

The rapid growth of Teotihuacan and its great size, both in absolute terms and relative to other Basin of Mexico settlements, suggest that political authority was already very strong in the Patlachique phase. Rulers probably resided somewhere within the main settlement of the city, but there seems little else to be said.

By the Tzacualli phase there is evidence for at least moderately intense occupation over nearly the whole region ever covered by the city of Teotihuacan. The population may have reached 60,000 to 80,000 (Cowgill 1979:55). East and south of the Sun Pyramid ceramic densities tend to be lower than in later phases, but the Ciudadela was no longer outside the main settlement. It was far from the region where the highest Tzacualli sherd densities were collected (around square N4W2), but relative to the outer margins of settlement, its location had become central. It is not at all clear where the rulers of Tzacualli phase Teotihuacan resided. The absence of evidence about Tzacualli architecture in the Ciudadela is inconclusive but this very lack of evidence suggests that the Tzacualli rulers probably did not live there. If they had, they would probably have built structures monumental enough to avoid being obscured by Miccaotli and Early Tlamimilolpa construction.

The innermost Moon Pyramid has been dated to the Tzacualli phase (Acosta 1967:46–47), but little is known about it. Data on the Sun Pyramid are much more ample (Millon, Drewitt, and Bennyhoff 1965; Rattray 1981; R. Smith n.d.). In material recovered from Mexican government tunnels through the base of the pyramid, nothing later than an early subphase of Tzacualli is represented. A very small proportion of ceramics from an INAH tunnel near the top of the pyramid appears to be Miccaotli. A Mapping Project excavation in the floor of this upper tunnel (TE 22) obtained nothing at all later than Tzacualli, although it is believed to represent a late subphase. This excavation also revealed tantalizing evidence of a structure not far below the top of the present Sun Pyramid, with hints that it may have been one of a pair of twin temples (R. Millon 1973:fig. 17*b*, 1976:238; Rattray 1981:36–38). Thus, during the Tzacualli phase, a pyramid nearly as large as the present one was completed. Evidently it was built on a very large base and was intended from the outset to be enormous. If it had grown by the accretion of a series of successively larger whole pyramids, the lower tunnel should have revealed a significant amount of late Tzacualli ceramics in the more recent parts farther away from the inner core. Although evidence about the very top of the Sun Pyramid has been thoroughly destroyed, there cannot have been any extensive post-Tzacualli additions there. Around the base of the pyramid, INAH excavations and a Mapping Project excavation (TE 16) show that relatively minor alterations and additions continued at least into Xolalpan times.

The significance of this evidence is that, during the Tzacualli phase, an immense Sun Pyramid, which completely overshadowed any structures likely to have existed then at the Ciudadela, was built within a very short time. It is impossible to say whether the Moon Pyramid also was already immense, but it may have been. It certainly seems likely that the persons who caused the Sun Pyramid to be built were people of the highest political, as well as ritual, importance. Construction of the Sun Pyramid may have been as much a political as a religious act (Millon 1981:235).

It is only a step from this observation to the conjecture that the high priests of the cult (or cults, since there were probably two temples) associated with the Sun Pyramid were also the heads of the Teotihuacan state.[5] This seems to me an altogether plausible guess, and it is consistent with the idea that religious authority is often a pathway to secular authority. However, I do not think we can yet rule out other possibilities. The priests associated with the cults centered on the Sun Pyramid must have been extremely important, but it is at least possible that the heads of the state were not among them. If they were not, then it is difficult to say much else about the rulers. William Sanders (personal communication) has suggested that they may have lived in the Xala Compound (Figs. 11.1 and 11.2, no. 32) where the density of Tzacualli ceramics is high.

In any case, it is important to remember that by this time Teotihuacan had already been an extremely large and important settlement for two or three centuries. René Millon has been at pains to point out that it is not clear that the early city was entirely laid out in accordance with a single, preconceived master plan (R. Millon 1973:43), but at least the laying out of the northern half of the Street of the Dead dates to the Tzacualli phase, and by this time more than 20 three-temple complexes had been built, some of them quite distant from the Street of the Dead (R. Millon 1973:52). The conception of the Pyramid of the Sun and the monumental avenue it faces, and the organization, authority, and resources to have carried this conception out imply that, whether or not much coercion was involved, there was an already quite developed political system and an already wealthy society. Millon (1973:52–55; 1981: 220–21, 235) has particularly emphasized this point.

It is not clear if East and West Avenues were also laid out by the Tzacualli phase, but René Millon (1973:52) mentions evidence that suggests this possibility, and he connects it with the possibility that there was already "a temple or shrine of some importance on the site of the later Ciudadela . . ., perhaps on the site of the present Temple of Quetzalcoatl."

In the Miccaotli phase the Ciudadela and the Quetzalcoatl Pyramid are clearly monumental, as discussed earlier. I conjecture that the Ciudadela, in the form we know it, was the physical realization of the vision of an extremely powerful ruler, who probably lived during the Miccaotli phase. By that time Teotihuacan had had a population of scores of thousands of people for centuries. The influence of the Teotihuacan state was already extensive and was rapidly expanding. It is likely that the heads of the Teotihuacan state had exercised strong authority for many generations. I do not think that construction of the Ciudadela marks the sudden imposition of strong or highly centralized control over a society that previously had not been very complex. The monumental plan of the Ciudadela *may* reflect a significant further increase in the centralization of political authority, significant changes in political structure, and conceivably in the ideological basis for rulership. More concretely, it is possible that it represents a shift in the physical locus of supreme political power away from the vicninity of the Sun and Moon Pyramids, or wherever the heads of state had previously resided. Whether it also meant a change in the cult with which the head of the state was associated is impossible to say. In textually documented states violent and abrupt shifts in occupancy of high office have been quite common. It is very unlikely that Teotihuacan politics somehow proceeded smoothly for six or eight centuries, never seriously complicated by palace intrigues, struggles over succession to high office, or widespread popular disorders and threatened (if not actual) rebellions. However, I can see no evidence about the timing or nature of such episodes, except for the final catastrophic collapse of the city at the end of the Metepec phase. It is at least as likely that the Miccaotli phase Ciudadela represents the relatively orderly intensification of long-term trends as that it reflects some revolution in Teotihuacan politics.

Two possible analogies that come to mind are the construction of Versailles by Louis XIV and the Escorial by Philip II. Neither represents a revolutionary break with the past. Both embody the personal intentions of powerful individuals. Earlier I noted the "impersonal" significance of the Ciudadela, and this may seem contradictory. Part of the resolution of this apparent contradiction is that both Louis and Philip intended their palatial complexes to be of national, not merely personal or dynastic, significance. Moreover, in both cases the edifices have in fact acquired national symbolic meanings that transcend the significance of the specific individuals who planned them and caused them to be built.

Insofar as one can read intention from architectural form, the designer of the Ciudadela apparently intended that it would remain the royal residence as long as the world lasted. At the same time, either the previous administrative experience of the designer did not suggest that a housing capacity of 200 to at most 400 would create any problems, or else administrative convenience was subordinated to other considerations.

But what became of these intentions? Throughout the Early Tlamimilolpa period, which lasted perhaps a century, there was active rebuilding within the Ciudadela palaces and at least one substantial change in room plans (Drucker 1974:113–14). After that, the room plans of these palaces, as well as the rest of the Ciudadela, seem to have remained unchanged, with only minor renovations and maintenance, until the Metepec phase. It seems certain that the symbolic value of the Ciudadela was too great to permit any changes in the plan.

In the case of any ordinary apartment compound, such a hiatus in major architectural activity would probably suggest a hiatus in occupation as well. But it scarcely seems possible that a structure as important as the Ciudadela would have been left wholly unoccupied. It is almost as difficult to believe that during the 350 years or so of Teotihuacan's greatest influence, in Late Tlamimilolpa and Xolalpan times, the political organization of the state did not change substantially, in fact if not in theory. Moreover, it seems highly probable that these political changes would be reflected in new architectural developments somewhere in the city. The conclusion I draw from putting these ideas together is that the Ciudadela remained symbolically very important after the Early Tlamimilolpa phase, but that it very probably became less closely connected with the everyday business of administration and political management.

This change could have occurred in many ways. René Millon (personal communication) suggests that the heads of state may have shifted their residence out of the Ciudadela and returned there only on state occasions, for ceremonial and ritual activities. An alternative that I find equally plausible (although Millon does not agree) is that the office of head of state remained in theory at the top of the political hierarchy, but in practice came to be involved primarily with state-related ceremonial, while it became customary for persons holding somewhat lesser offices to carry out most of the active decision-making and political management. In other words, some high minister or "second in command" may have taken over most of the actual management of the state. According to this hypothesis, the nominal head of state continued to reside in the Ciudadela palaces, carrying out his routine activities with a comparatively small resident staff and assembling a larger number of people only on special state occasions. The persons more actively involved in government lived elsewhere, in closer proximity to larger resident staffs. If such a shift in the locus of high political power occurred, it may have been gradual, or it might have come about through violence and intrigue—perhaps a coup d'état. However, it is well to remember that we do not yet have any evidence of such events. Both the possibilities I have mentioned are intended mainly to show that there are plausible explanations for the evidence provided by the Ciudadela. The alternatives mentioned—that the heads of state maintained effective political control, but lived outside the Ciudadela except on special occasions, or that they continued to reside in the Ciudadela but became less directly involved in active political management—are obviously not the only possible explanations.

Nor are these possibilities mutually exclusive. Actual events were probably far more complicated and may possibly have involved elements of both these and other alternatives. For example, perhaps the head of the state continued to reside in the Ciudadela, but on most days proceeded to some other section of the city to conduct most routine governmental business, using the Ciudadela primarily on special occasions. Something like this occurs in some nations today: the head of state leaves his residence each morning in a procession of limousines, with motorcycle escort, and makes his way to a government office building. At Teotihuacan the ruler might have traveled in a litter with an escort of spearmen, perhaps something like the figures on some Maya polychrome vessels. It is appealing to conjure up such a scene. However, the separation of residence from work place seems quite uncommon for specialists in nonindustrialized societies. For this reason, if no other, it is unlikely that Teotihuacan rulers customarily resided in one place and worked in another.

Evidence for renewed architectural activity in the Ciudadela in the Metepec phase suggests it may have returned to closer involvement with political management. This might reflect a consciously renewed emphasis on the Ciudadela as a symbol of the stability and majesty of the Teotihuacan state, in response to intensified threats to the actual survival of that state. However, if the renewed building activity in the Ciudadela reflected its symbolic significance, one would expect an even greater emphasis on keeping it exactly the way it was. The rooms in the north palace that Drucker (1974:115) thinks may be Metepec do, apparently, preserve the Early Tlamimilolpa layout, though at a substantially higher floor level. However, the pyramids on the great surrounding platforms on the north, east, and south have *talud-tablero* construction only in front, but only single, unbroken *taludes* in the rear. This is probably a late architectural innovation. Perhaps in Metepec times there was a renewed emphasis on the Ciudadela as the locus of active high-level political management, as much as or more than an increase in its symbolic importance.

Possible Major Political Loci Outside the Ciudadela

If for three or four centuries the physical locus of much high-level political management at Teotihuacan was not in the Ciudadela, then where was it? This question leads to further questions. What would one expect the archaeological manifestations of active political management to look like? In the language of "new archaeology," what are the archaeologically testable implications of the hypothesis that, around the middle of the Tlamimilolpa phase, political management largely shifted away from the Ciudadela to structures better suited to the activities of a large and complex political system?

In view of my earlier discussion, I would expect the new locus to include a large complex of structures, with some exceptionally large and fine apartments, and other much less fine residential areas. In the entire complex, there should be facilities to accommodate several hundred people, and perhaps as many as a few thousand. There would probably be at least some rooms whose functions were primarily administrative or civic rather than residential or ceremonial. Craft workshops might well be present or very close by. Pyramids might or might not be included; if present, they would not necessarily be of exceptional size. Finally, the structure of the complex should resemble the layers of an onion, that is, a very private core, progressively more accessible layers surrounding it, and a relatively accessible periphery. The entire complex, however, might be rather clearly bounded and marked off from neighboring structures. Great architectural stability is not likely. Indeed, frequent major alterations are probable and shifts to totally different locations within the city are possible.

When expectations are phrased in this way, almost all the great complexes of buildings within several hundred meters of the Street of the Dead, from the vicinity of the Moon Pyramid to the Great Compound, seem like reasonable candidates. However, I must confess that I did not first formulate the above implications of my hypothesis and then begin looking for a complex that would fit them. I had a favorite candidate already in mind: the "Street of the Dead Complex," or "Calle de los Muertos Complex," which I refer to as CMC henceforth (Figs. 11.1 and 11.2, the large complex centered on number 43). This was first recognized as what we call a "macrocomplex"—a very large complex of architectural complexes—by Bruce Drewitt and Matthew Wallrath in the course of the Mapping Project survey (R. Millon 1973:18, 35, 39). Wallrath (1967) has published a brief description of it, calling attention to many of its distinctive architectural features but failing to suggest that it might have had special political significance. Matos Moctezuma (1980) describes excavations in the 1960s in a northern section of the CMC. Other partially excavated complexes within the CMC include the "Superposed Buildings" and the "Explorations of 1917" (Fig. 11.2, nos. 45 and 44; Marquina 1922) and the Viking Group (Figure 11.2, no. 42; Armillas 1944). The CMC includes many temples, as well as a number of residential groups and some open spaces. It straddles the Street of the Dead. A freestanding wall bounds most of its margins (the thick line barely visible in Figure 11.1 but readily seen in Figure 11.2). The enclosed area is about 350 meters east-west, and varies from about 340 to 390 meters north-south. The total area is around 12 to 13 hectares, somewhat less than the Ciudadela's 16 hectares but with considerably more residential space. A large proportion of the room complexes remains unexcavated. Judging from the Mapping Project interpretations shown in Figure 11.2 (mainly by René Millon and Bruce Drewitt), I estimate that the entire CMC provides facilities for around 800 to 1,600 persons. This estimate may be conservative, since excavations by the current INAH project show that at least several areas shown as open spaces in Figure 11.2 actually contain rooms.

At first sight, the privacy of the CMC seems to be compromised by the fact that it is bisected by the Street of the Dead. However, the four southernmost of the six transverse platforms ("avenue dividers") that cross the Street of the Dead are parts of the CMC. One is at its southern edge, another at the northern edge, and two within it. These platforms had stairs running their length on both sides, and they need not have seriously impeded movement along the Street of the Dead. Nevertheless, they form obvious "thresholds," or limits, for ordinary traffic. Although there is now no evidence bearing on the question, it seems to me entirely possible that movable and perishable barriers of some sort might have been used at these points to create something like screens between parts of the CMC and between the CMC and the outside on ordinary occasions. My conjecture that the CMC was a center of high-level political management implies that movement along this segment of the Street of the Dead must have been restricted. But in fact *any* interpretation of the CMC that postulates its architectural integrity must assume this.

In general, structures within the CMC are exceptionally fine, strongly suggesting that important people lived in them, whether or not the CMC was, for a time, a locus of very high-level political management. Especially notable is the Viking Group, where extraordinary finds included unparalleled massive layers of mica (Armillas 1944). Also, as René Millon points out (personal communication), its rooms are the most spacious of any extensively excavated residence in Teotihuacan. Although the Viking Group (whose eastern limits are uncertain) was probably not as large as either one of the Ciudadela palaces, it may have rivaled or even possibly exceeded them in richness of construction materials. This question should be answerable when results of the current INAH excavations in the Ciudadela are available. In any case, it seems possible that, at least for a while, the apartment of the effective ruler of Teotihuacan was in the Viking Group.

A difficulty is that Millon further points out that a reassessment in terms of what is now known of the Teotihuacan ceramic chronology indicates that the lower level of the Viking Group was built in the Early Tlamimilolpa phase—as early as the south palace of the Ciudadela. The upper level of the Viking Group is Early or mid-Tlamimilolpa. There were apparently no further rebuildings. This leads Millon to wonder if the Ciudadela palaces were never intended to be the principal residence of the ruler. Perhaps instead they were designed for ceremonial and other state occasions from the outset, and conceivably the Viking Group was the principal residence of the head of state in Early Tlamimilolpa times.

However that may be, Mapping Project evidence indicates a great deal of Xolalpan and Metepec phase building activity in other parts of the CMC. Whether or not it had already begun to be the setting for very high-level political activities in the Early Tlamimilolpa phase, the CMC is a very strong candidate for having played this role during much of the time from Late Tlamimilolpa through Metepec. For this reason, among others, the current INAH excavations in the CMC are of extraordinary interest.

Other architectural complexes near the Street of the Dead should also be considered. If I am correct in thinking that the Ciudadela remained the stable physical embodiment of state-related symbolism, then the centers of active political management may have shifted location rather freely and may have occupied many different architectural complexes at different times. One such additional candidate for political importance is the so-called "House of the Priests" (Figs. 11.1 and 11.2, no. 41). Its rooms are directly atop the southern part of the platform surrounding the precinct of the Sun Pyramid, and at first sight the House of the Priests seems linked with that pyramid. But apparently it was not directly accessible from the Sun Pyramid precinct. In any case, the major orientation of the House of the Priests is southward, away from the Sun precinct and toward a large sunken plaza (Fig. 11.2, site 25:N3E1). This plaza is almost square, about 85 meters on a side. It is much larger than any of the patios or courts in apartment compounds, although much smaller than the main plaza within the Ciudadela. The configuration of the House of the Priests and the plaza it faces is not very much like the Ciudadela, but it is even less like ordinary Teotihuacan apartment compounds or temple complexes. The House of the Priests may have been of great political importance. It is even possible that the entire stretch of the Street of the Dead and regions near it, that includes the CMC, the two avenue dividers north of the CMC, and the House of the Priests, was a single very large macro-complex in which political activities were of major importance. This is in no way to suggest that religious rituals, of varying degrees of political significance, did not also occur regularly in this area.

Another region that has received little attention in this paper is the Moon Pyramid and Plaza. Doris Heyden (1975:143–44) suggests that the Moon Pyramid may have succeeded the Sun Pyramid as the most important sacred place in Teotihuacan. Her suggestion is affected by the mistaken belief that in early times the land around the Ciudadela was swampy and that the Ciudadela was not built until Late Tlamimilolpa and Xolalpan times. Nevertheless, the cult (or cults) associated with the Moon Pyramid must have been among the most important in Teotihuacan. The Moon Pyramid was already very large in the Miccaotli phase, and the outermost structure apparently dates to the

Tlamimilolpa phase (R. Millon 1973:55, 57). I know little reason to link it with a moon deity, except that much later Aztec traditions may preserve a kernel of accurate history. Michael Spence (1981) discusses evidence that the priests associated with the Moon Pyramid were involved in manufacture of obsidian artifacts for long-distance trade. However, the political role of the hierarchy (or hierarchies) associated with the Moon Pyramid and the other pyramids of the Moon Plaza is unclear.

Just off the southwest corner of the Moon Plaza are the Quetzalpapalotl Palace and the adjacent Palace of the Jaguars (Figs. 11.1 and 11.2, no. 29; Acosta 1964). They probably did not house the priests most directly associated with the Moon Pyramid. Nevertheless, they are exceptionally fine residences, and it is possible that their occupants played major political roles.

In contrast to all these sites, the Great Compound seems an unlikely spot for top-level political activity. As long as management was centered in the Ciudadela, the structures on the north and south platforms of the Great Compound would have been a sensible location for bureaucrats and officeholders at "second-from-the-top" and lower levels, as suggested by René Millon (1973:20, 1976:236). However, if the locus of highest level political management passed out of the Ciudadela, I have difficulty imagining it moving to the Great Compound. First, there are no pyramid temples at all in the Great Compound, and I doubt if political management had become so thoroughly secular that no pyramids at all would be closely associated with it. Furthermore, the central plaza of the Great Compound was probably a major marketplace. Locating such a marketplace in very close proximity to the political center is very plausible (there are many instances, for example, in early China), but locating it in the very middle of the political center is most improbable. If high-level political management was shifted outside the Ciudadela, as I believe it was, the Great Compound probably remained the same as before: the setting for a principal marketplace and for officials and others of less than the highest rank.

Epilog

In this paper I have refrained from much discussion of Teotihuacan iconography and symbolism. This is most emphatically not because of my views about method and theory, for I believe that attempts at strictly materialist understandings of sociocultural phenomena are fundamentally misconceived. On the contrary, research on the political meanings of various elements in Teotihuacan iconography, such as the study by Clara Millon (1973), are one of the most promising approaches for further investigation. My restraint here is partly due to space limitations and partly because of the complexity of the subject. I hope in the future, however, to be able to do justice to some of the many hypotheses suggested by the iconography and architectural symbolism of the Ciudadela and other Teotihuacan structures; hypotheses that for the moment I have had to leave undeveloped.

Notes

1. Support for this work has come from a series of National Science Foundation grants and from the National Endowment for the Humanities, the Wenner-Gren Foundation for Anthropological Research, the American Council of Learned Societies, the Canada Council, and the Ivey Foundation. I am grateful to Edward Calnek, Clemency Coggins, Richard Leventhal, Robert Zeitlin, Judith Francis Zeitlin, and an anonymous reader for helpful comments on one or another earlier version of this paper. I am especially indebted to René and Clara Millon for very extensive and extremely valuable discussions of several earlier drafts.

2. Table 11.1 implies a substantially higher density of Patlachique ceramics than is indicated by the map in Cowgill (1974). This is because Table 11.1 is based on the results of recent ceramic reanalyses under the direction of Evelyn Rattray. These reanalyses have increased the quantity of Patlachique ceramics mainly by reassigning some sherds to Patlachique that were originally assigned to Tzacualli.

3. Edward Calnek (personal communication) has provided a very useful assessment of reliable information on Aztec palaces.

4. René Millon prepared a tenative plan of the layout of these compounds in 1971, based on architectural evidence then visible. The current INAH excavations substantiate most of the major features of Millon's reconstruction.

5. There is, of course, no firm evidence for a cult of a sun deity at the so-called Sun Pyramid, although there are several lines of evidence that suggest this possibility (R. Millon, personal communication). If there were twin temples, at least one must have been dedicated to some other deity.

Twelve

Chan Chan and Cuzco: On the Nature of the Ancient Andean City

Alan L. Kolata, Field Museum of Natural History

Prologue

   In many ways, the nature of the ancient Andean city remains an enigma. The astonishing array of contradictory definitions, interpretations, and disquisitions on the forms and functions of cities in the Andes testifies to the intractability of the problem (Rowe 1963; Hardoy 1968; Morris 1972; Moseley 1975a). Several scholars have offered specific functional interpretations of Andean cities: Keatinge (1975, 1978) argues that Pacatnamu and Pachacamac were primarily centers of religious pilgrimage; Isbell and Schreiber (1978) regard Huari as a political center of empire; Núñez and Dillehay (1978) describe Tiwanaku as simultaneously a focus of pan-Andean ideological prestige and a nexus of long-distance llama caravan trade. However, no one has yet come up with a unified theory of urban evolution in the Andes that can embrace all of these varied functional categories. We lack a convincing portrait of the preindustrial Andean city that isolates its special economic and political character—a character that distinguishes it from its counterparts elsewhere in the world.
   Joyce Marcus (1983) states that she "hoped to discover some patterns shared by all Mesoamerican cities. . . . that would distinguish them from cities in other parts of the world," but instead she found that "what Mesoamerican cities shared, they also shared with cities elsewhere." I too have looked for certain

patterns or features in the pre-Columbian cities of Peru that imparted to them a special distinguishing character. However, unlike Marcus, who ultimately decided that Mesoamerican cities were as formally varied and as functionally eclectic as the preindustrial cities of the Old World, I believe that I have found exactly what I set out to discover.

Certainly, the ancient cities of Peru have some general features in common with preindustrial cities elsewhere. In this essay, however, I intend to bring into relief a special feature shared by two of the great capitals of the ancient Andean world, Chan Chan and Cuzco, which sets them apart from all other cities outside the Andes. Much of the following analysis, I believe, would also apply to the urban settlements of Moche, Huari, and Tiwanaku.

From the perspective presented here, the pre-Hispanic Andean city forms a distinct cultural unit reflecting the culmination of millennia of political and economic development adapted to the peculiar circumstances of the Andean social and physical environment. It must therefore be analyzed on its own terms.

Chan Chan and Cuzco as Cities of Empire

Chan Chan was the capital city and the tool of an expanding imperial power. The essential political and economic power of the Kingdom of Chimor was focused there. Thus, above all else, Chan Chan was a city of empire.

The bulk of the empire's population resided in dispersed rural villages engaged primarily in farming and fishing. The empire stimulated and controlled the production of surplus goods and services of these populations (agricultural produce, cloth, labor) by implanting elite administrative centers in each subject valley. These planned colonial settlements, of which Farfan in the Jequetepeque Valley is a prime example, politically dominated the surrounding countryside. Their purpose was simple: they were outposts of the central city charged with organizing the economic exploitation of the provinces. Nobles of Chimor resided in these centers as economic managers and were undoubtedly accountable to their superiors in Chan Chan for fixed quotas of goods to be funnelled back to the capital and for labor services to be performed for the state. Unlike Chan Chan, these colonial settlements were not self-sufficient, nor did they grow organically. They were artificially imposed expedients of the state, a means of organizing production in and assuring control over surrounding nonurban areas.

The same settlement network of a dominant capital city exercising control over several secondary colonial towns can be documented for both the Inca and Roman empires. I have no doubt that this type of network was a prominent feature of many other empires as well.

The Inca established many secondary towns as their conquests proceeded.

To service these new urban colonies, the Inca would require local populations to reside near the new towns or move entire foreign populations to the vicinity of the settlement (the *mitmaq* colonists). Morris (1972) aptly terms this population reduction a policy of "compulsory urbanism."

Cuzco-dominated secondary cities were established throughout Tawantinsuyu, the imperial realm of the Inca. Among the clearest examples of such cities are Huanuco Pampa, Tomebamba, and Incallacta in the Andean Cordillera of Peru, Ecuador, and Bolivia, respectively, and Tambo Colorado on the south coast of Peru. All these cities were the product of Inca imperial expansion between about A.D. 1450 and 1525. Moreover, like Huanuco Pampa (Morris) 1972), these sites were the residences of Inca elite: imperial governors and local *caciques* favored by Cuzco. They were all relatively short-lived, and most were abandoned after the Spanish conquest of the Inca. Like Farfan, the Inca colonial town was designed as a locus of political control and a tool of economic exploitation. It was an efficient means of extending the influence of Cuzco, the dominant urban power. As Brundage phrases it: ". . . administratively there were, of course, numerous and significant urban communities in Tahuantinsuyo, but there was only one capital, or *capac llacta;* thus it can be said there was only one true city" (1967:7).

The urban network of imperial Rome structurally paralleled that of the Inca (and Chimu), and apparently engendered similar attitudes toward the relationship between the capital and country in the ruling elite: "For the upper-class Roman, it would seem, the provincial towns did not exist: Rome's prestige held them [sic] To live well, he must dwell in Rome" (Mumford 1961:210). Yet colonies of Roman citizens in provincial new towns formed the cornerstone of the imperial economic enterprise.

These towns were regional centers of economic action organized on behalf of Rome: they were the prime instruments for extracting taxes in the provinces, but in return brought with them the political power, security, and prestige of the capital. Like Inca provincial towns, such as Tambo Colorado on the coast and Huanuco Pampa in the highlands, the new towns of the Roman empire were planned for a limited population (rarely exceeding 35,000 inhabitants) and constructed in a clear, regular layout. Most often the original plan of these towns was a simple rectangular grid, well suited to administrative efficiency. Autun in the west and Dura-Europos in the east are splendid examples of this kind of premeditated, symmetrical, almost obsessively formal design (see Mumford 1961; Saalman 1968: fig. 3).

The phenomenon of colonial new towns is not necessarily restricted to large empires, but it is invariably the product of a powerful, centralized authority. For instance, new towns "sprang up in the open country under the auspices of cities and princes in Italy, France and Germany from the twelfth century on" (Saalman 1968:114).

These towns were the instruments first of regional princes, who controlled large areas economically and politically from a dominant city, and later of "national governments exploiting the economic resources of an entire country under absolute central control" (Saalman 1968:114).

Across time, space, and cultural tradition, planned colonial towns share two essential features: (1) they are the product and tool of an organized political authority localized in a dominant city, and (2) they depend on this external authority for their continued existence. As Saalman remarks, "rigidly planned and controlled from the beginning, few of these new towns had the potential of becoming independent cities, and hardly any of them achieved major importance in later times" (1968:114). Although Saalman is specifically referring to the medieval new towns of Europe, I believe this characterization is valid cross-culturally.

In fact, it applies with even greater force to the state-founded colonial settlements of Chimor and Tawantinsuyo. When the powerful central authority of the Inca was truncated by the Spanish conquest, planned towns such as Huanuco Pampa were quickly abandoned. Many of these secondary cities had been established in regions that were either economically unable to support the settlement independently, or in which the settlement itself was incompatible with the traditional economic organization of the local populations.

When the political authority of both these empires was destroyed, their planned colonial towns (the physical tools of their power) became dysfunctional. That not a single state-inspired town of Cuzco or Chan Chan became an important, thriving settlement under Spanish rule is impressive testimony to this fact. Under Spanish hegemony, the old principles of national economic organization (taxation, labor service, and so forth) were greatly modified and entirely new ones instituted (Lockhardt 1968). The indigenous network of important cities and towns, which was both insufficient and unnecessary for the Spanish, could not adapt to the changing economic and political circumstances, so a different network began to form.

The *absolute* dependence of the planned administrative centers of Chimor and Tahuantinsuyo on the continued integrity of the political authority centered in their capital cities has implications for the nature of that authority and its influence on the form and internal organization of these dominant cities. There is a difference between the new towns of Rome and those of Chan Chan and Cuzco: the former at least carried the *potential* of becoming independent settlements; the latter never did. It is this difference that highlights the special character of these two Andean cities of empire.

The Andean City: Oikos Versus Marketplace

In an essay on the nature of the city, Max Weber (1951) distinguished two types of institutions regulating the exchange of goods and services that integrated the economic activity of preindustrial urban settlements: the *oikos* and the market. According to Weber, the city may be defined as both an economic and "politico-administrative" unit that satisfies the daily needs of a substantial (although numerically unspecified) population. The city has its origins in two kinds of economies.

The first of these is the household, or *oikos*, economy. In this economy the considerable political and economic needs of a feudal or princely estate stimulate "specialization in trade products . . . providing a demand for which work is performed and goods are bartered" (Weber 1951:66). Here the product and labor requirements of a large patrimonial or princely household exert a kind of centripetal force, attracting settlers to the estate. The household, or *oikos*, of the prince essentially creates and sustains the local economy. However, as Weber remarks:

> even though the *oikos* of a lord or prince is as large as a city, a colony of artisans and small merchants bound to villein services is not customarily called a "city" even though historically a large proportion of important "cities" originated in such settlements. In cities of such origin the products of a prince's court often remained a highly important, even chief, source of income for the settlers. (1951:66)

The second kind of economy important for the city is that of the market. In contrast to the household economy, the market economy encourages a free and regular exchange of goods and services. Economic activity in the market is more broadly based, in that the demand for goods and services is not restricted to or dominated by the needs of a single prominent household.

For Weber, one can speak of a "city" only when the local population and that of the immediate hinterland derive a substantial part of their income from, and satisfy a substantial part of their daily needs in, the market. The marketplace is the source of income for inhabitants of the city, in that they specialize in producing goods for sale or exchange in it. According to this view, the city is invariably linked to a market economy.

Weber goes on to note:

> Wherever it appeared as a configuration different from the country, it was normal for the city to be both a lordly or princely residence as well as a market place. It simultaneously possessed centers of both kinds, *oikos* and market, and frequently in

> addition to the regular market it also served as periodic foreign
> markets of travelling merchants. In the meaning of the word
> here, the city is a market settlement. (1951:67)

Thus the city can be based either on a pure market economy, divorced from any attachment to a princely estate, or on a combined *oikos* and market economy. According to Weber, this latter pattern of a large princely household with a conjoined market was by far the most common mechanism integrating the economy of cities in preindustrial Europe and Asia.

Yet Weber also argues that a city based on the combined *oikos* and market economy often experienced a gradual transformation in economic emphasis:

> In this case the eminent household as one contact point of the city
> could satisfy its wants either primarily by means of a natural
> economy (that is, by villein service or natural service or taxes
> placed upon artisans and merchants dependent on it) or it could
> supply itself more or less secondarily by barter in the local
> market as that market's most important buyer. The more
> pronounced the latter relation the more distinct the market
> foundation of the city looms and the city ceases by degrees to be
> a mere appendaged market settlement alongside the *oikos*.
> Despite attachment to the large household it then became a
> market city. As a rule quantitative expansion of the original
> princely city and its economic importance go hand in hand with
> an increase in the satisfaction of wants in the market by the
> princely household and other large urban households attached
> to that of the prince as courts of vassals or major officials. (1951:68)

As a politico-administrative concept, the Weberian city has a structure analogous to the economic distinction between *oikos* and market. Specifically, Weber differentiates cities on the basis of the type of regulations that governed the administration of urban economic policy, that is, those rules designed to maximize the production and exchange of goods and services in the local economy.

Weber states that the "urban economic policy itself may be the work of a prince to whom political dominion of the city with its inhabitants belongs. In this case when there is an urban economic policy, it is determined *for* the inhabitants of the city, not *by* them" (1951:74). Conversely, the urban economic policy might be determined entirely by the inhabitants themselves through decisions implemented by autonomous associations. A classic example is the occupational guild associations of medieval European cities. In theory these two ways of formulating urban economic policy parallel the division between *oikos* and market. In actuality, just as the economic underpinnings of most of Weber's cities were a mixture of *oikos* and market, the administration of economic policy was also a mosaic of decisions, some imposed from above (by the prominent household[s] with partial dominion over the city), others "democratically" devised by autonomous citizen groups (guild associations and the like).

Although Weber was concerned with urban settlements in the Old World, particularly the cities of ancient and medieval Europe, I believe that the political and economic concepts that he introduces to describe and explain the genesis of cities are more broadly applicable. Chan Chan and Cuzco, in fact, conform quite well to Weber's model of an urban settlement based on an *oikos* economy and politically dominated by that *oikos*.

Chan Chan and Cuzco as Cities of Oikos

I think there is little question that Chan Chan was constructed and maintained at the behest of a ruling dynasty of "princes" and their lineages. The ethnohistoric record explicitly describes Chimor as a kingdom controlled by a royal dynasty (Rowe 1948). In late Chimu times (after A.D. 1350), this dynasty was headed by a king who was perceived as a divine figure and who maintained absolute (divine) proprietary rights to the wealth of the state: land and labor. The needs of the king and his household (the *oikos*) literally created the economy that sustained Chan Chan (Kolata 1978).

The central importance of the king and his household to the development of Chan Chan is reflected with equal explicitness in the architectural record. The 10 great enclosures, or *ciudadelas,* that were the palaces of the royal household physically and visually dominate the city (Figs. 12.1, 12.2). An enormous amount of time, labor, and material were expended in the construction and maintenance of these palaces (Fig. 12.3). All other types of architecture were subsidiary to the palaces and involved in some way with the support of the royal household (Day 1973; Moseley 1975a; Conrad 1981, 1982; Klymyshyn 1982; Topic 1982).

The inhabitants of the residential barrios (Fig. 12.1) directly fulfilled the needs of the elite for both menial services and craft products of high quality, such as fine textiles, wooden sculptures, and emblems of gold (Topic 1982). Occupants of the various kinds of architecture intermediate in scale and elaboration between the royal palaces and the barrios acted as retainers of higher status or indirectly supported the royal household by helping manage the political and economic affairs of state (Klymyshyn 1982). In effect, the affairs of state were identical with the affairs of the royal household.

The way Chan Chan grew confirms the impression that the city was de-

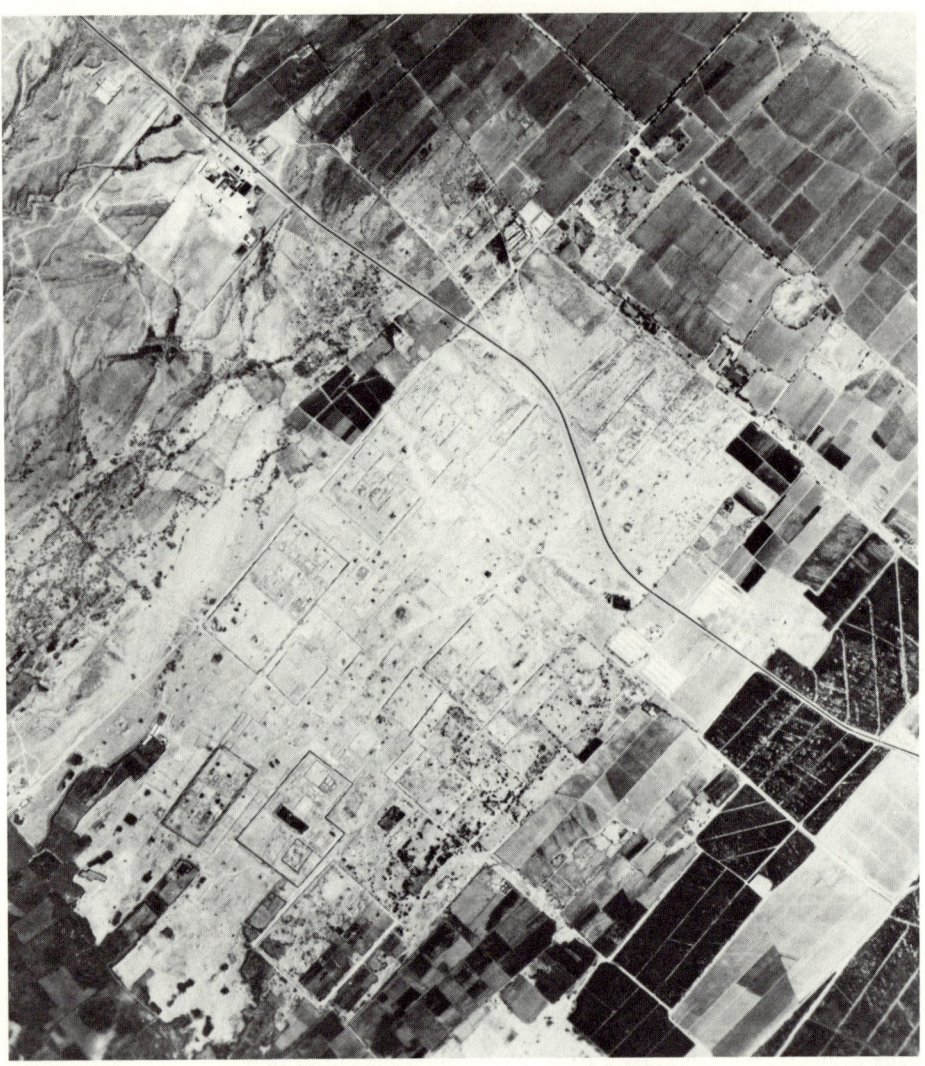

Figure 12.1. Aerial photograph of Chan Chan's core area.

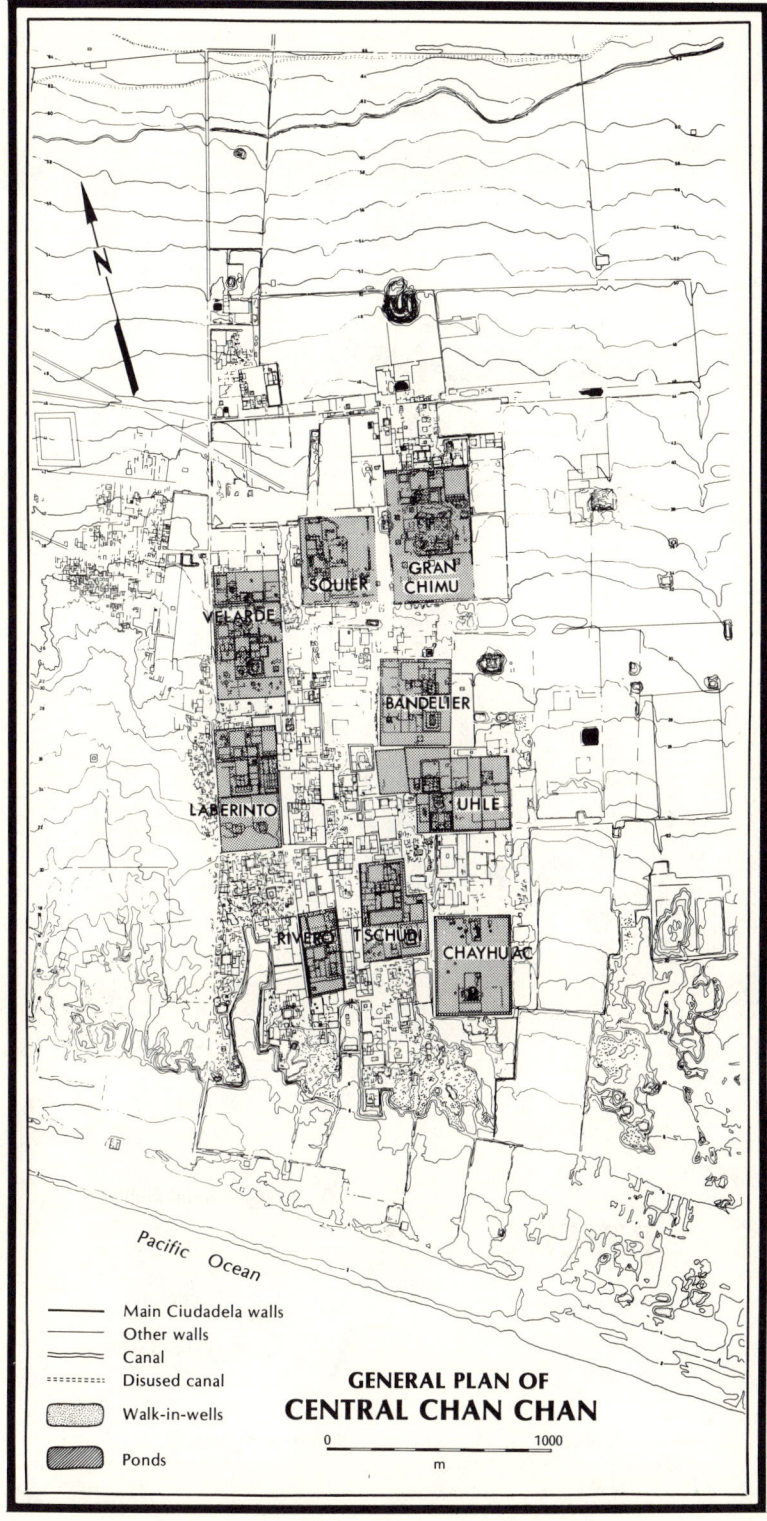

Figure 12.2. General plan of Chan Chan's core area.

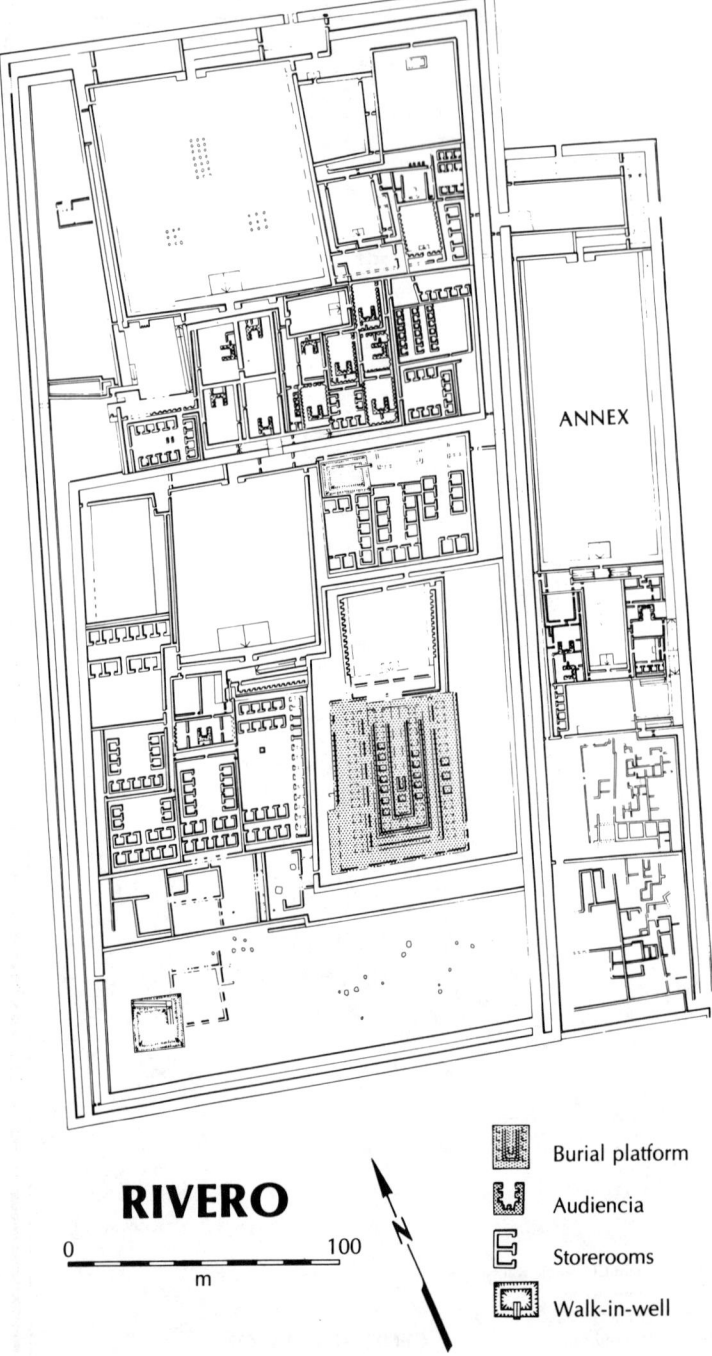

Figure 12.3. Plan of Ciudadela Rivero.

ABSOLUTE CHRONOLOGY	PHASE CHRONOLOGY	PALACE SEQUENCE
years A.D. 1400 - 1470	Late Chimu 2	Rivero Tschudi
1300 - 1400	Late Chimu 1	Bandelier Velarde
1150 - 1300	Middle Chimu	Squier Gran Chimu
1000 - 1150	Early Chimu 2	Laberinto Tello
900 - 1000	Early Chimu 1	Uhle Chayhuac

Figure 12.4. Chronological ordering of the principal architecture at Chan Chan.

pendent on and dominated by the *oikos* of a royal dynasty. As I have shown elsewhere, both the intermediate architecture and craft barrios developed as a result of specific social needs and expanded in response to particular political events (Kolata 1978, 1982, n.d.). Both types of architecture (and the people who inhabited them) were present throughout the history of the city. The earliest craft barrios, which were clustered to the east of *ciudadela* Chayhuac, and the earliest intermediate architecture, which appeared between Chayhuac and Uhle and immediately east of Tello, developed at the start of the Early Chimu 1 Phase (A.D. 950–1000) (Figs. 12.4, 12.5). A certain portion of this architecture evolved as a result of gradual population growth. But in great part, the growth of intermediate architecture and residential craft barrios was episodic, occurring in two temporally bounded bursts of construction activity:

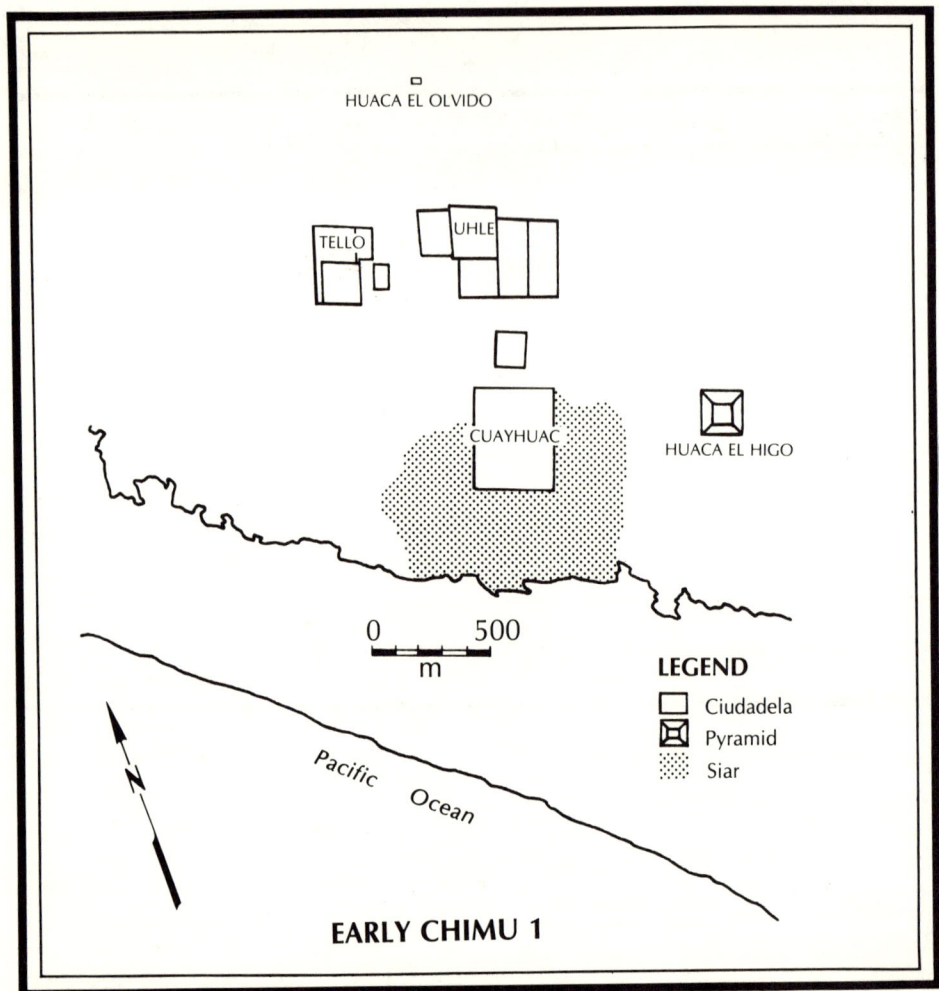

Figure 12.5. Chan Chan during Early Chimu 1 times.

(1) during Early Chimu 2 (A.D. 1000–1150) (Fig. 12.6), and (2) for a somewhat longer period, from Late Chimu 1 through Late Chimu 2 (A.D. 1300–1470) (Kolata 1978, n.d.) (Figs. 12.7, 12.8).

The evolution of intermediate architecture, in particular, was marked by periods of relative quietude punctuated by remarkable spurts of construction. The prime example of this kind of architectural evolution is the arc of intermediate architecture to the south and west of Tschudi and Rivero: these units, forming a substantial percent of the total universe of intermediate architecture, were built essentially all at once between about A.D. 1400 and A.D. 1470 (Late Chimu 2) (Fig. 12.8). Although the craft barrios were also subject to this abrupt, episodic type of architectural evolution, they seem to have been somewhat more stable. During periods of expansion, the rate of barrio construction was generally not as precipitous as the construction rate for intermediate architecture.

It is crucial to note that the two episodes of frenetic construction activity in intermediate architecture and residential barrios coincided with the two major episodes of Chimu military expansionism: first, the emperor Ñançen-pinco's initial conquests of the five north Peruvian coast valleys from Santa to Saña about A.D. 1050 (Anónimo Trujillano [1604], in Rowe 1948); second, the subjugation of the great Lambayeque Valley complex around A.D. 1300–1350 (Kolata 1978, n.d.). These military conquests by the kings of Chimor triggered the growth of the residential craft barrios and intermediate architecture. At Chan Chan, the location and density of the supporting architecture shifted as the royal palaces were sequentially built and occupied. On the whole, it was the political and economic success of the individual monarchs of Chimor that determined the size and complexity of this architecture, not internal or independent mechanisms of population growth.

The royal palaces of Chan Chan themselves provide some of the clearest evidence that this ancient city was the product and tool of an *oikos* economy, shaped by and maintained for the benefit of aristocratic households and their agents. Specifically, I believe it is possible to infer from certain modifications in the palace architecture that, over time, two important and complementary changes occurred in the political structure of Chimor, and that these changes indicate an *oikos* economy. First, the person of the king became increasingly distinguished in status and authority from the other members of the ruling elite. Second, the class of the ruling elite greatly expanded and became more complex. These changes in status relationships, essentially a restructuring of the governing hierarchy, substantially altered the architecture of the palaces and their annexes.

Several modifications to the *ciudadela* and its interior architecture directly

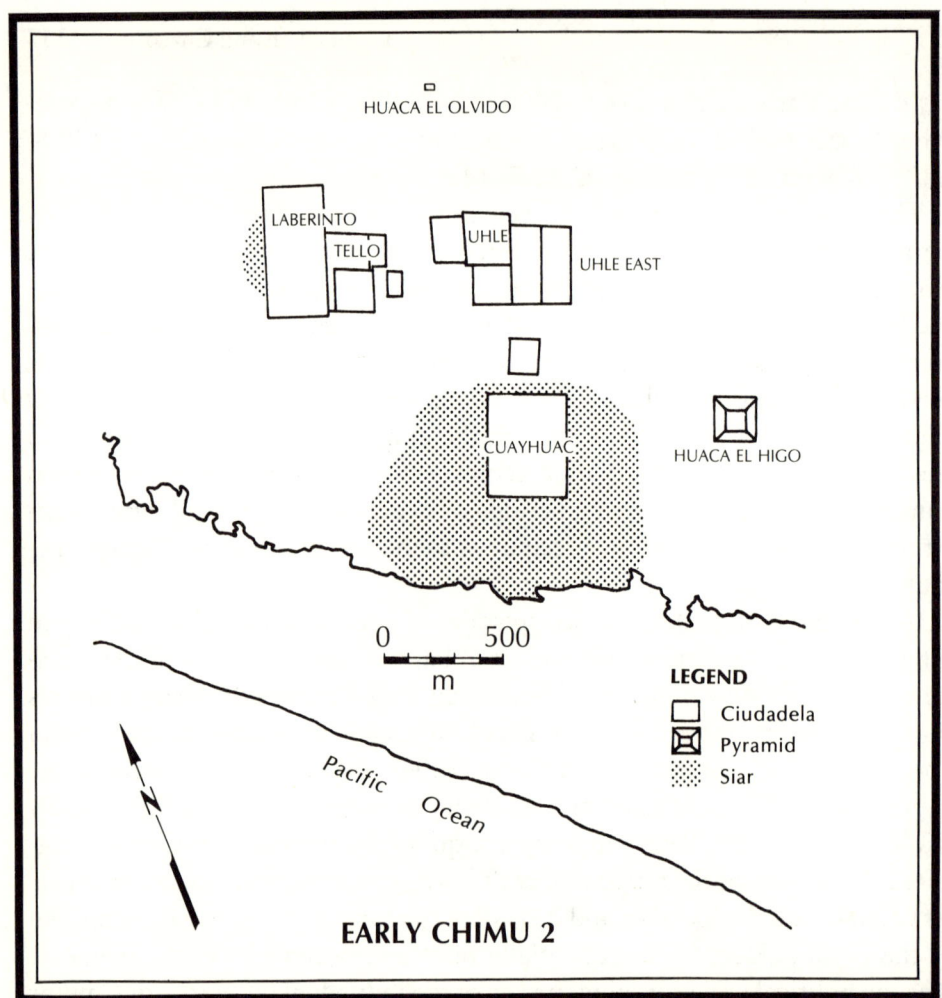

Figure 12.6. Chan Chan during Early Chimu 2 times.

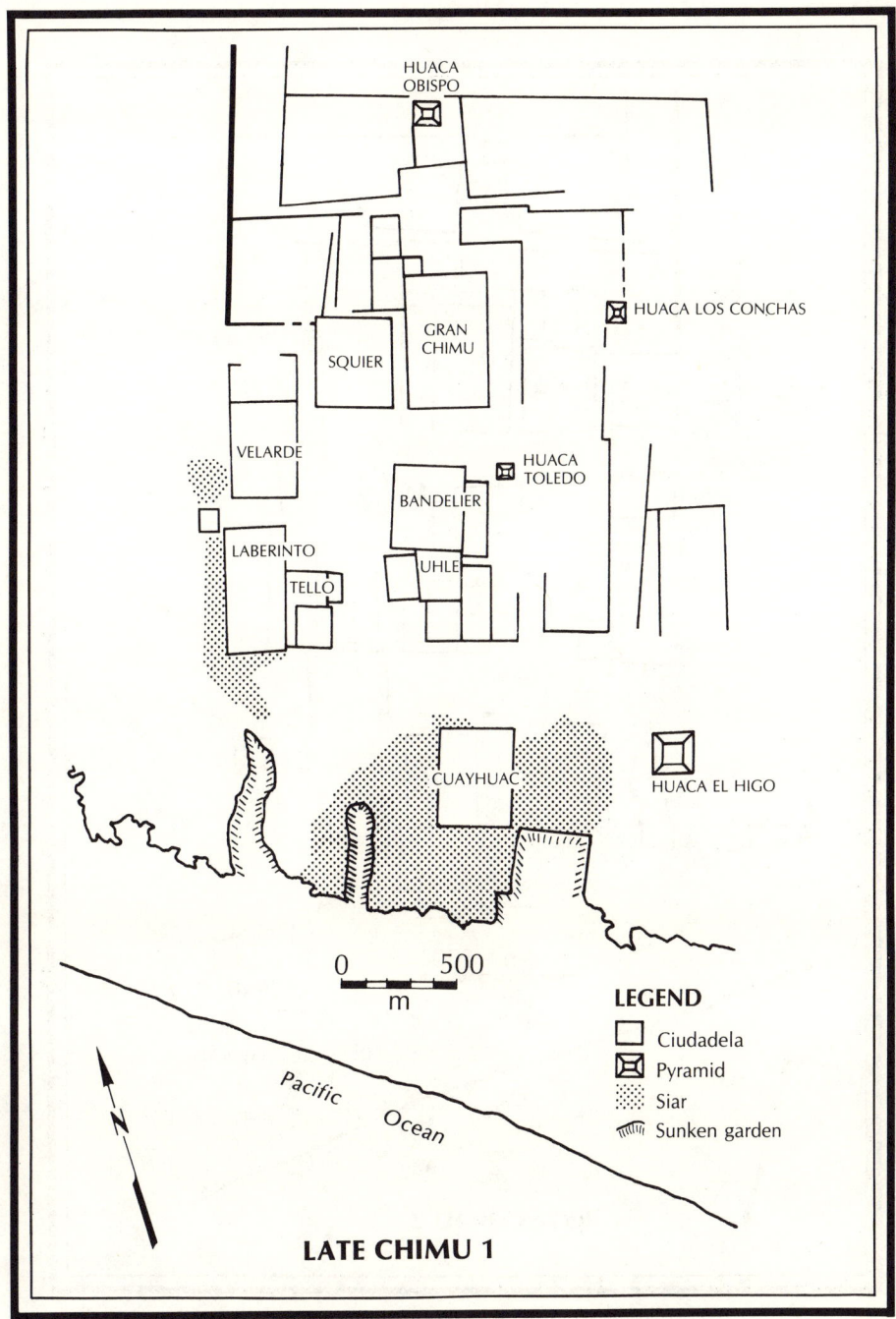

Figure 12.7. Chan Chan during Late Chimu 1 times.

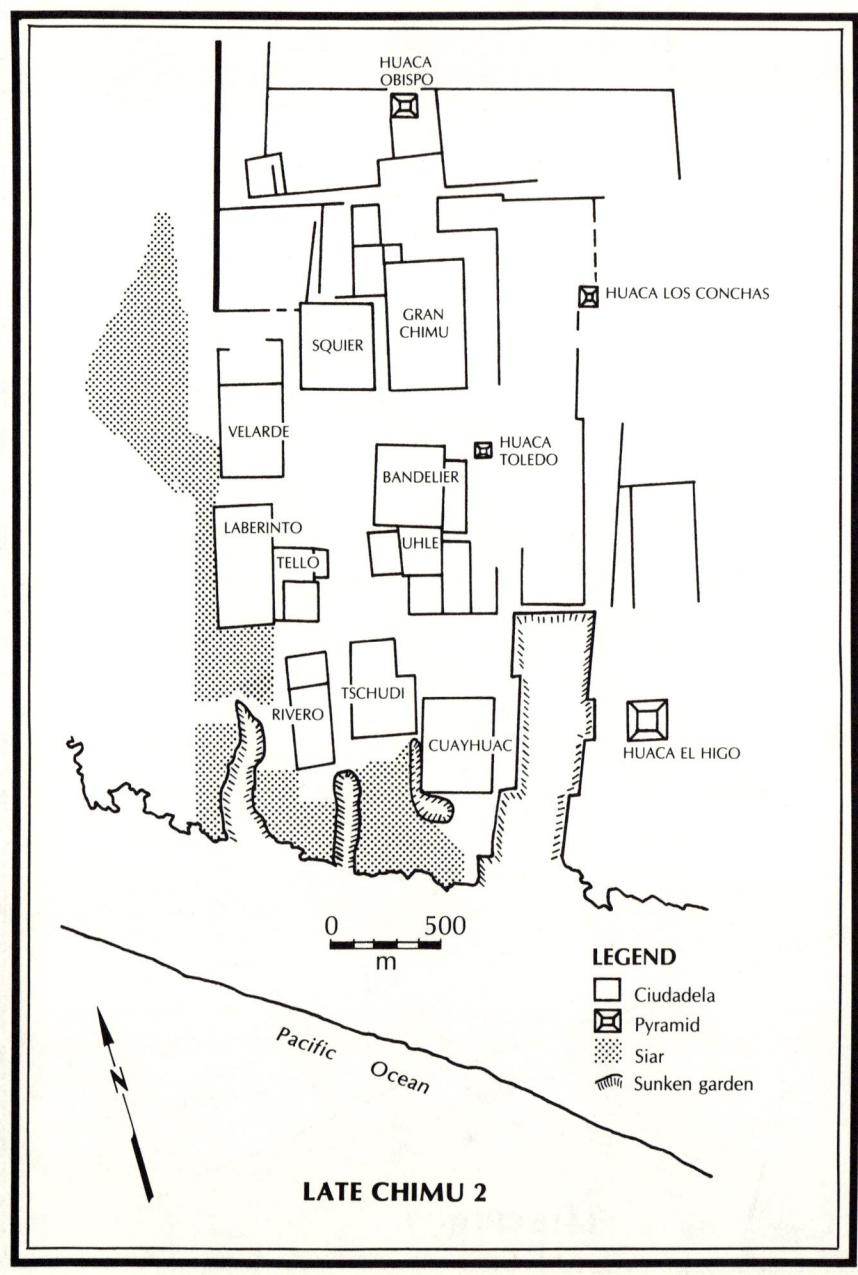

Figure 12.8. Chan Chan during Late Chimu 2 times.

reflect the heightened social differentiation between the king and his subjects. Perhaps the clearest of these is the change in the overall internal design of the *ciudadela*.

During what I have termed the Early Chimu 1 Phase of Chan Chan (ca. A.D. 850–1000), the *ciudadela* consisted of a simple, though exceptionally large, rectangle (Chayhuac), or an apparently ad hoc collection of such rectangles (Uhle, Tello) (Fig. 12.5). In many respects, Brundage's characterization of the imperial palaces of Cuzco also applies to these *ciudadelas:* "the palace proper generally resembled on an exaggerated scale its model, the traditional stone-walled Peruvian farm enclosure called the *cancha*" (1967:80).

The architecture within these initial *ciudadelas* exhibits no overall concern for internal ordering beyond a general north-south orientation. In both Chayhuac and Uhle, the first of Chan Chan's palaces, the bulk of the internal space is devoid of architecture (Figs. 12.2, 12.5), and the structures that are present occur in dense, well-defined nodes (enclosed on at least three sides by substantial adobe walls).

With the construction of Laberinto in Early Chimu 2 (A.D. 1000–1150), the interior design of the *ciudadelas* was changed radically to a sectorial, tripartite form. From this time and throughout the subsequent history of the city, each *ciudadela* was organized with a tripartite distribution of internal space (Figs. 12.1, 12.2, 12.6): a northern sector provided with a large entry court and smaller courts flanked by a variety of structures; a central sector provided with a second entry court, similar smaller courts, flanking structures, and generally a burial platform; a southern sector devoid of permanent adobe architecture but frequently containing walk-in wells and, at times, a congeries of vernacular structures built of perishable materials. This change in the organization of the royal palaces was accompanied by a gradual redistribution of administrative structures within the new sectors.

Over time, the central sectors of the palace enclosures became more insulated from the administrative activites associated with *audiencia* courts. (*Audiencias* are substantial, elevated, U-shaped structures found within the major architecture at Chan Chan.) The nature and context of *audiencias* suggest that they served administrative functions, perhaps primarily regulating the flow and storage of state-owned goods within the palaces. For a full discussion of *audiencias,* see Moseley and Day (1982). As the "public" activity of administration was progressively removed to the northern sector and annex of the palaces, the central sector became an increasingly private space, fitted with only one or two large *audiencia* courts, storerooms, and ultimately a royal burial platform. The central sector was almost certainly the specific locus of residence for the king and his harem. (An analogous identification of specific royal residence is made by Brundage [1967:80] for the Inca palaces; here the king's quarters were also toward the "back of the enclosure.") Therefore, I believe that the isolation of the central sector—the king's quarters—from public activities was a direct physical expression and symbol of increased social differentiation between the king and his subjects. In fact, I would go further and argue that the physical boundary drawn between the central sector and the rest of the *ciudadela* resulted from the evolution of a very specific institution: divine kingship.

We know that divine kingship was a prominent feature of Chimor on the eve of its conquest by the Inca (Rowe 1948). But when did this institution appear? Was it characteristic of Chimu social organization from the beginning? I believe the architectural evidence from Chan Chan shows that divine kingship was *not* a fixed and permanent feature of the political structure of Chimor, but rather evolved only gradually as the principal institution around which the political system came to be organized. Furthermore, this same evidence suggests that the concept of divine kingship crystallized relatively late, at some point after the subjugation of Lambayeque, around A.D. 1350 (Kolata 1978). It was at this time that access to the central sector was severely restricted. It had finally become inviolate to the public, the locus of the sacred. It was also at this time that a pattern of "one king–one palace–one burial platform," reflecting the principle of royal succession by split inheritance—a clear indication of the presence of divine kingship—became manifest in the architecture (see Demarest and Conrad this volume, also see Conrad 1981, 1982 for a detailed discussion of split inheritance in Chimor; Kolata n.d.). Prior to the Lambayeque conquest, *ciudadelas* were less standardized in overall design and interior architecture. Several appear to have housed more than one king and were occupied for a number of generations. All had administrative structures (*audiencias*) more evenly distributed throughout the enclosure. These patterns imply that effective political power was also more evenly distributed at this time, or at least had not yet been focused as sharply in the person of the king.

Expansion of the ruling hierarchy seems to have occurred episodically after major campaigns of imperial conquest. Annexation of foreign provinces opened up increasing numbers of managerial positions. Not surprisingly then, construction of residences for these new bureaucrats (the presumed tenants of Chan Chan's intermediate architecture) also increased substantially after each episode of conquest.

In addition, the gradual development of elaborate northern annexes to the palaces, annexes incorporated as wings of *ciudadelas,* and the more imposing units of "high" intermediate architecture, all point to progressive status differentiation within this growing elite class of managers. That is, as the state expanded through military conquest, creating more and different kinds of management positions, the lines of authority became increasingly complex. The Chimu solution to this complexity was to develop a clearly articulated political hierarchy in which each position was ascribed distinct obligations, privileges, status, and authority. These positions were probably hereditary, and vertical movement in the hierarchy was rare. Likewise, these positions enjoyed very specific rights of residence. In late Chan Chan the nobles of highest rank and authority probably resided in the elaborate northern annexes of the palace enclosures (present in Gran Chimu, Velarde, Tschudi, and Rivero), where they performed the daily administrative duties most closely affecting the king. Nobles of lesser rank and with fewer responsibilities were housed in various kinds of intermediate architecture, again arranged in a hierarchy determined by ascribed position.

Thus, both military expansionism and heightened status differentiation were among the prime determinants of change in the form of Chan Chan. Military expansionism was responsible for changing the configuration of the craft barrios and intermediate architecture, and status differentiation altered the form and distribution of activities in the palaces and their annexes. These two social phenomena were interrelated in that economic expansion brought on by military conquest created new positions of authority in an increasingly complex hierarchy of political power. Furthermore, the specific evolution of divine kingship, with the attendant principle of royal succession by split inheritance, was accompanied by an emerging ideology of conquest. That is, by the time the institution of divine kingship had fully developed in Late Chimu 1, military conquest had become both a prerogative and an obligation of the king. Conquest itself was justified by appeal to religious ideology; it was a sacred function of the divine ruler. However, the underlying impetus to military expansion was economic.

The changes in the form of Chan Chan are an architectural document of the birth, expansion, and ultimate contraction of the Chimu state and the empire it controlled. Trends in the development of the architecture draw a portrait of a bureaucratic state organization forming gradually and becoming increasingly complex and centralized over time. The principal force underlying growth in the size and complexity of the state was change in the economy, particularly that caused by military expansion.

The focal point of the state economy was the *ciudadela*. It was the residence of the royal dynasty, the seat of government, and the locus for the storage and redistribution of the kingdom's wealth. Over time, the *ciudadelas* and the structures they contained became increasingly standardized in form and function. This standardization was a reflection of the gradual growth in political and economic power vested in the king and his lineage, culminating in the institution of divine kingship.

The development of intermediate architecture and residential craft barrios was directly dependent on growth in the state economy: the varying economic and political fortunes of the kings of Chan Chan, ruling from their *ciudadelas*, determined the size and configuration of this architecture. The *ciudadela* and its supporting architecture were linked in a system of growth. This system was shaped primarily by economic forces generated and manipulated by the royal dynasties of Chimor. Unlike Weber's "emergent cities" of the preindustrial Old World, however, Chan Chan's state economy and its political structure were completely and inextricably bound to the royal household—that is, to the *oikos*.

Similar evidence reveals that Inca Cuzco was also the product of an *oikos* type of economy. Again, the ethnohistoric record, which is much more extensive and explicit for the Inca than for Chimor, portrays the economy of the Inca empire as focused on the household of the king. The wealth of the nation (surplus production extracted as taxes in the provinces) flowed back to Cuzco, the center and symbol of the royal dynasty. A few short sentences by Pedro Sancho de la Hoz, the "official" record of the first sighting of Cuzco by the Spanish, captures the very special character of the city:

> Cuzco, because it is the capital city and residence of the Inca nobles, is large enough and handsome enough to compare with any Spanish city. It is full of the palaces of magnates, for in it reside no poor folk. Each one of these Inca magnates, as well as all the *curacas*, erect there their dwellings, although they do not permanently occupy them. Most of the houses are of stone; others have stonework only half way up; many are of adobe and all are very regularly built. (Brundage 1967:8)

Like Chan Chan, Cuzco was constructed as the residence of a royal dynasty, a hereditary line of nobles and their households. Also like Chan Chan, this residential pattern is reflected architecturally in the presence of large palace enclosures that physically dominate the settlement (Fig. 12.9). Not all of the enclosures shown in the ground plan of Cuzco were strictly residences of the ruling elite, but all served functions directly related to this elite. Coricancha, for instance, was the most sacred temple of the state religion. It was dedicated to the god Inti but housed shrines to all the major gods and ancestral demigods of the Inca religion. A variety of nobles and their commoner retainers were attached to Coricancha to serve these gods in perpetuity: they fed, clothed, entertained, and in all ways served the gods as they would a living emperor. These people constituted state-created households of the divinities.

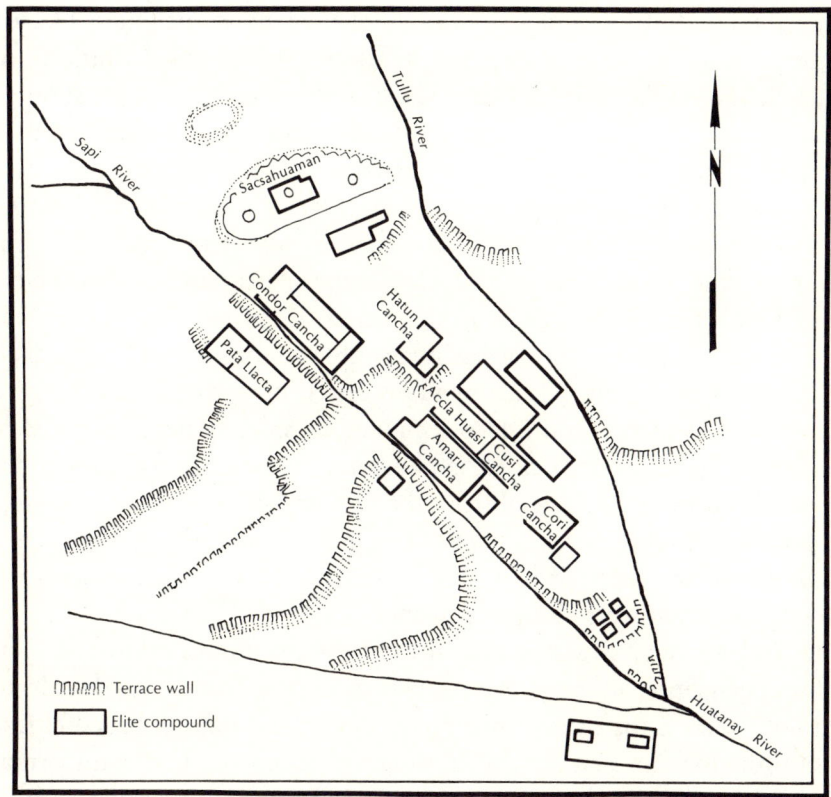

Figure 12.9. Ground plan of Cuzco (after Brundage 1967).

In actuality, these divine households were in service to the *living* emperor, because in Inca society there was no division between state and religion. That is, the emperor, as the direct descendant of the Inca gods through the line of his royal ancestors, held both the highest office of state and the most sacred office of religion. He was identified with Inti and, in a sense, was the living embodiment of that divinity. Thus, all the important structures in Cuzco, like those in Chan Chan, were related to the needs and activities of the royal dynasty in particular and the class of (Inca) elite in general.

In Weber's scheme Chan Chan and Cuzco would clearly be classed as *oikos*-based settlements, but would not be considered true cities, because they apparently lacked any admixture of the market type of economy. I believe the characterization of Chan Chan and Cuzco as *oikos*-type settlements is conceptually valuable, but I would also argue that they were true cities. I base this argument on a definition of city that differs from Weber's definition. In my view, lack of a market does not imply lack of cities; rather a city is simply any settlement that economically and politically dominates a significant rural hinterland. Chan Chan and Cuzco undeniably fit this criterion.

In a more specific Weberian attribution, these two Andean cities would be termed "pure *oikos* settlements." Their economy was structured *solely* around the needs of the princely household. Unlike the ancient and medieval cities of Europe studied by Weber, these Andean cities never supplied themselves by barter in local markets. They were invariably supported by a "natural economy," that is, by villein service or taxes levied on artisans and the general population. Chan Chan and Cuzco remained completely attached to the royal household. Unlike Weber's cities, expansion of these princely cities and their economic importance followed from the military success of the royal household and not from increasing investment in local markets by the large elite households of the cities. It is in this sense that the *oikos* settlements of the Andes are different from those of Europe.

The Andean cities began as and always remained pure *oikos*-based cities. The European cities, although they often began as pure *oikos*-based settlements, eventually were transformed into mixed *oikos* and market-based cities, often with the market element dominating the economy. This transformation affected the political administration of the city in that the economy became increasingly less subject to the demands of a prominent household. In short, the European type of city, with its mixed economy, was decidedly less authoritarian than the Andean type, which was based purely on the *oikos* of a prince.

I believe there is a second distinction between the Andean cities of *oikos* and those described by Weber. With this distinction I propose to extend his categories of city type. The original princely cities of ancient and medieval Europe were relatively self-contained. Their sphere of political influence and region of economic interaction were generally restricted to the city itself and a circumscribed rural hinterland. It was only during times of empire (such as with Rome) or with the development of centralized nation states (such as in the Baroque period) that this political and economic circumscription was broken down. Then the important urban settlements ceased to be cities of *oikos* and became part of a larger economic network dependent on mercantile activities.

Chan Chan and Cuzco never underwent this transformation in economic and political type. Metaphorically their evolution may be characterized as an unbroken linear progression: from relatively small *oikos*-dominated settlements controlling a circumscribed hinterland to exceptionally large *oikos*-dominated cities controlling far-flung empires. The key point is that when

Chan Chan and Cuzco entered into a broader economic network, their economic bases were not transformed by becoming centers of mercantile activity. Rather the household-dominated economies of these two cities were simply extended directly into the ever-growing provinces in the form of colonial secondary towns. These provincial towns were dominated by aristocrats who represented the royal household of the capital city: they were direct extensions of the political and economic policies of that household. There was a mechanical linkage between the capital city and its founded secondary settlements; the relationship was imposed, autocratic, and unequal.

The provincial colonial towns of Chimor and Tahuantinsuyo were, quite simply, repositories for the wealth of their capital cities, and, by extension, for the princely households that dominated and were symbolized by those cities. Therefore, the economies of Chan Chan and Cuzco can be characterized both as pure *oikos* and as what I would term *"hyper-oikos."* By this I mean that the economy of the princely household was extended far beyond the confines of the local circumscribed hinterland. The agents of that extension were the elites who governed the provincial settlements. These aristocratic managers were either directly or symbolically related to members of the royal household, and they worked to further the economic and political ends of that household. This is the meaning behind the Inca political device of installing "Incas by privilege." When incorporating new provinces into the empire, the Inca emperor would often elevate local *caciques* to "Inca status," allowing them to use the symbols of that status, such as earplugs, litters, and gold. In a symbolic sense—and perhaps more tangibly in the case of exceptionally powerful foreign lords, who were given Inca women of high caste as wives—these *caciques* were brought into the convoluted kinship system of the royal household. In return for their newly gained status, they were expected to act on behalf of their royal "relatives" at Cuzco.

I believe the economic and politico-administrative structure of Chan Chan and Cuzco as *hyper-oikos* truly distinguishes these two cities. The *hyper-oikos* was essentially a technique of building an empire by integrating a class of elite in an extended, fictive kinship system. These elite were bound in a complex network of privilege and obligation that was manipulated by the royal household residing in the capital city. I know of no other empire that relied as completely on this kind of centrally dominated kin (or pseudo-kin)-based system to exert control over its provinces.

Finally, the economic and politico-administrative structure of the *hyper-oikos* also distinguishes the colonial "new towns" of Chimor and Tahuantinsuyo. As we have seen, these secondary administrative centers were directly imposed in the provinces and staffed by a managing elite bound to the royal household of the capital city. They were, in effect, provincial manifestations of the capital, the one true city. The mechanical, *hyper-oikos* relationship between the capital and its secondary centers prevented the latter from developing an autonomous, internal economy. It was for this reason that the founded administrative centers of these two empires never became independent cities. In contrast, the new towns of the Roman empire at times did become independent cities because they had a more flexible economic structure: they carried out the economic policies of the Roman emperor, but they also engaged in independent mercantile activities. Thus, a mixed *oikos* and market-based city inherently possesses greater adaptability. It is more likely to survive changing political and economic circumstances and enjoy organic growth.

Oikos and Market in the Americas

If Chan Chan and Cuzco can be viewed as pure *oikos* and *hyper-oikos* settlements, what of the other pre-Columbian cities of the Americas? A comprehensive survey of these cities is not feasible here, but I will make a few brief comparisons.

The great cities of the Valley of Mexico, Teotihuacan and Tenochtitlan, were clearly different from Cuzco or Chan Chan, both in formal and presumably social composition. Perhaps the most important institution integrating the economic activity of the Mexican cities was the market. Both contained a vast central marketplace where a variety of local goods were exchanged. The market was supplied with local agricultural produce and with more exotic products brought in by the famous class of merchants, the *pochteca*. The *pochteca* formed a kind of "middle class" engaged not only in private entrepreneurship but also in service to the state government. They accompanied state military operations and often acted as informal ambassadors and spies.

Although mercantile activity was at the heart of the economic structure of these two Mesoamerican cities, they were not *pure* market cities. They were also attached to elite households that formed the ruling hierarchy and directed the activities of the merchant class. In other words, Teotihuacan and Tenochtitlan are classic examples of Weber's emergent cities: they were both lordly or princely residences as well as marketplaces. They possessed simultaneously centers of *oikos* and *market*. Furthermore, the needs of the princely household in these two Mexican cities were supplied both by villein service or taxes placed upon artisans and merchants and by barter or other forms of exchange in local and foreign markets.

The differences in economic structure between the Andean and Mexican cities are reflected in their architecture. Unlike the Andean cities, Teotihuacan and Tenochtitlan had a large and socially heterogeneous resident population. This population was housed in several different kinds of domestic structures, ranging from mean one- and two-room shacks to moderate-sized "apartment complexes" to palatial, elaborately furnished compounds (Millon 1973; Cowgill 1974, and this volume). The architectural bifurcation of monumental and nonmonumental structures characteristic of Chan Chan and Cuzco was absent in these Mexican cities. One can infer that they also lacked the severe social bifurcation of aristocracy and commoners that typified Chan Chan and Cuzco.

I believe that some Maya cities are more similar to Chan Chan and Cuzco in social composition, if not architectural form, than their counterparts in the Valley of Mexico. Like the Andean cities, Maya settlements such as Palenque, Kaminalyjuyu, and Copan appear to have lacked a large, concentrated resident population. Moreover, most of the structures in these cities were monumental, designed as elite residences, tombs, and places of worship. Like Chan Chan and Cuzco, these Maya cities were the economic, religious, and administrative centers of princely households. They were probably more closely attached to the elite households and more dependent on the stimulus of the *oikos* economy than either Teotihuacan or Tenochtitlan. The "stela-cult" supports this perspective in that these monuments appear to be concerned chiefly with recording the political exploits of Maya lords. That is, the stelae document the importance of the Maya lords and their households in the development of Maya cities.

Although the Maya settlements reflect an emphasis on an *oikos* economy, they were not entirely dependent upon it, as were Chan Chan and Cuzco. The Maya cities also had markets and merchant-traders, and mercantile activity was certainly an important element of their economy. Thus, the Maya cities had a mixed *oikos* and market-based economy. They never became the capitals of empires, nor were they ever the centers of a *hyper-oikos* type of economy.

The Stability of Cities in the Andes

Even this cursory comparison brings into relief some of the distinctive economic and political features of Chan Chan and Cuzco and the secondary settlements they controlled. The sharpest economic difference between the Mesoamerican cities and their Andean counterparts is that the former were engaged, to varying degrees, in mercantile activity. The development of a "class," or more accurately a guildlike organization of long-distance merchant-traders, was perhaps the strongest expression of the Mesoamerican concern for trade and exchange of goods in the market. In this respect, the Mesoamerican urban settlements were similar to the ancient and medieval cities of the Old World analyzed by Weber: in both areas, the market-merchant-trader complex was a crucial element integrating and sustaining the urban economy.

As we have seen, the architects of Chan Chan and Cuzco found other mechanisms for organizing the urban economy. Although there was undoubtedly some type of informal bartering, established trade routes and partners, and perhaps even ephemeral markets, this form of economic activity was never as well developed or as socially important as it was in the cities of Mesoamerica and Europe.

Private entrepreneurship was never part of the economic life of these Andean cities, unless this was entrepreneurship by members of the ruling households. The cities were tightly and completely tied to the needs and desires of these royal households. Expansion of the urban economy entailed incorporation of foreign provinces, which were taxed for labor and products. This expansion was attained by directly extending the economic prerogatives of the royal household: surrogates of the household were set up in the subject provinces to oversee the extraction of taxes and maintain political control over the surrounding nonurban countryside. Thus, required or desired goods and services were *directly* expropriated by the state (read: the princely household) rather than obtained through less secure trade networks. This was Weber's *oikos* economy writ large; it was the *hyper-oikos* economy.

What was the origin of this highly specialized type of economy? Was it characteristic only of Chan Chan and Cuzco or of empires in the Andean World? Did it have deeper roots in the Andean tradition? These are questions for another study. Here I would note only that a possible point of departure for such a study would be an analysis of the similarities between the *hyper-oikos* economy and the "vertical archipelago economy" of the Andes recognized by Murra (1972). Both emphasized economic self-sufficiency and direct expropriation of the resources needed to support the major centers of population. Murra maintains that the archipelago economy was characteristic of both highland and coastal Andean societies, and that this method of economic organization was probably very ancient. In effect, the *hyper-oikos* type of economy may be a more highly integrated, state version of the folk-based vertical archipelago economy described by Murra.

Several valleys along the central and north coasts of Peru have a general settlement pattern in which one exceptionally large site dominates all other sites in the valley during any given temporal horizon (Moseley and Day 1982). This pattern is well established in the Early Horizon and may have had its inception as early as late preceramic times. Perhaps this settlement pattern reflects an economic and political organization similar in principle to Murra's vertical economy or that of the *hyper-oikos*. Like Chan Chan and Cuzco, these large sites may have been the residences of politically dominant artistocratic households that directly controlled the surrounding countryside. If so, the remarkable similarities between Chan Chan and Cuzco may be explained, in part, as parallel developments from a common heritage of the pure *oikos* type of economy. The evolution of Andean cities might then be seen as a stable and gradual process operating within the parameters set by this distinctive type of economy.

Thirteen

Ideological Adaptation and The Rise of the Aztec and Inca Empires

Arthur Demarest, Harvard University
Geoffrey Conrad, Harvard University

Questions of causality in cultural evolution are a central concern of contemporary archaeology. Recent theoretical trends emphasize systemic models that integrate many variables in explaining the interplay of environment, technology, subsistence, and trade in the rise of civilization. However, these models generally have been limited to the material aspects of culture.

A small, but growing, group of scholars in New World archaeology and ethnohistory is beginning to call for explanations of cultural development that incorporate the *nonmaterial* aspects of culture (religion, cosmology, philosophy, and so forth) into holistic models of culture change. One of the strongest and clearest of these voices has come from Gordon Willey, who continues to challenge his colleagues to confront difficult questions:

> How do ideas, or ideologies, articulate with other cultural systems? This is a complex question, and archaeologists, in their study of the rise and growth of civilizations, have been hesitant to address it. . . . Still, if thinking human beings are the generators, as well as the carriers, of culture it seems highly probable that, from very early on, ideas provided controls for and gave distinctive forms to the materialist base and to culture, and that these ideas then took on a kind of existence of their own, influencing, as well as being influenced by, other cultural systems. If this is so, then it is of interest and importance to try to see how ideas were interrelated with other parts of culture

and how they helped direct the trajectories of cultural and civilizational growth. (Willey 1976:205)

Heeding Willey's call to arms on ideology, some scholars have begun to explore the importance of nonmaterial factors in regard to the development of specific cultures (for example, see Flannery 1972; Flannery and Marcus 1976; Blanton 1976a, 1978; Willey 1976; Cowgill 1979; Freidel 1979; Townsend 1979; Conrad 1981; Demarest 1981). Most archaeologists, however, still feel that they do not have the kind of data needed to interpret ancient belief systems. Ethnohistorians, who do possess such information, have been concerned primarily with specific details of history and religion. The construction of broader evolutionary models has been left to the archaeologists, who continue to rely heavily upon environment, technology, subsistence, and trade—the aspects of the past most easily revealed by archaeological research.

Yet some of the most important developments in New World prehistory defy evaluation in strictly material terms. Perhaps the most enigmatic in this respect are the Aztec and Inca empires. The sudden rise and explosive expansion of these two states, which rank among the most dramatic episodes in human history, provide us with an opportunity to answer Willey's challenge.

The Culture-Historical Problem

When Spanish conquistadors entered Mesoamerica in 1519 and the Central Andes in 1532, they found each area under the domination of a single people—the Mexica Aztecs of Mexico and the Incas of Peru. At the time of the conquest, the Mexica were leading the frenzied expansion of the Aztec Triple Alliance, the largest political hegemony in the history of Mesoamerica. They controlled a loosely knit empire stretching from the highlands of Central Mexico to the tropical coasts of Guatemala and inhabited by many millions of people. Mexica power rested upon a tripartite base of market exchange, state-regulated long-distance trade, and endless streams of tribute paid by the subject peoples of Mesoamerica. The imperial capital of Tenochtitlan-Tlatelolco, one of the richest and most populous urban centers of the preindustrial world, so impressed Cortez's men that at first glance they were unsure whether what appeared before them was real or a hallucination (Diaz del Castillo 1956:139).

No less astonishing to the Spanish were the splendors of the Inca empire. In 1532 the Inca realm, whose capital lay at Cuzco in the southern Peruvian highlands, sprawled across the Andean world, stretching over 4,300 kilometers from northern Ecuador to central Chile. Integrated by its famous network of roads, a large and highly organized administrative hierarchy, and state-controlled redistribution of certain goods, this empire of millions was the largest pre-Columbian state in the New World, and probably the largest ever found anywhere at a "Bronze Age" level of technology.

Yet both of these macro-states had been assembled in less than a century by the military expansions of groups that were initially tiny, marginal, and backward. The Mexica entered the Mesoamerican scene quite late as a small and despised group of northern barbarians. Driven from place to place by their more civilized neighbors, they were finally forced to settle on the swampy island of Tenochtitlan. In 1350 their future capital was merely one of the many local centers of the Valley of Mexico. Likewise, as late as 1400 the Inca were an unsophisticated chiefdom confined to a small mountain valley, where they struggled for survival and autonomy amid larger and stronger neighbors. They were overshadowed by the more powerful states of the Titicaca Basin and totally eclipsed by the brilliant Chimu civilization of north coastal Peru.

The rise of the Aztec and Inca empires has never been convincingly explained. How and why were two such unpromising groups able to rise to sudden dominance of their heartlands and then to extend their control into far-flung regions? Recent studies based on ethnohistorical and archaeological evidence shed new light upon specific aspects of these questions, demonstrating the importance of complex social, political, and ideological forces (for example, see Davies 1973; Berdan 1976; Broda 1978; Erdheim 1978; Townsend 1979; Conrad 1981; Demarest 1981). Previously environmental factors and materialist paradigms dominated discussions of causality in New World imperialism (for example, see Palerm and Wolf 1957; Sanders and Price 1968; Murra 1972; Paulsen 1976; Harner 1977; Harris 1977; Carrasco 1978; Isbell 1978a). Now it is realized that such material factors must be incorporated into broader interpretive structures if we are ever to understand these extraordinary expansions.

Environmental Pressures

In the past two decades, ecologically oriented studies have identified several selective pressures favoring the development of ever-larger political units in Central Mexico and the Andes. The most commonly cited factors are the agricultural potential and the environmental diversity of these two regions. The extraordinary fertility and resources of the Valley of Mexico and the Titicaca Basin provided the subsistence base that was necessary, but not sufficient, for the development of a series of expansionistic civilizations. Once these regions were controlled, their agricultural wealth could support further territorial growth.

Environmental diversity may have been more important than agricultural potential in generating expansionistic tendencies. Some scholars have argued that where there are many different microenvironments, producing different crops and offering localized resources, it is advantageous for polities to control as much territory as possible, insuring a balanced diet, access to necessary resources, protection against crop failure in any one zone, and so on. In the case of Central Mexico, Sanders and Price have developed this theory into a model of "economic symbiosis," which states that environmental diversity encourages "the economic interdependence of social and physical population units in a given region to the advantage of all" (Sanders and Price 1968:188). This induced interdependence favored the development of the Central Mexican pattern of a network of markets linking specialized communities. However, Sanders and Price go on to point out that networks of specialized communities linked into trade and market systems

> are difficult to maintain except when the communities are part of some larger sociopolitical structure such as a regional state. Wholly aside from the need of a peaceful and stable political climate for the successful establishment of such economic patterns, the traditional market encounters of people from different communities would tend to produce a feeling of community interests and social identification that should act as a subtle integrative factor. (Sanders and Price 1968:189)

In other words, environmental diversity is a selective factor favoring not only specialization, interdependence, and markets, but also state formation, as well as the economic development of even larger political units. Symbiosis brings direct economic benefits—and according to Sanders and Price, a sense of national unity—to polities that can bring larger, more diverse territories under their control.

Independently, yet through a parallel logic, John Murra, William Isbell, and others view environmental diversity as a critical factor favoring regional interdependence and, ultimately, expansionism in the Central Andes. The extreme "verticality" of Andean ecological niches results in altitudinally determined environmental diversity. Murra (1972) notes that the general cultural response to this ecological pattern is the development of a "vertical archipelago," in which a community maintains a string of satellite settlements at different elevations so as to exploit a maximum number of microenvironments. Isbell (1978a) has gone further to propose that verticality is a selective factor favoring large-scale polities with centralized authority. By giving access to a wide variety of environmental zones, conquest served as an "energy averaging mechanism" that helped to insure the economic welfare of the state as a whole.

Another factor favoring the evolution of larger polities, population pressure, is emphasized in some materialist models of cultural evolution. In such scenarios demographic growth requires agricultural intensification, which in turn demands more complex sociopolitical systems ("structures") to administer the more complicated subsistence strategies ("infrastructures"). However, even if one accepts the materialist proposition that economic infrastructure determines all other aspects of culture, the problem with this equation is that the prime mover, demographic increase, is not simply a natural tendency. It must be demonstrated that population pressure is present, and if present, its own causes must be elucidated. As Cowgill (1979) has noted, analogies with feudal China suggest that the increasing militarism of Mesoamerican culture may have been as much a cause as a result of population pressure. State propaganda and religious dogma may have encouraged population growth to provide an increased citizenry for armies, taxation, and the economic pursuits necessary to support military campaigns.

The effect of hydraulic agriculture, irrigation systems, is another material force often cited as a causal factor in the development of New World states. Drawing on Marx, Wittfogel (1957) elaborated the theory that irrigation stimulated the rise of despotic, centralized state structures, because only that type of political formation could coordinate the construction and maintenance of complex irrigation systems. Sanders (1956, 1968), Palerm (1972), Carrasco (1978), and others have used aspects of Wittfogel's theory to explain developments in Mesoamerica.

Recent evidence challenges the view that hydraulic agriculture was of primary importance in the cultural evolution of most regions (for example, see Adams 1965; Adams and Nissen 1972; Millon 1973; Moseley 1975b; Blanton 1978). Meanwhile, the reasoning underlying the theory has also been widely disputed (for example, see Adams 1966; Flannery 1972, 1977; Blanton 1976a, 1976b). In any case, it does not seem relevant to the Aztec and Inca empires, which were late *macro*-state formations, not pristine, initial state developments. Furthermore, any arguments regarding the causes and effects of hydraulic projects could have been more convincingly applied to the sophisticated neighbors of the Mexica and Inca. The hydraulic theory does not explain why the relatively backward Inca and Mexica became the imperial leaders.

Irrigation (like diversity, population pressure, or agricultural potential) has some explanatory power if seen as one of the elements providing the setting for imperialism. Conquest and its fruits, tribute and political subordination, were a, if not *the*, principal factor in the Aztec and Inca expansions. Material forces provided a general pressure for such expansionism. Yet any understanding of the expansions requires some knowledge of the nature, motivation, and success of the conquest *structure* itself.

Despite these objections to monocausal materialist theories, it is clear that the interplay of environment, demography, and political development was crucial to late pre-Columbian cultural evolution. In the centuries preceding the ascendancy of the Mexica and Inca, both Central Mexico and the Central Andes experienced increasing militarism, demographic stress, and agricultural intensification. Although largely a result of state policy, population growth also affected the many competing states of the region, accelerating the pace and scale of their military struggles. Reinforcing the feedback between militarism and population growth was the intensification of agricultural systems, a response which in turn led to greater community specialization and interdependence—thereby increasing the importance of the "diversity factor" (economic symbiosis or vertical control) in expansionism. Thus, regardless of the order of causality, the preimperial polities of Central Mexico and the Andes were caught in a cycle of environmental, political, military, and demographic pressures that built toward a staggering crescendo in the fierce struggles between the many pre-Columbian states of the fourteenth and early fifteenth centuries.

Even assuming that this cycle generated a competitive political situation and generally favored expansionism, it does not explain the phenomenal success of the Mexica and Inca response to existing pressures. We contend that even a combination of these material factors is an insufficient explanation for the Mexica and Inca achievements, because such forces did not affect those two peoples alone. Their neighbors, many of whom had initial advantages over the Mexica and Inca, felt the same pressures but failed to build such sweeping empires. The same argument applies to environmental diversity, agricultural potential, and hydraulic developments.

A satisfactory explanation of late pre-Columbian imperialism in Mexico and Peru must be truly multicausal. It must include *both* general, widely operating, selective forces and the specific factors that allowed the Mexica and Inca to surpass their neighbors. Such a broadened theoretical perspective guides the brief reconstructions of Mexica and Inca history that follow. These summary interpretations of the two expansions reflect our analysis of the interplay of specific material and nonmaterial factors. The reconstructions are drawn from the major chronicles and from recent ethnohistorical research. (For further documentation and discussion, see Demarest 1976; Conrad 1981, 1982a; Conrad and Demarest n.d.). Here we are interested primarily in highlighting the role of ideology and its interplay with political and economic institutions in the rapid evolution of these societies.

The Ideological Adaptation of the Mexica Aztec

THE EARLY MEXICA[1]

In the thirteenth and fourteenth centuries the Valley of Mexico was balkanized into competing city-states and fragile alliances, each battling militarily and ideologically for the claim to be the rightful heir of the earlier, by then legendary, Toltec state. By the beginning of the fourteenth century, two loose confederations of centers appeared to be heading toward a major confrontation. On the northwestern side of the lake system the Tepanecs, with their alliance centered on the town of Azcapotzalco, were rapidly expanding in influence, even though they lacked a legitimizing quasi-Toltec ancestry. On the eastern shore of Lake Texcoco another heterogeneous group, the Acolhua, had a more established hegemony, dominated by a sequence of capitals: Coatlichan, Huexotla, and finally, Texcoco. Between the growing alliances of the Tepanec and Acolhua, smaller polities fought for survival.

Among these lesser contenders were the Mexica, a group of "barbarians" from the north who had entered the Valley of Mexico relatively late. According to the chronicles,[2] the early Mexica were despised by their neighbors for their backwardness and savagery. They were driven from place to place in the valley until the mid-fourteenth century. At that time, seeking refuge from their persecutors, they settled on some marshy islands in western Lake Texcoco, their future capital. Here they managed to survive on a combined economy of fishing, lakebed *(chinampa)* agriculture, and mercantile activities. During this period the dominant institution of Mexica society was the *calpulli*, the basic Mexica social unit, whose precise nature has long been debated.[3] Most analysts agree that the *calpulli* was a localized, clanlike unit that held land corporately but also possessed internal social and economic stratification. Though the evidence in the chronicles (see note 1) is somewhat contradictory, the traditional governing body was generally said to have been a council of the heads of the *calpulli* units.

As the Mexica were drawn more deeply into the byzantine power struggles of the Valley of Mexico, wider involvement in regional politics altered the traditional leadership structure. At some point in the fourteenth century a position of temporary leader was transformed into the hereditary office of *tlatoani* ("chief speaker"). The Mexica leadership also intermarried with Culhua and Texcocan rulers in order to borrow the legitimizing Toltec roots needed by any claimant to power. The offspring of this quasi-Toltec dynasty would form the core of a developing upper class, the *pipiltin*.[4]

However, the political fortunes of the early Mexica were principally tied to the rising fortunes of the Tepanecs. The early Mexica were vassals of the

Tepanec alliance, for which the Mexica often fought in battles with other powers. Gaining a reputation as capable warriors, the Mexica were gradually drawn into the political schemes of the Tepanec tyrant Tezozomoc, ruler of Azcapotzalco. Under his tutelage the acculturation and cultural evolution of the Mexica accelerated. The Tepanecs trained the Mexica warriors for their later role as military imperialists. More important, they provided a model of a highly stratified society for the rapidly changing institutions of the Mexica and thus encouraged the ambitions of the Mexica warrior class.

The growing influence of warfare was also felt in religious institutions, as seen in the Mexica's somewhat obscure composite hero-god, Huitzilopochtli. This deity was gradually elevated into a militaristic patron god.[5] Like other Central Mexican peoples and in keeping with ancient traditions in Mesoamerica, the early Mexica practiced religious rituals of human sacrifice and cannibalism on a limited scale. This religious complex of the sacrifice of captured warriors continued to develop as militarism and political competition increased in Central Mexico.

By the end of the fourteenth century, the Mexica had undergone considerable cultural change since their entry into the Valley of Mexico. Yet Tenochtitlan's rising state structure was little more than a foreshadowing of its rapid transformation into an imperial juggernaut after the fall of their Tepanec overlords in 1428. Before that date, the power of the Mexica in valley affairs, their share of tribute, and their holdings in conquered lands were all limited by their vassalage to the Tepanec state. This external check on Mexica power was paralleled by internal restraints on the warrior elite. The development of elite authority was fettered by the traditional *calpullin* system, and the economic importance of warfare and tribute remained quite small in comparison to the intensive lakebed agriculture of the *calpullin* farmers and the regional marketing activities of the Mexica merchants of Tlatelolco.

THE TRANSFORMATIONAL CRISIS[6]

In 1418 the Tepanecs, aided by the Mexica *tlatoani* Chimalpopoca and his warriors, finally crushed their principal rivals, the Acolhua conferacy, led by the prestigious city of Texcoco. The king of Texcoco was slain and his son, the prince Nezahualcoyotl, driven into exile. For a period the Tepanec leader, Tezozomoc, became the dominant ruler in the Valley of Mexico. However, he had taken no great pains to legitimize his sovereignty by acquiring a Toltec ancestry. Furthermore, his macro-state lacked the unifying imperial cosmology that would later be the inspiration for the continuing expansion of the Aztec empire. It is not surprising, then, that upon his death in 1426 Tezozomoc's kingdom fell apart.

The complex and confusing accounts of the events of 1426–28 (see note 2) can be summarized as follows. Tezozomoc's death was followed by a war of succession at Azcapotzalco, which ended when a certain Maxtla seized the throne. Shortly thereafter the Mexica *tlatoani* Chimalpopoca died of "unnatural causes"—either suicide or murder.[7] A new *tlatoani*, Itzcoatl, succeeded to power in Tenochtitlan. Together with his nephews Moctezuma I and Tlacaelel, Itzcoatl led the militant faction favoring revolt against the Tepanecs. It seems likely that the new Mexica leaders perceived that civil strife had weakened the Tepanec alliance, giving them the opportunity for a daring bid for power. Itzcoatl's warrior faction prevailed in the debate at Tenochtitlan, and the Mexica, supported by the city-states of Texcoco and Tacuba, rose in revolt. The "Triple Alliance" of Tenochtitlan-Texcoco-Tacuba defeated the Tepanecs in 1428, falling heir to Tezozomoc's realm. This Triple Alliance, which came to be dominated by the Mexica Aztecs of Tenochtitlan, was the Aztec empire.

The ascendancy of Itzcoatl's warrior faction has many characteristics of a military coup designed to remove the internal and external checks on the power of the Mexica elite.[8] Regardless of the exact details of their victory, there is no question that after the triumph of the Triple Alliance the new leaders initiated a sweeping series of changes that transformed Mexica society. Most of the major chronicles (see note 2) mention the imperial "reforms" instituted by the principal figures of the new order: Itzcoatl, the *tlatoani;* Moctezuma I, his nephew and successor; and Tlacaelel, a larger-than-life figure said to have been the *cihuacoatl* (high priest and chief advisor) of the first four imperial rulers. It is reported that the new leaders ordered the burning of existing historical and religious texts (for example, see Sahagún bk. 10, ch. 29, 1950–65:191). Then they set about restructuring Mexica economic, political, social, and ideological institutions.

Modern analyses confirm that crucial changes in all aspects of Mexica society can be traced to these reforms. Castillo (1972:45,46,69,70, and *passim*) Katz (1966:33, 34, and *passim*), Davies (1974:78–82), and Berdan (1975: ch. 6) have described the economic restructuring of Mexica society that resulted from the unequal distribution of the lands and tribute gained by conquering the Tepanecs. Lopez Austin (1961:39–42) has shown that the concentration of power in a *tlatoani* and a Council of Four (all of whom were members of the imperial family) began during the reforms of Itzcoatl and his advisor, Tlacaelel. Many scholars (for example, Brundage 1972:82–91; Carrasco 1976; Bray 1978; Rounds 1979) have noted the great augmentation of the power and prestige of the military warrior class after their victory in the Tepanec war. Class distinctions were eventually formalized by Tlacaelel and by Moctezuma I, Itzcoatl's successor as *tlatoani,* who issued a series of

14 decrees (Duran 1964: ch. 26) defining the nobility *(pipiltin)* and commoners *(macehualtin)*. These elaborate sumptuary laws reinforced through dress, privileges, and religious ceremonies the new and more highly stratified social order.[9]

All of these changes were in the interest of the new leaders and the nobles. They concentrated wealth, social privilege, and political power in the hands of the ruling *tlatoani*, his warrior knights, and the noble *pipiltin* class. Tribute, distributed on the basis of birthright and military achievement, became one of the principal economic foundations of Mexica life.[10] Responsible for only a tiny portion of the vastly increased Mexica landholdings and virtually excluded from the new political structure, the *calpullin* organizations lost much of their traditional economic and political significance.[11] The social and economic foundations of the empire had been laid.

Yet the political, social, and economic changes resulting from Itzcoatl's coup only served to raise the Mexica abruptly to the level of the Tepanec macrostate under Tezozomoc. These reforms merely concluded the processes already well advanced by the beginning of the fifteenth century, completing the Mexica's adoption of the political and economic institutions of their more advanced neighbors and allies. Though perhaps slightly better structured than earlier city-states, the new institutions of Mexica society differed little from those of the capitals of previous Postclassic military alliances. However, the Mexica's precursors had never extended their control beyond Central Mexico and had quickly collapsed into small warring polities. In contrast, the Aztec Triple Alliance poured out of the Valley of Mexico and swept across much of Mesoamerica. Rather than quickly disintegrating into diffuse centers of power, the Triple Alliance hegemony gradually became more focused on the royal house of Tenochtitlan.

What was the critical difference, the competitive edge, responsible for the Mexica's phenomenal success? The answer to this question lies in an ideological transformation that assured Mexica victories while it stimulated expansionism.

THE IDEOLOGICAL ADAPTATION[12]

The original contribution of the Mexica to the evolution of Mesoamerican civilization was an ideology that successfully integrated religious, economic, and social systems into an imperialistic war machine. The ideological changes that completed this integration were the work of the same handful of men (Itzcoatl, Tlacaelel, Moctezuma I, and so forth) who had led the coup and instituted the other reforms. Some of their manipulations of historical and religious concepts were intended to justify their own actions and consolidate

Ideological Adaptation and the Rise of the Aztec and Inca Empires

their power; others were designed to combat neighboring peoples' rather low opinion of the Mexica. Above all, the new historians and mythographers set out to transform ancient myths and religious cosmology into an integrated cult that supported Mexica military imperialism.

This last set of reforms completed one of the Mexica's greatest achievements: the imperial ideology that elevated Huitzilopochtli and united the patron deity, Mexica military ambitions, and the sun in a vision of the constant struggle between the forces of the universe.[13] As we have seen, the preimperial Huitzilopochtli began as a late-developing and strictly local divine patron, possibly a union of a Mexica god-hero with a more ancient water deity of the southern lakes.[14] In the imperial period, in keeping with the new prominence of the Mexica themselves, Huitzilopochtli became one of the four "creation gods," the deities at the very top of the ancient Mesoamerican pantheon. He came to be identified with both Tezcatlipoca and Tonatiuh, the warrior sun. Huitzilopochtli took on roles and aspects of Tezcatlipoca, as the "young" sun of the spring and summer (Hunt 1977) and as the warrior sun (Tonatiuh) who battled his way across the sky every day.[15] To fortify himself for his daily combat and to stave off his inevitable destruction by the forces of darkness, Huitzilopochtli/Tonatiuh had to be "fed" with the precious source of vital energy—human blood (see notes 13, 15).

This elaboration of the state cult and its combination with more ancient beliefs had clear ramifications for the long-established cults of warfare and human sacrifice. The imperial cosmology held that the Mexica must relentlessly take captives in warfare and sacrifice them; the spiritual strength of the sacrificed enemy warriors would strengthen the sun, helping it prevail in its constant battle for survival. Furthermore, it was specifically the *Mexica's* sacred duty to pursue a course of endless warfare, conquest, and sacrifice to preserve the universe from the daily threat of annihilation. The new vision of the cosmos accelerated the pace and scale of human sacrifices beyond all previous measure and directly associated these ancient rites with the Mexica state and the imperial expansion of the Triple Alliance. Most of the elements of this vision of the universe were ancient Mesoamerican beliefs, but the new Mexica cosmology united them and aligned them with the national needs and imperial quest of the state.

Clearly, this new central role for the Mexica and their transformed patron deity was also the product of imperial reforms. Indeed, one chronicler specifically attributes the transformation of the cult of Huitzilopochtli to the ever-present high priest and chief advisor, Tlacaelel (Chimalpahin 1965:197). Even if such interpretations credit this semilegendary figure with a little too much creativity, it is certain that the transformation of the state religion does, in fact, date to this period of ideological reform and that it coincides perfectly with the needs of the new state and its rulers.

As we have seen, ideological manipulations were only one part of the changes instituted by the new regime. However, these religious reforms—the elevation of Huitzilopochtli and nationalization and elaboration of the sacrificial cult—were the most innovative and crucial elements of the entire transformation. The new ideology set the Mexica apart from their neighbors and predecessors, and it irrevocably altered the course of Aztec history.

Although Mesoamerican religions had always involved human sacrifice, the Mexica cosmology cast this need into a new, almost mechanistic, view of the universe. Appropriating aspects of Tonatiuh, the warrior-sun, the patron deity Huitzilopochtli required the blood and hearts of human victims to nourish him in his constant struggle with the forces of darkness and disorder. Thus, not only was the need for human sacrifice more pronounced, but there could now be no limits to its scale: the greater the number of captives offered on the sacrificial altar, the greater would be the strength (and gratitude) of the gods. Human sacrifices became more conspicuous in every major religious festival, and many thousands of victims were killed each year (see, for example, Cook 1946). In single ceremonies coinciding with major imperial victories, thousands of captives fell beneath the knife, and the flesh of their limbs was consumed in ritual feasts.

Some recent interpretations of Aztec human sacrifice and cannibalism seem as bizarre as the state cult itself. Despite overwhelming evidence, one scholar has even denied that such practices existed (Arens 1979). Others see the Triple Alliance as a "cannibal empire" driven by a mindless search for protein (Harner 1977, Harris 1977), and another characterization portrays the Mexica as a people enslaved by an irrational ideology (Brundage 1975).

A more holistic interpretation of Aztec warfare and human sacrifice can show that this sacred complex was a rational phenomenon, in terms of both the context of Mesoamerican belief systems and the specific political and economic interests of the people and the state. Looking first at its ideological context, we see that the Mexica cosmology was acceptable and effective only because it drew on established religious institutions and traditional myths. Human sacrifice was a long and venerated tradition in Mesoamerica, as it has been among many cultures in human history. The reformed imperial ideology merely altered the potential scale (and thus the consequences) of sacrifice by directly associating the strength of the astral gods with the offerings of their mortal collaborators, the Mexica. This superficially minor adjustment tied the ancient sacrificial complex to the imperial ambitions of the state.

Mexica warfare and the sacrificial cult were also quite rationally integrated with the political and economic needs of the state and its new leaders. On the collective level, the secular rationality of the state cult can be seen in the correspondence between ideological changes and immediate political pressures on the Mexica people. Initially, at the time of the Tepanec collapse, the ideological reforms fulfilled Tenochtitlan's suddenly critical need for legitimization. The reforms of myth and history gave the state the required cultural ancestry, a Toltec heritage. More important, the association of the myth of solar struggle with Huitzilopochtli gave the state a divine sanction, raising it to a level superior to its neighbors. The new cosmology conferred a sacred role on the Mexica people, giving them the national identity and collective zeal necessary for survival and success in the greater political arena into which they had been suddenly thrust. Thus, the state cult of accelerated warfare and mass sacrifice was a timely ideological adaptation to the political environment of fifteenth century Central Mexico. Well within the bounds of traditional Mesoamerican religious thinking, the modification of Mexica cosmology was a politically rational (indeed, astute) policy.

The state cult can also be seen as economically adaptive. Although they rested on a foundation of intensive agriculture, the economies of the Central Mexican city-states also relied heavily on tribute gained through military victories (see note 10). The Mexica's sacrificial cosmology gave them the competitive edge needed for such victories: fanaticism. The unending hunger of the gods for mass sacrifices fueled the Mexica armies, allowing them to wear down some of their most obstinate opponents. The Mexica economy reaped the benefits in vast new quantities of annual tribute and control over additional sources of labor.

Thus, in all respects the transformation of Mexica ideology was a successful adaptation to the political and economic world of fifteenth century Central Mexico, and ultimately to the environmental pressures that had formed that cultural landscape. The new ideology was a major cause of the Mexica's dramatic success in responding to the ecological pressures favoring expansionism.

The new cosmology and the rituals it demanded launched the Mexica armies on a divine quest, a quest resulting in the sprawling Aztec empire. After the victory of 1428 and the subsequent transformation of the Mexica, their history becomes a tale of ceaseless conquests. Led by the Mexica warriors, the armies of the Triple Alliance capitals marched outward, increasing with each campaign the number of centers and peoples pledging allegiance and tribute to Tenochtitlan and its Aztec allies. The reformed ideology was the driving force behind their campaigns. The *tlatoani* Itzcoatl, leader of the new order, was clearly aware of this fact as he announced the mission of their newly exalted patron, Huitzilopochtli:

This is also the task of our god Huitzilopochtli
And that is why he came to us.
He gathers, he draws to his service
All the nations with the strength of his chest and
   of his head.[16]

The Ideological Adaptation of the Inca

THE EARLY INCA[17]

In the thirteenth and fourteenth centuries the Inca situation paralleled that of the Mexica. Inca culture emerged in the context of a political power vacuum left by the breakup of the Tiahuanaco civilization in the Titicaca Basin. Piecing together the limited archaeological evidence and the believable bits of the imperially authorized version of Inca history, we can characterize the early Inca as a small-scale, rural society occupying a limited zone around Cuzco in the Vilcanota Valley. They were one of the least sophisticated and least promising of the many small polities struggling to assert themselves in the southern Peruvian highlands. The basic unit of early Inca society was the *ayllu*, a corporate landholding group tied together by reciprocal labor obligations, communal property ownership, endogamy, and the worship of a common ancestor.[18]

The early Inca shared the religious beliefs and institutions of their neighbors in the Central Andes. Like other Andean highland peoples, the Inca worshipped a host of deities, many of them sky gods. Foremost among the latter was a generalized god of sky and storm, a divinity with many aspects, incorporating the sun, celestial elements, and a creator-culture hero role in his manifold godhead. This celestial complex, much modified by time and imperial ambition, would later be seen in the upper pantheon of Inca state religion.[19]

Early Inca ancestor worship—the preservation and propitiation of ancestral mummies—was merely a chiefdom's version of this basic Andean religious institution. Ancestor worship had more spectacular manifestations elsewhere—for instance, in the north coastal Chimu empire—and would appear later as the lavish and costly Inca cult of the royal mummies. However, in the thirteenth and fourteenth centuries Inca religion in general and *ayllu* ancestor worship in particular were typical, and rather unimpressive, variations on general Andean religious themes.[20]

There is much less believable information on the preimperial Inca than on the Mexica. Some accounts implausibly project imperial institutions and activities back into preimperial times. The less reliable chronicles report vast Inca armies marching to battle in distant regions during the nascent years of Inca society. The more consistent historical sources and available archaeological evidence demonstrate that these tales are flagrant exaggerations of the petty raids of Inca *sinchis,* or elected war leaders.[21]

Nonetheless, in the competitive environment of the Central Andean world in the thirteenth and fourteenth centuries, the Inca were gradually drawn, probably as minor participants, into the quarrels of the more powerful groups surrounding them. By the fourteenth century *sinchis* were in power for longer and longer periods. As is the pattern with such temporary military leadership (even today), the *sinchi* gradually evolved into a permanent office, first a war chief, and ultimately a monarch, the *Sapa Inca* ("unique Inca"). As with the Mexica *tlatoani,* we can assume that the relatives and offspring of the *sinchis* formed the nucleus of a privileged class. With the rapid evolution and militarization of the Inca people, these privileged members probably acquired the status of an incipient nobility.[22]

In this sense the future institutions of the empire undoubtedly assumed their embryonic forms during the fourteenth century. Yet while the increasing militarism of Central Andean polities offset the inertia of tradition to some extent, the strongly conservative institutions of *ayllu* power, reciprocal obligations, and ancestor worship restrained the initial development of social stratification and political inequality among the Inca. Not until the turn of the fifteenth century would the acceleration of military rivalries in the Central Andes provide the Inca leadership with the opportunity to transform their society internally while breaking the restraining influence of the powerful alliances around them.

THE TRANSFORMATIONAL CRISIS[23]

In the early fifteenth century the Inca, under the leadership of ruler/*sinchi* Viracocha Inca, were beginning to assert themselves, widening their area of influence and alliance and possibly even meddling in the internal politics of the Titicaca Basin.[24] During the same period, a rival people, the Chanca, were increasing their own power. After conquering Quechua groups to the northwest of Cuzco, the Inca homeland, the Chanca began to menace Viracocha Inca's realm directly.

The situation became critical around 1438. Intent on crushing their rivals, the Chanca invaded Inca territory. Viracocha Inca had grown old and was nearing the end of his reign; by chance or design, the Chanca had chosen to launch their attack at a time when the Inca leadership was weak. The Chanca shattered the initial Inca resistance and laid seige to Cuzco. Convinced that Cuzco could not be held and that the Inca cause was hopeless, Viracocha Inca fled to the hills behind the capital district. His son and designated successor,

Inca Urcon, went with him. Command of the defense of Cuzco fell to another son of Viracocha Inca, Cusi Inca Yupanqui, who later renamed himself Pachakuti ("Cataclysm"). A vigorous warrior, he is said to have rallied the citizens of Cuzco after his father's desertion. To the astonishment of all, the beleaguered Inca triumphed. They drove the Chanca invaders from Cuzco and in later battles conquered the Chanca regions.

Seizing the opportunity afforded by his victory, Pachakuti and his warrior lieutenants assumed power. Pachakuti had himself crowned ruler in place of his father and brother. He then embarked on a series of internal reforms, rewriting Inca history and remodeling the social and political organization of the Inca state. The details of this period presented in the Inca oral histories are far more sketchy and even more contradictory than the accounts of the Mexica transformation, which were based upon written, pictographic records. However, it seems clear that, as with the Mexica, the reforms of the new military leaders abruptly consolidated and completed what had been a slow and limited development of class stratification. The acquisition of new territories around Cuzco and in the former Chanca homeland altered the balance of economic and political power. Claims to the tax revenues from these lands became the prerogative of the Inca ruler, his warrior leaders, and his kin. This new wealth undercut the traditional power of the *ayllu,* the councils of *ayllu* leaders, and the larger aggregates of traditional, kin-based groups. It also completed the process of shifting the Inca economy from a base of local farming and llama herding to dependence on the labor taxation of conquered peoples, the Andean analog of tribute.[25]

As among the Mexica, these fundamental shifts in the economic base were accompanied by a restructuring of the social and political order. Under the guidance of Pachakuti and his advisors, elaborate hierarchies were constructed to channel the heightened ambitions of the Inca nation. As the empire grew through conquest, this governmental structure grew with it, supervising the growing labor taxes that supported the ruling class and the state religion. Not surprisingly, this accelerated political stratification was reinforced by a reworking of oral history and traditional social codes. In the early decades of the empire both of these models of behavior were adjusted to legitimize the growing distance between *ayllu* commoners and the rising class of nobles and administrators. The revised myth and history also claimed that Inca militarism and imperialism were both the traditional way of life and a sacred obligation of Inca leadership.[26]

In the authorized version of Inca history, the reforms that followed Pachakuti's rise to power were described as unprecedented, and they were usually attributed to Pachakuti himself. In reality, most of these innovations consisted of "reorganization and projections onto a wider screen of old, deep-rooted

Andean techniques" (Murra 1958:31). Among the reworkings of traditional cultural elements, there were transformations of ideological institutions, particularly ancestor worship. These religious "reforms" were to have profound effects on Inca society, and they would become the competitive edge responsible for the Inca's imperial success.

THE IDEOLOGICAL ADAPTATION[27]

The principal product of the early imperial religious reforms was an elaborate cult centered upon the bodies of deceased Inca rulers. Royal mummy worship manifested itself in many spectacular ways and was a pervasive theme of court life in Cuzco. No manifestation, however, was more strange or significant than an institution that has been called "split inheritance," or "the property rights of the dead."

Upon the death of an Inca emperor the rights to govern, to wage war, and to impose taxes on the realm passed to one of his sons, who was his successor and principal heir. However, the chroniclers emphatically state that the new ruler received no material legacy from his predecessor. The deceased emperor's buildings, servants, chattel, and other possessions continued to be treated as his property and were entrusted to his *panaqa,* a corporate social group containing all of his descendants in the male line except his successor. These secondary heirs did not actually own the items named above. Ownership remained vested in the dead king, and the *panaqa* derived its support from its own holdings. Members of the *panaqa* managed their ancestor's property for him, using it to perpetuate his cult. They maintained the emperor's mummy in state, made sacrifices to it, consulted it in times of stress, and brought it out to take part in important state ceremonies. In short, an emperor's *panaqa* continued to treat him as if he were alive.

The most obvious physical manifestation of these property rights of the dead kings was the sequential construction of palaces in the capital city.[28] In imperial times each Inca ruler built one or more palaces for himself in Cuzco and its environs. After his death his mummy was kept in this building (or moved among these buildings) under the care of his *panaqa,* while his successor built the next palace(s). Each successive ruler was obliged to construct his own palace, develop his own court, and raise the economic support needed to maintain it.

In typical fashion, Inca oral history credited Pachakuti with the establishment of split inheritance, but his creativity need not be exaggerated. Such a royal cult of the dead had existed previously among the Chimu, whom the backward Inca probably consciously imitated. Furthermore, the property rights of dead kings, and the principle of split inheritance that assured them, resulted from an apparently minor manipulation of the ancient Andean institutions of ancestor worship.[29] Split inheritance simply applied this fundamental tenet of Inca religion to imperial rulers on an appropriately regal scale. If the dead bodies through which the local *ayllu's* ancestors spoke were sacred entities, the mummy bundles containing the spiritual essences of dead rulers were to be among the holiest objects in the realm. If the *ayllu's* progenitors received small sacrifices and occasional ritual remembrances, past kings were to be treated with all the pomp and ceremony they had enjoyed as living monarchs. If the *ayllu* supported its forebears by reserving a small portion of its fields for them, deceased emperors were to sustain themselves by keeping all of the property they had accumulated during their lifetimes.

In aggrandizing all of the basic political, social, and religious institutions, the new leaders also carefully sought to replace the Inca's obscure and unprepossessing origins with myths and legends more appropriate to their newly elevated political status. Pachakuti appears to have created, or at least reorganized, the ancestor cults of earlier *sinchi* warriors or legendary heroes. After this reshuffling, formal *panaqas*, each maintaining a palace, lands, and a mummy worship cult, existed for seven "kings" who had allegedly preceded Viracocha Inca and the mid-fifteenth century transformation of the Inca.[30] History and legend were appropriately reworked, giving an artificial time depth to the Inca dynasty and linking it directly to one aspect of the upper pantheon, a solar deity known as Inti.

Like the Mexica's Huitzilopochtli, the Inca patron god, Inti, had gradually evolved into both a sun god and a militaristic national patron (see note 19). His attributes confusingly overlap with the creator god, Viracocha, and other highland sky gods (Illapa, Thunapa, and so on), suggesting a certain degree of manipulation by Inca leaders. Such manipulations allowed them to segregate their own solarized patron from the other elements of the manifold celestial pantheon and to portray him as an evangelistic sponsor of Inca imperialism. Not surprisingly, Inca leaders also claimed direct descent from Inti. Hence, Inti justified not only Inca imperialism in general, but the dynasty's right to power and privilege.

The most important modification of state religion and official history was the elaborated royal manifestation of ancestor worship. Indeed, this change can be seen as the crucial element in the ideological adaptation of the Inca people in the early fifteenth century. For while the dogma of Inti and the reworking of myth and oral history motivated the Inca populace toward conquest, Inca *leadership* was driven by a far more direct consideration: the economic implications of split inheritance and property rights of the royal dead.

The basis of wealth and economic stratification among the Inca was agricultural land and the labor taxation needed to farm it.[31] Inca law required each taxpayer (able-bodied adult male head of household) to contribute a certain amount of labor to the state every year. Citizens complied with these obligations by cultivating state-owned lands for the support of civil and religious authorities, constructing all public works projects, and joining the Inca armies. Labor taxation also supported the Inca rulers themselves. This labor produced the agricultural support that sustained leaders and constituted their wealth. The leaders used this wealth to provide themselves with goods and services and to help support their own system of political patronage.

The important fact is that both land and labor tax rights continued to support the ruler, his patronage system, and his corporate ancestor cult (the *panaqa*) for all eternity! A king's private lands, as well as his labor tax support, were covered by the law of split inheritance; there is no doubt that an emperor retained his lands after his death. In fact, most of the chroniclers' explicit references to royal estates are specifically concerned with the lands owned by deceased rulers. This conclusion is confirmed by colonial legal records of disputes over land tenure and water rights. The exact amount of territory owned by any single ruler is unknown, but the total was obviously large: various sources name entire highland valleys that were the personal property of Inca sovereigns, and it is clear that each emperor owned lands in all the provinces of his realm. At least during the empire's early years, these royal estates were cultivated by taxpayers as part of their labor service obligations. All such labor taxes imposed by an emperor for his own benefit were also covered by this principle of split inheritance and remained in effect after his death.[32]

Thus, through split inheritance, the property rights of the deceased king were assured for all eternity, while his primary heir, the new head of state, was left without a palace, property, the means to support his imperial estate, or the land and labor needed to establish his own perpetual ancestor cult at death. In order to accumulate his own property, the new ruler had to extract more surplus labor from the present population through new labor tax obligations, owed directly to himself. However, this course of action would exhaust the surplus time of the people, strain the bonds of reciprocity between ruler and subjects, and clearly damage the new leader's public image. An alternative, and far less troublesome, strategy was to conquer new regions. Once subjected, they would owe their labor tax directly to the new emperor and not to some previous ruler. These new regions also allowed the conquering ruler to set aside lands for his own personal support without infringing on the perpetual rights of the dead kings. Hence, the grand version of ancestor worship applied by Pachakuti to the royal line forced each successive emperor to embark on a program of conquest.

The property rights of the dead were to alter Inca society irrevocably. Split inheritance would force each succeeding ruler into a constant search for new agricultural land—a drive that may have been intended from the beginning by the militant architects of the new imperial regime. Combined with their other religious reforms, the elevation of their jingoistic solar patron god, Inti, and the reworking of myth and history, the Inca ideological transformation drove both the leadership and the populace outward on the path to conquest, converting Inca society into one of history's most efficient imperial juggernauts.

The Interplay of Factors in Mexica and Inca Expansionism

These schematic reconstructions of the development of Aztec and Inca imperialism make it clear that the interweaving of environmental, economic, social, political, and religious factors could not be more complex. All the elements of this network of causality are indispensable. Above all, the development of these societies must be understood not by viewing the cultures as unified, single-minded, ecologically intuitive organisms, but rather by analyzing all levels—individual, class, and collective—of decisions and adaptations. Furthermore, these adaptations must be understood in terms of the cultural and political environments of the times, as well as the physical environment.

Both the Mexica and Inca empires arose from balkanized political situations that had characterized their respective areas for several hundred years. During the thirteenth and fourteenth centuries Central Mexico and the southern Peruvian highlands were fragmented among many small states and chiefdoms, each competing militarily and politically for the right to be the heir of the Toltecs or Tiahuanaco. In part, these conflicts were generated by long-term environmental pressures acting on the late pre-Columbian peoples of Central Mexico and the southern sierra.

Foremost among these pressures was environmental diversity, along with the concomitant tendencies toward economic symbiosis in Mesoamerica and verticality in the Andes. Both of these strategies conferred the advantage of a more productive and reliable subsistence base on any polity able to control access to multiple ecological niches. Coupled with this diversity factor was some degree of population pressure, leading to competition for resources. Responses to demographic problems—agricultural intensification and increased interregional exchange—augmented the importance of symbiosis/verticality and the benefits accruing to states able to establish dominion over varied environmental zones.

Nonetheless, environmental and demographic factors alone are insufficient explanations for late pre-Columbian imperialism. Population pressure was as much an effect as a cause of militaristic policies. Likewise, there is no necessary correlation between environmental diversity and empire building. Symbiosis and verticality were selective forces that favored, but did not require, imperial expansion. Furthermore, any attempt to explain the Inca empire and the Aztec Triple Alliance in terms of general environmental and economic pressures is based on a misleading biological metaphor. The implicit treatment of society as a single organism with one mind obscures the behavior of individuals and interest groups, whose desires and actions may be either complementary or contradictory. When unity of purpose exists, it is based on a multiplicity of motives that must be explicated if the rationale for cultural stability or change is to be understood.

This last consideration introduces politics into the argument. Success in war brought direct benefits to the leadership groups of Mesoamerican and Andean societies. Even if victory did not lead to permanent conquest, it produced booty, which increased the power and prestige of leaders. By distributing the spoils of war to his followers, a successful military leader could build a patronage network to serve as his power base. Maintenance of this patronage network required a continuing flow of loot from new victories. Thus, in late prehistoric times Mesoamerican and Andean rulers had strong vested interests in pursuing militaristic policies.

This complex of environmental, political, and economic factors led to an intensely antagonistic atmosphere in Central Mexico and the southern Peruvian highlands in the centuries immediately preceding the Spanish Conquest. Competition among local states and chiefdoms was the result of interrelated and inseparable historical, environmental, demographic, and political forces. The bellicosity they produced built toward a staggering crescendo in the fierce struggles of the fourteenth and early fifteenth centuries. These struggles formed the setting, the political environment, of the early Mexica and Inca. It was to this cultural environment that the Aztec and Inca societies adapted by means of internal transformations.

Mexica and Inca cultural evolution consisted of a series of adaptations to the conditions of their times. As we have seen, the internal transformations of both societies began during the preimperial epochs, as the institution of hereditary rulership developed from what had been the temporary office of elected war leader. Concomitantly, the authority of traditional kin group leaders began to be undercut. This process of centralization of power and incipient social stratification was itself a gradual adaptive response to the environmental, demographic, and political pressures made manifest in the threats posed by the larger and stronger societies surrounding the early Mexica and Inca.

These pressures eventually triggered what we have designated as the transformational crises—the Mexica's overthrow of the Tepanecs and the Inca's defeat of the Chanca. In both cases victory brought great power to a small group of leaders, who set about restructuring their societies by intensifying existing developmental trends. Survival of the military crises was followed by a series of reforms enacted by the new leadership. These changes resulted in further centralization of authority in the office of *tlatoani* or *Sapa Inca;* institutionalization of patronage networks through greater social stratification, consolidation of a hereditary nobility, and increasingly unequal distribution of wealth; and continuing drives for new conquests to support the system.

Again, these cultural changes were adaptive responses to the natural and social environments of fifteenth century Mexico and Peru, in that the initial expansions brought benefits to the Mexica and Inca nations as a whole. Yet viewed cynically, these collective benefits may have been more an effect than a cause of the shift to empire. The cause of the imperial reforms, in the sense of the *conscious* reason for which they were undertaken, probably lies in the fact that they served the ambitions of the new rulers. Moreover, the institution and maintenance of an imperial system demanded that the new leadership offer something to their followers in return for their support—that is, the creation of economic and social incentives for warriors, administrators, merchants, and commoners. Without offering such culturally defined rewards to interest groups and individuals, it would have been difficult for the Mexica and Inca elites to sustain their expansionistic policies.

As we have argued, the most critical measures enacted by the new leaders were religious reforms. Economic and political changes merely enabled the Mexica and Inca to compete with their neighbors on a roughly equal footing. Neither society rose to mastery until the sanctions and drives generated by a reformed state religion gave it a decisive advantage. It was this process of ideological adaptation that gave the Mexica and Inca states the competitive superiority that transformed them into empires.

The ideological adaptations of the Mexica and Inca peoples were of two main types: manipulations of the upper pantheons and reworkings of ancient, basic institutions. Within these broad categories were several specific changes in ritual and belief. Some may have been unconscious or unintentional, but it is clear that others were deliberately instituted to meet the goals of leadership groups.

Manipulations of the upper pantheons began in preimperial times with the crystallization of patron gods, the Mexica's Huitzilopochtli and the Inca's Inti, out of more fluid deities with many aspects. The Mexica and Inca had inherited long-standing traditions of manifold deities based on the movements and transformations of astronomical phenomena. Eventually both peoples emphasized the solar associations of the ancient divine complexes and isolated one solar aspect as a national symbol and dynastic ancestor.

Although the actual mechanics of these parallel pantheon shifts were somewhat different, in both cases as Huitzilopochtli and Inti became imperial patrons there was also a general "solarization" of religion. This emphasis on the solar aspects of the divine complexes is hardly surprising. Even in preimperial times, when the Mexica and Inca were small-scale societies, the sun was important to them as the source of agricultural life and growth. The transition to empire brought demands for the increased production of a mobile, storable food surplus—especially maize—to support the state and its projects. Agricultural intensification centered upon maize as the all-important staple crop. Hence, the great elaboration of ritual related to corn and the sun was economically logical.

However, religious reforms did not stop with the creation of solar patron deities. The most crucial ideological elements in the transition to empire were reworkings of fundamental religious institutions: human sacrifice in Mesoamerica and ancestor worship in Peru. We have seen how the Mexica molded Huitzilopochtli, the sun, and their own military ambitions into a vision of constant struggle among the forces of the universe, making the daily struggle of the sun not only parallel to, but actually dependent upon, Mexica militarism and human sacrifices. Likewise, the Inca aggrandized the fundamental Andean tradition of ancestor worship through their cult of the royal dead. By keeping most imperial property in the hands of the dead and their retainers, this cult forced each new Inca ruler to generate his own support system through new conquests.

Taken together, these pantheon shifts and manipulations of basic institutions had multiple consequences. First, they justified imperial expansion in ideological terms. The supernatural forces upon whom society's welfare—in fact, mankind's very existence—depended had to be supported in proper fashion. The Mexica's gods demanded daily rations of human blood, and the Inca's living dead demanded perpetual income. Only continual conquest could supply these paramount necessities.

Yet the need for expansion was not simply ideological. In each case the reformed state religion had economic and political side effects that perpetuated militarism. The Aztec economy and political patronage networks became increasingly dependent on the tribute that could be provided only by military victories, and each succeeding Inca emperor, through his conquests, had to provide for a patronage structure that would be comparable or superior to that of preceding rulers. Both empires needed a constant flow of goods and services through their patronage networks, so that the view of the state and its rulers as open and generous could be maintained. Furthermore, both societies were motivated by economic, social, and ideological rewards obtained through patronage. On the individual level, ferocity in combat earned a warrior not only a highly honored position in afterlife, but upward mobility in the form of sumptuary perquisites, greater access to property or labor, additional wives, and more prestigious roles in public and cult ceremonies. Finally, both state religions provided ample justifications for imperialism, giving the Mexica and the Inca, at least in their own eyes, the right to conquer.

All told, the ideological reforms carried out by the Mexica and Inca military leaders who came to power through the Tepanec and Chanca crises were nothing short of revolutionary. The new state religions achieved something that all previous cultural changes had not accomplished: the integration of economic, social, political, and religious factors into unified cults of imperial expansion. Manipulations of ritual and belief were undertaken to serve the ambitions of the new ruling cadres and were maintained through incentives to interest groups and individuals. Initially, the new religious orders also brought great benefits to the Mexica and Inca peoples as a whole. In that sense the transformations of traditional ideologies were masterful adaptive responses to the external pressures and selective forces described above.

Conclusion

Our evaluation of causality in Mexica and Inca expansionism suggests that several factors are critical to an understanding of cultural evolution in general. As is widely acknowledged, both multicausality and an understanding of ecological pressures and adaptations are fundamental elements of cultural change. However, a multicausal approach must be more than a cataloguing of the factors involved. Instead, it is necessary to plot the interplay of factors and to identify the particular social institutions affected. Avoiding the fallacy of the organic metaphor, analyses of cultural adaptations should specify the actual decision-making groups within the society and how the adaptive changes were perceived to be in their own interests. Thus, a social and political analysis of decision-making strategies within the culture can explain the specific nature of the responses to external cultural and ecological pressures. Indeed, it is only through such specific reconstructions of cultural change that archaeological and historical data can be used to test the ecological interpretations involved.

Another conclusion of our analysis of pre-Columbian imperialism concerns the controversial question of the role of ideology in cultural evolution. As we have seen with the Aztec and Inca, the interaction among events, institutions, and causal factors blurs the very distinctions made among categories of cultural phenomena (economic, political, ideological, and so on). Nonetheless, conscious manipulations of state religion, ritual, and cosmology can safely be termed "ideological" factors. These ideological adaptations initiated the rapid feedback cycles that transformed the Aztec and Inca states into empires. Such ideological factors—through their effects on political and economic institutions—were highly adaptive to the competitive cultural and ecological environment of the time. Thus, ideology played a critical role in the adaptive transformation of Mexica and Inca societies.

It appears then that it is useless to continue the long-standing debate between "idealists" and "materialists" on the nature of cultural evolution. Gordon Willey has pointed out (1976:205) that the interplay of all major cultural subsystems, regardless of how they are labeled, is the key to understanding the dynamics of cultural change. We have tried to give at least a preliminary analysis of this interplay of factors in the Mexica and Inca civilizations. We hope that others will respond to Willey's challenge to discover "how ideas were interrelated with other parts of culture and how they helped direct the trajectories of cultural and civilization growth" (1976:205).

Notes

1. The principal sources for the preimperial Mexica are Sahagún (bk. 10, ch. 29, 1950–65, pt. 11:189–97), Durán (chs. 2–7, 1964:13–46), Tovar (1944:24–51), *Relación de la Genealogía y Linaje* (1941:245–52), Tezozomoc (1975:11–100), *Historia de los Mexicanos por sus Pinturas* (chs. 9–20, 1941:218–28), *Origen de los Mexicanos* (1941:264–70), Ixtlilxochitl (1975, vol. 1:326–50, 433–39, 533–38; vol. 2:28–54), *Anales de Tlatelolco* (1948:31–54). See also Torquemada (bk. 2, chs. 1–24, 1975:113–66) and later historians.

2. E.g., Sahagún (bk. 10, ch. 29, 1950–65, pt. 11:196) and Durán (ch. 4, 1964:23).

3. For debate on the nature of the *calpulli,* see especially Morgan (1877), Bandelier (1878, 1880), Moreno (1931), Monzon (1949), Kirchhoff (1959), Caso (1963), Katz (1966), Carrasco (1967, 1971), Sanders and Price (1968:154–56), and Zantwijk (1975).

4. See note 1. Also see Leon-Portilla (1960), Katz (1966), Carrasco (1971, 1976), Gibson (1971), Davies (1972), Bray (1978), and Rounds (1979).

5. This interpretation of Huitzilopochtli—his origins, nature, and role in imperial myth—follows aspects of recent interpretations by Davies (1973:35–38), Lopez Austin (1973:*passim),* Brotherston (1974), Demarest (1976), Uchmany (1978, 1979), Carrasco (1979), and Zantwijk (1979).

6. The principal sources on the transformational crisis, the death of Chimalpopoca, and the subsequent establishment of the imperial order must be interpreted with considerable care (and skepticism) because of the many contradictions among different versions often attributable to regional biases. The "official" Mexica state version is given in accounts based on the lost *Cronica X,* Duran (1964: chs. 8–11), Tezozomoc

(1975:100–109), Tovar (1944:51–73). Other versions, often contradicting the state account of major events—such as the death of Chimalpopoca—include *Anales Mexicanos* (1903:49–55), Ixtlilxochitl (1975, vol. 1:350–81, 433–45, 538–44; vol. 2:55–105), *Anales de Tlatelolco* (1948:55), *Historia de los Mexicanos por sus Pinturas* (ch. 20, 1941:229–30), *Origen de los Mexicanos* (1941:271–73), *Anales de Cuauhtitlan* (1975:37–49), *Relación de la Genealogía y Linaje* (1941:252–53). Again, Torquemada (bk. 2, chs. 24–37, 1975:166–200) provides an excellent compilation based on earlier sources, though he apparently relies heavily on the Mexica version of events.

7. Compare, for example, the contradictory explanations of Chimalpopoca's death given by Durán (ch. 8, 1964:49), *Anales Mexicanos* (1903:50), Chimalpahin *(Séptima Relación,* 1965:191), and Torquemada (bk. 2, ch. 20, 1975:190).

8. Convincing arguments that the events of 1426–28 represent a takeover by militaristic factions within the Mexica polity have been given by Leon-Portilla (1958, 1959:162–66, 1960), Padden (1967:2–13, 50–66), Davies (1973:152–61), Demarest (1976), Bray (1978), and Rounds (1979).

9. On this sumptuary and ritual reinforcement of social stratification see especially Anawalt (1976, 1977, 1980) and Broda (1976, 1978).

10. The role of tribute as one of the fundamental bases of Mexica economics has been demonstrated by Berdan (1975: chs. 3, 6, 1976, 1977, 1978). See also Castillo (1972) and Carrasco (1978:43–49).

11. The eclipsing of the *calpullin* by the new land distribution is discussed further by Adams (1966: ch. 3), Katz (1966), Carrasco (1976, 1978), Bray (1978), and Rounds (1979).

12. The imperial state religion, nuclear sacrificial cult, and other aspects of Mexica cosmology are well known from a number of primary sources, including both pictorial manuscripts and written chronicles. Our own analyses (Conrad and Demarest, n.d.: ch. 2; Demarest 1976), rely heavily on Sahagún (1950–65, especially bks. 1, 2, and 3), Durán (1971), Motolinia (especially pt. 1, chs. 14–35, 1971), *Leyenda de los Soles* (1975), *Histoyre du Mechique* (1961), *Historia de los Mexicanos por sus Pinturas* (chs. 1–8, 1941), as well as numerous comments in the historical sources (see notes 1 and 2).

13. Our specific interpretations of the solar struggle myth, the nuclear cult, and the development of the imperial Huitzilopochtli follow aspects of the interpretations of Caso (e.g., 1927, 1945, 1953, 1966), Bernal (1957), Leon-Portilla (1958, 1959, 1960), Soustelle (1961), Zantwijk (1963, 1966, 1975, 1979), Lopez Austin (1973), Brotherston (1974), Townsend (1979), and Uchmany (1979).

14. See Seler (1960–1961, vol. 2:471), Zantwijk (1963, 1975), and Davies (1973: 35–38).

15. On the overlapping between Huitzilopochtli, Tezcatlipoca, and Tonatiuh in symbols, myths, and cosmology of sacrifice, see especially Caso (1945, 1953), Nicholson (1971:424–26), Brotherston (1974), Townsend (1979), and Uchmany (1979: 55–59). Also compare with the evolution of the Inca pantheon (Demarest 1981).

16. Durán (1964:69).

17. All of the primary sources on early (preimperial) Inca history are transcriptions of oral tradition and mix fact with myth, legend, propaganda, personal biases, misunderstandings, and so on. Our interpretations are based on the generally conser-

vative accounts of sixteenth-century chroniclers, most notably Sarmiento (1942) and Cieza de León (bk. 2, 1943, 1959). For modern analyses, see Rowe (1946), Brundage (1963), Katz (1972) and Schaedel (1978). Rowe (1944) discusses archaeological data from preimperial Inca sites; the evidence supports the picture of a small-scale, rustic society.

18. For a good capsule summary of the *ayllu,* see the seventeenth-century compilation by Cobo (bk. 12, chs. 25–26, 1890–95:III, 235–39; 1979:200–205); see also Garcilaso (bk. 4, ch. 8, 1945:I, 195; 1966:206). Murra (1980) provides a detailed analysis of Inca socioeconomic organization and an exhaustive list of references.

19. For the nature and historical development of the celestial high god, see Demarest (1981), as well as Conrad and Demarest (n.d.).

20. Some standard manifestations of ancestor worship are described in Polo de Ondegardo (1916a:7–10; 1916b:116–19), Pizarro (1844:264; 1921:251–52), Guaman Poma de Ayala (1936:256–57), Arriaga (chs. 2, 3; 1920:25, 32; 1968:27, 33), Hernández Príncipe (1923), and Cobo (bk. 13, ch. 10; bk. 14, ch. 19; 1890–95:III, 338–43; IV, 236–38). For modern analyses, see Bandelier (1904) and Zuidema (1973).

21. On early leadership by *sinchis,* see Sarmiento (ch. 8, 1942:56–57) and an anonymous sixteenth-century report (Anonymous 1920:106–7). Brundage (1963:13, 27, 74–75, 119–22) provides a modern analysis.

22. The Incas' increasing involvement in regional power struggles and the growth of hereditary leadership are described in Sarmiento de Gamboa (chs. 24–25; 1942: 91–96) and Cieza de León (bk. 2, chs. 34, 37, 41–43; 1943:184–85, 192–93, 205–15; 1959:201, 207, 215–21).

23. The Chanca crisis and the rise of Pachakuti's military faction are described in most of the standard sources, but with considerable variation in detail. For accounts that portray Pachakuti and his cohorts favorably, see Betanzos (chs. 6–9, 17; 1924: 105–29, 191–97) and Cieza de León (bk. 2, ch. 43–46; 1943:214–25; 1959:220–29). Anti-Pachakuti versions were recorded by Sarmiento de Gamboa (chs. 24–29, 32–33; 1942:93–105, 110–12) and Cabello Valboa (bk. III, ch. 14; 1951:296–303). We should also mention the generally discredited version of Garcilaso de la Vega (bk. 4, chs. 21–24; bk. 5, chs. 17–20; 1945: I, 217–24, 258–68; 1966:230–37, 276–87), in which the entire episode is moved back one generation and Viracocha Inca becomes the savior of Cuzco. Cobo's (bk. 12, ch. 10; 1890–95: III, 147–51; 1979:126–29) account was taken from Garcilaso.

24. Viracocha Inca's attempt to manipulate the internal politics of the Titicaca Basin is discussed by Cieza de León (bk. II, chs. 34, 37, 41–43; 1943:184–85, 192–93, 205–15; 1959:201, 207, 215–21) and Sarmiento de Gamboa (ch. 24; 1942:91–92).

25. For a detailed analysis of imperial Inca economic organization and an extensive list of primary sources, see Murra (1980).

26. Here we can only mention the social and political reforms undertaken by the new Inca leadership. Again, for detailed modern analyses, complete with extensive lists of references, see Rowe (1946), Murra (1958, 1980), Katz (1972:263–309), and Schaedel (1978).

27. Our discussion of split inheritance—the veneration of deceased Inca rulers, their retention of all their property after death, and the role of the *panaqas*—is based on Sancho (ch. 17; 1917:159; 1962:92), Cieza de León (bk. 2, ch. 11, 61; 1943:77–78,

284; 1959:188–89, 247), Castro and Ortega Morejón (1936:237–39), Santillán (no. 29; 1879:34), Polo de Ondegardo (1916b:123–25; 1917:134–36), Pizarro (1844: 238–40, 264; 1921:202–5, 251–52), Acosta (bk. 5, ch. 6; bk. 6, ch. 20; 1894: II, 24, 201–2), and Cobo (bk. 12, chs. 4, 9, 36; bk. 13, ch. 10; 1890–95: III, 131–32, 146–47, 290, 339–41; 1979: I, 125, 248).

28. Evidence for the sequential construction of palaces in Cuzco comes mostly from written sources; see note 27 and Rowe (1967). For an earlier archaeological manifestation of this pattern in Chan Chan, the capital of the northern coastal Chimu empire, see Conrad (1980, 1981, 1982).

29. On the origins of split inheritance through manipulation of traditional institutions during the reign of Pachakuti, see Betanzos (chs. 11–13, 16, 17; 1924:139–62, 178–86, 195–97) and Sarmiento de Gamboa (chs. 19, 30–34, 37; 1942:83, 106–12, 141).

30. Rowe (1967) argues that the first four "kings" in the traditional Inca dynastic list were mythical personages. For an even more skeptical view, see Zuidema (1962, 1964), who contends that the entire list has more to do with Inca cosmology and social structure than with actual history.

31. Again, for a detailed analysis, see Murra (1980).

32. On the royal estates and their retention by dead rulers, see note 27. On the ownership of entire highland valleys by Inca rulers, see Sarmiento de Gamboa (ch. 32; 1942:110) and Rostworowski de Diez Canseco (1962:136). On the distribution of a ruler's estates throughout all the provinces and their cultivation through labor taxation during the early stages of the empire's growth, see Castro and Ortega Morejón (1936:237–39), Ortiz de Zúñiga (1967:25–26), and Rowe (1967:61). This system was subsequently modified, and the cultivation of the royal estates was eventually assigned to full-time retainers; see Cieza de León (bk. 2, ch. 18; 1943:118; 1959: 164–65), Morúa (bk. 3, ch. 12; 1922–25: 4, 146), and Rostworowski de Diez Canseco (1962, 1966).

PART SIX

Bibliography of Gordon R. Willey

Bibliography of Gordon R. Willey

1937 "Notes on Central Georgia Dendrochronology," *Tree Ring Bulletin* 4, no. 2:6–8.
1938 "Time Studies: Pottery and Trees in Georgia," *Proceedings of the Society for Georgia Archaeology* 1, no. 2:15–22.
1939 "Ceramic Stratigraphy in a Georgia Village Site," *American Antiquity* 5, no. 2:140–47.
1939 "Chipped Stone Typology of Marksville, Troyville, and Coles Creek," *Newsletter, Southeastern Archaeological Conference* 2, no. 1:21–22.
1939 "Troyville and Coles Creek Pottery Types" (with James A. Ford), *Newsletter, Southeastern Archaeological Conference* 1, nos. 3–4.
1940 Review of *Prehistory in Haiti: A Study in Method*, by Irving Rouse, in *American Anthropologist* 42, no. 4:673–75.
1940 *Crooks Mound, A Marksville Period Site in La Salle Parish, Louisiana* (with James A. Ford), Louisiana Department of Conservation, Anthropological Study, no. 3 (Baton Rouge).
1941 Review of *The Wright Mounds* by W. S. Webb and associates, in *American Anthropologist* 43, no. 4:651–53.
1941 "An Interpretation of the Prehistory of the Eastern United States" (with James A. Ford), *American Anthropologist* 43, no. 3:325–63.
1942 "A Chronological Outline for the Northwest Florida Coast" (with R. B. Woodbury), *American Antiquity* 7, no. 3:232–54.
1943 *Excavations in the Chancay Valley, Peru,* Columbia University Studies in Archaeology and Ethnology, vol. 1, no. 3 (New York: Columbia University Press).
1943 *A Supplement to the Pottery Sequence at Ancon, Peru,* Columbia University

Studies in Archaeology and Ethnology, vol. 1, no. 4 (New York: Columbia University Press).

1943 Review of *Chavin Stone Carving* by W. C. Bennett, in *American Anthropologist* 45, no. 1:136–37.

1943 *Archaeological Notes on the Central Coast of Peru* (with W. D. Strong), Columbia University Studies in Archaeology and Ethnology, vol. 1, no. 1 (New York: Columbia University Press).

1944 Abstract of *Origen y Desarrollo de los Civilizaciones Andinas* by J. C. Tello, in *Acta Americana* 1, no. 3:405–13.

1944 Review of *Survey and Excavations in Southern Ecuador,* by D. Collier and J. Murra, in *American Anthropologist* 46, no. 1:129–31.

1944 "Negative Painted Pottery from Crystal River, Florida" (with Philip Phillips), *American Antiquity* 10, no. 2:173–85.

1945 "The Weeden Island Culture: A Preliminary Definition," *American Antiquity* 10, no. 3:225–54.

1945 "Horizon Styles and Pottery Traditions in Peruvian Archaeology," *American Antiquity* 11, no. 1:49–56.

1945 Review of *Archaeological Regions of Columbia, A Ceramic Survey and Excavations in the Vicinity of Cali, Colombia* by W. C. Bennett and J. A. Ford, in *American Antiquity* 10, no. 4:407–10.

1945 Review of *The Navajo Door: An Introduction to Navajo Life* by A. H. and D. C. Leighton, in *Social Forces* 23, no. 4:478–79.

1945 Review of *Peguche: A Study of Andean Indians* by E. C. Parsons, in *The Inter-American* 4, no. 12:32–33.

1946 "The Archaeology of the Greater Pampa," in *Handbook of South American Indians,* ed. J. H. Steward, vol. 1, pp. 25–46, Bureau of American Ethnology, Bulletin 143 (Washington, D.C.: Smithsonian Institution).

1946 "The Culture of La Candelaria," in *Handbook of South American Indians,* ed. J. H. Steward, vol. 2, pp. 661–72, Bureau of American Ethnology, Bulletin 143 (Washington, D.C.: Smithsonian Institution).

1946 "The Viru Valley Program in Northern Peru," *Acta Americana* 4, no. 4: 224–38.

1946 "Projecto de Investigaciones Andinas para El Valle del Viru," *Revista del Museo Nacional* (Lima), 15:47–71.

1946 "The Chiclin Conference for Peruvian Archaeology, 1946," *American Antiquity* 12:132–34.

1946 Review of *Plant Geography and Culture History in the American Southwest* by G. F. Carter, in *Geographical Review* 36, no. 1:132–34.

1946 Review of *Tihuanaca, the Cradle of American Man* by A. Posnansky, in *The Inter-American* 5, no. 1:34–35.

1946 Review of *Plant Geography and Culture History in the American Southwest* (Carter's Thesis in the Light of Archaeology: The Southeast) by G. F. Carter, in *American Antiquity* 11, no. 4:265–66.

1946 Review of *The North Highlands of Peru: Excavations in the Callejon de Huaylas and at Chavin de Huantar* by W. C. Bennett, in *American Anthropologist* 48:105–7.

1946 "The Leake Mounds, Barton County, Georgia" (with Pat Wofford, Jr.), *American Antiquity* 12:126–27.
1947 "A Middle Period Cemetery in the Viru Valley, Northern Peru," in *Journal of the Washington Academy of Science* 37, no. 2:41–47.
1947 "Ecuadorean Figurines and the Ceramic Mold in the New World," *American Antiquity* 13:85–86.
1947 "A Synopsis of the Archaeology," in *Indian Skeletal Material from the Central Coast of Peru* by M. T. Newman, Papers of the Peabody Museum of Archaeology and Ethnology, vol. 27, no. 4 (Cambridge, Mass.: Harvard University).
1947 Review of *Indians Before Columbus* by P. Martin, D. Collier, and G. I. Quimby, in *Science*, April 25:1449–50.
1948 "Culture Sequence in the Manatee Region of West Florida," *American Antiquity* 13, no. 3:209–18.
1948 "Anthropology, New World," *Americana Annual for 1948*.
1948 "The Cultural Context of the Crystal River Negative Painted Style," *American Antiquity* 13, no. 4:325–28.
1948 "A Functional Analysis of 'Horizon Styles' in Peruvian Archaeology," in *Reappraisal of Peruvian Archaeology*, ed. W. C. Bennett, pp. 8–15 (Menasha, Wis.: Society for American Archaeology).
1948 "A Proto-type for the Southern Cult," *American Antiquity* 13, no. 4:328–30.
1948 *Lowland Argentine Archaeology* (with G. D. Howard), Yale University Publications in Anthropology, no. 39 (New Haven).
1949 "Ceramics," in *Handbook of South American Indians*, ed. J. H. Steward, vol. 5, pp. 139–204, Bureau of American Ethnology, Bulletin 143 (Washington, D.C.: Smithsonian Institution).
1949 *Excavations in Southeast Florida*, Yale University Publications in Anthropology, no. 42 (New Haven).
1949 *Archaeology of the Florida Gulf Coast*, Smithsonian Miscellaneous Collection, vol. 113 (Washington, D.C.: Smithsonian Institution).
1949 "The Southeastern United States and South America: A Comparative Statement," in *The Florida Indian and His Neighbors*, pp. 101–16 (Winter Park, Fla.: Rollins College).
1949 "The Florida Indian and His Neighbors: A Summary," in *The Florida Indian and His Neighbors*, pp. 139–68 (Winter Park, Fla.: Rollins College).
1949 "Anthropology, New World," *Americana Annual for 1949*.
1949 "Inter-areal Relationships of New World Culture," *Philadelphia Anthropological Society Bulletin* 3, no. 2:1–2.
1949 Review of *Men Out of Asia* by H. S. Gladwin (with M. T. Newman), in *American Anthropologist* 51, no. 1:160–64.
1949 Review of *Highland Communities of Central Peru* by H. Tschopik, Jr., in *Boletín Bibliográfico de Antropología Americana* 11:277–78.
1949 Review of *Most of the World, Peoples of Africa, Latin America, and the East Today*, ed. R. Linton, in *Scientific Monthly* 69:204–5.
1949 Review of *Archaic Sites in McLean County, Kentucky* by W. S. Webb and W. G. Haag, in *American Antiquity* 15:68–69.

1949 Review of *The Fisher Site, Fayette County, Kentucky* by W. S. Webb and W. G. Haag, in *American Antiquity* 15:69–70.
1949 Review of *The Flint River Site, Ma°48* by W. S. Webb and D. L. DeJarrette, in *American Antiquity* 15:71.
1949 Review of *The Whitesburg Bridge Site, Ma^{v}10* by W. S. Webb and D. L. DeJarrette, in *American Antiquity* 15:71.
1949 "A Veraguas Grave" (with Karl P. Curtis), *Journal of the Washington Academy of Sciences* 39, no. 1.
1949 *Surface Survey of the Viru Valley, Peru* (with J. A. Ford), Anthropological Papers of the American Museum of Natural History, vol. 43, pt. 1 (New York).
1950 "Separate Migrations as an Explanation of Physical Variability Among American Indians," *Journal of the Washington Academy of Science* 40, no. 3:71–75.
1950 "Crystal River, Florida: A 1949 Visit," *The Florida Anthropologist* 2, nos. 3 and 4:41–45.
1950 "Growth Trends in New World Cultures," in *For the Dean: Essays in Honor of Byron Cummings*, pp. 223–48 (Santa Fe, N.M.).
1950 Review of *Andean Culture History* by W. C. Bennett and J. B. Bird, in *American Anthropologist* 52, no. 1:89–91.
1950 "Reconnaissance Notes on the Site of Huari, near Ayacucho, Peru" (with J. H. Rowe and D. Collier), in *American Antiquity* 16, no. 2:120–37.
1951 "Peruvian Horizon Styles," *American Antiquity* 16, no. 4:354.
1951 "South American Archaic Relations: Additional Comment," *American Antiquity* 16, no. 4:354–55.
1951 "American Archaeology," *Science* 114, no. 2959:3.
1951 "The Chavin Problem: A Review and Critique," *Southwestern Journal of Anthropology* 7, no. 2:103–44.
1951 "Peruvian Settlement and Socio-Economic Patterns," *Twenty-ninth International Congress of Americanists*, ed. Sol Tax, vol. 1, pp. 195–200 (Chicago: University of Chicago Press).
1951 "A Preliminary Report on the Monagrillo Culture of Panama," *Twenty-ninth International Congress of Americanists*, ed. So. Tax, vol. 1, pp. 173–80 (Chicago: University of Chicago Press).
1951 Review of *Maranga: Contribucion al Conocimiento de Los Aborigines del Valle del Rimac, Peru* by J. Jijon y Caamano, in *American Anthropologist* 53, no. 1:112–14.
1951 Review of *The Safety Harbor Site* by J. W. Griffin and R. Bullen, in *American Antiquity* 17, no. 1:64–65.
1951 Review of *Negative Painted Pottery of the Angel Mound Site and Its Distribution in the New World* by Hilda Curry, in *Boletin Bibliografico de Antropologia Americana* 14, pt. 2:68–71.
1952 "Some Aspects of American Culture History: A Review," *Antiquity*, no. 104:201–5.
1952 Review of *A Survey of Indian River Archaeology, Florida* by I. Rouse, and *Chronology at South Indian Field, Florida* by V. Masius, in *American Antiquity* 18:75–77.

1952 Review of *Middle American Research Records,* vol. 1, ed. R. Wauchope, (New Orleans: Tulane University), in *American Anthropologist* 54, no. 3:422–23.
1952 "Archaeology in Western Panama," (with C. R. McGimsey), *Archaeology* 5, no. 3:173–81.
1952 "The Kasita Site" (with W. H. Sears), *Southern Indian Studies* 4:3–18.
1953 "Archaeological Theories and Interpretation: New World," in *Anthropology Today,* ed. A. L. Kroeber et al., pp. 361–85 (Chicago: University of Chicago Press).
1953 *Prehistoric Settlement Patterns in the Viru Valley, Peru,* Bureau of American Ethnology, Bulletin 155 (Washington, D.C.: Smithsonian Institution).
1953 "A Survey of South American Archaeology," *Journal Royal Anthropological Institute* 83, pt. 1:58–64.
1953 "A Pattern of Diffusion-Acculturation," *Southwestern Journal of Anthropology* 9, no. 4:369–84.
1953 Review of *Excavations at Nebaj* by A. L. Smith and A. V. Kidder, in *American Anthropologist* 55:258–60.
1953 Review of *Archaeology of the Santa Elena Peninsula in Southwest Ecuador* by G. H. S. Bushnell, in *Antiquity* 105:61–63.
1953 Review of *Piedras Negras Archaeology: Part V* by L. Satterthwaite, in *American Anthropologist* 55, no. 1:129.
1953 Review of *The Civilizations of Ancient America, Selected Papers, Twenty-ninth International Congress of Americanists,* vol. 1, ed. Sol Tax, in *Antiquity* 107:183–84.
1953 Review of *Hopewellian Communities in Illinois,* ed. T. Deuel, in *Antiquity* 107:179–80.
1953 "Method and Theory in American Archaeology: An Operational Basis for Culture-Historical Integration" (with Philip Phillips), *American Anthropologist* 55, no. 5:615–33.
1954 "Tradition Trend in Ceramic Development," *American Antiquity* 20:9–14.
1954 "Comment on Southwestern Cultural Interrelationships and the Question of Area Co-Tradition," *American Anthropologist* 56, no. 4, pt. 1:589–90.
1954 "Burial Patterns in the Burns and Fuller Mounds, Cape Canaveral, Florida," *Florida Anthropologist* 7, no. 3:79–90.
1954 *Alfred Marston Tozzer, (1877–1954),* in *Teocintli,* No. 58.
1954 Review of *Prehistory in Porto Rico* by Irving Rouse, in *American Anthropologist* 56, no. 1:138–41.
1954 Review of *Paracas Cavernas and Chavin* by A. L. Kroeber, in *American Antiquity* 20:184–85.
1954 *Early Ancon and Early Supe Culture: Chavin Horizon Sites of the Central Peruvian Coast* (with J. M. Corbett), Columbia University Studies in Archaeology and Ethnology, vol. 3 (New York: Columbia University Press).
1954 *The Monagrillo Culture of Panama* (with C. R. McGimsey), Papers of the Peabody Museum of Archaeology and Ethnology, vol. 49, no. 2 (Cambridge, Mass.: Harvard University).
1954 "Cultural Stratigraphy in Panama: A Preliminary Report on the Giron Site" (with T. L. Stoddard), *American Antiquity* 19, no. 4:332–42.

1955 "Archaeology of the New World (and various topical sections)," *Colliers Encyclopedia*, pp. 123–34 (New York).
1955 "The Interrelated Rise of Middle and South American Civilizations," in *New Interpretations of Aboriginal American Culture History, 75th Anniversary Volume* pp. 28–45 (Washington, D.C.: Anthropological Society of Washington).
1955 "The Maya Community of Prehistoric Times," *Archaeology* 8, no. 1:18–25.
1955 "The Prehistoric Civilizations of Nuclear America," *American Anthropologist* 57, no. 3:571–93.
1955 Review of *Piedras Negras Archaeology: Part VI* by L. Satterthwaite, in *American Anthropologist* 57, no. 3:646.
1955 Review of *Excavations at Wari, Ayacucho, Peru* by W. C. Bennett, in *American Journal of Archaeology* 59:105–6.
1955 Review of *On the Excavation of a Shell Mound at Palo Seco, Trinidad, B.W.I.* by J. A. Bullbrook, in *Antiquity*, no. 113:50–51.
1955 Review of *Excavations at Wari, Ayacucho* by W. C. Bennett, in *Antiquity*, no. 113:51–52.
1955 "The Archaic Tradition in Puerto Rico" (with R. Alegría and H. B. Nicholson), *American Antiquity*, 21:113–21.
1955 "Method and Theory in American Archaeology II: Historical-Developmental Interpretation" (with Philip Phillips), *American Anthropologist* 57:723–819.
1956 "Archaeology of South America," *Encyclopedia Britannica*, pp. 259T–259W (Chicago).
1956 Introduction to *Prehistoric Settlement Patterns in the New World*, ed. G. R. Willey, vol. 23, pp. 1–2 (New York: Viking Fund Publications in Anthropology).
1956 "Problems Concerning Prehistoric Settlement Patterns in the Maya Lowlands," *Prehistoric Settlement Patterns in the New World*, ed. G. R. Willey, vol. 23, pp. 107–14 (New York: Viking Fund Publications in Anthropology).
1956 "Archaeology: The Snows of Yesteryear," in *The Frontiers of Knowledge*, ed. Lynn White, Jr., pp. 48–67 (New York: Harpers).
1956 "The Structure of Ancient Maya Society," *American Anthropologist* 58, no. 5:777–82.
1956 Review of *Tlatilco and the Pre-Classic Cultures of the New World* by Muriel Noe Porter, in *American Antiquity* 22, no. 1:88–89.
1956 "The Melhado Site, A House Mound Group in British Honduras" (with W. R. Bullard, Jr.), *American Antiquity* 22, no. 1:29–44.
1956 *Prehistoric Settlement Patterns in the New World*, ed., no. 23 (New York: Viking Fund Publications in Anthropology).
1956 "An Archaeological Classification of Culture Contact Situations" (ed. with D. W. Lathrap), in *Seminars in Archaeology: 1955*, ed. R. Wauchope, Memoirs of the Society for American Archaeology, no. 11 (Menasha, Wis.).
1957 "Archaeology, New World," in *Encyclopedia Americana*, pp. 162–64d (Danbury, Conn.: Grolier).
1957 Publisher's Preface to *Chichen Itza and Its Cenote of Sacrifice* by A. M. Tozzer, Memoir of the Peabody Museum of Archaeology and Ethnology, vol. 11, p. v (Cambridge, Mass.: Harvard University).

1957 *Selected Papers of the Harvard Middle American Archaeological Seminar, 1955–56: An Introduction,* Papers of the Kroeber Anthropological Society, vol. 17, pp. 1–6 (Berkeley, Calif.).

1957 Review of *Poverty Point, a Late Archaic Site in Louisiana,* by J. A. Ford and C. H. Webb, in *American Antiquity* 23, no. 2:198–99.

1957 Review of *Highway of the Sun* by Victor W. von Hagen, in *ISIS* 48, pt. 1:77–79.

1957 Review of *Toward Definition of the Nazca Style* by A. L. Kroeber, in *American Anthropologist* 59, no. 6:1131–32.

1957 *The Ormond Beach Site, East Florida* (with J. D. Jennings and M. T. Newman), Bureau of American Ethnology, Anthropological Papers, Bulletin 164, no. 49, pp. 1–28 (Washington, D.C.: Smithsonian Institution).

1957 "Comment on Method and Theory in American Archaeology" (with Philip Phillips), *American Antiquity* 23, no. 2:185.

1958 "Introductory Note" in *Middle American Anthropology,* ed. G. R. Willey; E. Z. Vogt; and A. Palerm, Social Science Monograph 5, Social Science Section, Pan American Union, pp. vii–viii (Washington, D.C.).

1958 "Estimated Correlations and Dating of South and Central American Culture Sequences," *American Antiquity* 23, no. 4:353–78.

1958 "Local Grouping in Melanesia: An Article of Theoretical Importance," *American Antiquity* 23, no. 3:312.

1958 "Archaeological Perspective on Algonkian-Gulf Linguistic Relationships," *Southwestern Journal of Anthropology* 14, no. 3:265–72.

1958 Review of *The Ancient Civilizations of Peru* by J. A. Mason, in *American Antiquity* 24:86–87.

1958 Review of *Ceramic Sequence at Uaxactun, Guatemala,* 2 vols., by R. E. Smith, in *American Journal of Archaeology* 62:256–57.

1958 *Method and Theory in American Archaeology* (with Philip Phillips), (Chicago: University of Chicago Press).

1959 "The Intermediate Area of Nuclear America: Its Prehistoric Relationships to Middle America and Peru," *Actas del 33rd Congreso Internacional de Americanistas,* vol. 1, pp. 184–94 (San Jose, Costa Rica).

1959 Review of *The Incas of Pedro de Cieza de Leon,* trans. Harriet de Onis, ed. V. W. von Hagen, in *Science:* 130, no. 3381:973.

1960 "Historical Patterns and Evolution in Native New World Cultures," in *Evolution After Darwin,* vol. 2, ed. Sol Tax, *The Evolution of Man,* pp. 111–41 (Chicago: University of Chicago Press).

1960 "Archaeological Studies of Nicaragua," *Year Book, American Philosophical Society,* pp. 495–99 (Philadelphia).

1960 "New World Prehistory," *Science* 131, no. 3393:73–83.

1960 Review of *Ancient Landscapes* by John Bradford, in *American Anthropologist* 62, no. 1:176–78.

1960 Review of *Indian Life in the Upper Great Lakes* by George I. Quimby, in *Science* 132: 1243–44.

1960 "Altar de Sacrificios, A Prehistoric Maya Crossroads" (with A. L. Smith; W. R. Bullard, Jr.; and John A. Graham), *Archaeology* 13, no. 2:110–17.

1960 "Informe Preliminar, Altar de Sacrificios, 1959" (with A. L. Smith; W. R.

Bullard, Jr.; and John A. Graham), *IDAEH, Instituto de Antropologia e Historia Nacional de Guatemala* 12, no. 1:5–16.

1960 "The Type-Variety Concept as a Basis for the Analysis of Maya Pottery" (with R. E. Smith and J. C. Gifford), *American Antiquity* 25, no. 3:330–40.

1961 "Developments in the Archaeology of Nuclear America: 1935–1960," *American Antiquity* 27, no. 1:46–55.

1961 Foreword to *The Ethnobotany of Pre-Columbian Peru* by M. A. Towle, Viking Fund Publications in Anthropology, no. 30, p. ix (New York).

1961 "Volume in Pottery and the Selection of Samples," *American Antiquity* 27:230–31.

1961 Review of *Evolution and Culture*, ed. M. D. Sahlins and E. R. Service, *American Antiquity* 26, no. 3:441–43.

1961 Review of *World Prehistory, An Outline* by Grahame Clark, in *American Anthropologist* 63:1377–79.

1961 "Altar de Sacrificios, Guatemala: Preliminary Map and Summary of Excavations" (with W. R. Bullard, Jr.), *Estudios de Cultura Maya* 1:81–85.

1961 "Pottery of the Holmul I Style from Barton Ramie, British Honduras" (with J. C. Gifford), *Essays in Pre-Columbian Art and Archaeology* by S. K. Lothrop et al., pp. 152–70 (Cambridge, Mass.: Harvard University Press).

1961 "Leocadio E. Hopun, 1894–1960" (with A. L. Smith; L. Satterthwaite; and W. R. Bullard, Jr.), *American Antiquity* 27, no. 1:101.

1961 Preface (with D. Z. Stone; J. B. Bird; and G. F. Ekholm) to *Essays in Precolumbian Art and Archaeology* by S. K. Lothrop et al. (Cambridge, Mass.: Harvard University Press).

1962 "Mesoamerica," in *Courses Toward Urban Life: Archaeological Considerations of Some Cultural Alternates,* ed. R. J. Braidwood and G. R. Willey, pp. 84–105, Viking Fund Publications in Anthropology, vol. 32 (New York).

1962 "The Early Great Styles and the Rise of the Precolumbian Civilizations," *American Anthropologist* 64, pt. 1:1–14.

1962 "Archaeology (its place in Anthropology)," *Colliers Encyclopedia*, vol. 2, pp. 303–5 (New York).

1962 "Comment" on *Archaeology and Epistemology* by G. Lowther in *Current Anthropology* 3, no. 5:509.

1962 Review of *Map of the Ruins of Tikal, El Peten, Guatemala* by R. F. Carr and J. E. Hazard, in *American Antiquity* 28, no. 1:117–19.

1962 "Conclusions and Afterthoughts" (with R. J. Braidwood), in *Courses Toward Urban Life: Archaeological Considerations of Some Cultural Alternates,* ed. R. J. Braidwood and G. R. Willey, pp. 330–59, Viking Fund Publications in Anthropology, vol. 32 (New York).

1962 "Introduction" (with R. J. Braidwood), in *Courses Toward Urban Life: Archaeological Considerations of Some Cultural Alternates,* ed. R. J. Braidwood and G. R. Willey, pp. v–viii, Viking Fund Publications in Anthropology, vol. 32 (New York).

1962 "History and Archaeology in the *Handbook of Middle American Indians*" (with G. F. Ekholm), *Proceedings of the Thirty-fourth International Congress of Americanists,* pp. 248–50 (Vienna).

1962 "Preliminary Report on Excavations at Altar de Sacrificios, Guatemala,

1959–60" (with A. L. Smith), *Proceedings of the Thirty-fourth International Congress of Americanists,* pp. 318–25 (Vienna).

1962 "Altar de Sacrificios, Cuarto Informe Preliminar, 1962" (with A. L. Smith and R. E. W. Adams), *IDAEH, Instituto de Antropologia e Historia Nacional de Guatemala* 14, no. 2:5–38.

1962 *Courses Toward Urban Life* (ed. with Robert J. Braidwood), Viking Fund Publications in Anthropology, no. 32 (New York).

1963 Review of *The Art and Architecture of Ancient America: The Mexican, Mayan, and Andean Peoples* by George Kubler, in *American Anthropologist* 65, no. 3, pt. 1:699–703.

1963 "Recent Discoveries at Altar de Sacrificios, Guatemala" (with A. L. Smith), *Archaeology* 16, no. 2:83–90.

1964 "An Archaeological Frame of Reference for Maya Culture History," in *Desarrollo Cultural de Los Mayas,* ed. E. Z. Vogt and Alberto Ruz L., Universidad Nacional Autonoma de Mexico, Seminario de Cultural Maya, pp. 137–75 (Mexico, D.F.).

1964 "Diagram of a Pottery Tradition," *Process and Pattern in Culture, Essays in Honor of J. H. Steward,* ed. R. A. Manners, pp. 156–72 (Chicago: Aldine Press).

1964 "Maya Archaeological Research at Harvard University," *Newsletter, Harvard Foundation for Advanced Study and Research,* Harvard University, March 20 (Cambridge, Mass.).

1964 "A Hypothesis on the Process of Mesoamerican Agricultural Development," *Homenaje a Fernando Marquez-Miranda,* pp. 378–87, Universidades de Madrid y Sevilla.

1964 "Archaeology," in *A Dictionary of the Social Sciences,* ed. J. Gould and W. L. Kolb, pp. 35–36 (Glencoe, Ill.: Unesco; The Free Press of Glencoe).

1964 Review of *Aboriginal Cultural Development in Latin America: An Interpretative Review,* ed. B. J. Meggers and C. Evans, in *American Anthropologist* 66, no. 2:443–46.

1964 Review of *Amerindia, No. 1,* Centro de Estudios Arqueologicos y Antropologicos Americanos, Montevideo, in *American Antiquity* 30, no. 2:228–29.

1964 "Patterns of Mesoamerican Farming Life and Civilization" (with G. F. Ekholm and R. F. Millon), *Handbook of Middle American Indians,* vol. 1, ed. R. Wauchope and R. West, pp. 446–500 (Austin: University of Texas Press).

1964 "Origins of Agriculture in Mesoamerica" (with P. C. Mangelsdorf and R. S. MacNeish), *Handbook of Middle American Indians,* vol. 1, ed. R. Wauchope and R. West, pp. 427–45 (Austin: University of Texas Press).

1965 "Middle America: Prehistory and Archaeology," *Encyclopedia Britannica,* vol. 15, pp. 404–7 (Chicago).

1965 "Chronological Distributions of Some Artifact Types at Altar de Sacrificios, Guatemala," *Estudios de Cultura Maya* 5:33–40.

1965 Foreword to *Life, Land and Water in Ancient Peru* by Paul Kosok (New York: Long Island University Press).

1965 Review of *The Living Races of Man* by Carleton Coon and E. E. Hunt, Jr., in *Gloucester Times,* December 11 (Gloucester, Mass.).

1965 "Prehistoric Settlement Patterns of the Maya Lowlands" (with W. R. Bullard,

Jr.), *Handbook of Middle American Indians,* vol. 2, *Archaeology of Southern Mesoamerica,* pt. 1, ed. R. Wauchope and G. R. Willey, pp. 360–77 (Austin: University of Texas Press).

1965 *Prehistoric Maya Settlements in the Belize Valley, British Honduras* (with W. R. Bullard, Jr.; J. B. Glass; and J. C. Gifford), Peabody Museum Publications in American Archaeology and Ethnology, vol. 54 (Cambridge, Mass.: Harvard University).

1965 *Archaeology of Southern Mesoamerica,* ed., *Handbook of Middle American Indians,* vols. 2–3 (Austin: University of Texas Press).

1966 *An Introduction to American Archaeology, Vol. I: North and Middle America* (Englewood Cliffs, N.J.: Prentice-Hall).

1966 "Prehistory of North and Middle America," in *Fischer Weltgeschichten Vol. I, Vorgeschichte, Nord-und Mittelamerika,* ed. M-H. Alimen and M-J Steve, pp. 302–19 (Frankfurt-am-Main).

1966 "Postlude to Village Agriculture: The Rise of Towns and Temples and the Beginnings of the Great Traditions," *Thirty-sixth International Congress of Americanists, Actas y Memorias,* vol. 1, pp. 267–77 (Sevilla).

1966 "New World Archaeology in 1965," *Proceedings of the American Philosophical Society,* vol. 110, no. 2, pp. 140–45 (Philadelphia).

1966 "Archaeology, New World," *Science Year, The World Book of Science Annual,* pp. 258–60 (Chicago: Field Enterprises Educational Corporation).

1966 "Ceibal, 1965: Segundo Informe Preliminar" (with A. L. Smith), *IDAEH, Instituto de Antropologia e Historia Nacional de Guatemala,* vol. 18, no. 2:71–80.

1966 "The Harvard University Explorations at Seibal, Department of Peten, Guatemala: The 1964 Season" (with A. L. Smith), *Thirty-sixth International Congress of Americanists, Actas y Memorias,* vol. 1, pp. 385–88 (Sevilla).

1966 *Archaeological Frontiers and External Connections,* ed. with G. F. Ekholm, *Handbook of Middle American Indians,* vol. 4 (Austin: University of Texas Press).

1967 "Alfred Vincent Kidder," *Biographical Memoirs,* National Academy of Sciences, vol. 39, pp. 293–322 (New York: Columbia University Press).

1967 "Archaeology, New World," *Science Year, 1967,* pp. 249–51 (Chicago: Field Enterprises).

1967 Review of *The Ceramic Sculptures of Ancient Oaxaca* by F. H. Boos, in *American Anthropologist* 69, nos. 3–4:406.

1967 "Maya Lowland Ceramics: A Report from the 1965 Guatemala City Conference" (with T. P. Culbert and R. E. W. Adams), *American Antiquity* 32, no. 3:289–315.

1967 "The Collapse of Maya Civilization in The Southern Lowlands: A Consideration of History and Process" (with J. A. Sabloff), *Southwestern Journal of Anthropology* 23, no. 4:311–36.

1967 "A Temple at Seibal, Guatemala" (with A. L. Smith), *Archaeology* 20, no. 4:290–98.

1968 "Settlement Archaeology: An Appraisal," in *Settlement Archaeology,* ed. K. C. Chang, pp. 208–26 (Palo Alto, Calif.: National Press Books).

1968 "One Hundred Years of American Archaeology," in *One Hundred Years of Anthropology,* ed. J. O. Brew, pp. 29–53 (Cambridge, Mass.: Harvard University Press).

1968 "Reconsiderations: 1966," Appendix to "The Prehistoric Civilizations of Nuclear America," republished in *Readings in Anthropology,* vol. 1, ed. M. H. Fried, pp. 602–6 (New York: Crowell and Co.).

1968 "Archaeology, New World," *Science Year, 1968,* pp. 266–67 (Chicago: Field Enterprises Educational Corporation).

1968 Review of *Conquistadores Without Swords: Archaeologists in the Americas* by Leo Deuel, in *American Antiquity* 33, no. 4:519–20 (New York: St. Martins Press, 1967).

1968 "Seibal," (with A. L. Smith), *Arqueologia,* no. 22:27–29.

1969 "James Alfred Ford 1911–1968," *American Antiquity* 34, no. 1:62–71.

1969 "The Mesoamericanization of the Honduran-Salvadoran Periphery: A Symposium Commentary," *Thirty-eighth International Congress of Americanists,* vol. 1, pp. 536–42 (Stuttgart-Munich).

1969 Review of "America's First Civilization," by M. D. Coe, in *Antiquity* 43, no. 172:323–24.

1969 Review of *The First Civilizations: The Archaeology of Their Origins* by Glyn Daniel, in *Antiquity* 43, no. 170:161–62.

1969 *The Ruins of Altar de Sacrificios, Department of Peten, Guatemala: An Introduction* (with A. L. Smith), Papers of the Peabody Museum vol. 62, no. 1 (Cambridge, Mass.: Harvard University).

1969 "Seibal, Guatemala in 1968: A Brief Summary of Archaeological Results" (with A. L. Smith), *Thirty-eighth International Congress of Americanists,* vol. 1, pp. 151–58 (Stuttgart-Munich).

1970 "Air Photography in Peru," in *Introductory Readings in Archaeology* by Brian M. Fagan, pp. 39–43a (Boston: Little Brown).

1970 "Type Descriptions of the Ceramics of the Real Xe Complex, Seibal, Peten, Guatemala," *Monographs and Papers in Maya Archaeology,* ed. W. R. Bullard, pp. 313–56, Papers of the Peabody Museum of Archaeology and Ethnology vol. 61 (Cambridge, Mass.: Harvard University).

1970 "Catherwood, Frederick (1799–1854)," *Encyclopedia Americana,* vol. 6, p. 21.

1970 "Philip Phillips: Two Memories, 1937 and 1957," In *Philip Phillips: Lower Mississippi Survey,* ed. Stephen Williams (Cambridge, Mass.: Peabody Museum, Harvard University).

1970 Review of *Everyday Life of the Aztecs,* by Warwick Bray, in *Antiquaries Journal* 50, no. 1.

1971 *An Introduction to American Archaeology, Vol. II: South America* (Englewood Cliffs, N.J.: Prentice-Hall).

1971 Addendum to "An Archaeological Frame of Reference for Maya Culture History," 2d ed., *Desarrollo Cultural de los Mayas,* ed. E. Z. Vogt and A. Ruz, pp. 137–86 (Mexico, D.F.: Centro de Estudios Mayas, Universidad Nacional Autonoma de Mexico).

1971 "A Commentary on: The Emergence of Civilization in the Maya Lowlands,"

Contributions of the University of California Archaeological Research Facility, no. 11, pp. 97–111, Department of Anthropology, University of California (Berkeley).

1971 Review of J. A. Ford's *A Comparison of Formative Cultures in the Americas, Diffusion or the Psychic Unity of Man,* in *American Journal of Archaeology* 75:115–18.

1971 Review of *The Upper Amazon* by D. W. Lathrap, in *Antiquity* 45, no. 178: 146–47.

1971 Review of *In Search of Maya Glyphs, From the Archaeological Journals of Sylvanus G. Morley,* ed. R. H. and F. C. Lister, in *American Anthropologist* 73, no. 6:1410.

1971 Review of *Dumbarton Oaks Conference on Chavin,* ed. E. Benson, in *Science* 74:1117–18.

1971 "The Collapse of Classic Maya Civilization in the Southern Lowlands: A Symposium Summary Statement" (with D. B. Shimkin), *Southwestern Journal of Anthropology* 27, no. 1:1–18.

1971 "Why Did the Pre-Columbian Maya Civilization Collapse?" (with D. B. Shimkin), *Science* 173:656–58.

1972 *The Artifacts of Altar de Sacrificios,* Papers of the Peabody Museum of Archaeology and Ethnology, vol. 64, no. 1 (Cambridge, Mass.: Harvard University).

1972 "Urban Trends of the Lowland Maya and the Mexican Highland Model," *Thirty-eighth International Congress of Americanists,* vol. 4, pp. 11–16 (Stuttgart-Munich).

1972 Review of *Art of the Americas: Ancient and Hispanic* by P. Kelemen, in *Archaeology* 25, no. 1:69.

1972 Review of *The First Americans* by C. W. Ceram, in *Antiquity* vol. 46, no. 182:159–60.

1973 *The Altar de Sacrificios Excavations: General Summary and Conclusions,* Papers of the Peabody Museum of Archaeology and Ethnology, vol. 64, no. 3 (Cambridge, Mass.: Harvard University).

1973 "William Rotch Bullard, Jr., 1926–1972," *American Antiquity* 38, no. 1:80–84.

1973 "Certain Aspects of the Late Classic-to-Postclassic Periods in the Belize Valley," in *The Classic Maya Collapse,* ed. T. P. Culbert, pp. 93–106 (Albuquerque: University of New Mexico Press, School of American Research).

1973 "Mesoamerican Art and Iconography and the Integrity of the Mesoamerican Ideological System," in *The Iconography of Middle American Sculpture,* pp. 153–61 (New York: Metropolitan Museum of Art).

1973 "John Ladd 1923–1971," *American Antiquity* 38, no. 3:315.

1973 "Man in the Americas," in *Civilization, Vol. I, The Emergence of Man in Society,* pp. 79–85, published but given no credit in volume, (Del Mar, Calif.: CRM Books).

1973 Introduction to a re-publication of *Archaeology of the United States* by S. F. Haven, pp. vii–ix, *Antiquities of the New World Series* (New York: AMS Press).

1973 Introduction to a re-publication of *Peru: Incidents of Travel and Exploration in the Land of the Incas* by E. G. Squier, pp. vii–x, *Antiquities of the New World Series* (New York: AMS Press).
1973 "George Clapp Vaillant," *Dictionary of American Biography: Supplement Three, 1941–1945,* pp. 786–87 (New York: Charles Scribner's Sons).
1973 "Man, Settlement, and Urbanism," *Antiquity* 47, no. 188:269–79.
1973 Preface in *Ancient Maya Pottery* by J. C. Gifford and Muriel Kirkpatrick, pp. i–ii (Philadelphia: Temple University).
1973 Review of *Precolumbian Cities* by J. E. Hardoy, in *Boston Globe,* 13 May.
1973 "The Maya Collapse: A Summary View" (with D. B. Shimkin), *The Classic Maya Collapse,* ed. T. P. Culbert, pp. 457–502 (Albuquerque: University of New Mexico Press, School of Advanced Research).
1973 "Aspero, Peru: A Reexamination of the Site and Its Implications" (with M. E. Moseley), *American Antiquity* 38, no. 4; 452–68.
1974 *A History of American Archaeology* (with J. A. Sabloff), The World of Archaeology Series (London: Thames and Hudson).
1974 "Precolumbian Urbanism: The Central Mexican Highlands and The Lowland Maya," in *The Rise and Fall of Civilizations, Modern Archaeological Approaches to Ancient Cultures,* ed. C. C. Lamberg-Karlovsky and J. A. Sabloff, pp. 134–44 (Menlo Park, Calif.: Cummings).
1974 Introduction *Archaeological Researches in Retrospect,* ed. G. R. Willey, pp. ix–xix (Cambridge, Mass.: Winthrop).
1974 "The Viru Valley Settlement Pattern Study," *Archaeological Researches in Retrospect,* ed. G. R. Willey, pp. 149–78 (Cambridge, Mass.: Winthrop).
1974 "Comments on 'The Prehistory of the Southeastern Maya Periphery' " by R. J. Sharer, *Current Anthropology* 15, no. 2:183–84.
1974 "New World Prehistory: 1974," *American Journal of Archaeology* 78, no. 4:321–31.
1974 Introduction to *Mesoamerican Archaeology, New Approaches,* ed. Norman Hammond, pp. xiii–xxiv (London: Duckworth).
1974 "The Classic Maya Hiatus: A 'Rehearsal' for the Collapse," in *Mesoamerican Archaeology, New Approaches,* ed. Norman Hammond, pp. 417–30 (London: Duckworth).
1974 *Das Alte Amerika,* Propylaen Kunstgeschichte, vol. 18 (Berlin: Propylaen Verlag).
1974 "A Summary of the Complex Societies Colloquium," in *Reconstructing Complex Societies,* ed. C. B. Moore, pp. 145–53, Supplement to the Bulletin of the American Schools of Oriental Research (Cambridge, Mass.).
1974 "Un Modelo de Difusión Culturación," *Museo del Hombre Dominicano, Boletín* 5:73–91.
1974 "Radiocarbon Chronology for Seibal, Guatemala" (with R. Berger, S. DeAtley, and R. Protsch), *Nature* 252, no. 5483:472–73.
1974 *Archaeological Researches in Retrospect,* ed. (Cambridge, Mass.: Winthrop).
1975 "Alfred Marston Tozzer and Maya Archaeology," in *The Maya and Their Neighbors, Buried Treasures Series,* no. 5, pp. 3–10, Peabody Museum of Archaeology and Ethnology (Cambridge, Mass.: Harvard University).

1975 Review of *Archaeological Atlas of the World* by David and Ruth Whitehouse, in *Science* 190:551.
1975 *Excavations at Seibal, Department of Peten, Guatemala. Introduction: The Site and Its Setting,* (with A. L. Smith, Gair Tourtellot, III, and Ian Graham), Memoirs of the Peabody Museum of Archaeology and Ethnology, vol. 13, no. 1 (Cambridge, Mass.: Harvard University).
1976 "The Earliest Americans," in *Physical Anthropology and Archaeology,* pp. 251–59 (New York: MacMillan).
1976 "Sir Eric Thompson (1898–1975)," *Archaeology,* 29, no. 1:57.
1976 "The Caribbean Preceramic and Related Matters in Summary Perspective," *Proceedings of the First Puerto Rican Symposium on Archaeology,* ed. L. S. Robinson, Informe no. 1, Report no. 1, pp. 1–8 (Puerto Rico, San Juan: Fundacion Arqueologica e Historica).
1976 Review of *Tikal,* directed and filmed by Karl Heider, *American Anthropologist* 78:378.
1976 Foreword to *Prehistoric Pottery Analysis and the Ceramics of Barton Ramie in the Belize Valley* by J. C. Gifford, Memoirs of the Peabody Museum of Archaeology and Ethnology, vol. 18, pp. vii–viii (Cambridge, Mass.: Harvard University).
1976 "A Peruvian Pottery Collection in the Teatino Style," *To Illustrate the Monuments, Essays on Archaeology Presented to Stuart Piggott,* ed. J. V. S. Megaw, pp. 301–8 (London: Thames and Hudson).
1976 Review of *Archaeoastronomy in Pre-Columbian America,* ed. A. F. Aveni, in *Times Literary Supplement,* no. 3883, 13 August, p. 1016 (London).
1976 "Mesoamerican Civilization and the Idea of Transcendence," *Antiquity* 50, nos. 199 and 200:205–15.
1976 "Samuel Kirkland Lothrop, 1892–1965," in *Biographical Memoirs,* vol. 48, pp. 253–72 (Washington, D.C.: National Academy of Sciences).
1976 Foreword to *Emblem and State in the Classic Maya Lowlands* by Joyce Marcus, pp. ix–xv (Washington, D.C.: Dumbarton Oaks).
1976 Review of *Archaeological Salvage in the Walter F. George Basin of the Chattahoochee River in Alabama,* in *Antiquaries Journal* 56, pt. 2:294–95.
1976 "Un Proyecto para el Desarrollo de Investigación y Preservación Arqueológica en Copan (Honduras) y Vecinidad, 1976–1981" (with W. R. Coe and R. J. Sharer), *Yaxkin,* vol. 1, no. 2:10–29.
1976 "Una Clasificación Preliminar Descriptiva de Cerámica de La Isla de Roatan, Honduras" (with Vito Veliz and Paul Healy), *Revista de La Universidad,* no. 11:19–29.
1977 Review of *Cultural Change and Continuity, Essays in Honor of James Bennett Griffin,* in *American Scientist* 65, no. 3:374–75.
1977 "The Rise of Classic Maya Civilization: A Pasión Valley Perspective," in *The Origins of Maya Civilization,* ed. R. E. W. Adams, pp. 133–58 (Albuquerque: University of New Mexico Press).
1977 "The Rise of Maya Civilization: A Summary View," in *The Origins of Maya Civilization,* ed. R. E. W. Adams, pp. 383–424 (Albuquerque: University of New Mexico Press).

1977 "A Consideration of Archaeology," *Daedalus* (Summer):81–95.
1977 "Origines et Destin des Anciens Mayas", *La Recherche,* no. 82:861–71.
1977 "Clasificación Descriptiva Preliminar de Ceramica de Roatan", *Yaxkin* 2, no. 1:5–18.
1977 "The Maya," "Copan," "Altar de Sacrificios," in *Encyclopedia of Archaeology* (New York: T. Y. Crowell).
1977 "El Asentamiento Maya del Valle de Copan" (with R. M. Leventhal and W. L. Fash, Jr.), *Yaxkin,* vol. 2, no. 2:99–116.
1977 "External Influences on the Lowland Maya: 1940 and 1975," in *Social Process in Maya Prehistory,* ed. Norman Hammond, pp. 57–75 (London: Seminar Press).
1978 "A Summary Scan", in *Chronologies in New World Archaeology,* ed. R. E. Taylor and C. W. Meighan, pp. 513–64 (New York: Academic Press).
1978 *Excavations at Seibal, Department of Peten, Guatemala: Artifacts,* Memoirs of the Peabody Museum of Archaeology and Ethnology, vol. 14, no. 1 (Cambridge, Mass.: Harvard University).
1978 Preface to *A Reconnaissance of Cancuen,* in *Excavations at Seibal,* ed. G. R. Willey, by G. Tourtellot III, J. A. Sabloff, and Robert Sharick, Memoirs of the Peabody Museum of Archaeology and Ethnology, vol. 14, no. 2 (Cambridge, Mass.: Harvard University).
1978 Preface to *A Brief Reconnaissance of the Ruins of Itzan* by G. Tourtellot III, N. Hammond, and R. M. Rose, in *Excavations at Seibal,* ed. G. R. Willey, Memoirs of the Peabody Museum of Archaeology and Ethnology, vol. 14, no. 3 (Cambridge, Mass.: Harvard University).
1978 "Prehispanic Maya Agriculture: A Contemporary Summation," *Prehispanic Maya Agriculture,* ed. P. D. Harrison and B. L. Turner II, pp. 325–36 (Albuquerque: University of New Mexico Press).
1978 Review of *The Rural Foundations for Urbanism, Economic and Stylistic Interaction between Rural and Urban Communities in Eighth-Century Peru* by W. H. Isbell, in *Man,* vol. 13, no. 3:479–80.
1978 "Developmental Stages in Ancient Mesoamerican Society: Reflections and Impressions," *Human Mosaic* 12:155–62.
1978 "Maya Settlement Study in the Copan Valley, Honduras" (with R. M. Leventhal and W. L. Fash, Jr.), *Archaeology* 31, no. 4:32–43.
1979 Foreword to *Fundamentals of Archaeology* by R. J. Sharer and Wendy Ashmore, pp. vii–viii (Menlo Park, Calif.: Cummings).
1979 Review of *Monte Alban: Settlement Patterns at the Ancient Zapotec Capital* by R. E. Blanton, in *The Hispanic American Historical Review* (August):505–6.
1979 Review of *Prehistoric Coastal Adaptations, the Economy and Ecology of Maritime Middle America,* ed. B. L. Stark and B. Voorhies, in *American Antiquity* 44, no. 1:850–51.
1979 "Prehispanic Maya Agriculture, A Summary," *Actes, Forty-second International Congress of Americanists,* vol. 8, pp. 449–53 (Paris).
1979 "A Commentary on Cultural Evolution in the Maya Highlands and Lowlands," *Actes, Forty-second International Congress of Americanists,* vol. 8, pp. 205–9 (Paris).

1979 "Highland Culture Contacts in the Lowland Maya Area: An Introductory Commentary," *Actes, Forty-second International Congress of Americanists,* vol. 8, pp. 213–20 (Paris).
1979 "The Concept of the 'Disembedded Capital' in Comparative Perspective," *Journal of Anthropological Research* 35, no. 2:123–37.
1979 "Maya Archaeology and Ethnohistory: An Introduction" (with Norman Hammond), *Maya Archaeology and Ethnohistory,* ed. N. Hammond and G. R. Willey, pp. xi–xvii (Austin: University of Texas Press).
1979 "Some Ideas Were More Efficient" (with Ulrika Junker), *Kontakt Stencil* 17:24–35.
1979 "A Preliminary Report on Prehistoric Maya Settlements in the Copan Valley" (with R. M. Leventhal), *Maya Archaeology and Ethnohistory,* ed. N. Hammond and G. R. Willey, pp. 75–102 (Austin: University of Texas Press).
1979 *Maya Archaeology and Ethnohistory,* ed. with Norman Hammond (Austin: University of Texas Press).
1980 Review of *Quiche Conquest* by J. W. Fox, in *Journal of Interdisciplinary History* 10, no. 3:570–71.
1980 "Toward a Holistic View of Ancient Maya Civilization," *Man,* vol. 15, no. 2:249–66; Royal Anthropological Institute: The Huxley Memorial Lecture for 1979 (London).
1980 "The Social Uses of Archaeology," Kenneth B. Murdock Lecture, Leverett House, Harvard University (Cambridge, Mass.).
1980 Foreword to *Prehistoric Andean Ecology,* ed. F. Engel (New York: Humanities Press, Department of Anthropology, Hunter College).
1980 "Precolumbian Taino Art in Historical and Socio-Cultural Perspective," *La Antropologia Americanista en la Actualidad,* vol. 1, pp. 113–28 (Mexico, D.F.: Editores Mexicanos Unidos).
1980 "The Maya," in *The Encyclopedia of Ancient Civilizations,* ed. Arthur Cotterell, pp. 336–42 (London: Rainbird Publishing Group).
1980 Review of *A History of Mexican Archaeology* by Ignacio Bernal, in *Antiquity* 54:238–39.
1980 Review of *Gordon Childe: Revolutions in Archaeology* by Bruce G. Trigger, in *Nature* 288:417–18.
1980 Foreword to *Archaeology of the Rivas Region, Nicaragua* by Paul Healy, pp. xxiii–xxiv (Waterloo, Ontario, Canada: Wilfrid Laurier University Press).
1980 *A History of American Archaeology* (with J. A. Sabloff), 2d ed. (San Francisco: W. H. Freeman).
1980 *Precolumbian Archaeology* (ed. with J. A. Sabloff) (San Francisco: W. H. Freeman).
1981 "Lowland Maya Settlement Patterns: A Summary Review," in *Lowland Maya Settlement Patterns,* ed. W. Ashmore, pp. 385–415 (Albuquerque: University of New Mexico Press).
1981 "John Eric Sidney Thompson, 1898–1975," *Proceedings of the British Academy,* vol. 65, pp. 783–98 (London).
1981 Foreword to *Mystery of the Maya* by Richard M. Leventhal, p. 3 (Boston: Boston Museum of Science).

1981 "Spinden's Archaic Hypothesis," *Antiquity and Man,* ed. J. D. Evans, B. Cunliffe, and C. Renfrew, pp. 35–42 (London: Thames and Hudson).
1981 Review of *The Ceramics of Kaminaljuyu, Guatemala* by R. K. Wetherington, in *Hispanic American Historical Review,* vol. 61, no. 3.
1981 "Recent Researches and Perspectives in Mesoamerican Archaeology: An Introductory Commentary", in *Supplement to the Handbook of Middle American Indians,* vol. 1, *Archaeology,* ed. V. R. Bricker and J. A. Sabloff, pp. 3–27 (Austin: University of Texas Press).
1981 "A Historical Introduction to the Study of Lowland Maya Settlement Patterns" (with Wendy Ashmore), *Lowland Maya Settlement Patterns,* ed. W. Ashmore, pp. 3–18 (Albuquerque: University of New Mexico Press).
1981 "Adolfo Molina Orantes, 1915–1980" (with W. R. Coe), *American Antiquity* 46, no. 1:127.
1982 "Maya Archaeology," *Science* 215:260–67.
1982 Review of *The World of the Ancient Maya* by John S. Henderson, in *Archaeology* 35, no. 2:79.
1982 "Dennis Edward Puleston (1940–1978): Maya Archaeologist," in *Maya Subsistence,* ed. K. V. Flannery, pp. 1–15 (New York: Academic Press).
1982 Foreword to *Archaeology of the Florida Gulf Coast* by Gordon R. Willey, reprint edition with an introduction by C. H. Fairbanks, pp. i–ii (Gainesville, Fla.: Florida Book Store).

References

ACOSTA, JORGE R.
1964   *El Palacio del Quetzalpapalotl,* Instituto Nacional de Antropología e Historia, Memorias, no. 10 (Mexico City).
1967   "Una Classificación Tentativa de los Monumentos Arqueológicos de Teotihuacan," in *Teotihuacan: Onceava Mesa Redonda,* vol. 1, pp. 45–55 (Mexico City: Sociedad Mexicana de Antropología).

ACOSTA, JOSEPH de
1894   *Historia Natural y Moral de las Indias* (1590). 2 vols. (Madrid: Ramón Angles).

ADAMS, RICHARD E. W.
1963   "The Ceramic Sequence at Altar de Sacrificios, Guatemala" (Ph.D. diss., Harvard University).
1969   "Maya Archaeology 1958–1968, a Review," *Latin American Research Review* 4, no. 2:3–45.
1971   *The Ceramics of Altar de Sacrificios, Guatemala,* Papers of the Peabody Museum of Archaeology and Ethnology, vol. 63, no. 1 (Cambridge, Mass.: Harvard University).
1973   "Maya Collapse: Transformation and Termination in the Ceramic Sequence at Altar de Sacrificios," in *The Classic Maya Collapse,* ed. T. P. Culbert, pp. 133–64 (Albuquerque: University of New Mexico Press, School of American Research Advanced Seminar Series).
1977a *Prehistoric Mesoamerica* (Boston: Little, Brown).
1977b "Rio Bec Archaeology and the Rise of Maya Civilization," in *The Origins of Maya Civilization,* ed. R. E. W. Adams, pp. 77–100 (Albuquerque: University

of New Mexico Press, School of American Research Advanced Seminar Series).
1977c "Comments on the Glyphic Texts of the 'Altar Vase,' " in *Social Process in Maya Prehistory*, ed. N. Hammond (New York: Academic Press).
1980 "Swamps, Canals, and the Locations of Ancient Maya Cities," *Antiquity* 54, no. 212:206–14.

ADAMS, R. E. W., W. E. BROWN, AND T. P. CULBERT
1981 "Radar Mapping, Archaeology, and Ancient Maya Land Use," *Science* 213:1457–63.

ADAMS, ROBERT McC.
1965 *Land behind Baghdad: A History of Settlement on the Diyala Plains* (Chicago: University of Chicago Press).
1966 *The Evolution of Urban Society* (Chicago: Aldine).

ADAMS, ROBERT McC., AND HANS J. NISSEN
1972 *The Uruk Countryside: The Natural Settling of Urban Societies* (Chicago: University of Chicago Press).

ALBA ALBA, WALTER
1978 "Las salinas de Chao: un complejo precerámico," in *El Hombre y la Cultura Andina, Actas y Trabajos del III Congreso Peruano del Hombre y la Cultura Andina*, ed. R. Matos M., vol. 1, pp. 275–76 (Lima: Instituto Nacional de Cultura).

ANALES DE CUAUHTITLAN
1975 "Anales de Cuauhtitlan," in *Codice Chimalpopoca*, trans. P. Feliciano Velazquez, pp. 3–118 (Mexico: Instituto de Investigaciones Historias).

ANALES DE TLATELOLCO
1948 *Anales de Tlatelolco*, ed. H. Berlin (Mexico: Antigua Librería Rebredo).

ANALES MEXICANOS
1903 Anales Mexicanos, Mexico-Azcapotzalco (1426–1589), *Anales del Museo Nacional de Mexico*, epoca 1, vol. 7, pp. 49–74.

ANAWALT, PATRICIA R.
1976 "Pan-Mesoamerican Costume Repertory at the Time of Spanish Contact" (Ph.D. diss., University of California, Los Angeles).
1977 "What Price Aztec Pageantry?" *Archaeology* 30:226–33.
1980 "Costume and Control: Aztec Sumptuary Laws," *Archaeology* 33, no. 1:33–43.

ANDREWS IV, E. WYLLYS
1940 "Chronology and Astronomy in the Maya Area," in *The Maya and their Neighbors*, ed. C. L. Hay, R. L. Linton, S. K. Lothrop, H. L. Shapiro, and G. C. Vaillant, pp. 150–61 (New York: D. Appleton-Century).
1943 *The Archaeology of Southwestern Campeche*, Carnegie Institution of Washington, Contribution 40, Publication 546 (Washington, D.C.).
1959 "Dzibilchaltun: Lost City of the Maya," *National Geographic* 115:91–109.
1965 "Archaeology and Prehistory in the Northern Maya Lowlands: An Introduction," in *Handbook of Middle American Indians*, vol. 2, ed. G. R. Willey, pp. 288–330 (Austin: University of Texas Press).
1968 "Dzibilchaltun: A Northern Maya Metropolis," *Archaeology* 21:36–47.

1969 *The Archaeological Use and Distribution of Mollusca in the Maya Lowlands,* Middle American Research Institute, Publication 34 (New Orleans: Tulane University).

1970 *Balankanche, Throne of the Tiger Priest,* Middle American Research Institute, Publication 34 (New Orleans: Tulane University).

1973 "The Development of Maya Civilization After Abandonment of the Southern Cities," in *The Classic Maya Collapse,* ed. T. P. Culbert, pp. 243–65 (Albuquerque: University of New Mexico Press, School of American Research Advanced Seminar Series).

ANDREWS IV, E. WYLLYS, AND E. WYLLYS ANDREWS V

1980 *Excavations of Dzibilchaltun, Yucatan, Mexico,* Middle American Research Institute, Publication 48 (New Orleans: Tulane University).

ANONYMOUS

1920 *Informaciones del Virrey Toledo, Verificados en Jauja, Cuzco, Guamanqa, y Tucay* (1570–72), Colección de Libros y Documentos Referentes a la Historia del Peru, ed. H. H. Urteaga, 2d series, vol. 3, pp. 103–44 (Lima: Sanmarti).

ARENS, WILLIAM

1979 *The Man-Eating Myth: Anthropology and Anthropophagy* (New York: Oxford University Press).

ARMILLAS, PEDRO

1944 "Exploraciones Recientes en Teotihuacan," *Cuadernos Americanos* 16, no. 4:121–36.

1947 "La Serpiente Emplumada, Quetzalcoatl y Tlaloc," *Cuadernos Americanos* 31, no. 1:161–78.

1964 "Northern Mesoamerica," in *Prehistoric Man in the New World,* ed. J. D. Jennings and E. Norbeck, pp. 291–329 (Chicago: University of Chicago Press).

ARNOLD, DEAN

1978 "Ethnography of Pottery Making in the Valley of Guatemala," in *The Ceramics of Kaminaljuyu, Guatemala,* ed. R. K. Wetherington, pp. 327–400 (University Park: Pennsylvania State University Press).

ARRIAGA, PABLO JOSEPH DE

1920 *La Extirpación de la Idolatría en el Peru* (1621), Colección de Libros y Documentos Referentes a la Historia del Peru, ed. H. H. Urteaga and C. A. Romero, 2d series, vol. 1 (Lima: Sanmarti).

1968 *The Extirpation of Idolatry in Peru* (1621), trans. and ed. L. C. Keating (Lexington: University of Kentucky Press).

ASHMORE, WENDY

1981 "Some Issues of Method and Theory in Lowland Maya Settlement Archaeology," in *Lowland Maya Settlement Patterns,* ed. W. Ashmore, pp. 37–70 (Albuquerque: University of New Mexico Press, School of American Research Advanced Seminar Series).

ASHMORE, WENDY, ed.

1981 *Lowland Maya Settlement Patterns,* (Albuquerque: University of New Mexico Press, School of American Research Advanced Seminar Series).

ASHMORE, WENDY, AND GORDON R. WILLEY
1981 "A Historical Introduction to the Study of Lowland Maya Settlement Patterns," in *Lowland Maya Settlement Patterns,* ed. W. Ashmore, pp. 3–18 (Albuquerque: University of New Mexico Press, School of American Research Advanced Seminar Series).

AVENI, ANTHONY R., ed.
1975 *Archaeoastronomy in Pre-Columbian America,* (Austin: University of Texas Press).

BADNER, MINO
1972 *A Possible Focus of Andean Artistic Influence in Mesoamerica,* Studies in Pre-Columbian Art and Archaeology, 9 (Washington, D.C.: Dumbarton Oaks).

BALL, JOSEPH W.
1977 *The Archaeological Ceramics of Becan, Campeche, Mexico,* Middle American Research Institute, Publication 43 (New Orleans: Tulane University).
1978 *Archaeological Pottery of the Yucatan-Campeche Coast,* Middle American Research Institute, Publication 46 (New Orleans: Tulane University).
1979 "Ceramics, Culture History, and the Puuc Tradition: Some Alternative Possibilities," in *The Puuc: New Perspectives,* Publication 1, Central College Scholarly Studies in the Liberal Arts, ed. L. Mills, pp. 18–35, (Pella, Iowa: Central College).

BANDELIER, ADOLPH F.
1878 "On the Distribution and Tenure of Lands and the Customs with respect to Inheritance Amoung the Ancient Mexicans," *Eleventh Annual Report of the Trustees of the Peabody Museum of American Archaeology and Ethnology,* vol. 2, pp. 385–448.
1880 "On the Social Organization and Mode of Government of the Ancient Mexicans," *Twelfth Annual Report of the Trustees of the Peabody Museum of American Archaeology and Ethnology,* vol. 2, pp. 557–699.
1904 "On the Relative Antiquity of Ancient Peruvian Burials," *Bulletin of the American Museum of Natural History,* vol. 20, pp. 217–26.

BARDAWIL, LAWRENCE W.
1976 "The Principal Bird Deity in Maya Art—An Iconographic Study of Form and Meaning," in *The Art, Iconography and Dynastic History of Palenque,* pt. 3, ed. M. Greene Robertson, pp. 195–209 (Pebble Beach, Calif.: Robert Louis Stevenson School).

BASTIAN, ADOLF
1878–
89 *Die Culturlander des Alten America,* 3 vols. (Berlin).

BAUDEZ, CLAUDE F., ed.
n.d. *Investigaciones en Copan: Resultados de la Primera Fase del Proyecto Arqueológico Copan* (San José, Costa Rica, forthcoming).

BAUMHOFF, MARTIN A., AND ROBERT F. HEIZER
1959 "Some Unexploited Possibilities in Ceramic Analysis," *Southwestern Journal of Anthropology* 15:308–16.

BAWDEN, GARTH
1977   "Galindo and the Nature of the Middle Horizon of the North Coast of Peru (Ph.D. diss., Harvard University).
1978   "The Social Context of Moche Ceramics," paper presented at the Forty-third Annual Meeting of the Society for American Archaeology, Tucson, Ariz.
1982a   "Galindo: A Study in Cultural Transition During the Middle Horizon," in *Chan Chan: Andean Desert City,* ed. M. E. Moseley and K. C. Day, pp. 285–321 (Albuquerque: University of New Mexico Press, School of American Research Advanced Seminar Series).
1982b   "Community Organization Reflected by the Household: A Study in Pre-Columbian Social Dynamics," *Journal of Field Archaeology* 9, no. 2:165–82.

BECKER, MARSHALL J.
1979   "Priests, Peasants and the Ceremonial Centers: The Intellectual History of a Model," in *Maya Archaeology and Prehistory,* ed. Norman Hammond, pp. 3–20 (Austin: University of Texas Press).

BENDER, BARBARA
1978   "Gatherer-Hunter to Farmer: A Social Perspective," *World Archaeology* 10, no. 2:204–22.

BENNETT, WENDELL C.
1939   *Archaeology of the North Coast of Peru,* Anthropological Papers of the American Museum of Natural History, 37, pt. 1:1–153.
1944   *The North Highlands of Peru: Excavations in the Callejon de Huaylas and at Chavin de Huantar,* Anthropological Papers of the American Museum of Natural History, 39, pt. 1.
1946   "The Archaeology of the Central Andes," in *Handbook of South American Indians, Vol. II: The Andean Civilizations,* ed. J. H. Steward, pp. 61–148, Bureau of American Ethnology, Bulletin 143 (Washington, D.C.: Smithsonian Institution).
1948   "The Peruvian Co-Tradition," in *A Reappraisal of Peruvian Archaeology,* ed. W. C. Bennett, Memoirs of the Society for American Archaeology, no. 4, pp. 1–8 (Menasha, Wis.).
1950   *The Gallinazo Group, Viru Valley, Peru,* Publications in Anthropology, no. 43 (New Haven: Yale University).

BERDAN, FRANCES
1975   "Trade, Tribute, and Market in the Aztec Empire" (Ph.D. diss., University of Texas).
1976   "La Organización del Tributo en el Imperio Azteca," *Estudios de Cultura Nahuatl* 12:185–96.
1977   "Distributive Mechanisms in the Aztec Economy," in *Peasant Livelihood: Studies in Economic Anthropology and Cultural Ecology,* ed. R. Halperin and J. Dow, pp. 91–101 (New York: St. Martin's Press).
1978   "Tres Formas de Intercambio en la Economia Azteca," in *Economía, Política e Ideología en el México Prehispánico,* ed. P. Carrasco and J. Broda, pp. 77–94 (Mexico City: Centro de Investigaciones Superiores).

BERLIN, HEINRICH
1958 "El Glifo 'Emblema' en las Inscripciones Mayas," *Journal de la Société des Americanistes (Paris)* 47:111–19.

BERNAL, IGNACIO
1957 "Huitzilopochtli Vivo," *Cuadernos Americanos* 16:127–52.
1963 *Teotihuacan: Descubrimientos, Reconstrucciones* (Mexico City: Instituto Nacional de Antropología e Historia).
1977 "Maya Antiquaries," in *Social Process in Maya Prehistory*, ed. N. Hammond, pp. 19–43 (New York: Academic Press).
1980 *The Vanished Civilizations of Middle America*, trans. R. Malet (London: Thames and Hudson).

BERNASCONI, ANTONIO, AND ANTONIO CALDERON
1946 *Expediente Relativo al Descubrimiento de las Ruinas del Palenque e Informes Referentes a Ellas.*

BETANZOS, JUAN DIEZ DE
1924 *Suma y Narración de los Incas* (1551), Colección de Libros y Documentos Referentes a la Historia del Peru, ed. H. H. Urteaga, 2d ser., vol. 8, pp. 75–208 (Lima: Sanmarti).

BINFORD, LEWIS R.
1962 "Archaeology as Anthropology," *American Antiquity* 28:217–25.
1968 "Post-Pleistocene Adaptations," in *New Perspectives in Archaeology* ed. L. R. Binford and S. R. Binford (Chicago: Aldine).

BINFORD, LEWIS R., AND SALLY R. BINFORD
1968 *New Perspectives in Archaeology* (Chicago: Aldine).

BIRD, JUNIUS B.
1948 "Preceramic Cultures of Chicama and Viru," in *A Reappraisal of Peruvian Archaeology*, ed. W. C. Bennett, Memoirs of the Society for American Archaeology, no. 4, pp. 41–28 (Menasha, Wis.).

BIRMINGHAM, JUDY
1975 "Traditional Potters of the Kathmandu Valley: An Ethno-Archaeological Study," *Man* 10:370–86.

BLANTON, RICHARD E.
1976a "The Role of Symbiosis in Adaptation and Sociocultural Change in the Valley of Mexico," in *The Valley of Mexico*, ed. E. R. Wolf, pp. 181–202 (Albuquerque: University of New Mexico Press, School of American Research Advanced Seminar Series).
1976b "Anthropological Studies of Cities," *Annual Review of Anthropology* 5: 249–64.
1978 *Monte Alban: Settlement Patterns at the Ancient Zapotec Capital* (New York: Academic Press).

BORAH, WOODROW, AND SHERBURNE F. COOK
1963 *The Aboriginal Population of Central Mexico on the Eve of the Spanish Conquest*, Ibero-Americana 45 (Berkeley and Los Angeles: University of California Press).

BORHEGYI, S.
1961 "Shark Teeth, Stingray Spines, and Shark Fishing in Ancient Mexico and Central Mexico," *Southwestern Journal of Anthropology* 17:273–96.

BOWDITCH, CHARLES P.
1901 "Memoranda on the Maya Calendars Used in the Books of Chilam Balam," *American Anthropologist* 3:129–38.
1910 *The Numeration, Calendar Systems, and Astronomical Knowledge of the Mayas* (Cambridge, Mass.).

BRAIDWOOD, ROBERT J.
1960 "The Agriculture Revolution," *Scientific American* 203, no. 3:130–48.

BRASSEUR DE BOURBOURG, C. E.
1857– *Histoire des nations Civilisés du Mexique et de l'Amerique-Centrale durant*
59 *les siècles anterieurs à Cristophe Colomb*, 4 vols. (Paris).
1864 *Relation des Choses de Yucatan de Diego de Landa . . . accompagné de Documents Divers Historiques et Chronologiques . . .* (Paris).

BRAUN, DAVID P.
1976 "Rim Form and Ceramic Vessel Use: Results of an Experiment with a Central Arizona Archaeological Collection," paper presented at the Forty-second Annual Meeting of the Society for American Archaeology, St. Louis.

BRAY, WARWICK
1978 "Civilising the Aztecs," in *The Evolution of Social Systems*, ed. J. Friedman and M. J. Rowlands, pp. 373–98 (London: Duckworth).

BRENNAN, CURTISS T.
1980 "Cerro Arena: Early Cultural Complexity and Nucleation in Northern Peru," *Journal of Field Archaeology* 7, no. 1:1–22.

BRICKER, VICTORIA R.
1973 *Ritual Humor in Highland Chiapas* (Austin: University of Texas Press).
1981 *The Indian Christ, the Indian King: The Historical Substrate of Maya Myth and Ritual* (Austin: University of Texas Press).

BRODA, JOHANNA
1976 "Los Estamentos en el Ceremonial Mexica," in *Estratificación Social en la Mesoamérica Prehispánica*, ed. P. Carrasco and J. Broda, pp. 37–66 (Mexico City: Centro de Investigaciones Superiores).
1978 "El tributo en Trajes Querreros y la Estructura del Sistema Tributario Mexica," in *Economía, Politíca e Ideología en el México Prehispánico*, ed. P. Carrasco and J. Broda, pp. 175–94 (Mexico City: Centro de Investigaciones Superiores).

BRONSON, BENNET
1966 "Roots and the Subsistence of the Ancient Maya," *Southwestern Journal of Anthropology* 22, no. 3:251–79.

BROTHERSTON, GORDON
1974 "Huitzilopochtli and What Was Made of Him," in *Mesoamerican Archaeology: New Approaches*, ed. N. Hammond, pp. 155–66 (London: Duckworth).

BROWN, KENNETH L.
1980 "A Brief Report on Paleoindian-Archaic Occupation in the Quiche Basin, Guatemala," *American Antiquity* 45, no. 2:313–24.

BRUNDAGE, BURR CARTWRIGHT
1963 *Empire of the Inca* (Norman: University of Oklahoma Press).
1967 *Lords of Cuzco* (Norman: University of Oklahoma Press).
1972 *A Rain of Darts: The Mexica Aztecs* (Austin: University of Texas Press).
1975 *Two Earths, Two Heavens: An Essay Contrasting the Aztecs and the Incas* (Albuquerque: University of New Mexico Press).

BRUNHOUSE, ROBERT L.
1971 *Sylvanus G. Morley and the World of the Ancient Mayas* (Norman: University of Oklahoma Press).
1973 *In Search of the Maya: The First Archaeologists* (Albuquerque: University of New Mexico Press).
1975 *Pursuit of the Ancient Maya: Some Archaeologists of Yesterday* (Albuquerque: University of New Mexico Press).
1976 *Frans Blom, Maya Explorer* (Albuquerque: University of New Mexico Press).

BRUSH, STEPHEN B.
1976 "Man's Use of an Andean Ecosystem," *Human Ecology* 4, no. 2:147–66.
1977 "Kinship and Land Use in a Northern Sierra Community," in *Andean Kinship and Marriage,* ed. R. Bolton and E. Mayer, American Anthropological Association Special Publication No. 7.

BUNGE, O. D. E.
1940 "Contribution a l'Astronomie Maya," *Journal de la Société des Americanistes de Paris* 32:69–92.

BUNGE, W.
1962 *Theoretical Geography,* Lund Studies in Geography, Series C, General and Mathematical Geography, vol. 1 (Lund, Sweden: Lund Series).

BUNZEL, RUTH
1952 *Chichicastenango: A Guatemalan Village,* Publications of the American Ethnological Society, vol. 22 (Washington, D.C.).

BUSHNELL, G. H. S.
1957 *Peru* (New York: Praeger Paperbacks).

CABELLO VALBOA, MIGUEL
1951 *Miscelanea Antartica* (1586) (Lima: Instituto de Etnología, Universidad Nacional Mayor de San Marcos).

CABRERA CASTRO, RUBEN
1981 "El Proyecto Arqueológico Teotihuacan," paper presented at the conference Teotihuacan: Nuevos Datos, Nuevas Síntesis y Nuevos Problemas, Mexico City, Universidad Nacional Autónoma de Mexico, Instituto de Investigaciones Antropología.

CANBY, JOEL S.
1951 "Possible Chronological Implications of the Long Ceramic Sequence Recov-

ered at Yarumela, Spanish Honduras, in *Twenty-ninth International Congress of Americanists 1949,* pp. 79–85 (New York).

CARDENAS MARTIN, MERCEDES
1977– "Obtención de Una Cronología del Uso de Los Recursos Marinos en el An-
78   tiguo Peru," *Arqueologia PUC* 19 and 20:3–26.

CARMICHAEL, ELIZABETH
1973   *The British and the Maya* (London: Trustees of the British Museum).

CARMICHAEL, PATRICK
1980   *"Prehistoric Sociopolitical Evolution of Small Polities in the Northern Sierra, Peru"* (M.A. thesis, Trent University).

CARR, A.
1952   *Handbook of Turtles* (Ithaca, N.Y.: Comstock).

CARR, A., AND L. GIOVANNOLI
1957   "The Ecology and Migrations of Sea Turtles," *American Museum Novitiates,* no. 1835.

CARR, H. S.
1980   "Faunal Remains from Cerros," paper presented at the Seventy-ninth Annual Meeting of the American Anthropological Association (Washington, D.C.).

CARR, ROBERT F., AND JAMES E. HAZARD
1961   *Tikal Report No. 11: Map of the Ruins of Tikal, El Peten, Guatemala,* Museum Monographs, University Museum (Philadelphia: University of Pennsylvania).

CARRASCO, PEDRO
1967   "Relaciones Sobre la Organización Social Indígena en el Siglo XVI, *Estudios de Cultura Nahuatl* 7:119–53.
1971   "Social Organization of Ancient Mexico," in *Handbook of Middle American Indians,* ed. R. Wauchope, vol. 10, pp. 349–75 (Austin: University of Texas Press).
1976   "Los Linajes Nobles del México Antiguo," in *Estratificación Social en la Mesoamérica Prehispánica,* ed. P. Carrasco and J. Broda, pp. 19–36 (Mexico City: Centro de Investigaciones Superiores).
1978   "La Economía del México Prehispánico," in *Economía, Politíca, e Ideología en el México Prehispánico,* ed. P. Carrasco and J. Broda, pp. 15–76 (Mexico City: Centro de Investigaciones Superiores).
1979   "Las Bases Sociales del Politeismo Mexicano: Los Dioses Tutelares," *Actes du 42e Congrès International des Americanistes,* vol. 6, pp. 11–17 (Paris).

CARRASCO, PEDRO, WALTER MILLER, AND ROBERTO J. WEITLANER
1961   "El Calendario Mixe," *El México Antiguo* 9:153–72.

CASO, ALFONSO
1927   *El Teocalli de la Guerra Sagrada* (Mexico City: Talleres Graficos de la Nación).

1928 *Las Estelas Zapotecas,* Monografías del Museo Nacional de Arqueología, Historia y Etnografía (Mexico City).
1945 *La Religión de los Aztecas* (Mexico City: Secretaría de Educación Pública).
1953 *El Pueblo del Sol* (Mexico City: Fondo de Cultura Económica).
1958 "Comentario al Códice Baranda," *Miscellanea Paul Rivet,* pp. 373–93 (Mexico City).
1960 *Interpretación del Códice Bodley 2858,* facsimile edition, (Mexico City: Sociedad Mexicana de Antropología).
1963 "Land Tenure Among the Ancient Mexicans," *American Anthropologist* 65:863–78.
1966 "El Culto al Sol," *Sociedad de Mexicana de Antropología, Traducciones Mesoamericanas* 1:177–90.
1967 *Los Calendarios Prehispánicos* (Mexico City: Instituto de Investigaciones).
1977 *Reyes y Reines de la Mixteca,* vol. 1 (Mexico City: Fondo de Cultura Económica).
1979 *Reyes y Reines de la Mexteca,* vol. 2 (Mexico City: Fondo de Cultura Económica).

CASO, ALFONSO, AND IGNACIO BERNAL
1952 *Urnas de Oaxaca,* Instituto Nacional de Antropología e Historia, Memorias, no. 2 (Mexico City).

CASTILE, GEORGE PIERRE
1980 "Purple People Eaters? A Comment on Aztec Elite Class Cannibalism a la Harris-Harner," *American Anthropologist* 82:389–91.

CASTILLO F., VICTOR M.
1972 *Estructura Económica de la Sociedad Mexica* (Mexico City: Instituto de Investigaciones Históricas).

CASTRO, CRISTOBAL, AND DIEGO ORTEGA MOREJON
1936 "Relación y Declaración del Modo que Este Valle de Chincha y sus Comarcanos se Governavan Antes Que/Oviese Yngas y Despues q(ue) los Yuo Basta q(ue) los (Cristian)os E(n)trarón en Esta Tierra (1558)," in *Quellen zur Kulturgeschichte des Prakolumbischen Amerika,* ed. H. Trimborn, Studien zur Kulturkunde, vol. 3, pp. 236–46 (Stuttgart: Strecker and Schroder).

CHANG, K. C.
1983 "Settlement Patterns in Chinese Archaeology: A Case Study for the Bronze Age," in *Prehistoric Settlement Patterns,* ed. E. Z. Vogt and R. M. Leventhal (Albuquerque: University of New Mexico Press; Cambridge, Mass.: Peabody Museum).

CHAPMAN, KENNETH
1970 *The Pottery of San Ildefonso Pueblo* (Albuquerque: University of New Mexico Press).

CHASE, DIANE Z.
1981 "The Maya Postclassic at Santa Rita, Corozal," *Archaeology* 34, no. 1:25–33.

CHILDE, V. GORDON
1951 *Man Makes Himself* (New York: Mentor).

CHIMALPAHIN CUAUHLTEHUANITZIN, DON FRANCISCO DE SAN ANTON MUNON
1965 *Relaciones Originales de Chalco Amaquemecan* (Mexico City: Fondo de Cultura Económica).

CIEZA DE LEON, PEDRO DE
1943 *Del Senorio de los Incas* (Segunda Parte de la Crónica del Peru, que Trata del Senorio de los Incas Yupanquis y de sus Grandes Hechos y Gobernación (1553) (Buenos Aires: Ediciones Argentinas Solar).
1959 *The Incas of Pedro de Cieza de León* (1553), trans. H. de Onis, ed. V. W. von Hagen (Norman: University of Oklahoma Press).

CIUDAD REAL, ANTONIO DE
1872 *Relación Breve y Verdadera de Algunas Coasas de las Muchas que Sucedierón al Padre Fray Alonso Ponce en las Provincias de la Nueva España* (Madrid).

CLARKE, DAVID L.
1968 *Analytical Archaeology* (London: Methuen).

CLIFF, MAYNARD B.
1981 "Excavations in a Late Preclassic Nucleated Village at Cerros, Northern Belize" (manuscript; Southern Methodist University).

CLOSS, MICHAEL
1976 "New Information on the European Discovery of Yucatan and the Correlation of the Maya and Christian Calendar," *American Antiquity* 41:192–95.
1977 "Decipherment of the Maya Zero Hieroglyph," paper presented at the International Symposium on Maya Art, Architecture, Archaeology, and Hieroglyphic Writing, Guatemala City.

COBO, BERNABE
1890– *Historia del Nuevo Mundo* (1653), ed. M. Jiménez de la Espada, 4 vols.
95 (Seville: Sociedad de Bibliofilos Andaluces).
1979 *History of the Inca Empire: An Account of the Indians' Customs and Their Origin Together with a Treatise on Inca Legends, History, and Social Institutions* (1653), trans. and ed. R. Hamilton (Austin: University of Texas Press).

CODEX VINDO BONENSIS MEXICANUS 1
1929 Facsimile, text by Walter Lehmann and Ottokar Smital (Vienna).

CODICE RAMIREZ. *see* TOVAR

COE, MICHAEL D.
1966 *An Early Stone Pectoral from Southeastern Mexico,* Studies in Pre-Columbian Art and Archaeology, no. 1 (Washington, D.C.: Dumbarton Oaks).
1973 *The Maya Scribe and His World* (New York: Grolier Club).
1975 *Classic Maya Pottery at Dumbarton Oaks* (Washington, D.C.: Dumbarton Oaks).
1978 *Lords of the Underworld: Masterpieces of Classic Maya Ceramics* (Princeton, N.J.: Princeton University).
1981 "Religion and the Rise of Mesoamerican States," in *The Transition to State-*

hood in the New World, ed. G. D. Jones and R. R. Kautz, pp. 157–71 (Cambridge: Cambridge University Press).

COE, WILLIAM R.
1959 *Piedras Negras Archaeology: Artifacts, Caches, and Burials,* Monograph 4, University Museum (Philadelphia: University of Pennsylvania).
1965a "Tikal: Ten Years of Study of a Maya Ruin in the Lowlands of Guatemala," *Expedition* 8, no. 1:5–56.
1965b "Tikal, Guatemala and the Emergent Maya Civilization," *Science* 147: 1401–19.

COGGINS, CLEMENCY C.
1975 "Painting and Drawing Styles at Tikal: An Historical and Iconographic Reconstruction" (Ph.D. diss., Harvard University).
1979 "A New Order and the Role of the Calendar: Some Characteristics of the Middle Classic Period at Tikal," in *Maya Archaeology and Ethnohistory,* ed. N. Hammond and G. R. Willey, pp. 38–50 (Austin: University of Texas).
1981 "Review of Maya Lords of the Jungle," *Archaeology* 34, no. 6:76–77.
1982a "The Temple of the Seven Dolls: The Stucco Decoration and Architectural Assemblage of Structure 1-sub, Dzibilichaltun, Yucatan, Mexico," manuscript forthcoming in Publication 49, Middle American Research Institute (New Orleans: Tulane University).
1982b "Wooden Objects from the Cenote of Sacrifice," paper presented at the Forty-seventh Annual Meeting of the Society for American Archaeology, Minneapolis.

COHEN, MARK N.
1972– "Some Problems in the Quantitative Analysis of Vegetable Refuse Illustrated
74 by a Late Horizon Site on the Peruvian Coast," *Nawpa Pacha* 10, no. 12: 49–60.
1977 *The Food Crisis in Prehistory* (New Haven: Yale University Press).

COHODAS, MARVIN
1978 *The Great Ball Court at Chichen Itza, Yucatan, Mexico,* Outstanding Dissertations in the Fine Arts (New York: Garland).

COLLIER, DONALD
1955 *Cultural Chronology and Change as Reflected in the Ceramics of the Viru Valley, Peru,* Fieldiana: Publications in Anthropology, 43 (Chicago: Chicago Natural History Museum).
1962 "The Central Andes," in *Courses Toward Urban Life,* ed. R. J. Braidwood and G. Willey, Viking Fund Publications in Anthropology, vol. 32, pp. 165–76 (New York).

CONRAD, GEOFFREY W.
1974 "Burial Platforms and Related Structures on the North Coast of Peru: Some Social and Political Implications" (Ph.D. diss., Harvard University).
1980 "Platformas Funerarias," in *Chan Chan: Metropoli Chimu,* ed. R. Ravines, pp. 217–30, Fuentes e Investigaciones para la Historia del Peru, 5 (Lima: Instituto de Estudios Peruanos).

1981 "Cultural Materialism, Split Inheritance, and the Expansion of Ancient Peruvian Empires," *American Antiquity* 46:3–26.
1982 "The Burial Platforms of Chan Chan: Some Social and Political Implications," in *Chan Chan: Andean Desert City,* ed. M. E. Moseley and K. C. Day (Albuquerque: University of New Mexico Press, School of American Research Advanced Seminar Series).

CONRAD, GEOFFREY W., AND ARTHUR DEMAREST
n.d. *Religion and Empire: The Dynamics of Aztec and Inca Expansionism* (Cambridge: Cambridge University Press, in press).

COOK DE LEONARD, CARMEN
1973 "A New Astronomical Interpretation of the Four Ballcourt Panels at Tajin, Mexico" (this unpublished ms. contains her new correlation, which is omitted in the version published in Aveni [1975:263–82]).

COOK, SHERBURNE F.
1946 "Human Sacrifice and Warfare as Factors in the Demography of Pre-Colonial Mexico, *Human Biology* 18:81–102.

COOKE, RICHARD G.
1977 "Maximizing a Valuable Resource: The White-Tailed Deer in Prehistoric Central Panama," paper presented at the Forty-third Annual Meeting of the Society for American Archaeology, Tucson.

COUPLAND, GARY
1979 "A Survey of Prehistoric Fortified Sites in the North Highlands of Peru" (M.A. thesis, Trent University).

COWGILL, GEORGE L.
1963 "Postclassic Period Culture in the Vicinity of Flores, Peten, Guatemala" (Ph.D. diss., Harvard University).
1974 "Quantitative Studies of Urbanization at Teotihuacan," in *Mesoamerican Archaeology: New Approaches,* ed. N. Hammond, pp. 363–96 (London: Duckworth).
1977 "Processes of Growth and Decline at Teotihuacan: The City and the State," in *Los Procesos de Cambio en Mesoamérica y Areas Circunvecinas, XV Mesa Redonda,* vol. 1, pp. 183–93 (Mexico City: Sociedad Mexicana de Antropología).
1979 "Teotihuacan, Internal Militaristic Competition, and the Fall of the Classic Maya," in *Maya Archaeology and Ethnohistory,* ed. N. Hammond and G. R. Willey, pp. 51–62 (Austin: University of Texas Press).

COWGILL, G. L., J. H. ALTSCHUL, AND R. S. SLOAD
n.d. "Spatial Analysis of Teotihuacan: A Mesoamerican Metropolis," in *Spatial Analysis in Archaeology,* ed. H. Hietala and P. Larson (Cambridge: Cambridge University Press, forthcoming).

CRAIG, ALAN K., AND NORBERT P. PSUTY
1971 "Paleoecology of Shell Mounts at Otuma, Peru," *Geographical Review* 61, no. 1:125–32.

CULBERT, T. PATRICK
1965   *The Ceramic History of the Central Highlands of Chiapas, Mexico*, papers of the New World Archaeological Foundation, Publication 14, no. 19 (Provo, Utah).
1974   *The Lost Civilization: The Story of the Classic Maya* (New York: Harper and Row).

CUSTRED, GLYNN
1977   "Peasant Kinship, Subsistence, and Economics in a High Altitude Andean Environment," in *Andean Kinship and Marriage*, ed. R. Bolton and E. Mayer, Special Publication 7, American Anthropological Association, pp. 117–35 (Washington, D.C.).

DAMON, P. E., C. W. FERGUSON, A. LONG, AND E. I. WALLICK
1974   "Dendrochronologic Calibration of the Radiocarbon Time Scale," *American Antiquity* 39, no. 2:350–66.

DANIEL, GLYN E.
1950   *A Hundred Years of Archaeology* (London: G. Duckworth).

DAVID, NICHOLAS
1972   "On the Life Span of Pottery Types, Type Frequencies and Archaeological Inference," *American Antiquity* 37, no. 1:141–42.

DAVID, NICHOLAS, AND HILKE HENNIG
1972   *The Ethnography of Pottery: A Fulani Case Seen in Archaeological Perspective*, Addison-Wesley Modular Publications in Anthropology, no. 21 (Reading, Mass.: Addison-Wesley).

DAVIDSON, W.
1976   "Black Carib (Garifuna) Habitats in Central America," in *Frontier Adaptations in Lower Central America*, ed. M. W. Helms and F. O. Loveland (Philadelphia: ISHI).

DAVIES, CLAUDE NIGEL
1972   "The Military Organization of the Aztec Empire," *Atti del 40 Congresso Internazionale degli Americanisti*, vol. 4, pp. 213–21 (Rome).
1973   *Los Mexicas: Primeros Pasos Hacía el Imperio* (Mexico City: Instituto de Investigaciones Históricas).
1974   *The Aztecs* (London: Macmillan).
1977   *The Toltecs, Until the Fall of Tula* (Norman: University of Oklahoma Press).

DAY, KENT
1973   "Architecture of Ciudadela Rivero, Chan Chan, Peru," (Ph.D. diss. Harvard University).

DEBOER, WARREN R.
1974   "Ceramic Longevity and Archaeological Interpretation: An Example from the Upper Ucayali, Peru," *American Antiquity* 39, no. 2:335–43.

DeHETRE, DEBORAH
1979   "Prehistoric Settlement and Fortification Patterns of La Libertad, Peru: An Aerial Photographic Analysis" (M.A. thesis, Trent University).

DEMAREST, ARTHUR A.
1976   The Ideological Adaptation of the Mexica Aztec, *Advanced Seminar on Mesoamerican Archaeology*, ed. G. R. Willey (Cambridge: Tozzer Library, Harvard University).
1981   *Viracocha: the Nature and Antiquity of the Andean High God*, Monographs of the Peabody Museum of Archaeology and Ethnology, no. 6 (Cambridge, Mass.: Harvard University).

DE ROSNY, LEON
1904   *L'Amerique precolombienne: Etudes d'histoire, de linguistique et de paleographie sur les anciens temps du nouveau monde* (Paris).

DIAZ DEL CASTILLO, BERNAL
1956   *The Discovery and Conquest of Mexico*, trans. A. P. Maudslay (New York: Farrar, Straus, and Cudahy).

DIESEDORFF, E. P.
1926   "Kunst und Religion der Mayavolker," *Sonderabdruck aus Zeitschrift fur Ethnologie*, vol. 1 (Berlin).

DILLEHAY, TOM D.
1979   "Pre-Hispanic Resource Sharing in the Central Andes," *Science* 204:24–31.

DITTRICH, ARNOST
1936   *Die Korrelation der Maya-Chronologie* (Berlin: Abhandlungen der Preussischen Akademie der Wissenschaften).

DONNAN, CHRISTOPHER B.
1968   "An Association of Middle Horizon Epoch 2A Specimens from the Chicama Valley, Peru," *Nawpa Pacha* 6:15–18.
1972   "Moche-Huari Murals from Northern Peru," *Archaeology* 25, no. 2:85–95.
1973   *The Moche Occupation of the Santa Valley, Peru*, University of California Publications, vol. 8 (Berkeley, Calif.).
1976   *Moche Art and Iconography*, University of California, Los Angeles, Latin American Series, vol. 33.

DRUCKER, R. DAVID
1974   "Renovating a Reconstruction: The Ciudadela at Teotihuacan, Mexico: Construction Sequence, Layout, and Possible Uses of the Structure" (Ph.D. diss. University of Rochester).

DUBY, GERTRUDE, AND FRANS BLOM
1969   "The Lacandón," in *Handbook of Middle American Indians*, vol. 7, ed. E. Z. Vogt, pp. 276–97 (Austin: University of Texas Press).

DUELLMAN, W. E.
1963   "Amphibians and Reptiles of the Rainforests of Southern El Peten, Guatemala," *University of Kansas, Museum of Natural History* 15:205–49.

DURAN, FRAY DIEGO
1964   *The Aztecs: The History of the Indies of New Spain*, trans. D. Heyden and F. Horcasitas (New York: Orion Press).
1971   *Book of the Gods and Rites and the Ancient Calendar*, trans. F. Horcasitas and D. Heyden (Norman: University of Oklahoma Press).

EASBY, ELIZABETH, AND JOHN F. SCOTT
1970   *Before Cortez: Sculptures of Middle America* (New York: Metropolitan Museum of Art, distributed by the New York Graphic Society).

EDMONSON, MUNRO S.
1971   *The Book of Counsel: The Popul Vuh of the Quiche Maya of Guatemala*, Middle American Research Institute, Publication 35 (New Orleans: Tulane University).

EGGAN, FRED
1934   "The Maya Kinship System and Cross-Cousin Marriage," *American Anthropologist* 36:188–202.

EISENSTADT, S. N.
1969   *The Political Systems of Empires* (New York: Free Press).

ENGEL, FREDERIC
1963   "A Preceramic Settlement on the Central Coast of Peru: Asia, Unit 1," *Transactions of the American Philosophical Society* 53, no. 3.
1966   *Paracas: Cien Siglos de Cultura Peruana* (Lima: Librería Editorial Juan Mejia Baca).
1967   "Le complexe preceramique d'El Paraiso (Perou)," *Journal de la Société des Americanistes* (Paris): 55:43–96.

EPSTEIN, JEREMY F.
1957   "Late Ceramic Horizons in Northeast Honduras" (Ph.D. diss., University of Pennsylvania).

ERDHEIM, MARIO
1978   "Transformaciones de la Ideología Mexica en Realidad Social," *Economía, Polítíca e Ideología en el México Prehispánico*, ed. P. Carrasco and J. Broda, pp. 221–55 (Mexico City: Centro de Investigaciones Superiores).

ERICSON, J. E., D. W. READ, AND C. BURKE
1972   "Research Design: The Relationship Between the Primary Functions and the Physical Properties of Ceramic Vessels and Their Implications for Ceramic Distributions on an Archaeological Site," *University of California at Los Angeles Publications in Anthropology* 3, no. 2:84–95.

ESCALONA RAMOS, ALBERTO
1940   *Cronología y Astronomía Maya-Mexica* (Mexico City).
1943   "Cronología y Astronomía Maya-Mexica: Un Nuevo Sistema de Correlación Calendárica," *Twenty-seventh International Congress of Americanists* vol. 27, no. 1, pp. 623–30 (Mexico).

ESPINOZA SORIONO, WALDEMAR
1971   "Geografía Histórica de Huamachuco," *Historia y Cultura* no. 5, pp. 5–96 (Lima: Museo Nacional de Historia).

FASH, WILLIAM L.
1980   "Random vs. Purposive Sampling in Maya Archaeology: A Test Case from the Copan Valley," paper presented at the Forty-fifth Annual Meeting of the Society for American Archaeology, Philadelphia.
n.d.a   "El Mapa de la Bolsa de Copan" (in Baudez, forthcoming).

n.d.b "Investigaciones en el Valle" (in Baudez, forthcoming).

FASH, WILLIAM L., RICARDO AGURCIA F., AND ELLIOT M. ABRAMS
n.d. "Investigaciones en el Sitio CV-36, 1980-1981," *Primer Simposio del I.H.A.H.,* ed. Vito Veliz (Tegucigalpa: Universidad Nacional Autonoma de Honduras, forthcoming).

FASH, WILLIAM L., AND SHEREE LANE
n.d. "El Juego de Pelota B, Copan" (in Baudez, forthcoming).

FELDMAN, ROBERT ALAN
1980 "Aspero, Peru: Architecture, Subsistence Economy, and Other Artifacts of a Preceramic Maritime Chiefdom" (Ph.D. Diss., Harvard University).

FLANNERY, KENT V.
1968 "Archaeological Systems Theory and Early Mesoamerica," in *Anthropological Archaeology in the Americas,* ed. B. J. Meggars, pp. 67–87 (Washington, D.C.: Anthropological Society of Washington).
1972 "The Cultural Evolution of Civilizations," *Annual Review of Ecology and Systematics* 3:399–426.
1973 "The Origins of Agriculture," *Annual Review of Anthropology* 2:271–310.
1977 Review of *The Valley of Mexico,* ed. E. R. Wolf, *Science* 196:759–61.

FLANNERY, KENT V., AND JOYCE MARCUS
1976 "Formative Oaxaca and the Zapotec Cosmos," *American Scientist* 64:374–83.

FLORES OCHOA, JORGE
1977 *Pastores de Puna* (Lima: Instituto de Estudios Peruanos).

FONCERRADA DE MOLINA, MARTA
1964 "Fechas de Radiocarbon en el area Maya," *Estudios de Cultura Maya* 4:141–66.

FONTANA, B. L. et al.
1962 *Papago Indian Pottery* (Seattle: University of Washington Press).

FORD, JAMES A.
1949 *Cultural Dating of Prehistoric Sites in Viru Valley, Peru,* Anthropological Papers of the American Museum of Natural History, 43, pt. 1.

FORSTEMANN, ERNST W.
1880 *Die Maya Hardschrift der Koniglichen Offentlichen Bibliothek zu Dresden . . . mit 74 Tafeln in Chromo-Lichtdruck* (Leipzig: Verlag der A. Naumann'schen Lichtdruckerei).
1906 *Commentary on the Maya Manuscript in the Royal Public Library of Dresden,* Papers of the Peabody Museum of Archaeology and Ethnology, vol. 4, no. 2 (Cambridge, Mass.: Harvard University).

FOSTER, GEORGE M.
1960 "Life-expectancy of Utilitarian Pottery in Tzintzunzan, Michoacan, Mexico," *American Antiquity* 25, no. 4:606–9.

FREIDEL, DAVID A.
1976 "Late Postclassic Settlement Patterns on Cozumel Island, Quintana Roo, Mexico" (Ph.D. diss., Harvard University).
1978 "Maritime Adaptation and the Rise of Maya Civilization: The View from

Cerros," in *Prehistoric Coastal Adaptations in Mesoamerica,* ed. Barbara Stark and Barbara Voorhies, pp. 239–65 (New York: Academic Press).

1979 "Culture Areas and Interaction Spheres: Contrasting Approaches to the Emergence of Civilization in the Maya Lowlands," *American Antiquity* 44, no. 1:36–54.

1981 "Civilization as a State of Mind: The Cultural Evolution of the Lowland Maya," in *The Transition to Statehood in the New World,* ed. G. D. Jones and R. R. Kautz, pp. 188–227 (Cambridge: Cambridge University Press).

FRY, E. I.
1956 "Skeletal Remains from Mayapan," Carnegie Institution of Washington *Current Reports,* no. 38, pp. 551–71, Department of Archaeology (Washington, D.C.).

FUNG PINEDA, ROSA
1969 "Las Aldas: Su Ubicación Dentro del Proceso Historico del Peru Antiguo," *Dedalo* (Sao Paulo) 5:9–10.

FUNG PINEDA, ROSA, AND CARLOS WILLIAMS LEON
1977 "Exploraciones y Excavaciones en el Valle de Sechin, Casma," *Revista del Museo Nacional* (Lima) 43:111–55.

GANN, THOMAS W. F.
1897 "The Contents of Some Ancient Mounds in Central America," *Proceedings of the Society of Antiquaries of London,* 2d ser., vol. 16, pp. 3–8.

1900 "Mounds in Northern Honduras," *Bureau of American Ethnology, Nineteenth Annual Report,* pt. 2, pp. 655–92 (Washington, D.C.: Smithsonian Institution).

1918 *The Maya Indians of Southern Yucatan and Northern British Honduras,* Bureau of American Ethnology, Bulletin 64, (Washington, D.C.: Smithsonian Institution).

1925 *Mystery Cities: Exploration and Adventure at Lubaantun* (New York: Charles Scribner's Sons).

GARCIA DE PALACIO, DIEGO
1860 *Carta Dirigida al Rey de España, 1576,* trans. E. G. Squier (New York: Charles Norton).

GARCILASO DE LA VEGA, "EL INCA"
1945 *Comentarios Reales de los Incas* (1609), 2 vols. (Buenos Aires: Emece Editores).

1966 *Royal Commentaries of the Incas and General History of Peru* (1609–17), trans. H. V. Livermore, 2 vols. (Austin: University of Texas Press).

GIBSON, CHARLES
1971 "The Structure of the Aztec Empire," in *Handbook of Middle American Indians,* ed. R. Wauchope, vol. 1, pp. 376–94 (Austin: University of Texas Press).

GIFFORD, JAMES C.
1976 *Prehistoric Pottery Analysis and the Ceramics of Barton Ramie in the Belize Valley,* Memoirs of the Peabody Museum of Archaeology and Ethnology, vol. 18 (Cambridge, Mass.: Harvard University).

GINZEL, F. K.
1906/ *Handbuch der Mathematischen und Technischen Chronologie,* 3 vols. (Liep-
1958 zig: J. C. Hinrichs Buchhandlung).

GIRARD, R.
1962 *Los Mayas Eternos* (Mexico City: Antigua Librería Robredo).
1966 *Los Mayas* (Mexico City: Libro Mex Editores).

GOODMAN, J. THOMPSON
1905 "Maya Dates," *American Anthropologist* 7, no. 4:642–47.

GORDON, G. B.
1896 *Prehistoric Ruins of Copan, Honduras,* Memoirs of the Peabody Museum of Archaeology and Ethnology, vol. 1, no. 1 (Cambridge, Mass.: Harvard University).
1898a *Caverns of Copan, Honduras,* Memoirs of the Peabody Museum of Archaeology and Ethnology, vol. 1, no. 5, (Cambridge, Mass.: Harvard University).
1898b *Researches in the Uloa Valley,* Memoirs of the Peabody Museum of Archaeology and Ethnology, vol. 1, no. 4 (Cambridge, Mass.: Harvard University).
1902 *The Hieroglyphic Stairway, Ruins of Copan,* Memoirs of the Peabody Museum of Archaeology and Ethnology, vol. 1, no. 6 (Cambridge, Mass.: Harvard University).

GOSSEN, GARY H.
1974 *Chamulas in the World of the Sun* (Cambridge, Mass.: Harvard University Press).

GRAHAM, ELIZABETH
1976 *Archaeology of the Stann Creek District, Belize,* Stann Creek Project 1975, Interim Report (Cambridge: Centre of Latin American Studies, University of Cambridge).

GRAHAM, IAN
1963 "Juan Galindo, Enthusiast," *Estudios de Cultura Maya* 3:11–35.
1971 *The Art of Maya Hieroglyphic Writing* (Cambridge, Mass.: Peabody Museum Press).
1977 "Alfred Maudslay and the Discovery of the Maya, *British Museum Yearbook II: Collections and Collectors,* pp. 137–55 (London).

GRAHAM, JOHN A.
1979 "Maya, Olmecs and Izapans at Abaj Takalik," in *Forty-second International Congress of Americanists, Paris 1976, Actes du XLII,* vol. 8, pp. 179–88 (Paris: Societe des Americanistes).

GREENE ROBERTSON, MERLE
1979 "A Sequence for Palenque Painting Techniques," in *Maya Archaeology and Ethnohistory,* ed. N. Hammond and G. R. Willey, pp. 149–71 (Austin: University of Texas Press).

GRUHN, RUTH, AND ALAN L. BRYAN
1977 "Los Tapiales: A Paleo-Indian Campsite in the Guatemalan Highlands," *Proceedings of the American Philosophical Society* 121, no. 3, pp. 235–73.

GUAMAN POMA DE AYALA, FELIPE
1936 *Nueva Coronica y Buen Gobierno . . .,* Codex Peruvien Illustré, ca. 1610–15, Travaux y Memoires de l'Institut d'Ethnologie, no. 23 (Paris).

HABEL, S.
1878 *The Sculptures of Santa Lucia Cosumalwhuapa in Guatemala,* Smithsonian Contributions to Knowledge, vol. 22 (Washington, D.C.).

HAGGETT, PETER, ANDREW D. CLIFF, AND ALLAN FREY
1977 *Locational Analysis in Human Geography,* 2d ed. (London: Edward Arnold).

HALEY, SHAWN D.
1979 "Late Intermediate Period Settlement Patterns on the Carabamba Plateau, Northern Peru" (M.A. thesis, Trent University).

HAMBLIN, N. L.
1980 "Animal Utilization by the Cozumel Maya: Interpretation through Faunal Analysis" (Ph.D. diss., University of Arizona).

HAMMOND, NORMAN
1972 "Locational Models and the Site of Lubaantun: A Classic Maya Centre," in *Models in Archaeology,* ed. D. L. Clarke, pp. 757–800 (London: Methuen).
1975 *Lubaantun, A Classic Maya Realm,* Monograph of the Peabody Museum of Archaeology and Ethnology, vol. 2 (Cambridge, Mass.: Harvard University).
1977a "The Earliest Maya," *Scientific American* 236, no. 3:116–33.
1977b "Sir Eric Thompson, 1898–1975," *American Antiquity* 42, no. 2:180–90.
1978 "The Myth of the Milpa: Agricultural Expansion in the Maya Lowlands," in *Pre-Hispanic Maya Agriculture,* ed. P. D. Harrison and B. L. Turner II, pp. 23–34 (Albuquerque: University of New Mexico Press).
1980 "Early Maya Ceremonial at Cuello, Belize," *Antiquity* 54, no. 212:176–90.

HAMMOND, NORMAN, D. PRING, R. WILK, S. DONAGHEY, E. WING, A. V. MILLER, F. P. SAUL, AND L. H. FELDMAN
1979 "The Earliest Lowland Maya: Definition of the Swasey Phase," *American Antiquity* 44, no. 1:92–110.

HAMMOND, NORMAN, ed.
1973 *Corozal Project, 1973 Interim Report* (Cambridge: Cambridge University, Centre of Latin American Studies).
1974 *Mesoamerican Archaeology: New Approaches* (London: Duckworth).
1977 *Social Process in Maya Prehistory* (New York: Academic Press).

HARDOY, JORGE
1968 *Urban Planning in Pre-Columbian America* (New York: Brazilier).

HARNER, MICHAEL
1977 "The Ecological Basis for Aztec Sacrifice," *American Ethnologist* 4:117–35.

HARRINGTON, M. R.
1909 "The Last of the Iroquois Potters," *New York State Museum, Bulletin 133,* pp. 399–407.

HARRIS, MARVIN
1968 *The Rise of Anthropological Theory* (New York: Thomas Y. Crowell).
1977 *Cannibals and Kings: The Origins of Cultures* (New York: Random House).

HARRISON, PETER D.
1981   "Some Aspects of Preconquest Settlement in Southern Quintana Roo, Mexico," in *Lowland Maya Settlement Patterns,* ed. W. Ashmore, pp. 259–87 (Albuquerque: University of New Mexico Press).

HARRISON, PETER D., AND B. L. TURNER II, eds.
1978   *Pre-Hispanic Maya Agriculture* (Albuquerque: University of New Mexico Press).

HATT, R. T.
1953   *Faunal and Archaeological Researches in Yucatan Caves,* Cranbrook Institute of Science, Bulletin 33 (Bloomfield Hills, Mich.).

HAVILAND, WILLIAM A.
1963   "Excavations of Small Structures in the Northeast Quadrant of Tikal" (Ph.d. diss., University of Pennsylvania).
1970   "Tikal, Guatemala, and Mesoamerican Urbanism," *World Archaeology* 2:186–98.
1977   "Dynastic Genealogies from Tikal, Guatemala: Implications for Descent and Political Organization," *American Antiquity* 42, no. 1:61–67.
1981   "Dower Houses and Minor Centers at Tikal, Guatemala: An Investigation into the Identification of Valid Units in Settlement Hierarchies," in *Lowland Maya Settlement Patterns,* ed. W. Ashmore, pp. 89–117 (Albuquerque: University of New Mexico Press, School of American Research Advanced Seminar Series).

HEALY, PAUL F.
1973   "Archaeological Reconnaissance in the Department of Colon, Northeast Honduras" (manuscript, Harvard University).
1974a "The Cuyamel Caves: Preclassic Sites in Northeast Honduras," *American Antiquity* 39:435–47.
1974b "An Olmec Vessel from Northeast Honduras," *Katunob* 8:73–79.
1975   "H-CN-4 (Williams Ranch Site): Preliminary Report on a Selin Period Site in the Department of Colon, Northeast Honduras," *Vinculos* 1:61–71.
1977   "The Archaeology of Northeast Honduras: Preliminary Report on the 1975 and 1976 Research," paper presented at the Forty-second Annual Meeting of the Society for American Archaeology, New Orleans.
1978a "Excavations at Selin Farm (H-CN-5), Colon, Northeast Honduras," *Vinculos* 4:57–79.
1978b "Excavations at Rio Claro (H-CN-12), Northeast Honduras: Preliminary Report," *Journal of Field Archaeology* 5:15–28.

HELLMUTH, NICHOLAS
1977   "Cholti-Lacandon (Chiapas and Peten-Ytza Agriculture, Settlement Pattern and Population)," in *Social Process in Maya Prehistory,* ed. N. Hammond, pp. 421–48 (New York: Academic Press).
1978   *Maya Archaeology: Tikal, Copan Travel Guide* (Guatemala City: Foundation for Latin American Anthropological Research).

HELMS, MARY W.
1971   *Asang: Adaptations to Culture Contact in a Moskito Community* (Gainesville, Fla.: University of Florida Press).

HERNANDEZ PRINCIPE, RODRIGO
1923 "Mitología Andina (1621–22)," *Inca* 1:25–68.

HESTER, THOMAS R.
1979 "Colha, Belize: Preliminary Comments on the 1979 Season" *Cerámica de Cultura Maya* 10:63–71.

HESTER, T. R., J. D. EATON, AND H. J. SHAFER
1980 *The Colha Project, Second Season, 1980 Interim Report* (San Antonio: University of Texas, Center for Archaeological Research).

HESTER, THOMAS R., AND NORMAN HAMMOND, eds.
1976 *Maya Lithic Studies: Papers from the 1976 Belize Field Symposium* (San Antonio: University of Texas, Center for Archaeological Research).

HEYDEN, DORIS
1975 "An Interpretation of the Cave Underneath the Pyramid of the Sun in Teotihuacan, Mexico," *American Antiquity* 40, no. 2:131–47.

HEYDEN, DORIS, AND PAUL GENDROP
1975 *Pre-Columbian Architecture of Mesoamerica* (New York: Harry M. Abrams).

HISTORIA DE LOS MEXICANOS POR SUS PINTURAS
1941 "Historia de los Mexicanos por sus Pinturas," in *Nueva Colección de Documentos para la Historia de México*, pp. 209–40 (Mexico City: Editorial Chávez Hayhoe).

HISTOYRE DU MECHIQUE
1961 "Histoyre du Mechique," trans. J. Meade, *Memorias de la Academia Mexicana de la Historia* 20:183–210.

HOCHLEITNER, FRANZ J.
1970 "An Attempt at a Chronological-Astronomical Interpretation of the Numbers and Day-Signs of the Dresden Codex," *Boletín Informativo de Escritura Maya*, Universidad Nacional Autónoma de México (Mexico City).
1972 "The Correlation Between the Mayan and the Julian Calendars," *Fortieth International Congress of Americanists*, pp. 413–417 (Rome).

HOLLAND, WILLIAM
1963 *Medicina Maya en los Altos de Chiapas: Un Estudio del Cambio Socio-Cultural*, Colección de Antropología Social, vol. 2 (Mexico: Instituto Nacional Indigenista).

HOLMES, W. H.
1895–97 *Archaeological Studies Among the Ancient Cities of Mexico*, Field Columbian Museum, Publications 8, 16, Anthropological Series, vol. 1 (Chicago).

HOOTON, E. A.
1940 "Skeletons from the Cenote of Sacrifice at Chichen Itza," in *The Maya and Their Neighbors*, ed. C. L. Hay, R. L. Linton, S. K. Lothrop, H. L. Shapiro, and G. C. Vaillant, pp. 272–80 (New York: D. Appleton-Century).

HUAPAYA MANCO, CIRILO
1977–78 "Vegetales Como Elementos Antisísmico en Estructuras Prehispánicas," *Arqueología PUC* 19 and 20:27–38.

HUMBOLDT, ALEXANDER, BARON VON
1816   *Vues des Cordilleres et Monuments des Peuples Indigenes de l'Amerique* (Paris: Librairie Grecque-Latine-Allemande).

HUNT, EVA
1977   *The Transformation of the Hummingbird* (Ithaca: Cornell University Press).

ISBELL, WILLIAM H.
1978a   "Environmental Perturbations and the Origin of the Andean State," in *Social Archeology* ed. C. Medman et al., pp. 303–13 (New York: Academic Press).
1978b   "Cosmological Order Expressed in Prehistoric Ceremonial Centers," *Actes du XLII Congrès International des Americanistes*, pp. 269–97 (Paris: Société des Americanistes).

ISBELL, WILLIAM H., AND KATHARINA SCHREIBER
1978   "Was Huari a State?" *American Antiquity* 43, no. 3:372–90.

ISHIDA, EIICHIRO, K. AKI, T. YAZAWA, S. IZUMI, H. SATO, I. KOBORI, K. TERADA, AND T. OBAYASHI
1960   *Andes I: Report of the University of Tokyo Scientific Expedition to the Andes in 1958* (Tokyo: Kadokawa Publishing Co.).

IXTLILXOCHITL, FERNANDO DE ALVA
1891   *Obras Históricas*, 2 vols., ed. Alfredo Chavero (Mexico City).
1975   *Obras Históricas*, 2 vols. (Mexico City: Instituto de Investigaciones Históricas).

JIMENEZ MORENO, WIGBERTO
1961   "Diferente Principie del Ano Entre Diversos Pueblos y sus Consecuencias para la Cronología Prehispánica," *El Mexico Antiguo* 9:137–52.

JOHNSON, FREDERICK, AND RICHARD S. MACNEISH
1972   "Chronometric Dating," in *The Prehistory of the Tehuacan Valley*, vol. 4 ed. F. Johnson, pp. 3–58 (Austin: University of Texas Press).

JOHNSON, FREDERICK, ed.
1972   *The Prehistory of the Tehuacan Valley*, vol. 4 (Austin: University of Texas Press).

JOHNSON, JAY K.
1976   "Chipped Stone Artifacts from the Western Maya Periphery" (Ph.D. diss., Southern Illinois University).

JONES, CHRISTOPHER
1977   "Inauguration Dates of Three Late Classic Rulers of Tikal, Guatemala," *American Antiquity* 42:28–60.

JORALEMON, DAVID
1971   *A Study of Olmec Iconography*, Studies in Pre-Columbian Art and Archaeology, 7 (Washington, D.C.: Dumbarton Oaks).
1974   "Ritual Blood-Sacrifice Among the Ancient Maya: Part 1," in *Primera Mesa Redonda de Palenque*, pt. 1, ed. M. Greene Robertson, pp. 59–76 (Pebble Beach, Calif.: Robert Louis Stevenson School).

JORDON D. S., AND B. W. EVERMAN
1963   *The Fishes of North and Middle America* (Jersey City, N.J.: T. F. H. Publishing).

JOYCE, THOMAS A.
1914   *Mexican Archaeology* (New York: G. P. Putnam's Sons).
1926   "Report on the Investigations at Lubaantun, British Honduras in 1926," *Journal of the Royal Anthropological Institute* 56:207–30.

KATZ, FRIEDRICH
1966   *Situación Social y Económica de los Aztecas durante los Siglos XV y XVI* (Mexico City: Instituto de Investigaciones Historicas).
1972   *The Ancient American Civilizations* (New York: Praeger).

KAUCHER, CARL D.
1980   "Maya Chronology and the Conjunction of Mars," manuscript.

KAUTZ, ROBERT E.
1976   "Late-Pleistocene Paleoclimates and Human Adaptation on the Western Flank of the Peruvian Andes" (Ph.D. diss., University of California, Davis).

KEATINGE, RICHARD W.
1975   "From the Sacred to the Secular: First Report on a Prehistorical Architectural Transition on the North Coast of Peru," *Archaeology* 28, no. 2:128–29.
1978   "The Pacatnamu Textiles," *Archaeology* 31, no. 2:30–41.

KELLEY, DAVID H.
1960   "Calendar Animals and Deities," *Southwestern Journal of Anthropology* 16, no. 3:317–37.
1967   "Grant No. 676—Johnson Fund." *Yearbook of the American Philosophical Society,* pp. 552–53.
1972   "The Nine Lords of the Night," *Contributions of the University of California Archaeological Research Facility,* 5, no. 16:53–68.
1974   "Eurasian Evidence and the Mayan Correlation Problem," in *Mesoamerican Archaeology: New Approaches,* ed. N. Hammond, pp. 135–42 (London: Duckworth).
1975   "Planetary Data on Caracol Stela 3," in *Archaeoastronomy in Pre-Columbian America,* ed. A. F. Aveni, pp. 257–62 (Austin: University of Texas Press).
1976   *Deciphering the Maya Script* (Austin: University of Texas Press).
1977   "Maya Astronomical Tables and Inscriptions," in *Native American Astronomy,* ed. A. F. Aveni, pp. 57–73 (Austin: University of Texas Press).
1980   "Astronomical Identities of Mesoamerican Gods," *Archaeoastronomy Supplement to the Journal for the History of Astronomy* 2:S1–S54.
n.d.   "Notes on Puuc Inscriptions and History," in *Scholarly Studies in the Liberal Arts* (Pella, Iowa: Central College, forthcoming).

KELLEY, DAVID H., AND K. ANN KERR
1973   "Mayan Astronomy and Astronomical Glyphs," in *Mesoamerican Writing Systems,* ed. E. P. Benson, pp. 179–215 (Washington, D.C.: Dumbarton Oaks).

KENDRICK, THOMAS D.
1950   *British Antiquity* (London: Methuen).

KENNEDY, E. S., AND DAVID PINGREE
1971   *The Astrological History of Masha Allah* (Cambridge, Mass.: Harvard University Press).

KIDDER, A. V.
1947   *The Artifacts of Uaxactun, Guatemala,* Carnegie Institution of Washington, Publication 576 (Washington, D.C.).

KIDDER, A. V., J. D. JENNINGS, AND E. M. SHOOK
1946   *Excavations at Kaminaljuyu, Guatemala,* Carnegie Institution of Washington, Publication 561 (Washington, D.C.).

KIDDER, A. V., AND C. SAMAYOA C.
1959   *The Art of the Ancient Maya* (New York: Thomas Y. Crowell).

KINDT-JENSEN, OLE
1976   *A History of Scandinavian Archaeology* (London: Thames and Hudson).

KINGSBOROUGH, LORD EDWARD KING
1831–48   *Antiquities of Mexico, Comprising Facsimiles of Ancient Mexican Paintings and Hieroglyphs,* 9 vols. (London).

KIRCHHOFF, PAUL
1949   Paper on Maya Katun counts presented at the New York Academy of Sciences.
1950   "The Mexican Calendar and the Founding of Tenochtitlan-Tlatelolco," *Transactions of the New York Academy of Sciences,* ser. 2:126–32.
1955   "Calendarios Tenochca, Tlatelolca y Otros," *Revista Mexicana de Estudios Antropológicos* 14, no. 2:257–67.
1959   "The Principles of Clanship in Human Society," in *Readings in Anthropology,* ed. M. H. Fried, pp. 259–70 (New York: Thomas Y. Crowell).

KLEIN, C. F.
1976   *The Face of the Earth: Frontality in Two-Dimensional Mesoamerican Art,* Outstanding Dissertations in the Fine Arts (New York: Garland).
1980   "Who was Tlaloc?" *Journal of Latin American Lore* 6:155–204.

KLUCKHOLN, CLYDE
1940   "The Conceptual Structures in Middle American Studies," in *The Maya and Their Neighbors,* ed. C. L. Hays, R. L. Linton, S. K. Lothrop, H. L. Shapiro, and G. C. Vaillant, pp. 41–51 (New York: D. Appleton-Century).

KLYMYSHYN, ALEXANDRA ULANA
1982   "Elite Compounds in Chan Chan," in *Chan Chan: Andean Desert City,* ed. M. E. Moseley and K. C. Day, pp. 119–45 (Albuquerque: University of New Mexico Press, School of American Research Advanced Seminar Series).

KNOROZOV, YURII
1952   "Drevnyaya Pis'menost Tsentralnoy Ameriki" (The Ancient Script of Central America), *Sovietskaya Etnografiya* no. 3:100–118.
1955   *La Escritura de los Antiguos Mayas (Ensayo de Descrifado)* (Moscow: Inst. Etnografi Akad. Nauk.).
1963   *Pismennost' Indeitsev Maiia* (Writing of the Maya Indians) (Moscow-Leningrad: Academy of Sciences).

KOEPPEN, W.
1948   *Climatología* (Mexico).

KOLATA, ALAN L.
1978 "Chan Chan: The Form of the City in Time," (Ph.D. diss., Harvard University).
1982 "Chronology and Settlement Growth at Chan Chan," in *Chan Chan: Andean Desert City*, ed. M. E. Moseley and K. C. Day, pp. 67–86 (Albuquerque: University of New Mexico Press, School of American Research Advanced Seminar Series).
n.d. *An Architectural History of Chan Chan* (Washington, D.C.: Dumbarton Oaks Research Library and Collection, Harvard University, forthcoming).

KOSOK, PAUL
1965 *Life, Land and Water in Ancient Peru* (New York: Long Island University Press).

KREICHGAUER, DAMIAN
1927 "La Correspondencia Entre la Cronología Maya de el Computo Europeo," *Investigación y Progresso* 1, no. 7.

KROEBER, ALFRED L.
1925 "The Uhle Pottery Collections from Moche," *University of California Publications in American Archaeology and Ethnology* 21:191–234.
1926 *Archaeological Explorations in Peru, Part I, Ancient Pottery from Trujillo,* Field Museum of Natural History, Anthropology Memoirs, vol. 2, no. 1 (Chicago).
1930 *Archaeological Explorations in Peru, Part II, the Northern Coast,* Field Museum of Natural History, Anthropology Memoirs, vol. 2, no. 2 (Chicago).
1944 *Peruvian Archaeology in 1942,* Viking Fund Publications in Anthropology, no. 4 (New York).
1963 *An Anthropologist Looks at History* (Berkeley: University of California Press).

KRZANOWSKI, ANDRZEJ
1977 "Yuraccama: The Settlement Complex in the Alto Chicama Region (Northern Peru," *Polish Contributions in New World Archaeology*, no. 16:29–58.

KURJACK, EDWARD B.
1974 *Prehistoric Lowland Maya Community and Social Organization,* Middle American Research Institute, Publication 38 (New Orleans: Tulane University).

KURJACK, EDWARD B., AND SILVIA GARZA T.
1981 "Precolumbian Community Form and Distribution in the Northern Maya Area," in *Lowland Maya Settlement Patterns*, ed. W. Ashmore, pp. 287–309 (Albuquerque: University of New Mexico Press, School of American Research Advanced Seminar Series).

LA FARGE, OLIVER
1947 *Santa Eulalia: The Religion of a Cuchumatan Indian Town* (Chicago: University of Chicago Press).

LA FARGE, OLIVER, AND DOUGLAS BYERS
1931 *The Year Bearer's People* (New Orleans: Middle American Research Institute).

LAND, H.
1970 *Birds of Guatemala* (Wynwood, Pa.: Livingston).

LANNING, EDWARD P.
1967　　*Peru Before the Incas* (Englewood Cliffs, N.J.: Prentice-Hall).

LARCO HOYLE, RAFAEL
1938–
39　　*Los Mochicas*, 2 vols. (Lima: Casa Editora "La Cronica y Variedades").
1944　　*La Cultura Salinar* (Buenos Aires: Sociedad Geográfica Americana).
1945a　*Los Mochicas* (Buenos Aires: Sociedad Geográfica Americana).
1945b　*La Cultura Viru* (Buenos Aires: Sociedad Geográfica Americana).
1946　　"A Culture Sequence for the North Coast of Peru," in *Handbook of South American Indians, Vol. II: The Andean Civilizations*, ed. J. H. Steward, pp. 149–75, Bureau of American Ethnology, Bulletin 143 (Washington, D.C.: Smithsonian Institution).
1966　　*Peru* (Geneva: Nagel; Cleveland: Third World Publishing Company).

LAUGHLIN, ROBERT M.
1969　　"The Tzotzil," in *Handbook of Middle American Indians*, vol. 7, ed. E. Z. Vogt, pp. 152–94 (Austin: University of Texas Press).
1976　　*Of Wonders Wild and New: Dreams from Zinacantan*, Smithsonian Institution Contributions to Anthropology, no. 22 (Washington, D.C.).

LEHMANN, HENRI
1968　　*Arts Maya du Guatemala* (Paris: Grand Palais).

LEHMANN, WALTER
1912　　"Enige Probleme des Centralamerikanischen Kalenders," *Eighteenth International Congress of Americanists*, vol. 18, pp. 155–63 (London).

LEON-PORTILLA, MIGUEL
1958　　"Itzcoatl Creador de Una Cosmovisión Místico-Guerrera," in *Siete Ensayos sobre Cultura Nahuatl*, pp. 117–43. (Mexico City: Universidad Nacional Autónoma de México).
1959　　*La Filosofía Nahuatl Estudiada en sus Fuentes* (Mexico City: Instituto de Investigaciones Historicas).
1960　　"The Concept of the State Among the Ancient Aztecs," *Alpha Kappa Deltan* 30, no. 1:7–13.

LEVENTHAL, RICHARD M.
1979　　"Settlement Patterns at Copan, Honduras" (Ph.D. diss., Harvard University).
1981　　"Settlement Patterns in the Southeast Maya Area," in *Lowland Maya Settlement Patterns*, ed. W. Ashmore, pp. 187–209 (Albuquerque: University of New Mexico Press, School of American Research Advanced Seminar Series).
1983　　"Household Groups and Classic Maya Religion," in *Prehistoric Settlement Patterns*, ed. E. Z. Vogt and R. M. Leventhal (Albuquerque: University of New Mexico Press; Cambridge, Mass.: Peabody Museum).

LEVENTHAL, RICHARD M., AND WILLIAM L. FASH
1981　　"The Political Economy of Copan," paper presented at the Eightieth Annual Meeting of the American Anthropological Association, Los Angeles.

LEYENDA DE LOS SOLES
1975　　"Leyenda de los Soles," in *Codice Chimalpopoca*, trans. P. Feliciano Velazquez, pp. 119–42 (Mexico City: Instituto de Investigaciones Historicas).

LINARES, OLGA F.
1976 "Garden Hunting in the American Tropics," *Human Ecology* 4:331–49.
1979 "What is Lower Central American Archaeology?" *Annual Review of Anthropology* 8:21–43.

LINTON, RALPH
1944 "North American Cooking Pots," *American Antiquity* 9, no. 4:369–80.

LISCHKA, JOSEPH J.
1978 "A Functional Analysis of Middle Classic Ceramics at Kaminaljuyu," in *Ceramics of Kaminaljuyu, Guatemala,* ed. R. K. Wetherington, pp. 223–78 (University Park: Pennsylvania State University Press).

LITTLEHALES, B.
1961 "Treasure Hunt in the Deep Past," *National Geographic* 120:550–61.

LOCKHARDT, JAMES M.
1968 *Spanish Peru, 1532–1560* (Madison: University of Wisconsin Press).

LOGAN, MICHAEL H., AND WILLIAM T. SANDERS
1976 "The Model," in *The Valley of Mexico,* ed. E. R. Wolf, pp. 31–58 (Albuquerque: University of New Mexico Press, School of American Research Advanced Seminar Series).

LONGYEAR, JOHN M.
1952 *Copan Ceramics: A Study of Southeastern Maya Pottery,* Carnegie Institution of Washington, Publication 597 (Washington, D.C.).

LOPEZ AUSTIN, ALFREDO
1961 *La Constitutión Real de México-Tenochtitlan* (Mexico City: Universidad Nacional Autónoma de México).
1973 *Hombre-Dios: Religión y Política en el Mundo Nahuatl* (Mexico City: Instituto de Investigaciones Históricas).

LOPEZ DE COGOLLUDO, D.
1971 *Los Tres Siglos de la Dominación Española en Yucatan o sea Historia de Esta Provincia,* 2 vols., (Graz: Akademische Druck, Verangsanstalt).

LOTHROP, J. M.
1982 "Textiles from the Cenote of Sacrifice at Chichen Itza," paper presented at the Forty-seventh Annual Meeting of the Society for American Archaeology, Minneapolis.

LOTHROP, S. K.
1924 *Tulum: An Archaeological Survey of the East Coast of Quintana Roo,* Carnegie Institution of Washington, Publication 335 (Washington, D.C.).
1952 *Metals from the Cenote of Sacrifice, Yucatan,* Memoirs of the Peabody Museum of Archaeology and Ethnology, vol. 10, no. 2 (Cambridge, Mass.: Harvard University).

LOUNSBURY, FLOYD G.
1973 "On the Derivation and Reading of the "Ben-Ich" Prefix" in *Mesoamerican Writing Systems,* ed. E. P. Benson, pp. 99–143 (Washington, D.C.: Dumbarton Oaks).

1978 "Maya Numeration, Computation, and Calendrical Astronomy," *Dictionary of Scientific Biography,* vol. 15, supplement, pp. 759–818.

LUDENDORFF, HANS
1938 *Contribuciones a la Interpretación Astronómica de las Inscripciones Mayas* (Mexico City: Editorial Cultura).

LUMBRERAS, LUIS G.
1974 *Peoples and Cultures of Ancient Peru,* trans. B. J. Meggers (Washington, D.C.: Smithsonian Institution).
1977 "Excavaciones en el Templo Antiguo de Chavin (Sector R); Informe de la Sexta Campana," *Nawpa Pacha* 15:1–38.

LUTHER, E.
1974 "Faunal Material," in *Excavations at Actun Polbilche, Belize* by David Pendergast, Monograph 1, Royal Ontario Museum of Art and Archaeology Monograph, pp. 62–80.

MCCOWN, T. D.
1945 *Pre-Incaic Huamachuco, Survey and Evacuations in the Region of Huamachuco and Cajabamba,* University of California Publications in American Archaeology and Ethnology 39, no. 4 (Berkeley).

MACKENZIE, JANET
1980 "Coast to Highland Trade in Precolumbian Peru: Dendritic Economic Organization in the North Sierra" (M.A. thesis, Trent University).

MACLEOD, BARBARA, AND DENNIS E. PULESTON
1978 "Pathways into Darkness: The Search for the Road to Xibalba," in *Tercera Mesa Redonda de Palenque,* vol. 4, ed. M. Greene Robertson and D. C. Jeffers (Monterey, Calif.: Pre-Columbian Art Research).

MACNEISH, RICHARD S., S. JEFFREY K. WILKERSON, AND ANTOINETTE NELKEN-TERNER
1980 *First Annual Report of the Belize Archaic Archaeological Reconnaissance* (Andover: Robert S. Peabody Foundation for Archaeology).

MAKEMSON, MAUD W.
1943 *The Astronomical Tables of the Maya,* Carnegie Institution of Washington, Contribution 42, Publication 546 (Washington, D.C.).
1946 *The Maya Correlation Problem,* Publications of the Vassar College Observatory, no. 5 (Poughkeepsie, N.Y.: Vassar College).
1957 *The Miscellaneous Dates of the Dresden Codex,* Publications of the Vassar College Observatory, no. 6 (Poughkeepsie, N.Y.: Vassar College).

MALER, TEOBERT
1901 *Researches in the Central Portion of the Usumatsintla Valley: Report of Explorations for the Museum 1898–1900,* Memoirs of the Peabody Museum of Archaeology and Ethnology, vol. 2, no. 1 (Cambridge, Mass: Harvard University).
1903 *Researches in the Central Portion of the Usumatsintla Valley: Report of Explorations for the Museum 1898–1900,* Memoirs of the Peabody Museum of Archaeology and Ethnology, vol. 2, no. 2 (Cambridge, Mass: Harvard University).
1908a *Explorations of the Upper Usumatsintla and Adjacent Regions: Altar de Sacri-*

ficios; Seibal; Itsimté-Sácluk; Cankuen, Memoirs of the Peabody Museum of Archaeology and Ethnology, vol. 4, no. 1 (Cambridge, Mass: Harvard University).

1908b   *Explorations in the Department of Peten, Guatemala, and Adjacent Regions: Tópóxte; Yaxhá; Benque Viejo; Naranjo. Reports of Explorations for the Museum*, Memoirs of the Peabody Museum of Archaeology and Ethnology, vol. 4, no. 2 (Cambridge, Mass: Harvard University).

1910   *Explorations in the Department of Peten, Guatemala, and Adjacent Regions: Motul de San José; Peten-Itza, Reports of Explorations for the Museum*, Memoirs of the Peabody Museum of Archaeology and Ethnology, vol. 4, no. 3 (Cambridge, Mass.: Harvard University).

1911   *Explorations in the Department of Peten, Guatemala, Report of Explorations for the Museum*, Memoirs of the Peabody Museum of Archaeology and Ethnology, vol. 5, no. 2 (Cambridge, Mass.: Harvard University).

MALMSTROM, VINCENT H.
1978   "A Reconstruction of the Chronology of Mesoamerican Calendrical Systems," *Journal of the History of Astronomy* 9:105–16.

MARCUS, JOYCE
1976   *Emblem and State in the Classic Maya Lowlands* (Washington, D.C.: Dumbarton Oaks).
1983   "On the Nature of the Mesoamerican City," in *Prehistoric Settlement Patterns*, ed. E. Z. Vogt and R. M. Leventhal (Albuquerque: University of New Mexico Press; Cambridge, Mass.: Peabody Museum).

MARDEN, L.
1959   "Dzibilchaltun: Up from the Well of Time," *National Geographic* 115: 110–29.

MARQUINA, IGNACIO
1922   "Arquitectura y Escultura. Primera Parte—Arquitectura," in *La Población del Valle de Teotihuacan*, ed. M. Gamio, pp. 99–164 (Mexico City).
1951   *Arquitectura Prehispánica*, Memorias, Instituto Nacional de Antropología e Historia, no. 1 (Mexico City).

MARTINEZ HERNANDEZ, JUAN
1926   "Paralelismo Entre los Calendarios Maya y Azteca," *Diario de Yucatan*, February 7 (Merida).

MASON, J. ALDEN
1968   *The Ancient Civilizations of Peru* (Harmondsworth, England: Penguin Books).

MATHENY, RAYMOND T.
1970   *The Ceramics of Aguacatal, Campeche, Mexico*, Papers of the New World Archaeological Foundation, no. 27 (Provo, Utah).
1980   *El Mirador, Peten, Guatemala: An Interim Report*, Papers of the New World Archaeological Foundation, no. 45 (Provo, Utah).

MATHEWS, PETER, AND LINDA SCHELE
1974   "Lords of Palenque: The Glyphic Evidence," in *Primera Mesa Redonda de Palenque*, pt. 1, ed. M. Greene Robertson, pp. 63–76 (Pebble Beach, Calif.: Robert Louis Stevenson School).

MATOS MOCTEZUMA, EDUARDO
1978 "The Tula Chronology: A Revision," in *Middle Class Mesoamerica: A.D. 400–700,* ed. E. Pasztory, pp. 172–177 (New York: Columbia University Press).
1980 "Teotihuacan: Excavaciones en la Calle de los Muertos (1964)," *Anales de Antropología* 17, no. 1:69–90.

MATSON, FREDERICK R.
1965 "Ceramic Ecology: An Approach to the Study of the Early Cultures of the Near East," in *Ceramics and Man,* ed. F. R. Matson, pp. 202–17 (Chicago: Aldine).

MAUDSLAY, ALFRED P.
1889–
1902 "Archaeology," in *Biologia Centrali-Americana,* 4 vols. (London: R. H. Porter).

MAYER, ENRIQUE
1977 "Beyond the Nuclear Family," in *Andean Kinship and Marriage,* ed. R. Bolton and E. Mayer, pp. 60–80, American Anthropological Association, Special Publication No. 7 (Washington, D.C.).

MEEK, S. E.
1907 "Synopsis of the Fishes of the Great Lakes of Nicaragua," *Field Columbian Museum,* Publication 121, vol. 7, pp. 97–132 (Chicago).

MEIGHAN, CLEMENT E.
1969 "Molluscs as Food Remains in Archaeological Sites," in *Science in Archaeology,* ed. D. Brothwell and E. Higgs, pp. 415–22 (New York: Praeger Publishers).

MENDELSON, E. M.
1958 "Guatemalan Sacred Bundle," *Man* 58:121–26.

MENDELSSOHN, KURT
1971 "A Scientist Looks at Pyramids," *American Scientist* 59:210–20.

MENZEL, DOROTHY
1964 "Style and Time in the Middle Horizon," *Nawpa Pacha* 2:1–106.
1968 "New Data on the Huari Empire in the Middle Horizon Epoch 2A," *Nawpa Pacha* 6:47–115.
1977 *The Archaeology of Ancient Peru and the Work of Max Uhle* (Berkeley: University of California, R. H. Lowie Museum of Anthropology).

MERCER, H. C.
1975 *The Hill-Caves of Yucatan,* with a new introduction by Sir J. E. S. Thompson (Norman: University of Oklahoma).

MERWIN, RAYMOND E.
1913 "The Ruins of the Southern Part of the Peninsula of Yucatan with Special Reference to Their Place in the Maya Culture" (Ph.D. diss., Harvard University).

MERWIN, R. E., AND G. C. VAILLANT
1932 *The Ruins of Holmul, Guatemala,* Memoirs of the Peabody Museum of Archaeology and Ethnology, vol. 3, no. 2 (Cambridge, Mass.: Harvard University).

MICHAEL, HENRY N., AND ELIZABETH K. RALPH
1971   *Dating Techniques for the Archaeologist* (Cambridge, Mass.: M.I.T. Press).

MICHELS, JOSEPH W.
1973   *Dating Methods in Archaeology* (New York: Seminar Press).

MICHELS, JOSEPH W., AND C. BEBRICH
1971   "Obsidian Hydration Dating," in H. N. Michael and E. K. Ralph, *Dating Techniques for the Archaeologist,* pp. 164–221.

MICHELS, JOSEPH W. AND WILLIAM T. SANDERS
1973   *The Pennsylvania State University Kaminaljuyu Project: 1969, 1970 Seasons, Part I - Mound Excavations,* Occasional Papers in Anthropology, no. 9 (University Park: Pennsylvania State University Press).

MICHELS, JOSEPH W., AND WILLIAM T. SANDERS, EDS.
1977–79   Monograph Series on Kaminaljuyu (University Park: Pennsylvania State University Press).

MILES, SUZANNA W.
1952   "An Analysis of Modern Middle American Calendars: A Study in Conservatism," *Twenty-ninth International Congress of Americanists,* vol. 2, pp. 273–84 (New York).
1965   "Sculpture of the Guatemala-Chiapas Highlands and Pacific Slopes, and Associated Hieroglyphs," in *Handbook of Middle American Indians,* vol. 2, ed. G. R. Willey, pp. 237–75 (Austin: University of Texas Press).

MILLER, ARTHUR G.
1977   "Captains of the Itza: Unpublished Mural Evidence from Chichen Itza," in *Social Process in Maya Prehistory,* ed. N. Hammond, pp. 197–225 (London: Academic Press).

MILLON, CLARA
1973   "Painting, Writing, and Polity in Teotihuacan, Mexico," *American Antiquity* 38, no. 3:294–314.

MILLON, RENE
1973   *Urbanization at Teotihuacan, Mexico,* vol. 1, *The Teotihuacan Map, Part One: Text* (Austin, University of Texas Press).
1974   "The Study of Urbanism at Teotihuacan, Mexico," in *Mesoamerican Archaeology: New Approaches,* ed. N. Hammond, pp. 335–62 (London: Duckworth).
1976   "Social Relations in Ancient Teotihuacan," in *The Valley of Mexico,* ed. E. R. Wolf, pp. 205–48 (Albuquerque: University of New Mexico Press, School of American Research Advanced Seminar Series).
1981   "Teotihuacan: City, State, and Civilization," in *Supplement to the Handbook of Middle American Indians,* vol. 1, *Archaeology,* ed. J. A. Sabloff, pp. 198–243 (Austin: University of Texas Press).

MILLON, RENE, BRUCE DREWITT, AND JAMES A. BENNYHOFF
1965   *The Pyramid of the Sun at Teotihuacan: 1959 Excavations,* American Philosophical Society, Transactions, vol. 55, pt. 6 (Philadelphia).

MILLON, RENE, BRUCE DREWITT, AND GEORGE L. COWGILL
1973   *The Teotihuacan Map, Part Two: Maps* (Austin: University of Texas Press).

MILLS, LAWRENCE, ed.
1979 *The Puuc: New Perspectives,* Scholarly Studies in the Liberal Arts, Publication 1 (Pella, Iowa: Central College).

MOHOLY-NAGY, HATTULA
1963 "Shells and Other Marine Material from Tikal," *Estudios de Cultura Maya* 3:65–84.
1975 "Obsidian at Tikal, Guatemala," *Actas del XLI Congreso Internacional de Americanistas,* vol. 1, pp. 511–18 (Mexico City).
1978 "Social and Ceremonial Uses of Mollusks at Tikal, Guatemala," paper presented at the Forty-third Annual Meeting of the Society for American Archaeology, Tucson.
1982 "Artifacts of Shell, Bone, and Ground Stone from the Cenote of Chichen Itza," paper presented at the Forty-seventh Annual Meeting of the Society for American Archaeology, Minneapolis.

MOLLOY, JOHN, AND DAVID H. KELLEY
1981 "A Toltec Dynastic Sequence" (manuscript).

MONZON, ARTURO
1949 *El Calpulli en la Organización Social de los Tenocha* (Mexico City: Instituto de Historia).

MORAN, HUGH A., AND DAVID H. KELLEY
1969 *The Alphabet and the Ancient Calendar Signs,* 2d ed. (Palo Alto, Calif.).

MOREAU, JEAN-FRANCOIS
1978 "L'analyse des coquillages préhistoriques," *Recherches Amerindiennes au Québec* 8, no. 1:53–63.

MORENO, MANUEL
1931 *La Organización Política y Social de los Aztecas* (Mexico City: Universidad Nacional Autonoma).

MORGAN, L. H.
1877 *Ancient Society* (New York: Henry Holt).

MORLEY, SYLVANUS G.
1907 "On a Nephrite Statuette from San Andres Tuxtla, Vera Cruz, Mexico," *American Anthropologist* 9:696–700.
1909 "The Inscriptions of Naranjo, Northern Guatemala," *American Anthropologist* 2:543–62.
1915 *An Introduction to the Study of the Maya Hieroglyphs,* Bureau of American Ethnology, Bulletin 57 (Washington, D.C.: Smithsonian Institution).
1920 *The Inscriptions at Copan,* Carnegie Institution of Washington, Publication 219 (Washington, D.C.).
1946 *The Ancient Maya* (Stanford, Calif.: Stanford University Press).

MORLEYANA
1950 *A Collection of Writings in Memoriam, Sylvanus Griswold Morley, 1883–1948* (Santa Fe: School of American Research and Museum of New Mexico).

MORRIS, CRAIG
1972 "State Settlements in Tawantinsuyu: A Strategy of Compulsory Urbanism," in *Contemporary Archaeology: A Guide to Theory and Contributions,* ed. M. P. Leone, pp. 393–401 (Carbondale: Southern Illinois University Press).

MORRIS, E. H., J. CHARLOT, AND A. A. MORRIS
1931 *The Temple of the Warriors at Chichen Itza,* Carnegie Institution of Washington, Publication 406 (Washington, D.C.).

MORRIS, W.
1980 "Warping Glyphs: A Reading of Maya Textiles," paper presented at the Cuarta Mesa Redonda de Palenque, Palenque, Chiapas.

MORUA (MURUA), MARTIN DE
1922– *Historia de los Incas, Reyes del Peru, de sus Hechos, Costumbres, Trajes y*
25 *Manera de Gobierno* (ca. 1600), Colección de Libros y Documentos Referentes a la Historia de Peru, ed. H. U. Urteaga and C. A. Romero, 2d ser., vol. 4, pp. 1–253, vol. 5, pp. 1–72 (Lima: Sanmarti).

MOSELEY, MICHAEL E.
1968 "Changing Subsistence Patterns: Late Preceramic Archaeology of the Central Peruvian Coast" (Ph.D. diss., Harvard University).
1972 "Demography and Subsistence: An Example of Interaction from Prehistoric Peru," *Southwestern Journal of Anthropology* 28, no. 1:25–49.
1975a "Chan Chan: Andean Alternative of the Preindustrial City," *Science* 187: 219–25.
1975b *The Maritime Foundations of Andean Civilization* (Menlo Park, Calif.: Cummings).
1978 *Peru's Golden Treasures* (Chicago: Field Museum of Natural History).
1983 "Patterns of Settlement and Preservation in the Viru and Moche Valleys," in *Prehistoric Settlement Patterns,* ed. E. Z. Vogt and R. M. Leventhal (Albuquerque: University of New Mexico Press; Cambridge, Mass.: Peabody Museum).

MOSELEY, MICHAEL E., AND KENT C. DAY, eds.
1982 *Chan Chan: Andean Desert City* (Albuquerque: University of New Mexico Press, School of American Research Advanced Seminar Series).

MOSELEY, MICHAEL E., ROBERT E. FELDMAN, AND CHARLES T. ORTLOFF
1981 "Living with Crises: Human Perceptions of Process and Time," in *Biotic Crises in Ecological and Evolutionary Time,* ed. M. Nitiecki, pp. 231–67 (New York: Academic Press).

MOSELEY, MICHAEL E., AND GORDON R. WILLEY
1973 "Aspero, Peru: A Reexamination of the Site and Its Implications," *American Antiquity* 38, no. 4:452–68.

MOTOLINIA, TORIBIO DE BENAVENTE
1971 *Memoriales, o Libro de las Cosas de la Nueva España y de los Naturales de Ella* (Mexico City: Instituto de Investigaciones Historicas).

MUKERJI, DHIRENDRA NATH
1936 "A Correlation of the Mayan and Hindu Calendars," *Indian Culture* 2, no. 4:685–92.

MUMFORD, LEWIS
1961 *The City in History* (New York: Harcourt, Brace, and World).

MUNOZ, JUAN BAUTISTA
1946 "Informe," in *Las Ruinas de Palenque* ed. R. Castañeda P., pp. 41–44 (Guatemala City).

MURPHY, ROBERT C.
1926 "Oceanic and Climatic Phenomena Along the West Coast of South America During 1925," *Geographic Review* 16:26–54.

MURRA, JOHN V.
1958 "On Inca Political Structure," in *Systems of Political Control and Bureaucracy in Human Societies,* ed. V. F. Ray, pp. 30–41, *Proceedings of the 1958 Annual Spring Meeting of the American Ethnological Society.*
1972 "El 'Control Vertical' de un Máximo de Pisos en la Economía de las Sociedades Andinas," in *Visita de la Provincia de Leon de Huanuco (1562),* by Inigo Ortiz de Zuniga, vol. 2, pp. 427–76 (Huanuco, Peru: Universitario Nacional H. Valdizan).
1980 *The Economic Organization of the Inka State* (Greenwich: JAI Press).

MURUA, MARTIN DE
See Morua, Martin de

MYERHOFF, B. G.
1974 *Peyote Hunt: The Sacred Journey of the Huichol Indians* (Ithaca, N.Y.: Cornell University Press).

NELSON, F. W., R. B. SIDRYS, AND R. D. HOLMES
1978 "Trace Element Analysis by X-Ray Fluorescence of Obsidian Artifacts from Guatemala and Belize," in *Excavations at Seibal, Department of Peten, Guatemala: Artifacts* by G. R. Willey, pp. 153–61, Memoirs of the Peabody Museum of Archaeology and Ethnology, vol. 14, no. 1 (Cambridge, Mass.: Harvard University).

NEWELL, H. P., AND A. D. KRIEGER
1949 *The George C. Davis Site, Cherokee County, Texas,* Memoirs of the Society for American Archaeology, vol. 14, no. 4 (Salt Lake City).

NIALS, FRED L., ERIC E. DEEDS, MICHAEL EL MOSELEY,
SHELIA G. POZORSKY, THOMAS G. POZORSKY, AND ROBERT A. FELDMAN
1979a,b "El Niño: The Catastrophic Flooding of Coastal Peru, Parts I and II," *Field Museum of Natural History Bulletin* 50, no. 7, pp. 4–14, and 50, no. 8, pp. 4–10 (Chicago).

NICHOLSON, HENRY B.
1971 "Religion in Pre-Hispanic Central Mexico," in *Handbook of Middle American Indians,* vol. 10, ed. R. Wauchope, pp. 395–445 (Austin: University of Texas Press).

NIETSCHMANN, B.
1973   Between Land and Water: The Subsistence of the Moskito Indians, Eastern Nicaragua (New York: Seminar Press).

NORMAN, V. GARTH
1973   Izapa Sculpture: Album, Papers of the New World Archaeological Foundation 30 (Provo, Utah: Brigham Young University).

NOYES, E.
1932   Fray Alonso Ponce in Yucatan (1588), Middle American Research Institute, Publication 4 (New Orleans: Tulane University).

NUNEZ, LAUTARO, AND THOMAS DILLEHAY
1978   Movilidad Giratoria, Armonia Social y Desarollo Meridionales: Patrones de Tráfico e Interacción Económica (Antofagasta, Chile: Universidad del Norte).

OAKES, MAUD
1951   The Two Crosses of Todos Santos: Survivals of Mayan Religious Ritual (New York: Pantheon Books).

OBREGOSO R., EFRAÍN
1967   Otuzco, Ciudad Andina (Lima: Editorial Jurídica).

OLSEN, STANLEY J.
1971   Zooarchaeology: Animal Bones in Archaeology and Their Interpretation, Addison-Wesley Module no. 2 (Reading, Mass.: Addison-Wesley).
1972   "Animal Remains from Altar de Sacrificios," in The Artifacts of Altar de Sacrificios by G. R. Willey, Papers of the Peabody Museum of Archaeology and Ethnology, vol. 64, no. 1, pp. 243–46 (Cambridge, Mass.: Harvard University).
1978   "Special Problems of Faunal Analysis in the Maya Area," paper presented at the Forty-third Annual Meeting of the Society for American Archaeology, Tucson.

OPPOLZER, T. R.
1962   Canon of Eclipses, trans. O. Gingerich (New York: Dover Press).

ORIGEN DE LOS MEXICANOS
1941   "Origen de los Mexicanos," in Nuevo Colección de Documentos para la Historia de México, pp. 256–80 (Mexico City: Editorial Chavez Hayhoe).

ORTIZ DE ZUNIGA, INIGO
1967   Visita de la Provincia de Leon de Huanuco en 1562, ed. J. V. Murra, Documentos para la Historia y Etnología de Huanuco y la Selva Central 1 (Huanuco, Peru: Universidad Nacional Hermilio Valdizan).

OSBORN, ALAN J.
1977a   "Prehistoric Utilization of Marine Resources in Coastal Peru: How Much Do We Understand?" paper presented at the Seventy-sixth Annual Meeting of the American Anthropological Association, Houston.
1977b   "Strandloopers, Mermaids, and Other Fairy Tales: Ecological Determinants of Marine Resource Utilization—the Peruvian Case," in For Theory Build-

ing in Archaeology, ed. L. R. Binford, pp. 157–205 (New York: Academic Press).

OWEN, NANCY K.
1975 "The Use of Eclipse Data to Determine the Maya Correlation Number," in *Archaeoastronomy in Pre-Columbian America,* ed. A. Aveni, pp. 237–46 (Austin: University of Texas Press).

PADDEN, R. C.
1967 *The Hummingbird and the Hawk,* (Columbus: Ohio State University Press).

PAHL, GARY
1977 "The Inscriptions of Rio Amarillo and Los Higos, Secondary Centers of the Southeastern Maya Frontier," *Journal of Latin American Lore,* 3:133–54.

PALERM, ANGEL
1972 *Agricultura y Sociedad en Mesoamérica* (Mexico City: Centro de Investigaciones Superiores).

PALERM, ANGEL, AND ERIC R. WOLF
1957 "Ecological Potential and Cultural Development in Mesoamerica," in *Social Science Monographs,* vol. 3, pp. 1–32 (Washington, D.C.: Pan American Union).

PARMALEE, P. W., AND W. E. KLIPPEL
1974 "Freshwater Mussels as a Prehistoric Food Source," *American Antiquity* 39:421–34.

PARSONS, LEE A.
1967 "An Early Maya Stela on the Pacific Coast of Guatemala," *Estudios de Cultura Maya* 6:171–98.
1967– *Bilbao, Guatemala, Part II,* Publications in Anthropology, no. 12 (Milwaukee:
69 Milwaukee Public Museum).
1973 "Iconographic Notes on a New Izapan Stela from Abaj Takalik," *Atti del XL Congresso Internazionale Degli Americanisti,* vol. 1, pp. 203–12 (Rome).
1980 *Pre-Columbian Art,* The Morton D. May and the Saint Louis Art Museum Collections (New York: Harper and Row).
in *A Study of the Monumental Stone Sculpture of Kaminaljuyu, Guatemala and*
press *the Southern Pacific Coast* (Princeton University Press).

PASZTORY, ESTER, ed.
1978 *Middle Classic Mesoamerica:* A.D. *400–700* (New York: Columbia University Press).

PAULSEN, ALLISON C.
1976 "Environment and Empire: Climatic Factors in Prehistoric Andean Culture Change, *World Archaeology* 8:121–32.

PENDERGAST, DAVID M.
1964 "Excavaciones en la Cueva Eduardo Quiroz, Districto Cayo, Honduras Británica," *Estudios de Cultura Maya* 4:119–39.

1967 *Palenque: The Walker-Caddy Expedition to the Ancient Maya City, 1839–40*. (Norman: University of Oklahoma Press).
1969a *Altun Ha, British Honduras (Belize): The Sun God's Tomb*, Royal Ontario Museum of Art and Archaeology, Occasional Papers, no. 19 (Toronto).
1969b *The Prehistory of Actun Balam, British Honduras*, Royal Ontario Museum of Art and Archaeology, Occasional Papers, no. 16 (Toronto).
1971 *Excavations at Eduardo Quiroz Cave, British Hondruas*, Royal Ontario Museum of Art and Archaeology, Occasional Papers, no. 21 (Toronto).
1974 *Excavations at Actun Polbilche, Belize*, Royal Ontario Museum of Art and Archaeology, Monograph no. 1 (Toronto).
1979 *Excavations at Altun Ha, Belize, 1964–1970*, vol. 1 (Toronto: Royal Ontario Museum of Art and Archaeology).
1981 "Lamanai, Belize: Summary of Excavation Results 1974-1980," *Journal of Field Archaeology* 8:29–53.

PIÑA CHAN, R.
1970 *Informe Preliminar de la Reciente Exploración del Cenote Sagrado de Chichen Itza*, Instituto Nacional de Antropología e Historia, Investigaciones 24 (Mexico City).

PINGREE, DAVID
1963 "Astronomy and Astrology in India and Iran," *ISIS* 54:229–46.

PIO PEREZ, JUAN
1843 "Ancient Chronology of Yucatan; or a True Exposition of the Method Used by the Indians for Computing Time," in *Incidents of Travel in Yucatan*, by J. L. Stephens, vol. 1, pp. 434–59; vol. 2, pp. 465–69.

PIZARRO, PEDRO
1844 *Relación del Descubrimiento y Conquista de los Reinos del Peru, y del Gobierno y Orden que los Naturales Tenian (1571)*, Colección de Documentos Ineditos para la Historia de España, compiled by Martín Fernández Navarrete; Miguel Salva; and Pedro Sainz de Baranda, vol. 5, pp. 201–388. (Madrid: Imprenta de la Viuda de Calera).
1921 *Relation of the Discovery and Conquest of the Kingdoms of Peru (1571)*, trans. P. A. Means, Documents and Narratives Concerning the Discovery and Conquest of Latin America, no. 4, 2 vols. (New York: Cortés Society).

POGO, ALEXANDER
1937 "Maya Astronomy," *Yearbook* 36:24–35, Carnegie Institution of Washington (Washington, D.C.).

POHL, J.
1979 "Rain Gods and Flayed Skins: A Costume Element Complex Associated with Arrow and Spear Sacrifices," paper presented at the Dumbarton Oaks Conference on Ritual Sacrifice in Precolumbian Mesoamerica, Washington, D.C.

POHL, MARY
1976 "The Ethnozoology of the Maya: An Analysis of Faunal Remains from Five Sites in Peten, Guatemala" (Ph.D. diss., Harvard University).
1980 "The Terminal Classic Period Economy at Tikal," paper presented at the

Forty-fifth Annual Meeting of the Society for American Archaeology, Philadelphia.
1981a "The Deer as a Major Supernatural Being in Ancient Maya Religion" (manuscript).
1981b "Ritual Continuity and Transformation in Mesoamerica: Reconstructing the Ancient Maya *Cuch* Ritual," *American Antiquity* 46:513–29.

POHL, MARY, AND J. POHL
1981 "Deciphering Ancient Maya Art," paper presented at the Forty-sixth Annual Meeting of the Society for American Archaeology, San Diego.
n.d. "Ancient Maya Cave Rituals," *Archaeology*, forthcoming.

POLLOCK, H. E. D.
1940 "Sources and Methods in the Study of Maya Architecture," in *The Maya and Their Neighbors*, ed. C. L. Hay et al., pp. 179–201 (New York: D. Appleton-Century).

POLLOCK, H. E. D., AND D. E. RAY
1957 *Notes on Vertebrate Animal Remains from Mayapan*, Carnegie Institution of Washington, Report no. 41 (Washington, D.C.).

POLLOCK, H. E. D., R. L. ROYS, T. PROSKOURIAKOFF, AND A. L. SMITH
1962 *Mayapan, Yucatan, Mexico*, Carnegie Institution of Washington, Publication 619, (Washington, D.C.).

POLO DE ONDEGARDO, JUAN
1916a *Los Errores y Supersticiones de los Indios, Sacadas del Tratado y Averiquación que Hizo el Licenciado Polo* (1559), Colección de Libros y Documentos Referentes a la Historia del Peru, ed. H. H. Urteaga and C. A. Romero, vol. 3, pp. 1–43 (Lima: Sanmarti).
1916b *Relación de los Fundamentos Acerca del Notable Dano que Resulta de No guardar a los Indios sus Fueros* (1571), Colección de Libros y Documentos Referentes a la Historia del Peru, ed. H. H. Urteaga and C. A. Romero, vol. 3, pp. 45–188 (Lima: Sanmarti).
1917 *Translado de un Cartapacio a Manera de Borrador que Quedo en los Papeles del Licenciado Polo de Ondegardo . . .* (1567), Colección de Libros y Documentos Referentes a la Historia del Peru, ed. H. H. Urteaga and C. A. Romero, vol. 4, pp. 95–138 (Lima: Sanmarti).

PORTER, P.
1965 "Environmental Potentials and Economic Opportunities: A Background for Cultural Adaptation," *American Anthropologist* 67:409–20.

POZORSKI, SHELIA G.
1976 "Prehistoric Subsistence Patterns and Site Economics in the Moche Valley, Peru" (Ph.D. diss., University of Texas).

POZORSKI, SHELIA, AND THOMAS POZORSKI
1979a "Alto Salaverry: A Peruvian Coastal Preceramic City," *Annals of the Carnegie Museum* 48:337–75.
1979b "An Early Subsistence Exchange System in the Moche Valley, Peru," *Journal of Field Archaeology* 6, no. 4:413–32.

POZORSKI, THOMAS G.
1976   "Caballo Muerto: A Complex of Early Ceramic Sites in the Moche Valley, Peru" (Ph.D. diss., University of Texas).

PRESCOTT, W. H.
1844   *History of the Conquest of Mexico with a Preliminary View of the Ancient Mexican Civilization and the Life of the Conqueror Hernando Cortez,* 3 vols., (London).

PRING, DUNCAN C.
1977   "Influence or Intrusion? The Protoclassic in the Maya Lowlands," in *Social Process in Maya Prehistory,* ed. N. Hammond, pp. 136–66 (New York: Academic Press).

PROSKOURIAKOFF, TATIANA
1946   *An Album of Maya Architecture,* Carnegie Institution of Washington, Publication 558 (Washington, D.C.).
1950   *A Study of Classic Maya Sculpture,* Carnegie Institution of Washington, Publication 593 (Washington, D.C.).
1960   "Historical Implications of a Pattern of Dates at Piedras Negras, Guatemala," *American Antiquity,* 25:454–75.
1973   "The Hand-grasping-fish and Associated Glyphs on Classic Maya Monuments," in *Mesoamerican Writing Systems,* ed. E. Benson, pp. 165–78 (Washington, D.C.: Dumbarton Oaks).
1974   *Jades from the Cenote of Sacrifice, Chichen Itza, Yucatan,* Memoirs of the Peabody Museum of Archaeology and Ethnology, vol. 10 (Cambridge, Mass.: Harvard University).

PULESTON, DENNIS E.
1968   "*Brosimum Alicastrum* as a Subsistence Alternative for the Classic Maya of the Central Southern Lowlands" (M.A. thesis, University of Pennsylvania).
1974   "Intersite Areas in the Vicinity of Tikal and Uaxactun," in *Mesoamerican Archaeology: New Approaches,* ed. N. Hammond, pp. 303–34 (London: Duckworth).

PULGAR VIDAL, JAVIER
1972   *Geografía del Perú: Las Ocho Regiones Naturales del Peru,* 7th ed. (Lima: Editorial Universo).

PROULX, DONALD
1973   *Archaeological Investigations in the Nepena Valley, Peru,* Research Reports, Department of Anthropology, University of Massachusetts, no. 13 (Amherst).

QUIRARTE, JACINTO
1973   "Izapan-Style Art: A Study of Its Form and Meaning," *Studies in Pre-Columbian Art and Archaeology,* no. 10 (Washington, D.C.: Dumbarton Oaks).
1976   "Izapan Style Antecedents for the Maya Serpent in Celestial Dragon and Serpent Bar Contexts," *Actas del XXIII Congreso Internacional de Historia del Arte: España Entre el Mediteraneo y el Atlantico,* vol. 1, pp. 227–37 (Granada: Universidad de Granada, Departmento de Historia del Arte).

RABIN, EMILY
1981 "Oconana in the Valley of Oaxaca," paper presented at the Twenty-ninth Annual Meeting of the American Society for Ethnohistory, Colorado Springs.

RANDALL, J. E.
1968 *Caribbean Reef Fishes* (Jersey City, N.J.: T. F. H. Publishing).

RATHJE, WILLIAM L.
1970 "Socio-Political Implications of Lowland Maya Burials: Methodology and Tentative Hypotheses," *World Archaeology* 1, no. 3:359–74.

RATTRAY, EVELYN CHILDS
1981 "The Teotihuacan Ceramic Chronology: Early Tzacualli to Metepec Phases," manuscript for pt. 1 of *Ceramics and Chronology,* vol. 4 of *Urbanization at Teotihuacan,* ed. Rene Millon (Austin: University of Texas Press).

RAY, C. E.
1956 "Preliminary Checklist of Vertebrate Remains from Mayapan, Yucatan," manuscript.

REDFIELD, ROBERT
1941 *The Folk Culture of Yucatan* (Chicago: University of Chicago Press).

REDFIELD, ROBERT, AND A. VILLA-ROJAS
1962 *Chan Kom: A Maya Village,* 2d ed. (Chicago: University of Chicago Press).

REINA, RUBEN E.
1967 *The Law of the Saints: A Pokomam Pueblo and Its Community Culture* (New York: Bobbs-Merrill).
1969 "Eastern Guatemalan Highlands: The Pokomames and Chorti," in *Handbook of Middle American Indians,* vol. 7, ed. E. Z. Vogt, pp. 101–32 (Austin: University of Texas Press).

REINA, RUBIN E., AND ROBERT M. HILL II
1978 *The Traditional Pottery of Guatemala* (Austin: University of Texas Press).

RELACION DE LA GENEALOGIA Y LINAJE
1941 "Relación de la Genealogía y Linaje," in *Nueva Colección de Documentos para la Historia de México,* pp. 240–56 (Mexico: Editorial Chavez Hayhoe).

RENFREW, COLIN
1972 *The Emergence of Civilization: The Cyclades and the Aegean in the Third Millennium B.C.* (London: Methuen).
1974 "Beyond a Subsistence Economy: The Evolution of Social Organization in Prehistoric Europe," in *Reconstructing Complex Societies,* ed. C. B. Moore, American Schools of Oriental Research Bulletin, no. 20.

RICE, DONALD S., AND PRUDENCE M. RICE
1981 "Muralla de Leon: A Lowland Maya Fortification," *Journal of Field Archaeology* 8:271–88.

RICHARDS, H. G.
1962 "Studies on the Marine Pleistocene: Part 1, The Marine Pleistocene of the Americas and Europe," *Transactions of the American Philosophical Society* 52, no. 3.

RICHARDSON, JAMES B., III
1974   "Holocene Beach Ridges Between the Chira River and Punta Parinas, Northwest Peru, and the Archaeological Sequence," paper presented at the Thirty-ninth Annual Meeting of the Society for American Archaeology, Washington, D.C.
1981   "Maritime Adaptations on the Peruvian Coast: A Critique and Future Directions," paper presented at the Annual Meeting of the Society for American Archaeology (San Diego).

RICKETSON, OLIVER G., AND E. A. RICKETSON
1937   *Uaxactun, Guatemala: Group E—1926–1931,* Carnegie Institution of Washington, Publication 477 (Washington, D.C.).

RIO, ANTONIO DEL
1822   *Description of the Ruins of an Ancient City, Discovered New Palenque, in the Kingdom of Guatemala in Spanish America,* trans. Dr. Paul Felix Cabrera (London).

ROBERTSON, ROBIN A.
1973   "Cooking Practices as Detected in Animal Bone Coloration at Dun Ailinne, Ireland," paper presented at the Thirty-ninth Annual Meeting of the Society for American Archaeology, Washington, D.C.
1980   "Late Preclassic Ceramics from Cerros, Belize: Their Importance for Interpreting the Protoclassic," paper presented at the Seventy-ninth Annual Meeting of the American Anthropological Association, Washington, D.C.

ROBERTSON-FREIDEL, ROBIN A.
1980   "The Ceramics from Cerros: A Late Preclassic Site in Northern Belize" (Ph.D. diss., Harvard University).

ROBICSEK, F.
1975   *A Study of Maya Art and History: The Mat Symbol* (New York: Museum of the American Indian, Heye Foundation).

ROSTWOROWSKI DE DIEZ CANSECO, MARIA
1962   "Nuevos Datos Sobre Tenacia de Tierras Reales en el Incario," *Revista del Museo Nacional* (Lima) 31:130–64.
1966   "Las Tierras Reales y su Mano de Obra en el Tahuantinsuyu," *Actas y Memorias del 36 Congreso Internacional de Americanistas,* vol. 2, pp. 31–34 (Seville).
1973   "Plantaciones Prehispánicas de Coca en la Vertiente del Pacifico," *Revista del Museo Nacional* (Lima) 39:193–224.

ROUNDS, J.
1979   "Lineage, Class, and Power in the Aztec State," *American Ethnologist* 6:73–86.

ROWE, JOHN H.
1944   *An Introduction to the Archaeology of Cuzco,* Papers of the Peabody Museum of Archaeology and Ethnology, vol. 22, no. 2 (Cambridge, Mass.: Harvard University).
1946   "Inca Culture at the Time of the Spanish Conquest," in *Handbook of South*

American Indians, Vol. II: The Andean Civilizations, ed. J. H. Steward, pp. 183–330, Bureau of American Ethnology, Bulletin 143 (Washington, D.C.: Smithsonian Institution).
1948 "The Kingdom of Chimor," *Acta Americana* 6:26–59.
1956 "Archaeological Explorations in Southern Peru, 1954-1955," *American Antiquity* 22, no. 2:135–50.
1962 "Stages and Periods in Archaeological Interpretations," *Southwestern Journal of Anthropology* 18, no. 1:40–54.
1963 "Urban Settlements in Ancient Peru," *Nawpa Pacha* 1:1–27.
1966 "Diffusionism and Archaeology," *American Antiquity* 31, no. 3:334–37.
1967 "What Kind of a Settlement Was Inca Cuzco?" *Nawpa Pacha* 5:59–77.

ROYS, RALPH L.
1931 *Ethnobotany of the Maya,* Middle American Research Institute, Publication 2 (New Orleans: Tulane University).
1933 *The Book of Chilam Balam of Chumayel,* Carnegie Institution of Washington, Publication 438 (Washington, D.C.).
1943 *The Indian Background of Colonial Yucatan,* Carnegie Institution of Washington, Publication 548 (Washington, D.C.).
1949 "The Prophecies for the Maya Tuns or Years in the Books of Chilam Balam of Tizimin and Mani," Carnegie Institution of Washington, *Contribution* 51, no. 10, pp. 153–86 (Washington, D.C.).
1965 *Ritual of the Bacabs* (Norman: University of Oklahoma Press).

RUBIN DE LA BORBOLLA, DANIEL F.
1947 "Teotihuacan: Ofrendas de los Templos de Quetzalcoatl," *Anales del Instituto Nacional de Anthropología e Historia* 2:61–72.

RUPPERT, K.
1935 *The Caracol at Chichen Itza, Yucatan, Mexico,* Carnegie Institution of Washington, Publication 454 (Washington, D.C.).

RUPPERT, KARL, AND JOHN H. DENISON, JR.
1943 *Archaeological Reconnaissance in Campeche, Quintana Roo and Peten,* Carnegie Institution of Washington, Publication 543 (Washington, D.C.).

RUZ LHUILLIER, ALBERTO
1968 *Costumbres Funererias de los Antiguos Mayas* (Mexico: Universidad Nacional Autónoma de México, Seminario de Cultura Maya).
1973 *El Templo de las Inscripciones* (Mexico City: INAH).

SAALMAN, HOWARD
1968 *Medieval Cities* (New York: Braziller).

SABLOFF, JEREMY A.
1970 "Type Descriptions of the Fine Paste Ceramics of the Bayal Boca Complex, Seibal, Peten, Guatemala," in *Monographs and Papers in Maya Archaeology,* ed. W. Bullard, pp. 357–404, Papers of the Peabody Museum of Archaeology and Ethnology, vol. 61 (Cambridge, Mass.: Harvard University).
1973 "Continuity and Disruption During the Terminal Late Classic Times at Seibal: Ceramic and Other Evidence," in *Classic Maya Collapse,* ed. T. P. Culbert,

pp. 107–32 (Albuquerque, University of New Mexico Press, School of American Research Advanced Seminar Series).

1975   *Excavations at Seibal: The Ceramics,* Memoirs of the Peabody Museum of Archaeology and Ethnology, vol. 13, no. 2 (Cambridge, Mass.: Harvard University).

SABLOFF, JEREMY A., AND WILLIAM L. RATHJE
1975   "The Rise of a Maya Merchant Class," *Scientific American* 233, no. 4:72–82.

SABLOFF, JEREMY A., AND WILLIAM L. RATHJE, eds.
1975   *A Study of Changing Pre-Columbian Commercial Systems: Cozumel, Mexico,* Monographs of the Peabody Museum of Archaeology and Ethnology, no. 3 (Cambridge, Mass.: Harvard University).

SABLOFF, JEREMY A., AND GORDON R. WILLEY
1967   "The Collapse of Maya Civilization in the Southern Maya Lowlands: A Consideration of History and Process," *Southwestern Journal of Anthropology* 24, no. 4:311–36.

SAHAGUN, FRAY BERNARDINO DE
1950–65   *Florentine Codex: General History of the Things of New Spain,* trans. C. E. Dibble and A. J. O. Anderson, 11 vols. (Santa Fe: School of American Research and University of Utah).

SAHLINS, MARSHALL D.
1958   *Social Stratification in Polynesia* (Seattle: University of Washington Press).

SANCHO (DE LA HOZ), PEDRO
1917   *An Account of the Conquest of Peru (1534),* trans. Philip A. Means, Documents and Narratives Concerning the Discovery and Conquest of Latin America, no. 2 (New York: Cortes Society).

1962   *Relación de la Conquista del Peru (1534),* ed. Joaquín García Icazbalceta, Biblioteca Tenanitla, no. 2 (Madrid: Ediciones José Porrua Turanzas).

SANDERS, WILLIAM T.
1956   "The Central Mexican Symbiotic Region," in *Prehistoric Settlement Patterns in the New World,* ed. G. R. Willey, pp. 115–27 (New York: Wenner-Gren Foundation).

1968   "Hydraulic Agriculture, Economic Symbiosis and the Evolution of States in Central Mexico," in *Anthropological Archaeology in the Americas,* ed. B. Meggers, pp. 88–107 (Washington, D.C.: Anthropological Society).

1981a   "Ecological Adaptation in the Basin of Mexico 23,000 B.C. to the Present," in *Supplement to the Handbook of Middle American Indians, Vol. I, Archaeology,* ed. J. A. Sabloff, pp. 147–97 (Austin: University of Texas Press).

1981b   "Classic Maya Settlement Patterns and Ethnographic Analogy," in *Lowland Maya Settlement Patterns,* ed. W. Ashmore, pp. 351–69 (Albuquerque: University of New Mexico Press, School of American Research Advanced Seminar Series).

n.d.   "Program for Investigations in the Second Phase of the Proyecto Arqueologico Copan" (manuscript).

SANDERS, WILLIAM T., JEFFREY R. PARSONS, AND ROBERT S. SANTLEY
1979 *The Basin of Mexico: Ecological Processes in the Evolution of a Civilization* (New York: Academic Press).

SANDERS, WILLIAM T., AND BARBARA J. PRICE
1968 *Mesoamerica: The Evolution of a Civilization* (New York: Random House).

SANDERS, WILLIAM T., AND ROBERT S. SANTLEY
1977 "A Prehispanic Irrigation System Near Santa Calra Xalostoc in the Basin of Mexico," *American Antiquity* 42:582–88.

SANDERS, WILLIAM T., AND DAVID WEBSTER
n.d. "El Reconocimiento del Valle," in *Primer Simposio del I.H.A.H.*, ed. Vito Veliz (Tegucigalpa: Universidad Nacional Autonoma de Honduras, forthcoming).

SANTILLAN, FERNANDO DE
1879 "Relación de Origen, Descendencia, Política y Gobierno de los Incas (1563–64)," in *Tres Relaciones de Antiguedades Peruanas*, ed. M. Jiménez de la Espada, pp. 1–133 (Madrid: Imprenta y Fundición de M. Tello).

SAPPER, KARL
1895a "Altindianische Ansiedlungen in Guatemala und Chiapas," *Veroffentlichungen aus dem Koniglichen Mueum fur Volkerkuunde* 4:13–20.
1895b "Altindianische Ansiedlungen und Bauten in Nordlichen Mittelamerika," *Globus* 68:165–69, 183–89.
1898 "Die Ruinen von Mixco (Guatemala)," *Internationales Archiv fur Ethnographie* 11:1–6.

SARMIENTO DE GAMBOA, PEDRO
1942 *Historia de los Incas (1572)*, collección Horreo, no. 10 (Buenos Aires: Emece Editores).

SATTERTHWAITE, LINTON
1947 *Concepts and Structures of Maya Calendrical Arithmetics*, University of Pennsylvania Museum and the Philadelphia Anthropological Society, no. 3 (Philadelphia).
1962 "An Appraisal of a New Maya-Christian Calendar Correlation," *Estudios de Cultura Maya* 2:251–76.
1964 "Long Count Positions of Maya Dates in the Dresden Codex, with Notes on Lunar Positions and the Correlation Problem," *Proceedings of the Thirty-Fifth International Congress of Americanists*, pt. 2, pp. 47–67 (Mexico City).
1965 "Calendrics of the Maya Lowlands," in *Handbook of Middle American Indians*, vol. 3, ed. Gordon R. Willey, pp. 603–31 (Austin: University of Texas Press).
1967 "Radiocarbon and Maya Long Count Dating of 'Structure 10' (Str. 5d-52, first story), Tikal," *Revista Mexicana de Estudios Antropológicas* 21:225–49.

SATTERTHWAITE, LINTON, AND ELIZABETH K. RALPH
1960 "Radiocarbon Dates and the Maya Correlation Problem," *American Antiquity* 26:165–84.

SAUL, FRANK P.
1975 "The Maya and Their Neighbors (1974): As Recorded in Their Skeletons," in *The Maya and Their Neighbors,* Peabody Museum of Archaeology and Ethnology, Publication 5 (Cambridge, Mass.: Harvard University).

SAVAGE, H.
1978 "Faunal Findings in Cave Sites in Belize," paper presented at the Forty-Third Annual Meeting of the Society for American Archaeology, Tucson.

SAVILLE, MARSHALL H.
1892 "Explorations on the Main Structure of Copan, Honduras," *Proceedings of the American Association for the Advancement of Science* 41:271–75.

SCARBOROUGH, VERNON L.
1980 "The Settlement System in a Late Preclassic Maya Community: Cerros, Northern Belize" (Ph.D. diss., Southern Methodist University).

SCHAEDEL, RICHARD P.
1951a "Major Ceremonial and Population Centers in Northern Peru," *Selected Papers of the Twenty-Ninth International Congress of Americanists,* ed. S. Tax, vol. 1, pp. 232–43.
1951b "Mochica Murals at Panamarca," *Archaeology* 4:145–54.
1978 "Early State of the Incas," in *The Early State,* ed. H. Claessen and P. Skalnik, pp. 289–320 (The Hague: Mouton).

SCHELE, LINDA
1974 "Observations on the Cross Motif at Palenque," in *Primera Mesa Redonda de Palenque,* pt. 1, ed. M. Greene Robertson, pp. 41–61 (Pebble Beach, Calif.: Robert Louis Stevenson School).
1976 "Accession Iconography of Chan-Bahlum in the Group of the Cross at Palenque," in *The Art, Iconography and Dynastic History of Palenque (Mesa Redonda de Palenque),* pt. 3, ed. M. Greene Robertson, pp. 9–34 (Pebble Beach, Calif.: Robert Louis Stevenson School).
1977 "Palenque: The House of the Dying Sun," in *Native American Astronomy,* ed. A. Aveni, pp. 42–56 (Austin: University of Texas Press).

SCHELLHAS, PAUL
1904 *Representations of Deities of the Maya Manuscripts,* Papers of the Peabody Museum of Archaeology and Ethnology, vol. 4, no. 1 (Cambridge, Mass.: Harvard University).

SCHOLES, F. V., AND RALPH L. ROYS
1948 *The Maya Chontal Indians of Acalan-Tixchel,* Carnegie Institution of Washington, Publication 560 (Washington, D.C.).

SCHOLES, F. V., AND E. B. ADAMS, eds.
1938 *Don Diego de Quijada, Alcalde Mayor de Yucatan 1561–1565* (Mexico: Antigua Librería Robredo).

SCHOVE, DEREK J.
1976 "Maya Chronology and the Spectrum of Time," *Nature* 261:471–73.
1977 "Maya Dates, A.D. 352–1296," *Nature* 263:670.
1980 "Maya Correlations Quantitatively Evaluated" (manuscript).

SCHRAM, R.
1908   Kalendariographische und Chronologiscge Tafeln (Leipzig).
SCHULZ, R. P. C.
1955   "Dos Variantes Nuevas del Calendario Chinanteco," *El Mexico Antiguo* 8:233–46.
SCHULTZE-JENA, L.
1946   *La Vida y las Creencias de los Indígenos Quiches de Guatemala*, trans. A. G. Carrera and H. D. Sapper, Publicaciones Especiales del Instituto Indigenista Nacional, no. 1 (Guatemala).
SEJOURNE, LAURETTE
1966   *Arquitectura y Pintura en Teotihuacan* (Mexico City: Siglo Veintiuno).
SEJOURNE, LAURETTE, AND GRACIELA SALICRUP
1965   "Arquitectura y Arqueología," *Revista de la Universidad de México* 19, no. 7:4–8.
SELER, EDUARD
1895   *Wandmalerei von Mitla: Eine Mexikanische Biderschrift in Fresko, Nach Eigenen, An Ort und Stelle Aufgenommenen Zeichnungen Herausgegeben und Arlautent* (Berlin).
1902–   *Gesammelte Abhandlungen zur Amerikanischen Sprachun Altertumskunde*
23   (Berlin).
1915   "Beobachtungen und Studien in den Ruinen von Palenque," *Einzelausgabe aus den Anhandlungen der Koniglichen Preussichen Akademie der Wissenschaften*, Akademie der Wissenschaften, no. 5 (Berlin).
1917   "Die Ruinen von Uxmal," *Einzelausgabe aus den Anhandlungen der Koniglichen Preussischen Akademic der Wissenschaften*, Akademie der Wissenschaften, no. 3 (Berlin).
1960–   *Gesammalte Abhandlungen*, 5 vols. (Graz, Austria: Akademischen Druk-
61   und Verlagsanstalt).
SERVICE, ELMAN R.
1962   *Primitive Social Organization* (New York: Random House).
SEVERIN, GREGORY M.
1981   *The Paris Codex: Decoding an Astronomical Ephemeris*, American Philosophical Society, Transactions 71, pt. 5 (Philadelphia).
SHARER, ROBERT J.
1978a   "Archaeology and History at Quirigua, Guatemala," *Journal of Field Archaeology* 5:51–70.
1978b   *The Prehistory of Chalchuapa, El Salvador*, vol. 3 (Philadelphia: University of Pennsylvania Press).
SHARER, ROBERT J., AND JAMES C. GIFFORD
1970   "Preclassic Ceramics from Chalchuapa, El Salvador, and Their Relationship with the Maya Lowlands," *American Antiquity* 35, no. 4:441–62.
SHARER, ROBERT J., AND CHRISTOPHER JONES
1980   "Archaeological Investigations in the Site Core of Quirigua," *Expedition* 23, no. 1:11–19.

SHEETS, P. D., AND D. C. BATHGATE
1982 "Ritual and Utilitarian Aspects of the Chipped Stone Artifacts from the Sacred Cenote at Chichen Itza," paper presented at the Forty-Seventh Annual Meeting of the Society for American Archaeology, Minneapolis.

SHIMADA, IZUMII
1978 "Commodity and Labor Flow at Moche V Pampa Grande," *American Antiquity* 43, no. 4:569–93.

SHOOK, E. M., AND A. V. KIDDER
1952 *Mound E-III-3, Kaminaljuyu, Guatemala,* Carnegie Institution of Washington, Contribution 53, Publication 596 (Washington, D.C.).

SIDRYS, RAYMOND V.
1976 "Classic Maya Obsidian Trade," *American Antiquity* 41:449–64.

SIEMENS, ALFRED H. AND DENNIS E. PULESTON
1972 "Ridged Fields and Associated Feature in Southern Campeche: New Perspectives on the Lowland Maya," *American Antiquity* 37:228–39.

SMILEY, CHARLES H.
1960 "A New Correlation of the Mayan and Christian Calendars," *Nature* 188: 215–16.
1961 "Bases Astronómicas para una Nueva Correlación entre los Calendarios Mayas y Cristianos," *Estudios de Cultura Maya* 1:237–42.

SMITH, A. LEDYARD
1950 *Uaxactun, Guatemala: Excavations of 1931–1937,* Carnegie Institution of Washington, Publication 588 (Washington, D.C.).
1962 "Residential and Associated Structures at Mayapan, Yucatan, Mexico," in *Mayapan, Yucatan, Mexico,* H. E. D. Pollock et al., Carnegie Institution of Washington, Publication 619 (Washington, D.C.).
1972 *Excavations at Altar de Sacrificios,* Papers of the Peabody Museum of Archaeology and Ethnology, vol. 62 (Cambridge, Mass.: Harvard University).
1982 *Excavations at Seibal, Department of Peten, Major Architecture and Caches,* Memoirs of the Peabody Museum of Archaeology and Ethnology, vol. 15, no. 1 (Cambridge, Mass.: Harvard University).

SMITH, A. L. AND A. V. KIDDER
1943 *Explorations in the Motagua Valley, Guatemala,* Carnegie Institution of Washington, Contributions to American Anthropology and History, no. 41 (Washington, D.C.).

SMITH, JOHN WILLIAMSON, JR.
1978 "The Recuay Culture: A Reconstruction Based on Artistic Motifs" (Ph.D. diss., University of Texas).

SMITH, ROBERT E.
1953 "Cenote X-Coton at Mayapan," Carnegie Institution of Washington, Department of Archaeology, *Current Reports,* no. 5, pp. 67–81 (Washington, D.C.).
1954 "Cenote Exploration at Mayapan and Telchaquillo," Carnegie Institution of Washington, *Current Reports,* no. 12, pp. 222–33 (Washington, D.C.).
1955 *Ceramic Sequence at Uaxactun, Guatemala,* Middle American Research Institute, Publication 20 (New Orleans: Tulane University).

1971   *The Pottery of Mayapan,* Papers of the Peabody Museum of Archaeology and Ethnology, vol. 66 (Cambridge, Mass.: Harvard University).

n.d.   *A Ceramic Sequence from the Pyramid of the Sun at Teotihuacan, Mexico,* Papers of the Peabody Museum of Archaeology and Ethnology, vol. 75 (Cambridge, Mass.: Harvard University, forthcoming).

SMITH, ROBERT E., AND JAMES C. GIFFORD
1966   *Maya Ceramic Varieties, Types and Wares at Uaxactun,* Middle American Research Institute, Publication 28 (New Orleans: Tulane University).

SOLHEIM, WILLIAM G., II
1960   "The Use of Sherd Weights and Counts in the Handling of Archaeological Data," *Current Anthropology* 1, no. 4:325–29.
1965   "The Functions of Pottery in Southeast Asia: From the Present to the Past," in *Ceramics and Man,* ed. F. R. Matson, pp. 254–73 (Chicago: Aldine).

SOUSTELLE, JACQUES
1961   *The Daily Life of the Aztecs on the Eve of the Spanish Conquest,* trans. P. O'Brian (Stanford: Stanford University Press).

SPENCE, MICHAEL W.
1981   "Obsidian Production and the State in Teotihuacan," *American Antiquity* 46, no. 4:769–88.

SPINDEN, HERBERT J.
1913   *A Study of Maya Art,* Memoirs of the Peabody Museum of Archaeology and Ethnology, vol. 6 (Cambridge, Mass.: Harvard University).
1924   *The Reduction of Maya Dates,* Papers of the Peabody Museum of Archaeology and Ethnology, vol. 6, no. 4 (Cambridge, Mass.: Harvard University).
1925   "The Chorotegan Culture Area," *Proceedings of the Twenty-first International Congress of Americanists* (Goteborg).
1928   *Maya Inscriptions Dealing with Venus and the Moon,* Buffalo Society of Natural Sciences, Bulletin 14, no. 1 (Buffalo, N.Y.).
1930   *Maya Dates and What They Reveal,* Brooklyn Institution of Arts and Sciences, vol. 4, no. 1 (Brooklyn, N.Y.).

STAHLMAN, WILLIAM D., AND OWEN GINGERICH
1963   *Solar and Planetary Longitudes for Years -2500 to $+2000$* (Madison: University of Wisconsin Press).

STARK, BARBARA L. AND BARBARA VOORHIES
1978   *Prehistoric Coastal Adaptations: The Economy and Ecology of Maritime Middle America* (New York: Academic Press).

STARR, F.
1904   "Notes Upon the Ethnography of Southern Mexico," *Proceedings of the Davenport Academy of Sciences* 9, pp. 63–85.

STEPHENS, JOHN L.
1841   *Incidents of Travel in Central America, Chiapas and Yucatan* (New York: Harper & Bros.).
1843   *Incidents of Travel in Yucatan,* 2 vols. (New York: Harper & Bros.).

STEWARD, JULIAN H.
1948 "A Functional-Developmental Classification of American High Cultures," in *A Reappraisal of Peruvian Archaeology*, ed. W. C. Bennett, pp. 103–5, Memoirs of the Society for American Archaeology, no. 4 (Menasha, Wis.).
1949 "Cultural Causality and Law: A Trial of the Development of Early Civilizations," *American Anthropologist* 51:1–25.

STONE, DORIS Z.
1941 *Archaeology of the North Coast of Honduras*, Memoirs of the Peabody Museum of Archaeology and Ethnology, vol. 9 (Cambridge, Mass.: Harvard University).

STONE, ANDREA, DORRIE REENTS, AND ROBERT COFFMAN
1980 "Genealogical Documentation of the Middle Classic Dynasty of Caracol, El Cayo, Belize," paper presented at the Fourth Mesa Redonda of Palenque.

STRONG, WILLIAM DUNCAN
1948 "Cultural Epochs and Refuse Stratigraphy in Peruvian Archaeology," in *A Reappraisal of Peruvian Archaeology*, ed. W. C. Bennett, Memoirs of the Society for American Archaeology, no. 4, pp. 93–103 (Menasha, Wis.).

STRONG, WILLIAM DUNCAN, AND CLIFFORD EVANS, JR.
1952 *Cultural Stratigraphy in the Viru Valley, Northern Peru*, Columbia University Studies in Archaeology and Ethnology, vol. 4 (New York: Columbia University Press).

STUART, GEORGE E., ET AL
1979 *Map of the Ruins of Dzibilchaltun, Yucatan, Mexico*, Middle American Research Institute, Publication 47 (New Orleans: Tulane University).

STUART, L. C.
1934 *A Contribution to a Knowledge of the Herpetological Fauna of El Peten, Guatemala*, Occasional Papers of the Museum of Zoology, University of Michigan, 292, pp. 1–8 (Ann Arbor).

SULLIVAN, T.
1977 "Tlazolteotl-Ixcuina: The Great Spinner and Weaver," paper presented at the Dumbarton Oaks Conference on Art and Iconography of Late Post-Classic Central Mexico, Washington, D.C.

TASCHEK, J. T.
1982 "Specialized Precolumbian Offertory Activities at Cenote Xlacah, Dzibilchaltun," paper presented at the Forty-seventh Annual Meeting of the Society for American Archaeology, Minneapolis.

TAYLOR, D.
1978 "The Cauac Monster," in *Tercera Mesa Redonda de Palenque*, vol. 4, ed. M. Greene Robertson and D. C. Jeffers, pp. 79–90 (Monterey, Calif.: Pre-Columbian Art Research Center; Palenque: Herald Printers).

TEEPLE, JOHN E.
1926 "Maya Inscriptions: The Venus Calendar and Another Correlation," *American Anthropologist* 28:402–8.
1930a "Factors Which May Lead to a Correlation of Maya and Christian Dates,"

Proceedings of the Twenty-third International Congress of Americanists, New York, pp. 136–39.
1930b   *Maya Astronomy,* Carnegie Institution of Washington, Contributions to American Archaeology 1, no. 2 (Washington, D.C.).

TELLO, JULIO C.
1943   "Discovery of the Chavin Culture in Peru," *American Antiquity* 9, no. 1:135–60.
1956a   *Arqueología del Valle de Casma, Culturas Chavin, Santa o Huaylas Yunga y Sub-Chimu,* Publicación Antropologica del Archivo "Julio C. Tello," vol. 1 (Lima: Universidad de San Marcos).
1956b   *Arqueologia del Valle de Casma* (Lima: Editorial San Marcos).

TEZOZOMOC, FERNANDO ALVARADO
1943   *Crónica Mexicana* (Mexico City: Universidad Nacional Autonoma).
1975   *Crónica Mexicayotl* (Mexico City: Instituto de Investigaciones Historicas).

THATCHER, JOHN P., JR.
1972–74   "Early Intermediate Period and Middle Horizon 1B Ceramic Assemblages of Huamachuco, North Highlands, Peru," *Nawpa Pacha* 10 and 12, 109–29.

THOMAS, CYRUS
1882   "A Study of the Manuscript Troano," *Contributions to North American Ethnology,* vol. 5, pp. 1–237 (Washington, D.C.: U.S. Department of the Interior).

THOMPSON, DONALD E.
1964   "Formative Period Architecture in the Casma Valley, Peru," *Actas y Memorias XXXV Congresso Internacional del Americanistas* vol. 1, pp. 205–12 (Mexico).

THOMPSON, EDWARD H.
1886   "Archaeological Research in Yucatan," *Proceedings of the American Antiquarian Society* 4, pp. 248–54 (Worcester, Mass.).
1892   "The Ancient Structures of Yucatan Not Communal Dwellings," *Proceedings of the American Antiquarian Society* 8, pp. 262–69 (Worcester, Mass.).
1938   *The High Priests' Grave, Chichen Itza, Yucatan, Mexico,* Field Museum of Natural History, Anthropological Series, vol. 27 (Chicago).

THOMPSON, J. ERIC S.
1927   "A Correlation of the Mayan and European Calendars," *Field Museum of Natural History, Anthropological Series,* vol. 17, no. 1, pp. 1–22 (Chicago).
1930   *Ethnology of the Mayas of Southern and Central British Honduras,* Field Museum of Natural History, Anthropological Series, vol. 17, no. 2 (Chicago).
1931   "Archaeological Investigations in the Southern Cayo District, British Honduras," *Field Museum of Natural History, Anthropological Series,* vol. 17, no. 3 (Chicago).
1935   *Maya Chronology: The Correlation Question,* Carnegie Institution of Washington, Contribution 14, Publication 456 (Washington, D.C.).
1938   "Sixteenth- and Seventeenth-Century Reports on the Chol Mayas," *American Anthropologist* 51:584–605.

1939 *Excavations at San Jose, British Honduras,* Carnegie Institution of Washington, Publication 506 (Washington, D.C.).
1940 *Late Ceramic Horizons at Benque Viejo, British Honduras,* Carnegie Institution of Washington, Contribution 35, Publication 528 (Washington, D.C.).
1950 *Maya Hieroglyphic Writing: Introduction,* Carnegie Institution of Washington, Publication 539 (Washington, D.C.).
1962 *A Catalog of Maya Hieroglyphs* (Norman: University of Oklahoma Press).
1963 *Maya Archaeologist* (Norman: University of Oklahoma Press).
1970 *Maya History and Religion* (Norman: University of Oklahoma Press).
1972a *A Commentary on the Dresden Codex, A Maya Hieroglyphic Book,* Memoirs of the American Philosophical Society, no. 93 (Philadelphia).
1972b *Maya Hieroglyphs Without Tears* (London: British Museum).
1973 *The Civilization of the Mayas,* Natural History Museum, Popular Series, Anthropology, no. 25 (Chicago).
1974 "Maya Astronomy," *Philosophical Transactions of the Royal Society of London,* A276:83–98.
1975 Introduction to *The Hill-Caves of Yucatan* by H. C. Mercer (Norman: University of Oklahoma Press).

THOMPSON, J. ERIC S., AND DONALD E. THOMPSON
1955 "A Noble's Residence and Its Dependencies at Mayapan," Carnegie Institution of Washington, Historical Research, *Current Reports,* no. 25, pp. 225–51 (Washington, D.C.).

THOMPSON, RAYMOND H.
1958 *Modern Yucatecan Mayan Pottery Making,* Memoirs of the Society for American Archaeology, no. 15 (Salt Lake City).

TOLKIEN, J. R. R.
1965 *The Fellowship of the Ring* (New York: Ballantine Books).

TOPIC, JOHN
1982 "Lower-Class Social and Economic Organization at Chan Chan," in *Chan Chan: Andean Desert City,* ed. M. E. Moseley and K. C. Day, pp. 145–76 (Albuquerque: University of New Mexico Press, School of American Research Advanced Seminar Series).

TOPIC, JOHN R., AND THERESA LANGE TOPIC
1979 "Prehistoric Fortifiaction Systems of Northern Peru: Preliminary Report on the Third Field Season, May–August 1979" (manuscript).

TOPIC, THERESA LANGE
1977 "Excavations at Moche," (Ph.D. diss., Harvard University).
1982 "The Early Intermediate Period and Its Legacy," in *Chan Chan: Andean Desert City,* ed. M. E. Moseley and K. C. Day, pp. 255–84 (Albuquerque: University of New Mexico Press, School of American Research Advanced Seminar Series).

TORQUEMADA, FRAY JUAN DE
1975 *Monarquia Indiana,* vols. 1–5 (Mexico City: Instituto de Investigaciones Históricas).

TOURTELLOT, GAIR, III
1970   "The Peripheries of Seibal: An Interim Report," in *Monographs and Papers in Maya Archaeology,* ed. William R. Bullard, Jr., pp. 405–21, Papers of the Peabody Museum of Archaeology and Ethnology, vol. 61 (Cambridge, Mass.: Harvard University).

TOVAR, JUAN DE
1944   *Codice Ramírez: Relación del Origen de los Indios que Habitan Esta Nueva España, Sequn sus Historias* (Mexico: Editorial Leyenda).

TOWNSEND, RICHARD F.
1979   *State and Cosmos in the Art of Tenochititlan,* Studies in Pre-Columbian Art and Archaeology, no. 20 (Washington, D.C.: Dumbarton Oaks).

TOZZER, ALFRED M.
1907   *A Comparative Study of the Maya and the Lacandones* (New York: Archaeological Institute of America).
1911   *A Preliminary Study of the Prehistoric Ruins of Tikal, Guatemala,* Memoirs of the Peabody Museum of Archaeology and Ethnology, vol. 5, no. 2 (Cambridge, Mass.: Harvard University).
1913   *A Preliminary Study of the Prehistoric Ruins of Nakum, Guatemala,* Memoirs of the Peabody Museum of Archaeology and Ethnology, vol. 5, no. 3 (Cambridge, Mass.: Harvard University).
1957   *Chichen Itza and Its Cenote of Sacrifice: A Comparative Study of Contemporaneous Maya and Toltec,* Memoirs of the Peabody Museum of Archaeology and Ethnology, vols. 11–12 (Cambridge, Mass.: Harvard University).

TOZZER, A. M., AND G. M. ALLEN
1910   *Animal Figures in the Maya Codices,* Papers of the Peabody Museum of Archaeology and Ethnology, vol. 4 (Cambridge, Mass.: Harvard University).

TOZZER, ALFRED M., ed.
1941   *Landa's Relacion de las Cosas de Yucatan,* Papers of the Peabody Museum of Archaeology and Ethnology, vol. 18 (Cambridge, Mass.: Harvard University).

TRIK, A. S.
1963   "The Splendid Tomb of Temple I at Tikal, Guatemala," *Expedition* 6:1–18.

TURNER, C. G., AND L. LOFGREN
1966   "Household Size of Prehistoric Western Pueblo Indians," *Southwestern Journal of Anthropology* 22, no. 2:117–32.

TURNER, B. L., II
1974   "Prehistoric Intensive Agriculture in the Mayan Lowlands," *Science* 185: 118–24.

TURNER, B. L., II et al.
n.d.   "Informe Sobre la Ecologia del Valle" (in Baudez, forthcoming).

UCHMANY, EVA A.
1978   "Huitzilopochtli, Dios de la Historia de los Azteca-Mexitin," *Estudios de Cultura Nahautl* 13:211–38.

1979 "Las Características de un Dios Tutelar Mesoamericano: Huitzilopochtli," *Actes du 42e Congrès International des Americanistes,* vol. 6, pp. 49–62 (Paris).

UHLE, MAX
1903 "Ancient South American Civilizations," *Harper's Monthly* 107:780–86.
1913 "Die Ruinen von Moche," *Journal de la Société des Americanistes de Paris* 10:95–117.
1925 "Report on Explorations at Supe," in *The Uhle Pottery Collections from Supe,* by A. L. Kroeber, University of California Publications in American Archaeology and Ethnology, vol. 21, pp. 257–64 (Los Angeles).

VALENTINI, PHILIP J. J.
1879 "The Katunes of the Maya History," Proceedings of the American Antiquarian Society (Worcester, Mass.).

VAUGHAN, H. H.
1979 *Prehistoric Disturbance of Vegetation in the Area of Lake Yaxha, Peten, Guatemala* (Ph.D. diss., University of Florida).

VELAZQUEZ V., RICARDO
1980 "Recent Discoveries in the Caves of Loltun, Yucatan, Mexico," *Mexicon* (Berlin) 2, no. 4:53–55.

VILLA ROJAS, ALFONSO
1945 *The Maya of East Central Quintana Roo,* Carnegie Institution of Washington, Publication 559 (Washington, D.C.).
1947 "Kinship and Nagualism in a Tzeltal Community, Southeastern Mexico," *American Anthropologist* 49:578–87.
1969a "The Maya of Yucatan," in *Handbook of Middle American Indians,* vol. 7, ed. E. Z. Vogt, pp. 244–75 (Austin: University of Texas Press).
1969b "Maya Lowlands: The Chontal, Chol, and Kekchi," in *Handbook of Middle American Indians,* vol. 7, ed. E. Z. Vogt, pp. 195–225 (Austin: University of Texas Press).

VILLACORTA CALDERON, J. A., AND C. A. VILLACORTA
1930 *Codices Mayas: Dresdensis-Peresianus-Tro-Cortesianus* (Guatemala: Tipografía Nacional).

VIVO ESCOTO, J. A.
1964 "Weather and Climate of Mexico and Central America," in *Handbook of Middle American Indians,* vol. 1, ed. R. West, pp. 187–215 (Austin, University of Texas Press).

VLCEK, DAVID T., AND WILLIAM L. FASH
1980 "Survey in the Outlying Region and the Copan-Quirigua 'Connection,'" paper presented at the Forty-fifth Annual Meeting of the Society for American Archaeology, Philadelphia.

VOGT, EVON Z.
1969 *Zinacantan: A Maya Community in the Highlands of Chiapas* (Cambridge, Mass.: Harvard University Press).

VOLLEMAERE, ANTOON
1972 "Problème des calendriers mayas et la correlation," *Proceedings of the Fortieth International Congress of Americanists* 1, pp. 419–26.

VON HAGEN, VICTOR W.
1947 *Maya Explorer* (Norman: University of Oklahoma Press).

WAGLEY, CHARLES
1949 *The Social and Religious Life of a Guatemalan Village,* Memoirs of the American Anthropological Association, no. 71 (Menasha, Wis.).

WAGNER, PHILIP L.
1964 "Natural Vegetation of Middle America," in *Handbook of Middle American Indians,* vol. 1, ed. R. West, pp. 216–64 (Austin: University of Texas Press).

WALDECK, JEAN-FREDERIC
1838 *Voyage Pittoresque et Archeologique dans la Province d'Yucatan Pendant les Annees 1834 et 1836* (Paris).

WALLRATH, MATHEW
1967 "The Calle de los Muertos Complex, in *Teotihuacan Onceava Mesa Redonda,* vol. 1, pp. 113–22 (Mexico City: Sociedad Mexicana de Antropología).

WAUCHOPE, ROBERT
1934 *House Mounds of Uaxactun, Guatemala,* Carnegie Institution of Washington, Contribution 7, Publication 436 (Washington, D.C.).
1938 *Modern Maya Houses: A Study of Their Archaeological Significance,* Carnegie Institution of Washington, Publication 502 (Washington, D.C.).
1948 *Excavations at Zacualpa, Guatemala,* Middle American Research Institute, Publication 14 (New Orleans: Tulane University).

WEBER, MAX
1951 *The City* (Glencoe, Ill.: Glencoe Press).

WEBSTER, DAVID L.
1977 "Warfare and the Evolution of Maya Civilization," in *The Origins of Maya Civilization,* ed. R. E. W. Adams, pp. 335–72 (Albuquerque: University of New Mexico Press, School of American Research Advanced Seminar Series).

WEITZEL, ROBERT B.
1945 "Inscriptions at Chichen-Itza and the Maya Correlation Problem," *American Antiquity* 11, no. 1:27–31.

WENDT, W. E.
1964 "Die Prakermaische Siedlung am Rio Seco," *Baessler Archiv* 11, no. 2:225–75.

WHALLON, ROBERT
1969 "Rim Diameter, Vessel Volume, and Economic Prehistory," *The Michigan Academician* 2, no. 2:89–98.

WHORF, BENJAMIN L.
1933 *The Phonetic Value of Certain Characters in Maya Writing,* Papers of the Peabody Museum of Archaeology and Ethnography, vol. 13, no. 2 (Cambridge, Mass.: Harvard University).

WILLARD, T. A.
1926   *The City of the Sacred Well* (New York: Century).

WILLEY, GORDON R.
1948   "Functional Analysis of Horizon Styles in Peruvian Archaeology," in *A Reappraisal of Peruvian Archaeology*, ed. W. C. Bennett, Memoirs of the Society for American Archaeology, no. 4, pp. 8–16 (Menasha, Wis.).
1953   *Prehistoric Settlement Patterns in the Viru Valley, Peru*, Bureau of American Ethnology, Bulletin 155 (Washington, D.C.: Smithsonian Institution).
1968   "One Hundred Years of American Archaeology," in *One Hundred Years of Anthropology*, ed. J. O. Brew, pp. 29–56 (Cambridge, Mass.: Harvard University Press).
1970   "The Real Xe Ceramics of Seibal, Peten, Guatemala," in *Monographs and Papers in Maya Archaeology*, ed. William R. Bullard, pp. 313–55, Papers of the Peabody Museum of Archaeology and Ethnology, vol. 61 (Cambridge, Mass.: Harvard University).
1973   *The Altar de Sacrificios Excavations: General Summary and Conclusions*, Papers of the Peabody Museum of Archaeology and Ethnology, vol. 64, no. 1 (Cambridge, Mass.: Harvard University).
1974   "Precolumbian Urbanism: The Central Mexican Highlands and Lowland Maya," in *The Rise and Fall of Civilizations* ed. C. C. Lamberg-Karlovsky and J. A. Sabloff, pp. 134–54 (Menlo Park, Calif.: Benjamin Cummings).
1976   "Mesoamerican Civilization and the Idea of Transcendence," *Antiquity* 50:205–15.
1977a "External Influences on the Lowland Maya: 1940 and 1975 Perspectives," in *Social Process in Maya Prehistory*, ed. N. Hammond, pp. 58–75 (London: Academic Press).
1977b "The Rise of Maya Civilization: A Summary View," in *The Origins of Maya Civilization*, ed. R. E. W. Adams, pp. 383–423 (Albuquerque: University of New Mexico Press, School of American Research Advanced Seminar Series).
1980   "Towards a Holistic View of Maya Civilization," *Man*, no. 15:249–66.
1981   "Maya Lowland Settlement Patterns: A Summary Review," in *Lowland Maya Settlement Patterns*, ed. W. Ashmore, pp. 385–415 (Albuquerque: University of New Mexico Press, School of American Research Advanced Seminar Series).

WILLEY, GORDON R., AND WILLIAM R. BULLARD, JR.
1965   "Prehistoric Settlement Patterns in the Maya Lowlands," in *Handbook of Middle American Indians*, vol. 2, ed. R. Wauchope and G. R. Willey, pp. 360–77 (Austin: University of Texas Press).

WILLEY, G. R., W. R. BULLARD, JR., J. B. GLASS, AND J. C. GIFFORD
1965   *Prehistoric Maya Settlements in the Belize Valley*, Papers of the Peabody Museum of Archaeology and Ethnology, vol. 54 (Cambridge, Mass.: Harvard University).

WILLEY, GORDON R., AND JOHN CORBETT
1954   *Early Ancon and Early Supe Culture: Chavin Horizon Sites of the Central Peruvian Coast*, Columbia Studies in Archaeology and Ethnology 3 (New York: Columbia University Press).

WILLEY, G. R., T. P. CULBERT, AND R. E. W. ADAMS
1967 "Maya Lowland Ceramics: A Report from the 1965 Guatemala City Conference," *American Antiquity* 32:289–315.

WILLEY, GORDON R., AND JAMES C. GIFFORD
1961 "Pottery of the Holmul I Style from Barton Ramie, British Honduras," in *Essays in Pre-Columbian Art and Archaeology*, ed. S. K. Lothrop, pp. 152–70 (Cambridge, Mass.: Harvard University Press).

WILLEY, GORDON R., AND RICHARD M. LEVENTHAL
1979 "Prehistoric Settlement at Copan," in *Maya Archaeology and Ethnohistory*, ed. N. Hammond and G. R. Willey, pp. 75–102 (Austin: University of Texas Press).

WILLEY, GORDON R., RICHARD M. LEVENTHAL, AND WILLIAM L. FASH
1978 "Maya Settlement in the Copan Valley," *Archaeology* 31:32–43.

WILLEY, GORDON R., AND JEREMY A. SABLOFF
1974 *A History of American Archaeology* (London: Thames and Hudson).
1980 *A History of American Archaeology*, 2d ed. (London: Thames and Hudson).

WILLIAMS LEON, CARLOS
1972 "La Difusión de los Pozos Ceremoniales en la Costa Peruana," *Apuntes Arqueologicos* 2:1–9.

WILLSON, ROBERT W.
1924 *Astronomical Notes on the Maya Codices*, Papers of the Peabody Museum of Archaeology and Ethnology, vol. 6, no. 3 (Cambridge, Mass.: Harvard University).

WILSON, DAVID J.
1981 "Of Maize and Men: A Critique of the Maritime Hypotheses of State Origins on the Coast of Peru," *American Anthropologist* 83, no. 1:93–120.

WING, ELIZABETH S.
n.d. "Animal Remains Associated with the Formative Occupation at Cuello in Northern Belize" (manuscript).

WING, ELIZABETH, AND NORMAN HAMMOND
1974 "Fish Remains in Archaeology: A Comment on Casteel," *American Antiquity* 39:133–35.

WING, E. S., AND D. STEADMAN
1980 "Faunal Remains from the Dzibilchaltun Site," in *Excavations at Dzibilchaltun, Yucatan, Mexico* by E. Wyllys Andrews IV and E. Wyllys Andrews V, pp. 326–31, Middle American Research Institute, Publication 48 (New Orleans: Tulane University).

WISDOM, CHARLES
1940 *The Chorti Indians of Guatemala* (Chicago: University of Chicago Press).

WITTFOGEL, KARL
1957 *Oriental Despotism* (New Haven: Yale University Press).

WOLF, ERIC R., ed.
1976 *The Valley of Mexico: Studies in Pre-Hispanic Ecology and Society* (Albu-

querque: University of New Mexico Press, School of American Research Advanced Seminar Series).

WOLFMAN, DANIEL
1973 *A Re-evaluation of Mesoamerican Chronology: A.D. 1–1200* (Ph.D. diss., University of Colorado).

WOODBURY, R. B., AND A. S. TRIK
1953 *The Ruins of Zaculeu, Guatemala,* 2 vols. (Richmond, Va.: William Byrd Press).

XIMENEZ, F.
1967 *Historia Natural del Reino de Guatemala,* Publicación Especial 14, (Guatemala: Sociedad de Geografia e Historia).

ZAKI, ANDRZEJ
1978 *Ayangay: Polskie Odkrycia Archeologiczne W Peru* (London: Polski Uniwersytet Na Obczyznie).

ZANTWIJK, RUDOLF VAN
1963 "Principios Organizadores de los Mexicas," *Estudios de Cultura Nahuatl* 4:187–220.
1966 "Los Seis Barrios Sirvientes de Huitzilopochtli," *Estudios de Cultura Nahuatl* 6:177–87.
1975 "La Organización Social de Mexico-Tenochtitlan Naciente," *Actes du 42e Internacional Congreso des Americanistas,* vol. 2, pp. 188–208 (Mexico City).
1979 "El Parentesco y la Afiliación Etnica de Huitzilopochtli," *Actes du 42e Internacional Congreso des Americanistas,* vol. 6, pp. 63–68 (Paris).

ZUIDEMA, REINER TOM
1962 "Reflections on Inca Historical Conceptions," *Akten des 34 Internationalen Amerikanistenkongresses,* pp. 718–21 (Vienna).
1964 *The Ceque System of Cuzco: The Social Organization of the Capital of the Inca,* trans. E. M. Hooykaas, International Archives of Ethnography, supplement to vol. 50 (Leiden: E. J. Brill).
1973 "Kinship and Ancestorcult in Three Peruvian Communities: Hernandez Principe's Account of 1622," *Bulletin de l'Institut Francais d'Etudes Andines* 2, no. 1:16–33.

Index

Acalan, 265
Acolhua, the, 379–80
Acosta, Jorge, 27
Actun Balam cave, 87, 89
Actun Ceh cave, 87
Actun Polbilche cave, 89, 90
Aegean culture, 300
agriculture, 292–93, 303–10
Aguan River Valley, 39, 40, 48
Akbal, 153, 155
aldea, 267–68, 278
Almendariz, Ricardo, 9
Altar de Sacrificios, 16, 25–26, 73, 75, 78, 79, 81, 108–10, 140
Altun Ha, 27, 73, 98, 102
Alva Ixtlilxochitl, 159
American Antiquity, 24
Andrews, E. Wyllys, IV, 27, 157, 158, 162
Andrews, E. Wyllys, V, 162
Apollo, 198
aguadas, 101
arable land, 247
Arenal phase, 146, 153

armadillo: in Maya diet, 44, 46, 51; in Maya ritual, 65, 79
Aspero, 289–93, 295–303
audiencia, 361
Aztec, the: deities, 324; empire, 163, 373–86; expansion, 377–86; temple, 329; tradition, 342; Triple Alliance, 374, 381–5

bajo, 276
Bajo de Santa Fe, 81
balam, 73
Balankanche cave, 87
balche, 136–38
Barton Creek, 161
Barton Ramie, 25, 161, 162
Baudez, Claude F., 261, 263
Belize, 23, 27, 29, 89
Belize River Valley, 23, 25–26
Bender, Barbara, 304–5
Berlin, Heinrich, 24–25
Bernasconi, Antonio, 8–9
Bienvenida, Lorenzo de, 5–6
Bird, J. B., 39

birds: in Maya diet, 42, 44, 46, 48; in Maya ritual, 83–84, 89–90, 96–98; in Peruvian diet, 292, 294
Blackfeet Indians, 101
Boekelman Shell Heap Expedition, 35
Bowditch Chair, 25
Bowditch, Charles P., 18, 25
Brasseur de Bourbourg, Charles Etienne, 14, 158
Breton, Adela, 16
Brundage, Burr Cartwright, 347, 361
Burgh, Robert, 282

Caban, 251
Cabot, Samuel, Jr., 13
Cabrera Castro, Rubén, 313
Cajamarca, 241, 247, 248, 251, 252, 257, 258
Cajamarquilla, 225
Calcehtok, 87
Calderón, Jose, 8
calendar, Maya, 157–208; compared with Hindu and Siamese calendars, 200–201; reform, 194–200
Calle de Los Muertos (Street of the Dead) Complex, 316–22, 331–33, 335, 339–41
Callejón de Huaylas, 241, 248, 252, 257–58
Campeche, 83
Canby, Joel, 158
Cancuc, 265
cannibalism, 384
Cañon del Pato, 243
Canterbury Cathedral, 329
Caracol, 75, 171, 184–93, 202
Carnegie Institution, 5, 20–25, 158, 282
Casma, 251
Caso, Alfonso, 166–68, 195, 196, 324
Castañeda, José, 9–10
Castillo de Tomoval, 258
Catalog of Maya Hieroglyphs, 24
Catherwood, Frederick, 10–14
caves, 86–91, 99–100, 102
Caves Branch caves, 90

cenotes, 86–87, 91–98, 101, 102
cercadura, 231
ceremonies, Maya, 55–102, 136–37; armadillo in, 65, 79; birds in, 83–84, 89–90, 96–98; *Chac chac,* 136; crocodile in, 65, 79–81; deer in, 62–65, 79, 81, 87, 89, 91; dog in, 65, 70–71, 89, 91–94; felines in, 65, 71–74, 79, 89, 101–2; fish in, 65, 74–78; human remains in, 85, 86, 89, 90, 91, 96; manatee in, 75, 98; monkey in, 65–66; opossum in, 65, 79; *Pacum chac,* 136–37; peccary in, 65, 66–70, 89, 91, 94; shellfish in, 55, 66, 75–78, 90–91, 94–96, 98, 102; small animals in, 85–86, 90; snakes in, 65, 78–79, 81, 90; turkey in, 65, 82–83, 96; turtle in, 65, 81–82, 90, 96, 98, 100–101
Cerro Arena, 217, 228
Cerro Blanca de León, 255
Cerro Chino, 283
Cerro Oreja, 257
Cerros, 75, 105–42
chala, 240, 248
Chalchuapa, 110
Chamula, 90
Chan Chan, 231, 251, 330, 345–71
Chan Kom, 85, 96, 132, 266
Chanca, 387–88
Chao Valley, 242, 251
Chapagua River, 39, 48, 49
Charles III (King of Spain), 8–9
Charles IV (King of Spain), 8, 9
Charnay, Désiré, 15
Ch'en Mul cenote, 91, 94
Chetumal Bay, 105
Chiapas, 8, 63, 85, 86, 110, 146
Chicama River Valley, 216, 250, 251
Chicanel Ceramic Sphere, 108
Chicanel period, 21–22
Chichen Itza, 7, 13, 14, 17, 21, 22, 81, 84, 86, 87, 91, 94, 96, 98, 99, 100, 102, 161, 166, 168, 171, 172, 202, 205, 208

chiefdom, 299, 300
Chilam Balam of Tizimin, Book of, 73, 79
Chimor, 346, 348, 351, 357, 362, 364, 367
Chimu Capac, 225
Chimu culture, 212, 216–18, 231, 249–51, 352, 357, 362–63, 375, 389
Chiquimula, 74
Chocola, 154
Chorro, 287
Chuen, 153
chultun, 17
Chumayel, chronicles of, 165–66
Ciudad Real, 9, 78, 86
ciudadela, 231
Ciudadela, the, 313–43
Civilization of the Mayas, The, 23
Closs, Michael, 158
cluster (Maya social group), 262, 272
Coastal Chavin style, 212
coastal uplift, 307–8
Coba, 16, 22
Cocal Period, 53
Coe, Michael, 31, 324
Coe, William, 26
Coggins, Clemency, 31, 324
C'oh Complex, 108, 111, 113–18, 120, 123–25, 128, 132, 136, 140–41
Colha, 30
Comedero, 283, 286
Commentary on the Dresden Codex, 24
Coner phase, 281–82, 286–87
Copan, 7, 10–12, 15, 18, 21, 66, 70, 74, 78, 81, 84, 89, 90, 94, 99, 100, 261–87, 369
Copan pocket, 261–87
Corbett, John M., 289
corporate labor, 298
Cozumel, 28, 62, 70, 71, 82–83, 86, 89, 93, 101
crocodile: in Maya diet, 44, 47, 51; in Maya ritual, 65, 79–81

Crónica de Okutzcab, 164
cross, ancestral, 266
Cruz Blanca, 253–58
cu, 74
cuch (new year or renewal) rite, 56, 62–70, 73, 74–78, 82, 87, 91, 93, 94, 98, 99, 100, 102
Cuello, 29, 62, 75, 98, 101
cultural reconstitution, 235
Cuscatlan, 74
Cuzco, 345–71, 374, 386–89

dating methods: astronomical, 172–201; C-14, 161–63; Caracol Stela 3, 184–93; documentary, 163–66; Dresden Ring Numbers, 193–94; Dresden tables, 173–79; geophysical, 160–63; historical, 166–72, 194–201; Kaliyuga era, 200–201; obsidian, 160–61; paleomagnetic, 161; tropical year, 179–84
deer: in Maya diet, 44, 46, 48, 51; in Maya ritual, 62–65, 74, 79, 81, 87, 89, 91
dog in Maya ritual, 65, 70–71, 89, 91–94
domestic group, Maya, 264
Dresden Codex, 15, 62, 75, 79, 82, 84: astronomical tables in, 173–79; Ring Number dates, 193–94
Drewitt, Bruce, 339
Dupaix, Guillermo, 9–10
Dzibilchaltun, 75, 90, 94, 96, 98, 262

economic symbiosis, 376
Eduardo Quiroz cave, 89, 90
El Bosque, 276, 286
El Cedral, 62, 83
El Niño, 294
El Salvador, 74
epigraphy, 14
Epstein, J. F., 40
Escorial, the, 336
Esperanza phase, 155

Estachería, Jose de, 8
ethnoarchaeology, 329

fanaticism, 385
faunal analysis, 40–45
felines: in Maya diet, 44; in Maya ritual, 65, 71–74, 79, 89, 101–2
field exploration, 14
Finca Solola, 146–52
fish: in Maya diet, 43–44, 47, 48–49, 51; in Maya ritual, 65, 74–78; in Peruvian diet, 292–94
Floral Park Ceramic Sphere, 139, 142
Flores, 70
Förstemann, Ernst, 15–16
Fortifications Project, 237–59

Galindo, 216, 218, 221–24, 228–33
Gallinazo, 212, 217, 228, 241, 251–55, 257–58
Gann, Thomas, 18, 48
García de Palacio, Diego, 7–8, 74, 89
gods and goddesses (Maya): Bacabs, 79; Four Crocodile, 197; Four Earthquake, 197; Four House, 197, 198; Four Rabbit, 198; GI, 78; God D, 91; God N, 75, 79; Itzam Na, 79, 81, 99; Ix Chebel Yax, 87; Ix Chel, 75; Kinich Kakmo, 84; One Death of Sun Mountain, 197; Principal Bird Deity, 154, 155; rain (*chacs*, God B), 56, 63, 74, 78, 81, 85, 87, 89, 91; Serpent-Winged Deity, 145–55; sun gods, 27, 62, 85, 197–99; Ten Eagle, 198; Three Monkey, 197, 198
Goodman, Joseph T., 15–16
Gordon, George Byron, 16, 18
Graham, Ian, 31
Great Compound, 342
group residential unit (Maya), 262, 272
Gauimoreto Lagoon, 39, 47–49, 51, 52
Guatemala, 8–9, 10, 15, 17, 78, 81, 145–55, 162
Guatemala City, 145, 146

Hairs, Joya, 146, 155*n*, 156*n*
Harvard University, 16–26, 282
Hieroglyphic Stairway, 185, 287
Holmul, 18–19, 21, 73, 79
Honduras, 16, 18, 23, 35–53
House of the Priests, 341
Huaca de la Luna, 217–21, 228–30
Huaca de los Idolos, 295–302
Huaca de los Reyes, 298
Huaca de los Sacrificios, 295–98, 300–302
Huaca del Sol, 212, 214, 216–18, 228–30, 251
Huaca San Jose, 300
Huacaloma, 252
Huamachuco, 241, 245, 247–51
Huancaco, 222
Huancayo Alto, 256
Huarez, 247, 252
Huichol Indians, 98
Huitzilopochtli, 380, 383–86
human sacrifice, 383–84
Hunter, Annie, 15–16
hunting, 293

iguana: in Maya diet, 44, 47, 51, 91; in Maya ritual, 103*n*
Inca, the: empire, 346–48, 364–65, 373–78, 386–92; expansion, 249–50, 346–47, 362, 367, 377–78, 386–92; highway system, 247, 374–75; religious beliefs, 386, 389–90
Incidents of Travel in Central America, Chiapas and Yucatan, 12
Incidents of Travel in Yucatan, 14
Inquisition of 1562, 62, 63, 81, 86, 87, 91
Institute of Andean Research, 289
Instituto Nacional de Antropología e Historia, 313
Inti, 364–65, 390
irrigation, 308–9
Isbell, William, 376
itzam, 103*n*
Itzcoatl, 381–82, 385–86
Iximche, 5

Ixtabai, 108, 113–16, 120, 123–25, 128, 132–34, 136, 141
Izamal, 84
Izapa, 146, 154
Izapan dragon, 152, 153
Izapan horizon, 146, 154

Jaguar House, 73
Jefferson, Thomas, 6
Jenney Creek, 161
Jequetepeque, 250, 346
Jocotan, 267, 268

Kabah, 13
Kaminaljuyu, 110–11, 145–55, 369
kan, 70, 75, 153
katun, 158, 159, 163, 164–66
Kidder, Alfred V., 21
kin, 62, 84, 153, 155
Knorosov, Yurii, 24
koben, 17
Kroeber, A. L., 235
Kurjack, Edward B., 263
kurus ko mam, 266

La Cuesta, Rio, 253–55
Labna, 17
lagarto, 103n
Lambayeque Valley, 214, 218, 229, 241, 248, 357, 362
Landa, Bishop Diego de, 4, 6–8, 15, 48, 62, 70, 74, 89, 91, 136, 165
Las Sepulturas, 272, 276, 282–83, 286
Leventhal, Richard M., 263, 272, 281
Leyenda de los Soles, 168–71
Lineage of the Lords of Totonicapan, 73
Loltun Cave, 29
Lounsbury, Floyd, 158
Lowry's Bight, 123
Lubaantun, 18–19, 22, 28, 102
Ludendorff, Hans, 158, 172

Macal-Tipu, 101
Madrid Codex, 14, 15, 63, 79, 81, 82, 84, 85, 87, 94

Makemson, Maud, 158, 172, 177
Maler, Teobert, 15, 16
Malta, 299, 300
Mamom period, 21
manatee: in Maya diet, 48, 51; in Maya ritual, 75, 98
Manchan, 225
Marañon River Valley, 250
Marcahuamachuco, 251
Marcus, Joyce, 345
market economy, 349
Maudslay, Alfred, 15–16
Maya Chronology: The Correlation Question, 157
Maya collapse, 204–5
Maya Hieroglyphic Writing: Introduction, 24
Maya people: Cakchiquel Maya, 66; Chol, 265; Chontal, 265; Chorti Maya, 76, 81, 84, 100, 261, 265, 267, 268, 272; Cozumel Maya, 83; Lacandon, 63, 71, 265, 266; Mam Maya, 86; Putun Maya, 140; Quiche Maya, 62, 78, 116; Tzeltal, 86, 265; Tzotzil, 85, 86, 265; Tzutuhil Maya, 71; Yucatec Maya, 265
Mayapan, 13, 20, 24, 25, 70, 71, 75, 82, 87, 89, 90, 91, 93, 94, 98, 101, 102, 110, 165
Mérida, 5, 7, 82, 165
Merwin, Raymond, 18–19
Mesa de Petapilla, 276–77, 280, 282
Mexica, the, 374, 375, 377–85, 392
Mexico, 9, 10, 373–86; Valley of, 375, 379, 380, 382
Middle Horizon, 213–35, 314
Miles, Suzanna, 146, 155n
militarism, 100, 377–86, 387, 390–92, 393, 395
Millon, René, 313, 324, 331, 335, 337, 340
minimum residential unit (Maya), 262, 272
Miraflores (Verbena) phase, 146, 153, 154
Mixcoatl, 202, 205

Mixtec, the, 166–68, 195, 196
Moche culture, 212–35
Moche Valley, 214–18, 228–31, 237–43, 248–55, 257–58
Moctezuma, 331
Moctezuma I, 381–82
Molloy, John, 163, 168
monkey: in Maya diet, 46; in Maya ritual, 65–66
Moon Pyramid, 324, 331, 332, 334, 341–42
Morley, Sylvanus G., 19–24, 157
Moseley, Michael, 290
Moskito coast, Nicaragua, 39, 49–50, 52
Moskito Indians, 48, 52
Motul dictionary, 73, 84
Muluc, 153
mummy worship, 389
Murra, John V., 255–56, 370, 376

naguals, 100
Naranjo, 185
National Geographic Society, 27
National Science Foundation, 28
Nebaj, 66, 93, 162
Nepena Valley, 214
network design, 243–47
New World Archaeological Foundation, 31
Newman, Marshall T., 289
Numeration, Calendar Systems, and Astronomical Knowledge of the Mayas, The, 18

Oaxaca, 123
Ocosingo, 12
oikos, 349; *hyper-oikos*, 367
Olmec art, 146, 154
Olopa, 267, 268
opossum in Maya ritual, 65, 79
Ordoñez y Aguiar, Ramón, 8, 9
Ostuman, 279–81
Otuzco, 240–41, 252–55, 257–58
Oxchuc, 265

Pachakuti, 388–91
Palenque, 7, 9–10, 11, 12, 15, 27, 30, 62, 73, 85, 100, 155, 369
Pampa de las Llamas, 225
Pampa Grande, 218, 221–24, 228–31
Panamarca, 221–22
Pasión Valley, 25
Patlachique, 326–27, 332–33
Peabody Museum, 16–26, 263
peccary: in Maya diet, 44, 46, 51; in Maya ritual, 65, 66–70, 89, 91, 94
Pech, Nakuk, 165
Pendergast, David, 27, 89
Pennsylvania, University of, 20, 21, 24–27
Perez, Pio, 14, 15, 158
Peru, 211–59, 289–310
Peten, 18–19, 25, 79, 161, 162, 263
Petroglyph Cave, 90, 91
Piedra Parada, 290, 300, 302–3
Piedras Negras, 16, 21, 24
Pikillagta, 225
Pogo, Alexander, 158
Polynesia, 299
Popol Vuh, 14, 31, 62, 73, 84, 99
Poroto, 243
pottery, Maya, 105–42; *apaste*, 116; *batidor*, 116; bucket, 131–32; Chicanel Ceramic Sphere, 108; chronology, 105–8; *comale*, 120; dry storage vessels, 124; eating and ritual offering, 132–34; Floral Park Ceramic Sphere, 139, 142; *florero*, 126–27; functional classification, 108–42; jar, 124–26; *jarro*, 116; *lec-i-uah*, 127; mixing bowl, 123; *ocliz*, 116; ritual vessel, 134–38; serving dishes, 127–31; soaking vessel, 121–23; special forms, 138; stationary cooking vessels, 120–21; *tamalero*, 116; utilization, 108–42. *See also* pottery type names
pottery type names (Maya): Bobche Smudged, 127, 137; Bribri Black, 138; Cabro Red, 117, 124, 126, 130, 133, 138; Canxun Red, 124,

129, 133; Cassada, 116, 129; Chactoc, 118, 130; Chahmah, 121, 127; Chiculte, 123, 124, 138; Cockscomb Buff, 129, 130, 133; Conop, 116, 130; Crabboe, 121, 127; Hokab Impressed, 117, 124, 125; Hole Dull, 117, 132, 134, 136; Kuxche Orange, 133, 136; Laguna Verde, 124, 129; Lanillo Groove, 129; Liscanal, 117, 130; Matamore, 116, 118, 126–27, 130, 133; Munequita, 118, 138; Nictaa Buff, 126, 130, 133; Pahote, 117, 124, 125, 130, 133; Paila, 128; Pixoy, 130; Poknoboy, 120, 132, 138; Remax, 124, 133; Sangre Red, 118, 138; Sapote, 123, 124; Savannah Bank, 130, 132, 133; Sierra Red, 117, 123, 124, 129, 130, 134, 136, 141; Taciste, 118, 138; Teabox, 120, 132; Tinta Usulutan, 116, 130; Tuk, 130, 133; Yaxnik, 116, 130; Zapatista, 136; Zorra, 116, 130. *See also Table 4.3, 129, and Table 4.4, 133*
pottery, Peruvian, 252–55, 258, 293; kaolin, 252–55, 258; types, 252
Price, Barbara J., 376
Proskouriakoff, Tatiana, 24
Projecto Arqueológico Copan, 261, 263, 269, 281
Puerto de Supe, 289–92
Puuc, 14, 171, 205

quebrada, 272, 277
Quechua, the, 387
quechua zone, 240, 247
Quetzalcoatl, 202, 205; Pyramid (Temple) of, 316, 322–25, 328, 335
Quintana Roo, 16, 28, 132, 266
Quirigua, 12, 19, 287

Rabin, Emily, 166–68
Rabinal-Achi, 14
Ramirez-Horton, Susan, 259*n*

Relación de las Cosas de Yucatán, 6–7, 14
Renfrew, Colin, 299–300, 302
residential pattern, Maya, 265–66
Ricketson, Oliver G., Jr., 22
Río, Captain Antonio del, 9
Rio Saco de Léon, 290
Roman empire, 346, 347
Rosny, Leon de, 14–15
route location theory, 241–43
Rowe, J. H., 211, 213
Roys, Ralph, 164–65
Ruz Lhuillier, Alberto, 27

Sac Balam, 83
sacbe, 282–83
St. Andrew's cross, 154, 155
St. Ursula, 94
Salinar culture, 212
Salinar settlement, 217
San Antonio, 23
San Augustín Acasaguastlan, 66, 78, 87
San Cristóbal de Las Casas, 9
San Gervasio, 70
San José, 23, 75
Sanders, William, 263, 335, 376
Santa, 250, 251, 357
Santa Eulalia, 98
Santa Lucia phase, 162
Santa Rita, 18, 81
Santa River Valley, 221, 242, 243, 251
Santiago Atitlan, 71
Santiago Chimaltenango, 265
Sapper, Karl, 18
Satterthwaite, Linton, 158; calendar studies, 184
Saville, Marshall, 18
Schove, J. D., 157, 162, 163, 183
Seibal, 16, 25–26, 70, 78–79, 82, 89, 90, 101, 139, 140, 204, 205, 269
Selin Farm site, 35–53
Selin Period, 40, 51
Severin, Gregory, 158
shellfish: in Maya diet, 42, 45–46, 49,

51, 121; in Maya ritual, 55, 66, 75–78, 90–91, 94–96, 98, 102; in Peruvian diet, 292–94
Shepard, Anna O., 24
shicra, 300
Shook, Edwin, 26
sian otot, 267, 268, 272, 287
Sinsicap, Rio, 253
small animals: in Maya diet, 44, 46–47; in Maya ritual, 85–86, 90. *See also individual species names*
Smiley, Charles, 158, 159, 173, 175
Smith, A. Ledyard, 26
Smith, Robert, 21
snake: in Maya ritual, 65, 78–79, 81, 90
Spanish conquest, 348, 374
Spanish Lookout, 161
Spinden, H. J., 39; calendar studies, 158, 160, 162–64, 166, 172–75, 177–78, 182–83
split inheritance, 389–92
Stephens, John Lloyd, 4, 7, 10–14
Stone, D. Z., 39
Stromsvik, Gustavus, 21
stylistic analysis, 211–35
subsistence, 290–95
Sun Pyramid, 324, 332, 334–35, 341
suni, 240, 247
Supe culture, 289
Supe Valley, 225, 290, 300

Tabay, 62
Tahuantinsuyo, 347–48, 367
Teeple, John, 158, 176–77
Tello, Julio C., 289
Temple of the Cross, 10, 155
Temple of the Foliated Cross, 85, 155
Temple of the Inscriptions, 12, 27
Tenochtitlan, 329, 368–69, 374, 375, 380–82, 385
Teotihuacan, 205, 313–43, 368–69
Teotihuacan Mapping Project, 313
Tepanec, the, 379–82, 385
Texcoco, 379–81
Thomas, Cyrus, 15

Thompson, Edward H., 16–17
Thompson, J. Eric S., 22–24; calendar studies, 157–60, 162–64, 166, 172–75, 177–78
Tiahuanaco, 386
Tiahuanacoid culture, 212–14
Tihoo, 5, 7
Tikal, 16, 26–27, 70, 71, 81, 83, 101, 102, 127, 162, 262, 269
Tilantongo, 166–68
Titichon, 277–80
Tixpayan, 86
Tlacaelel, 381–83
Tlaloc (Aztec rain god), 56, 87, 99, 324
Tlatelolco, 374
Toltec, the, 163, 168–72, 202, 205–8, 379–80, 385
Toral, Bishop, 165
travel time, 243
Trujillo, Honduras, 39
Trujillo, Peru, 245, 251
Tula, 171–72, 205–8
Tulane University, 27
Tulix Complex, 108, 112–18, 120, 123–26, 128, 130, 132–35, 136, 141
Tulum, 14, 75, 82, 102
tun, 66, 164
turkey: in Maya diet, 91, 101; in Maya ritual, 65, 82–83, 96
turtle: in Maya diet, 44, 47–48, 49–50, 90, 101; in Maya ritual, 65, 81–82, 90, 96, 98, 100–101
Tzacualli, 326–27, 333–35

Uaxactun, 20, 21–22, 73, 79, 81
Uhle, Max, 289
Utatlan, 12
Uxmal, 6, 7, 8, 10, 13, 15, 82

Valliant, George C., 19, 23, 158, 163
vega, 278
Vega, Bishop Nuñez de la, 86
Versailles, 333, 336
vertical archipelago, 256, 376

verticality model, 255–56, 376
Viking Group, 340
Viracocha Inca, 387–88, 390
Viru Valley, 214, 216, 217, 221, 227, 228, 237–40, 242, 249–55, 257–58

Waldeck, Jean-Frédéric, 9, 10
Wallrath, Matthew, 339
war with heaven, 197–98
Wari culture, 213–35
Wauchope, Robert, 22, 28, 158
Weber, Max, 349–51
Webster, David, 263
Whorf, Benjamin, 24
Willey, Gordon R., 25–26, 28, 32, 204, 225, 261–63, 276, 287, 289–90, 373–74, 397
Willson, R. W., 158, 178
Wiracocha Pampa, 225, 228

Wisdom, Charles, 265–66, 267–68, 278, 281
Wolfman, Daniel, 157, 158

X-Coton cenote, 91
Xiu, D. Juan, 164
Xiu lineage, 82
Xiucoatl, 324
Xlacah, Cenote, 94, 96–98
Xochicalco, 172, 198
xtol dance, 82

Yaxcaba, 81
Yaxchilan, 15, 71, 99
Yucatan, 5–14, 17, 73, 83, 85, 89, 90, 91, 99, 161–66, 171
yungas, 240, 247

Zaculeu, 83, 286
Zinacantan, 86, 96, 266
Zinacanteco domestic groups, 264